Bulgaria

THE ROUGH GUIDE

There are more than sixty Rough Guide titles covering
destinations from Amsterdam to Zimbabwe

Forthcoming travel titles include
Bali • Costa Rica • Goa • Hawaii • Majorca
Rhodes • Singapore • Vietnam

Rough Guide Reference Series
Classical Music • World Music

Rough Guide Phrasebooks
Czech • French • German • Greek • Italian • Spanish

Rough Guide Credits

Text Editor:	Jack Holland
Series Editor:	Mark Ellingham
Editorial:	Martin Dunford, Jonathan Buckley, Graham Parker, Jo Mead, Samantha Cook, Alison Cowan, Amanda Tomlin, Annie Shaw, Lemisse al-Hafidh, Catherine McHale
Production:	Susanne Hillen, Andy Hilliard, Melissa Flack, Alan Spicer, Judy Pang, Link Hall, Nicola Williamson
Publicity:	Richard Trillo (UK), Jean-Marie Kelly (US)
Finance:	John Fisher, Celia Crowley, Simon Carloss

The authors would like to thank Angel Angelov of the Bulgarian National Tourist Office in London, Brenda Walker of Forest Books, Aglika Markova, cultural attache at the Bulgarian Embassy, London, Manol Dimitrov and Valentina Kanazirska of *Turistreklama* in Sofia, Bogdana Dimitrova Lilova of the Iskra museum in Kazanlâk, Stoyka Kairakova in Stara Zagora, Rositsa Simeonova in Sofia, and all in Sozopol. Thanks to everyone at the Rough Guides, especially Jack Holland for skilled and patient editing.

Thanks, too, to everyone who has written in with various comments and additions: I. Parker, Larry Ray, S.J.W. Squires, Keith Crane, Basil G. Twigg, Simon Branch, Peter Tucker, David Main, Joanne Rushby, Denise Searle and Mike Power.

The poems reproduced in the *Contexts* section of this book – *November, Epoch, November 3rd* and *A small anonymous song about the big Old Organ-grinder* – were originally published by Forest Books and are © Jusautor, Sofia. *November* was originally also co-published by UNESCO. The short story *Shibil* was published by Slavica Books, translation © John Burnip 1990.

This first edition published March 1993 and reprinted twice in 1994 and in June 1995 by Rough Guides Ltd, 1 Mercer Street, London WC2H 9QJ.

Distributed by the Penguin Group:

Penguin Books Ltd, 27 Wrights Lane, London W8 5TZ
Penguin Books USA Inc., 375 Hudson Street, New York 10014, USA
Penguin Books Australia Ltd, 487 Maroondah Highway, PO Box 257, Ringwood, Victoria 3134, Australia
Penguin Books Canada Ltd, 10 Alcorn Avenue, Toronto, Ontario, Canada M4V 1E4
Penguin Books (NZ) Ltd, 182–190 Wairau Road, Auckland 10, New Zealand

Typeset in Linotron Univers and Century Old Style to an original design by Andrew Oliver.
Printed in the United Kingdom by Cox and Wyman Ltd (Reading).
Maps by Micromap, 1 Nursery Gardens, Romsey, Hampshire SO51 8UU.
Illustrations in Part One and Part Three by Ed Briant.
Illustrations on p.1 and p.285 by Henry Iles.

368pp. Includes index.

British Library Cataloguing in Publication Data.
A catalogue record for this book is available from the British Library.

ISBN 1-85828-047-8

Bulgaria

THE ROUGH GUIDE

Written and researched by

Jonathan Bousfield and Dan Richardson

With additional research and writing by

Simon Broughton, Kim Burton and Jill Denton

THE ROUGH GUIDES

CONTENTS

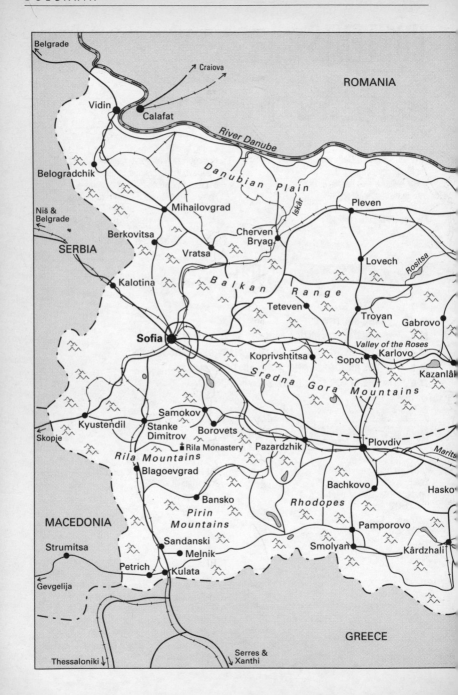

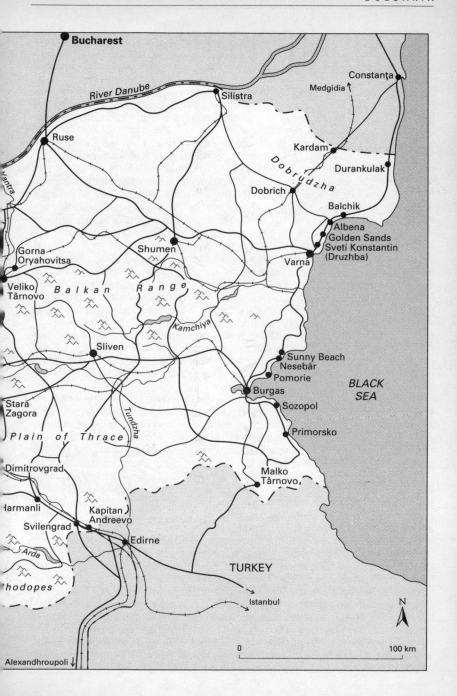

INTRODUCTION

I n many ways, **Bulgaria** is the forgotten country of the Balkans. Back in the days when it was one of the Soviet Union's most loyal east European allies, mention of the country brought few distinct images to mind. Despite being known as the site of extensive Black Sea package resorts and the source of several good wines, Bulgaria was too often dismissed as a dour, inward-looking place peopled by officious bureaucrats. If westerners remained in the dark about the real Bulgaria however, this was largely because the country's rulers didn't seem to want anybody to see it. Bizarre currency regulations, arbitrary border hassles, and restrictions on where you were allowed to stay, made Bulgaria one of the most infuriating countries to visit. Happily all this has changed, but the new, post-totalitarian Bulgaria still finds it difficult to emerge from the smokescreen imposed by over four decades of Communist-inspired dullness. The process of democratic reform here (although never lacking in drama) proved to be less newsworthy than the chaos and violence experienced by some of the country's Balkan neighbours, reinforcing the impression that nothing much ever happened here. Worse still, the war in the former Yugoslavia disrupted Bulgaria's land links with western Europe, leaving the country cut off from a continent it was increasingly eager to join.

Bulgarians are frustrated by their country's lack of a clearly defined image abroad. Heirs to one of Europe's great civilizations, and guardians of Balkan Christian traditions, they have a keen sense of national identity distilled by centuries of turbulent history. In a constantly repeating cycle of grandeur, decline and national rebirth, successive Bulgarian states have striven to dominate the Balkan peninsula before succumbing to defeat and foreign tutelage, only to be regenerated by patriotic resistance to outside control.

The Bulgarian nation was formed in the seventh and eighth centuries when the **Bulgars**, warlike nomads from central Asia, assumed the leadership of Slav tribes in the lower Danube basin and took them on a spree of conquest in southeastern Europe. The resulting **First Bulgarian Empire**, after accepting Orthodox Christianity as the state religion, became the centre of Slavonic culture and spirituality before falling victim to a resurgent **Byzantine** Empire in the eleventh century. Recovery came a century later when the local aristocracy broke free from Constantinople and restored past glories in the shape of the **Second Bulgarian Empire**. However the rise of Ottoman power in the fourteenth century ushered in the 500-year-long period of *Tursko robstvo* or "**Turkish bondage**" when the achievements of the medieval era were extinguished. Bulgarian art and culture recovered during the nineteenth-century **National Revival**, and the emergence of a fearsome revolutionary movement prepared the ground for Bulgaria's eventual **Liberation** in 1878, achieved with the help of Russian arms. However, Europe's other Great Powers conspired to limit the size of the infant state at the Berlin Congress of 1878, the first of a series of betrayals which denied Bulgarian claims to a territory which had long been considered an integral part of the historical Bulgarian state, **Macedonia**. In the present century Bulgaria went to war three times (in the Balkan Wars of 1912–13, World War I, and World War II) to try and recover Macedonia, and was defeated on each occasion. By 1945 it seemed like a country which had somehow missed out on its destiny, and rapidly turned in on itself during the subsequent deep sleep of Communism.

The end of Communist Bulgaria

Back in the momentous winter of 1989, it looked as if Bulgaria was dragging its feet on the road to democracy while others forged ahead. The Communist Party ditched a few of the old guard, changed its name to the Socialist Party, promptly won the country's first multi-party elections for over forty years, and attempted to carry on as if little had changed. It took over a year of further struggle and political infighting before the opposition Union of Democratic Forces secured an electoral victory in October 1991 – and even then by the narrowest of margins.

The 1990s had begun with symbols of westernization everywhere apparent. Bulgaria's traditionally reserved young spent their time acquiring the latest western sounds or shortening the lengths of their miniskirts, while Sofia's taxi drivers wouldn't be seen dead without miniature star-spangled banners and union jacks fluttering from their dashboards. The ensuing plunge into market economics led to hitherto undreamt of opportunities for some, but plummeting living standards for the majority. The result was a certain amount of schizophrenia, with a messianic faith in the redemptive power of private enterprise co-existing with a more resigned acceptance of the sacrifices that the new religion entailed – and a fatalistic recognition that for most individuals, the dream of personal wealth would never be realized. However it's a tribute to Bulgarian moderation and forbearance that political change has been achieved here without much social unrest or serious violence. In a region notorious for its propensity to descend into chaos, Bulgaria is fast gaining respect as a model of democracy and stability.

Where to go and when

Bulgaria has a **continental climate**, with long, hot, dry summers and – in the interior at least – bitterly cold winters. July and August can be oppressively hot in the big cities, and a little crowded on the Black Sea coast – elsewhere, you won't have to worry about being swamped by fellow visitors, and those who travel through Bulgaria too far out of season will find many tourist facilities shut. Using public transport is reasonably easy throughout the year, although the highest cross-mountain routes will be closed during the coldest months.

Bulgaria's most obvious urban attractions are **Sofia**, a set-piece capital city whose centre was laid out by successive regimes as an expression of political power; and the second city **Plovdiv**, home to what is arguably the finest collection of nineteenth-century architecture in the Balkans. Both are increasingly cosmopolitan places offering a range of street cafés and nightlife opportunities in short supply elsewhere in the country. They each form important cultural centres well endowed with museums and galleries, and are good bases from which to visit the rest of the interior. The Danube town of **Ruse** has a relaxed air of turn-of-the-century elegance which shouldn't be missed if you're entering Bulgaria from the north.

Most foreign visitors still make a beeline for the **Black Sea**, formerly the summer playground of the entire eastern bloc. The big purpose-built resorts like **Sunny Beach** and **Golden Sands** can be rather characterless, and tend to isolate the tourist from Bulgarian life and culture. Although package tours based at these resorts present a cheap and easy way of getting to Bulgaria, it's best to steer clear of them once you arrive. The main resort-city of **Varna** is the liveliest place along the coast, while small peninsula settlements like **Nesebâr** and **Sozopol** provide a more relaxing fishing-village atmosphere. Beaches are magnificent, especially in the south, and private enterprise is more developed here than anywhere else in the country – ensuring a plentiful supply of private rooms and good seafood restaurants. The climate remains mild all the year round, the Black Sea becomes deserted outside the main tourist season, which runs from July to September – outside that period, everything will be closed.

Some of the finest highland scenery in Europe is found in the **Rila**, **Pirin** and **Rhodope** mountain ranges, where a burgeoning winter tourist industry is taking shape in resorts like **Borovets**, **Malyovitsa**, **Bansko** and **Pamporovo**. Snow is thick on the ground from late November through to mid-March, and in summer the mountain resorts are taken over by climbers and ramblers. The mountains are pretty deserted in late spring and throughout the autumn.

Elsewhere, few places are geared up to cater to western-style, consumer-oriented tourism, although the rugged highlands which cut across central Bulgaria are the best places to explore the heartlands of Bulgarian history and culture. The crafts towns and monasteries of the central **Balkan Range** were the places where Bulgarian culture recovered during the nineteenth-century National Revival, and are easily explored from the dramatically situated, citadel-encrusted town of **Veliko Târnovo**, medieval capital of the Second Bulgarian Empire. **Shumen**, main town of the northwest, is dour in comparison; but allows access to the remains of the Bulgarian state's first two capitals, **Pliska** and **Preslav**. South of the Balkan Range, the **Sredna Gora** hills retain memories of Bulgaria's nineteenth-century struggles against Turkish oppression, with the agricultural village of **Koprivshtitsa** surviving as a living memorial to the April Rising, which broke out here in 1876. Between the Balkan Range and the Sredna Gora lies the **Valley of the Roses**, spectacular in late May and early June when Bulgaria's renowned rose crop is harvested, and lined by a string of historic market towns.

BULGARIA'S CLIMATE											
Average temperatures °F (°C)											
Jan	Feb	Mar	Apr	May	June	July	Aug	Sept	Oct	Nov	Dec
Borovets											
30	33	41	48	59	65	71	74	61	54	42	33
(-1)	(1)	(5)	(9)	(15)	(19)	(22)	(23)	(16)	(12)	(6)	(1)
Plovdiv											
33	34	44	54	62	73	74	76	65	55	45	36
(1)	(3)	(7)	(12)	(17)	(23)	(23)	(24)	(19)	(13)	(8)	(3)
Varna											
36	43	43	54	62	70	75	74	68	60	49	39
(3)	(6)	(6)	(12)	(17)	(22)	(24)	(23)	(20)	(16)	(10)	(4)

PART ONE

THE
BASICS

GETTING THERE

Given Bulgaria's location on the southeast fringes of Europe, the overland journey from the UK can be both time consuming and costly – however rewarding the trip may be. By far the most convenient way to get there is to fly, although scheduled airline services to Bulgaria tend to be expensive. Alternative options include flying to another city in southeast Europe and continuing your journey by land, or signing up for an inexpensive package holiday. You'll have less freedom on the latter, but at least it will get you to Bulgaria for a reasonable price.

FLIGHTS

The sad fact is that unlike Athens, Istanbul or even Budapest there's not enough volume in air traffic to Sofia to have created a discount market: finding the least expensive seat is a matter of scouring the newspapers, checking the independent travel specialists and utilizing any student/youth bargains you may be eligible for.

FROM LONDON
BALKAN, the Bulgarian national airline, operate **scheduled flights** between London Heathrow and Sofia three times a week. An Apex fare (which must include at least one Saturday night away, with a maximum stay of three months) currently costs about £275 return, more in summer. Cheaper options may be available from ticket agents (independent travel specialists such as **Campus** and **STA Travel** may have discounts for the under-26s – see addresses below), although these will probably involve flying with another European carrier (such as *Austrian Airlines, Swissair* or *Finnair*) and will involve at least one change.

The **package tour** operators *Balkan Holidays* may have a few discount flights to Sofia, Burgas or Varna over the summer; but these are rarely advertised in the press and you'll have to contact operators direct to find out what's on offer. Similarly, you may find packages that fly from a regional airport that's more convenient than London – see "Package Tour Operators", p.6.

One option is to fly to another destination in southeast Europe, such as Budapest, Bucharest or Istanbul, and continue to Bulgaria overland. Flights to the Romanian capital Bucharest can be as expensive as those to Sofia, but cheap flights to Budapest and Istanbul are frequently advertised in the press – check out *Time Out* or the *Evening Standard* if you're in London, or the travel pages of Sunday newspapers.

FROM OUTSIDE EUROPE
There are no direct flights **from the USA or Canada** to Bulgaria, although a newly formed private airline, *Jes-Air*, is hoping to begin services between Sofia and North American

TRAVEL OPERATORS

AGENTS
Campus Travel, 52 Grosvenor Gardens, London SW1 0AG (☎071/730 3402); and offices all over the country.

Canterbury Travel, 248 Streatfield Rd, Kenton, Harrow, HA3 9BY (☎081/206 0411).

STA Travel, 86 Old Brompton Rd, London SW7 3LQ (☎071/937 9921); and offices nationwide.

Travelines, 154 Cromwell Rd, London SW7 4EF (☎071/370 6131).

AIRLINES
BALKAN, 322 Regent St, London W1 (☎071/637 7637). Ticket sales in the UK are handled by **British Airways**, 156 Regent St, London W1 (☎081/897 4000).

cities in the near future. Other airlines operate indirect flights (with *KLM*, for example, flying from New York to Sofia via Amsterdam), with return tickets costing around $900–1000 depending on the time of year – they can be booked through the *Bulgarian Tourist Office* in New York (161 East 86th Street; ☎212/722 1110).

Travellers **from down under** will have to consult local travel agents about services connecting with *BALKAN*'s weekly flights from Bangkok and Kuala Lumpur.

BY TRAIN

The most direct overland **rail routes** to Bulgaria (Dieppe–Paris–Milan–Venice–Zagreb–Belgrade–Sofia or Ostende–Munich–Zagreb–Belgrade–Sofia) were disrupted by the outbreak of civil war in Yugoslavia. Initially, passengers were able to bypass the main trouble spots by travelling via Vienna, Budapest and Belgrade, but at the time of writing UN sanctions against Serbia have rendered this impossible. All that remains is the significantly longer route looping through Hungary and Romania before entering Bulgaria at the northern town of Ruse – a journey requiring two and a half days and a transit visa for Romania, available at the border or from the Romanian consulate in your home country for £20.

A standard second-class return from London to Sofia weighs in at £231, so it makes sense to opt for an **InterRail pass** instead (currently £175 for a month or £145 for 15 days if you're under 26 or over 65; £235 for a month, £175 for 15 days if you're not), which gives you unlimited travel on all continental European railways – including Bulgaria – and half-price discounts in Britain and on Channel ferries.

Under-26s are also eligible for discounted **BIJ** tickets from *Eurotrain* or *Wasteels*. These can be booked for journeys from any station in Britain to any major station in Europe; they remain valid for two months and allow as many stopovers as you want along a pre-specified route. However, at £212 for a return ticket from London to Sofia, this will only save you money if you plan to be in Bulgaria for more than a month.

If you're travelling on from Bulgaria to another country, remember that international tickets purchased in Bulgaria can be very expensive; another argument for opting for either InterRail or BIJ tickets.

RAIL AND COACH ENQUIRIES

British Rail European Travel Centre, Victoria Station, London SW1 (☎071/834 2345).
Eurotrain, 52 Grosvenor Gardens, London SW1 (☎071/730 3402).
Wasteels, 121 Wilton Rd, London SW1 (☎071/834 7066).
Eurolines, 52 Grosvenor Gardens, London SW1 (☎071/730 8235).

BY COACH

There are no direct **coaches** from the UK to Bulgaria, and services to cities in neighbouring Turkey, Greece and Yugoslavia have been disrupted by instability in the latter. However, it's worth contacting the UK's main international coach operators *Eurolines* to see whether any services are running to Balkan destinations, or scanning the rear pages of *Time Out* or other London listings magazines for news of what other companies are offering. *Eurolines* run a weekly service to Budapest (currently the nearest you can get), departing on Thursday evenings and arriving some 36 hours and a change at Frankfurt later. This costs £94 single, £149 return.

APPROACHING FROM TURKEY

Travellers approaching Bulgaria from Turkey will find that several Turkish coach operators run regular **services from Istanbul** to Plovdiv, Sofia, Varna, Burgas and elsewhere. Numerous travel agents in the central Sultanahmet district of town will reserve seats; otherwise head for west Istanbul's main bus station at Topkapi, where most of the coach operators have offices. Bear in mind, however, that Bulgarian–Turkish border crossings are clogged up with east European coach parties travelling to or from the Bosphorus, and long queues at the frontier (a wait of 5 to 8 hours for coaches is not uncommon) ensure that coach travel can be long, tedious, and difficult to timetable.

DRIVING AND HITCHING

Driving to Bulgaria is not an easy option. The most direct route is **through Yugoslavia**, following the E5 from Belgrade down to the Dimitrovgrad/Kalotina border crossing. However, until UN sanctions against Serbia are lifted and the internal conflict is resolved, this is most definitely *not* an advisable route to follow. Most travellers instead opt to drive **through Austria/ Hungary/Romania**, heading for the two main frontier crossings at Calafat-Vidin and Giurgiu-Ruse. The E5 runs from the Belgian coast to Budapest, passing through Brussels, Köln and Vienna on the way. From here, the road crossing into Romania at Nadlac and continuing to Arad, Timisoara and Dobreta-Turnu Severin is probably the quickest way of getting to the Bulgarian frontier. Be warned, however, that the trip can be a gruelling experience. Road conditions deteriorate markedly east of Budapest, and the vast increase in transit traffic crossing Romania in order to avoid Yugoslavia has rendered traditionally overloaded border crossings even more nightmarish.

If you do decide to undertake the journey, you'll need an **international driving licence**, available from the motoring organizations in your home country for a small fee, together with an **international Green Card** from your insurance company. Both documents are obligatory in Hungary and recommended in the other countries you'll be driving through.

HITCHING

Even when fully traversable the road down through Yugoslavia was notoriously awful for **hitching**, and the long route through Hungary and Romania is, if anything, worse. However, hitching **from Turkey or Greece** is quite feasible. Otherwise, the best idea seems to be to hitch as far as you can on the western European motorway network, heading through Germany and Austria as far as the Hungarian border and making for Budapest, from where you can complete the journey reasonably cheaply by public transport.

PACKAGE DEALS

The main advantage of **package holidays** is their low cost. Flight-plus-accommodation deals are often cheaper than the price of a scheduled air fare on its own, and even the most independent of travellers should consider the package option. Although they tie you down to staying in one or two centres, there's nothing to prevent you from absenting yourself for a few days and indulging in a little exploration of your own. A different type of package deal is the **study tour**, specialized holidays for those with particular interests – monasteries, ornithology, archaeology, folk dancing and so on. *Balkan Holidays* and *Sunquest*, for example, both offer two-week coach tours taking in Bulgarian monasteries and historic towns. If you merely fancy a city break in Sofia, try *Balkan Holidays*, or *Peltours*, a company specializing in travel to eastern Europe, who will tailor a flight-plus-accommodation deal to your needs.

The main **disadvantage** of Bulgarian package holidays is the nature of the principal holiday resorts themselves. The purpose-built complexes on the Black Sea coast are often over-large and too far away from the nearest town or village, ensuring that you experience little of Bulgarian life. **Beaches**, however, are generally spotless, and coastal waters both warm and clean. *Sunny Beach* (*Slânchev Bryag*) and *Golden Sands* (*Zlatni Pyasâtsi*) are the biggest (and the most soulless) of the tourist complexes along the coast, but are well served by restaurants, bars, discos and other social activities. Villa complexes and holiday villages (like *Dyuni*, south of Burgas) will appeal to holiday makers in search of something more tranquil. Fuller descriptions of both the Black Sea resorts and the winter skiing centres appear in the guide.

Food and drink **prices** in package resorts are usually twice as high as those in the rest of Bulgaria – still cheap by western standards of course, but worth bearing in mind when working out your budget.

HOLIDAYS ON THE COAST

The main summer package tour **operators** are *Balkan Holidays*, *Sunquest* and *Enterprise*, although you should look out for new operators joining the market in future seasons. All of them offer 7- and 14-day holidays in *Sunny Beach*, *Golden Sands*, *Albena* and *Dyuni*, with peak-season prices hovering around £350–400 per person for two weeks – prices are about £100 lower in May and September. *Balkan Holidays* travel to the widest choice of resorts, and also arrange numerous two-centre holidays combining coastal and mountain resorts, Bulgarian and Romanian, or Bulgarian and Turkish destinations. For those wishing to avoid big resorts and modern hotels, the *Balkan Holidays* brochure also offers holiday flats in the old houses of Nesebâr – for about £275–300 per person for 7 days in the high season, or as little as £150 in May or September.

SKIING HOLIDAYS

Balkan, Inghams, Enterprise, Neilson and *Crystal Holidays* all offer 1- and 2-week winter holidays at Borovets in the Rila mountains, or the Rhodope resort of Pamporovo – British tourists make up about 75 percent of foreign guests at the latter. *Balkan Holidays* also sell packages to *Mount Vitosha*, which has the added attraction of being next door to the urban delights of Sofia. Expect to pay £275–375 for a week's holiday in the mid-February peak season, less in early January or March, and much less if you stay in apartments or chalets instead of hotels. Remember though that equipment and tuition will be extra: about £40 a week for a lift pass, £40 for ski and boot hire, and £60 for 7 days' worth of skiing lessons.

PACKAGE TOUR OPERATORS

SUMMER

Balkan Holidays, 19 Conduit St, London W1R 9TD (☎071/493 8612).

Enterprise, Groundstar House, London Rd, Crawley, West Sussex RH10 2TB (☎0293/560777).

Sunquest, 9 Grand Parade, Green Lanes, London N4 1JX (☎081/800 8030).

WINTER

Balkan Holidays (see above).

Crystal Holidays, Crystal House, The Courtyard, Arlington Rd, Surbiton, Surrey KT6 6BW (☎081/399 5144).

Enterprise (see above).

Inghams, 10–18 Putney Hill, London SW15 6AX (☎081/789 3331).

Neilson, 1–4 Argyll St, London W1V 1AD (☎0532/394555).

SPECIALIST TOUR OPERATORS

ACE Study Tours, Babraham, Cambridge CB2 4AP (☎0223/835055). 15-day tours of Bulgaria including selected monasteries, archaeological sights and folk architecture.

British-Bulgarian Society, c/o Finsbury Library, 245 St John St, London EC1V 4NB (☎071/837 2304). Membership (£7 a year) gives you access to numerous special-interest tours, including ornithology, botany, archaeology, embroidery and folk dancing.

Contiki, Wells House, 15 Elmfield Rd, Bromley, Kent BR1 1LS (☎081/290 6422). Grand tours of Europe which include a couple of days' stay in Sofia.

Exodus Expeditions, 9 Weir Rd, London SW12 0LT (☎081/673 0859). Hiking tours.

Explore Worldwide Ltd, 1 Frederick St, Aldershot, Hants GU11 1LQ (☎0252/344161). 14-day hiking tour in the Pirin and Rila mountains southeast of Sofia.

Peltours, Sovereign House, 11/19 Ballards Lane, Finchley, London N3 1UX (☎081/346 9144). Tailor-made flight-plus-accommodation deals to Sofia.

RED TAPE: VISAS AND CARTES STATISTIQUES

A full (not Visitor's) **passport** is needed to enter Bulgaria, and unless you go on a package tour it's necessary to have a **visa**. These are in theory available on arrival at Sofia airport and at major road frontier crossings, but you should check the precise situation with the Bulgarian embassy in your home country before setting out.

Bearing in mind the changeable nature of Bulgaria's frontier regulations, it's much safer to obtain a visa in advance. **Tourist visas** (issued in 7 working days for £20, issued on the spot for £40) are valid for 3 months and entitle you to 30 days' stay. **Transit visas** (issued on the spot for £20)

are good for 30 hours' stay. If you're passing through Bulgaria and then returning by the same route, make sure you ask for a double-entry transit visa; otherwise you'll end up paying twice. Whatever your plans it's best to get a tourist visa, since Bulgarian customs sometimes view transit ones as an implied slight on their country, and have been known to pester holders to change large sums into leva as the price for gaining entry.

If **applying by post** you should enclose your passport, a note specifying the type of visa required, and an SAE. Payment must be in cash or by postal order, and one photograph is required.

The procedure for acquiring **visa extensions** is currently under review, so you should seek advice from your embassy in Sofia before proceeding further.

THE CARTE STATISTIQUE

Something of a hangover from the over-bureaucratic Communist era, the *carte statistique* is issued to all independent travellers on arrival. This must be date-stamped at reception whenever you check into and out of a hotel or campsite (where staff sometimes keep the *carte* meantime); or at the tourist office responsible for booking you a private room. The procedure is designed to ensure that you only stay in official accommodation – accept an unlicensed room

---

BULGARIAN EMBASSIES AND CONSULATES

Argentina Calle Manuel Oballio 2967, PO Box 238, Buenos Aires (☎802 92 51).

Australia 1–4 Carlotta Rd, Double Bay, Sydney, NSW 2028 (☎2/36 75 81).

Austria 1040 Wien, Schwindgasse 8, Vienna (☎505 2557).

Belgium 58 Avenue Hamoir, UCCLE, Brussels 1180 (☎374 5963).

Canada 325 Steward Street, Ottawa, Ontario K1H 6K5 (☎232 3215).

Denmark A.N. Hansens allee 5, 2900 Hellerup, Copenhagen (☎01/64 24 84).

France 1 Avenue Rapp, Pariss 75007 (☎455 18 590).

Germany Leipziger Str. 22, 1080 Berlin (☎30/200 09220

Greece Akadimias 12, Athens (☎64 78 105/6/7).

Italy Via Pietro P.Rubens 21, Rome 00197 (☎322 4648).

Romania Str. Rabat 4, Bucuresti (☎0/332 150).

Spain Santa Maria Magdalena 11, Madrid 16 (☎457 6651).

Sweden Karlavagan 29, Stockholm 11431 (☎8/209 038).

Turkey Kavakli dere, Ataturk bulvari 124, Ankara (☎4/267 455); Zinzirlik koyu caddesi 44, Ulus-Ortaköy, Istanbul (☎1/169 2216); Talat pasa caddesi 31, Edirne (☎181/1069).

UK 186–188 Queen's Gate, London SW7 5HL (Mon–Fri 9.30am–12.30am; ☎071/584 9400).

USA 1621 22nd Street NW 667 3870 (☎202/387 7969).

from a private individual and you will have to forgo a stamp for that night. Those who have gaps in their record are liable to a fine upon leaving the country. Considering the fuss they make about stamps, it's ridiculous how small this vital document is – they usually become an illegible mess of stamps after a week, to the ill-natured consternation of more than one receptionist.

Matters are complicated by the fact that many smaller hotels and hostels either don't have the relevant stamps or simply don't take the stamping process seriously any more, believing it to be a relic of the past which will soon be on the way out. Admittedly, most border guards check the *carte statistique* much less rigorously than they used to and adopt a lenient attitude towards transgressors, but it still seems a good idea to keep the document safe, and make sure that you have at least a few "official" accommodation stamps to your credit.

HEALTH AND INSURANCE

Inoculations aren't required for travel in Bulgaria, but if you're heading on to Turkey, especially the southeast, jabs for cholera and typhoid may be worth considering. The most common complaints are diarrhoea and sunburn, so stock up on *Diocalm* (or, with a prescription, *Lomotil*) before you leave home, and don't expose yourself rashly to the sun while in Bulgaria. It is safe to drink tap **water** everywhere.

Minor complaints can be solved at a pharmacy or **Apteka** (Аптека, see the guide for addresses), but if you require a doctor (*lekar*) or dentist (*zâbolekar*) head for the nearest **Poliklinika** or health centre, whose staff might well speak English or German. Urgent cases go to hospitals (*bolnitsa*) courtesy of the *bârza pomosht* or ambulance service (☎150 in most towns, service free), and emergency treatment is free of charge although you must pay for **medicines**. In Sofia there's a pharmacy selling Western drugs for hard currency at the *Tsentâr po Higiena*, and a special clinic for foreigners in the *Mladost 1* suburb (1, Ul. Evgeni Pavlovski, ☎ 75 361).

INSURANCE

On production of a passport, British citizens and nationals of other countries with which Bulgaria has a reciprocal health agreement receive all treatment free of charge, so it's not absolutely essential to carry **insurance**. However, taking out a policy before you leave home will normally give you cover for theft and/or damage to your gear and enable you to claim for any medicines you have to buy, so it's definitely worthwhile. Any travel agent will sell you a policy over the counter (for about £30 for a month's cover); otherwise contact a specialist low-priced firm like *Endsleigh Insurance* (97 Southampton Row, London WC1; ☎071/436 4451). To claim compensation back home you'll need receipts for any medicines purchased, or in the case of theft, an official police report. If local police are unwilling to issue one, be persistent and invoke the name of your embassy (*posolstvo*).

COSTS, MONEY AND BANKS

Bulgaria always was a relatively cheap country for Western visitors, and has been made more so by the sudden lurch towards market economics and the fall in value of the national currency – the lev (*leva* in the plural) – which under the previous regime was always artificially overvalued. The outlook is less bright for Bulgarians themselves, who find their living standards increasingly eroded by high inflation – something the tourist is protected against by the constant slide of the lev against hard currencies.

COSTS

Despite constant price rises and comparatively high costs in Sofia, Plovdiv and along the coast, life's essentials remain cheap. If you're camping and buying food in local markets, you can live on under £6 a day. Staying in 2-star hotels, the occasional private room where available, and eating out regularly, £10–12 should be sufficient. A daily budget of anything above £15 should provide you with a very good life indeed.

The one item of expenditure likely to play havoc with your daily budget estimates is **accommodation**. Hotel prices vary widely, and in some Bulgarian towns the choice of accommodation boils down to a single hotel which, knowing full well that the traveller has no choice but to stay there, simply charges what the market will bear. In general however, 2-star hotels charge between £6–12 per head; considerably cheaper are hostels (£1–2), chalets (£1–2), camp-

sites (£1–2) and private rooms (as little as £2–3 per head in some areas, going up to £4–6 in Sofia, Varna and Plovdiv), although these less costly alternatives won't be available in all areas.

Once you've sorted out a bed for the night, your remaining daily costs can be very slight. All forms of public **transport** are cheap, with flat fares of about 5 pence on most urban transport and inexpensive rates on intercity buses and trains (travelling by rail second class, you can traverse the country from east to west for less than £3 – international services are another matter, however: see p.12). Providing you avoid deluxe hotel restaurants, **eating** should likewise prove to be an economical business. An average evening meal with drinks will set you back £2–3, less if you stick to standard local fare like simple grills and salad. **Drinking** Bulgarian wine or spirits (about £1 and £2 a bottle respectively) will hit your liver harder than your wallet. Snatching a quick cup of coffee or a sandwich won't set you back more than about 10p respectively.

Many Bulgarian museums and tourist attractions charge foreigners about five times the amount paid by the natives, but with this higher rate rarely exceeding 25p, this shouldn't deter you from seeing any of the sights.

MONEY

The currency in Bulgaria is the *lev* (literally, lion), subdivided into 100 *stotinki*. There are notes of 1, 2, 5, 10, 20, 50, 100 and 200 leva; and coins of 1, 2 and 5 leva, and 1, 2, 5, 10, 20 and 50 stotinki. At the time of writing there are 43 leva to the pound sterling – how much this has risen by the time you read this largely depends on the fortunes of the Bulgarian economy.

Although almost all goods and services can be paid for in leva, **hard currency** (known as *valuta*) is often required in paying for international train and bus services, airline tickets, and hotel bills in a few of the more upmarket establishments.

> Because of the rapid rate of inflation of the lev, we've deliberately avoided quoting food, drink and museum prices in the guide: you'll find the key to hotel prices explained in "Accommodation", p.17.

BANKS AND EXCHANGE

Although the value of the lev is now free to slide against that of other currencies, the lev is still unavailable in banks outside Bulgaria. Once inside Bulgaria, money can be changed in banks, tourist offices, reception desks of the bigger hotels, and a growing number of private exchange bureaux in the more touristed areas. There's usually a slight difference in the rates offered, with the ultra-competitive private bureaux offering the most generous terms, if you fancy shopping around. **Banks** are usually open Monday to Friday 9am–4pm, although foreign exchange facilities at many of them are only available until about 2pm. Private exchange bureaux are usually open until 5–6pm, longer in summer. It makes sense to request a receipt (*smetka*) – surplus leva can in theory be re-exchanged for hard currency at the frontier before leaving if you have the receipts, but don't bank on it. You can usually buy dollars (and, on occasion, pounds and deutschmarks) from private exchange bureaux with your excess leva, but the exchange rate may be disadvantageous.

THE BLACK MARKET

The realistic exchange rates now available in banks and exchange bureaux have all but demolished the appeal of the **black market** to visitors, but the demand for hard currency among Bulgarians remains strong. At the time of writing, Bulgarians are officially allowed to buy no more than $500 dollars' worth of hard currency a year, ensuring that illegal money-changing remains a highly visible feature of street life in Sofia, Plovdiv and the coastal cities. "Freelance" money-changers may well offer you a slightly higher rate than the best of the exchange bureaux, but it's best to resist the temptation – the high proportion of crooks among them will attempt to cheat the customer either by a sleight-of-hand trick or rushing the transaction by pretending that the police are just around the corner.

TRAVELLERS' CHEQUES & CREDIT CARDS

Although tourist offices and the bigger bank branches in Sofia, Plovdiv and the coast will cash any of the better-known brands of **travellers' cheques**, they are of little use elsewhere. **Credit cards** can be used to pay for car rental, topnotch hotels, and luxury goods in a small number of shops in the bigger towns and resorts, but are otherwise virtually useless. You can in theory get **cash advances** in leva with Eurocard, Access, Visa, Diners Club and Mastercard, but most banks are still either inequipped to deal with the procedure or simply too lazy to bother. Expect to wait 30 minutes or longer while they check things out, after which the answer may still be in the negative. In Bulgaria, therefore, you'll need to carry much of your money around in cash – whatever the security risk. Buying a discreet money-carrying belt prior to departure seems wise.

INFORMATION AND MAPS

It's worth contacting the Bulgarian Tourist Office before you leave, where you'll be provided with a generous selection of booklets and brochures, although much may be out of date. Most of the publications are designed to whet your appetite rather than impart practical information, but the motoring and camping maps and the *Tourist Calendar* (a list of festivals and other events) are worth taking to Bulgaria. Ask in particular for town plans of any major cities you are visiting – with the exception of Sofia and Plovdiv, these are only sporadically available once in the country itself.

BULGARIAN TOURIST OFFICES ABROAD

DENMARK 6 Vester Farimagsgade, 1606 Copenhagen V (☎01/123 510).

GERMANY 1-3 Stefanstrasse, 6 000 Frankfurt/Main I (☎069/29 52 84 6).

THE NETHERLANDS 43 Leidsestraat, 1017 Amsterdam (☎020/24 84 31).

SWEDEN 30 Kungsgatan, III 35 Stockholm (☎8/115 191).

UK 18 Princes Street, London W1R 7RE (☎071/499 6988).

USA 161 East 86th Street, New York, NY10028 (☎212/722 1110).

INFORMATION IN BULGARIA

Once inside the country, **tourist information offices** in the western European sense are rather thin on the ground, and are really only found in major cities and on the coast. In the past, almost all services for foreign tourists, including tourist information, were run by the centralized, state-owned travel company **Balkantourist**. Two other bureaucratic dinosaurs, **Orbita**, dealing with youth travel, and **Pirin**, responsible for hostels and hikers' chalets, had offices throughout the country. All three organizations still exist, but decentralization, privatization, and the need for each of them to compete in the marketplace have led to a redefinition of their basic roles. Most importantly, they are increasingly operating as travel agents selling foreign holidays to the native Bulgarians, but are less well equipped to dole out information to foreign visitors. To make things worse, there is a shortage of tourist literature; due to financial restrictions, few brochures or maps have been printed in recent years.

Balkantourist are still your most likely source of information. As well as running accommodation bureaux in Sofia, Varna, Burgas and many other areas, they are also responsible for the 24-hour information bureaux at Bulgaria's main border crossings, which can book rooms and furnish information nationwide. Much of the *Balkantourist* empire is being broken up into autonomous, regional firms (such as *Balkan Tours* in Sofia, *Pâldin Tour* in Plovdiv, or *Dunav Tours* in Ruse), which tends to make information-gathering more difficult. However, the main disadvantage of *Balkantourist* and its successors is that they only provide information and make reservations for their own facilities – they'd rather that you didn't know about new private hotels and restaurants which don't fall under their aegis. It will be some time yet before an unbiased system of tourist information comes into being.

Most of the hotels previously owned by *Balkantourist* will still advertise "tourist services" in the lobby, although the services in question are often limited to changing money and selling places on sightseeing tours. However, people are usually sufficiently friendly and helpful to answer the enquiries of any stray tourists, providing that you can find a common language: although staff in Sofia and the main coastal and ski resorts generally speak English, their colleagues elsewhere are likelier to understand German, French or Russian. Addresses of tourist offices appear in the guide.

MAPS

The best general **map** currently available in western Europe is the *Kümmerly and Frey* or *Freytag and Berndt*'s 1:1,000,000 combined map of Romania and Bulgaria. If you can read the Cyrillic alphabet (p.335) there's more information to be gleaned from the Bulgarian-made *Pâtna Karta* ("road map"), available from bookstalls once in the country. The *Bulgarian Tourist Union* produces maps covering principal **mountainous areas** – notably the Rila, Pirin, Rhodope and Vitosha ranges – which are sporadically available in bookshops. Although good for general touring, they're not detailed enough to be of much help to serious walkers. **Town plans** are conspicuous by their absence. Maps of Sofia and Plovdiv are widely available in the respective cities (there's also a good *Falk* plan of Sofia available outside Bulgaria), but plans of Varna, Ruse, Veliko Târnovo and other towns haven't been reprinted for years; remaining stocks of them may turn up in hotels hundreds of kilometres away, but rarely in the places themselves. If you do succeed in finding maps, bear in mind that streets named after illustrious Communists may well have changed since the map was printed.

If you want maps of the Balkans before you go, *Stanfords*, 12–14 Long Acre, London WC2 (☎071/836 1321), have the best selection.

GETTING AROUND

Bulgaria is covered by a comprehensive rail and bus network, and even the remotest villages are accessible, if only by a single daily minibus. Public transport is very cheap but can also be time consuming. Both trains and buses are notoriously slow, a failing compounded by the demands of Bulgaria's mountainous terrain – journeys on a north-south axis are particularly prone to roundabout routes and numerous changes. Bear in mind also that public transport timetables are designed to fit in with the working day. There may be plenty of departures in the early morning, then nothing for several hours until mid-afternoon, often leaving you stranded waiting for a connection in between.

Both rail and bus stations should have prominently displayed **timetables** (расписание, *raspisanie*), with arrivals listed on one side, departures on the other. "Departures" can be rendered as Тръгва, *trâgva* (abbreviated to Тр) or Заминаване, *zaminavane*; and "Arrivals" as Пристига, *pristiga* (Пр) or Пристигане, *pristigane*. It's rare to see timetables in anything but Cyrillic, so to make things easier we've included a list of town names in that script at the end of each chapter.

TRAINS

Bulgarian State Railways (БДЖ – *BDZh*) can get you to most towns mentioned in this book, although trains are very slow by Western standards and delays are common on the longer routes. Express **services** (*Ekspresen vlak*) are restricted to trunk routes, but on everything except the humblest branch lines you'll find so-called Rapid (*bârz vlak*) trains. Use these rather than the snail-like *pâtnicheski* services unless

you're planning to alight at some particularly insignificant halt. On timetables, the three types of services are indicated by the abbreviations Е, Б and П; and express services are usually lettered in red.

Long-distance/overnight trains have a wagon with reasonably priced **couchettes** (*kushet*) and/ or **sleepers** (*spalen vagon*). For these, and on all expresses and many rapids, you need a seat **reservation** (*zapazeno myasto*).

Commonly, a single sign halfway down the platform is all that identifies a **station** (*gara*). You won't see this until the train starts up if you're sitting at the back, so the wise traveller will sit up front. Most stations have a **left-luggage office** (*garderob*); in the large ones it may be necessary to complete a form before stowing your gear. Charges should come to no more than a few pence.

TICKETS

Tickets (*bileti*) can be bought at the station just before travel (in out-of-the-way places, a ticket window will only open a few minutes before the train is due), although in many large towns, it's usually easier to obtain tickets and reservations from **railway bookings offices** (*BDZh*) or **comprehensive transport services bureaux** (*Tsentâr za kompleksno transportno obsluzhvane na naselenieto*, or *TsKTON*, ЦКТОН, sometimes referred to as simply *kompleksni transportni uslugi*) rather than the station; and it is wise – if not always essential – to book a day in advance.

INTERNATIONAL TICKETS

Advance bookings are required for **international tickets**, which are handled by a separate organization, the *Rila Agency*. (Addresses of their offices are detailed in the text). Bulgaria overcharges for all international services – the fare from Sofia to Budapest is twice what the Hungarians charge for a ticket from Budapest to Sofia – so it's always worth buying a return ticket outside Bulgaria if you're planning to travel back along the same route. The Bulgarians make most money from those travellers **heading on to Turkey**, with *Rila* charging around £60 for a ticket on the *Istanbul Express*. The Bulgarians discourage the hoary dodge of paying to ride only

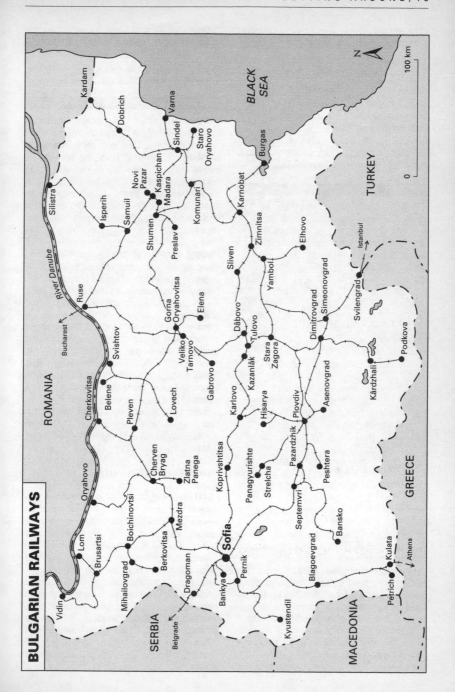

BULGARIAN RAILWAYS

100 km

0

N

BLACK SEA

TURKEY

ROMANIA

GREECE

SERBIA

MACEDONIA

River Danube

Kardam
Dobrich
Varna
Sindel
Staro Oryahovo
Burgas
Silistra
Isperih
Samuil
Novi Pazar
Kaspichan
Madara
Komunari
Karnobat
Shumen
Preslav
Zimnitsa
Elhovo
Istanbul
Sliven
Yambol
Simeonovgrad
Svilengrad
Ruse
Gorna Oryahovitsa
Elena
Dăbovo
Dimitrovgrad
Podkova
Bucharest
Swishtov
Veliko Tarnovo
Tulovo
Stara Zagora
Kărdzhali
Belene
Gabrovo
Kazanlăk
Pleven
Lovech
Karlovo
Hisarya
Plovdiv
Asenovgrad
Cherkovitsa
Oryahovo
Cherven Bryag
Zlatna Panega
Koprivshtitsa
Panagyurishte
Pazardzhik
Peshtera
Lom
Strelcha
Septemvri
Bansko
Vidin
Brusartsi
Boichinovtsi
Mezdra
Berkovitsa
Dragoman
Bankya
Sofia
Pernik
Blagoevgrad
Kulata
Mihailovgrad
Kyustendil
Petrich
Belgrade
Athens

as far as the border by refusing to sell tickets to Svilengrad (although guards may be bribable). Once the train is inside Turkey, buying a ticket to Istanbul (for the equivalent of £5) is quite straightforward.

Most railway stations sell a paperback national **timetable** (пътеводител, *pâtevoditel*), an essential purchase if you're travelling a great deal. International services are printed in the Roman alphabet. Trains running on a particular day only are indicated by a numeral in a circle: for example, 1 = Monday, 2 = Tuesday, etc.

BY BUS

Practically everywhere is accessible **by bus** (*avtobus* or, more colloquially, *reis*), though in remoter areas there may only be two or three services a day. Each town of any size will have a bus station (*avtogara*) from which services radiate outwards to the outlying villages. There are also regular inter-city services on routes ill-served by rail. **Tickets** are sold at the *avtogara* up until five minutes before departure, although it's advisable to buy them an hour or two in advance if travelling on a route serving major towns – especially during summer or at weekends. Some towns contain a comprehensive transport service bureau (*kompleksni transportni uslugi*, see p.12) where bus tickets can be bought up to seven days in advance. Addresses of these appear in the text. If hoping to catch a bus which originates elsewhere, tickets are only sold when the bus arrives, in which case people queue outside the shuttered ticket hatch. *Tova li e gisheto za bileti za...?* means "Is this where I get tickets to...?" (remember that a shaken head means "yes" and a nod "no"). Almost invariably, more tickets are sold than there are seats, so either arrive early or be prepared to stand. On **rural routes**, tickets are often sold by the driver rather than at the terminal. If you're aiming for a campsite or monastery along a bus route, ask the driver for the *spirkata za kâmping* (or *manastir*), or call *Spri!* ("Stop!") as it hoves into sight.

On **urban transport** there's a flat fare (seldom more than 5 pence) on all routes, so it's sensible to buy a bunch of 10 tickets (from street kiosks next to tram and bus stops) whenever you arrive somewhere, which must then be punched on board the bus. Fare-dodgers risk a spot-fine. Routes are usually displayed at each bus stop (*spirka*) together with the times of the first and last services. Some municipal authorities have already permitted the introduction of private operators, and on some routes you'll encounter a plethora of differently coloured buses and mini-buses – the drivers of which take cash rather than pre-purchased tickets.

DRIVING AND HITCHING

A current UK or other foreign **driving licence** is acceptable in Bulgaria (though not in most neighbouring countries), but third-party **insurance** plus a "Green" or "Blue" card – the latter can be bought at the frontier – are obligatory. Entering Bulgaria, your vehicle will be registered with a special **"visa tag"** which must be presented on leaving the country – a rule intended to prevent foreigners from flogging their cars when in the country.

PETROL, MAPS AND SIGNS

The days are over when Bulgaria could rely on cheap oil supplies from the Soviet Union, and the country is now suffering a **petrol** shortage. Some petrol stations (*benzinostantsiya*) have closed down due to inadequate deliveries; others are prone to long queues. You'll find filling stations on the main roads leaving most towns and spaced 30–40km apart along the highways, as shown on the Cyrillic-script **motoring maps** (*Pâtna Karta*) available from bookshops. Names signposted along the highways appear in both alphabets, and although the system of transliteration is slightly different from the one used in this book, they're recognizably similar. Other **signs** are basically identical to those employed in the West.

ROADS AND SPEED LIMITS

Roads are inconsistently numbered (some highways carry two or three designations), but as a general rule trunk routes – marked in red on maps – are reasonably surfaced, whereas minor roads – indicated in yellow – are gravelly, bumpy or both. **Traffic** is pretty light everywhere and drives on the right; at crossroads, vehicles approaching from that direction have right of way. Right turns and moving on are forbidden when the traffic light is red. In urban areas buses have the right of way and parking is restricted to specified spots. **Speed limits** in built-up areas (60 kph), on the open road (80 kph) and highways (120 kph) are reduced to 50 kph, 70 kph or 100 kph for minibuses or cars with caravans or trailers.

STREET NAMES

Any visitor to Bulgaria in the near future is bound to experience at least some confusion over **street names**. During the Communist period, towns vied with each other to name their principal thoroughfares or main squares after revolutionary personalities or events. Thus there's hardly a settlement in the country which didn't have at least something named after the unholy trinity of **V.I. Lenin**, **Georgi Dimitrov** (first leader of the postwar socialist state), and **Vasil Kolarov** (Dimitrov's loyal disciple); not to mention the key date in Bulgarian Communist history **9 septemvri** (the day on which the Monarchy was toppled in 1944).

Since November 1989, when the Bulgarian Communists were finally forced to proceed with democratic reforms, the removal of ideologically loaded street names obviously became an issue. So far, however, progress in changing them has been inconsistent. In a few cases, both the street name and the appropriate street sign have been changed; in others, the name has been changed but the old signs have remained; while in many cases a decision is still pending. We've included new names in the guide where possible, but be on the lookout for further changes. Many streets which were named after Georgi Dimitrov at the time that this book was researched may carry a new name by the time you visit.

Generally speaking, anything named after Lenin has already disappeared, but the fates of many other names from the Communist period are currently in the hands of the local councils. Chances are that the towns and villages run by the Bulgarian Socialist Party (ie the ex-Communists) will be less likely to do away with street names pertaining to left-wing heroes than those in the hands of their adversaries.

ACCIDENTS AND FINES

Mountainous Bulgaria has lots of hairpin bends, and in rural areas it's important to watch out for donkeys, farm animals and carts. Motorists are legally obliged to report **accidents** and, in case of injury, render assistance where appropriate while awaiting the Militia. **Spot-fines** for trival offences are common practice, and the police have been known to abuse this by demanding payment in dollars and pocketing the cash. Requests for a receipt might put a stop to this – or make things worse. In the event of arrest, insist on being allowed to contact your embassy (see Sofia "Listings" for addresses). Although the Bulgarian government is currently considering a change in the law, **drinking and driving** is for the time being absolutely prohibited, and offenders are punished with a heavy fine or imprisonment.

CAR HIRE

Car hire can be arranged through *Balkantourist*, who act as agents for *Hertz*, or another nation-wide agency *Interbalkan*, who have a similar arrangement with *Europcar*. Expect to pay £15 per day for a cronky Lada and upwards of £20 for a Western car, plus 15–30 pence per kilometre. Insurance and driving licence regulations are as described opposite.

HITCHING

Hitching is fair to good in most parts of Bulgaria, and it's unusual to have any problems with the police. Bulgarians themselves often resort to thumbing a lift when left stranded by the deficiencies of a local bus service, and drivers are on the whole eager to help travellers reach somewhere inaccessible or badly served by public transport. Drivers may be less accommodating on busier routes, when it's generally assumed that trains or buses are cheap enough for you not to bother hitching. Women travelling alone should still exercise the usual caution about which lifts to accept.

It's advisable to carry a sign in Cyrillic if you're heading for somewhere distant, while a clue to drivers' movements may be gained from their number plates, the first letter(s) of which indicate their home town (П = Plovdiv; C = Sofia; Бл = Blagoevgrad, etc).

INTERNATIONAL CAR HIRE RESERVATIONS

Avis ☎081/848 8733
Budget ☎0800/181 181
Europcar 081/950 5050
Hertz ☎081/679 1799

BY BOAT

Between May and September, passenger **hydro-foil** services operate along the Black Sea (they used to serve the River Danube as well, but were discontinued in 1992 due to lack of trade – it's worth looking out to see if they've started up again). Sailings may be limited to one or two a day, and tickets are more expensive than either bus or train – although not prohibitively so: a one-way trip between Varna and Burgas costs about £3. Locations of hydrofoil stations are given in the guide where relevant. It's not possible to book hydrofoil tickets in advance, and ticket counters usually only open an hour or two before departure.

BY AIR

Daily **Balkan** **flights** are the quickest way to travel between Sofia and the Danubian and Black Sea ports, and given the length of the railway journey a flight to Varna or Burgas is worth considering. Fares from Sofia to Varna work out at about £40 one way for non-Bulgarians, payment in hard currency only. Book the day before (since most flights leave around 7–8am) if not two or three days in advance for services to the coast.

FINDING A PLACE TO STAY

All accommodation in Bulgaria is up to three times more expensive for foreign guests than it is for the natives, but costs are still cheap by west European standards. Most towns can be relied upon to have at least one reasonably comfortable 2-star hotel charging £6–10 per person; while private rooms, where available, give even better value. Although prices are usually quoted in dollars, you can nowadays pay in leva. Very occasionally, a hotel or accommodation bureau will request payment in hard currency and will only relent if you show them an exchange receipt proving that you've acquired your leva legally. They aren't supposed to do this any more, and you're perfectly entitled to kick up a fuss if they try it.

HOTELS

Under the Communist regime, westerners were restricted to **hotels** run by the state-owned chains *Balkantourist* and *Interhoteli*. Cheaper establishments frequented by Bulgarians were off limits, although they would often claim to be full up rather than admit this. These days, although you may be turned away by cheaper establishments – often because the facilities are so bad that they can't believe you'd want to stay there – you can, in theory, stay where you wish.

Most of Bulgaria's hotel accommodation nevertheless boils down to the establishments previously under the aegis of *Balkantourist* and *Interhoteli*. They're predominantly clean, modern, high-rise affairs save for those at the bottom end of the price scale, which often occupy older (and grimier) buildings. They're seldom difficult to find – it seems to have been an axiom of postwar urban planning to place a large 2- or 3-star hotel on each town's main square; if you head for the centre it will never be very far away – and in most cases (save Sofia, Plovdiv and the coast) it's seldom neccessary to book a room in advance. Hotels usually charge a standard rate per person, regardless of whether you occupy a single or double room. Most 1-, 2-, and even some 3-star hotels refuse to accept credit cards.

PRICES

Most ex-*Balkantourist* hotels are now financially independent, and their attempts to survive in free-market conditions may mean that **prices and**

standards will be a little unpredictable for some time to come. For the time being, however, hotels are graded according to a fairly rigid system of star ratings, from 1 star up to 5. Generally speaking, 1-star hotels may have a sink in the room, but toilet facilities and showers are in the hallway; 2-star establishments have en-suite bathrooms; and anything above this is getting quite luxurious. Breakfast is usually included in the price in 3-star hotels and above, but is rare elsewhere. Prices can vary widely within each category, although upper limits to each band are set by the national Committee for Tourism; thus you're unlikely to come across a 2-star hotel which costs more than £15 a head outside Sofia and Plovdiv, and most of them are significantly cheaper than that.

Most of Bulgaria's purpose-built **coastal resorts** have now become independent, self-administering companies which fix their own prices. Each resort will have a central accommodation office responsible for handling bookings in all of the resort's hotels (the locations of these are described in the text), although it's worth remembering that the independent traveller arriving on spec will pay much more for a room here than those who opt for an all-in package tour.

A small number of **privately owned hotels** are beginning to appear on the coast and in the busier inland spots, often offering friendly bed-and-breakfast style accommodation at about the same price as a regular 2-star hotel. With the reorganization of Bulgaria's tourist industry, however, it can be difficult to get information about these places other than from roadside advertisements. **Motels** along the main highways cost roughly the same as 2-star hotels.

OTHER OPTIONS

Bulgaria has a whole range of **other accommodation facilities** which currently face an uncertain future, but which may in time be made available to foreign tourists. *Orbita*, the state-run

agency for youth tourism, used to run a chain of **"youth hotels"** which traditionally looked after the large number of young travellers who came to Bulgaria from fellow socialist countries. Now that much of this inter-Communist tourism has dried up, *Orbita* have lost their *raison d'être*, though it seems that most of their facilities will be refurbished and transformed into "normal" hotels.

More uncertain is the future of the many *pochivni stantsii*, or **rest homes**, mostly to be found on the Black Sea and in inland spa resorts, owned by trade unions and offering cheap holidays to their members. Many of these were no more than frugal holiday camps, but those establishments catering for the upper managerial echelons of socialist society could be quite sumptuous. Some are already opening their doors to foreign travellers, and Bulgaria's spa resorts in particular may soon be blessed with a wide choice of affordable, good-quality accommodation.

The quality of hotel accommodation often depends on the **time of year** at which you travel. In 1- and 2-star hotels, hot water may only be available in the morning and evening. This is rarely a problem at the height of summer, but can be a bit tiresome in winter, when rooms in many 1-, 2-, and even 3-star establishments can be very poorly heated. If travelling at this time of year, it's a good idea to opt for private rooms (see below) if available, where the provision of basic comforts can be taken for granted.

PRIVATE ROOMS

Private rooms (*chastni kvartiri*) are available in Sofia, Plovdiv, Ruse, Varna and a number of other specific tourist destinations, especially on the coast. They're bookable through the local tourist offices; accommodation bureaux (квартирно бюро, *kvartirno byuro*); and on the coast, a small but growing number of private or cooperative firms which specialize in renting out rooms:

addresses are given in the guide. In the smaller coastal towns, some bureaux are closed from early September onwards, after which it shouldn't be too difficult to find a room unofficially, simply by asking around – although this will mean forgoing a date stamp on your *carte statistique* (see p.7). **Costs** for double rooms range from about £2–3 in smaller towns, up to about £5 in Sofia and Plovdiv. As single rooms are quite rare, sole travellers should expect to pay the full fee. Prices are up to 30 percent cheaper out of season.

The size and quality of private rooms vary enormously (it's rarely possible to inspect the place first), but they are always clean. Spacious rooms in nice old houses seem to be the rule in smaller resorts such as Sozopol and Nesebâr on the coast, and Koprivshtitsa inland; while in the cities private rooms are almost invariably situated in apartment blocks.

If you stay in someone's home as a guest, you're technically required to **register with the police** within 24 hours, but few hosts will bother taking these formalities seriously.

CAMPSITES, HOSTELS AND MOUNTAIN CHALETS

Most towns of interest have a **campsite**, (*Kâmping*) on the outskirts, the majority of which have two-person **chalets** (£1–2 per night).

Beware that many campsites, especially on the coast, close down in early ot mid-September, as soon as the summer rush has slackened. **Camping rough** is illegal and punishable with a fine.

Two further types of accommodation are mainly found in the mountains or small towns. Dirt-cheap, very basic **hostels** (Туристическа спалня, *Turisticheska spalnya*) run by the Bulgarian Tourist Union lurk in the backstreets of many provincial towns, usually offering a bunk in a large, 20-bed dormitory. In highland areas favoured by hikers there are scores of mountain **chalets** (хижи, or *hizhi*), some primitive, others comfy hotels in all but name. Both hostels and chalets tend to fill up quickly with Bulgarian walking enthusiasts and school parties. The **Pirin Travel Agency** in Sofia (bul. Stamboliiski 30; ☎870 687) used to handle bookings for mountain *hizhi*, and are the best source of information.

The larger of Bulgaria's **monasteries** traditionally accommodate guests in their cells, but closed their doors to Westerners in the early 1980s. Nowadays it's up to the individual monastery to decide who they will or won't admit, and many have yet to formulate a clear policy on the subject. It's worth enquiring about rooms at heavily touristed monasteries such as Rila, Troyan, Bachkovo and Rozhen – alternative accommodation is nearby should you be turned away.

EATING AND DRINKING

Bulgaria is stuffed full of vegetable plots and orchards ("Bulgar" used to be a synonym for

"market gardener" in several Balkan countries), and fresh fruit and vegetables are half the secret of Bulgarian food. However, 45 years of collectivized agriculture and catering have conspired to impose a certain conformity on Bulgarian restaurants, and the high quality and range of cooking you would be likely to experience as a guest in a Bulgarian home is rarely reflected in the country's eating establishments. Grilled meat dishes everywhere predominate, and vegetarians will be frustrated by the frequent lack of animal-free alternatives. Now that privatization is under way more variety can be expected, and the impact of market economics is already evident in the increasing variety of street food available.

The average Bulgarian supermarket (*magazin na samoobsluzhvane*) or food shop (*hranitelni stoki*) receives irregular supplies of fresh produce, and shelves tend to be lined with jars of fruit conserves, packets of dry biscuits, and little else. However, most towns or villages will have an outdoor **market**, or *pazar*, where smallholding peasants from the outlying districts sell whatever fruit and vegetables are currently in season. Many towns also have old-style, municipally run, **indoor markets** (*hali*), though these are nowadays sad, half-abandoned affairs with little to offer. Most things of value are sold on the streets, and ad-hoc street stalls are the best place to look for foreign produce imported by a growing breed of entrepreneurs: bananas, coffee and chocolate predominate. Private enterprise is yet to make much of an impact on **bakeries**, however: for the time being shops selling bread (*hlyab*) stand empty for much of the day, until an arbitrarily timed delivery attracts lengthy queues of shoppers.

BREAKFASTS, SNACKS AND STREET FOOD

Traditionally, food was eaten in the fields or pastures, or consumed on returning home – which meant subsisting on bread, cheese, vegetables and fruit throughout the day until an evening meal of stew or grilled meat. Nowadays, people eat rather less frugally, but the habit of picking up a bite to eat in the morning and continuing to nibble at snacks throughout the day still remains.

BREAKFAST

Many restaurants (see p.20), especially self-service ones, open for **breakfast**, although the most popular and convenient places to pick up snack food are the street stalls and small kiosks which tend to congregate around main thoroughfares, railway and bus stations.

Pastries, cakes and bread-based snacks are also available throughout the day in a *sladkarnitsa*, or patisserie, where they are often washed down with one of two traditional breakfast drinks: yoghurt (*kiselo mlyako*); or *boza*, a browny-coloured millet drink. In general, the best advice is to keep an eye out for signs advertising закуски, *zakuski*, a generic term meaning either breakfast or any other daytime snack.

SNACKS

The most common type of Bulgarian snack food is *banitsa* (often referred to by its diminutive form, *banichka*, or known in some areas as *byurek*), a flaky pastry filled with cheese or, on occasion, meat. At its best, the *banitsa* is a delicious light snack, although it occasionally gets a bit stodgy by the time it reaches the streets. *Mlechna banitsa* (literally "milk banitsa") is a richer, sweeter version made using eggs and dusted off with icing sugar.

Equally popular is the *kifla*, a small bread roll usually made from slightly sweetened dough and with a vein of marmalade running through the middle, although you will probably encounter more savoury variants, filled either *sâs sirene*, with cheese; or *s krenvirsh*, a small hot-dog-type sausage. Similar is the *sirenka*, a small bread bun with a cheese filling.

Other favourites among street vendors are *ponichki*, deep-fried lumps of dough – not unlike doughnuts; *palachinki* or pancakes, usually stuffed with cheese; and *pici* (pizzas), which are generally pretty basic cheese and tomato combinations.

Street stands also sell *kebapcheta*, little wads of grilled mincemeat (traditionally a combination of lamb, pork and veal, although the precise mix will depend on what's available) served with a hunk of bread; or variations on the theme such as *kyufte*, with the same ingredients in meatball form. The grill repertoire occasionally includes *nadenitsa*, a spicy sausage, while in autumn and winter, street vendors emerge peddling corn on the cob (*tsarevitsa*).

SANDWICHES

Sandvichi, open sandwiches (usually toasted) are sold at many kiosks, cafés and bars. Typical toppings are *kashkaval*, a hard, cheddar-like cheese; *salam*, a salami-like slice of pinkish meat; *kayma*, a mincemeat paste; *shunka*, ham; or *kombiniran*, a mixture of two or more of the above. Bulgarian *hamburgeri* tend to be the same as *sandvichi*, but encased in a bread bun – only on coastal resorts do they resemble their Western namesake.

Incorrigible snack-munchers will be able to find solace in two further regulars on the street food scene: *fâstâtsi*, or roast nuts; and *semki*, sunflower seeds sold everywhere in little paper cones.

RESTAURANTS AND MAIN MEALS

Although Bulgarian restaurants (ресторант, *restorant*) vary widely in terms of decor and service, the range of food on offer can be pretty limited wherever you eat. Although you'll encounter printed menus in tourist restaurants and on the coast, in most cases the choice of available dishes is so meagre that the waiter will rattle through a brief list of what's on offer that evening. Higher prices in topnotch restaurants don't necessarily imply a wider choice – usually merely a higher quality of meat. Restaurants are usually open between about 11.30am and 3pm for lunch, and 6pm and 11pm for dinner. It's very difficult to get food after 11pm outside big city hotels or package resorts, and in some provincial towns you'll be lucky to find anywhere open after 10pm.

Restaurants in big **hotels** are often the best, if often rather characterless. In Sofia and Plovdiv these can often be overpriced, international affairs; while in provincial centres they often provide a focus for the social life of the local elite. A **han** (жан) or **hanche** (жанче) – literally an "inn" – is usually a recently-built folk-style restaurant, though a few are ensconced within sumptuously appointed mansions dating back to the nineteenth century. Usually popular with both tourists and locals, the cooking in these establishments should be a cut above that of most ordinary restaurants. **Mehanas** (механа) are also usually quite folksy, although they tend to be less predictable: although their grills and salads can be excellent, some are just places to drink wine or spirits. The same applies to **skara-bira joints** (скара-бира) a lower form of culinary life serving little more than beer and kebabs – which are, in rural areas at least, a males-only preserve. In towns, you'll also find **self-service** restaurants (*ekspres-restorant*): invariably cheap, but often with reason.

With the exception of deluxe hotel restaurants in the capital, none of these should **cost** the earth, and providing you avoid imported drinks, the bill should be very modest indeed: in most cases, a three-course meal for two, with a bottle of wine, will rarely exceed £5, except in Sofia, Plovdiv and the coastal resorts.

WHAT TO EAT

Salads in Bulgaria are usually eaten as a starter, or as the accompaniment to a stiff aperitif, rather like *meze* in Turkey. Most common are those formed from the following vegetables, whether singly or in combination: cabbage (*zele*), tomatoes (*domati*), cucumber (*krastavitsi*) and peppers (*piperki* or *chushki*). *Salata shopska* is a mixture of the whole lot topped with a layer of crumbled white cheese. There are various kinds of *mlechna salata*, or yoghurt-based salad, of which the most common are *snezhanka* (pickled cucumbers covered in yoghurt) and *tarator* (a cold cucumber soup-cum-salad). Another oft-encountered starter is *lukanka*, a spicy salami-like sausage.

Mainstay of any Bulgarian restaurant menu are the **grilled meats**, of which *kebapcheta* and *kyofte* (see "Snacks", p.19) are the most common. More substantial are chops (*pârzhola* or *kotlet*), or fillets (*file*), invariably *teleshko* (veal) or *svinsko* (pork). In the grander restaurants the main course will be accompanied by potatoes (*kartofi*) and a couple of vegetables, as well as bread: sometimes a *pitka* or small bread bun, or more rarely a *simitla*, a glazed bun made from chickpea flour. Lower down the scale, you may just get chips (*pârzheni kartofi*) and a couple of slices of a stale loaf.

Touristy folk-style restaurants are the likeliest places to find **traditional Bulgarian dishes** baked and served in earthenware pots. The best known is *gyuvech* (which literally means "earthenware dish"), a rich stew comprising peppers, aubergines, and beans, to which are added either meat or meat stock. *Kavarma*, a spicy meat stew (often pork), is prepared in a similar fashion. Two other traditional recipes which you may come across if you're lucky are *sarmi*, cabbage leaves stuffed with rice and mincemeat; and *imam bayaldi*, aubergine stuffed with all manner of vegetables, meat and herbs – a Turkish dish, whose name translates as "the priest burst".

Finally, along the coast and around the highland lakes and reservoirs there's **fish** (*riba*) – most often fried or grilled, but sometimes in a soup or stew.

VEGETARIAN OPTIONS

Traditional Bulgarian cuisine excels in vegetable dishes; the snag is trying to find a place which serves them. Vegetarian restaurants (вегетариански ресторант, *vegetarianski restorant*) used to exist in most major towns, but began to lose their appeal in the mid-1980s as supplies of agricultural produce from the countryside deteriorated. With privatization in the offing, they may be refurbished and given a new lease of life, or simply turned into something else.

Standard restaurant menus usually include omelettes (*omlet*), either with cheese or mushroom fillings; along with *kashkaval pane*, hard cheese fried in breadcrumbs or batter; and *pâleni chushki*, peppers stuffed with cheese. Any of these would suffice as a main meal; otherwise you're limited to choosing from vegetable side dishes, many of which won't be available in most restaurants. You may with luck encounter fried courgettes (*pârzheni tikvichki*) and peppers (*pârzheni chushki*), purée of aubergines (*kyopolu*) or potatoes (*pyure ot kartofi*), eggs fried on spinach (*pârzheni yaitsa s pyure ot spanak*) or scrambled with peppers and tomatoes into aptly named *mish-mash*. Also popular is *gyuvech-zarzavat*, the herbivorous version of a quintessentially Bulgarian dish, consisting of vegetables baked in an earthenware pot.

SWEETS

Cakes and pastries are sold throughout the day in a **patisserie** or s*ladkarnitsa* (сладкарница), also a popular venue for daytime drinking. Many of Bulgaria's sweet dishes were originally imported from the Middle East by the Turks – the syrupy *baklava* (referred to in some establishments as a *triguna*), the nut-filled *revane*, and the gooey rich *kadaif* being the most common. Turkish Delight (*lokum*) and *halva* are also firm favourites. Betraying a more central European ancestry are the variety of cakes (*torta*) on offer; with buttercream (*maselna*), fruit (*frukti*) or chocolate (*shokoladova*) filling. *Garash*, a layered chocolate cake, is the most widely available. Ice cream – *sladoled* – is sold everywhere on the streets in summer.

DRINKING

The advent of private enterprise in Bulgaria has led to a rapid increase in the number of **drinking venues**. Most town centres now have a healthy sprinkling of kiosks serving coffee, soft drinks and basic snack food, usually with chairs and tables scattered across the adjoining pavement. A few of them serve beer, vodka, and other strong drinks, and stay open well after nightfall, but for the most part these kiosks are a daytime, fair-weather phenomenon. A more traditional venue is the *sladkarnitsa*, a Bulgarian version of the central European café. Again, a *sladkarnitsa* rarely serves alcohol, and most are closed by 8pm.

Evening drinking tends to take place in restaurants (where it's quite common for tables to be monopolized by drinkers rather than diners), or in the growing number of privately owned bars (normally operating under the generic title of кафе-аперитиф or *kafe-aperitif*), some of which are no more than a converted garage or basement room. Here you can get the full range of domestic alcoholic and non-alcoholic drinks, as well as imported spirits and canned beers.

Coffee (кафе, *kafe*) almost invariably comes in the form of strong, sweet *espresso* (specify *bez zahar* if you prefer it without sugar), although you'll sometimes encounter *kapuchino*, *nes* (Nescafé, or a similar instant coffee), or *tursko* (Turkish coffee). To balance the strong taste of the coffee, it's often drunk alongside a glass of juice (*sok*), usually a pretty artificial concoction such as *tropik*, a cocktail of citrus fruits; or the sickly green *kivi* (kiwi). Delicious natural fruit juices (*nektar*, or *fruktovi sok*) are sold bottled in supermarkets and food shops, but rarely appear in cafés or bars. Other *bezalkoholni* (non-alcoholic) choices include *gazirana voda* (gaseous mineral water), or international beverages such as Coca Cola or Pepsi. Imported tea bags from China are usually available in the shops, but ask for **tea** (*chay*) in a *sladkarnitsa* and you're more likely to receive some herbal concoction.

WINE

From having an insular **wine** industry before World War II, Bulgaria has muscled its way into the forefront of the world's export market, specializing in robust red wines of basic but solid quality. Tried and tested grapes like Cabernet Sauvignon and Merlot have been planted in different regions (such as Pomorie, Haskovo, Asenovgrad or Suhindol), under whose name they're sold with phenomenal success abroad. Inside Bulgaria there's a greater variety and more differentiation between the various blended wines, all of which cost less than £1 a bottle in supermarkets and mehanas.

Amongst the **reds** are full-bodied *Cabernet*; heavier, mellower *Melnik* and *Gâmza*; rich, dark *Mavrud*; and the smooth, strawberry-flavoured *Haskovski Merlot*. Sweet *Pamid*, first grown by the Thracians and verging on rosé, is blended with Mavrud to produce *Trakiya*, or with Melnik wine to make *Pirin*, while *Madara* is obtained from concentrated Gâmza and Dimyat grapes (a similar mix is used for the more acidic *Târnovo*).

Asenovgradski Mavrud and the red Muscatel Slavyanska are both dessert wines.

The sweeter **whites** are preferable to Dimyat unless you like your wine very dry; Karlovski Misket (Muscatel) and Tamyanka are widely available, but the golden-coloured Evksinograd is much harder to find.

SPIRITS

Native **spirits** are highly potent and cost very little; they are drunk diluted with water in the case of mastika (like ouzo in Greece or raki in Turkey), or downed in one, Balkan-style, in the form of rakiya, or brandy. Slivova rakiya is made from plums, and grozdova from grapes – Pliska cognac is a particularly fine example of the latter. Vodka is also widely drunk, although with the collapse of trade between former Communist lands, you're now more likely to find domestic

brands like Tsarevets rather than the Soviet variety. Imported whisky is widely available, bottles of which are sold openly by street traders at duty-free prices. Obscure brands such as "Green Park" and "Wells" are much in evidence.

BEER

Bulgarian **beer** (bira) is pretty unexciting, unless you chance upon one of the few places where it's served from a cask. Among the bottled brands, Zagorka, from Stara Zagora, is considered by natives to be the best, although the smoother Haskovo, from the town of the same name (an export version is sold under the name of Astica), will appeal more to west European tastes. German, Austrian, and even Turkish beers are increasingly common along the coast and in the more expensive restaurants inland, as well as in small private food stores and on the streets.

BULGARIAN FOOD AND DRINK TERMS

Basics

Imate li...?	Do you have...?	Mlyako	milk
Molya, donesete mi/ni...	Please bring me/us....	Kifli	rolls
Az sâm vegetarianets/ vegetarianka	I am a vegetarian	Kiselo Mlyako	yoghurt
		Piper	pepper
Imate li neshto bez meso?	Do you have anything without meat ?	Sol	salt
		Zahar	sugar
Listata	the menu	dve biri	two beers
Hlyab	bread	Nazdrave!	Cheers!
Maslo	butter	Smetkata, molya	The bill, please
Med	honey	Yaitse	egg

Appetizers, Soups (supi) and Salads (salati)

Chorba	broth, thick soup	Postna supa	vegetable soup
Kyopolu	aubergine, pepper and tomato salad	Salata shopska	Shoppe salad, topped with grated cheese
Lyutenitsa	piquant sauce of red peppers and herbs	Supa s meso	consommé
		Tarator	yoghurt and cucumber soup

Meat (meso)

Ezik	tongue	Mozâk	brains
Gyuvech	stir-fried veg, baked with meat	Musaka	moussaka
		Pârzhola	grilled cutlet
Imam Bayaldi	stuffed aubergines (lit. "the Imam burst")	Pile	chicken
		Salam	salami
Kebapche	shish kebab	Shishcheta	lamb or pork shish
Kebapcheta	grilled, spicy sausage-shaped meatballs		kebabs
		Shkembe chorba	tripe soup
Kyufteta	meatballs	Slanina	bacon
		Svinsko (s kiselo zele)	pork (and sauerkraut)

Terms

cheverme	barbecue	*pecheno*	roast
divech	game	*ptitsi*	poultry
na skara	grilled	*zadusheno*	braised
pârzheni	fried		

Fish (*riba*)

Byala riba	pike perch	*Palamud*	tuna
Chiga	sterlet	*Pâstârva*	trout
Esetra	sturgeon	*Popche*	bullhead
Haiver	roe	*Skumriya*	mackerel
Kalkan	turbot	*Som*	sheatfish
Kefal	grey mullet	*Sharan*	carp
Midi	mussels		

Vegetables (*zelenchutsi*)

Chesân	garlic	*Morkovi*	carrots
Chushki/piperki	peppers	*Pârzheni kartofi*	chips
Domati	tomatoes	*Praz*	leeks
Grah	peas	*(Presen) luk*	(spring) onions
Gâbi	mushrooms	*Sini domati*	aubergines
Karfiol	cauliflower	*Spanak*	spinach
Kartofi	potatoes	*Tikvichki*	courgettes
Krastavitsa	cucumber	*Zelen fasul*	runner beans

Fruit (*plodove*) and cheese (*sirene*)

Chereshi	cherries	*Slivi*	plums
Dinya	watermelon	*Vishni*	morello cherries
Grozde	grapes	*Yabâlki*	apples
Kaisii	apricots	*Yagodi*	strawberries
Krushi	pears	*Sirene*	salty, feta-type cheese
Limon	lemon	*Pusheno sirene*	smoked cheese
Malini	raspberries	*Kashkaval*	hard, Edam-type
Praskovi	peaches		cheese

COMMUNICATIONS: POST, PHONES AND MEDIA

POST OFFICES

Most **post offices** (Поща, *poshta*) are open from 8.30am to 5.30pm Monday to Saturday, although those in the larger towns tend to be open an extra thirty minutes or so either side. It's not always easy to identify the right counter (*gishe*) to queue up at; look for signs advertising the sale of *marki* (stamps) or the despatch of *pisma* (letters) and *koleti* (parcels). Stamps are best bought at the post office, although envelopes (*plikove*) are sold at street kiosks. **Mail** can take 10–14 days to reach the UK and three weeks to the US; or less than half that time if you send it *bârza* (express) or *vâzdushna* (airmail). It's reasonably cheap to send **parcels** home from Bulgaria, although items have to be brought into the post office and a customs declaration filled out before being wrapped up on the premises (only books and magazines are exempt from this procedure).

Poste restante services are available at the major post office of every sizable town. Mail can be claimed by showing your passport (ask *Ima li pisma za mene?*), and letters should be addressed писма до поискване централна поща, followed by the name of the town. However, letters from western Europe generally take around a week to arrive in Bulgaria, and Bulgar postal officers are apt to misfile or return mail to the sender if it's not claimed immediately, so don't hold high hopes for poste restante communications.

PHONES

Bulgaria's **public telephones** are usually just about reliable for local calls (currently requiring a 20-stotinki piece), despite appearances to the contrary. Calls between one town and another seem dogged with problems, and it's much better to head for the telephone (Телефон, *telefon*) section of the local post office, where you are assigned a cabin and pay for your call afterwards. The telephone section is usually open longer than other parts of the post office, often as late as 11pm in the major cities.

This is also the best place from which to attempt **international phone calls** in order to avoid the extortionate surcharges levied by most hotels. In the cities and resorts you might find international call boxes, taking either one- and two-leva coins (now so rare that the call boxes have become almost useless), or a new breed of phonecard (available from the post office). To dial direct, first use the international code and then the STD (area) code, remembering to omit the initial 0.

INTERNATIONAL TELEPHONE CODES
UK ☎0044
EIRE ☎00353
AUSTRALIA ☎0061
NEW ZEALAND ☎0064
USA & CANADA ☎001

THE MEDIA

English-language newspapers and magazines are less widely available than German titles, although you may find recent copies of the *Financial Times* and the *Herald Tribune* on the bigger newsstands in Sofia, Plovdiv and Varna. English tabloids appear regularly at the big package-tourist resorts along the coast.

THE BULGARIAN PRESS
The collapse of censorship after November 1989 and the disappearance of turgid, pro-regime propaganda organs such as the former party newspaper *Rabotnichesko Delo* ("Workers' Deeds") have resulted in a lively domestic media scene. The two principal **daily newspapers** are Дума (*Duma*, "The Word"), organ of the Bulgarian Socialist Party, and Демокрация (*Demokratsiya*, "Democracy"), mouthpiece for the governing Union of Democratic Forces; although serious journalistic content is often undermined by frequent political slanging matches between the two. Refreshingly lacking in party affiliations is the much breezier, tabloid-size 24 Часа (*24 Chasa*, "24 Hours"), although its messianic commitment to popular capitalism places it firmly on the right.

A gaggle of lesser, predominantly weekly, titles have emerged offering a hitherto forbidden diet of celebrity gossip, lurid crime stories, and improbable tales of the paranormal. The most obvious beneficiary of new press freedoms, however, has been soft porn. Widely read weeklies such as *Adam i Eva* (Adam and Eve) and *Az i Ti* (Me and You) look pretty tame by western standards, and publishers claim that they're performing a much-needed educational role, introducing both male and female readers to a sexual revolution taken for granted by westerners since the Sixties. Others, however, disagree: town councils in both Plovdiv and Veliko Târnovo were provoked into banning the open sale of several titles in November 1991 after a series of increasingly explicit front covers.

TV AND RADIO
Bulgaria's two domestic **TV channels** are augmented by two foreign stations picked up here; TV5 Europe, an international French-language channel, and Russian TV. The latter, originally imported to foster Bulgarian–Soviet friendship, was becoming an embarrassment by

the mid-Eighties, when it provided Bulgarians with a window on *glasnost* denied to them by their own government.

Best ways to catch up on news are the **BBC World Service** on short wave (available on the following frequencies, depending on the time of day: Mhz 15.07, 12.09, 9.41, 6.18); and, if you're in Sofia, the **Voice of America**, which broadcasts on VHF – predominantly pop music, but with news in English on the hour.

HOLIDAYS, FESTIVALS AND ENTERTAINMENT

ous church festivals and saint's days, occasions marked by the holding of special services, feasting, or simply by lighting candles next to the icon of the appropriate saint – traditions which are resurfacing after decades of state-inspired indifference.

FESTIVALS

Despite Bulgaria's well-deserved reputation for preserving folk culture, whether music, dance or costume, **festivals** as such are less frequent and less spontaneous than in its Balkan neighbours. State funding for the arts has dropped dramatically over the past three years, and many arts festivals in smaller towns have either disappeared entirely or been postponed indefinitely until private sponsorship can be found.

Nevertheless three events stand out: the great **Koprivshtitsa Folklore Festival**, Bulgaria's largest gathering of traditional musicians and singers, held every five years (next due in 1996; see pp.184–85); the **Burgas International Folk**

With the collapse of the Communist system, several ideological holidays have disappeared from the calendar to be replaced by more traditional festivities, such as Easter (*Velikden*) and Christmas (*Koleda*). There's an increasing awareness too of the numer-

NATIONAL HOLIDAYS

You'll find shops, banks and restaurants closed on major national holidays, although the occasional privately owned café, exchange bureau or provision shop may open up in big cities or resorts.

Jan 1 New Year's Day
March 3 Liberation of Bulgaria
Easter Sunday

Easter Monday
May 1 Labour Day
May 24 Day of Bulgarian Education and Culture

Dec 25 Christmas Day
May 6 St George's Day (*Gergyovden*; the traditional end of spring)

PROMINENT SAINT'S DAYS

May 11 SS Cyril and Methodius
May 21 SS Constantine and Elena
July 20 St Elijah's Day (*Ilinden*)
Sept 8 Birth of the Virgin (*Rozhdestvo na Presveta Bogoroditsa*)

Oct 19 John of Rila (Ivan Rilski)
Oct 26 St Demetrius (*Dimitrovden*)
Nov 8 The Archangels Michael and Gabriel (*Arhangelovden*)
Dec 6 St Nicholas (*Nikulden*)

MUSIC FESTIVALS

Plovdiv
Festival of orchestral music, early January.
International festival of chamber music, mid-June.

Ruse
March Music Days (classical music), last two
weeks in March.

Shumen
Festival of classical music, April.
Festival of piano music, late September.

Sofia
Sofia Music Weeks (classical music and ballet),
late May to late June.
International Jazz Festival, second week in
November.

Varna
Varna Summer (classical music, opera and ballet),
mid-June to mid-July.

Festival held annually in the second half of
August; and **Kazanlâk's Festival of the Roses**
in early June (see p.192). Slightly more frivolous is
the internationally renowned **Gabrovo's
Biennial Festival of Humour and Satire** in
mid-May (on odd-numbered years, see p.159). All
Bulgaria's major cities hold annual musical events
of some kind or another; see above for details.

RURAL CELEBRATIONS AND SEASONAL RITES

The nearest most tourists get to Bulgaria's
annual cycle of **rural celebrations** is a glimpse
of the festive costumes displayed in local
museums. However, a surprising number of
village customs are still in use, although you will
have to be in rural areas at the right time of year
in order to see them. Most Bulgarian festivals are
associated with the different stages of the agricultural year, although the pantheon of Orthodox
saints has been recruited in order to provide a
Christian framework to seasonal merrymaking.

CELEBRATIONS THROUGH THE YEAR

The festival calendar begins with **New Year's
Day** or St Basil's Day (also known as *survaki*),
when young children go from house to house
offering New Year wishes to the householders by
slapping them on the back with a *survaknitsa* – a
bunch of twigs adorned with brightly coloured
threads and dried fruit. In some western areas,
New Year's Day is also marked by processions of
villagers wearing animal masks, a ritual similar to
those performed on *Kukerov den*, of which more
below.

In wine-producing areas festivities take place
on February 14, or *Trifon Zarezan*, St Tryphon's
Day, traditionally the time of year when the vines
are pruned. Another, more widespread festival

associated with the start of the agricultural year
is *Kukerov den* on the first Sunday before lent.
Processions are led through the village by the
dancing, leaping *kukeri*, men dressed up in
animal costumes and grotesque masks, often
augmented by a girdle of goat or sheep bells and
extravagantly tasselled trousers. Examples of
kukeri costume are a regular sight in Bulgaria's
provincial museums.

The advent of **spring** is celebrated on March 1
(aka *Baba Marta*, Granny March), when peasant
households embark on a round of spring-cleaning
– symbolically sweeping the winter months away.
On the same day people present each other with a
martenitsa (or alternatively hang them on trees), a
good-luck charm made up of red and white
woolen threads with tassles or furry bobbles on
the end. One typical springtime fertility rite is
lazaruvane on St Lazar's Day (eight days before
Easter), when village maidens considered fit for
marriage perform ritual dances, songs and games.

The coming of **summer** is traditionally marked
on May 21st, the day of SS Constantine and
Elena, characterized by **fire-dancing** (ie barefoot
on hot coals) in some of the remoter villages of
southeast Bulgaria's Strandzha hills (see p.282).

Sundry other **church holidays** coincide with
the changing of the seasons: St Marina's Day on
July 17th has always been a popular Midsummer
feast day, while *Golyama Bogoroditsa* (the day of
the Dormition of the Virgin) on August 28 traditionally marks the beginning of **autumn**. The end
of the farming year is celebrated on October 26 or
Dimitrovden, St Demetrius's Day. Characteristic
of the Bulgarian Christmas (*koleda*) is the *koleduvane*, when young men of the village go from
house to house singing carols. The leader of the
carol singers, the *stanenik*, is charged with the
baking of a specially decorated loaf of bread,

HOLIDAYS AND FESTIVALS/27

which the singers take with them on their rounds. Again, examples of typical Christmas loaves are fairly ubiquitous in Bulgaria's museums.

MUSLIM FESTIVALS

Religious festivals are widely observed by Bulgaria's Muslim minority, with the faithful converging on the major mosques and holy sites in order to celebrate the more important holidays. If you're in Bulgaria at the right time, you'll observe these gatherings at the city-centre mosques in Sofia and Plovdiv, or in the cities nearest to areas of Muslim settlement: for example, Shumen, Razgrad and Dobrich in the north; Pazardzhik, Kârdzhali, Haskovo and Harmanli in the south. Since the **Islamic calendar** is lunar, dates of festivals tend to drift backwards eleven days each year relative to the Gregorian calendar. See below for the specific dates of forthcoming religious festivals.

The most important Muslim festival is **Ramadan** (*Ramazan*), the month of daylight abstention from food, water, tobacco or sexual relations, occuring during the late winter in the 1990s. The more devout inhabitants of Bulgaria's Muslim areas observe the fast, but you'll find most restaurants and cafés open nevertheless. The three-day **Sheker Bayram** (Sugar Holiday) is held at the end of Ramadan, celebrated by family get-togethers and the giving of presents and sweets to children. The four-day **Kurban Bayram**

UPCOMING MUSLIM RELIGIOUS FESTIVALS

Sheker Bayram	*Kurban Bayram*
24–26 March 1993	1–4 June 1993
13–15 March 1994	21–24 May 1994
2–4 March 1995	10–13 May 1995

(Festival of the Sacrifice) celebrates the offering of a sheep in place of Abraham's son Ismael – a Koranic version of the biblical story – and is marked by the ritual slaughter of sheep and goats.

ENTERTAINMENT

Compared to western Europeans, most Bulgarians have little surplus spending power, and the range of **entertainment** on offer reflects this. However, a tradition of state subsidies to the arts means that most provincial towns will have a theatre and most big cities will have an opera house, resulting in a substantial and cheap diet of "high culture". The removal of cold war cultural barriers is expressed in the range of drama currently on offer. Bulgarian translations of the West End farces of Ray Cooney seem to have taken the country by storm recently. Local storytelling traditions find expression in the work of puppet theatres (*kuklen teatâr*), popular with children and found in most of the bigger cities.

Although Bulgaria is well known for its **folk music**, it's difficult for the uninitiated visitor to discover places where this might be performed – unless you're on a package tour, in which case colourfully dressed singing and dancing troupes may well form part of the entertainment laid on. If young Bulgarians listen to folk music at all, it tends to be the pop-folk crossover music of neighbouring Serbia rather than the home-grown stuff.

There's little in the way of a domestic rock tradition, and regular gig venues are few and far between, although big sports halls in Sofia sometimes play host to foreign touring bands. Most Bulgarian radio stations play predominantly western pop (including a lot of speed metal, popular among young males), and stalls selling cheap cassettes of western bands are a feature of most street markets.

MUSEUMS, CHURCHES AND MOSQUES

Bulgaria's museums and art galleries were quite well provided for by a postwar state eager to instil in its inhabitants a strong sense of history and a pride in national culture. Civic pride comes into it too: every town in the country was determined to display at least some evidence of its contribution to Bulgarian history, whether in the shape of a small archaeological museum, a restored nineteenth-century house, or the former home of a famous revolutionary. Religious monuments fared less well: while the most prestigious of them were paraded as examples of Bulgarian achievement, the vast majority were allowed to fall into neglect and disuse.

MUSEUMS

Most towns and cities will have a central **history museum** or Исторически музей, *istoricheski muzei* (bigger centres will have an *arheoloshki muzei* as well) designed to showcase the achievements of the ancient Thracians, the medieval Bulgarian empires, and the struggles of the Bulgarian peoples to overcome Turkish oppression. The style is often didactic, relying on sequences of texts and photographs past which schoolchildren slowly file, and English-language translations are extremely rare. However, presentation is usually good, and the wealth of Neolithic and Thracian artefacts which tend to turn up in Bulgarian museums make the effort worthwhile.

The same may be said of Bulgaria's outstanding **ethnographic museums** (етнографски музеи, *etnografski muzei*), where rural traditions are faithfully documented with an array of folk costumes and craft implements – although texts explaining their use are often in short supply. Localities of particular ethnographic importance have been preserved, either whole or in part, as **heritage villages** or **museum towns** (old Plovdiv, Tryavna, Nesebâr and Sozopol are just four examples). Buildings falling within such an *arhitekturen rezervat* are carefully reconstructed according to traditional building methods, and the best examples of vernacular architecture are often opened to the public as a *kâshta-muzei* (къща-музеи), or museum house.

OPENING TIMES AND ENTRANCE FEES

Opening times vary widely, although the working hours of Tuesday–Sunday 8am–noon & 2pm–5.30pm seem to be most common. Big museums in Sofia, Plovdiv and Varna tend to open later and do without the break for lunch. Museums may stay open until 6 or 7pm during the summer, but once the tourist season is over opening times begin to get very unpredictable – some establishments close up altogether after September because of the lack of visitors. **Entrance fees** are rarely more than a few pence, although foreigners often pay several times more than the locals (possession of a student card will sometimes secure admission at the lower rate). Many museums offer a *beseda* or guided tour with commentary for an extra 25 pence or so, and if you can find an English-speaking member of staff this is well worth taking advantage of.

CHURCHES AND MONASTERIES

During the Communist period, **religious buildings** considered to be of particular architectural or cultural importance were removed from church control and taken under the government's wing. Although their transformation into "museums" was at odds with their spiritual purpose, this policy did ensure that large amounts of cash were channelled into their restoration and upkeep. Now that ecclesiastical properties are being returned to the ownership of the Bulgarian Orthodox Church, many historical churches and chapels, previously visited as exhibition halls or tourist attractions, are being transformed into places of worship again. This often entails a short period of closure, so don't be too surprised if some of the museum-churches described in the guide turn out to be inexplicably locked up.

Another reason why you'll find the doors of many churches firmly shut is general unease about **rising crime**. Many Bulgarian priests don't like the idea of their precious icons being half-inched, and only open up shop when services draw near. The period between about 4–5pm, just before the evening service, tends to be the best time for looking around.

The gates of **monasteries** tend to be open to all-comers from dawn until dusk. The more famous monasteries such as Rila, Troyan, Bachkovo, Dryanovo and others are used to receiving visitors all the year round, and you can wander round the galleried monastery courtyards more or less at will. Some of the smaller foundations, however, will only have a handful of monks or nuns in residence, so you may again discover that churches and chapels within the monastic precinct are locked. Somebody will probably open things up if you show persistent interest.

MOSQUES

Five hundred years of Turkish occupation left Bulgaria with some of the finest **Islamic architecture** in the Balkans. Prestige mosques (such as the *Tombul Dzhamiya* in Shumen) were restored and opened to the public by the Communist authorities, but the vast majority suffered as a result of the government's anti-Turkish policies. Many were left to slide into disrepair, while others were deliberately demolished – especially during the mid-1980s, when the *vâzroditelniyat protses* or "Regeneration Process" (see p.316) was at its height. Surviving mosques in areas where Muslims live are now being returned to the Islamic community, although the delapidated state of many minor mosques will require a good deal of time and money to put right. Mosques in non-Muslim parts of the country (such as the one currently occupied by the archaeological museum in Kyustendil) are unlikely to revert to their original use.

Like so many churches, working mosques in Bulgaria are rarely found to be open outside prayer times. Theft is a problem for the Islamic authorities too, with mosque kilims being spirited across the border to be sold to dealers in Istanbul.

ARCHITECTURE AND ETIQUETTE

The **basic layout** of a mosque is a carpet-covered square with a *mihrab* cut into the eastern end facing Mecca; from this niche the *imam* or priest leads the congregation in prayer, the women grouped behind the men on a balcony or behind a low balustrade. Occasionally, particularly in those towns in the Rhodopes and the southeast which are almost purely Muslim, you'll hear the *muezzin* singing the *ezan*, or call to prayer, from a minaret, though these days it's more usually relayed by a loudspeaker. The Islamic faith prohibits reproduction of the human form, with the result that the richest mosques are covered in passages from the Koran and non-figurative decoration of tiles and ornamented plaster. Normally it's only this and the size that distinguishes one mosque from the next. Visitors are allowed in major mosques, but are expected to observe **certain proprieties**: shoes should be removed before entering, women must cover their heads, and you may be asked to leave a small donation.

POLICE, TROUBLE AND SEXUAL HARASSMENT

Modern Bulgaria is a refreshingly unthreatening country in which to travel, and most tourists will have little or no contact with the Bulgarian **Militia** (Милиция, *Militsiya*). Everyone is required to carry ID at all times, so it's a good idea to carry your passport, together with your *carte statistique* (see p.7).

Of the things you're likely to do once in Bulgaria, **camping rough** is likely to attract the disapproval of officialdom, and driving with any quantity of **alcohol** in the blood whatsoever is strictly forbidden and carries stiff penalties. Given Bulgaria's position on the overland route to Turkey and beyond, an equal lack of mercy is shown to anyone caught in possession of **drugs**, for whom years in jail are likely. The only negative stories relating to Bulgarian police concern motorists in transit between Yugoslavia and Turkey, whom **traffic cops** sometimes book for spurious speeding or safety violations and then charge on-the-spot fines. Over the past two years society has become much more aware of the abuses committed by those in uniform, although it will take some time yet before all the bad habits of the past are abandoned.

TROUBLE

Bulgaria's **crime rate** has mushroomed since the collapse of the totalitarian system, a phenomenon which has engendered a great deal of fear and insecurity among the law-abiding majority. The situation is still nowhere near as serious as in the urban centres of the West, and is largely restricted to petty offences rather than crimes of violence. However, it's from the small-time thief that travellers are most at risk, so it's wise to take the obvious precautions: flaunt cameras and other material goods as little as possible, always carry your valuables with you, and keep large wads of foreign cash well out of sight. The most obvious precaution against theft is to take out insurance (see p.8). If you do have anything stolen, go to the police immediately, and get a report detailing the things you've lost.

If you're unfortunate enough to be arrested yourself, wait until you can explain matters to someone in English if at all possible (misunderstandings in a foreign language can make things worse), and then request that your consulate be notified. **Consulates** may be helpful in some respects, but will never lend cash to nationals who've run out or been robbed. You'll find the addresses in Sofia Listings.

SEXUAL HARASSMENT

Modern feminism has made few inroads into what is a predominantly patriarchal society, and **women** travelling alone can expect to encounter stares, comments and sometimes worse from macho types. A firm response should be enough to cope with most situations – if not, holler *Pomosht!* ("Help!") or *Militsiya*.

Remember that local **attitudes** are often conservative, particularly in rural areas, and "immodest" attire can sometimes arouse strong feelings. However, most young, especially urban, natives have spent the last two years casting off Bulgaria's erstwhile sartorial straitjacket, and Western fashions and hairstyles no longer attract particular disapproval.

DIRECTORY

ADDRESSES are normally written in the Cyrillic alphabet, like everything else in Bulgaria. In the text, they're transcribed into Roman script according to the system in "Language", p.335. The most common abbreviations are ул. (*ul.)* for "street" (*ulitsa*), пл. (*pl.)* for "square" (*ploshtad*) and бул. (*bul.)* for *bulevard*, although these designations are omitted altogether when the meaning is clear from the context. The street number of a building is given after the name of the street. Addresses in the high-rise suburbs (*kvartal*, abbreviated to кв, *kv)* include the block number (*blok*, shortened to бл, *bl)* a letter denoting the entrance (*vhod*), Roman numerals signifying the floor (*etazh*), and finally the number of the apartment itself.

BODY LANGUAGE Although a shake of the head means **yes** and a nod means **no** according to local custom, natives sometimes shake or nod their head in the "usual" way when talking with foreigners. Bulgarians are tolerant of misunderstandings over gestures, but it must be disconcerting for them to have a chat with someone who constantly nods "no, no". Anyone **waving** at you is probably signalling "come here" or "step inside", not "goodbye". Flashing the lights of your car does not mean "I am prepared to give way to you" but "get the hell out of my way".

BRING camera film, camping gas cartouches, razor blades, contraceptives, which are either unavailable or difficult to procure. Instant coffee is less common than unground beans, and tea is either Chinese or herbal, so it's wise to bring both if you're planning on self-catering.

CHILDREN Many package deals offer child reductions, and the main Black Sea resorts are well-equipped for kids. Imported baby milk is sold sporadically by street traders – best to bring your own, along with baby food and disposable nappies.

CIGARETTES Western *tsigari*, or cigarettes (predominantly *Marlboro*, *Rothmans* and *HB*), are sold on street stalls and in kiosks for around 75p a packet; Greek brands cost slightly less. Bulgarian brands such as *Arda*, *Feniks* and *Rodopi* cost next to nothing but are fairly rough in comparison. Matches are called *kibrit*. Smoking is prohibited in public buildings (notably rail and bus terminals) and in many self-service restaurants and patisseries. Elsewhere, however, non-smokers may find Bulgarian social life fairly oppressive.

ELECTRICITY is 220 volts. Round two-pin plugs are used, so bring an adaptor.

EMBASSIES (*Posolstvo*) and consulates are all in the capital; see the listings at the end of the Sofia chapter for addresses.

GAY LIFE The mere idea of homosexuality raises hackles in what is essentially a conservative and patriarchal society. Although some open discussion of gay issues are beginning to surface in the media, gays themselves continue to keep a low profile. While homosexual acts between men over the age of 21 are not officially illegal, there are heavy restrictions on vague things like "scandalous homosexuality" or "homosexual acts leading to perversions" – which basically means that the authorities have the right to arrest you for any homosexual act.

LAUNDRY Laundrettes (*peralnya*), let alone *himichesko chistene* (dry cleaners), are exceedingly rare. At the larger hotels, it's sometimes possible to have cleaning done on the premises.

LEFT LUGGAGE Most railway stations have a left-luggage office or гардероб (*garderob*); in the larger towns these will be open 24hrs. Bus stations will usually have a *garderob* as well, but opening times are more restricted and staff take more frequent breaks (*pauza*). Each item of baggage should cost no more than a few pence.

NATURISM was once forbidden on the Black Sea's beaches, and the sight of naked foreigners being bundled into police cars provided frequent amusement for the locals. Topless bathing is now pretty much *de rigeur* among young Bulgarian holidaymakers, and nude sunbathing quite common on the quieter beaches. "Official" nudist beaches are yet to be established, although the naturist lobby in Varna is pressing for recognition of its own favoured stretch of the seafront (see p.243).

POWER CUTS Bulgaria now has to pay in hard currency for the electricity it once acquired so cheaply from the former Soviet Union, and the

resulting energy shortage has led to the introduction of power cuts (*rezhim na toka*) in recent winters. Electricity is rationed according to the *3-1 system* – for every three hours you spend with electricity, you have to spend one without. Big hotels and ski centres are usually exempt from these privations, but if you're travelling away from the big resorts, be sure to pack the odd candle.

SHOPPING HOURS Big city shops and supermarkets are generally open Monday to Friday from 8.30am (or earlier) through until 6pm (or later, in the case of neighbourhood supermarkets); on Saturdays until 2pm. In rural areas and small towns, a kind of unofficial siesta may prevail between noon and 3pm.

SKIING Several UK operators offer excellent value skiing holidays (see "Getting There", p.6) at the main resorts of Pamporovo (p.233) and Borovets (p.78). Aleko-Vitosha near the capital, and Bansko and Malyovitsa in the mountains of the southwest, are up-and-coming resorts.

TAMPONS Imported tampons (*tamponi*) and sanitary towels (*damski prevrâzki*) are available in many of the newer, privately owned kiosks and shops in big towns, but the selection will be limited. Best bring your own.

TIME Two hours ahead of GMT and BST; Bulgarian Summer Time lasts from the beginning of April to the end of September.

TOILETS Public toilets (тоалетни, *toaletni*) are found at all railway stations, most bus stations, and in central parks in towns. They're usually badly maintained, and cleanliness depends on the caretaker or cleaner, to whom you pay a small fee (*taksa*) on entering. Mâzhe (Мъжи, or М) are men; zheni (Жени, or Ж) or dami (Дами, Д) are women.

WATER (*voda*) is safe to drink from all taps, but supplies may be restricted to set periods (*rezhim na vodata*) during the summer.

PART TWO

THE

GUIDE

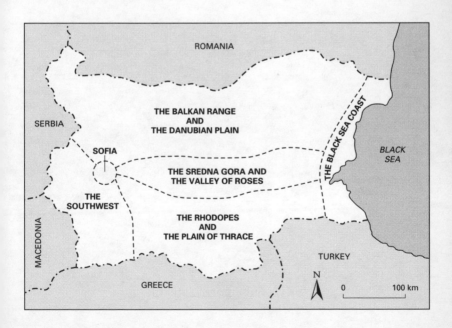

ROMANIA

SERBIA

THE BALKAN RANGE
AND
THE DANUBIAN PLAIN

SOFIA

THE
SOUTHWEST

THE SREDNA GORA AND
THE VALLEY OF ROSES

BLACK
SEA

THE BLACK SEA COAST

MACEDONIA

THE RHODOPES
AND
THE PLAIN OF THRACE

TURKEY

GREECE

N

0   100 km

CHAPTER ONE

SOFIA

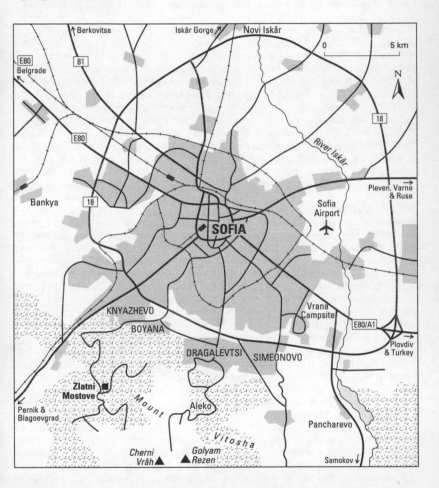

A ccording to its motto, **SOFIA** "grows but does not age": a tribute to the mushrooming suburbs occupied by one-tenth of Bulgaria's population, and a cryptic reference to its ancient origins. Although various Byzantine ruins and a couple of mosques attest to a long and colourful history, little else in the city is of any real vintage. Sofia's finest architecture post-dates Bulgaria's liberation, when the capital of the infant state was laid out on a grid pattern in imitation of Western capitals – although the peeling stucco of its turn-of-the-century buildings lends an air of Balkan delapidation to the capital's wide, tree-shaded boulevards. The close historical relationship between Bulgaria and Russia reveals itself in the capital's public buildings, foremost of which is the **Aleksandâr Nevski church**, a magnificent Byzantine-Muscovite confection. The socialist era, too, produced its shrines – most notably the ghoulish **mausoleum of Georgi Dimitrov** on the recently renamed Aleksandâr Batenberg square.

Gone, however, are the days when the city resembled a kind of Communist Geneva, with fresh wreathes laid before its monuments and a police force that one could imagine clubbing litterbugs or jaywalkers. The downtown streets and parks are still fairly spruce, but the sudden emergence of free-enterprise culture, with traders hawking Western goods from pavement stalls and privately owned cafés crammed into alleyways, has given the capital a new vigour. Now that the Party is no longer around to fulminate against drinking, pop music and jeans, Sofian society has loosened up considerably, with a desire to emulate the West most evident in the fashions of the capital's youth. However, their spending power is limited, and entertainment still revolves around an evening promenade in one of the city's parks, followed by a coffee in a nearby café. Nightlife boils down to folklore shows, the odd disco and a few bars, plus lots of drama and serious music, especially during the *Sofia Music Weeks*, which take place each June.

Sofia in history

Sofia's first inhabitants were the **Serdi**, a Thracian tribe who settled here some 3000 years ago. Their Roman conquerors named the town *Serdica*, a walled city which reached its zenith under Emperor Constantine in the early fourth century. Serdica owed its importance to the position it occupied on the *diagonis*, the Roman road which linked Constantinople with modern Belgrade on the Danube, providing the Balkans with its main commercial and strategic artery. However, the Empire's foes also used the road as a quick route to the riches of Constantinople, and Serdica was frequently under attack – most notably from the Huns, who sacked the city in the fifth century. Once rebuilt, the town became one of the Byzantine Empire's most important strongpoints in the Balkans.

Migrating Slavs began to filter into the town in the seventh century, becoming the dominant force in the region after the town's capture by the Bulgar Khan Krum in 809. The town continued to flourish under the Bulgarians, although few medieval cultural monuments remain, save for the thirteenth-century **Boyana church**. Initially named *Sredets* by the Slavs, the town became known as Sofia sometime in the fourteenth century, most probably taking its name from the ancient church of **Sveta Sofia** (Holy Wisdom) which still stands in the city centre. Five centuries of Turkish rule began with the town's capture in 1382, during which time Sofia thrived as a market centre, though little material evidence of the Ottoman period remains save for a couple of **mosques**.

Economic decline set in during the nineteenth century, and Sofia was little more than a minor provincial centre at the time of the Liberation in 1878, when defeat of the Turks by Russian forces paved the way for the foundation of an independent Bulgarian state. Sofia was chosen to become the new capital of the coun-

The phone code for Sofia is ☎02.

try in preference to more prestigious centres (such as Târnovo in central Bulgaria) because of its geographical location: situated on a wide plain fringed by mountains, Sofia combined defensibility with the potential for future growth. It was also thought that Sofia would occupy a central position in any Bulgarian state which included (as was then hoped) Macedonia. The town underwent rapid development from the Liberation onwards, although progress sometimes sat uneasily beside backwardness and poverty.

Sofia experienced even more frenetic growth in the postwar era of "socialist construction", and a veneer of Stalinist monumentalism was added to the city centre in the shape of buildings like the **Party House**, a stern-looking expression of political authority. Sofia's rising population was housed in the endless high-rise suburbs (suburbs with declamatory names like *Mladost* – "youth" – and *Nadezhda* – "hope") which girdle the city today. Most of the capital's inhabitants are of *Shop* descent – the Shops being the original peasant population of the surrounding countryside who migrated to the city in vast numbers over the past hundred years. Owners of an impenetrable dialect, the Shops are much maligned by their fellow Bulgarians for being the worst speakers of Bulgarian in the land.

Arrival, information and city transport

Sofia is a surprisingly well-organized city when it comes to **getting about**. An extensive bus, trolleybus and tram network extends to just about everywhere you're likely to want to go, and inexpensive taxis fill in the gaps. Getting official **information** about the city, however, isn't so easy.

Arrival

Bus #84, running every thirty minutes, connects **Sofia airport**, 10km west of town, with the Orlov Most (p.56), from where you can walk into the city centre; the last buses leave the airport at 10pm and midnight. Taxi drivers tend to charge foreigners fresh off the plane a straight $10 for the ride into town. If you utter the odd word of Bulgarian or appear to know where you're going, you'll pay the regular fare – about £3. See also "Airlines" and "Airport" in the Listings section at the end of this chapter.

Trains
Trains arrive at the Central Station (*Tsentralna gara*), a concrete barn twenty minutes north of the city centre by foot. Trams #1 and #7 will take you from the station forecourt to pl. Sveta Nedelya, within easy reach of tourist offices, central hotels and the important sights. If you're merely pausing in Sofia between trains, the Central Station is not the kind of place where you would want to sleep rough. By day it's pretty civilized, but by night the dimly lit underground walkways begin to fill up with teenage runaways, the homeless, and other displaced characters, making it a target for regular police raids.

Train tickets
When leaving Sofia by train, remember that **tickets** for Lom, Vidin, Ruse and Varna are sold on the ground floor; all others in the basement. The system of plat-

Vidin ↖

N

0   500 m

Tsentralna
Gara

Novotel
Evropa

BULEVARD SLIVNITSA

LÁVOV
MOST

Belgrade ←

Dimitrov
Memorial
House

ULITSA TSAR SIMEON

Open-air
Market

BULEVARD HRISTO BOTEV

ULITSA GEORGI KIROV

BULEVARD KNYAGINYA MARIYA LUIZA

ULITSA GEORGI SAVA RAKOVSKI

BULEVARD L

Banya Bashi
Mosque

Hotel
Iskår

ULITSA
EXZARH IOSIF

Synagogue

Hali

Turkish
Baths

Balkantours

KNYAZ DONDUKOV

ULITSA OPÁLCHENSKA

Restaurant
Vietnam

TsUM

Party
House

National
Art Gallery

SS C
Meth
Found

BULEVARD ALEKSANDAR STAMBOLIISKI

THE LARGO

Russian
Church

Aleksa
Nevski C

Hotel
Balkan

St Nedelya
Church

BULEVARD TSAR OSVOBODITEL

Dimitrov
Mausoleum

BALKAN
(external

HRISTO MIHAILOV

National History
Museum

Evropa
Palace
Hotel

US
Embassy

City
Garden

ULITSA G. S. RAKOVSKI

Hotel
Slavyanska-Be

International
Bus terminal

ULITSA ALABIN

BALKAN
(internal)

Rila
Ticket Agency

Hotel
Sevastopol

Central
Post Office

ULITSA IVAN VA

ULITSA GENERAL GURKO

BULEVARD HRISTO BOTEV

BULEVARD VITOSHA

ULITSA GRAFIGNATIEV

BULEVARD

Hotel
Rodina

BULEVARD MAKEDONIYA

GENERAL SKOBELEV

BULEVARD PATRIARH EVTIMII

Avtogara
Ovcha Kupel
& Hotel Slaviya

Museum of
Military History

1300 Years
Monument

British
Embassy

BULEVARD BĂLGARIYA

National
Palace
of Culture

Yuzhen Park

Hotel
Hemus

Tihiya Kåt &
Zlatni Mostove ←

Hotels Vitosha
& Orbita ↓

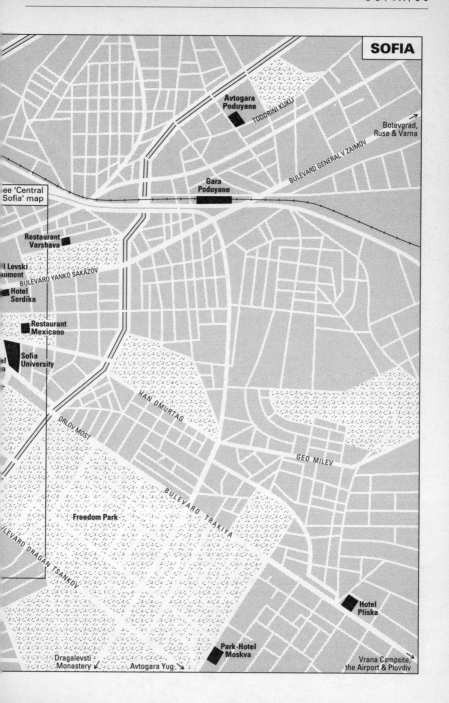

SOFIA

Avtogara
Poduyane

TODORINI KUKU

Botevgrad,
Ruse & Varna

BULEVARD GENERAL V ZAIMOV

ee 'Central
Sofia' map

Gara
Poduyane

Restaurant
Varshava

l Levski
ument

BULEVARD YANKO SAKAZOV

Hotel
Serdika

Restaurant
Mexicano

Sofia
University

HAN OMURTAG

ORLOV MOST

GEO MILEV

BULEVARD TRAKIYA

Freedom Park

LEVARD DRAGAN TSANKOV

Hotel
Pliska

Park-Hotel
Moskva

Dragalevsti
Monastery

Avtogara Yug

Vrana Campsite,
the Airport & Plovdiv

form numbering is incredibly confusing (each platform is also divided into *iztok* – eastern – and *zapad* – western – sections, referred to as *i* and *z* respectively on the departures board), so allow plenty of time to catch your train. To beat the queues, make **advance bookings** at the *BDZh* office at bul. Knyaginya Mariya Luiza 23; unless you want a sleeper, in which case head for bul. Knyaginya Mariya Luiza 79 (☎833416).

Tickets and bookings for **international services** are handled by the *Rila Bureau* (General Gurko 5; ☎870777; Mon–Sat 8am–7pm). All the above ticket services are available at the *TsKTON*, or transport service centre (Mon–Fri 7am–7pm, Sat 8am–2pm) located beneath the National Palace of Culture (NDK). Sleeping cars on international services must be booked through the *Bureau Wagon Lits*, ul. Lege 10 (☎873452).

Buses

International **buses** arrive at a small terminus at Hristo Mihailov 38 (☎525004), ten minutes west of the city centre. There are three main stations serving **domestic routes**, all of them some way out from the centre. Services for points north and northeast of Sofia use the *Avtogara Poduyane* terminal on ul. Todorini Kukli (tram #20 from the Levski monument to Gara Poduyane, followed by bus #120); buses from the southwest use *Ovcha Kupel*, halfway down bul. Deveti Makedoniya (tram #5 from behind the National History Museum); buses from the southeast use the *Yug* terminal, on bul. Bålgarsko Såvetska Druzhba, beneath an underpass just beyond the park na svobodata (tram #14 from pl. Sveta nedelya). In all cases, the best place to get information and tickets is the *TsKTON* underneath the NDK.

Some **private bus operators** are beginning to run express services between Sofia and major provincial cities, with buses departing from a car park behind the Hotel Novotel Evropa – just across the square from the Central Station. Destinations, departure times and prices are usually displayed on a sign in the windscreen.

Information

Although a small counter in the lobby of the Central Station advertises itself as a **tourist information office** (daily 8am–8pm), it seems to concentrate exclusively on changing money and booking rooms in top-price hotels. It's best to head straight into town, where the *Balkantours* office at Vitosha 1 (daily 8am–8pm; ☎43331) handles info, hotel reservations, car hire and touts costly excursions. The same services are on offer at another *Balkantours* office at Knyaz Dondukov 37 (daily 8am–9pm; ☎880655), which is also the main bureau for handling **private rooms** (see opposite). There's also an **information desk** inside the *TsKTON* beneath the NDK.

As elsewhere in Bulgaria, there's a distinct shortage of tourist leaflets and **maps** on offer. Little has been printed in recent years because of financial restraints, and places advertising tourist information will seldom have very much to hand out. An acceptable tourist map of Sofia (but with pre-1989 street names) is usually available at newstands and street stalls. A shop at Triaditsa 4 belonging to *Turistreklama*, the state agency responsible for publicizing tourism, is perhaps the only reliable source of maps and brochures covering the whole country – it's a good idea to stock up here before you head off into the country.

City transport

Public transport is cheap and reasonably efficient, with intertwining networks of buses (*avtobus*), trolleybuses (*troleibus*) and, slowest of all, trams (*tramvai*). Most services run from about 4am until midnight. Triple-digit route numbers indicate express buses, which stop less frequently and are useful for travelling across town in a hurry. All routes are marked on the tourist map of Sofia (see opposite).

There's a flat fare on all urban routes (currently about 3 pence); **tickets** (*bileti*) are sold from street kiosks and must be punched on board the vehicle (inspections are frequent and there are spot-fines for fare-dodgers – a crippling 25 pence at present). Though few visitors find it worthwhile to buy one, you can also purchase monthly season tickets, valid for a single route or the whole city transport system. Private companies are soon to be given the go-ahead to operate some of Sofia's bus routes – you'll probably be expected to pay in cash when riding on these services.

Taxis aren't particularly expensive either, charging about 20 pence per kilometre until 10pm, after which the rate is 30 pence per kilometre until 5am. Expect a small surcharge if you order by telephone (☎142).

Accommodation

Accommodation prices are significantly higher in Sofia than elsewhere in the country. However, there's a reasonable stock of budget accommodation – establishments previously off limits to Westerners no longer discriminate – but facilities in the cheaper hotels may be a little basic and run-down. More promisingly, small family-run hotels are beginning to appear in the suburbs, offering comfortable rooms at bargain rates (see below). That said, most of the central hotels remain expensive, so a **private room** is still the best-value way of getting a place close to the action. Centrally located private rooms are available from *Balkantours* at Knyaz Dondukov 37 for £4 a double; the *Orbita* youth travel bureau at bul. Stamboliiski 45a (Mon–Fri 9am–noon & 1–7pm) also has private rooms for around the same price. New, independent, room-letting bureaux are beginning to emerge which may offer better deals. The *Markela* bureau, bul. Knyaginya Mariya Luiza 17 (the office is in a small kiosk opposite the Largo, set back from the road), have rooms for £2 a night, although they tend to be located some distance from the centre.

PRIVATE GUESTHOUSES IN SIMEONOVO

Private enterprise has yet to make an impact on the hotel business in central Sofia, but small **family-run guesthouses** charging about £4 a night are beginning to crop up in the suburbs below Mount Vitosha. Unfortunately, the *Balkantours* accommodation office in the centre of town doesn't work on behalf of these private hoteliers, thus making it extremely difficult for the traveller to get any information about them. The suburb of **Simeonovo** (tram #2 to the Hladilnika terminus, then bus #98) has become the centre of the guesthouse trade, and with the mountain resort of Aleko only a chair-lift ride away, it's a good place to escape from the hubbub of downtown Sofia. The Simeonovo guesthouse phenomenon is so recent that it's difficult to give concrete recommendations, but with an estimated 160 establishments already in existence, it should be feasible to arrive on spec and start asking around – or merely wander the streets until you spot something that you like.

Hotels

Your choice of hotel will depend a great deal on how much you are prepared to pay in order to be near the centre of things. Hotels within walking distance of the centre tend to charge western European prices without neccessarily offering the same degree of service, and the handful of budget alternatives are rather dingy affairs with poor facilities. You may therefore have to settle for something outside the inner city and rely a great deal on public transport. Good hotel rooms at affordable prices (and often in idyllic surroundings) are reasonably plentiful just outside the city limits on Mount Vitosha to the south – bear in mind, however, that these will fill up with tour groups during the winter season. Although accessible by public transport, the journey time can be long, and services to the Vitosha area run less frequently than those serving the city centre, especially in the evenings and at weekends.

Central Sofia

Balkan Sheraton, pl. Sveta Nedelya 5 (☎876541; ⑥). Sofia's most expensive and luxurious hotel; a newly refurbished Stalinist pile occupying a prime site on the city's central square.

Bulgaria, bul. Tsar Osvoboditel 4 (☎871977; ⑤). Located in the midst of the city's main tourist sights. Slightly older than other "international" hotels in the same price range, it preserves something of its old central European charm.

Edelvais, bul. Knyaginya Mariya Luiza 79 (②). Centrally placed, but grotty.

Evropa Palace, ul. Kaloyan 6 (☎881861; ⑥). Well-appointed business hotel. Slap in the heart of things but somewhat lacking in atmosphere.

Grand Hotel Sofia, pl. Narodno Sâbranie 1–A (☎878821; ⑤). Very comfortable modern hotel opposite the Bulgarian National Assembly.

Iskâr, ul. Iskâr 9 (②). A bit run-down and gloomy, but a convenient bolt-hole if your budget won't stretch to the other downtown hotels.

Novotel Evropa, bul. Knyaginya Mariya Luiza (☎31261; ⑥). A snooty, costly tower block next to the main station.

Rodina, bul. Totleben 8 (☎51631; ⑥). Another business travellers' preserve; on the southwest fringes of the city centre and therefore slightly inconvenient for walking in.

Serdika, bul. Yanko Sakâzov 1 (☎443411; ④). Cheapest of those central hotels which have en-suite bathrooms.

Sevastopol, ul. Rakovski 116 (☎875941; ③). A little noisy, but the best of the cheapies.

Slavyanska Beseda, ul. Slavyanska 3 (☎880441; ④). A bit lacking in character, but like the *Serdika*, an affordable mid-range choice.

The suburbs

Hemus, bul. Cherni Vrâh 31 (☎63951; ⑤). Pretty unremarkable international-style hotel. Tram #6 or #9 from the NDK.

Orbita, bul. Anton Ivanov 7 (☎63931; ④). Situated between Yuzhen park and the suburban foothills of Mount Vitosha. Tram #2 from pl. Sveta Nedelya or #9 from *Tsentralna gara*.

Park Hotel Moskva, ul. Nezabravka 25 (☎71261; ⑥). Modern, high-rise affair much patronized by tour groups. Nice wooded location on the fringes of park na svobodata. Tram #14 from pl. Sveta nedelya.

HOTEL ROOM PRICES

For a fuller explanation of these codes, see p.16 of *Basics*.

① £4–6 ② £6–12 ③ £12–25 ④ £25–40 ⑤ £40–60 ⑥ over £60

Pliska, bul. Trakiya 87 (☎71281; ⑤). Unprepossessing but comfortable modern place, on the southeastern fringes of town and handy for the airport. Bus #80 from Orlov Most.

Sara, ul. Asen Velchev 58 (☎720352; ④). A friendly, pension-style small hotel hiding within a characterless office block. A 20–min ride by tram #20 from the Levski monument – alight at the *Elektronika* stop.

Slaviya, ul. Sofiiski Geroi 2 (☎443441; ④). Amid modern residential suburbs southwest of the city centre. Tram #5 from behind the National History Museum.

Vitosha New Otani, bul. Anton Ivanov 100 (☎62451; ⑥). Near the foothills of Mount Vitosha itself, this is Sofia's most palatial tower block, featuring a multitude of restaurants and sporting facilities. In 1980, the Pope's would-be assassin, Mehmet Ali Agca, stayed in room 911 under the name of "Yogander Singh".

Mount Vitosha

Kopitoto (☎575051; ③). In the foothills of Mount Vitosha above the suburb of Knyazhevo. Tram #5 from behind the National History Museum to Ovcha kupel, then bus #62.

Moreni (☎671059; ③). Above the suburb of Dragalevtsi in the heart of the best skiing terrain. Tram #2 from pl. Sveta Nedelya or tram #9 from *Tsentralna gara* as far as the Hladilnika terminus; then bus #66 to the end.

Prostor (☎671173; ④). Best of the Aleko ski resort hotels, a popular package-holiday base over the winter. For public transport details, see *Moreni*.

Shtastlivetsa (☎665024; ③). Highest up the mountain, above the *Prostor* and *Moreni*. Like the latter, at the end of bus route #66.

Motels

Motorists might consider one of the **motels** on Sofia's outskirts, which charge between £6 and £12 per head.

Boyana (☎563035). Located in the southern suburb of the same name, just below Mount Vitosha. Signposted off the outer ring road.

Gorublyansko Hanche (☎723720). Southeast of town just off the E80 highway to Plovdiv.

Iztok (☎741151). Twelve kilometres out of town, is 500m past the junction with the outer ring road, just off the Plovdiv highway.

Tihya Kât (☎571401). Cheapest of the motels, stands just off the main E79 route to Greece, on the road leading to Zlatni Mostove on Mount Vitosha.

Hostels and campsites

Although slightly more expensive than elsewhere in the country, Sofia's hostels and campsites are still remarkably cheap by Western standards. However, they are likely to be some way from the city centre, and what you gain in purely budgetary terms may not warrant the hassle involved in busing in and out of town.

There's one **hostel** in Sofia proper, and a couple of others in the Vitosha national park to the south. Often packed with vacationing Bulgarians throughout both summer and winter seasons, it's best to call in at the *Pirin Travel Agency* at bul. Stamboliiski 30 (☎870687) to see about securing a place. Prices for a dorm bed hover around £1.

All of Sofia's **campsites** also rent out **chalets**. Sleeping two, these go for around £2 per night, while campers are charged around £1 per head and £1 for ground space. All have a rudimentary restaurant, a snack bar and cooking facilities, but site shops won't stock much save for booze, cigarettes and soft drinks.

Hostels

Aleko, Vitosha (☎671113). In the heart of the popular winter sports area above the suburbs of Dragalevtsi and Simeonovo. Tram #2 from pl. Sveta Nedelya to the terminus, then bus #66.

Planinets, Vitosha (☎574310). Between Boyana suburb and Zlatni mostove. Just off the #62 bus route to the Hotel Kopitoto.

Turisticheska spalnya, ul. Rilksi prohod 1 (☎205014). Spartan dorms in a western suburb of town; tram #4 from behind the National History Museum as far as bul. Ovcha Kupel.

Campsites

Bankya (☎98/32509). Northwest of town in the suburban spa resort of Bankya, 7km off the E80 Belgrade–Sofia highway. Open May 1 to September 30. Bankya is linked to Sofia by half-hourly commuter train; the last one leaves *Tsentralna gara* at 11.30pm.

Vrana Camping (☎781213). Ten kilometres east of town on the E80 to Plovdiv, this is the best-equipped and most expensive of the sites. Catering largely for travellers in transit to Turkey, it has a certain soullessness which is only slightly remedied by the live musical entertainments laid on for campers. Open all year round. Accessible by bus #5 from Orlov Most. To get to the site from the Central Station, take bus #213 as far as the Plovdiv highway, then change to the #5.

Cherniya Kos (☎571129). Eleven kilometres out towards Pernik on the E79 highway, beneath the Vitosha range. Open May 1 to October 30. Take tram #5 to the end of the line, then bus #59 or #58.

Lebed (☎773045) Chalets only, and furthest from the city, beside Lake Pancharevo on the road to Samokov. Tram #20 from the Levski monument to the Geo Milev suburb, then bus #1, #2 or #3.

THE CITY

The heart of Sofia fits compactly within the irregular octagon formed by the city's inner ring road. Most of the sights are found inside this **central area** within easy walking distance of each other, and the grid-like pattern of streets radiating outwards from ploshtad Sveta Nedelya makes orientation relatively easy. Sveta nedelya is the obvious place from which to begin explorations of the capital, although there's no single obvious sightseeing route to follow. It's a good idea to sample the area around Sveta nedelya first, before embarking on a trip to the set-piece public buildings and squares to the east. Within striking distance are the refreshing open spaces of the city's main parks, a brisk walk or tram ride away from the centre. Expeditions to Mount Vitosha and the suburbs nestling in its foothills require more time and reliance on public transport.

Around the centre

Ploshtad Sveta Nedelya – Sveta Nedelya square – is Sofia's central hub, straddling the capital's principal north–south and east–west thoroughfares and providing easy access to the main business and shopping districts. Centred around the church of Sveta Nedelya, the square elongates to join bul. Knyaginya Mariya Luiza to the north, and bul. Vitosha to the south. Until very recently the square carried the name of Lenin, whose huge statue – now demolished – used to dominate the square's southern end. With his removal, the central focus of the square has returned northward to the church after which it was originally named.

The church of Sveta Nedelya

Trams rattle round a paved island that bears the **church of Sveta Nedelya**. Standing upon the former site of Serdica's chief crossroads, the current building was constructed after the Liberation as the successor to a line of churches that has stood here since medieval times. In those days aristocratic families built private chapels and endowed the monastic schools which formed the nucleus of the *Varosh* – the old Bulgarian quarter. During the Ottoman period it was known as the church of Sveti Kral – the "Blessed King" – on account of the remains of the Serbian monarch, Stefan Urosh, kept here. In 1925 it almost claimed another king, when bombs exploded among high dignitaries attending a funeral mass, killing 123 people but failing to harm their intended victims, Tsar Boris and his cabinet. The Communists – whose attempted revolution had been crushed in 1923 – were naturally blamed but denied all responsibility. Leading revolutionary Georgi Dimitrov later laid claim to the attack, but the postwar Communist regime tended to ascribe it to "ultra leftists". Until recently the cupola of the church was occupied by a surveillance team from the *DS* – Bulgaria's secret police. Packed with zoom cameras and high-tech listening devices, the cupola was the ideal place for keeping tabs on central Sofia.

North of the Sveta Nedelya church, the *Balkan Sheraton Hotel* and the *Tsum* department store guard the entrance to the broad street-cum-square known as the Largo, main route to the tourist attractions of east central Sofia, of which more on p.50. Continuing north from the square towards the railway station is bul. Knyaginya Mariya Luiza, the "most horrible street in Europe" for Arthur Symons when he was here in 1903, a "kind of mongrel East" existing "between two civilizations . . . a rag-heap for the refuse of both". Though it has been considerably cleaned up since then you can see what he was getting at, if only in the delapidated mixture of buildings which line the street.

The Banya Bashi mosque and the Turkish baths

Most eye-catching of bul. Knyaginya Mariya Luiza's buildings is the **Banya Bashi mosque**: a "Sultan style" edifice with one large dome and a single minaret, built in 1576 by Hadzhi Mimar Sonah, who also designed the great mosque at Edirne in Turkey. In 1960, Bernard Newman noted "scarcely enough Turks in Sofia to make up a congregation"; and in subsequent years the mosque fell into disuse as the Communist regime turned against the country's Muslim population. Now the mosque is once again open for worship, and the discreet call of the muezzin occasionally wafts above the heads of bemused city-centre shoppers.

As the name *Banya* suggests, the mosque stands near Sofia's **mineral baths**, which occupy a stately mock-oriental building overlooking the rear of the park. It's now pretty derelict with clumps of weeds growing from gaps in the tiled roof: don't expect to be able see the marble pillars and domed ceiling of the interior for some time yet. Outside, people lounge on benches gossiping and spitting sunflower seeds or fragments of *kebabcheta*, or come with jugs to collect mineral water from public taps.

The Hali and the synagogue

Facing the mosque is the market hall or **Hali**, an elaborately carved structure crowned by a clock tower. Currently closed for restoration, it used to play host to the city's state-run central market – a dull affair with drab stands and limited

CENTRAL SOFIA

Hotel Edelvais

Mineral Baths

Banya Bashi Mosque

TsUM

THE LARGO

Party House

Archaeological Museum

National Gallery

Natural History Museum

Russian Church

Church of Sveta Sofia

SS Cyril and Methodius Foundation

Alexander Nevsky Church

Vasil Levski Monument

Sofia University

National Assembly

Kristal

Dimitrov Mausoleum

National Theatre

City

Archaeological Museum

Rotunda of St George

Church of Sveta Nedelya

National Historical Museum

ULITSA GEORGI KIRKOV
BULEVARD KNYAGINYA MARIYA LUIZA
EKZARH JOSIF
KIRIL I METODII
ULITSA GEORGI SAVA RAKOVSKI
EKZARH JOSIF
ISKAR
ZNYAZ DONDUKOV
TRIYADITSA
BULEVARD LEVSKI
MOSKOVSKA
PL ALEXANDER NEVSKI
BULEVARD TSAR OSVSBSDITEL
PL NARODNO SABRANIE
BULEVARD YANKO SAKAZOV
AL STAMBOLIISKI
AL BATENBERG
IL LEVSKI
POZITANO
PL SVETA NEDELYA
SLAVE
LEGE

Vasil Levski Stadium

Memorial to the Soviet Army

BULEVARD BĂLGARIYA

BULEVARD DRAGAN TSANKOV

BULEVARD MARSHALL TOLBUHIN

200 m

N

0

ULITSA IVAN VAZOV

Ivan Vazov Museum

ULITSA GENERAL GURKO

ULITSA GEORGI SAVA RAKOVSKI

Church of Sveti Sedmochislentsi

ULITSA GRAF IGNATIEV

HAN KRUM

BULEVARD BĂLGARIYA

BULEVARD PATRIARH EVTIMII

F NANSEN

SOLUNSKA

PARCHEVICH

NEOFIT RILSKI

HAN ASPARUH

Yuzhen Park

National Palace of Culture

BULEVARD VITOSHA

PL BABA NEDELYA

stocks. Whether the new boom in private enterprise culture will brighten up the atmosphere of the *Hali* once reopened remains to be seen; for the time being, Sofian shoppers head for the lively outdoor market a block or two west, past the **Sofia synagogue**. This, a fanciful structure seemingly upheld by its dome, which might have been conceived by some Moorish Leonardo with a premonition of airships, was actually built in 1910, and is the main centre of the country's small Jewish community. Notwithstanding Bulgaria's historical tolerance of Jews (a tolerance which manifested itself in World War II, when popular pressure forced the government to back down from the deportation programme demanded by their Nazi allies), large numbers emigrated to Palestine in the late 1940s – which accounts for the discreet "Israel Contact Office" around the back of the synagogue.

The backstreets

Continuing westwards along Ekzarh Iosif, you'll pass unpretentious shops and cheap restaurants which ultimately merge with the **fruit and vegetable market** on Georgi Kirkov: an intensely crowded affair that quietens down around the far line of stalls, of which one end sells flowers while the other displays heaps of raw wool, which serve the robust women vendors as cushions. The backstreets north and west of the market comprise one of Sofia's **older quarters**, with rutted cobblestones and low houses built around courtyards: a far cry from the modern housing estates which girdle the town.

Bulevard Vitosha and the National History Museum

The silhouette of Mount Vitosha surmounting the rooftops is the first thing you see on **bul. Vitosha**. Its foothills are hazy beyond the boulevard's trolleybus wires and exhaust fumes, the vanishing point of parallel lines of greyish buildings, many of which date from the 1950s when the thoroughfare was called bul. Stalin. Lined with pavement cafés and the capital's more stylish shops, it's an invigorating street to stroll along. However, save for the unmissable National History Museum, there's little in the way of things to see.

The National History Museum

The **National History Museum** (Tues–Thur, Sat & Sun 10.30am–6.30pm, Fri 2pm–6.30pm) occupies the former Palace of Justice at the northern end of the boulevard. Some are insisting on the return of the building to its former function, forcing the museum to seek premises elsewhere, although such an expensive and disruptive changeover is unlikely to take place for a number of years. The museum is, at least in its current home, a superbly arranged affair marred only by the lack of catalogues and captions in foreign languages. The archaeological relics on the ground floor cover the history of the Bulgarian lands up until the medieval period, while the first floor concentrates on the politics and culture of Bulgaria's nineteenth-century renaissance.

ANCIENT ARTEFACTS

Halls 1–4 contain artefacts left by various Neolithic cultures between the seventh and third millennia BC – including stone **goddess figures** found near Varna and inscribed with rams, birds, chevrons, labyrinths and other motifs associated with the Great Earth Mother. Pride of place, however, goes to the great gold and silver hoards associated with the **Thracians**, who inhabited the eastern Balkans during the pre-Christian era. Earliest of these is the hoard of golden vessels found near the village of **Vâlchitrân** in northern Bulgaria, and thought to date from about 1300 BC. The various cups and goblets appear quite simple and functional, save for one item consisting of three small containers linked by a trident-like handle. Possibly intended for the ceremonial mixing of liquids, this triple-vessel no doubt had ritual significance for the tribal chieftain who owned it.

THE ROGOZEN TREASURE

Next comes the **Rogozen treasure**, a hoard of 165 silver vessels unearthed in the village of Rogozen near Vratsa. This was in all probability a family treasure, accumulated by wealthy nobles of the Triballi tribe somewhere between the years of 500 and 350 BC. The scenes which decorate many of the vessels portray typically Thracian concerns: hunting trips involving a variety of wild beasts, and archetypal goddess figures – one in a chariot drawn by winged horses, another riding a golden-headed lioness.

THE PANAGYURISHTE TREASURE

More sumptuous still is the golden **treasure of Panagyurishte**, a collection of eight *rhyta* (drinking vessels) and one *phiale* (a kind of plate) made by Greek artisans of the Dardanelles area and imported into Thrace by a wealthy chieftain. Each *rhyton* is designed in the shape of an animal's head, with mythological scenes shown in relief around the side. One amphora-shaped *rhyton* features handles in the form of centaurs and a procession of naked warriors round the main body of the vessel. Originally on show in the town of Panagyurishte itself, the treasure was snapped up by the archaeological museum in Plovdiv before cultural bigwigs in Sofia finally got their hands on it. As Bulgaria slowly moves away from the enforced centralization of the past, it remains to be seen whether the Panagyurishte and other treasures will remain in the capital or return to the regions from which they were unceremoniously plucked.

Further artefacts and jewellery from the Thracian period include a series of fourth-century BC horse trappings found at **Letnitsa** near Lovech: small silver plaques with gilded images of mythical beasts and hunters on horseback.

BULGARIAN TREASURES

Bas reliefs, ceramics, silverware and frescoes (halls 10–11) give some idea of the artistic heights attained during the medieval era, when Pliska, Preslav and Veliko Târnovo enjoyed their heyday as capitals; although these pale before the superb collection of **ecclesiastical art** (jewellery, frescoes and icons) displayed in halls 12–14 upstairs. Centuries of Ottoman rule are ignored in favour of the National Revival of the nineteenth century, when progressive Bulgarians struggled for education, civic reforms and, ultimately, independence, giving rise to revolutionaries like Vasil Levski and Hristo Botev, whose banners and proclamations are prominently featured.

The upper floor also exhibits a wonderful collection of nineteenth-century **folk costumes** (hall 22) and **carpets** (in the corridor); plus two beautiful and very cosy-looking **rooms from Bansko and Tryavna**, furnished in the National Revival style.

The Largo

The broad road stretching eastward from pl. Sveta nedelya, **the Largo**, was one of the major showpieces of postwar Sofia, not least because of the political symbolism embodied in its most imposing edifice: the Communist Party head-quarters. Flanked on three sides by severely monumental buildings, this elon-gated plaza was built on the ruins of central Sofia, which had been pulverized by British and American bombers in the autumn of 1944. Its yellow-painted stones are the start of a kilometre-long stretch of seemingly golden cobblestones which, leading through pl. Aleksandâr Batenberg and along bul. Tsar Osvoboditel, forms a kind of processional way linking many of the capital's key sights.

The Rotunda and the church of Sveta Petka Samardzhiiska

On the south side of the Largo, the *Hotel Balkan Sheraton* casts its sombre wings around a courtyard containing the fourth-century **Rotunda of Saint George's church**. This brick building has been under restoration for years, and the court-yard (with a public entrance on bul. Stamboliiski) may still be officially closed. On the northern side of the Largo an equally large structure houses the Council of Ministers (Bulgaria's cabinet) and Sofia's main department store, the **TsUM** (ЦУМ, pronounced "Tsoom"), alongside which runs an arcade lined with the stalls of street traders.

Another underpass gives access to a sunken plaza laid out with café tables, whose bright awnings contrast with the weathered brick and stone **church of Sveta Petka Samardzhiiska** (Tues–Sat 10.30am–1pm & 3.30–6pm), girded with concrete platforms, its tiled rooftop poking above street level. Originally built in the fourteenth century, the church gained the epithet *samardzhiiska* in the late 1900s, when it was adopted by the Saddlers' Guild as their private chapel.

The Party House

Of the buildings surrounding the Largo, the white, colonnaded supertanker of the **Party House**, or *partiinyat dom*, is by far the most arresting structure. Besides housing sporadic Communist Party congresses, the building accommodated the office of the Central Committee (*Tsentralen Komitet*), and featured in a popular joke. A man cycles up to the building and leans his bike against it, whereupon a policeman shouts: "Hey! You can't leave that there, a high Soviet delegation is due to arrive any minute." "That's okay," replies the cyclist, "I'll chain it up".

After November 1989, public pressure mounted to have the Communists evicted from the building: initially without much success. Anti-Communist demonstrations in August 1990 did, however, succeed in getting rid of the enor-mous **red star** traditionally perched above the roof. When the National Assembly decided on August 24 to have all Communist iconography removed from public buildings, the red star atop the Party House failed to disappear. Within two days the building had been torched by an angry mob – smoke-blackened walls at the rear of the building still bear testimony to their discontent.

The Bulgarian Socialist Party (as the Communists renamed themselves) attempted to soften the building's image by adorning it with voter-friendly posters of red roses and an enormous sign bearing the legend "central club" – but ulti-mately to no avail. They were finally given their marching orders in early 1992, and the Party House was turned (for the time being at least) into a cinema, show-ing the kind of flashy American movies that would send Bulgaria's former moral guardians into shock. The cellars of the building are said to be packed with hundreds of artworks requisitioned by the country's erstwhile rulers to decorate their offices – experts are currently trying to identify both the paintings and their previous owners.

Immediately in front of the Party House, a pedestrian subway contains some **ruins of Serdica**. The underpass gives onto the brick stumps of walls (originally 8–12m high) from fifth- and sixth-century Byzantine fortifications, a section of original pavement and, eventually, the Eastern Gate of the city. Most of the ruins here, and in other parts of Sofia, post-date the devastating fifth-century Hun invasion; the majority are fragments of the new walls and buildings that were raised during the reign of the Byzantine Emperor Justinian.

Aleksandâr Batenberg square

If the Bulgarian Communist Party had a soul it would doubtless still hover over the cobbled expanse of **ploshtad Aleksandâr Batenberg**, formerly ploshtad Deveti Septemvri or 9 September square – where major anniversaries used to be celebrated with **parades**. These took place on May 1 and September 9 (the date of the Communist coup in 1944), and featured a familiar repertoire of Communist spectacle: red-scarved Young Pioneers, brigades of workers bearing portraits of their leaders, mass callisthenics, and floats carrying tableaux symbolizing the achievements of socialist construction. The anniversary of the Bolshevik Revolution (November 7) was marked by soldiers goose-stepping and armoured vehicles grinding across the plaza in emulation of mightier parades in Moscow. Militia cordons kept the uninvited at a distance (events were televized nation-wide), and the regimented proceedings – known as "spontaneous demonstrations of the people" during the Stalinist era – were a tiresome obligation for many participants. "We have seen so many of these demonstrations which humiliate human dignity, where normal people are expected to applaud some paltry medi-ocrity who has proclaimed himself a demi-god and condescendingly waves to them from the heights of his police inviolability", wrote dissident writer Georgi Markov (criticisms like these eventually cost Markov his life, killed by a Bulgarian agent wielding a poisoned umbrella in 1978).

The square is still the obvious venue for mass gatherings, although nowadays they're of a less disciplined, more spontaneous nature – whether election rallies or public lectures given by visiting evangelists from North America. Hastily renamed "Democracy Square" after November 1989, the square has now reverted to its original prewar title, honouring the young German aristocrat who was chosen to be the newly independent country's first monarch in 1878. As an idea-listic 22-year-old Aleksandâr had volunteered to fight alongside Bulgaria's Russian liberators during the War of Independence, yet it was his loss of Russian backing in 1886 – when Bulgaria declared union with Eastern Roumelia without first securing the approval of her big Slav brother – that brought his six-year reign to a premature close.

The Archaeological Museum
At the square's western end, on the corner of ul. Lege, stands an ivy-clad nine-domed building, formerly the *Buyuk Djami* or "Big Mosque", dating from 1494, and now housing the **National Archaeological Museum** (Tues–Sun 10am–noon & 1.30–6pm). Bulgaria's most valuable treasures have been

concentrated in the National History Museum, and the Thracian pottery and silverware on display here has a more workaday feel. However, some individual items stand out, such as an eighth-century BC bronze figurine of a stag found at Sevlievo near Pleven; and there are plentiful Greek and Roman finds from around the country. Most famous of these is the **Stela of Anaxander**, a sixth-century BC gravestone from the ancient Greek colony of Apollonia (now Sozopol) on the Black Sea coast.

Dimitrov's mausoleum

Party leaders used to take the salute from atop the austere white mausoleum on the southern side of the square. Now standing empty and daubed with graffitti, the mausoleum was built to house the embalmed body of **Georgi Dimitrov**, the first leader of the People's Republic of Bulgaria (see box below). Following his death in July 1949 while on a visit to Moscow, **Dimitrov's Mausoleum** was erected in six days and nights, in time for the body's return. Watched over by goose-stepping sentries wearing red-braided tunics and plumed hats, the mausoleum used to be open to visitors three afternoons a week. Suitably reverential citizens would file through antiseptic corridors into the dim, guarded vault where Dimitrov's corpse was displayed (though it was said that only the arms and head were original; the rest was wax). In July 1990, Dimitrov's body was quietly removed from the mausoleum and cremated; the future of his erstwhile tomb remains uncertain, although it is coveted by the National History Museum as a potential exhibition space.

GEORGI DIMITROV (1882–1949)

Born into a humble background in 1882, **Georgi Dimitrov** was a teenage apprentice printer when he converted to Communism, and, with characteristic nerve, he doctored the speeches of reactionary MPs before they went to press – the prelude to a lifelong militant career. He organised Party cells, unions, strikes and propaganda inside Bulgaria, emigrating to Moscow after the failure of the September Uprising of 1923. Once in the Soviet Union he rose quickly through the ranks of the *Comintern* or Communist International, and it was while on Comintern business in Berlin that he was arrested by the Nazis on March 9 1933 and charged with instigating the Reichstag fire. The subsequent show trial in Leipzig became an international cause célèbre, with Dimitrov (despite months of maltreatment by the Gestapo) conducting his own defence and succeeding in making Herman Goering, his prosecutor, seem both a liar and a fool. This, and the international attention the trial had received, ensured his acquittal in February 1934. He again took refuge in Moscow, survived Stalin's purges (probably by betraying fellow Bulgarians also exiled in the USSR), and became Secretary-General of the Comintern in 1935. During World War II he masterminded the Bulgarian Communist Party's strategy of infiltrating and gaining control of the anti-fascist opposition, returning to the country himself in November 1945. He was prime minister from 1946 until his death in 1949, presiding over a period of intense social change: sweeping nationalization and industrialization proceeding hand-in-hand with the crushing of all political opposition.

Until recently every town in Bulgaria had at least one street named after Dimitrov. Nowadays, memories of the man are fast disappearing from national life, but his paternal visage can still be seen peering from 10- and 20-leva banknotes.

The National Art Gallery

Opposite the mausoleum stands the former royal palace, which was once so delapidated that a ceiling came down upon the head of Tsar "Foxy" Ferdinand, who had just taken up residence. The palace was built on the site of the former Ottoman *Konak* where Vasil Levski (see p.191) was tortured prior to his execution. Inside is the **National Art Gallery** (Tues–Sun 10am–6pm), a fairly uninspiring collection which reveals how dependent on Western models Bulgarian painting has been. The works that stand out are those which heavily exploit the nostalgia for folk styles and motifs: notably Tsanko Lavrenov's pictures of old Plovdiv, and the near-naive canvases of fellow Plovdivite Zlatyu Boyadzhiev. More European in inspiration are the Bulgarian village landscapes painted in the Thirties and Forties by Vasil Barakov. Housed in the same building is a small **Ethnographic Museum** (Wed–Sun 10am–12.30pm & 1.30–6pm), with changing exhibitions of folk costumes and crafts.

Bulevard Tsar Osvoboditel and around

Bul. Tsar Osvoboditel heads out of ploshtad Aleksandâr Batenberg's eastern end, an attractive thoroughfare partially lined with wild chestnut trees. The **Natural Science Museum** (Wed–Fri 9am–noon & 1–6pm, Sat & Sun 9am–noon & 3–6pm) is at no. 1, presenting a thorough cataloguing of Bulgarian and worldwide wildlife, both stuffed and pickled. Among the exhibits are an insect collection of over 500,000 different species. Immediately beyond, the **Russian church** (Tues–Sat 7.30am–7.30pm; Sun 7.30am–4.30pm) is an unmistakable, zany firecracker of a building with an exuberant exterior of bright yellow tiles, five gilded domes and an emerald spire, concealing a dark, candlewax-scented interior. Officially dedicated to St Nicholas the Blessed, the church was built in 1913 at the behest of a Tsarist diplomat, Semontovski-Kurilo, who feared for his soul to worship in Bulgarian churches, which he believed to be schismatic.

Cut down ul. Rakovski just beyond the Russian church and it's impossible to miss the **statue of Aleksandâr Stamboliiski** near the neoclassical opera house, moustaches bristling and chest braced. A fiery orator, Stamboliiski led the Agrarian Party's campaign to assert "peasant power" over the the bourgeoisie and state bureaucracy, turning the established order upside down during the brief period of Agrarian government (1919–23) and propounding a "Green Alliance" of peasant parties throughout the Balkans. Stamboliiski's renunciation of Bulgarian claims on Macedonia – the cause of two wars with Serbia – united conservative factions with the fanatical separatist group, IMRO (see p.307), who staged a coup in June 1923. Peasants were murdered by the thousand, and the IMRO amputated Stamboliiski's hand (which had signed the treaty of Niš with Serbia) before killing him.

Around Kristal

Continuing eastward along bul. Ruski are the **military club**, where the *Zveno* (a radical political group which attracted young right-wing officers) hatched several conspiracies in the inter-war years, and a small square of greenery known popularly as **Kristal**, after the café which shelters on its southern flank. The area around *Kristal* is fast becoming the antiques quarter of Sofia; the square itself plays host to a daily **fleamarket**, selling reproduction icons, militaria and other ephemera; while more established dealers are increasingly setting up showrooms in the surrounding streets. Further along at no. 14, the erstwhile Museum of Revolutionary Movements – currently operating under the name of the **Museum of Political Parties and Movements** – remains closed pending agreement on what should be included among the exhibits.

National Assembly square

Bul. Tsar Osvoboditel opens out into ploshtad Narodno sâbranie – **National Assembly square**. On the northern side stands a cream building housing the *Narodno sâbranie* itself – Bulgaria's **National Assembly**, the facade of which bears the motto *sâedinenieto pravi silata* ("unity is strength"). Directly opposite a semicircular plaza encloses the Monument to the Liberators, which gives pride of place to a statue of the *Tsar Osvoboditel*, or "Tsar Liberator" himself, Alexander II of Russia.

Aleksandâr Nevski square

The area immediately north of bul. Ruski is dominated by another of Sofia's set-piece squares, an expanse of greenery and paving stones (overlaying what was, in Roman times, the necropolis of Serdica) overlooked by the twinkling domes of the Aleksandâr Nevski memorial church. Entering the square from the western end, however, you first encounter the brown brick **church of Sveta Sofia**. Raised in the sixth century during the reign of Justinian, it stands on the site of two earlier churches and follows the classic Byzantine plan of a regular cross with a dome at the intersection. Sofia means "wisdom", and the name of the saint was adopted by the city towards the end of the fourteenth century. Around the back an engraved boulder marks the **grave of Ivan Vazov** (p.190), who requested that he be buried amid the daily life of his people; you'll notice his statue, seated with book in hand, in a park nearby. Set beside the southern wall of the church is the Tomb of the Unknown Soldier, flanked by two recumbent lions.

Immediately opposite Sveta Sofia, shielded by trees, a beige building sporting a stripe of brightly coloured ceramic tiles houses the Bulgarian church's **Holy Synod**. In May 1992 the building was occupied by reformist priests eager to purge the church of those who had collaborated with the former regime, and guards were posted at the doorway to prevent any members of the "old synod" from getting back in. Led by Bishop Hristofor Sâbev, a well-known former dissident who holed up in the American Embassy in the late Eighties in order to escape the clutches of the Security Police, the reformists aimed most of their criticism at the Bulgarian patriarch, Maksim, maintaining that he had been a docile servant of the Communists.

The Aleksandâr Nevski cathedral

Arguably the finest piece of architecture in the Balkans and certainly Sofia's crowning glory, the **Aleksandâr Nevski memorial church** honours the 200,000 Russian casualties of the 1877–78 War of Liberation, particularly the defenders of the Shipka pass. Financed by public subscription and built between 1882 and 1924 to the designs of Saint Petersburg architect Pomerantsev, it's a magnificent structure, bulging with domes and half domes and glittering with 18lbs of gold leaf donated by the Soviet Union in 1960. Within the cavernous interior, a white-bearded God glowers down from the main cupola, an angelic sunburst covers the central vault, and as a parting shot a *Day of Judgement* looms above the exit. Expressive frescoes lacking the stiffness of Byzantine portraiture depict episodes from the life of Christ in rich tones, and the grandeur of the iconostasis is enhanced by twin thrones with columns of onyx and alabaster.

Orthodox congregations stand or kneel during services, although the weak and the elderly traditionally lean or sit on benches round the side. The church's capacity of 5000 souls is ample for daily **services** (9.30–11.30am). At such times sightseers are technically forbidden, although unobtrusive ones might gain admission to appreciate the spectacle, rich with incense, candlelight and sonorous chanting.

The **crypt**, entered from the outside, contains a superb **collection of icons** (Wed–Sun 10.30am–6.30pm) from all over the country, mostly eighteenth- and nineteenth-century pieces – though look out for some medieval gems from the coastal town of Nesebâr, home to a prolific icon-painting school.

The SS Cyril and Methodius Foundation

An imposing gallery on the northeastern edge of the cathedral square houses the **SS Cyril and Methodius Foundation** (Wed–Mon 10am–6.30pm), an international art collection largely based on the donations of rich Bulgarians living abroad (and the occasional philanthropic foreigner – Robert Maxwell was one early benefactor). The ground floor contains a sizable collection of Indian miniatures, manuscripts and sculpture. Next door, a series of eighteenth-century Japanese woodblock prints includes a variety of landscapes and scenes from courtesan life. Upstairs, second-division French artists take up a lot of space, though there are a couple of Delacroix sketches, a small Picasso etching (*The Visions of Count d'Orgas* of 1966), and a mesmerizing *Lucifer* by turn-of-the-century German symbolist Franz von Stück. For the most part, the contemporary art on display still reflects the tastes of Bulgaria's erstwhile socialist elite, typified by Cuban artist Carmelo Gonzales Iglesias' *Poetry, Socialism* – a still-life featuring machine gun, hammer, and loaf of bread.

The City Garden

Sofia's southeastern quarter is probably the liveliest part of the inner city, its City Garden and pavement cafés providing the focus for social life during the day, its theatres and restaurants in the evening. Free (for the time being at least) of rubbish, hustlers, punks or sex shows, the area is more decorous than its counterpart in any Western capital and quite safe at night. It can be approached from more or less any angle, and the best way to appreciate the area is to just walk in and wander as you will.

With its well-tended flowerbeds and shady paths, the **City Garden** invariably attracts courting couples and office workers taking their lunch break. Several fountains splash opposite the **Ivan Vazov National Theatre**, a handsome neoclassical edifice decked out in red, white and gold with Gobelin tapestries and Panagyurishte hangings inside, which provides a welcome contrast to the other, sombrely ministerial buildings along ul. Vasil Levski. At the southern end of this is ul. General Gurko, where you'll find the **City Art Gallery** on the edge of the park (daily 8am–3.30pm), a showcase for contemporary paintings, drawings and sculpture by Bulgarian artists.

Ulitsa G.S. Rakovski is one of Sofia's longest streets, extending north and south from bul. Tsar Osvoboditel, although from a visitor's standpoint only the latter section really merits attention, with a scattering of **patisseries** (*sladkarnitsi*), **restaurants** and **theatres** (see p.61 & p.63). Further down it joins **Graf Ignatiev**, a meandering thoroughfare lined with shops, named after the Russian count who persuaded Tsar Aleksandâr to support Bulgarian liberation. In the small garden beside the intersection with ul. Tsar Shishman stands the **church of Sveti Sedmochislenitsi**, literally the "Holy Seven", referring to Cyril, Methodius and their followers, the seven saints who brought Christianity to the Slavs. Built on the site of the so-called "Black Mosque" where the Turks imprisoned Bulgarians during the struggle for liberation, the church is another building designed by Pomerantsev.

The inner ring road and beyond

Girdling the city centre is the broad sweep of Sofia's inner ring road, built in imitation of the wide boulevards of other European capitals such as Paris, Vienna and Budapest. There's little of architectural interest along its length, save for a scattering of monuments and buildings around the eastern end of pl. Aleksandâr Nevski and bul. Tsar Osvoboditel. A hundred metres north of the Nevski church, at the intersection with Yanko Sakâzov, stands the weathered stone **Vasil Levski Monument**, marking the spot where the "Apostle of Freedom" (p.191) was hanged by the Turks in 1873.

From there it's a brief stroll southwards to **Sofia University**, the country's most prestigious. Founded a decade after the Liberation, it was named after *Kliment Ohridski*, a pupil of Cyril and Methodius, who as ninth-century bishop of Ohrid in western Macedonia had an important impact on the flowering of Slav culture. Not previously known for their radicalism, Sofia's students were at the heart of demonstrations in June 1990 protesting at the alleged unfairness of Bulgaria's first post-Communist elections. Barricades went up in front of the university, provoking fears that Bulgaria's nascent democracy would descend into confrontation, but government concessions to the opposition prevented any real violence.

Immediately opposite the university to the south stands the towering **Monument to the Soviet Army**, erected in honour of the "liberation" of Bulgaria in 1944. Although allied to Nazi Germany during World War II, the Bulgarians always shrank from declaring war on the Soviet Union, mindful of the long tradition of Russo-Bulgarian friendship. The Soviets, however, regarded Bulgaria as a hostile power, and despite desperate attempts by the latter to change sides as the war neared its end, occupation of the country by the Red Army proved inescapable. Centrepiece of the monument is a Red Army soldier flanked by a worker and a peasant woman with a child, an archetypal symbol of Bulgaro-Soviet friendship: you'll see it in monuments and fading propaganda billboards throughout the land.

Orlov Most and Freedom Park

To the east, the modest dribble of the Perlovska River is spanned by **Orlov Most** or Eagle Bridge, crowned with four ferocious-looking birds of prey. Set amid weeping willows, the bridge marks the spot where liberated prisoners of war were greeted by their victorious Russian allies and compatriots in the war of

1878. From here the main highway to Plovdiv (formerly bul. Lenin, it has now reverted to the original name of bul. Trakiya) heads southeast, flanked on one side by **park na svobodata** (Freedom Park), Sofia's oldest and largest. Partially influenced by St James' in London, it has a rich variety of flowers and trees, becoming more densely wooded the further southeast you go.

Yuzhen park and the NDK

As an evening parade ground for the city's burgeoning youth culture, park na svobodata is outshone by **Yuzhen park** (literally, Southern Park) at the southern end of bul. Vitosha. On summer evenings city centre office workers, shoppers and youngsters pour down the boulevard en route to the park to drink coffee or stroll between impeccably manicured flowerbeds.

The park also serves as the setting for two structures symbolizing Bulgaria's achievements. The **Thirteen Hundred Years Monument** is boldly modernist (some say hideously): huge wrench-shaped blocks emerging from a pit which represents centuries of servitude, garnished with anguished-looking figures (one of whom has Zhivkov's features, it's rumoured) and bearing Levski's maxim: "We are in time and time is in us" ("We transform it and it transforms us" he continued, to clarify the message).

At the top end of the park, the gleaming **NDK** or **National Palace of Culture** (*Natsionalen Dvorets na Kulturata*) rears up like a Dalek spaceship come to earth. Covering an area of 17,000 square metres, the complex contains concert halls, congress facilities, press centres, a mall of overpriced shops, a disco and an unusually-efficient **tourist bureau** in its subterranean arcade. As a tribute to her cultural work, the building originally bore the name of Lyudmila Zhivkova, the former Party leader's daughter, who died in her thirties of a brain tumour. But the most telling aspect of the NDK was its colossal cost, and with this in mind, Sofians invented a sarcastic pun on its initials, which can also stand for "another hole in the belt".

The popularity of the park as a strolling area has drawn a sizable number of street hawkers, illegal currency dealers and petty **hustlers** to the upper stretches of bul. Vitosha, which runs along the park's western side. Most tend to congregate in the vicinity of the *Magura* ice cream parlour, formerly a favourite hang-out of the trendy. Now dubbed "Magura Street", this particular stretch of pavement has entered modern Bulgarian folklore as the epitome of the new black market culture.

Mount Vitosha

A wooded mass of granite 19km long by 17km wide, **MOUNT VITOSHA** is very much a part of the capital and is the source of its pure water and fresh breezes. *Sofiantsi* come here for picnics, solitude, the magnificent views or to ski, and the ascent of its highest peak, Cherni Vrâh, has become a traditional test of stamina for hikers. If you're seeking absolute tranquility it's best to come on a weekday, or at least get some distance from the chair-lift terminals. Most people approach Mount Vitosha by way of one of the villages (really suburbs) at its foothills: Knyazhevo and Boyana are the starting points for the popular *Zlatni Mostove* ("golden bridges") area, while Dragalevtsi and Simeonovo provide access to the winter sports centre of Aleko.

Boyana and Knyazhevo

To reach Knyazhevo and Boyana, take tram #5 from behind the National History Museum to Ovcha Kupel, then change to bus #61, #62 or #107. These skirt the walled *Rezidentsiya Boyana* where Zhivkov and other top-ranking Communist functionaries used to have their villas, before reaching the village of **BOYANA** itself. There, follow Belite Brezi uphill and you'll come to a small garden surrounding **Boyana church** (Mon–Fri 8.45am–5pm), home to a recently restored set of **medieval frescoes**, largely executed in 1259. With their realism and rejection of the Byzantine style, these anticipate the work of Giotto, which heralded the beginning of the Italian Renaissance. As well as biblical themes, the unknown artist drew on contemporary life for inspiration: clothing the saints in medieval Bulgarian dress and setting garlic, radishes and bread – the peasants' staples – on the table in the *Last Supper*. Perhaps the finest portraits are those of Boyana's patrons, Desislava and Sebastocrator Kaloyan (depicted holding the church in the customary fashion), and the haloed figures of the king and queen, Asen and Irina.

Bus #61 continues on to **KNYAZHEVO**, from where there's a cabin-lift up to the *Hotel Kopitoto*, while bus #62 ascends through the forests past the *Tihya Kât* motel to *Zlatni Mostove*, a restaurant just to the east of the so-called **Stone River**. Beneath the large boulders running down the mountainside (the moraine of an ancient glacier) burbles a rivulet which once attracted gold-panners; today the area is a popular place for picnics.

Dragalevtsi

Another route to the mountain runs via **DRAGALEVTSI** village, which you can reach by taking tram #2 from Graf Ignatiev or Patriarh Evtimii to the Hladinka stop on bul. Cherni Vrâh, and then bus #66. Climbing the road beyond the village the bus passes three old mills now serving as the *Vodenicharski Mehani* restaurant (p.62), near which begins a chair-lift to the *Shtastlivetsa Hotel*. Situated in a beech wood 2–3km further on, **Dragalevski monastery** (Mon–Fri 9am–5pm) is the patriachal residence, with a fourteenth-century church – the only part of the original monastery that remains – and cells around its leafy courtyard which often sheltered the revolutionary Vasil Levski during the nineteenth century.

Aleko

Some twenty minutes later bus #66 arrives at **ALEKO**, an expanding **winter sports centre** which has a range of pistes to suit all grades of skiers and operates from November through late spring. The resort takes its name from nineteenth-century writer Aleko Konstantinov (see Svishtov, p.116): in 1895, back in the days when hill-walking was an expression of love for the country rather than mere recreation, Konstantinov led a party of 300 idealistic young Bulgarians in an assault on Vitosha's highest point, Cherni Vrâh – a climb that marked the beginning of alpine pursuits in Bulgaria.

Around the end of March and the first week of April there's a competition for the **Aleko Cup**, with slalom and giant slalom races open to all; qualifying heats for the European Cup may also take place here at the beginning of March. Tuition at the national **ski school** is of a high standard but organized primarily for package tourists (see "Getting There" in *Basics*), who also have first claim on skiing equipment, which is rented from the *Prostor* and *Shtastlivetsa* hotels. In the vicinity of these hotels are the chair-lifts up to the Stena crag or Malâk and Golyam Rezen. Vitosha's loftiest "Black Peak", **Cherni Vrâh** (7513ft), is accessible by a trail from the Rezen heights or by ski-drag.

Nightlife centres around the restaurants, discos and bars of the two main hotels (the Prostor also has a pool and sauna), and there's a **carnival** arranged for skiers with *Balkan Holidays*. Finally, lovers of long and vertiginous rides should enjoy the **cable-car** linking Aleko and the suburb of SIMEONOVO (bus #98 from Dragalevtsi).

Other museums, galleries and memorial houses

The lack of foreign-language captions and catalogues is the main problem with Sofia's **museums and galleries**. If you're lucky, there might be a tour-group doing the rounds with a guide giving commentary in a language that you can understand; otherwise, until the situation is remedied, the exhibits have to speak for themselves. A fair proportion of places seem likely to be shut pending repairs or relocation. Expect to pay a miniscule admission fee in museums and memorial houses; galleries are sometimes free.

Museums and galleries

Military History Museum, bul. Skobelev 23 (Mon–Fri 9am–noon & 2pm–6pm; Sun 1pm–7pm). Bulgaria has fought few wars abroad; banners proclaim the slogan "Liberty or Death" rather than the names of foreign battles. The prolonged "people's war" against Turkish domination during the nineteenth century and the partisan campaigns of World War II used to feature heavily in the displays here; present-day Bulgaria's desire to reassess the latter is one reason why this museum was closed for reorganization at the time of writing.

Museum of Physical Education and Sport, Vasil Levski stadium, park na svobodata (Tues–Sun 10am–6pm). Devoted to Bulgarian sports and sportspersons of the twentieth century.

Permanent Exhibition "Saving the Bulgarian Jews", 5th floor, bul. Stamboliiski 50 (Mon–Fri 9am–noon, 2–5pm). Bulgaria's wartime government was forced by the Germans into ordering the deportation of the Jews in 1943, then failed to carry it out after popular demonstrations in the Jews' favour. The museum looks back at the history of Bulgarian Jewry (most of the prewar population of 50,000 have now emigrated, leaving just 5000), who largely originated from the expulsion of the Jews from Spain in 1492.

Applied Arts Gallery, Rakovski 117 (Mon–Sat 10am–6pm). Another commercial gallery, with the emphasis on ceramics, sculpture and textiles.

Gallery of the Union of Bulgarian Artists, Shipka 6. Good place to check up on up-to-date trends in Bulgarian art.

Graphic Art Gallery, General Gurko 62. Possibly the best of Sofia's galleries, if only because Bulgarian graphic artists during the socialist era seemed to have been allowed a greater freedom of expression than contemporary painters.

Permanent Art Gallery, Rakovski 133 (daily 10am–6pm). Contemporary artworks and crafts for sale.

Memorial houses

Several houses and flats once inhabited by famous writers and politicians have been turned into museums and filled with artefacts (furniture, books, personal effects) related to the life of the great one in question. However, many of the figures thus honoured have socialist connections, and in the current political climate Sofia's city leaders may be unwilling to provide the funds necessary to keep such memorial houses open. Be on guard for sudden closures.

Dimitâr Blagoev, Kossuth 34 (Tues–Sat 10am–6pm). Residence of the founder of Bulgarian Marxism – was still open at the time of writing, but with increasingly unpredictable opening hours.

Georgi Dimitrov, Opâlchenska 66 (daily 10am–6pm). The residence of the Dimitrov family from 1888–1923. The ground floor where his parents lived until 1906 is small and folksy, featuring the loom on which Dimitrov's mother, "Granny" Parashkeva, used to weave. Dimitrov and his wife, Lyuba Ivosevits, also a revolutionary, lived upstairs. Their library of 3000 volumes, Georgi's pipe and slippers, and other personal effects are displayed; while Dimitrov's political career is the subject of a memorial hall adjoining the house. The museum faces an uncertain future.

Petko and Pencho Slaveykov, Rakovski 138. A reconstruction of the room which used to stand here, belonging to the liberal politician and writer Petko and his son Pencho, who was nominated for the Nobel Prize in 1912.

Hristo Smirnenski, Shekerdzhiiski 116. Twentieth-century poet with leftist leanings. His literary reputation (and therefore this memorial house) is likely to survive the downfall of Communism.

Aleksandâr Stamboliiski, Suhodolska 22. Ill-fated Agrarian leader and prime minister, overthrown by military coup in 1923 (see p.53).

Nikola Vaptsarov, Angel Kânchev 37. Working-class poet of the inter-war years whose work documents proletarian life. Shot in 1942 for being a Communist subversive (see p.86), Vaptsarov's socialist background may possibly lead to a reassessment of the role of this museum.

Ivan Vazov, Ivan Vazov 10 (Mon 1–5pm, Tues & Wed 1pm–8pm, Thurs–Sat 9am–5pm). Author of *Pod Igoto* or "Under the Yoke", the classic novel of nineteenth-century Bulgarian life, Vazov lived in this house from 1895 until his death in 1921.

Peyu Yavorov, Rakovski 136. Symbolist poet, socialist and Macedonian freedom-fighter, Yavorov tried to kill himself several times in an attempt to join his suicide-wife Laura. He finally succeeded in 1914.

EATING, DRINKING AND ENTERTAINMENT

Sofia was never the liveliest of Balkan capitals, its social life suffering from the endless moralizing of a regime which frowned on ostentation and promoted modesty of habits. Things are now beginning to improve, with state-owned restaurants and cafés attaining financial independence and having to attract custom in order to stay afloat, and the emergence of a few new privately owned establishments. Summer brings out the best in the city, when cafés and restaurants with outdoor seating remain packed well into the evening. In winter time, perhaps chastened by declining living standards, many *Sofiantsi* are increasingly staying at home. For the Westerner, if not for the locals, the costs of food, drink and entertainment remain relatively low.

Eating

Although Sofia would be lucky to get one star if Egon Ronay graded cities according to gastronomic merit, there's generally a wider range of culinary choices available in the capital than in the provinces. Prices are fairly reasonable if you stay out of deluxe hotels and avoid imported drinks; even in the topnotch establishments, a three-course meal with drink rarely exceeds £4–5 per person. Most places are open for lunch (11.30am–3pm) and in the evenings (6–11pm).

Almost all of Sofia's hotels of 3-star standard and above have **restaurants** pitched midway between Bulgarian and international tastes; tower-block hotels such as the *Vitosha*, *Rodina* and *Moskva* all have "panorama" restaurants on the top floor which tend to be popular with the local business class. Less well-heeled citizens tend to frequent the cheap-and-cheerful city centre **mehanas**, which sell predominantly grilled food and also serve as popular drinking venues; or the slightly more costly foreign-cuisine restaurants which, although few would pass muster in their homelands, form one of the more endearing legacies of socialist internationalism. Popular at weekends are a number of out-of-town places in the foothills of Mount Vitosha: though hard to get back from at night without private transport, they're often the best places to sample traditional Bulgarian cooking. Most restaurants now feature live music – usually an inoffensive mixture of folk and international easy-listening tunes.

For quick daytime eating, many locals frequent the cheap **self-service** places near the open-air market on Georgi Kirkov; or the slightly more salubrious **fast-food** joints along bul. Vitosha, which serve up *kyofteta*, *kebapcheta* and chips in Western-style surroundings. *Boyana* at no. 37 is one of the biggest.

In the city

Bålgarska Gozba, bul. Vitosha 34 (☎879162). Good range of Bulgarian dishes in comfortable surroundings; but very crowded due to its central location. Arrive early or try to book a table.

Berlin, bul. Yanko Sakâzov 2 (☎443411). Inside the Hotel *Serdika*. A few vaguely Germanic dishes on a schnitzel-dominated menu.

Budapest, Rakovski 145 (☎872750). Possibly the best of central Sofia's restaurants, with a comparatively varied menu of central European dishes. Elegant decor, and a selection of Danubian waltzes performed by live musicians.

Cheshka Birariya, Graf Ignatiev 12 (☎870022). Unpretentious place (the name means "Czech beer-hall") serving good draught beer and little else, save for grilled chicken.

Forum, bul. Vitosha 64 (☎521119). French-based international cuisine.

Havana, bul. Vitosha 27 (☎800544). The Havana's claim to serve Cuban cuisine has now all but been dispensed with, although a certain Caribbean ambience lives on in the vaguely tropical plants surrounding the dining area. Live music.

Gambrinus, Tsar Simeon 80 (☎835174). The oldest of central Sofia's restaurants, although nowadays a little delapidated and down-market.

Ko-op, bul. Vitosha 57. Straightforward food and uninspiring decor, slightly cheaper than others on the main boulevard.

Krim, Slavyanska 17 (☎870131). Delicious Russian food served in a nineteenth-century mansion, although the atmosphere is quite snooty – best reserve in advance. Summer garden.

Melnik, bul. Hristo Botev 48 (☎878142). Basic *mehana* serving grills.

Mexicano, Evlogi Georgiev 1 (☎446598). New, top-class restaurant (dress smart and make a reservation) situated in the headquarters of the Union of Bulgarian Architects.

Peking, inside the *Hotel Rodina*, bul. Totleben 8 (☎51631). Chinese restaurant with Chinese kitchen staff – so expect some reasonably authentic food.

Rozhen, bul. Vitosha 74 (☎521131). Bulgarian cuisine in elegant surroundings, specializing in dishes from the Rhodope region, such as *agneshko cheverme* – barbecued lamb.

Piccola Italia, Yanko Sakâzov 20. More of a fast-food joint than a restaurant; solid pasta and pizza fare at rock-bottom prices.

Rubin, pl. Sveta Nedelya (☎874704). Standard Bulgarian food in a central location; therefore somewhat touristy and overpriced. Serves as the meeting-place for local wheeler-dealers and small-time business types.

Sekura, in the Hotel Vitosha, bul. Anton Ivanov 100 (☎62451). Top-class Japanese restaurant: a meal with sake will set you back a small fortune by any standards.

Varshava, bul. Yanko Sakâzov 17 (☎442369). Set back from the main road on the edges of a tower-block housing estate. Vaguely Polish dishes and loud live music.

Vietnam, bul. Georgi Kirkov 1 (☎874502). An attempt to recreate Vietnamese food with Bulgarian ingredients. Peaceful atmosphere, somnolent service.

Out of town

Boyansko Hanche, Boyana (☎563016). Just below the Boyana church and therefore a popular stop-off with sightseers, the hanche is a custom-built "inn" with folklore shows in the evenings. Bus #63.

Vodenicharski Mehani, Dragalevtsi (☎671021). Housed in three renovated mills and serving up traditional millers' nosh, such as *kachamak* (fried maize dough with meat). bus #93.

Zlatni Mostove (☎773004). Situated in the popular Vitosha recreation area of the same name. Bus #62.

Drinking

For most of the capital's citizens **drinking** is a predominantly daytime or early evening activity which centres on the city's numerous cafés or the ubiquitous kiosks which dole out coffee, juice and sometimes alcohol. However, cafés tend to close at around 8–9pm, and night-time imbibing traditionally takes place in restaurants and hotel bars – western-European-style bars remain few and far between.

Most drinking venues lie on or near central Sofia's main thoroughfares, and there's little point in straying beyond this area.

Cafés and bars

Galeriya, Solunska. Quiet, intimate café just off bul. Vitosha.

Havana, bul. Vitosha 27. Largest café on the main street, with a warren of bars inside.

Kristal, Aksakov 10. Favourite hang-out of fashion-conscious youth in the early 1980s, although the plush fittings now look a bit dated.

Magura, bul. Vitosha 80. Has a reputation for serving the city's best ice cream, its position next door to Yuzhen park making it a popular stop-off for evening strollers.

Panorama, NDK, 8th floor. Unparalleled views across the Sofia skyline, and excellent ices.

Praga, Rakovski 145. Big central-European-style café.

Renesans, pl. Vâzrazhdane. Daytime venue behind the cultural institute of the same name.

Solun, Solunska. Small café just behind bul. Vitosha.

Union Jack Pub, Sveta Sofia 5. Housed in the basement of an office block on the western side of pl. Sveta Nedelya, it's not much like a pub – pool table, dart board and draught beer in pint mugs notwithstanding. Quiet café-like atmosphere during the day, transforms itself into a raucous meeting-place for the city's anglophile youth in the evening. Open until 2am.

Entertainment

Sofia's real forté is **drama, ballet and classical music,** all of which are of a high standard and very inexpensive. **Youth culture** is less prevalent, although it is beginning to make its presence felt in the more relaxed atmosphere of the post-Communist era. Cultural listings are usually to be found in the back pages of the daily press; otherwise **information and tickets** for most venues are available from the *Concert Bureau* at bul. Tsar Osvoboditel 2.

The most popular form of entertainment for many locals is the **cinema** – and the flood of (subtitled) American movies sweeping the country since the collapse of state cultural policy means that you won't have any problems understanding the dialogue. Biggest of the cinemas in the city centre are the *Serdika*, bul. Yanko Sakâzov 1; *Rex*, bul. Vitosha 37; and *Kultura*, Graf Ignatiev 11. For those with children there's a **circus** with attendant funfair on ul. Pozitano; and **bowling alleys** in both the *Hotel Vitosha* and the NDK.

Theatre

Plays are, naturally, performed in Bulgarian, so not knowing the language is a distinct drawback, but the general standard of performances can make a visit to the theatre rewarding. Works by eminent Bulgarians and classical writers are performed by the national theatre company at the *Naroden Teatâr Ivan Vazov*, Vasil Levski 1A. Visiting companies often appear at the *Dramatichen Teatâr Sofia*, bul. Yanko Sakâzov 23A. The next-door *Malâk gradski teatâr "zad kanala"*, bul. Yanko Sakâzov 25, is the best place to see modern works in a small, intimate auditorium, while the *Mladezhki teatâr*, or youth theatre, pl. Narodno sâbranie, often has the best of the avant-garde stuff. The *Satirichen teatâr Aleko Konstantinov*, Stefan Karadzha 26, is the place to go for **comedy and cabaret**. *Sâlza i Smyah*, Slavyanska 5, is the oldest professional theatre company in Sofia, dating from 1892, and it still has a reputation for challenging drama. Performances at the *Kuklen teatâr*, or puppet theatre, General Gurko 14, seem to be the choicest entertainments for children.

Music

The National Palace of Culture or NDK is the venue for many of the bigger symphonic concerts or operatic productions; otherwise **symphonic music** can be heard at the *Zala Bâlgariya*, Benkovski 1; or the *Zala Slaveykov*, pl. Slaveykov. Traditional home of **opera and ballet** is the *Narodna Opera*, bul. Dondukov 58 (☎877011). The *Stefan Makedonski State Musical Theatre*, Panayot Volov 3 (☎442321), tends to concentrate on lighter operetta and musicals. **Festivals** to look out for are the **Sofia Music Weeks** (late May–late June), featuring international soloists and ensembles; the **Music Evenings** (early December), concentrating on the best native classical musicians; and the November **Jazz Festival**. Festival events take place in the NDK and in the *Zala Universiada*, Shipchenski prohod 2.

Popular music and discos

Apart from the glut of easy-listening bands playing cover versions to the diners of Sofia's hotels and restaurants, there's very little in the way of a local contemporary **music scene**. There's a lot of enthusiasm for Heavy and Thrash Metal among the young, and a small number of domestic acts have emerged, but regular venues have yet to establish themselves. The best you can do for the time being is to look out for street posters advertising gigs in student halls. Bigger local acts or foreign bands on tour sometimes play in the NDK or in the large multipurpose halls such as *Zala Universiada*, Shipchenski prohod 2 (tram #20 from the Levski monument); *Festivalna Zala*, Vasil Vodenicharski 2 (bus #72 from Orlov Most); or *Sporten Kompleks Hristo Botev*, in the *Studentski kompleks*, or student village, southeast of town (bus #80 from the University).

Friendly and boisterous student **discos** can be found in almost every block of the *Studentski kompleks* during term time, although specific venues change: look out for posters or ask around. Western-style discos in the city centre are few in number and short on style. Those in the NDK centre attract a mixed clientele; while the one in the *Mladezhki teatâr* on pl. Narodno sâbranie attracts a younger crowd. Children of Sofia's emerging middle class tend to favour the *Yalta*, ul. Aksakov 31, a purple paradise opposite the university; and the *Orbilux*, opposite the hotel Vitosha on bul. Anton Ivanov. In the winter, look for *aprés ski* nightlife in the Mount Vitosha hotels: the *Prostor* usually hosts discos.

Listings

Airlines *Balkan*, pl. Narodno sâbranie 12 (☎881180, 885406) for international services, ul. Batenberg 10 (☎884436, 881394) for internal flights; *Aeroflot*, bul. Tsar Osvoboditel 2 (☎879080); *Air France*, bul. Stamboliiski 2 (☎872686); *Austrian Airlines*, bul. Knyaginya Mariya Luiza 68 (☎327057); *Lufthansa*, bul. Stamboliiski 9 (☎882310); *Swissair*, bul. Knyaginya Mariya Luiza 66 (☎328181).

Airport Ring ☎451113 for information on domestic flights, ☎722414 for international services. The airport is situated 10km east of the city and accessible by #84 bus from Orlov Most (runs about every 30min; allow 30min for the trip). The last bus leaves the airport at midnight. The taxi fare is around £3.

American Centre bul. Stamboliiski 1, adjacent to the US Embassy. Contains a library, a video and a range of Western newspapers. Open more frequently than the advertised time – Wed 8am–1pm – suggests.

Books The *Vicho Ivanov* second-hand bookshop at Alabin 40 has a selection of English and French paperbacks. Outdoor bookstalls along Graf Ignatiev and in the pedestrian subway outside Sofia University often have foreign-language books or out-of-print art books and dictionaries unavailable elsewhere. Serious bibliophiles should check out the *Antikvarium* at Graf Ignatiev 18.

Bulgarian Hikers' Union Contact the *Pirin Travel Agency* branch of the Union (bul. Stamboliiski 30, ☎870687) **for information** on potholing, hiking and caves; or to reserve **beds** in the cheap chalets (*hizha*) and hostels (*turisticheska spalnya*) in Bulgaria's highland regions.

Car rental *Hertz* at *Balkantours*, bul. Vitosha 1 (☎874480) and at the airport (☎791506); *Europcar* at *Interbalkan*, bul. Stamboliiski 11 (☎877788) and at the airport (☎720157).

Car repairs BMW, Fiat, Opel, Peugeot, Renault and Volvo at *Balkanautoservis*, Botevgradsko shose 239 (☎455005). Otherwise seek advice at the *Union of Bulgarian Motorists*, ul. Sveta Sofia 6 (☎883856); dial 146 for their **breakdown service**. Repairs might be possible at the *Iztok* service centre (17km along the Plovdiv highway) or at *Bozhur* (18km out on the Kalotina road).

Circus At the intersection of ul. Positano and bul. Hristo Botev (☎880000); see below for bookings.

Concert Tickets Bookings at bul. Tsar Osvoboditel 2 (Mon–Fri 8am–noon, 3–7pm), or in the NDK centre. Information on theatres and concerts can be obtained by telephoning ☎171, but don't bank on getting a foreign-language speaker.

Embassies and consulates *Albania*, Dimitâr Polyanov 10 (☎443349, 441110); *Denmark*, bul. Tsar Osvoboditel 10 (☎880455); *Germany*, Shipka 48 (☎443239); *Greece*, bul. Klement Gotvald 68 (☎443770); *Hungary*, ul. 6 Septemvri 57 (☎662021); *Netherlands*, Denkoglu 19a (☎874186); *Romania*, Shipchenski prohod 1 (☎706448); *Turkey*, bul. Tolbuhin 23 (☎ 872306); *UK*, bul. Tolbuhin 65 (☎885361 – open Mon–Thurs 9am–noon, 2–3.30pm, Fri 9am–noon); *USA*, bul. Stamboliiski 1 (☎884801; Mon–Fri 8.30am–1pm); *Yugoslavia*, Veliko Târnovo 3 (☎443237). Australians, Canadians and New Zealanders have no representation in Sofia but the British Embassy might help out; Denmark will do the same for other Scandinavian nationals.

Emergencies Medical treatment for foreigners at the clinic at Evgeni Pavolvski 1 (☎75361) in the Mladost I housing estate (bus #75 from Orlov Most). Dial ☎150 for an ambulance and ☎160 for the Militia.

Football Sofia's has two sides with a mass following. *CSKA-Sredets*, the nation's most successful in recent years, are the Bulgarian army team, and play at Stadion narodna armiya in the middle of park na svobodata; their rivals *Levski* (formerly owned by the internal security forces) are based at Stadion Levski northeast of the city centre on Todorini kukli – tram #20 from the Levski monument, then bus #120. The national side play at the similarly named Stadion Vasil Levski, at the western end of park na svobodata.

Markets The main fruit & vegetable market is on Georgi Kirkov; there's a smaller one on ul. Hristo Smirnenski.

Opticians bul. Vitosha 14; and ul. Graf Ignatiev 7.

Pharmacies 24-hour service at Alabin 29 (☎879029); Rakovski 159 (☎879206); Yanko Sakâzov 102 (☎441867), or Hristo Botev 123 (☎835651). Medicines manufactured in the West are available for hard currency at the International Pharmacy in the *Tsentâr po Higiena*, open Mon–Fri 7.30am–1pm & 2–4.30pm (trolleybus #4 or #7 from the university).

Photographic supplies Western brands of film are available from *TsUM* (on the ground floor), or from the many photographic processing shops which are springing up all over the capital.

Post office General Gurko 6 (daily 7am–9pm).

Shopping The main stores are all located around the bul. Vitosha, bul. Stamboliiski, Graf Ignatiev area. *TsUM* at the western end of the Largo stocks everything from shoelaces to satellite dishes, and although breadth of choice has never been its strong point, it's still the best place to seek imported Western consumer goods. There are few obvious souvenir-buying opportunities in Sofia, although shops selling luxury goods congregate around the southern end of bul. Vitosha and in the NDK centre. The *Bulgarian Association of Craftsmen* have shops selling folksy gifts at bul. Vitosha 14 and pl. Makedoniya 6. Cassette tapes of folk and popular music are best bought either in *TsUM* or from street hawkers along bul. Vitosha. For those addicted to vinyl or in search of serious music, try the *Balkanton* record shops at bul. Knyaginya Mariya Luiza 29 and Graf Ignatiev 53; or *Maestro Atanasov* at bul. Tsar Osvoboditel 8.

Sport Swimming pool, sauna, gym, bowling alley and tennis courts are open to non-residents at the *Hotel Vitosha*, bul. Anton Ivanov 100; but facilities are generally cheaper at sports halls such as *Zala Universiade*, ul. Shipchenski prohod 2 (tram #20 from the Levski monument) and *Slivnitsa*, bul. Slivnitsa 186 (tram #3 from *Hali*). In summer, try the open-air pool at the northern end of park na svobodata, where there are also some public tennis courts (☎653 169 for reservations). For skiing on on Mount Vitosha see p.55.

Taxi ☎142.

Visa extensions Enquire at your embassy first, who will either initiate the process for you, or offer advice on the current procedure.

travel details

Trains

From Sofia to Bankya (every 30min; 30min); Burgas (6 daily; 6hr 30min); Kazanlâk (6; 3–4hr); Koprivshtitsa (5; 1hr 40min); Pleven (hourly; 3hr); Plovdiv (8 daily; 2hr 30min); Ruse (5; 7hr); Varna (5; 8hr 30min); Vidin (5; 5hr).

Buses

From Avtogara Ovcha Kupel to Bansko (5; 3hr); Blagoevgrad (10; 2hr); Gotse Delchev (4; 4hr); Kyustendil (4; 2hr); Rila monastery (2; 2hr 30min); Sandanski (3; 3hr 30min); Stanke Dimitrov (hourly; 1hr).

From Avtogara Poduyane to Botevgrad (every 30min; 45min); Etropole (8 daily; 1hr 30min); Koprivshtitsa (1; 1hr 30min); Kozlodui (1; 3hr); Lovech (3; 3hr); Oryahovo (2; 3hr); Plovdiv (1; 2hr); Pravets (10; 1hr); Teteven (5; 2hr); Troyan (3; 3hr); Veliko Târnovo (2; 4hr).

From Avtogara Yug to Asenovgrad (2 daily; 2hr 30min); Haskovo (1; 3hr); Kârdzhali (2; 4hr); Pamporovo (1; 4hr); Panagyurishte (7; 2hr); Plovdiv (2; 2hr); Samokov (every 30min; 1hr); Smolyan (2; 4hr); Stara Zagora (1; 3hr 30min); Velingrad (2; 2hr 30min).

International trains

From Sofia to Athens (1 daily; 19hr); Bucharest (2; 10hr); Istanbul (1; 15hr); Moscow (1; 45hr); Thessaloniki (2; 10hr).

International buses

From Sofia to Athens (every Wed & Fri); Istanbul (every Sun); Skopje (daily); Tirana (every Sun).

Domestic flights

From Sofia to Burgas (1 daily; 1hr); Gorna Oryahovitsa (1; 45min); Kârdzhali (3 weekly; 1hr); Ruse (1 daily; 45min); Varna (2 daily; 1hr).

CYRILLIC PLACE NAMES

SOFIA	СОФИЯ	BUL. TSAR	БУЛ. ЦАР
ALEKO	АЛЕКО	OSVOBODITEL	ОСВОБОДИТЕЛ
BANKYA	БАНКЯ	BUL. VITOSHA	БУЛ. ВИТОША
BOYANA	БОЯНА	PLOSHTAD	ПЛОЩАД
DRAGALEVTSI	ДРАГАЛЕВЦИ	SVETA NEDELYA	СВЕТА НЕДЕЛЯ
KNYAZHEVO	КНЯЖЕВО	PLOSHTAD	ПЛОЩАД
SIMEONOVO	СИМЕОНОВО	ALEKSANDÂR	АЛЕКСАНДЪР
VITOSHA	ВИТОША	BATENBERG	БАТЕНБЕРГ
ZLATNI MOSTOVE	ЗЛАТНИ	THE LARGO	ЛАРГОТО
	МОСТОВЕ	TSENTRALNA	ЦЕНТРАЛНА
BUL. KNYAGINYA	БУЛ. КНЯГИНЯ	GARA	ГАРА
MARIYA LUIZA	МАРИЯ ЛУИЗА	UL. G.S.	УЛ. Г. С.
BUL.	БУЛ.	RAKOVSKI	РАКОВСКИ
STAMBOLIISKI	СТАМБОЛИИСИ		

CHAPTER TWO

THE SOUTHWEST

The landscape of Bulgaria south of the capital is dominated by the River Struma, which rises on the southern slopes of Mount Vitosha before sweeping west then south through a changing sequence of arid gorges and fertile flood plains. Both the main southbound rail route and the E79 highway to Greece follow the Struma valley for much of its length, skirting some of the country's most grandiose scenery on the way. Although the major towns along the route are pleasant enough, most of the area's real attractions lie in the mountains to the east.

Formerly noted for their bandits and hermits, the **Rila and Pirin ranges** contain Bulgaria's highest, stormiest peaks: swathed in forests and dotted with alpine lakes awaiting anyone prepared to hike or risk their car's suspension on the backroads. **Borovets** and **Malyovitsa** are major winter sports centres in the Rila range, both within easy striking distance from Sofia. Approaches to these resorts pass through the historic crafts town of **Samokov**, whose artists adorned **Rila monastery**, the most revered of Bulgarian holy places. The Pirin range is wilder and less developed, although hiking on and around its highest peak, Mount Vihren, is accessible from **Bansko**, a nest of old stone houses, the most attractive of the mountain towns. On the southern fringes of the Pirin range near the Greek border, the monastery of **Rozhen** lies at the end of a great hike from the village of **Melnik**, known both for its wine and its vernacular architecture.

Slightly nearer to Sofia, the route leading west towards Macedonia takes you past the ancient **monastery of Zemen** and the spa town of **Kyustendil**, which retains much of its nineteenth-century Turkish character. Destinations like these – along with many others in the southwest – are sufficiently accessible from the capital to make day trips a possibility.

If you're planning any **hiking** in the Rila or Pirin mountains, it's worth calling in at the *Pirin Travel Agency* in Sofia (bul. Stamboliiski 30; ☎02/870 687) first. As well as being the people most likely to stock detailed maps, they may also be able to reserve beds in the hikers' chalets or *hizhi* dotted around the mountains.

SOUTHWEST OF THE CAPITAL

Zemen monastery, some lovely wild countryside and the old Ottoman spa town of Kyustendil can be reached **by car** from Sofia in 1–2 hours by taking the E870 highway (which leaves the main southbound E79 at Pernik), although Zemen requires a small detour, leaving the highway at IZVOR and then following minor roads. **Trains** (leaving the capital at 7am, 9am, 7pm and 9pm) run from Zemen to Kyustendil, thus making it just about possible to include both places in a long day excursion from the capital. The route initially passes through some of Bulgaria's most unattractive areas of urban-industrial sprawl, centred around the mining and smelting settlements of Pernik and Radomir – neither of which, however, are without historical interest.

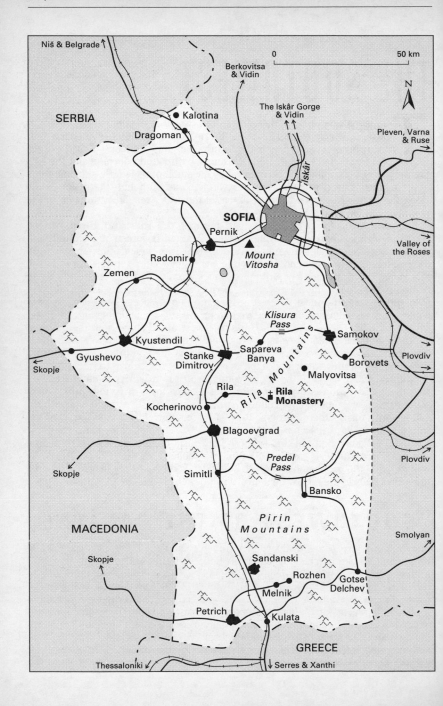

Niš & Belgrade

Berkovitsa
& Vidin

The Iskâr Gorge
& Vidin

0   50 km

N

Pleven, Varna
& Ruse

SERBIA

Kalotina

Dragoman

Iskâr

SOFIA

Pernik

Mount
Vitosha

Valley of
the Roses

Radomir

Zemen

Klisura
Pass

Samokov

Kyustendil

SaIareva
Banya

Rila Mountains

Borovets

Plovdiv

Gyushevo

Stanke
Dimitrov

Malyovitsa

Skopje

Rila

Rila
Monastery

Kocherinovo

Blagoevgrad

Predel
Pass

Plovdiv

Skopje

Simitli

Bansko

MACEDONIA

Pirin
Mountains

Smolyan

Skopje

Sandanski

Rozhen

Gotse
Delchev

Melnik

Petrich

Kulata

GREECE

Thessaloniki

Serres & Xanthi

Pernik and Radomir

Although both have played a significant role in Bulgarian history neither **Pernik** nor **Radomir** are attractive towns in any sense, and if you can avoid them, so much the better. While motorists on the E79 can escape with a brush of Pernik's eastern outskirts, travellers **heading south** by rail will – at least briefly – find themselves in both towns, since the line from Sofia passes through Pernik and divides at Radomir en route to Kyustendil (see p.70) or Stanke Dimitrov (p.79). Happily, though, you can minimize contact; you don't need to get off at Pernik and at Radomir you shouldn't have to wait more than an hour or so for a connection.

Pernik

The remains of a fortress on Krakra Pernishki hill and the derivation of its name – from the Slav god Perun – are the sole traces of antiquity in **PERNIK**. After 1891 this hitherto agricultural village became Bulgaria's largest centre of coal mining – an industry that still employs 90 percent of the workforce, although nowadays Pernik also produces power and cement. From the beginning, rampant exploitation forced the **miners** to organize a union, which was grudgingly recognized in 1905 following a 35-day strike led by Georgi Dimitrov. An almost entirely working-class town, Pernik was also one of the strongholds of the Communist-led **1923 uprising**, and suffered the worst police repression as a consequence. During the Communist period, miners received wages almost 70 percent higher than other industrial workers and enjoyed early retirement, subsidized holidays and other benefits. Today, however, the Bulgarian mining industry is overstaffed and underproductive; and with the current emphasis on privatization and profitability, places like Pernik look set to suffer.

For all its modern amenities, Pernik's only real source of excitement is an ancient one: the **Festival of the Kukeri**, a re-enactment of the old *survakari* and *kukeri* rites, originally intended to ward off evil spirits and promote fertility respectively. About 3500 dancers participate, wearing terrifying or grotesque masks, yelling and chanting. The festival supposedly takes place every five years some time during the second half of January; the scheduling of the next event, however, remains uncertain. The **town museum** (Tues–Sun 9am–noon & 2–5pm), ul. Fizkultura 2, holds ethnographical oddments relating to the rites, as well as a collection of ancient Thracian grave tablets found at a nearby sanctuary.

Radomir

On the slopes of "Bare Mountain" in a valley to the southwest, **RADOMIR** has developed in conjunction with Pernik, on whose coal and power its industries depend. The Machine-Building Works – here nicknamed "Goliath" – specializes in the production of heavy cranes, blast furnaces and open-cast mining gear. Historically, the town is renowned as the site of the short-lived **Radomir Republic**, proclaimed by soldiers returning from the front in 1918, who began

---

HOTEL ROOM PRICES

For a fuller explanation of these codes, see p.16 of *Basics*.

① £4–6 ② £6–12 ③ £12–25 ④ £25–40 ⑤ £40–60 ⑥ over £60

marching on Sofia to punish those responsible for Bulgaria's entry into World War I. Prevented from doing so by German troops, they so alarmed the government that it released the Agrarian leader Stamboliiski to avert a revolution. Radomir's socialist credentials were enhanced by the town's proximity to the **birthplace of Georgi Dimitrov**, located in the village of KOVACHEVTSI 10km to the west.

Zemen monastery

Lacking the high walls, tiers of cells and decorative facades that make Rila outstanding, **ZEMEN MONASTERY** (*Zemenski Manastir*) seems humble by comparison, and its small twelfth-century cruciform church of St. Ivan the Theologian appears similarly modest from the outside. Inside, however, are some of Bulgaria's finest surviving **medieval frescoes**, sensitively restored between 1970 and 1974. The frescoes – produced by anonymous artists during the 1350s for local noble Konstantin Deyan – are examples of the Macedonian School of painting, which was somewhat cruder and less formalized than the predominant style of Târnovo. Against a background of cool blues and greys, the saints with their golden haloes and finery are depicted in hierarchies (including Deyan and his wife Doya); while the narrative scenes are mainly rendered in ochrous hues, with dark blues and reds employed to highlight the gravity of episodes like the *Treason of Judas* and the *Judgement of Pilate*. The monastery is 3km southwest of Zemen itself, overlooking the town from a secluded hillside site. It's easy to find, however: on leaving the railway station simply bear right into the main street (the erstwhile ul. Georgi Dimitrov) and keep going.

To the southwest of Zemen, the River Struma has carved a rugged 19km-long defile between two massifs, known as the **Zemenski Prolom**. Various **rock formations** – dubbed the Cart Rails, the Dovecote, and so on by locals – are visible from the carriage window when the trains aren't plunging through a series of tunnels to escape the precipitous gorge. On inaccessible bone-dry crags you can also see the ruins of ancient forts, believed to have once defended the long-vanished town of Zemlen against incursions by the Byzantine empire. The gorge ends near the village of Râzhdavitsa, beyond which lies the broad **Kyustendil plain** – which locals proudly describe as the "largest orchard in Bulgaria". Fragrant in spring, the plain is richly coloured during autumn by the red apples, yellow pears and lustrous grapes which hang profusely in the **orchards** and vineyards.

Kyustendil

Bisected by the Bansko River, the town of **KYUSTENDIL**, with its fertile plain and thermal springs, has attracted conquerors since Thracian times. The Romans developed this into the "town of baths", and the Turks who settled here in large numbers after the fourteenth century constructed the *hamams* and mosques that gave Kyustendil its oriental character. Some of this atmosphere lingers on in the old backstreets, although the centre of town has undergone considerable modernization. Most of this has been tasteful: the town's wide, tree-shaded avenues lined with cafés help to make it one of the most pleasant and relaxing urban environments that Bulgaria has to offer.

The centre

From the railway station, the tree-lined bul. Bâlgaria leads south towards **the centre**. After first crossing a pair of fowl-infested circular ponds (designed at the turn of the century to resemble the cyrillic letter ф, or "F", when viewed from above – a tribute to long-serving monarch Ferdinand) the boulevard passes the **Strimon museum complex** (Tues–Sat 8am–noon & 1–5.30pm), a humble collection of Roman-era funerary finds. A few blocks further on, ul. Krakra leads left towards an impressive modern art gallery devoted entirely to the work of local painter **Vladimir Dimitrov-Maistor** (Tues–Sun 9.30–11.45am & 2–6.15pm), who earned the honourific title of "Master" by treating standard uplifting themes in a vigorous if rather uniform style. The archetypal Dimitrov-Maistor picture features an oddly sexless peasant girl, halfway between saintly icon and socialist heroine, standing against a background scene of agricultural plenty.

The bathhouse and town museum

Near the gallery is the overgrown brick dome of a small Turkish bath (open 7am–5pm), which admits men on Tuesdays and Thursdays and women on other days. Kyustendil's much larger municipal **bathhouse** (daily 5.30am–8.30pm except Sun & Wed 5.30am–12.50pm) lies a couple of blocks to the south, fronted by a fountain with three kitsch statues of babies. For a tiny fee you can bathe in its hot (74°C), sulphate-rich waters – waters which are used in several union-run sanatoria for the treatment of gynaecological and nervous disorders, including the heavy-metal poisoning that is an occupational hazard for certain miners.

Behind the baths stands the sixteenth-century Mosque of Ahmed Bey, now the **town museum** (Tues–Sun 8am–noon & 1–5.30pm). An array of archaeological trinkets awaits inspection inside, highlights of which are a couple of Neolithic dwellings, transferred here from the place they were excavated near Slatino, 40km southeast of Kyustendil; and an abstract late-Roman floor mosaic. Immediately outside the mosque, the foundations of the Roman baths have been uncovered.

A church, a mosque and the market

A few steps west of here is the predominantly modern main square, pl. Velbâzhd. Lurking at the southern end of the square, beneath chestnut trees, is the triple-domed **church of Sveta Bogoroditsa**. The peeling lime-green paintwork of the sunken interior provides some idea both of the delapidation into which Bulgarian orthodox churches were allowed to fall during the Communist period, and the sums of money which will be required to restore them. Right behind the church is the **Maiorska kâshta**, a National Revival-style house where the local artists' association holds occasional displays of members' work.

The main boulevard which heads eastwards from here soon leads to the tumbledown, overgrown **Mosque of Fetih Mehmed**, its minaret etched with hexagonal patterns, an effect achieved by inserting red tiles into the darker brown brickwork. There's a daily **market** just east of this on ul. Pârvi Mai, south of which pathways begin the ascent of **Hisarlâk hill**, shrouded in wooded parkland. In its eastern sector you can see the **ruins** of what was originally an extensive Roman settlement around the *Asclepion*, the sacred baths where Emperor Trajan cured his skin complaint and renamed the town *Ulpia Pautalia* to mark the occasion. Intermingled are the remains of a medieval fortress once occupied by the boyar Deyan. The Ottomans, who supplanted his rule over the region during the mid-fourteenth century, designated their new acquisition "Konstantin's land" – *Kostandinili* in Turkish – which eventually gave rise to the name of the town.

Practicalities

If you fancy staying the night here, **private rooms** may be available from the tourist office at the southern end of the main square at ul. Demokratsiya 37 (Mon–Fri 8am–noon & 3–5.30pm). Of the town's **hotels**, the *Pautalia*, pl. Velbâzhd 1 (☎ 078/24561; ③), and the *Velbâzhd*, bul. Bâlgariya 4 (☎ 078/20246; ④) are both comfortable and central. The *Hisarlâka* (☎ 078/25606; ③) is above the town in Hisarlâk park. Two **hikers' chalets** within striking distance of Kyustendil are the *Osogovo* and *Trite Buki*, both situated about four hours' walk from town en route to Mount Ruen – at 2252m the highest point around. A picnic on the Osogovo massif is one of the **excursions** sporadically advertised at the reception desks of the local hotels; look out too for day trips to Rila, Melnik, Rozhen and Sofia; or Skopje across the border in Macedonia. The *Pautalia* and *Velbâzhd* hotels are the best places in which to sample meagre nightlife; the former has a taverna open until midnight and a lively café.

On from Kyustendil

Assuming you don't drive 22km or catch a train to GYUESHEVO, the Bulgarian checkpoint where the road crosses **into Macedonia,*** it's fairly certain you'll end up heading **towards Stanke Dimitrov**, a place that's easy to reach by bus or hitching (by rail you have to backtrack and change at Radomir).

Just beyond NEVESTINO (14.5km from Kyustendil), the road crosses a famous old **bridge over the Struma**, the *Kadin Most*. Supported by five arches, the 330ft-long bridge was constructed between 1463 and 1470 to guarantee the Ottoman lines of communication and convey caravans en route between the Danube and Salonika, although **local legends** advance different explanations. According to one story, the Turkish Vizier Isak Pasha took pity on a maiden separated from her betrothed by the river, and had it built as a wedding present – hence its original name, the Bride's Bridge. Another tale has it that the builder, Manuil, suggested to his brothers that they appease the river god by offering one of their wives as a sacrifice, the victim being whichever woman arrived first with her husband's lunch. Manuil's wife turned up and was promptly imurred, weeping and begging that they leave holes so that she might see daylight and continue to suckle her child.

---

*At the time of writing, travel from Bulgaria to the former Yugoslav republic of Macedonia appears to be fairly risk-free. Bulgarian holidaymakers are still in the habit of making cross-border excursions, implying a certain confidence in Macedonia's ability to keep itself isolated from the violence raging elsewhere. However, the main road from Kyustendil to Skopje passes through Kumanovo, a Macedonian town with an ethnic Serb population – if relations between Serbia and Macedonia do become tense, this is the region most likely to experience unrest.

THE RILA MOUNTAINS

South of Sofia, Mount Vitosha gives way with barely a pause to the RILA MOUNTAINS, an area of wild highlands enclosing fertile valleys. If you're heading down the main southbound route towards Greece you'll only really see the lowland town of Stanke Dimitrov and the western fringes of the range, although this is the best direction from which to approach Rila monastery, the finest in Bulgaria. The region's ski resorts and hiking centres are easier to reach via the town of Samokov to the northwest.

Samokov and the ski resorts

Motorists can visit the historic town of **Samokov** and the mountain resorts **Borovets** and **Malyovitsa** during a day's outing from Sofia, but to appreciate them – and for anyone reliant on public transport – it's more realistic to allow at least two days. Reasonably priced **accommodation** is scarce here (though you might strike lucky with unofficial lodgings or beds in hikers' chalets), so it's worth considering the *Shtârkelovo gnezdo* ("Stork's nest") chalet-complex on Lake Iskâr, 10km north of Samokov, as a possible base camp. Anyone planning to visit Rila monastery afterwards should bear in mind that it's almost easier to *walk* across the mountains than get there by bus from Malyovitsa or Samokov.

Happily, the journey **from Sofia to Samokov** isn't difficult, with half-hourly buses from the capital's *Yug* bus terminal following the Iskâr River past **Lake Pancharevo**, a centre for watersports. Entering the defile between the Lozhen and Plana massifs, you should be able to glimpse the ruined fortress of **Urvich**, where Tsar Shishman allegedly withstood the Turks for seven years: on the opposite bank, **Zheleznitsa monastery** lurks deep in the forest. Beyond the defile lies the massive **Iskâr Dam** and **Lake Iskâr** – an artificially created body of water 16km long, sometimes known as the "Sea of Sofia". It might be advisable to leave the bus at this point and rent a chalet at the *Shtârkelovo Gnezdo* motel and campsite before proceeding on another 10km, up onto the highland plateau of Samokov.

Samokov

Though it lacks the cachet of antiquity, **SAMOKOV** has a tradition of skilled work, artistic achievement and popular socialism second to none in Bulgaria. Founded as a mining community in the fourteenth century, it soon became one of the busiest manufacturing centres in the Turkish empire – the name of the town derives from the Bulgarian verb "to forge". All kinds of crafts guilds flourished here, particularly weavers and tailors, who turned flax (still a major product) into uniforms for the Ottoman army. From the seventeenth century until the end of Turkish rule, Samokov's stature eclipsed that of Sofia and Kyustendil – a prestige which was raised even higher by the artistry of its woodworkers and painters, who decorated Bulgaria's finest monasteries. The town's working-class and artisan traditions also gave rise to one of Bulgaria's most interesting experiments with socialism, the Samokov Commune (see p.76).

↑ Sofia

Samokov ↗

Saparevo

Sapareva
Banya

Stanke
Dimitrov

Resilovo

Ovchartsi

Samoranovo

Bistritsa

Skakavitsa

Vada

← Blagoevgrad

Lovna

Otovitsa

Komsomolets

Sedemte ez
(Seven Lake

Ivan
Vazov

Malyovitsa

Dodov
Vrâh

Malyo

John of Ri
Tomb

Church of
St Luke

Rila

Pastra

Rila
Mona

← Kocherinovo

N

0   5 km

Bistritsa

Blagoevgrad

🏠 Tourist Chalets

∷ Places of interest

- - - Footpaths

↓ Sandanski

Samokov ↑   ↑Samokov

Kostenets →

Mala
Tsârkva   ● Beli Iskâr

Govedartsi   Borovets
        Madzhare

        Sitnyakovo

Mechit   Yastrebets   Chakâr
                                Voivoda

alyovitsa

        Musala

        Mt Musala

Dry
ake
Partisan
Meadow
                        Zavrachitsa

                Boris
Ribni ezera   Hadzhisotirov
(Fish Lakes)

                Semkovo

Makedoniya
                                Velingrad

                        Yakoruda

Razlog   Razlog
                & Bansko

THE RILA MOUNTAINS

THE SAMOKOV COMMUNE

Like many other Bulgarian towns, the election of a non-Communist town council in October 1991 has led to a revision of Samokov's political history. However, this is one place where the role of the Left in the town's development is too great to be ignored. Social progress was slow in the region until 1910, when a slump in the local ironworking industry provoked the declaration of the **Samokov Commune**. Within months of coming to power the socialist-dominated council inspected factory conditions, supplied workers' quarters with sewers and electricity, granted books and clothing, and levied a progressive income tax. It also flew a red flag from the town hall until ordered to desist by the Interior Minister, and claimed rent for a palace built on municipal land, which so infuriated Tsar Ferdinand that he had a new road built to bypass Samokov en route to Borovets.

Even though it increased its vote during the 1912 election, the Commune was overthrown by the police and conservatives, but the ideals behind it remained in the popular consciousness, helping to inspire another left-wing victory in the local elections of 1919. The history of the Commune was of course tailored to suit the needs of postwar Communist propaganda: Georgi Dimitrov called it the "first practical attempt of the working people to govern themselves in the name of their own interests, against the blood-suckers, *chorbadzhii* and capitalists".

The centre

There's plenty of evidence of Samokov's past in and around the town **centre**, although modern urban planning seems to have left ancient monuments stranded in a sea of crumbling paving stones. The town's bus station lies immediately below the main square, where a large fountain or *cheshma* trickles water: a legacy of the Turks, who considered running water inseparable from civilized living. Close by stands the only one of Samokov's once-numerous mosques to survive, the **Bairakli dzhamiya** (8am–noon & 1.30–5.30pm, closed Wed), preserved as a monument to the skills of local builders rather than as a place of worship. Commissioned by the pasha in 1840, the mosque's design betrays Bulgarian influences: its roof-line mimics the shape of the *kobilitsa* (a yoke used for carrying buckets); while the interior decoration relies upon plant motifs rather than arabesques, with a magnificent sunset beneath the dome – a piece of orthodox iconography.

Just off the main square to the east, the town **history museum** (Tues–Sun 7.30am–noon & 1.30–5.30pm) traces Samokov's evolution up to the present day. The town's industrial past is remembered in a sequence of models illustrating the mining and smelting of iron ore: one shows a gargantuan, waterwheel-powered set of bellows used for forcing air into the furnaces. Elsewhere the accent is on the various trades which made Samokov famous as a craft centre, with displays of ceramics, ironmongery, engraving and printing – the latter started by one Nikola Karastoyanov, who opened Bulgaria's first printing house here in the early nineteenth century.

However, it's the **Samokov school of icon painters** which receives the most attention, with pictures and personal effects of the Vienna-trained Hristo Dimitrov and his sons Dimitâr and Zahari. The latter, subsequently known as **Zahari Zograf**, is remembered as the greatest and most prolific of Bulgarian nineteenth-century painters. A few of his personal belongings are here, and his gravestone, now so worn as to be virtually illegible, lies in the museum corridor. A gallery of icon painting upstairs contains many works by Zahari's lesser-known colleagues, as well as examples of the growing number of secular subjects tackled by the same generation of painters: note especially the animated, Brueghelesque figures of Nikola Obrazopisov's 1892 painting *Peasants dancing the Horo*.

Woodcarving, icons and frescoes

Ul. Boris Hadzhisotirov leads south from the main square towards the old Bulgarian residential quarter of town, and the **Convent of Sveta Bogoroditsa** at no. 77. Inside the convent church are some colourful murals, while outside a cobbled alley leads past a ramshackle collection of nunnery buildings. A little way further on, the walled **church of Sveti Nikolai** features cast-iron weathercocks on each of its three cupolas.

Although such skilful wrought-ironwork embodied the fusion of art and industry during the town's commercial heyday, greater fame accrued to the **Samokov school of woodcarvers**. Collectively, this refers to local artisans (some of whom studied on Mount Athos in Greece in the late eighteenth century), in particular to a group formed in the early nineteenth century, primarily to make the iconostasis for Rila monastery. Although executed in 1793, the iconostasis of Samokov's **Metropolitan church** on ul. Zahari Zograf, a couple of blocks south of Sveti Nikolai, is characteristic of their work. It's covered with intricate figures linked by plant-like traceries, interspersed with rosettes – which sometimes took the form of a six-petalled narcissus. The church's collection of icons present the Samokov painting school at its best, with Hristo Dimitrov's *Enthroned Jesus* standing out.

Barring the occasional angel, Samokov woodcarvers generally avoided depicting human figures, preferring to represent eagles, sparrowhawks, dragons, falcons and, above all, plants. A large iconostasis would require several years work, and most woodcarvers probably undertook less ambitious commissions, such as fitting couches (*minderi*) and panelled ceilings in the homes of wealthy citizens. These still exist in a few **old houses** among the backstreets south of ul. Hadzhisotirov, which are known after the names of their onetime owners: Marikin, Ksenofontov, Obrazopisov and Kokoshov.

Frescoes by Samokov artists decorate the **Belyova church**, 4km south of town on the Borovets road, most notably the serried ranks of saints provided by Nikola Obrazopisov, the most sought-after of Samokov painters after Zahari Zograf himself.

Practicalities . . . and moving on

Samokov lacks tourist **accommodation**, so the nearest sources of hotel beds are either Borovets or Malyovitsa. Apart from the chalets at Lake Iskâr (see p.73), there's a motel and campsite at Govedartsi, 11km out along the road to Malyovitsa; and the *Belchanitsa* hostel in the small spa resort of BELCHINSKI BANI, 15km west of town, served by buses plying the Samokov-Stanke Dimitrov route. There are frequent **buses** to Borovets, 10km south of town, and services to Malyovitsa at around 11.30am, 1.40pm & 4.10pm.

Travellers hoping to make the 40km journey from **Samokov to Stanke Dimitrov** by bus will probably have an easier time if they reserve seats and board at the terminal rather than use the local buses which run sporadically between villages. Some services go by way of SAPAREVA BANYA, Bulgaria's most ferocious **mineral baths**. The hottest spring is fed by a super-heated geyser (102°C), which gushes 550 gallons of sulphurous water every minute.

Borovets: winter sports and hiking

Near the turn of the century, Prince Ferdinand of Bulgaria built three villas and a hunting lodge among the aromatic pine woods covering the northern slopes of Mount Musala, a mile above sea level. The Mamrikoff family – after whom a verb meaning "to steal from an exalted position" was coined – and other wealthy folk did likewise, founding an exclusive colony, Tchamkoria, from which **BOROVETS** has developed. Effectively nationalized for the benefit of union and Party members in 1949, Borovets has become a major **winter sports resort** in recent years, increasingly geared towards package tourism.

Competitively priced **package holidays** (see *Basics* p.5) ensure that you get lodgings, skiing equipment and a high standard of tuition – though none of this is assured if you just turn up in Borovets. Also, since most companies offer lift-passes and "ski packs" (covering equipment rental) for a lower cost than you pay on the spot, you might as well take a package in the first place.

Skiing

From mid-November through until late April the fountains in the centre of Borovets are frozen into icy cones, and snow blankets everything. The resort is wholly given over to **skiing**, which can be practised as late as May, or even June, on the upper slopes. Off to the west of the *Hotel Rila* are the nursery slopes, served by ten drag lifts (operating 9am–4.45pm), overlooked by a steep slope down from *Sitnyakovo*, once one of Ferdinand's villas (accessible by chair-lift; same hours). Experienced skiers favour the pistes on the western ridge of the mountain, which can be reached by a 5km-long gondola lift (9am–4.30pm) running up to *Yastrebets*, the former royal hunting lodge (now a hotel with a café nearby). Another chair-lift serves the two ski jumps (55m & 75m long). There are also buses to the start of three cross-country runs (3, 5 & 10km long), 2km away.

Hiking

Balkantourist, who have a desk in the *Hotel Bor*, organize various excursions, including **hikes from Borovets** during the summer months, which at least guarantee beds in mountain chalets if these are required. The *Yastrebets* chalet (3 hours' walk or 20 minutes by gondola from Borovets) is the starting point for the ascent of **Mount Musala**, the highest peak in Bulgaria (2295m), which takes about two and a half hours; get a weather forecast before you set off. From Mount Musala it's 6 hours trek southwards to the *Boris Hadzhisotirov* chalet, where one path leads down to YAKORUDA on the railway line **to Bansko**; the other trail runs **to the Fish Lakes** (5 hours). From here, having stayed overnight at the *Ribni Ezera* chalet, hikers usually push on to **Rila monastery** next morning (5–6 hours).

Accommodation

Borovets has seven 3-star hotels, all of which are grouped around the central bus terminal, but finding **accommodation** from December through to April can still be a problem if you're not on a package or haven't booked in advance. At any other time of year, there should be plenty of beds, although places may close for a while during the off season. *Balkantourist* deal with reservations for the whole resort. Remember, however, that rooms cost significantly more for those who arrive on spec – about £35 a double – than for those on a package. Cheaper are the two "vacation villages" at the northeastern end of the resort: *Yagoda*, a huddle of wooden villas with pointed rooves, and *Malina*, where you can rent log cabins – many of which have saunas. *Chuchiliga* (open 8am–11pm) offers the best value of all the various **restaurants** and tavernas, while *Chaina* – with jolly folklore performances – is liveliest. **Discos** take place on its second floor, and in the snack bar near the *Hotel Rila* (11pm–2am), and the *Rila* has a nightclub and a casino.

Malyovitsa and beyond

Beyond Govedartsi to the southwest of Samokov, a branch road snakes up to **MALYOVITSA**, 1750m above sea level, another ski resort with all mod cons, and pistes, a slalom track and nursery slopes on the neighbouring peak from which its name derives. However, Malyovitsa doesn't really compare with Borovets as a **skiing** centre, but it's a good starting point for **walks in the mountains**, particularly the trek to Rila monastery. Climbers' huts and the trails themselves are marked on *BTS* maps of the Rila Mountains, which should be available from the *Hotel Malyovitsa*. The ascent to the *Malyovitsa* chalet above the resort constitutes the first leg of several hikes, for from here it's 4–5 hours' walk to the beautiful **Seven Lakes** (*Sedemte ezera*) cabin, or 6 hours to the *Ivan Vazov* lodge, depending on which trail you follow after the Urdin Lakes. Blasted crags surround another lake, *Strashnoto ezero*, which lies to the east of the Malyovitsa cabin. Refuges there, and to the north of the Dry Lake (*Suhoto ezero*), serve as way-stations along the route to the chalet beside the **Fish Lakes**: 9 hours' hike in all. But the most popular trail leads south to **Mount Malyovitsa** and **Rila monastery**. Climbing the 2799m mountain takes about 3 hours, an easier ascent than by the steeper southern face. After, follow the path westwards along the ridge before taking the trail branching left, which leads to the monastery in the thickly wooded valley below (a further 3–4 hours).

Stanke Dimitrov and around

It's tempting to dismiss **STANKE DIMITROV** (known by the locals simply as "Stanke", although the town's pre-Communist name of *Dupnitsa* may make a return to everyday usage) as a stepping-stone to other, more attractive destinations. It has a good hotel, the *Rila* (☎ 0701/25011; ③), pleasantly situated on the landscaped Drenski Rid hill, but otherwise nothing to recommend it except for its **transport facilities**. This is the railway junction between Sofia and places further south, and the terminal for buses to Samokov and villages in the foothills of the Rila Mountains, from where hikes can be made. Stanke Dimitrov's other claim to fame is its **tobacco** industry: every year some eight million kilos of the stuff pass through the town's warehouses and processing plants, the river is tinted a nicotine yellow, and you can see huge quantities of the weed growing, or spread out to dry, throughout the surrounding countryside.

The Samokov road offers several **routes into the Rila Mountains**, but hiking trails begin just a few kilometres southeast of town at the village of BISTRITSA (accessible from Stanke Dimitrov by bus). From there, the shortest most southerly trail leads to the *Komsomolets* chalet, while the right-hand route runs to the *Otovitsa* hut, and it's about seven hours' walk, following the central path, up to another lodge, *Ivan Vazov*. This is well placed for various **hikes** – for example to Mount Damga (1hr 30min), the Seven Lakes (2hr 30min), or Mount Malyovitsa (6hr 30min). The average altitude is well over 1524m, so be sure to ask about weather conditions and travel properly equipped.

Boboshevo

Travellers **heading south** might consider a stopover at **BOBOSHEVO**, a village situated 3km west of the railway line, where trains halt briefly. Cherry orchards abound here, while during autumn the vines overhanging the streets are heavy with grapes destined for Boboshevo's extensive wine cellars. The **monastery of Sveti Dimitâr** contains some fifteenth-century frescoes, while paintings by Stanislav Dospevski can be seen in the church of the Virgin. Twelve kilometres from the Boboshevo turn-off, the main road encounters KOCHERINOVO, the start of the road to Rila monastery.

Rila monastery

As the best known of Bulgaria's monasteries – justly famed for both its architecture and its mountainous setting – **Rila** receives a stream of visitors, most of whom now arrive by coach or car rather than on foot or by mule, as did pilgrims in the old days. There are several ways of **getting there from Sofia**. The day-excursions advertised by *Balkantourist* and the capital's bigger hotels, which basically involve hiring a car, driver and guide, are the most expensive option at about £40 a head. Alternatively two direct **buses** to Rila monastery run from Sofia's Ovcha Kupel bus terminal: the first, leaving at 6.30am, just about enables you to "do" Rila as a day trip. All **trains** on the Sofia–Kulata line stop at KOCHERINOVO, where each is met by a bus service which conveys you up through the town of Kocherinovo to the village of RILA, 12km short of the monastery itself. From here about six buses a day run to the monastery. Approaching Rila from elsewhere, best places to head for are either Stanke Dimitrov or Blagoevgrad, both of which have regular bus links with Rila village.

Though the monastery buildings are open daily from dawn till dusk, if you want to see (or take part in) a service, morning prayers start at 8am, evening prayers at 5pm. Arrive on 19 October and you can enjoy the monastery's celebrations of the feast day of John of Rila.

The road to the monastery – and John of Rila

The single road leading to the **Rila Monastery** runs above the foaming River Rilska, fed by innumerable springs from the surrounding pine- and beech-covered mountains, beneath peaks flecked with snow. Even today there's a palpable sense of isolation, and it's easy to see why **John of Rila** (*Ivan Rilski*) chose this valley to escape the savagery of feudal life and the laxity of the established monasteries at the end of the ninth century. To disciples drawn to his hermit's cell, John preached that "he who would be chief among you must be as he that doth serve"; and while monasticism was condemned as escapism and selfishness by Presbyter Cosmas – the scourge of the Bogomils (see p.148) – after John's death in 946, the hermitage became an important spiritual centre. The monastery, established in 1335, forged links with others in Serbia and played a major role in Bulgarian Christianity throughout the Middle Ages.

The monastery

Founded 4km from the original hermitage, the monastery was plundered during the eighteenth century, and repairs had hardly begun when the whole structure burned down in 1833. Its rebuilding was presented as a religious and patriotic duty: urged on by Neofit Rilski, public donations were plentiful and master craftsmen such as Aleksii Rilets and Pavel Milenkov gave their services for free. Work continued in stages throughout the nineteenth century, while the east wing was built as recently as 1961 to display the monastery's treasures, which UNESCO has recognised as part of the World Cultural Heritage. Like the old monastery, it's ringed by mighty walls, giving it the outward appearance of a fortress.

Once through the west gate, however, this impression is dispelled by the harmonious beauty of the interior, which even the milling crowds don't seriously mar. Graceful arches surrounding the flagstoned courtyard support tiers of monastic cells, and stairways ascend to top-floor balconies which – viewed from below – resemble the outstretched petals of flowers. Bold red stripes and black-and-white check patterns enliven the facade, contrasting with the sombre mountains behind, and creating a visual harmony between the cloisters and the church within.

The monastery church

The **monastery church** has undulating lines, combining red and black designs with arches and a diversity of cupolas. Richly coloured frescoes shelter beneath the porch and within the interior – a mixture of scenes from rural life and the usual Orthodox iconography, executed by muralists from Razlog, Bansko and Samokov, including Zahari Zograf. Scenes on the outside of the church include archetypal scenes of cataclysm: the fall of Constantinople, various apocalypses, and visions of hell, many of which are peopled by the bat-winged curly-tailed demons which seem to play such a prominent part in the nineteenth-century Bulgarian imagination. Inside, the iconostasis is particularly splendid: almost 10m wide and covered by a mass of intricate carvings and gold leaf, it's one of the finest achievements of the Samokov woodcarvers. Beside the church rises **Hyrelo's Tower**, the sole remaining building from the fourteenth century, which you can ascend in order to visit the top-floor chapel. Its founder – a local noble – apocryphally took refuge as a monk here and was supposedly strangled in the tower; hence the inscription upon it: "Thy wife sobs and grieves, weeping bitterly, consumed by sorrow".

Other parts of the monastery

Huge cauldrons that were once used to feed pilgrims occupy the old **kitchen** on the ground floor of the north wing, where the soot-encrusted ceiling has the shape and texture of a gigantic termites' nest. Various rooms await inspection on the floors above, where the spartan refectory contrasts with the more salubrious, panelled guest rooms, named after the towns which endowed them.

The **ethnographic collection** on the second floor of the north wing (daily 8am–5pm) is most notable for its carpets and silverware, while beneath the modern east wing there's a wealth of objects in the **treasury** (same times). These include icons and medieval Gospels; Rila's charter from Tsar Ivan Shishman, written on leather and sealed with gold in 1378; the door of the original monastery church; and a miniature **cross** made by the monk Raphael during the 1970s. Composed of 140 biblical tableaux containing more than 1500 human figures (each the size of a grain of rice), this took twelve years for Raphael to carve with a needle, and cost him his eyesight.

Around the monastery

If you are into a spot of **walking**, the shortest trail begins by the roadside about 2km beyond the monastery and leads up to the **church of Sveti Luka** (St Luke), near **John of Rila's tomb** and the **"Miracle Hole"**, where he spent his last twenty years. Pilgrims were required to enter the hole before proceeding to the monastery, and the conscience-smitten were regularly unable to do so. These people were judged as sinners and were forced to go home to repent for a year before coming back to Rila.

Practicalities

Although Rila is out of the way, it has the basic amenities to make a short stay comfortable, if not particularly luxurious. As most visitors come on packaged day trips, hotel accommodation is sparse, and little goes on after dark – but then, no-one ever came to Rila for the nightlife.

Accommodation

Sadly, it's no longer possible for visitors to stay in Rila's cells, and the only **rooms** on offer are either at the *turisticheska spalnya* just down the hill from the monastery's eastern gate, or at the 3-star *Hotel Rilets* (☎2106; ③), a further 2km eastwards and across the Rilska river. Near the hotel is *Bor* **camping**, a fairly primitive and unsupervized site with campers lighting fires amid the rugged scenery. There's also the 2-star *Orbita* hotel (☎93754/2167; ③) back down the valley in Rila village.

HIKING IN THE RILA MOUNTAINS

Immediately north of Rila monastery, two hiking trails (which later diverge at Dodov Vrâh) lead to a hut called Ivan Vazov – about six hours' hard slog. From the right-hand path a trail branches off towards Mount Malyovitsa, which can also be approached from Suhoto Ezero, or "Dry Lake" (you'll need to camp overnight there), or by bus from the direction of Samokov. Paths to the Dry Lake itself begin at the Partisan Meadow east of the monastery, and the walk takes about five hours. To the southeast of Rila, the Ribni ezera ("Fish Lakes") are another feasible destination, with a mountain chalet nearby. You can reach them by following the road to its end, and then hiking up alongside the Rilska to its source in the mountains, or by a trail bearing southeast about halfway along the road, which crosses the ridge and passes some smaller lakes en route. Both walks take roughly six hours. Due south of Rila is another chalet, *Makedoniya*, accessible by several paths originating from the minor road which forks off a few kilometres west of the monastery. From the chalet it's a day's hike west down to Bistritsa (from where buses run to Blagoevgrad), or a few hours' walk eastwards to the *Semkovo* hut.

This can also be reached from the Fish Lakes, and may serve as a way-station for walkers making longer hikes (2–3 days) towards the Pirin and Rhodope mountains adjoining the Rila range. Semkovo lies on the way to Belitsa and Yakoruda, two villages linked by bus and rail to Razlog, Bansko and Velingrad; the Boris Hadzhisotirov hut situated east of the Fish Lakes serves hikers bound for Mount Musala and Borovets, or those pursuing a more easterly path down to Yakoruda. For any of these hikes food supplies and a map of the Rila Mountains are essential, and it's prudent to pack a tent in case the chalets are full.

Eating

For **snacks**, delicious bread can be had from the bakery (run by monks) just outside the monastery's east gate. A *skara-bira* den and a *sladkarnitsa* are situated a few metres up the hill, although the grilled dishes at the *Bachkova Cheshma* are tastier, 2km away on the road east. Slightly more pricey **restaurant fare** is available at the *Rila* restaurant just beyond the east gate, which has a disco downstairs. **Nightlife** is limited to the disco and the plush bar of the *Hotel Rilets*.

THE PIRIN RANGE AND THE FAR SOUTH

Like the Rila Mountains, the **Pirin range** can be approached from two directions. If you head down the Struma valley towards the Greek border you'll pass through the towns of Blagoevgrad and Sandanski – both provide access to the Pirin's western foothills, while the latter is also near to the strange rock formations of the "sandstone sea" around **Melnik**. Road and rail communications with Pirin's eastern flank tend to gravitate towards Plovdiv and other towns in southeastern Bulgaria, although some buses do make their way across the Predel pass to the village of **Bansko**, the region's best base for hiking and skiing.

From Blagoevgrad to Sandanski

Continuing further south on the main route towards Greece, you're bound to pass Blagoevgrad and Sandanski, the main towns in the Struma valley. Neither place is much to get worked-up about, but should you feel like taking a break, there could be worse stopovers.

Blagoevgrad

Administrative capital of the Pirin region, **BLAGOEVGRAD**'s concrete suburbs and factories suggest a workaday town with little to tempt you away from the southbound highway. Nevertheless, the town's older quarter provides some incentive to linger, and the establishment here in 1991 of the brand-new, English-language **American University in Bulgaria** gives the town added vitality.

Most sights are just east of the modern centre, around the River Bistritsa. Several pseudo-National Revival-style buildings and a brightly painted nineteenth-century church adorn the far bank, where the stump of a bridge now serves as a monument to Macedonia, while further downriver lies the slummy but picturesque remains of the former **"Turkish quarter"**. Previously known as *Gorna Dzhumaya*, Blagoevgrad was an important crafts' town, predominantly inhabited by Turks from the sixteenth century until their mass flight in 1912, after which Bulgarian peasants and displaced Macedonians moved in. Since 1950, when it was renamed in honour of the founder of Bulgarian Marxism, Dimitâr Blagoev, Blagoevgrad has switched to producing textiles and loudspeakers – and, above all, tobacco.

Both rail and bus stations are 2km southwest of town, a dull walk or short hop by bus down bul. Nikola Vaptsarov to the centre. There are two central hotels:

THE MACEDONIAN QUESTION

This southwestern corner of Bulgaria was only incorporated into the country after the First Balkan War of 1912. As the easternmost part of the former Ottoman province of **Macedonia**, it was originally ceded to Bulgaria by the Treaty of San Stefano in 1878, only to be returned to Turkey by the Congress of Berlin later that year. Originally stretching from the area around Kyustendil and Skopje in the north to Thessaloniki and the Aegean Sea in the south, Ottoman Macedonia was a multi-ethnic unit comprising a whole host of nationalities – for the most part Slavs, Greeks, Albanians and Turks. The Slavs of Macedonia share so many cultural, linguistic and religious affinities with the Bulgarian people that the latter have always considered the Macedonians to be merely "western" Bulgarians. Consider the fact that much of Macedonia was incorporated into Bulgaria during the heyday of medieval empire and it becomes clear why aspirations for a future "reunion" between Bulgaria and Macedonia have lurked constantly beneath the surface of modern Bulgarian politics.

Nowadays, the territory of historic Macedonia is split between Bulgaria, Greece and the former Yugoslav Republic of Macedonia. The postwar rulers of the latter have gone to great pains to establish that Macedonia is a nation in its own right: an idea fiercely contested by successive generations of Bulgarian nationalists. However, the emergence of an independent Macedonian state in what used to be Yugoslavia may encourage the growth of Macedonian feeling elsewhere, perhaps reawakening long-dormant regionalist sentiments in the Pirin area. For the time being, most people in the region tend to regard themselves as Bulgarians first and Macedonians second, but the Pirin has a long history of murderous disputes on that very issue (see the note on IMRO, p.95).

A lot will depend on the fortunes of the ex-Yugoslav Republic of Macedonia: if it survives and prospers as an independent unit, it may well attract the admiration of people in the Pirin region eager to rediscover their Macedonian identity. If, however, it proves to be untenable (and there are those in Greece and Serbia who would dearly love to strangle it at birth), then it will be the youth of Skopje who begin to look towards Bulgaria with a renewed sense of common ancestry. (For more on the Macedonian Question see *Contexts* p.305).

the *Alen Mak* (☎073/23373; ③) is the town's showpiece establishment and a little on the expensive side; the *Hotel Bor* (☎073/22491; ②) is a cheaper if less salubrious option. The *Riltsi* motel (☎073/7079; ③) is north of town on the main Sofia–Kulata highway.

South of Blagoevgrad

The Struma valley beyond Blagoevgrad is one of the most arid regions in Bulgaria, with terraces of sandy scrubland hovering above the more fertile valley floor. Fields of tobacco line the route during the 50km journey south to **SIMITLI**, a small thermal spa, just beyond which a branch road heads off towards Bansko (p.85). Once past Simitli the southward route becomes more scenic, whether you follow the road through the Kresna gorge or take the train, which forges its way through thirteen tunnels before reaching Sandanski.

From Blageoevgrad buses also run up to **BISTRITSA** village, whence it's about eight hours' walk eastwards to the *Makedoniya* chalet in the Pirin Mountains (for walks, see "Further into the Pirin Range" p.88).

Sandanski

A modernized town producing cigarettes and hothouse vegetables, **SANDANSKI** is believed to have been the birthplace of **Spartacus**, who led the great slave revolt against the Roman empire in the first century BC. The revolt originated in Sicily, where Spartacus – like others of the Thracian Medi tribe – had been deported to labour on the island's big agricultural estates following the Roman conquest of Thrace.

You can see the Spartacus monument from the highway, but most people come for the **Sandanski Hydro**, east of the centre, the largest health complex in the Balkans – with hot mineral baths, 4-star lodgings and diverse treatments (including massage and electro-acupuncture). There's been a spa here since Roman times, and it was known to the Slavs as *Sveti Vrach*, or "Blessed Doctor". Sveti Vrach languished during the Middle Ages, since the early Bulgars hardly swore by baths, but was revived as a provincial *chiflik* under Turkish rule, rivalling Melnik as a market town during the nineteenth century, when a great fair was held here every Monday. The town's current name, dating from 1949, derives from Yane Sandanski, nineteenth-century freedom fighter from the Pirin region.

In town

Sandanski's **railway station** is 4km west of town, but services are met by a bus into the centre. A couple of blocks uphill from the bus station is ul. Blagoev, the sterile pedestrianized main street. A ten-minute walk eastwards along this will take you past a few Roman and Byzantine ruins to the town's **Archaeological Museum** (Tues–Sun 9am–noon & 2–6pm), built over a late Roman/early Byzantine villa and featuring a walk-round display of the floor mosaics found *in situ*. The upper floor is filled with funerary stoneware from the necropolis of nearby Muletarovo, including the small sarcophagus of a child ringed with bull and ram head reliefs. Votive tablets to various deities abound; most of them feature either Zeus and Hera or a hunter figure presumed to be Artemis – all of them chiselled out in a vigorous, almost naive style which suggests that *Desudava* (as ancient Sandanski was known) was always a predominantly Thracian, rather than a Roman or Hellenic, town.

The town has just two **hotels** to choose from: the *Spartak* on ul. Blagoev (☎0746/2405; ③), and the *Sandanski*, a luxury spa hotel east of town (☎0746/2106; ⑤). A *kvartirno byuro* next door to the *Spartak* may be able to help with private rooms.

Bansko and the Pirin range

Bansko, the nicest of the small Pirin mountain towns, can be reached by train from Septemvri or Velingrad (see p.207), or by buses from Blagoevgrad or Simitli, which follow the valley down to the Gradevska River which divides the Rila and Pirin ranges. Cultivatable land is so scarce in this area that there's only one village between Simitli and the next town, RAZLOG, 36km away on the other side of the 1140m-high Predel Pass. From here it's just a short bus ride on to Bansko.

Bansko

Winter lasts for almost half the year in **BANSKO**, a town of 12,000 people nestled amongst greenery in the shadow of ice-capped Mount Vihren, the highest peak in the Pirin range. In recent years Bansko has shrewdly promoted itself as a winter sports resort, but its attractions aren't limited to skiing. The atmosphere here is mellow yet invigorating, and the community is tightly knit and proud of its achievements. Founded by exiled clans in the fifteenth century, Bansko has lived by trade and hard graft – growing tobacco at an altitude of 1000m above sea level – and has the lowest divorce rate in Bulgaria. This might be a result of sobriety, for Bansko's women had all the pubs shut down between 1946 and 1947, but most locals attribute it to their clannishness, and believe that divorces would be still rarer were it not for the presence of 2000 "outsiders" – immigrants from other Bulgarian towns.

Unlike many Bulgarian towns, Bansko's largely modernized centre exists easily with the older quarters, a maze of cobbled lanes where the timber-framed stone houses hide behind walls with stout double doors, as if built for siege. During the centuries of Ottoman rule Christian households were required to provide "hospitality" to travellers bearing the Sultan's *firman* (or seal of authorization), and worse still, were preyed upon by the rapacious Bashibazouks – irregular Ottoman troops charged with keeping the native Christian population quiet. It's still a traditional agricultural centre, its narrow streets jammed with goats and the horse-drawn carts of farmers bringing in produce from the outlying fields.

Around ploshtad Nikola Vaptsarov

Bansko is centred around the modern pl. Nikola Vaptsarov, with the largely pedestrianized maze of the old town lying to the south. On one corner of the main square stands the **Nikola Vaptsarov Museum** (Tues–Sat 9am–noon & 2–5pm), honouring the local-born revolutionary poet. An engineer by training, he shared the Futurists' enthusiasm for the machine age and joined the wartime resistance in the courage of his Communist convictions. Vaptsarov's final poem was composed in a Sofia prison as he awaited execution:

> *The fight is hard and pitiless*
> *The fight is epic, as they say:*
> *I fell. Another takes my place –*
> *Why single out a name!*

> *After the firing squad – the worms.*
> *Thus does the simple logic go.*
> *But in the storm we'll be with you*
> *My people, for we loved you so.*

A few steps south of here is the smaller pl. Vâzrazhdane, dominated by a statue of an even more renowned local, Otets ("Father") Paisii. Although the monasteries preserved religious arts and Orthodoxy, and Bulgars nursed memories of resistance with their songs of Haiduks and King Marko, the history of Bulgaria before the conquest was almost submerged by 1762, when Bansko-born **Paisii of Hilendar** (1722–73) completed his seminal *Slav-Bulgarian History*. Started after 1745, when Paisii became a monk at the monastery on Mount Athos, it both exalted past glories and the task of National Revival. Circulated in manuscript form for decades before its publication, Paisii's history inspired generations of Bulgarian nationalists.

BANSKO

0   200 m

N

Razlog

Bus Station

Railway Station

PL MAKEDONIYA

GEORGI DAMYANOV

Church of Sveta Bogoroditsa

Town Cemetery

River Glazne

Gotse Delchev

PL NIKOLA VAPTSAROV

Momini Dvori Tavern

Nikola Vaptsarov Museum

PIRIN

NIKOLA VAPTSAROV

YANE SANDANSKI

Icon Museum

Tourist Service Office

Church of Sveta Troitsa

VELYAN OGNEV

Neofit Rilski Museum House

The Velyanova House

Hotel Pirin

PIRIN

NEOFIT RILSKI

The Pirin Mountains

Neofit Rilski and the church of Sveta Troitsa

Just above pl. Vâzrazhdane is the **church of Sveta Troitsa**, the existence of which owes a great deal to the efforts of another patriot associated with Bansko, **Neofit Rilski**. Born in 1793, Neofit was a key figure in the nineteenth-century resurgence of Bulgarian education and church life, in the face of Turkish restrictions and Greek influence, and led the campaign to restore Rila monastery and build the local church. To accomplish this required a bribe to the governor and to the official witness of the "discovery" of an icon on the site (which qualified it as "holy ground" suitable for a Christian place of worship). A wall was then raised to conceal the townsfolks' enlargement of the church beyond the size set by Turkish clerks – for which the mayor of Bansko was jailed for five years in Thessaloniki.

One monument in the churchyard remembers Peyo Yavorov, poet and *Voyvoda*, or war leader, who liberated Bansko from the Turks on October 5, 1912, proclaiming "Throw away your fezzes, brothers! From today you are free Bulgarians". Behind the church is the **Neofit Rilski house** (Tues–Sat 9am–noon & 2–5pm), with re-created period rooms and a display illustrating Rilski's career.

The icon museum and old village houses

Near the northern end of pl. Vâzrazhdane is an **icon museum** (Tues–Sat 9am–noon & 2–5pm) grouped around the galleried courtyard of a former nunnery. The works on display illustrate the careers of Bansko's nineteenth-century icon painters – a school largely centred around the Vienna-educated painter Toma Vishanov, who together with pupils Dimitâr and Simeon Molerov travelled from village to village decorating the region's churches. One highlight of the museum is an anonymous *Wheel of Time*, in which everyday village scenes are encircled by portrayals of the different ages of man.

The nearby **Velyanova kâshta** (or Velyanov House) at Velyan Ognev 5 is a typical stone-built house now open to the public, with nineteenth-century furnishings and rugs on display inside. The **Hadzhivâlchova kâshta** at no. 11 remembers the late-eighteenth-century Bansko merchant Hadzhi Vâlcho, who exploited the village's position midway between Danube and Aegean to build up a minor trading empire, with offices in Vienna. He was a major patron of the arts (his wealth was instrumental in encouraging the early flowering of the Bansko icon school), and donated large sums to both Rila monastery and Zografski monastery – the Bulgarian foundation on Mount Athos in Greece.

On the other side of town, just east of the rail and bus stations, the town cemetery holds the early nineteenth-century **church of Sveta Bogoroditsa**: formerly home to an exquisite iconostasis carved by local artisans, it was gutted by fire a couple of years ago and the church may still be closed. In the meantime the central doors of the church's iconostasis (or *tsarskite dveri*), decorated with paintings by Toma Vishanov, can be seen in the icon museum.

Practicalities

Both **bus and rail stations** are on the northern fringes of town, from where it's a short walk to pl. Vaptsarov. A right turn here brings you shortly to the *Tourist Service Centre*, which has a range of **private rooms** in Bansko and may also have up-to-date info on the accommodation currently being built outside the town for winter holidaymakers. Immediately opposite the office is the *Hotel Pirin*, ul Dimitrov 8 (☎07443/2295; ③). There's a *turisticheska spalnya* on pl. Vâzrazhdane.

Despite Bansko's ambitions as a winter holiday centre, there is as yet very little in the way of *après-ski*. Numerous small cafés line the main street, but most young Bansko-ites seem to head for the *Momini Dvori* bar on pl. Vaptsarov. Places **to eat** are the *Orlovo Gnezdo* on the main square, or the restaurant of the *Hotel Pirin*.

Skiing is practised just outside town from December until March: facilities include one 1500m ski run with chair-lifts and two 300m practice slopes with ski-tows. Instructors speak various foreign languages (although Bansko has yet to become a centre of package tourism), and there's a range of equipment for hire – for details of this, check at the *Tourist Service Centre* in town.

Further into the Pirin range

Both Bansko and Dobrinishte (6km east by bus or rail) serve as starting points for excursions into the **Pirin Mountains**, Bulgaria's wildest range. The heart of the massif consists of 45 peaks all of which are over 2590 metres tall, snow-capped for much of the year and subject to such powerful winds and violent storms that the Thracians were convinced that this was the abode of the Thunder God, Perun. Pure water tarns and short-lived wildflowers abound in the highland valleys, and the slopes are a botanist's delight, with clumps of Scots, Corsican,

Macedonian and white pine. The highest peaks and most of the lakes are in the northern Pirin, which is criss-crossed with hiking trails between *hizhi* – simple hostels with rooms and bunk beds (and perhaps food and drink).

Hiking notes

If you're considering **hiking**, the first requirement is a map published by the *BTS* – clear enough although the text is in Bulgarian only, and available from Bansko's tourist office, where it's also important to make enquiries about staying in *hizha* – and to reserve beds in advance, if possible. Besides this, stout boots, warm clothing, a sleeping bag and food are **essential**. You can camp at designated spots (not within nature reserves), but only during the summer; inexperienced hikers should avoid high peaks and snowy ground and, ideally, join a group familiar with the mountains.

Beginning **from Bansko**, take the minor road heading directly south, which forks after 6km. The right-hand, better surfaced fork leads to the *Bunderitsa* hut 8km away, and on past the **Baikushev Fir** – a mighty tree 1200 years old – to the larger *Vihren* chalet, 2km on. From here on the scenery is magnificent, whether you make the two and a half hour walk northwards to **Mount Vihren** (2914m), Bulgaria's second highest peak, or trek for six hours in the opposite direction via Lake Tevetno to the *Begovitsa* chalet or the larger *Yane Sandanski* – which serves meals and attracts weekend hikers from Sandanski, 18km to the southwest. A third trail from the *Vihren* chalet runs eastwards, past two lakes and **Mount Todorin** (2746m) to the *Demyanitsa* cabin four and a half hours away, which awaits folks who've conquered the 11km ascent by way of the left-hand fork of the road leaving Bansko. Heading south from *Demyanitsa*, the second turn-off to the east leads to the **Balyavishki Lakes**, while the main trail reaches Lake Tevetno in three hours. If the weather's good and there's time to spare, consider pushing on from there to reach the *Pirin* or *Begovitsa* chalets (3–4 hours), or head north from Balyavishki Ezero to the *Bezbog* hut.

You can, alternatively, start **from Dobrinishte**, from where it's 11km by mountain road (petering out into a track) to the *Gotse Delchev* chalet, and a further two and a half hours' walk to the *Bezbog* cabin – whence you can hike to most of the places mentioned above. Few foreigners go further south into the Pirin range,

---

GOTSE DELCHEV (1872–1903)

Inspired by Balkan revolutionaries Vasil Levski and Hristo Botev, **Gotse Delchev** dedicated himself to the achievement of a free Macedonia, laboriously organizing a network of underground cells for the IMRO (p.95), while publicly leading the life of a penurious teacher. An enlightened and unusually liberal revolutionary, Delchev was similar to his idol Levski in refusing to target local Turks, declaring that they too were victims of Ottoman oppression. His dream of an autonomous Macedonia governed according to socialist principles was anathema to the right-wing, Sofia-based *Vârhovisti*, who urged an indiscriminate campaign of terror and sought the region's fusion with Bulgaria. Killed in a skirmish with Turkish troops, Delchev never witnessed the failure of the long-awaited uprising nor the IMRO's decline into sectarian butchery.

Nowadays Delchev is honoured as a hero in both Bulgaria and the ex-Yugoslav Republic of Macedonia, where his moustached portrait hangs from the wall of many a café. He was buried in the Macedonian capital Skopje, where his tomb can still be visited in the courtyard of the church of Sveti Spas.

although there are sporadic buses down the Mesta valley to the small town of **GOTSE DELCHEV**, a place rather less remarkable than its namesake, the revolutionary **Gotse Delchev** (see p.89). Previously known as *Nevrokop*, the town is a sleepy place engaged in tobacco-growing, with the **remains of Nicopolis ad Nestrum**, a staging-point on the Roman road from Constantinople to the Adriatic, standing nearby. From town a minor road runs through the mountains to KULATA on the Greek border.

Melnik and Rozhen monastery

Five buses daily run **from Sandanski to Melnik**, past tobacco fields hugging the roadside above the fertile bed of the Struma valley, between hills that become arid and rocky, swelling into desolate mountains which stretch towards the Greek and Macedonian frontiers. Off the highway, roads deteriorate and villages seem like triumphs of tenacity, clinging to hilltops burrowed with bunkers, or crouched around waterholes.

Melnik

Approaching **MELNIK** you'll catch glimpses of the wall of mountains which allowed the townsfolk to thumb their noses at the Byzantine Empire in the eleventh century. The town itself hides until the last moment, encircled by hard-edged crags, scree slopes and rounded sandstone cones. Its straggling square is lined with tavernas, whitewashed stone houses on timber props festooned with flowers and vines overhanging cobbled alleys and narrow courtyards, through which even tourist crocodiles don't manage to upset the local drinkers' equanimity. Visually, Melnik is stunning – marred only by the *Balkantourist* hotel on the hillside – but socially and economically it's fast becoming its own monument, a living fossil. In 1880 Melnik had 20,000 inhabitants, 75 churches and a thriving market called the *Charshiya* on the main street, where camels and horses departed for foreign lands, laden with wine. The economy waned towards the end of the nineteenth century, and the Second Balkan War of 1913 destroyed the town and sundered its trade routes. Nowadays, despite its central core of immaculately restored vernacular architecture, Melnik is a town where ruins outnumber inhabited houses. The town has barely 600 people living in it, who survive on wine-making – the traditional stand-by – and tourism.

The Pashov house

Melnik's backstreets invite aimless wandering and guarantee a succession of eye-catching details. The town's layout is fairly simple, with a main street running from west to east, where it divides into two tracks heading up parallel gulleys. Standing above the main street's western end is the **Pashov house**, a venerable nineteenth-century mansion now housing the **town museum** (Tues–Sun 8am–noon & 2–6pm). The creaking stairways and elegant rooms are more arresting than most of the exhibits – though photos and engravings of old Melnik manage to leap the language barrier. The high point is the top-floor room decked out with the accoutrements of Melnik's *haute-bourgeoisie* at the turn of the century – lace gloves, plush armchairs with antimacassars, the frock coats and ball gowns all redolent of a Slavonic *Forsyte Saga*.

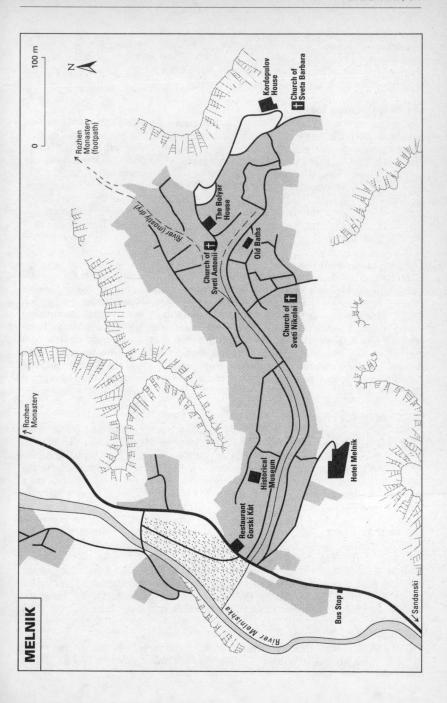

MELNIK

0   100 m

N

Rozhen Monastery (footpath)

↑ Rozhen Monastery

River (mostly dry)

River Melnishka

Kordopulov House

Church of Sveta Barbara

The Bolyar House

Church of Sveti Antonii

Old Baths

Church of Sveti Nikolai

Historical Museum

Restaurant Gorski Kât

Hotel Melnik

Bus Stop

↙ Sandanski

In a lovely **church** clinging to the hillside opposite, the nineteenth-century iconostasis is painted in a bold, almost naive style, the lowest row of panels depicting the Fall, while scaly fishes – a traditional motif – flank the crucifix topping the altar screen. There are turbaned Turkish gravestones in the crypt museum and medieval frescoes inside the nave.

The Bolyarskata kâshta

The single surviving wall of Melnik's oldest ruin – known as the **Bolyarskata kâshta** or Bolyar house – is sited on a hill overlooking the main street's eastern end, and was clearly built between the tenth and fourteenth centuries with defence in mind. It was probably the residence of Melnik's thirteenth-century overlord, Alexei Slav, who invited rich Greeks – then persecuted in Plovdiv – to settle here, thereby ensuring investment in the town in the form of businesses, churches and residences. Many of these now lie in ruins, as the dusty, stone-scattered hill above the Bolyar house attests, although several churches still survive to serve their tiny congregations – among them, the unadorned basilica of Sveti Antonii just below.

The church of Sveti Nikolai

Opposite the Bolyar house narrow alleyways head up the hill towards the angular stone bulk of Melnik's eighteenth-century metropolitan church, **Sveti Nikolai** (Tues–Sun 10am–noon & 2–5pm). Its exterior is characterized by the two-headed eagles which adorn its window frames and an almost minaret-like balustraded tower. Inside, a wooden bishop's throne decorated with light blue floral patterns offsets a fine iconostasis. Saint Nicholas himself is portrayed seated on a throne; and there's an eighteenth-century John the Baptist holding his own severed head. A panel below bears a narrative sequence of paintings set in the Garden of Eden, one of which features Eve covering her modesty with what appears to be a grass skirt.

The Kordopulov house

Below the church, a dirt road follows a gulley southeastwards past the now derelict Turkish bathhouse into an area of some of Melnik's most picturesque nineteenth-century town houses. Pride of place goes to the **Kordopulov house** (Tues–Sun 8am–noon & 1.30–6pm), protruding from a rocky shoulder above the gulley, its 24 windows surveying every approach. Above the ground floor, now a *mehana*, the spacious rooms are intimate, the reception room a superb fusion of Turkish and Bulgarian crafts, with painted panelling, rows of cushioned *minder* (long strips of seating) lining three walls, an intricate lattice-work ceiling and a multitude of stained glass windows. Kordopulov was a rich merchant of Greek extraction known for his anti-Ottoman sympathies – you can see the secret room he added to the house as a refuge for the family in case of emergencies. Below ground are the wine cellars, enormous wooden barrels occupying vast caverns cut from the hillside, and connected to the vineyards to the rear of the house by a network of tunnels. Further up the valley are yet more ruins, including the abandoned shell of the medieval church of Sveta Barbara.

Practicalities

There's an **accommodation bureau** on the main street offering rooms in old houses, although this often closes from mid-September onwards: if it is shut, a

MELNIK WINE

Full-bodied red **Melnik wine** is justly famed throughout Bulgaria and once enjoyed an international reputation through the wine trade organized by the merchants of Dubrovnik, which enriched Alexei Slav and continued under Ottoman rule when Melnik was a tribute-paying *kaza* town (the Turks weren't fundamentalists when fine wine and healthy profits were involved). Nowadays it provides a modest livelihood – restaurants and tavernas slosh it around and locals are keen to flog tourists their homebrew – but the wine sold here isn't much cheaper than in a Sofia supermarket, and can be more expensive. The vineyards laden with small, dark grapes (of the variety known as Melnik Broad Vine) are ritually pruned and sprinkled with wine on February 14 to ensure a bumper crop – an event known as **Vinegrowers' Day** (*Trifon Zarezan*) – while the harvest time is decided a week beforehand, and can sometimes occur as late as the middle of October if the summer has been particularly dry and sunny. The grapes are allowed to cool in basements before being pressed and left to ferment in the chilly cellars that riddle the hills around – every family has at least one, and casks of wine for the consumption of "insiders" only, which is better than the stuff sold to visitors. Melnik is also a fine place to drink *Mastika* (similar to Greek ouzo), which packs a delayed-action punch.

few casual enquiries about *chastni kvartiri* should secure you a bed. If not, there's a rough-and-ready *turisticheska spalnya*, signposted at the eastern end of the main street; or the 3-star *Hotel Melnik* (☎9972 7437/272; ③), overlooking the town centre from a hillside to the south. *Kâmping Melnik*, 500m north of Melnik on the Rozhen road, is fairly basic and doesn't have any chalets.

Of the half-dozen **places to eat**, the *Chinarite* is a fairly basic *mehana* just beyond the bridge at the top end of the square; the food is pretty standard fare, but the staff are friendly and the place buzzes until closedown at 11pm. The *Paskaleva Kâshta* on the opposite side of the valley offers the slightly more atmospheric surroundings of a reconstructed nineteenth-century house. Both of the above also serve as good **drinking venues**; otherwise try the *Vinarna* directly opposite the *Hotel Melnik*.

Rozhen monastery

Although the bus from Sandanski continues on to Rozhen, turning off the Pirin road at Kârlanovo to reach the village, it's more fun to walk over the mountains to the monastery. The six and a half kilometre footpath ascends the river gully – follow the right-hand fork after about a kilometre and a half – and up into the hills, offering great views of the valleys around Melnik. Scrambling up a mountain ridge is the only hard part of the journey, and the scenery repays any effort. Rippling sandstone mountains ranged behind the mushroom-like slabs of hard rock poised upon eroded columns of softer sandstone make up a surreal landscape reminiscent of *Dune*. In Robert Littell's novel *The October Circle*, it's here that the blind Witch of Melnik resides, fortelling the townsfolks' destiny for lumps of sugar in lieu of silver coins – a scenario that seems quite possible in the eerily unreal surroundings. Suddenly, the descent onto a grassy plateau reveals the monastery.

The monastery

Rozhen monastery (*Rozhenski manastir*) is small and – outwardly at least – austere, having survived looting and burning many times since its foundation in the twelfth century, on the site of an earlier monastery. Rozhen is dedicated to the "Mother of God's Nativity" and its name derives from the ancient form of the word *roden*, meaning "born". The irregular courtyard is intimate and unadorned, save for wooden trestles supporting a canopy of vines. In the **bakery** the oven and walls consist of the same mud-and-straw bricks, giving the entire room the texture of a very coarse wholemeal loaf. Only at the far end, where cell is stacked upon cell, does the woodwork display the finesse found at Rila. The **cells** themselves are arranged to give some idea of monastic life through the ages. The accent is on severe asceticism, although the vivid colours of rugs and cushions counterpoint the simplicity of the furnishings. It's also clear that leading clerics led a somewhat softer life than their charges, enjoying the use of silver coffee sets and book-holders inlaid with mother of pearl.

The monastery church

The **church of the Birth of the Holy Virgin**'s single cloister shelters a battered *Judgement Day*, which shows the righteous assisted up one side of the ladder to heaven by angels; while sinners attempting to climb the other side are tossed by demons into the mouth of a large red serpent. The torments of hell are vividly depicted on the right, where the damned meet a gory end (prodded by toasting forks and suchlike). Inside the narthex, delicately restored murals include the varied sea-beasts of a *Miraculous Draught of Fishes*, and a splendid *Dormition of the Virgin*. Once in the church itself, the endless ranks of saints covering the walls are if anything eclipsed by a magnificent iconostasis, the work of Debâr artisans. Flowers, birds, fishes and flounces swirl about the richly coloured icons, and the whole screen – unusually wide in proportion to its height – is a triumph of the woodcarver's art.

Outside the monastery – and Rozhen village

Beyond the monastery is a larger nineteenth-century church, with crudely "marbled" columns, cumbersome fittings and a brash iconostasis. Behind the church is the grave of Macedonian freedom fighter Yane Sandanski (1872–1915), inscribed with one of his favourite rallying-cries and a fitting epitaph: "To live is to struggle: the slave struggles for freedom; the free man, for perfection!". The track descends to **Rozhen village** in the valley; conspicuously poorer than Melnik, with houses like overgrown chicken-coops, a shop, a *mehana* and little else. The villagers can be amazingly friendly and might invite you to join the dancing (which is similar to that in northern Greece) if they're having a bash; try the local **strawberries**, which are delicious.

Petrich and the borderlands

If your ultimate destination is Greece, there's little of interest south of Melnik: the frontier town of **KULATA** has a motel and an all-year campsite if you need to stop off, but little else to detain you from heading straight for the 24-hour border checkpoint. If heading for the Macedonian Republic, the town of Petrich (15km west of the main north–south Struma valley route and accessible by train changing at General Todorovo) is more likely to warrant a stop-off. The border crossing is 22km further on.

Petrich and around

PETRICH contains few reminders of the past, having been reconstructed at the foot of Mount Belasitsa on the site of the old town destroyed during World War I, but the town harbours a respect for ancient traditions. There's been a succession of **oracles** here over the years, most recently a woman named Vanga, who at the age of six witnessed an angel who offered her the choice between sight and clairvoyance, and went blind after she chose the latter. Her subsequent prophecies gained a wide following (including Politburo members), and her vision of Varna engulfed by water was vindicated when it was discovered that the city stood upon an underground lake, following which additional high-rise buildings were prohibited.

PETRICH AND THE IMRO

Nowadays there's little reminder of the years between 1923 and 1934, when Petrich was the "murder capital" of Bulgaria, rife with so many hired killers that the price of an assassination dropped to £4. The warring factions then controlling the region descended from the most legendary of Balkan revolutionary movements, the **IMRO**. The **Internal Macedonian Revolutionary Organisation** was founded in Salonika in 1893 by two schoolmasters, Damian Gruev and Hristo Tatarchev, to liberate Macedonia from Ottoman rule by means of a mass insurrection. To prepare for this, the later leader, Gotse Delchev, and his supporters painstakingly constructed an underground "shadow" administration complete with schools, elected committees, taxation and a postal service, besides arming *komitadzhi* to wage guerilla war in the hills.

From the beginning, however, the IMRO was crippled by internal dissention, and soon became divided between those who regarded Macedonia as a natural part of Bulgaria and those who saw it as an autonomous unit, either within Bulgaria or some future Balkan federation. Following the assassination of Gotse Delchev, the Sofia-based *Vârhovisti* (the Supremists – those who aimed to incorporate Macedonia into Bulgaria) persuaded the IMRO to launch the Macedonian uprising on *Ilinden* (St Elijah's Day) in August 1903. This was premature: despite three months' heroic resistance they were defeated by the Turks, who took savage revenge on the populace.

Regrouped around Petrich and Kyustendil, the surviving IMRO members became increasingly dominated by the Supremists. The Turks were finally driven from the region in 1912 but the Greeks, Serbs and Bulgarians quarrelled over the spoils, and Macedonia was partitioned among the three states – Greece and Serbia taking the lion's share. In these conditions Macedonian nationalism became internecine, and the IMRO turned in on itself as the Supremists battled to purge the organization of the "Federalists" – those who pursued the original goal of an autonomous Macedonia. Mussolini secretly supported the latter to undermine Yugoslavia, while Bulgarian conservatives used the IMRO to crush the 1923 uprising and overthrow the Agrarian government. Finally, the IMRO's terrorist activities exceeded the tolerance of its right-wing backers, and in 1934 "bloody" Tsankov sent in troops to end the organization's power over southwestern Bulgaria.

Many of the townsfolk are fairly recent migrants from the surrounding villages, which perch upon volcanic cones overlooking the fertile **Strumeshnitsa valley**. Thanks to its excellent climate the valley produces Bulgaria's earliest crops of cherries, melons and grapes, and the experimental orchards planted in 1951 now yield superb **peaches** in vast quantities. Petrich itself is a vivacious town full of pavement cafés, although relatively lacking in specific attractions. There's a small **museum** beneath the town hall on the main square, which although currently undergoing reorganization, seems the most likely place at which to find reminders of Romano-Thracian Petra, administrative centre of the Medi tribe.

Samuel's fortress and Basil the Bulgar-slayer

Remains of Petra dot the slopes of the Kozuh Mountains (near the Petrich mineral baths), and in a park 15km west of town near the border stand the remains of **Samuilova krepost**, or "Samuel's fortress", site of a monument to perhaps the most infamous event in Bulgarian history. After being defeated in battle at Strumitsa in 1014, 14,000 Bulgarian prisoners were blinded on the orders of the Byzantine emperor **Basil the Bulgar-slayer**, except one man in every hundred to guide the victims back to Tsar Samuel in Ohrid (now in ex-Yugoslav Macedonia), who died of apoplexy at the horrible sight. Two buses a day link Petrich with the fortress, although take the morning one and you could be left several hours waiting for the evening return.

Practicalities

Petrich's only tourist **accommodation** is the 3-star *Hotel Bâlgariya*, Dimo Hadzhidimov 5 (☎0745/2233; ③), directly opposite the bus station. If you're heading for ex-Yugoslav Macedonia, there's a weekly bus (currently at 8am on Saturday) to the town of Strumitsa on the other side of the border. Otherwise there's a dearth of public transport to the frontier, and lack of traffic on the Strumitsa-bound road makes hitching a bit risky – be prepared to fork out for a taxi.

travel details

Trains

From Blagoevgrad to Kocherinovo (8 daily; 15min); Sandanski (8; 1–2hr 15min); Sofia (8; 2hr 30min–3hr 30min); Stanke Dimitrov (9; 45min).

From Kyustendil to Gyueshevo (3; 1hr 15min); Pernik (9; 1hr 30min–2hr); Radomir (8; 1hr 15min–1hr 30min); Sofia (7; 2hr 15min–3hr); Zemen (10; 30min–1hr).

From Sandanski to Blagoevgrad (8 daily; 1hr–2hr 15min); Kulata (7; 1hr 30min); Petrich (7; 45min); Sofia (7; 3hr 30min–4hr 45min); Stanke Dimitrov (7; 45min).

From Sofia to Kocherinovo (6 daily; 2hr 15min–3hr 15min); Kyustendil (4; 2hr); Pernik (every 30min; 45min); Sandanski (5; 3–5hr); Stanke Dimitrov (7; 2hr–2hr 45min); Zemen (5; 1hr 30min–

1hr 45min). For trains **to other parts of Bulgaria** see the *Travel Details* at the end of each chapter.

From Stanke Dimitrov to Kocherinovo (8; 15–30min); Kulata (7; 2hr–3hr 45min).

Buses

From Bansko to Blagoevgrad (9 daily); Gotse Delchev (11); Petrich (1); Plovdiv (2); Razlog (11).

From Blagoevgrad to Gotse Delchev (10 daily); Kyustendil (4); Petrich (4); Plovdiv (1); Rila village (9); Sandanski (4); Samokov (1); Simitli (every 30min); Stanke Dimitrov (5); Velingrad (1).

From Petrich to Gotse Delchev (2 daily); Kulata (5).

From Samokov to Borovets (every 30min); Malyovitsa (3 daily); Stanke Dimitrov (5).

From Sandanski to Melnik (5 daily).
From Sofia (*Avtogara Yug*) to Samokov (every 30min); (*Avtogara Ovcha Kupel*) to Bansko (1 daily); Blagoevgrad (10); Gotse Delchev (4);

Kyustendil (4); Rila monastery (2); Sandanski (3); Stanke Dimitrov (hourly).
From Stanke Dimitrov to Bistritsa (5–6 daily).

CYRILLIC PLACE NAMES

BANSKO	БАНСКО	PETRICH	ПЕТРИЧ
BLAGOEVGRAD	БЛАГОЕВГРАД	RADOMIR	РАДОМИР
BOROVETS	БОРОВЕЦ	RILA	РИЛА
DRAGOMAN	ДРАГОМАН	ROZHEN	РОЖЕН
DOBRINISHTE	ДОБРИНИЩЕ	SAMOKOV	САМОКОВ
GOTSE DELCHEV	ГОЦЕ ДЕЛЧЕВ	SANDANSKI	САНДАНСКИ
KALOTINA	КАЛОТИНА	SAPAREVA BANYA	САПАРЕВА БАНЯ
KOCHERINOVO	КОЧЕРИНОВО	SIMITLI	СИМИТЛИ
KYUSTENDIL	КЮСТЕНДИЛ	SOFIA	СОФИЯ
MALYOVITSA	МАЛЬОВИЦА	STANKE DIMITROV	СТАНКЕ ДИМИТРОВ
MELNIK	МЕЛНИК		
PERNIK	ПЕРНИК	ZEMEN	ЗЕМЕН

CHAPTER THREE

THE BALKAN RANGE AND THE DANUBIAN PLAIN

T he **Balkan Range** cuts right across the country, a forbidding swathe of rock known to the Bulgarians as the *Stara planina* – the "Old Mountains". To the ancients they were the *Haemus*, lair of brigands and supposed home of the North Wind. In the seventh and eighth centuries, the Balkan Mountains were the birthplace of the Bulgarian nation-state. It was here, first at **Pliska**, and later at **Preslav**, that the Bulgar khans established and ruled over a feudal realm – the "First Kingdom". Here too, after a period of

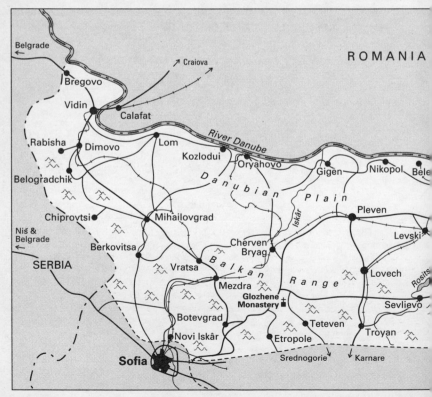

Byzantine control, the Bulgarian nobility (the *bolyari*) proclaimed the "Second Kingdom" and established a new and magnificent capital at **Veliko Târnovo**. During the Ottoman occupation, the **villages and monasteries** of the *Stara planina* helped to preserve Bulgarian traditions, preparing the ground for the re-emergence of native culture during the nineteenth-century National Revival.

Given the mountainous topography and the vagaries of the road and rail network, **routes** through the Balkan Range are many and complex. East–west routes between Sofia and the sea skirt the highest peaks and tend to be much quicker than north–south routes across the backbone of the Balkan Range. Hence many people approach the area from either the Sofia-Burgas line through the Valley of the Roses (see Chapter Four), or the Sofia-Varna line which arcs round the mountains to the north. The latter passes near three obvious bases for exploration: **Pleven**, whose numerous museums commemorate a celebrated episode from the War of Liberation, when Bulgarian independence was wrested with the aid of Russian arms; the aforementioned medieval capital of Veliko Târnovo, one of Bulgaria's most visually impressive cities and a convenient base for visiting a string of nearby medieval **monasteries** and a yet more brilliant ensemble of craftworking towns; and **Shumen**, close to the First Kingdom capitals of Pliska and Preslav, as well as the enigmatic cliff-face sculpture of the **Madara Horseman**.

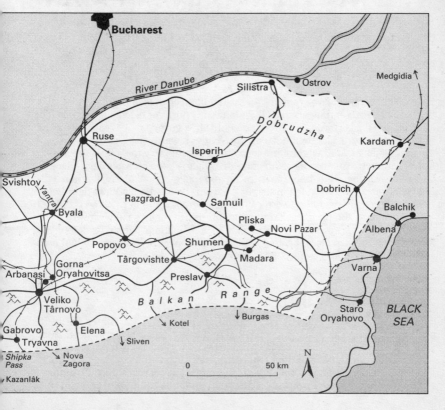

The Sofia-Varna route also skirts the **Danubian plain** (*Dunavska ravnina*), stretching from the northern foothills of the Balkan Range down to the banks of the river, which forms a natural boundary with Romania. Despite the name it's by no means uniformly flat, although this rich agricultural area of rolling hills lacks major attractions save for the River Danube itself. The citadel town of **Vidin** and the central-European ambience of **Ruse** will be the likely highlights of any trip along the river.

Travelling from the Danube towards the Black Sea coast you'll pass through the relatively unknown **Dobrudzha**, a hot, dusty region which lies at the southernmost limits of the Eurasian Steppe. Although short on specific sights, its wide-open skies nevertheless exert a certain fascination.

THE WESTERN BALKAN RANGE

Travelling between Sofia and the Danube takes you across the western spur of the **Balkan Mountains**, an area of forested highlands scattered with tortuous rock formations. Although not as high as the Rila or Pirin ranges to the south, the peaks of northwest Bulgaria present some of the country's most rewarding walking and rambling areas. Practical maps of the area are, however, thin on the ground, and serious hikers will have to pick up local knowledge from the Bulgarians patronizing the region's many mountain chalets or *hizhi*.

There are several routes across the mountains north of the capital: if travelling by train, you'll pass through the magnificent **Iskâr gorge** before reaching the rail junction at Mezdra, and then heading via **Vratsa** towards the Danube plain, with the mountains to your left. Much road traffic goes this way too, although an alternative route crosses the rugged terrain of Bulgaria's western borderlands. This takes you via the **Petrohan pass** to the mountain resort of **Berkovitsa** (also reachable via a rail line which branches off from the main Sofia-Vidin line) before rejoining the main road northwards at Mihailovgrad. From here it's a straightforward trip across the plains to Vidin, although minor roads head westward to the town of **Belogradchik**, whose spectacular rock formations demand a detour. For those who want to explore the area using public transport, Vratsa and Vidin probably offer the best bus connections to outlying towns.

The Iskâr Gorge

The **ISKÂR GORGE** is the most scenically impressive of the routes north. It's also within easy enough reach of Sofia to be a popular day-trip destination, although only the slow *pâtnicheski*, or local, trains (most of which run early in the morning and late in the afternoon) stop at the small settlements along the gorge. Beware too that the gorge is almost totally devoid of tourist **accommodation** – Sofia and Vratsa are the nearest places of note, although the one-horse town of

Mezdra at the gorge's northern end does have a basic hotel (see p.102) – so you really have no choice but to make a fleeting visit. The most breathtaking stretches of the gorge, where the river is squeezed beneath soaring crags, lie between **Gara Lakatnik** and **Lyutibrod**; and it's feasible to stop off at one of the halts between these places, indulge in a spot of walking, and pick up another train later in the day. There don't seem to be any distinct footpaths along the valley bottom, but it's possible to walk along stretches of the riverbank, rejoining the roadway above whenever the valley gets too narrow.

Things begin to get interesting just beyond the town of NOVI ISKÂR, 10km north of the capital, where the gorge burrows north into the Balkan massif, gradually becoming narrower and deeper, the road and railway competing for space above the river. Strewn with boulders and scored by gullies, it's archetypal partisan country. There's a monument near BATULIYA village commemorating the 24 partisans who clashed with local police in May 1944, and a train halt called *Tompsân* after **Major Frank Thompson** (brother of left-wing historian and veteran CND campaigner E.P. Thompson) who fought and died with them. A member of the British mission sent to observe the effectiveness of Bulgaria's antifascist fighters (and evaluate their suitability to receive Allied aid), Thompson was fondly remembered by the postwar Bulgarian regime, and his uniform used to be exhibited in Sofia's now defunct Museum of the Revolution. How Bulgaria's post-1989 generation of historians chooses to deal with his legacy, and that of the partisan movement as a whole, remains to be seen.

Around Gara Lakatnik

The **GARA LAKATNIK** halt stands opposite a precipitous knuckle of rock which harbours two **caves** known as *dupki* or "dens", around which (if numbers are sufficient) guides conduct short tours. *Temnata dupka* is the larger of the two, extending for nearly 3km over four levels and including several lakes fed by a subterranean river. Just south of the caves a track follows the River Proboinitsa up a scenic side valley surrounded by mountains – good hiking territory. At the end of the trail, about 10km away, stands the *Proboinitsa* chalet, the base for assaults on the 1785m-high TODORINI KUKLI, from which paths descend to the Petrohan pass on the other side. South of Gara Lakatnik, a more serviceable road heads for the pastoral highland village of LAKATNIK itself, 8km away, and beyond that, the *Trâstena* chalet, again the start of numerous walking possibilities.

This part of the Balkan Range also harbours two **monasteries**: **Sedmete prestola** (named after its seven altars), 10km south by minor road from ELISEYNA village, and the more accessible **Cherepish monastery** near the halt of the same name, midway between the villages of Zverino and Lyutibrod. Both date from the Second Kingdom, but Cherepish – with icons by Father Vitan of Tryavna and frescoes by the Macedonian Iliev – is the more rewarding. At the end of a track which descends from the halt, the monastery buildings form an untidy huddle at the base of a sheer limestone cliff on the west bank of the river. Founded in the fourteenth century, Cherepish was sacked by the Turks almost as soon as it was built, and most of the current monastery buildings date from seventeenth- and nineteenth-century rebuildings. The frescoes in the monastery church are in desperate need of restoration, but the intricate woodcarving of the bishop's throne stands out. A nearby grotto known as **Shishman's Cave** recalls Tsar Ivan Shishman, whose forces campaigned unsuccessfully in the area to stem the Ottoman advance.

The Iskâr gorge ends with a final geological flourish nicknamed *Ritlite* or the "Cart Rails": three parallel ribs of fissured rock up to 198m high which you'll see to the west of LYUTIBROD, a few miles before the road and railway enter **MEZDRA**. A useful transport hub at the junction of the Sofia-Vidin and Sofia-Pleven-Varna lines, Mezdra has little else to offer save for **rooms** at the *Hotel Rodina* in the town centre (☎0910/2445; ③).

Vratsa

Approaching from the south, arrival in **VRATSA** is presaged by the steaming pipelines and storage tanks of a vast chemical plant, which does much to detract from the undoubted beauty of the town's situation, standing at the base of a wall of mountains known as the *Vrachanska planina*. Vratsa's valued collection of **Thracian treasures** is the main attraction for visitors, but the town also gives access to a beautiful rocky hinterland, starting with the **Vratsata** defile which ascends into the mountains just west of the town centre. Overlooking Vratsa to the south is **Mount Okolchitsa**, where **Hristo Botev**, one of the more romantic figures in Bulgaria's struggle for liberation, met his death. An inspiring revolutionary leader as well as a poet known for his patriotic verses, Botev formed a *cheta*, or band of guerilla fighters, to lend assistance to the April Rising in 1876. Botev's men marched south into the Balkan Mountains from Kozlodui on the Danube, but were constantly harried by Ottoman forces. After days of running battles, Botev finally perished along with the remnants of his *cheta* on Okolchitsa on June 2.

The town

Vratsa's **rail and bus stations** stand together just east of the centre, from where the pedestrianized ribbon of bul. Nikolai Voivodov curves its way northwest to meet the main thoroughfare, ul. Georgi Dimitrov. Turn left into this and you'll pass a plaza built around the *kula na meschiite*, a seventeenth-century fortified tower. Such towers were built as family dwellings by local feudal lords who wanted to intimidate their exploited subjects with a suitable symbol of invincibility. Shortly afterwards ul. Târgovska breaks off to the left, a side street blessed with a picturesque collection of pastel-coloured nineteenth-century town houses. At the end of the street stands a monument to **Sofronii Vrachanski**, local church leader and key figure in the Bulgarian Renaissance (see opposite).

The ethnographic museum and complex
Immediately behind the statue is the **ethnographic museum** (summer Tues–Sun 9am–1pm & 3–7pm; winter Tues–Sun 9am–noon & 2–6pm) housed in a National Revival-period former girls' school, a fine half-timbered structure vaguely reminiscent of Tudor architecture. Inside is one of provincial Bulgaria's best collections of folk costumes and crafts, strong on local marriage customs: exhibits include the enigmatic *svatbeni bardeta* or "wedding pitchers", twelve earthenware jugs hanging from a 2m-long wooden pole. The first floor is devoted to brass band instruments, imported from central Europe by village ensembles at the turn of the century; while outside a pavilion displays nineteenth-century carriages and carts (and a particularly ornate bright-blue ceremonial sled) built by the local Orazov factory, Bulgaria's leading coachmakers.

SOFRONII VRACHANSKI (1739-1813)

Sofronii Vrachanski was born Stoiko Vladislavov in the central Bulgarian village of Kotel in 1739. He entered the priesthood in his home town and rose gradually through the ecclesiastical ranks, becoming *igumen*, or abbot, of Kapinovo monastery near Veliko Târnovo in the 1780s. During these years he was one of the most enthusiastic copiers and promoters of Otets Paisii's seminal manuscript, the *Slav-Bulgarian History*, a key text in the awakening of Bulgarian national consciousness.

Sofronii was appointed bishop of Vratsa in 1794, only to be chased into exile by the local *kârdzhali* (Turkish outlaws) then in alliance with the wayward Ottoman ruler of Vidin, Osman Pazvantoglu. He spent the rest of his life in Wallachia where he continued to work for the Bulgarian cause, dying in 1813. He is primarily remembered for his literary works, which include a translation of Aesop's *Fables* and the first autobiographical novel in Bulgarian, *The Life and Suffering of the Sinner Sofronii*, both of which assisted in the development of a standard written form of the Bulgarian language.

Next door to the museum is an **ethnographic complex**: a clutch of National Revival-style houses grouped around the *Vâznesenska* (Ascension) church. A couple of the houses are open to the public (same times as museum); one displays the work of local jewellers, while the other contains memories of Vratsa's **silk industry**. Silk was the region's major source of income a century ago, when each family would keep a tree for silkworms in the yard – a practice which still lives on in a few outlying villages. Examples of Vratsa-made fabrics are on show, alongside fading English-language posters offering handy hints on how to tend the worms.

The historical museum

Back on bul. Georgi Dimitrov, it's a short southward stroll to another seventeenth-century tower, the *Kula na Kurt Pashovtsi*, and another modern plaza, pl. Hristo Botev; this time holding the *Hotel Hemus* and the excellent **historical museum** (same times as ethnographic museum). Predictably, it harbours a "Botev Room" full of reminders of the warrior-poet's fateful march into Ottoman territory, but the real delights lie downstairs in the archaeological section. Hordes of Neolithic and Bronze Age idols, including well-endowed fertility figures, point to the long history of civilization in the Vratsa area.

Pride of place, however, goes to **Thracian finds**, the most valuable of which come from *Mogilanskata mogila*, a large *tumulus* unearthed in 1965. Three tombs were found here, dating from the fourth century BC, the largest of which contained a chieftain accompanied by two young women, both of whom appear to have suffered violent deaths at the time of the burial – possibly consorts of the deceased (one of them was sufficiently bejewelled to be a princess) who were required to accompany him into the afterlife. Three horses, two of them harnessed to a ceremonial chariot, completed the burial party. The latter were provided with decorative horse armour, their silver buckles depicting swirling animals. The more elaborately dressed of the women sported a pair of exquisitely filigreed earrings and a **golden laurel wreath** of great delicacy, featuring eighty finely sculpted leaves grouped around little berries. Most distinctive of the treasures is a **silver greave**, or shin guard, belonging to the chieftain. The upper part of the greave bears the face of a warrior, gold inlay highlighting the tattoos worn proudly by the Thracian aristocracy – swirling floral patterns decorating the forehead, and lateral stripes covering the left side of the face. It's thought that these artefacts, rather than being imports from the Hellenistic world, were the products of local gold and silversmiths.

Practicalities . . . and the Ledenika cave

The *Hotel Hemus* (☎092/24150; ③) is conveniently located on the town's central square, pl. Hristo Botev, although more frugal **accommodation** can be found up in the hills which provide Vratsa with such a stunning backdrop. Dorm beds are available at the *Alpiiski dom*, 2km east of town in the Vratsata gorge. Climbing out of the gorge, a road forks left towards Ledenika, 16km northwest of town and accessible by bus, site of the Ledenika *hizha* (☎092/24411) and the **Ledenika cave**. The cave gets its name from the icicles which form here during the winter – *leden* means icy – and its largest chamber has been dubbed the "Great Temple"; of the twenty-three species inhabiting the cave, ten are purely troglodyte.

Another geological curiosity can be seen from the minor road heading north from town, just outside the village of CHIREN: a rock tunnel about 25m wide, 20m high and 100m long, which locals call **Bozhiya most** – "God's Bridge".

The Petrohan Pass and Berkovitsa

The road that heads northwest from Sofia, route 81, skirts round the western edges of the Balkan Range en route for the mountain health resort of **Berkovitsa**. Few if any buses travel this way, so you'll be dependent either on your own transport or the vagaries of hitching – remember that if you're solely interested in visiting Berkovitsa itself, you can reach it from Vratsa, Mihailovgrad or Vidin by bus; and by train from BOICHINOVTSI, a rail junction on the Sofia-Vidin line.

After about 65km the road begins to ascend the *Petrohanski prohod* or **PETROHAN PASS**, 1446m above sea level, which sits between Mount Zelena glava (literally "green-head") and the jagged **Todorini Kukli**. Deer, rabbits and roe deer reportedly abound here, and for the hardy souls who wish to stay, **accommodation** can be found at the *Petrohan* campsite (open June–Sept) and the *Petrohan hizha* (☎096/25251), which is rumoured to contain a disco. From the pass the road zigzags down into the valley of the northward-flowing Bârziya, from where it's a short 20km ride to Berkovitsa.

Berkovitsa

Surrounded by orchards, raspberry plantations, rest homes and hills, **BERKOVITSA** is a strange combination: one part given over to its health resort that faces Mount Kom, where Bulgaria's wrestlers and weightlifters train, the other to an old maze of narrow streets, high walls and anonymous-looking doorways. Many people visit Berkovitsa simply for the local **strawberry wine** (*yagodovo vino*), which is difficult to get hold of elsewhere in Bulgaria, but can be bought in town here or sampled at the state winery. Other wines, made from raspberries (*malinovo*), blackcurrants (*kâpinovo*), and a grape-and-blackcurrant mixture, are also produced here.

Aside from the wine, and the lovely view from Mount Kom, Berkovitsa's charm lies chiefly in its old quarter. The town's eighteenth-century clocktower stands here, and just north of it, the sunken **church of Sveta Bogoroditsa**, featuring icons by Dimitâr and Zahari Zograf. Near the town centre (ask at the train or bus station for directions) is the **Ivan Vazov museum** (Tues–Sun 8am–noon & 2–5pm), occupying the house where Bulgaria's "national writer" spent two years as the local magistrate. Having come here to die of tuberculosis, Vazov was so improved by the climate and peaceable environment that he made a complete recovery, going on to write *Under the Yoke* and die at the ripe old age of 71. Extolling Vazov's literary and patriotic endeavours, the museum omits to mention the story (related to Leslie Gardiner by his guide) that local admirers who "knew his tastes so well" would "catch a young Turkish girl and tie her up in a sack" and throw her over Vazov's wall as a "token of their esteem" twice a week.

Practicalities...and moving on

Accommodation in Berkovitsa is provided by the *Hotel Mramor* (③), although there are several trade union rest homes which may open their doors to foreigners in the future. There are two **chalets** (both called *Kom*) near the summit of Mount Shtârkovitsa, a four-hour uphill struggle to the southwest. The **nearest camp sites** are at Petrohan (see opposite) or at Mihailovgrad, 24km northeast on the main Sofia-Vidin road, and served by regular trains and buses from Berkovitsa.

If travelling towards Mihailovgrad, you'll see the **Gramada** by the roadside leaving town, a pile of stones immortalized by Vazov's poem of the same name. It was accumulated over the years as local people threw down a rock here – accompanied by a muttered curse – to vent their resentment of Berkovitsa's middle class, the *chorbadzhii*, and the Turks with whom they collaborated.

Mihailovgrad and around

Bulgarian towns with a revolutionary tradition tend to look drably modern or prettily archaic, and **MIHAILOVGRAD** – largely rebuilt in concrete – belongs to the former category. Formerly Kutlovitsa, the town's present name and many of its monuments commemorate the September **1923 Uprising**, when local workers led by **Hristo Mihailov** rose against the right-wing Tsankov regime which had overthrown the Agrarian government three months earlier. Historians in postwar socialist Bulgaria subsequently overestimated the level of support for the revolt and elevated its participants to folk-hero status – perhaps understandable when one considers the violence used by the state to crush the rebellion, massacring 30,000 Bulgarians within a couple of weeks. The poet Geo Milev spoke out against the massacre in his poem *September*, for which he was murdered by Tsankov's police:

> *Uprooted from villages*
> *Peasants are followed by troops*
> *In grim convoy*
> *To be shot.*

A locomotive and a cannon from the time stand just outside the railway station, near the bus terminal, which is a couple blocks east of the centre. On the town square a monument bears three flames, symbolizing the town's struggles in 1688,

1923 and 1944. Photographs and memorabilia connected with the rising were exhibited in Mihailov's former **house** (he was killed fighting in Sofia in 1944), currently closed undergoing reassessment, and in the town's **museum**. There are the remains of Roman temples and a necropolis around the **Kaleto**, a fortress in the park beside the river.

Mihailovgrad doesn't really merit more than a fleeting visit, unless you're using it as a base from which to venture forth to Chiprovtsi (see below), in which case the *Hotel Zhitomir* (☎096/29186; ③) provides **beds**. Two **campsites** in the vicinity are the *Chernila* (open April–Oct; ☎096/26955), 3km south of town on the Berkovitsa road; and the *Pâstrina* (open June–mid Oct), 6km south on the E79 to Sofia.

Chiprovtsi and Midzhur

Regular buses make the 25km journey from Mihailovgrad to the carpet-making village of CHIPROVTSI, nestling beneath the highest mountains of the northeast, their lofty peaks marking the frontier between Bulgaria and Serbia. Chiprovtsi was the centre of an uprising in 1688, put down with customary viciousness by the Ottoman authorities, who burned down the nearby **CHIPROVSKI MONASTERY** as a token of their disapproval. About 6km out of town on the Mihailovgrad road, the most recent incarnation of this little-visited foundation dates mostly from the early nineteenth century, a clump of lumpish off-white outbuildings surrounding a dainty monastery church.

Much less visited, but worth a trip if you have your own transport, is **Lopushina monastery**, situated in one of the area's prettiest valleys, the Dâlgodelska ogosta, 10km to the east of Chiprovtsi. You'll find the monastery just beyond the village of GEORGI-DAMYANOVO, lurking in a grove of pine trees – a tranquil location which provided Ivan Vazov with the peace and quiet he needed to complete several chapters of *Under the Yoke*. The monastery church is particularly noted for two icons by Samokov master Stanislav Dospevski, the *Virgin and Child* and *Christ Pantokrator* – both works showing an almost portrait-like realism.

Twelve kilometres due west of Chiprovtsi is **MIDZHUR**, at 2168m the highest of a whole series of densely wooded hills which have only recently been made accessible to hikers. For decades they were considered off limits because of the supposedly sensitive nature of the border with Yugoslavia, and there's a corresponding lack of chalets or tourist facilities in the region. If you do fancy exploring, the foothill villages of GORNI LOM and CHUPRENE, both lying midway between Chiprovtsi and Belogradchik, are the starting points for footpaths into the mountains. Nearest **accommodation**, however, is about 20km to the north in Belogradchik itself.

Belogradchik and around

Lying in a bowl beneath the hills just east of the Serbian border, **BELOGRADCHIK** (literally "small white town") gives its name to Bulgaria's most spectacular rock formations, the *Belogradchishkite skali*, which cover an area of ninety square kilometres to the west. The limestone rocks greatly impressed French traveller Adolph Blanqui in 1841, who described them as an "undreamt landscape" rising to heights of 200m in shades of scarlet, buff and grey, with shapes suggestive of "animals, ships or houses, Egyptian obelisks" and "enormous stalagmites".

The towering rocks nearest the town form a natural fortress whose defensive potential has been exploited since ancient times. Begun by the Romans, continued by the Bulgars during the eighth century, and completed by the Turks a millennium later, the castle at Belogradchik used to command the eastern approaches to the Belogradchik pass. Although no longer in use, the pass was for centuries the main trade route linking the lower Danube with the settlements of Serbia's Morava valley. In Ottoman times the citadel and its garrison served to intimidate and control the local populace, and hundreds of Bulgarian insurgents were held here after the failed uprising of 1850. One particularly unsavoury tale relates that many of the prisoners were slaughtered when the Ottomans forced them to pass through a low doorway, only to have their heads lopped off by swordsmen lurking on the other side.

Lying just off the main E79 between Mihailovgrad and Vidin, Belogradchik is easily reached by bus from the latter. Otherwise trains on the Sofia-Vidin line stop at ORESHETS station 10km to the east, from where there are regular buses. **Accommodation** is provided by the 2-star *Belogradchishkite skali* (☎0936/3151; ③) on the main square; or the *Madona* campsite (open May–Aug) at the southern end of town.

The town and the rocks

Ruddy pinnacles of rock are immediately visible on arrival, glowering over the town from the hilltop around which Belogradchik is draped. The town's **bus station** lies immediately below the town's main street, which winds up towards the summit, passing on the way a small **art gallery** with modest exhibitions of local work, a **town museum** (Tues–Sun 9am–noon & 2–5pm) strong on local folklore, and the almost derelict **Huseyn Pasha mosque**, its former glory recalled in the delicate green-and-purple abstract swirls adorning the main entrance. Before long you'll reach the entrance of the **citadel** (daily 8am–noon & 2–5pm), three levels of fortifications representing different periods of occupation. The lowest two levels are Ottoman: solid, utilitarian blocks of stone enlivened here and there by the occasional floral-patterned relief. A steep climb between two enormous pillars of rock leads to the highest and oldest level, occupied by the medieval Bulgarian stronghold. The rocks themselves provided the perfect fortified enclosure, and apart from the tumbledown wall of a medieval reservoir there's little man-made to see. Enjoy instead the marvellous panorama of surrounding hills.

Another way of approaching the rocks begins at the opposite end of the main street, opposite the *Hotel Belogradchishkite skali*, where concrete steps lead down into a dry valley overlooked by some of the more spectacular rock formations. A path continues along the valley floor for several kilometres, providing views of a whole series of extravagantly weathered pillars – two of which are associated with misogynistic **legends**: the *Nun*, who was supposedly turned into stone for becoming pregnant by a knight; and the *Schoolgirl*, who was likewise afflicted after she was deserted by her husband.

The Magura Cave

There are about five buses a day from Belogradchik to the village of RABISHA, a couple of kilometres short of the much-publicized **MAGURA CAVE** (daily 7.30am–7.30pm). The cave was occupied by hunters as early as 2700 BC, traces of whom are now displayed in a small museum. It's best known, though, for its **rock paintings** excecuted in bat-droppings, which depict a giraffe, hunting scenes and a fertility rite, with some of the other chambers – with names like the "Hall of the Poplar" and the "Hall of the Fallen Pine" – equally interesting. Guided tours last about ninety minutes, and from the hill there's a fine view of the Belogradchik rocks to the southeast.

Accommodation at Magura will one day be provided by a deluxe vacation complex currently being planned by American investors. For the time being, however, you'll have to make do with camping at *Rabisha* (open May–mid Sept), near the entrance to the cave.

THE DANUBIAN PLAIN

The **River Danube** runs from the Black Forest to the Black Sea for about 3000km, about 480km of which form Bulgaria's frontier with its northern neighbour, Romania. The shorelines possess different characters: the Bulgarian side is buttressed by steep bluffs and tabletop plateaus, while the opposite bank is low-lying and riven by shallow lakes called *baltas*, which merge first with marshes, then the Wallachian plain. Between the two lies a shoal of wooded islands which provide a haven for local birdlife, a population sustained by the river's rich stocks of fish.

In ancient times the Danube was one of Europe's most important **frontiers**, a natural barrier separating the riches of southern Europe from the barbarian tribes to the north. The Macedonian kings tried to make the Danube the northern boundary of their domains, with Alexander the Great campaigning against the *Getae* here in 335 BC, but their hold on the area was always superficial. The **Romans** were the first to turn the Danube into a permanent, fortified line of defence, building a series of garrison towns and administrative centres along its length. By the second century, thriving civilian towns such as *Ratiaria, Oescus, Novae* and *Durostorum* were beginning to emerge alongside the armed camps. By the fifth century, however, the frontier was being breached by raiders from the north, many of whom (including the *sklaveni*, ancestors of the Balkan slavs) increasingly chose to settle down south of the river once their plundering days were over. Justinian attempted to stem the tide in the sixth century, refortifying the old Roman sites and establishing new garrisons along the river, but Byzantine diplomacy subsequently concentrated on paying off the barbarians to keep them sweet rather than attempting to shut them out altogether.

With the decline of the lower Danube's strategic importance the settlements along its banks began to decay, only to revive when the last of the Bulgarian kings, the **Shishmanids**, fought a delaying action against the advancing Turks from Danubian strongholds such as Nikopol and Vidin. The Ottomans themselves were great fortress builders, erecting the great eighteenth-century citadels of Ruse and Silistra in an attempt to strengthen the Danube frontier against the advance of Russian power.

During the nineteenth century, increased river transport brought the goods and culture of central Europe down the valley, turning the towns along its banks into cosmopolitan outposts of *Mitteleuropa*. European fashions and styles often arrived here first before being transmitted to the rest of Bulgaria, turning towns such as **Lom** and **Svishtov** into unlikely centres of elegance and sophistication. With the development of railways, however, the river trade went into decline, and nowadays most of Bulgaria's Danubian towns are quiet, provincial places, focusing their attention not on the river itself, but on the bigger cities inland. The only real exceptions are **Vidin**, **Silistra** and most of all **Ruse** – an important cultural centre which commands the major road and rail route to Bucharest and the north.

Travelling from the Danube towards the coast you'll pass through an extension of the Danube plain known as the Dobrudzha, a vast expanse of grain-producing flatland which extends from Silistra to the Black Sea. The region's administrative centre, the former Ottoman market town of **Dobrich**, provides the only potential stopoff en route.

Travelling down the Danube

The best way to travel the river used to be the **hydrofoil services** which plied between Vidin and Ruse during the summer. These were cut back in 1991 due to low water levels on the river, and were suspended altogether in 1992 because of lack of custom. It's worth keeping a look out for river transport, however, as services (perhaps under private ownership) may revive in the future. Locations of hydrofoil terminals are detailed in the text, just in case.

Attempting to follow the course of the river **by land** is less straightforward. The road is poorly surfaced in parts, and skirts inland much of the way. Making your way downriver by **bus** will be a time-consuming exercise and may involve a sequence of changes: although settlements along the river are linked by regular buses to inland cities like Mihailovgrad, Pleven and Veliko Târnovo, services between the Danube towns themselves are few and far between – perhaps limited to one or two a day. Look out, however, for posters advertising buses run by private companies – occasional express services linking Vidin and Ruse are beginning to fill the gap left by the hydrofoils.

CRUISING DOWN THE DANUBE

Several travel companies offer cruises covering long stretches of the River Danube, although recent years have seen a decrease in the number of tours including the lower (Bulgarian-Romanian) stretch – largely because of problems in neighbouring Serbia. With prices starting at around £1000 per person (more in July and August), most tours last 10–14 days and include flights to and from the cruise's starting and finishing points (Bucharest and Vienna, for example), and usually a couple of nights' hotel accommodation at either end.

Inghams Travel (10–18 Putney Hill, London SW15 6AX; ☎081/785 7777) offer a 12-day cruise beginning in Romania and culminating in Vienna, calling at Ruse, Belgrade and Budapest on the way.

Canterbury Travel (248 Streatfield Rd, Kenton, Harrow HA3 9BY; ☎081/206 0411) offer a wider choice, ranging from 17-day trips starting in Vienna and taking in Yalta and Istanbul to more modest 10-day affairs running between Giurgiu in Romania and Passau on the Austro-German border.

Vidin

"One of those marvellous cities of eastern fairytale which, secure behind their fortress walls, is decorated with spires and cupolas and minarets piled one upon another in a fantastic medley of creeds, ages and styles." So **VIDIN** was rather fancifully described by Lovett Edwards in his book *Danube Stream* in 1941. Nowadays you'll find that the truth is more prosaic: Vidin's modern skyline leaves a lot to be desired, and although the great sweep of the fortress walls still dominates much of the riverfront, the spires and minarets characteristic of Edwards' day have largely gone, to be replaced by utilitarian housing projects. Ample reasons for visiting are, however, still provided by the showpiece medieval **citadel of Baba Vida**, presiding over riverside parklands on the northern edge of town.

Some history

Vidin's potential as the guardhouse of the lower Danube was exploited by successive waves of Celts, Romans and Byzantines, but it was under the Bulgarian tsars and their Ottoman conquerors that the most frenzied fortress building took place. However, Vidin's relative isolation from major power centres like Târnovo and Constantinople made the place into a breeding ground for semi-independent local kinglets, and the citadel they built was much-coveted by neighbouring powers. In the fourteenth century it was the power base of **Mihail Shishman**, whom the nobles elected tsar rather than see Vidin secede from Bulgaria, and after 1371 it was the capital of an independent kingdom ruled by Mihail's grand-nephew **Ivan Stratsimir**. Vidin fought a rearguard action against Ottoman expansion in the Balkans, grudgingly accepting Turkish suzerainty in the 1390s – only to throw it off again as soon as help emerged from the west in the shape of the Crusade of 1396. The city was recaptured by Sultan Bajazet's army two years later.

In the late eighteenth century Vidin was the capital of **Osman Pazvantoglu**, a local ruler who rebelled against the reforms of Sultan Selim III in 1792. Energetic, despotic and fond of inventing tortures, Pazvantoglu pillaged as far afield as Sofia in defiance of the Sultan, and strengthened Vidin's fortifications with the assistance of French engineers sent by Napoleon, who envisaged him as a potential lever for toppling the Ottoman empire.

These days Vidin is comparatively quiet, but with the Romanian town of Calafat just across the river, and the Serbian border 30km northwest, the town still retains a little of its former cosmopolitan feel.

Around town

Vidin's modern heart stands at the southern end of the fortified old town, based around a flagstoned central square which is dominated by customary examples of socialist urban planning: the tower-block-style former headquarters of the Communist party vying for attention with the equally brutal modernism of the *obshtinski sâvet*, or town council building, next door. Somewhat less imposing are the structures lining the main downtown streets which radiate outwards from here – drab lumps of ochre and grey which reveal little of the town's former glory.

The archaeological museum

The only real interest in this part of town is provided by the **archaeological museum** (Tues–Sun 9am–noon & 2–6pm), housed in a pagoda-like nineteenth-century *konak* west of the main square at the end of ul. Blagoev. The display begins with prehistoric bone and stone tools found in the Mirizlivka cave near the village of Oreshets, but most space is devoted to Roman-period finds from the regional centre of *Ratiaria*, founded by Trajan in about 107 AD near the modern village of Archar, 25km southeast of Vidin. A floor mosaic on which a stag is chased by a wild cat, and a fine second-century marble sculpture of a pensive Hercules toying with his club, reveal something of the sophistication and comfort of life in this otherwise rather provincial outpost. Sarcophagi and gravestones from Ratiaria's necropolis litter the lawn outside. An adjoining section of the museum deals with the National Revival period, with particular reference to the local peasant uprising of 1850, centred on the towns of Gradets and Belogradchik.

The old town

On the northern side of the main square the borders of old Vidin are marked by the **Stambul kapiya** or Istanbul Gate, a stocky portal in the Turkish style. Beyond it lies a pleasant turn-of-the-century residential district with an extensive riverside **park** to the east. On the edge of the park stands the **Osman Pazvantoglu mosque**, the only surviving mosque in the city – most of the others were knocked down in the 1970s and 1980s. To one side is the squat, domed *kitabhane* or Koranic library, currently pressed into service as an art gallery. Immediately opposite is the modern **church of Sveti Nikolai**, inside which Cyril, Methodius and other saints are rendered in colourful turn-of-the-century realist frescoes, rather like illustrations in a children's encyclopaedia. More interesting is the **church of Sveti Panteleimon** hidden round the back, an austere twelfth-century basilica made from heavy stone.

From Sveti Nikolai, ul. Vitko Ivanov hugs the park's western flank, leading past an ensemble of sorry-looking buildings along the way: the whitewashed **Starata poshta**, or old post office, the peeling ochre plaster of the **banya** or town baths, and the shell of a derelict **synagogue**. Parallel to Vitko Ivanov to the east is ul. Boyan Chonos, site of Pazvantoglu's **Krastata Kazarma** (the "cross-shaped barracks"), now a museum covering local history. Considering that the museum used to contain a rather unsympathetic history of capitalism, it's not surprising that it's currently undergoing long-term reorganization. Across the road, stranded behind railings in a patch of wasteland between two school playgrounds, is the seventeenth-century **church of Sveta Petka**, an unassuming, sunken structure, traces of bright blue on the exterior giving some idea of its former appearance.

From the northern end of the riverside park stone ramparts run alongside the shoreline for over a kilometre, largely overgrown and deserted, eventually curving inland to protect the **Fortress of Baba Vida** (Tues–Sun 8am–noon & 1.30–5.30pm). Surrounded by huge walls and a deep moat, the fortress dates from the thirteenth century, although the brutal, blockhouse appearance of its turrets and towers owes more to the continuous improvements carried out by the Turks and the Habsburgs, who briefly occupied the town in the sixteenth century. Once inside, you can scramble around an extensive network of courtyards and ramparts, and survey the Danube from gun positions overlooking the river. Further stretches of wall extend well to the west of the citadel, and crumbling gates stand surrealistically amid the modern housing estates.

Practicalities

Most points of **arrival** lie in the modern centre a short distance from the main square: bus and train stations are a couple of blocks to the west, while the hydrofoil station is two blocks south, just off Todor Petrov, the main Sofia road. Approaching **from Romania** you'll arrive at the grandiosely named International Dock 2km north of town (connected to the town centre by sporadic bus or taxi). A ferry *(feribot)* shuttles between Vidin and Calafat half-hourly between about 7am and 7pm (times posted in Vidin hotel lobbies), and the border post – complete with **tourist information** office – is open roughly between these times. Once in town, info can be hard to find. Although the staff are friendly, the *raison d'être* of the *Balkantourist* office at General Dondukov 2 seems to be to help the locals leaving town rather than interlopers coming in, and the odd German-language brochure will be all you're offered.

There are two fairly basic 2-star **hotels** in town, the *Bononia* (③) on the main square; and the *Rovno*, ul. T. Petrov 4 (☎094/24402; ③), the latter with good views across the river; while **dorm beds** are on offer at the *turisticheska spalnya* (☎094/22813) further down T. Petrov. **Campers** can choose between the *Nora* site (open May–Oct; has bungalows) in a park on the western edge of town – take a bus out along bul. Lenin and alight just before the level-crossing; or the *Dunav* (open June–Aug; with bungalows), 8km north of town on the river bank, just off the road to Koshava.

Daytime drinking and snack-nibbling tends to take place in the cafés along ul. Blagoev, or in the riverside park. For live folk/pop music and reasonable food, try the restaurant of the *Hotel Bononia*.

Down the Danube: Vidin to Ruse

The road to Ruse passes through a string of settlements which, despite an often dramatic history, lack the kind of attractions – save for the river itself – which would warrant anything more than the briefest of halts. Much of archaeological or historical interest has been carted off to be displayed in provincial capitals to the south, such as Pleven or Veliko Târnovo, leaving perhaps only **Lom** and **Svishtov** with worthwhile museums. These two towns also offer hotel accommodation, a rare commodity along this stretch of the river.

From Vidin to Lom

Thirty or so kilometres downriver from Vidin, the village of ARCHAR was once the site of *Ratiaria* – the capital of Upper Moesia, from where the Emperor Trajan consolidated Roman rule over what's now the Romanian side of the Danube – though there's little to see beyond the relics now on show in Vidin's archaeological museum (see p.111). A kilometre or two after the village of Dobri Dol look out for signs leading to DOBRODOLSKI MONASTERY, home to the curious mid-nineteenth-century **church of Sveta Troitsa**. A buff-coloured structure topped off by an unusually tall drum, the exterior is unadorned save for a series of reliefs executed in a deliberately primitivist style, harking back to medieval, almost pre-Christian, Bulgarian models. A carving above the door shows a man fighting a dog-headed snake, flanked on either side by figures of the

THE VLACHS

Another minority living along Bulgaria's riverine border are the *Vlasi* or **Vlachs**, who speak a dialect of Romanian and are to be found in isolated villages throughout north Bulgaria, eastern Serbia, Macedonia and northern Greece.

Precise definitions of who is a Vlach and who isn't vary from area to area. To many Balkan Slavs, a Vlach is merely a Romanian-speaker who lives outside Romania. Elsewhere (notably in Croatia, Slovenia and Czechoslovakia), the term "Vlach" is used to designate transhumant shepherds, without necessarily denoting a particular ethnic origin. The Vlachs of the Balkans are traditionally nomadic sheep farmers, pasturing their flocks on the lowlands during the winter and moving to the mountains in the summer. Nowadays, however, the attractions of urban life, and the restrictions on movement imposed by modern bureaucratic states (not least socialist ones), have meant that most Balkan Vlachs lead an increasingly sedentary lifestyle.

The origins of the Vlachs have been the cause of much inconclusive debate, but the fact that they speak a Latin tongue suggests that they are descended either from second- and third-century Roman settlers or from the native Balkan peoples – whether Dacians, Thracians, or Illyrians – who came into contact with these settlers and adopted their language. With the collapse of Roman and Byzantine power, hastened by the successive deluges of Slavs, Magyars and Turks, the Vlachs somehow ensured the survival of their tongue by retreating into highland regions and reverting to nomadism. The most enthusiastic proponents of this version of Vlach history are the Romanians, who point to the existence of the modern Romanian nation as proof that the ancient, Latinized population in the Balkans was able to retreat into the hills, only to re-emerge centuries later with its language and culture intact. Nationalist historians from other Balkan countries sometimes beg to differ, arguing that Vlachs are either ethnic Slavs or ethnic Greeks, learning Latin from their Roman or Byzantine masters, and somehow clinging on to the language due to the isolated nature of their lifestyle.

Bulgaria's Vlachs are found along the Danube, in the Dobrudzha, and in the Balkan Mountains, where they are known as the *karakachani*. During the Communist period Bulgaria's Vlachs were encouraged to assimilate with the Slav majority, thus threatening the long-term survival of their language. The scattered nature of Vlach settlement makes it difficult to ascertain exactly how many of them there are in the country, and despite the new opportunities afforded by the advent of democracy, it's hard to say whether they will have the cohesiveness to develop strong cultural organizations of their own.

Archangel Michael and the builder of the church himself. Beyond here the road runs behind a wooded cliff over a hundred metres high which continues in an unbroken line for about 20km.

During the last century this stretch of the Danube shore was chosen by the Turks to accommodate the *cherkezi* or **Circassians**, Muslim refugees from the Caucasus who had been expelled from their homelands by the armies of Imperial Russia. Used by the Ottomans to keep the local Bulgarians under control, many of them fled after the Liberation to escape reprisals, although a few small communities still remain. Many of those who stayed were assimilated into Bulgaria's Turkish minority, with the result that surviving pockets of Circassians tend to be categorized (both by themselves and their Bulgarian neighbours) as Turks.

Lom

The first major town east of Vidin is **LOM**, a town renowned throughout Bulgaria for the watermelons grown in the surrounding fields. Citizens of Sofia used to come up to Lom in order to stock up on the local produce – the kind of fresh fruit of which urban dwellers were often deprived – thus leading the locals to dub the rail link between Lom and the capital as the *mazen vlak* – the "gravy train". Slightly closer to Sofia by rail than Vidin, Lom has traditionally rivalled its western neighbour as the capital's port on the Danube. Although river trade with central Europe has slackened due to the unwillingness of barge captains to sail through Serbia, Lom's harbours are still frequented by the Ukranian ships bringing coal and pig iron to feed the blast furnaces of Kremikovtsi, a vast steel mill on the outskirts of Sofia.

Aside from the industrial and port facilities hogging the east bank of the River Lom, the town amounts to little save for a single main street which drives its way southward from the hydrofoil jetty (you'll find **bus** and **train stations** at the southern end of town, a couple of blocks east of the main street). Traces of the Roman settlement of *Almus* lie to the east between blocks of flats, although there's precious little to see amid the long, rubbish-strewn grass. Gravestones and statuary from the site are to be found in the **historical museum** (currently undergoing renovation; will probably be open Tues–Sun), one block west of the main street on Eremiya Bålgarov. Most valuable of the museum's exhibits is the collection of **Bronze Age pottery** unearthed in the riverside marshes north of Orsoya, a village to the west. The people who lived here belonged to the Urnfield culture, a civilization which spread itself across central and eastern Europe in the second millennium BC, deriving its name from the way in which the ashes of the dead were buried in richly patterned funerary urns. The museum displays examples of these alongside the votive offerings which usually accompanied them – predominantly clay figurines and vessels in the shape of animals. Here too are memories of Lom's modest cultural renaissance in the nineteenth century. In 1857 the town provided the venue for Bulgaria's first-ever theatrical performance – a melodrama, *The Misfortunes of Genevieve*.

Accommodation boils down to two options: the murky *Hotel Dunav* (③) opposite the hydrofoil jetty, and the *Chaika* campsite just west of town.

Kozlodui, Oryahovo and Nikopol

The next place of any size is **KOZLODUI**, where a monument near the small harbour commemorates the **"landing of 1876"**. On hearing of a rebellion against the Turks deep in the Balkan Mountains (in what subsequently became known as the April Rising – see p.180), Hristo Botev assembled 200 volunteers from the Bulgarian émigré community in Romania, who boarded the Austrian steamer *Radetzky* disguised as market-gardeners, hijacked the vessel and disembarked at Kozlodui under the banner "Liberty or Death". But by this time the Turks had already crushed the uprising, and on learning of Botev's partisans, harried them through the mountains until their death near Vratsa.

More recently Kozlodui has become notorious as the site of Bulgaria's first and only **nuclear power station**, built with Soviet help in the 1970s. Throughout 1991 international observers became increasingly worried about the plant's safety, not least because the Soviet technicians who used to run it were being replaced by insufficiently qualified Bulgarian staff. The Bulgarian government are hoping that European aid will be forthcoming in order to fund a complete over-haul of the plant, and Western firms are competing for the job of making it safe. In the meantime, beset by energy problems brought about by the sudden curtail-ment of cheap electricity supplies from the former Soviet Union, the Bulgarians have little choice but to keep Kozlodui going as best they can.

Oryahovo

Forty kilometres downriver, **ORYAHOVO** slopes up the hillside overlooking a port used for the export of grain and grapes. In 1396, the Bulgarians holding Oryahovo's fortress, *Rachova*, surrendered willingly to the Crusaders rather than fight for the Turks, but the French contingent in the crusading army pillaged and burned the town anyway, later justifying their action by claiming that they had had to take the town by force. Oryahovo is nowadays useful as a railway junction, with a couple of trains a day departing for CHERVEN BRYAG on the Sofia-Pleven-Varna line.

At the confluence of the Iskâr and the Danube beyond BAIKAL, the ruins of Roman *Oescus* can be found about 2km north of GIGEN village. Excavations have uncovered ramparts, foundation walls, drains and large paving-slabs that give a fair idea of the layout of the ancient town, though the site's rich yield of statuary and mosaics is now displayed in Pleven's history museum. Like other Danubian settlements, Oescus was razed by the Huns in the fifth century, rebuilt during the reign of Justinian and destroyed again by the Avars, so it's hardly surprising that nothing remains of the great bridge over the Danube built for the Emperor Constantine. Reportedly 3800ft long, it was abandoned after less than forty years.

Nikopol

NIKOPOL, further downstream, is chiefly known for its ruined **fortress** glower-ing from a crag. Founded in 629 by Emperor Heraclius I, *Nikopolis* was consid-ered impregnable until its capture by the Turks in 1393, and the threat of further incursions by Sultan Bajazet frightened the Christian powers into organizing a crusade to retake the lower Danube.

Feasting and pillaging their way south, the Crusaders treated the campaign as a sport, bringing "wines and festive provisions" instead of siege weapons. Unable to storm Nikopolis's 26 mighty towers, they instituted a blockade and began squabbling among themselves (the French, in particular, resented the fact that Sigismund of Hungary had been chosen by the pope to be supreme commander). Pigheadedness and disunity proved fatal on November 25, 1396, when Bajazet's army appeared on the neighbouring plateau. Against Sigismund's orders the French cavalry charged uphill after fleeing irregulars, only to be impaled on hidden stakes and then butchered by the Turkish cavalry. The Crusaders' defeat was shattering, and no further attempts were made to check Turkish expansion until the battle of Varna fifty years later, by which time the Ottomans were entrenched in the Balkans.

Beyond Nikopol the road loops inland for the 60km journey to the next major Danube port, Svishtov, although a small side road does descend to the riverfront at BELENE, a small agricultural town. The town stands opposite **Belene island**, the river's biggest, now notorious in Bulgaria for being the site of one of the coun-try's biggest labour camps (see p.116). More happily, the island is a favoured nesting ground of **spoonbills** in May and June.

BELENE LABOUR CAMP

Between Nikopol and Svishtov lies a cluster of green islands whose name is now notorious in Bulgaria – **Belene**, the site of an infamous labour camp. Established in 1947 (together with a smaller women's camp which was soon closed), Belene held both political prisoners and dangerous criminals. The latter were reportedly favoured by the guards, who apparently permitted them to tyrannize the "politicals" according to Stalinist practice. During the 1950s when the purges were at their height, hundreds of Bulgarians perished here through a combination of malnutrition, overwork and brutality. Prisoners directed to woodcutting on neighbouring Bârzina Island had to chop 1120 cubic metres per day before receiving their rations, and inmates who violated camp rules (by scavenging for food, or addressing a guard as "comrade", for example) were used for target practice or marooned on rafts to freeze or suffer clouds of mosquitoes.

Conditions improved somewhat during the 1960s following a limited amnesty, but Belene remained a savage place. During the 1970s many of the inmates were Pomaks, Slav Muslims from western Rhodopes who were being pressured to drop their Islamic-sounding names and adopt Bulgarian ones instead – those that resisted ended up in Belene. Ethnic Turks who objected to the revitalized name-changing campaign of the mid-1980s were sent here too.

The camp was closed down swiftly after November 1989, but the "socialist" (i.e. ex-Communist) administration which ruled Bulgaria until October 1991 dragged its feet in investigating the truth behind the previous regime's penal system. Even now, mountains of evidence need to be examined before public prosecutors can decide who, if anyone, should be brought to justice for the crimes perpetrated against the inmates of Belene.

Svishtov

Coyly encircled by the Danube and surrounding hills, **SVISHTOV** is a long-established port and crafts town which grew just to the west of the former Roman city of *Novae*. As the easiest place to cross the Danube it witnessed the arrival of the Russian liberators in 1877 and the invasion of Romania by German and Bulgarian forces in 1916.

Bus, rail and hydrofoil terminals are all located in a drab riverside area just below the bluff upon which Svishtov is built. Roads curl up into the hilltop town, passing a shabby overgrown park in the midst of which lurk remains of the medieval *kale*, or fortress. Just below the *kale*, the modern facade of the **church of Sveti Dimitâr** obscures a ramshackle seventeenth-century nave, brightened up by some colourfully naive nineteenth-century frescoes.

Beyond lies the main square, presided over by the *Hotel Dunav* (③) and most other amenities. Head right along Tsar Osvoboditel and right again into ul. Konstantinov to reach the **church of Sveta Troitsa**. Just beyond is the former **house of Aleko Konstantinov** (daily 9am–noon & 1–5pm), a satirist remembered for creating *Bay Ganyu*, an itinerant peddler of rose oil and rugs who remains one of the most popular characters in Bulgarian fiction. Konstantinov himself was never afraid to enter public controversies, and was gunned down in 1897 by political opponents. A jar holding his heart, complete with ragged bullet hole, is the museum's most striking exhibit.

By returning to Tsar Osvoboditel and following it further west, you'll come across a large open-air market, behind which lies the **Sveto uchilishte** (daily 9am–noon & 1–5pm). A rather lumpish stone construction dating from 1815, this was the country's first secular school, and harbours some restored period classrooms.

Ruse

"Everything I experienced later in life had already happened in **RUSE**", wrote Elias Canetti in the autobiographical *Tongue Set Free*, remembering his childhood home as an invigorating city of different races and creeds, whose cosmopolitan culture placed it firmly in the orbit of *Mitteleuropa*. Although the ethnic mix of Canetti's day has long since disappeared, travellers continue to be surprised by Ruse's central European elegance. Despite being blighted by the customary concrete-and-steel overlay provided by Bulgaria's postwar urban planners, it's still a city of peaceful residential streets, where Art Nouveau-inspired ornamentation drips from delicate turn-of-the-century houses. Ruse bears a similarity to Bulgaria's other Danubian towns in lacking a riverfront of any great beauty, but a scattering of historic sights and the relaxed feel of its downtown streets more than compensate. An important cultural centre with an animated café life, the city also plays host to an evening *korso* which is one of the liveliest in Bulgaria.

Some history

Apart from the fortress and a sprinkling of stately mosques (the former blown up by Marshal Kutuzov in the Russo-Turkish war of 1806–12, the latter demolished by post-Liberation Bulgarians), Ruse (*Ruschuk* to the Turks) was an unremarkable Ottoman provincial town until the enlightened governorship of **Midhat Pasha** (1864–68), who provided the town with schools, hospitals, factories and, most importantly, the British-financed Ruse-to-Varna railway line – Bulgaria's first. Until the construction of the more direct Belgrade-Sofia-Istanbul line in the 1880s, travellers flooded through Ruse on their way from central Europe to Constantinople. A "European quarter" grew up rapidly along the river bank, although the speed at which the whole place was constructed gave the place a rather tacky, boom-town appearance.

Trade received a further boost after the Liberation, and for many years Ruse had more inhabitants, consulates, factories, hotels and banks than Sofia. The city's economic and cultural wealth owed a lot to the merchant families – including Germans, Greeks and Armenians – who settled here. Most numerous, however, were the **Sephardic Jews** (of whom Elias Canetti was one, born here in 1905), descendants of those Jews given refuge in the Ottoman Empire after their expulsion from Spain in 1492, and speaking Ladino, a mixture of archaic Spanish and Portuguese with numerous borrowings from the Turkish and Hebrew tongues.

The telephone code for Ruse is ☎082.

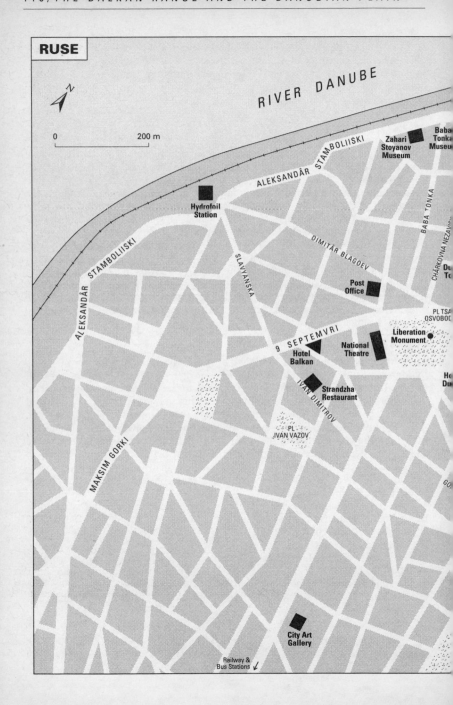

RUSE

RIVER DANUBE

0   200 m

ALEKSANDÅR STAMBOLIISKI

Zahari
Stoyanov
Museum

Bab
Tonka
Museu

Hydrofoil
Station

ALEKSANDÅR STAMBOLIISKI

DIMITÅR BLAGOEV

SLAVYANSKA

BABA TONKA

CHÅRKOVNA NEZAVI

D
To

Post
Office

PL TSA
OSVOBOD

9 SEPTEMVRI

Liberation
Monument

National
Theatre

Hotel
Balkan

H
Du

IVAN DIMITROV

Strandzha
Restaurant

PL
IVAN VAZOV

MAKSIM GORKI

GO

City Art
Gallery

Railway &
Bus Stations ↙

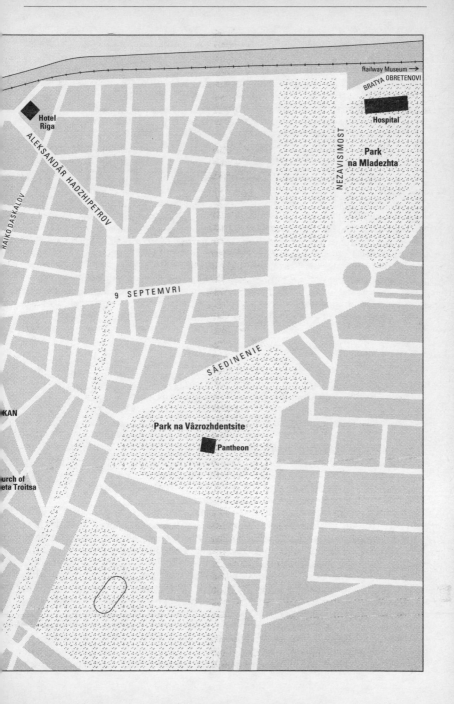

Railway Museum →

BRATYA OBRETENOVI

Hotel
Riga

Hospital

ALEKSANDAR HADZHIPETROV

NEZAVISIMOST

Park
na Mladezhta

MAIKO DASKALOV

9 SEPTEMVRI

SÂEDINENIE

KAN

Park na Vâzrozhdentsite

Pantheon

urch of
eta Troitsa

CHEMICAL EMISSIONS FROM GIURGIU

The citizens of Ruse played an important part in the democratizing tide of the late 1980s, when local people began to protest against the ecological damage caused by the **chemical plant** just across the river in Romanian **Giurgiu**. *Rusentsi* had been conscious of the regular chlorine gas emissions wafting over the river from Giurgiu – and the corresponding rise in respiratory complaints among the city's children – for over a decade. Bulgaria's Communist rulers nevertheless tried to keep the problem quiet, unwilling to compromise their good relations with Ceauşescu's Romania. Protests first took place in 1987, and in March 1988 a Committee for the Protection of Ruse was formed in Sofia. Prominent Party members who took part in this initiative were subsequently removed from their posts – a purge which made public for the first time the growing disagreements among the ruling socialist elite.

Despite Romanian protestations that the plant in question has ceased production, the problem of chlorine pollution still hovers over Ruse – and is becoming a major hindrance to Bulgarian-Romanian relations. In October 1991 Bulgarian newspapers reported a serious fire at the Giurgiu chemical plant which had claimed two lives and come within a hair's breadth of causing an enormous explosion. Romanian sources remained silent on the issue for two weeks before finally confirming the story. A month later, on November 7, ecological groups in Bulgaria organized an (overtly anti-Romanian) day of protest in Ruse, with crowds massing to hear politicians speak and rock bands perform next to the bridge marking the border between the two countries. The Romanians protested about the disruption caused to frontier traffic and called off bilateral ecological discussions between the two countries due the next day. The Romanians also compared the issue of Giurgiu with that of the Bulgarian nuclear power station at Kozlodui – the latter, they argued, was the *real* threat to the region's ecology.

Since then Bulgarian-Romanian relations have become more cordial again, perhaps in recognition of the fact that they share a similar predicament: without first attracting substantial Western aid, neither country can afford to move away from the environmentally harmful industrial projects bequeathed to them by previous regimes.

Arrival and accommodation

Trolleybuses #1, #11, #12 and #18 head up bul. Dimitrov from the rail and bus stations to the main square, pl. na Svobodata. The hydrofoil station is ten minutes downhill from here at the bottom of ul. Blagoev.

Town plans and **information** are available from *Dunav Tours* (Mon–Fri 8am–noon & 1–5.30pm) at Daskalov 1, a block north of the main square. The latter also handle **private rooms** in central locations, a much better bet than Ruse's **hotels**, which tend to be either on the expensive side or uncomfortably poky. Top of the range is the 3-star *Riga*, Stamboliiski 22 (☎2181; ④); while a mid-price alternative is the 2-star *Dunav*, pl. na Svobodata 7 (☎26518; ③). Less salubrious rooms without en-suite bathrooms can be had at the 1-star *Balkan*, Han Krum 1 (☎22837; ②); or at a couple of unclassified hotels previously unwilling to admit Westerners, the *Splendid*, 9 Septemvri 49 (☎24230; ②), and the *Sevastopol* (☎26637; ②).

Otherwise you could rent a chalet or **camp** at the mosquito-prone *Ribarska koliba* (open May–Oct), 6km west of town, which can by reached by boarding a #6 or #16 bus on bul. Maksim Gorki. The only other site in the vicinity is the *Kladenetsa* (open mid April–Oct), 20km south of town on the Ruse-Varna highway.

The town

A spacious mixture of concrete and greenery bordered by open-air bookstalls and flower sellers, the central **pl. na Svobodata** ("Freedom Square") is watched over by one of Ruse's trademarks, the 1908 **Freedom Monument**: a classical pillar surmounted by an allegorical figure of Liberty. Occupying the southwest side of the square is Ruse's **Drama Theatre**, a once-magnificent neo-Renaissance pile currently lying gutted as a prelude to complete restoration. Cutting across the square is the city's main commercial and social artery, ul. 9 Septemvri – venue for most shopping, drinking and aimless strolling. Both north and south of pl. na Svobodata lies a patchwork of residential streets lined with nineteenth-century bourgeois residences, nowadays divided up into flats. Hidden away among them is one reminder of Ruse's cosmopolitan past, the former **synagogue** on pl. Ivan Vazov, which currently serves as the regional headquarters of *Sport-totalizator*, Bulgaria's equivalent of the football pools.

Along the riverfront

Ul. Blagoev leads downhill from the square towards the hydrofoil station and the former merchants' quarter of town, an area of dust-laden stuccoed buildings where Elias Canetti's family used to have a warehouse – just round the corner from ul. Blagoev at Slavyanska 12. Unfortunately the Ruse historical museum at Blagoev 4 has long been closed due to earthquake damage sustained in 1977, and its collections have been dispersed to other centres in the city. Two of these lie on or near Aleksandâr Stamboliiski, a cobbled road which runs along the **waterfront** – a singularly unattractive area save for a few Art-Nouveauish town houses and the odd stretch of riverside parkland.

The **house of Zahari Stoyanov** (Tues–Sun 9am–noon & 2–5pm) at Stamboliiski 15 commemorates the journalist, politician and author best remembered for *Notes on the Bulgarian Uprisings*, a record of Stoyanov's own experiences during the 1870s. Inspired by the heroic suicide of Angel Kânchev (see p.156), the young Stoyanov joined the revolutionary movement and toured Bulgaria helping to set up clandestine patriotic cells. By the time of the April Rising of 1876 he was attached to the rebel group commanded by Georgi Benkovski, a leader of the Rising in the Koprivshtitsa area (see p.180). Stoyanov's subsequent account served to immortalize both Benkovski and many other leading personalities of April 1876, and helped enshrine the Rising as the crucial event in the nation's liberation. Aside from the books and manuscripts recalling Stoyanov's work, the house is now home to most of the historical museum's ethnographic collection, featuring a dazzling array of ceremonial blouses embroidered by the unmarried girls of the region – traditionally considered part of a young woman's upbringing. Much of the house is, however, devoted to **Panaiot Hitov**, the Sliven-born Haiduk and freedom fighter who retired to Ruse with his Serbian wife. Guerilla life in the forests is remembered through items such as Hitov's embroidered tobacco pouch, his secret money belt, and numerous antiquated pistols and shotguns.

Zahari Stoyanov married the youngest daughter of **Baba Tonka**, whose **Memorial House** (Tues 3–6pm; Wed–Sun 9am–noon & 3–6pm) is a few steps away at ul. Baba Tonka 40. A formidable matriarch, Baba ("Granny") Tonka Obretenova was at the forefront of revolutionary activity in nineteenth-century Ruse, offering her home to the patriotic underground as a safe-house and arms dump, smuggling rifles through swamps, and leading Ruse's women in an armed assault on the town prison. She raised her children as fervent patriots, her five sons taking part in the April Rising. Assembled here are the effects of several great revolutionaries, including the skull of Stefan Karadzha, preserved as a *momento mori* by Tonka after the illustrious Haiduk leader was executed in Ruse in 1868. Tonka's house also displays photos and prints of the town as it looked in the twilight years of Ottoman rule, when the humble single-storey dwellings occupied by Bulgarians and Turks alike contrasted sharply with the symbols of Europeanization hurriedly introduced by Midhat Pasha.

Midhat's crowning achievement, the establishment of the Ruse-Varna railway, is commemorated at the **transport museum** (daily 8am–noon & 2–5.30pm), which occupies the original station building at Bratya Obretenovi 13. The lines of historic locos and rolling stock parked outside include Locomotive no. 148, one of the initial set of steam engines built for the railway by a Manchester firm in 1866; and the sumptuous *Sultaniye* sleeping-carriage, used by Empress Eugenie of France in 1869 when on her way southwards to open the Suez Canal.

The Cathedral church and the Pantheon

A couple of blocks east of pl. Svoboda on ul. Gorazd is the **Cathedral church of Sveta Troitsa**, dating from 1632 and twice rebuilt in successive centuries. The resulting building borrows liberally from Russian models, sporting a curious Baroque facade and a medieval Muscovite spire. Steps descend into an icon-rich subterranean nave, its stuccoed ceiling supported by trompe l'oeil marble-effect pillars crowned with Corinthian capitals. Further east across bul. Tsar Osvoboditel is **Park na vâzrozhdentsite** ("Park of the Men of the Revival"), where the **Ruse Pantheon**, a mausoleum devoted to nineteenth-century revolutionary heroes (Tues–Sun 9am–noon & 3–6.30pm), squats on a flagstoned plaza. It's a grossly overstated building: a kind of high-tech Mayan temple surmounted by half a giant ping-pong ball covered in gold. Its cool vault has four sepulchral effigies keeping watch over an eternal flame while hushed crocodiles of schoolkids pass by graves of National Revival heroes, among them Stefan Karadzha and several members of Baba Tonka's family. The whole thing seems rather vulgar when compared to the smaller, more tasteful nineteenth-century chapels – honouring, among others, Zahari Stoyanov – which lie under the trees of the surrounding park.

North of here is **park na mladezhta**, or "Youth Park", where tree- and shrub-lined avenues provide a popular strolling area. Steps at the northern end of the park descend to the riverfront and the transport museum (see above).

There's little incentive to stray too far **south of the town centre**, save for the **City Art Gallery** (Tues–Sun 9am–noon & 3–6pm) at bul. Dimitrov 39, a largely parochial collection of local artists enlivened by a couple of eulogies to peasant toil from popular postwar painter Zlatyu Boyadzhiev; and the **Kyuntukapu gate**, sole remainder of the Turkish fortress, which lies just off Alei Osvobozhdenie 300m west of the railway station.

Eating, drinking and entertainment

Daytime drinking and snack-nibbling take place on or around the café-lined bul. 9 Septemvri. *Sladkarnitsa Teteven*, an almost Viennese-style coffee house and patisserie on the corner of 9 Septemvri and pl. na Svobodata, has been attracting

Ruse's more stolid, middle-class burghers since the inter-war years. The café in the *Hotel Dunav* across the square is more rough-and-ready, and seems very much a male preserve; while the *Budapeshta* ice-cream salon at Georgi Dimitrov 13 has a more relaxed family atmosphere.

Swishest place to **eat** in town is the restaurant of the *Hotel Riga*, Stamboliiski 22, where a three-course meal for two shouldn't set you back more than £6–7. Also popular with local diners are *Strandzhata*, Ivan Dimitrov 3, a cosy basement tavern with wooden folksy decor; the *Potsdam*, 9 Septemvri 77, offering good beer and vaguely Germanic cuisine; and the *Gyurgevo*, in the *Hotel Balkan*, which has a few Romanian dishes. Slightly further afield are *Leventa*, a popular weekend venue in the southern outskirts just off the Razgrad/Varna road (bus #18 from the railway station); and the *Ribarska Koliba*, a good place to sample fish from the Danube, 6km west of town in the campsite of the same name. All of the above feature live music and are good places to enjoy a **nighttime drink**. Otherwise try the bar of the *Hotel Riga*, which is also the venue for regular **discos**.

Ruse's **opera**, pl. na Svobodata, is one of the best in Bulgaria. Other types of classical music are showcased in the annual **March Music Weeks**, which attract some of the best ensembles, soloists and conductors in Europe.

Listings

Airport Out on the Razgrad/Varna road. Bus #101 from the railway station.
Airlines *Balkan*, pl. Dimitrov (☎24161).
Hospital Main polyclinic on Bratya Obretenovi at the edge of park na mladezhta.

MOVING ON

If you're **entering or leaving Bulgaria** by way of Ruse you'll first cross the 3km-long **Dunav Most** or "Danube Bridge" (known as "Friendship Bridge" back in the days of socialist brotherhood) spanning the Danube on the outskirts of Ruse and Giurgiu, an ugly yet technically impressive structure built by both countries (with Soviet assistance) between 1952 and 1954. The border is open 24 hours a day, and for those entering by road a *Tourist Service Office* on the Bulgarian side offers information and a hotel booking service. Be warned that traffic on the bridge can be heavy: the situation in Yugoslavia has meant that much of the traffic between central Europe and Turkey now passes through Romania and Bulgaria – and most of it is forced through the bottleneck of Dunav Most. Crossing from Bulgaria to Romania shouldn't involve too many problems, but when coming the other way expect to queue for several hours – anecdotal evidence suggests that Romanian frontier personnel will speed up the process in return for a few Deutschmarks or dollars.

Travellers **leaving Bulgaria by rail** have a choice of trains and destinations. The following services currently run once a day, although be careful to check precise timings and routes (uncertainties in the former Soviet Union may lead to several changes in itinerary in the near future): the *Pannonia* currently calls at Bucharest, Budapest, Prague, Dresden and Berlin; the *Bâlgariya* runs through Bucharest, Chernovtsy and Kiev; the *Vitosha* through Bucharest, Lvov and Saint Petersburg; and the *Sofia* connects Ruse with Bucharest, Kiev and Moscow.

Journeying from Ruse deeper into Bulgaria, there are direct trains to Sofia and Varna, although those travelling south into the Balkan Range will probably have to change trains at Gorna Oryahovitsa.

Market Fruit and veg, as well as diverse street traders, along the eastern stretches of 9 Septemvri.

Pharmacies Main central pharmacies are at 9 Septemvri 26, 9 Septemvri 97, and G. Dimitrov 113. These take it in turns to be on duty at night.

Post office and telephones pl. na Svobodata.

Rail ticket agents *BDZh*, ul. Blagoev 39 (☎22845); international tickets from *Rila*, ul. Blagoev 27 (☎29790).

Around Ruse

Silistra, Lake Srebârna and the Thracian tomb at Sveshtari (see p.173) are feasible destinations for **day excursions from Ruse** if you've got a car or if *Dunav Tours* are running any trips, but if you're relying on public transport an overnight stay is probably inescapable. However, three more sights – much closer to Ruse – might merit your attention. **Lipnik park**, 12km away near the commune of NIKOLOVO, is a half-tamed forest where the townsfolk go for picnics and strolls at the weekends, reachable by bus from the main terminal, or by driving out of town along Angel Gechov.

Slightly further afield, the Rusenski Lom national park holds two sets of **medieval Bulgarian ruins**, neither of which is easy to visit, but both rewarding if you make the effort. Both lie just off the main E85 road from Ruse to Veliko Târnovo. If travelling this route by private car, you'll be able to take a quick look at both of them before pressing on to the celebrated nineteenth-century bridge at **Byala**, 50km south of Ruse.

The Rock monastery of Ivanovo

The more famous of the ruins is the so-called **Rock monastery of Ivanovo** located near IVANOVO village 18km south of Ruse, among the rocks on the left bank of the River Rusenski Lom. The monastery is one of several hewn into the craggy gorge whose caves provided shelter for Stone Age tribes and medieval hermits alike. Monks first arrived at this remote gorge in the thirteenth century, a royal donation enabling one Yoakim of Târnovo to establish an extensive monastery complex dedicated to the Archangel Michael, its churches, cells and galleries cut from the sheer cliff. Inside, the fourteenth-century *Tsârkvata* cave features murals which have impressed art historians with their use of a realism unusual for the period. Scantily draped muscular figures crowd a scene depicting Christ's betrayal of Judas, which is followed by a grisly portrayal of the latter's suicide. *The Beheading of John the Baptist* betrays a similar lack of squeamishness.

The so-called **Buried church** features a damaged mural of Tsar Asen presenting a model of the church to the Archangel, and a depiction of Michael's miracles on the ceiling. Nearby is another, more derelict **rock church** decorated with a scene of the visions of Saint Peter of Alexandria. Along the same bank are **Chapel of Gospodev Dol,** or "The Lord's Valley" (with portraits of its patron saints, Vlassius, Spiridon and Modestus), and the accurately named **Demolished church**, all containing murals, variously faded by time.

Over the years the paintings have suffered greatly from the graffiti of visiting vandals, and visitors are now discouraged from approaching the monastery on their own. If you do attempt the journey independently, taking one of the eight daily trains to Ivanovo village and hiking up into the gorge, you'll probably find the whole place locked up. Trips to the monastery are organized by *Dunav Tours* in Ruse over the summer: if you arrive out of season they will hire a car and guide for you. As you might expect, this won't come cheap – about £15 excluding tips.

Cherven

Fifteen kilometres south of Ivanovo, a fork in the gorge provides a niche for the **ruins of CHERVEN**, clinging to the rock like Tsarevets at Veliko Târnovo. Formerly known as the "City of churches" or "City of bishops", Cherven was founded in the sixth or seventh century when recurrent barbarian invasions compelled the inhabitants of Ruse to seek a more defensible site inland. The citadel was devastated by the Turks, but Cherven survived as the region's administrative centre for some time, with Ottoman governors and Orthodox bishops coexisting here until the seventeenth century, when they both relocated to Ruse. Nowadays Cherven resembles a desolate and brutish version of Machu Picchu, with meagre remains standing high above the valley on a rocky table flanked on three sides by unscalable cliffs. You can still make out the ground plans of its many churches, although the biggest of the town's structures was the fortified complex of the local *bolyarin*, Cherven's feudal lord. A still-discernable main street runs past his palace and on towards the rude dwellings of his underlings.

Accessible by road for those with a private car, Cherven is less easy to reach if you're reliant on public transport. Sporadic buses to the village of Cherven may be running from Ruse's bus terminal; otherwise take a train to the town of DVE MOGILI 35km south of Ruse, and pick up a local bus to Cherven from there.

The bridge at Byala

Midway between Ruse and Veliko Târnovo is the market town of BYALA, unremarkable save for the **bridge over the River Yantra** 2km to the west of town on the E85 road. Built in 1867 by the National Revival's most prolific architect Kolyo Ficheto (see p.155), the structure originally rested on fourteen ornate piers – ten of which were subsequently washed away by floodwaters. The fluid, baroque forms of the remaining four are still intact, as are the reliefs of swans, nymphs and dragons which adorn the main body of the bridge.

Silistra

Regular buses continue eastwards from Ruse to the last town on the Bulgarian stretches of the Danube, **SILISTRA**. It's also accessible by rail, lying at the end of a branch line which leaves the Ruse-Varna line at SAMUIL. The site of Roman *Durostorum* and an important garrison town in Turkish times, Silistra is nowadays a sleepy border settlement lacking in the vigour and comparative sophistication of Ruse. Economic activity in the town revolves around the port, main outlet for the grain of the Dobrudzhan plain to the southeast. For the traveller, a fine late-Roman tomb and the nearby nature reserve at Srebârna provide the main reasons to visit, but there's little to justify a stay of any length.

Like their counterparts in Ruse, the citizens of Silistra also complain about foul-smelling chemicals wafting over the river from the north, producing skin complaints among the local children. The alleged culprit in this case is a metallurgy plant in the nearby Romanian town of Calaraş, but you're unlikely to experience any ill effects if you're just passing through.

The town

From the rail and bus stations on the town's western outskirts, ul. Dimitrov winds its way eastwards through the town centre before arriving at a typically flagstoned and flowerbedded town square, flanked by a sixteenth-century **mosque** on one side and a modern **art gallery** on the other. A few steps beyond at G. Rakovski 24 is the **archaeological museum** (Tues–Sun 8am–noon & 2–6pm), where a rich fund of material on life in *Durostorum* includes the epigraph-laden tombstones of the soldiers stationed here with the XI Legion. To the north, nineteenth-century residential houses occupy a grid of tree-shaded streets which separate central Silistra from the river. It's among these modest turn-of-the-century mansions, many with Art Nouveau details such as caryatids peering from upper storeys, that you get some impression of the elegance once enjoyed by the Danubian towns.

Bits of Roman ruin lie scattered on both sides of ul. Tolbuhin, which runs eastwards from the town centre towards the Romanian frontier in Silistra's suburbs. However, the town's main antique attraction is the **Roman tomb** (Tues–Sun 8.30am–noon & 1.30–5.30pm), south of the centre on ul. 7 Septemvri, just off the main Dobrich road. A modestly sized, vaulted structure dating from the twilight years of Imperial rule, the tomb is chiefly known for its **paintings**, probably executed in the late third or early fourth century during the reign of Theodosius I. Immediately opposite the entrance are portraits of the interred couple, flanked by male and female retainers bringing them sumptuous objects as indication of their wealth and status. The ceiling is decorated with octagons and circles containing bird figures, hunting scenes or plant motifs, while the portrait of the owners is surmounted by the image of two peacocks and a bronze vase.

Occupying a hill 3km south of town (best reached by walking along ul. Vasil Kolarov from the centre) are the remains of the Turkish fortress of **Medzhitabiya**, another corner of the defensive quadrilateral built by the Ottomans, and one that was frequently attacked in the course of successive Russo-Turkish wars. The hilltop park also features a TV tower complete with revolving café.

Practicalities and the border crossing

Silistra's **accommodation prospects** are modest: apart from a few **private rooms** available from *Istâr Tours*, Trâg na svobodata 7 (☎22392), the only place to stay in town is the nearby *Zlatna Dobrudzha* **hotel** (③), on the corner of G. Dimitrov and Otets Paisii.

The **border crossing** on Silistra's eastern fringes is relatively quiet, and opening times change according to the volume of traffic. The local frontier guards won't be equipped to hand out **visas** on the spot, so if you're entering Bulgaria here, make sure you get one before leaving home. Travelling in the other direction remains very much an untested possibility – on the Romanian side baksheesh in hard currency may smooth out some problems.

Lake Srebârna

Nineteenth-century Hungarian traveller Felix Kanitz called **Lake Srebârna**, 17km west of Silistra near the Danube shore, "the Eldorado of wading birds". An expanse of a reedy marshland spreads around the lake itself, providing ninety species of wildfowl (including seventy different types of heron) with a secure habitat. The lake is also frequented by around eighty migratory species, and there's a fair likelihood of being able to see **egrets** in the summer and **pelicans** in the autumn. In recent decades growing silt deposits have cut the lake off from the cleansing waters of the River Danube, causing Srebârna to stagnate. There's a consequent decline in the numbers of fish upon which the birds can feed, and local biologists reckon that the reserve's best days could be over – unless a lot of money is spent on new irrigation channels.

The reserve is approached from the villages of SREBÂRNA to the west or POPINA to the northwest (both are served by bus #22 from Silistra, and the latter is sometimes visited by hydrofoils from Ruse during the summer), but tourists are discouraged from penetrating the reserve on their own, so you may not see very much if you come independently. **Day trips** are organized by *Istâr Tours* in Silistra.

Dobrich and the Dobrudzha

Beyond Silistra the Danube swings north into Romania, leaving travellers with the choice of heading south across the Ludogorie hills towards Shumen (see p.162), or continuing eastwards towards the Black Sea Coast. The latter route takes you through the **Dobrudzha**, Bulgaria's main grain-producing region. Despite its agricultural wealth the Dobrudzhan plain remains dully flat and heat-hazed, with few centres of much size or historical interest. Regional capital **Dobrich**, 50km short of Varna and the coast, is the only worthwhile stopoff.

Dobrich (Tolbuhin)

Principal town of the eastern Dobrudzha, **DOBRICH** is an obvious place to break your journey if travelling between the Danube and the coast, or if heading towards the Romanian border at KARDAM, 35km to the north. Between 1949 and 1990 it carried the name of the Soviet marshal who "liberated" the area in 1944, *Tolbuhin* (and it appears as such on most postwar road signs and maps), but the town started life as *Hadzhioglu Bazardzhik*, supposedly named after itinerant merchant Hadzhi Oglu Bakal, who built the first house here in the sixteenth century. Circassians and Tatars formed the majority of the pre-Liberation population, and although many families fled south to avoid advancing Russian armies in 1877, the area retains a strong Muslim element. In the nineteenth century Dobrich was famous for its autumn horse fair, and horse rearing remains an important part of the local economy.

Around town

Travelling through here in the 1870s, Felix Kanitz said that he knew of no other town in Bulgaria whose "Asiatic character . . . was so typical and unadulterated in appearance". Nowadays central Dobrich is resolutely modern, with stark concrete piles and plazas, although something of the nineteenth-century artisans' quarter has been rather antiseptically re-created in the **Stariyat Dobrich** ("Old Dobrich") quarter just off the central pl. na svobodata. Visitors can see demonstrations of traditional crafts in some twenty workshops, including pottery, blacksmithing, woodcarving, bookbinding and jewellery. The town's only other real sight is the **Yordan Yovkov museum** at General Gurko 1, celebrating the Zheravna-born poet who spent many years in the Dobrudzha as a schoolteacher.

THE DOBRUDZHA IN HISTORY

"A wintry land deficient in cultivated grains and fruit", inhabited by a people "who are barbarous and lead a bestial existence" was how, according to Diodorus, third-century BC Thracian chieftain Dromichaetes described the **Dobrudzha** to his Macedonian captive Lysimachus, berating him for bothering to invade such a barren region in the first place.

Windswept in winter and parched in summer, the Dobrudzha has always had a reputation for harshness and inhospitability. Geographically speaking, it stretches from the mouth of the Danube in the north to the Gulf of Varna in the south, marking the southwestern extremity of the great **Eurasian steppelands** which sweep uninterruptedly round the north coast of the Black Sea and eastwards towards Central Asia and Mongolia. Successive generations of horseriding invaders have used the steppe as a corridor leading to the riches of southeastern Europe, and faced by such recurring dangers, Western civilization's hold on the region has always been tenuous. Successive Macedonian, Roman, Byzantine and Bulgarian empires always found the Dobrudzha to be the most difficult part of the northern frontier to defend, and by the thirteenth century, when **Tatar bands** were beginning to roam the region with impunity, the area was well on the way to becoming a lawless desert.

Arab chronicler Ibn Battuta, crossing the Dobrudzha in the fourteenth century, was struck by its desolate appearance, describing it as "eighteen days of uninhabited wasteland, for eight days of which there is no water". By the time the Ottoman Sultan Mehmet I conquered the Dobrudzha in 1416, the region was so depopulated that he had to colonize it with **Turkish settlers** in order to provide the newly won province with inhabitants capable of defending it – with the result that the local ethnic mix still includes a fair proportion of Turks. These are intermingled with the Turkish-speaking **Dobrudzha Tatars**, descendants of Crimean Tatars who were expelled from the Russian empire in the wake of the Crimean War.

The ethnic balance of the region was altered yet again during the inter-war period, when the Dobrudzha was part of Romania. Eager to boost the Latin element among the population, the government encouraged the immigration of Romanian-speaking **Vlachs** (see p.113) from Macedonia. After regaining the territory in 1941, the Bulgarian authorities imported Slav colonists to redress the ethnic balance, but the existence of so many non-Bulgarian minorities in an area so crucial to the economy was a source of concern to the country's postwar Communist bosses. Special attention was paid to the Dobrudzha during the 1980s, when the controversial *Vâzroditelniyat protses* or Regeneration Process tried to force local Muslims to speak only the Bulgarian language in public and to adopt Bulgarian names. Nowadays you'll find inter-ethnic relations more relaxed, with the babble of Bulgarian and Turkic tongues heard on the streets of Dobrich reflecting the meeting of cultures from the Dobrudzha's turbulent past.

Practicalities – and northwards to the border

Dobrich's **rail and bus** stations are on the western and eastern edges respectively of the downtown area – both involve a pretty straightforward ten-minute walk into the centre. Information of a sort may be available from a *Balkantourist* office at ul. Dimitrov 3; otherwise the hotels *Bâlgariya* (④); *Moskva* (②); and *Dobrudzha* (②) provide the choice of **accommodation**.

Crossing into Romania from Dobrich can be problematic for those without their own transport. Buses from here run only to KARDAM, 5km short of the border, and trains are few and far between. The Bulgarians run a *Cherno More* express train during the summer (beginning in Varna and calling at Dobrich before moving on to Medgidia, Kiev and Moscow), but times and frequencies change from year to year. Get information and **tickets** at *TsKTON*, ul. Marx 1A.

THE CENTRAL BALKAN RANGE

For over a thousand years, the **Balkan Range** (in Bulgarian, the Stara planina or "Old Mountains") has been the cradle of the Bulgarian nation and the cockpit of its destiny. Sloping gently towards the Danube plain, the Balkan's fertile valleys supported the medieval capitals of **Pliska** and **Preslav** (mere ruins today) and **Veliko Târnovo** (still a thriving city), while steep ranges with defensible passes shielded them to the south. Much was destroyed during the Ottoman conquest, but the thread of culture was preserved by monasteries and the crafts centres that re-established themselves under the Turkish yoke.

The range's gentler slopes lie just **east of Sofia**, where small towns like **Etropole** and **Teteven** provide a measure of rural tranquility lacking in the more touristed Balkan centres further east. First of these is **Lovech**, a well-preserved nineteenth-century town which lies in striking distance of **Troyan monastery**, and **Pleven**, site of a crucial battle in the Russo-Turkish War, to the north.

However, the best touring base in the **central part of the range** is Veliko Târnovo. A beautiful city in its own right, with a medieval citadel and several historic churches, Târnovo has good transport links with villages rich in vernacular architecture like **Arbanasi**, **Elena**, **Tryavna** and **Etâr**; as well as a whole cluster of monasteries: **Preobrazhenski**, **Dryanovo** and **Kilifarevo** are the big three, but numerous smaller foundations await further exploration.

The main urban centre of the **eastern Balkan Range** is **Shumen**, site of a fine medieval fortress and close to Bulgaria's first two capitals at **Pliska** and **Preslav**, and the enigmatic rock sculpture of the **Madara Horseman**. From here routes towards the Danube and the Dobrudzha pass through the Ludogorie hills, where **Razgrad** and the **Thracian tomb at Sveshtari** provide the targets for travels.

Towns in the western part of the central Balkan Range can be easily reached **by bus** from Sofia. The **Sofia-Varna railway line**, skirting the mountains to the north, is the fastest way of accessing places further afield. It passes through **Pleven**, from whence buses depart to Lovech and Troyan; **Gornya Orahovitsa**, with regular rail and bus connections to Veliko Târnovo, Tryavna and Gabrovo; and **Shumen**, before forging onwards to the coast. Once established in any of the above places, you can explore neighbouring attractions using **local bus services**.

East of Sofia

The foothills of the central Balkan Range northeast of Sofia are completely bypassed if you're travelling eastward by rail. However, the main Sofia-Veliko Târnovo-Varna highway (a gorge-defying dual carriageway for the first 60km or so) heads straight across the westernmost shoulder of the range, passing a handful of worthwhile villages and monasteries along the way. The market town of **Teteven** is the most attractive of the region's settlements if you need a base from which to explore. Otherwise, most of the area's worthwhile sights are accessible by bus either from Sofia, or Lovech to the east.

Botevgrad, Pravets and Etropole

An hour's drive beyond Sofia the highway bypasses **BOTEVGRAD**, hardly worth a detour unless you're aiming for the E79 to Vratsa, Mihailovgrad and Vidin, which heads northward from here. Once a thriving market town, profiting from its position at the northern end of the (no longer used) *Baba Konak* pass, Botevgrad is nowadays a sterile modern place whose main claim to fame is the *Chavdar* factory – makers of the buses and coaches which clatter their way across Bulgaria. Attractions are limited to a nineteenth-century **clock tower** on the main square, a couple of blocks east of the bus station; and a **town museum** at Vasil Kolarov 8, whose prize exhibit is a fourteenth-century Bulgarian inscription found among the ruins of the Bozhenski Urvich fortress, 29km north of town. There's a **hotel**, the 3-star *Botevgrad* (☎0723/831; ③), on the central square.

Pravets

About 10km after the turn-off to Botevgrad, another minor road forks eastwards to **PRAVETS**, a previously unremarkable village whose status as the birthplace of former dictator **Todor Zhivkov** made it into one of the most prosperous communities in Bulgaria. Although his modest childhood home is no longer open to the public as a museum, other aspects of the Zhivkov legacy will prove more lasting: high-tech industries, elite foreign-language schools, an ultra-modern cultural centre and, most importantly, the **holiday complex and artificial lake** on the town's western outskirts. Complete with tennis courts, restaurants, boating, waterskiing facilities and fishing opportunities, this is a popular stopoff for travellers – fringed by the mountains of the *Etropolska planina* to the south, it's quite an idyllic spot. There's a **motel** (☎07133/2754; ③) and **campsite** by the lake, as well as the *Shatra* restaurant and disco, a curious pagoda-like construction jutting out into the water.

Etropole

Thirteen kilometres southeast of Pravets is **ETROPOLE**, a quiet agricultural village surrounded by subalpine pastures. The centre, a couple of blocks west of the bus station, harbours the usual eighteenth-century **clock tower** and a small **town museum**, the latter containing memorabilia of Etropole's past as a wealthy mining town which attracted Saxon immigrants in the Middle Ages. The main attraction, however, is the **monastery of Sveta Troitsa** 4km to the east above the village of RIBARITSA. Founded in 1158, the monastery was a well-known literary centre in the sixteenth and seventeenth centuries, when monks copied and distributed Bulgarian manuscripts. Nowadays it's a little-visited foundation populated by four nuns, with a grassy courtyard surrounding the four hexagonal towers of the monastery church.

Getting to the monastery is fairly easy; about five daily buses run from Etropole to Ribaritsa, but these are usually early in the morning or late in the afternoon. Alternatively, it's an hour's **walk**: turn right out of Etropole bus station into ul. Partizanska, walk to the end of the street where the Ribaritsa road forks right, then after 50m bear right onto a partly asphalted track which takes you over the hills to Ribaritsa itself – where a signposted lane climbs to the monastery. If you need **to stay** in Etropole (and the fresh mountain air and numerous walking possibilities would make it worthwhile), the 3-star *Hotel Etropole* (☎0712/3616; ③) is just above the bus station.

TODOR ZHIVKOV

Born into a peasant family in 1911, **Todor Zhivkov** joined the Young Communists in 1928 while a print worker and became Mayor of Sofia after wartime service with the Chavdar partisan brigade. In 1954, within three years of joining the Politburo, he secured the post of First Secretary or Party leader with the approval of Moscow, and elbowed aside the old Stalinist, Anton Yugov, to claim the premiership in 1962. He survived a coup in 1965 – a murky affair blamed on "ultra-leftists" at the time, but subsequently attributed to nationalist army officers.

Zhivkov slavishly followed the Soviet line in foreign policy, enthusiastically sending troops to help crush the Prague Spring in 1968. He tried to counterbalance this closeness to the USSR by pumping up Bulgarian nationalism at home, presenting Communist Bulgaria as the natural culmination of the national struggles of the past. Consistent with this policy were the extravagant celebrations marking 1300 years of the Bulgarian state in 1981, and persecution of Bulgaria's ethnic Turkish population in the years that ensued. It's for this abuse of Turkish human rights that the Zhivkov years will be long remembered in Turkey and the West.

When "reform Communists" ditched Zhivkov in November 1989, it suited them to make the erstwhile dictator the scapegoat for all that was wrong in Bulgarian society. He was accordingly arrested on a charge of "embezzling state funds" and sentenced to seven years' imprisonment, though more charges are pending. The right-of-centre government elected in October 1991 has ordered the investigation of so many abuses of Communist power (notably Bulgarian support for international terrorism and Bulgaria's repression of ethnic Turks) that the potential list of charges against Zhivkov and his colleagues seems endless.

Zhivkov himself remains in combative spirits, accusing Mikhail Gorbachev of being the one who orchestrated his downfall. According to Zhivkov, a skilful self-publicist to the end, his own form of *perestroika* was much more logical and consistent than the "anarchy" brought forth by the former Soviet leader: hence Gorbachev's desire to be rid of him.

Yablanitsa and its caves

Assuming that you stick with the main highway, the next place of any importance is **YABLANITSA**, the "town of apples", which also produces Bulgaria's finest *halva* and acts as the lynchpin of the regional bus network. It's a good place from which to investigate neighbouring **caves**, although the nearest **accommodation** is in Teteven, 20km to the southeast.

South of the village of BRESTITSA, 11km beyond Yablanitsa on the E771, a backroad runs southwards for about a mile to the **Sâeva Dupka cave** (guided tours daily 9am–5pm). The 205m-long cave consists of five halls dripping with water and stalactites. On the Yablanitsa side of the massif (6km northeast of town) there's another subterranean shaft known as the **Bezdanniya pchelin** or "Bottomless Beehive". Since it's over 400ft deep and off limits to casual visitors, anyone interested in exploring this should contact the potholing section of the Bulgarian Hiking Union (see Sofia listings) beforehand. The main chamber, 30m by 40m, has a profusion of stalactites and stalagmites, which are also much in evidence at **Haidushka peshtera** ("Haiduk's Cave") and **Temna dupka** ("Deep Den") – a couple of other caves further to the northwest near the villages of KAMENO POLE and **Karlukovo**. The latter (served by local trains between Mezdra and Cherven Bryag) lies at the centre of a karst area pockmarked with more than a hundred caves and pots. Dorm accommodation in the village is provided by the *Natsionalen peshteren dom* ("National cavers' home"; ☎0697/ 3647), although this tends to fill up with Bulgarian groups during school and college holidays.

Teteven and around

If heading directly east along the E771 for Târnovo and Varna, about 5km beyond Brestnitsa you'll pass the entrance to the Vit valley, near the head of which stands the highland market town of Teteven. The river is a favourite of Bulgarian anglers, and runs alongside the *Balkan* campsite (open mid-May–Oct), which has a restaurant and chalets, near the junction where the E771 meets the Teteven road. The bus station opposite is the place to pick up regular buses along the valley.

Entering the Vit valley, the Teteven road passes a turn-off to the left running up to the village of GRADEZHNITSA, where locals will direct you to the **Gradezhnitsa cave**. Almost half a mile deep in all, this contains underground lakes and a small river, with karst formations bearing names like *Petrified Curtains* and *Fairyland*.

Ten kilometres up the valley the road hits **GLOZHENE**, a drab industrialized village known chiefly for the nearby **monastery**, perched high above and practically invisible from the valley. It's a small monastery, a tiny nineteenth-century church enclosed by fortress-like living quarters with stone ground-floor walls and overhanging timber upper storeys. Track-suited monks will show you round a small museum containing the church silver, and you can enjoy views of the surrounding countryside from the monastery's cliff-top eyrie. Most vehicles will balk at the gravelled roadway which winds the long way up to the monastery from town. If you fancy walking, a shorter route (for which you should allow fifty minutes) takes you south from Glozhene's central bus stop along the Teteven road, right across a footbridge spanning the Vit, through the *Spartak* sports field, up the cobbled hillside path, then fork right up a wooded ravine.

Teteven

Surrounded by imposing mountains further up the valley, **TETEVEN** once inspired writer Ivan Vazov to declare that had he not come here, "I should regard myself as a stranger to my native land . . . Nowhere have I found a place so enchanting as this". Vazov's endorsement seems a shade too fulsome for modern Teteven, but the town is certainly appealing in a laid-back way. Teteven comes to life on Saturday mornings, when the town **market** precipitates a deluge of visitors from surrounding villages – most notably the local Pomaks, easily recognizable by their *shalvari*, the brightly coloured trousers worn by the women.

Despite the undoubted prettiness of the pastel-coloured houses ranged above the **main square** (a couple of blocks south of the bus station), there's little in the way of specific sights, save for a small town **museum** (Tues–Sun 9am–noon & 2–5pm) on the square itself, with a small display of local crafts; and the re-created nineteenth-century interiors of the **Bobevska kâshta** (Tues–Sun 2–5pm), just to the north at ul. Ivan Vazov 83. **Rooms** are available at the *Hotel Teteven* (☎0678/ 3222; ③) just uphill from the square, while the *Dvata Bora* **restaurant** a few metres beyond offers basic grilled nosh in a fine National Revival-period house.

Ribaritsa

Twelve kilometres beyond Teteven at the end of the valley lies **RIBARITSA**, a popular mountain village with a couple of nearby campsites, the *Skribnata* (open June–Aug) 5km south, and the *Ribaritsa* (open May–Oct) in the village itself. **Walks** from Ribaritsa head either southwestwards up the Kostina valley, where, after 4km, there's a monument to **Georgi Benkovski**, the Koprivshtitsa-born revolutionary killed here in 1876; or southward up the Zavodka valley towards MOUNT VEZHEN, which at 2198m above sea level is the highest point in the *Tetevenska planina*.

The road to Pleven

Back to the main Yablanitsa-Pleven road. Karstic limestone formations lurk underground throughout the region, and the river running beneath the **junction of the Pleven and Veliko Târnovo highways** emerges as the **Glavna Panega** spring near ZLATNA PANEGA on the Pleven road (bear right just before the village), where it forms two lakes whose waters remain at an even temperature (10°–12.5°C) whatever the season. The Roman legend of the fair but afflicted Panega, who was cured by bathing here, seems to have been the model for apocryphal stories relating to other spas – the "Virgin's Pass" near Kostenets, for example.

The last stage of the route to Pleven is pretty straightforward, and after passing through CHERVEN BRYAG (the junction for trains to Oryahovo on the Danube), the E83 highway follows the same course as the Sofia-Pleven railway. Although trains don't stop there, motorists can visit **Lavrov Park** near the village of GORNI DUBNIK en route. On October 24, 1877, during the War of Liberation, the Russians flung themselves upon the Turkish redoubt that stood here guarding the road to Plevna, inspired by the suicidal heroism of General Lavrov, their commander. There's now a small museum near the park entrance exhibiting the kind of plans beloved of wargamers, and a statue of a Bulgarian and a Soviet soldier entitled "Eternal Friendship". On the opposite side of the road, an ossuary contains the bones of Lavrov and his men.

Pleven

Sited where the foothills of the Balkan Range descend to meet the Danube plain, **PLEVEN** isn't particularly appealing unless you're keen on war memorials and military history, since most of the old buildings and parks that mitigate its concrete sterility contain monuments or museums honouring the **siege of Plevna** – probably the most decisive episode of the War of Liberation. When the Russians crossed the Danube at Svishtov in 1877, their flank was threatened by the Turkish forces entrenched at Plevna (as the town was then known), which resisted three assaults that cost the Russians thousands of casualties. In response to Grand Duke Nicholas's pleas, Romanian reinforcements came with King Carol I, who personally led his troops into battle (the last European sovereign to do so) crying "This is the music that pleases me!" Russia's top generals, Skobelev and Totleben, then arrived to organize a professional siege, weakening the defenders by starvation and blasting each redoubt with artillery before the attackers made repeated bayonet charges, finally compelling the Turks to surrender on December 10. Over 40,000 Russians and Romanians and uncounted numbers of Turks and civilians died, but as a consequence of Plevna's fall and its shattering effect on Ottoman morale, northern Bulgaria was swiftly liberated.

Easily reached from Sofia, Varna or Ruse by rail, Pleven stands at the centre of an extensive local **bus network** which serves the smaller towns along the Danube to the north as well as Lovech and Troyan to the south.

Around town

Arriving at the bus or train station at the northern end of town, follow bul. Lenin (or take any bus) southwards until you come across a paved plaza containing the sunken **church of Sveti Nikolai**. A nineteenth-century portrait of the saint himself presides over the doorway of this simple structure, belived to date from the 1300s. Inside is a collection of icons, including works by the Samokov masters Stanislav Dospevski and Zahari Zograf. Beyond the church lies Kosta Zlatarev, Pleven's main downtown street. Follow this south and you'll pass the **museum of Liberation** (Tues–Sun 9am–noon & 2–5.30pm) in an adjoining park, occupying the house where the Turkish commander, Osman Pasha, formally surrendered to Tsar Aleksandr II. Here you'll see weaponry, mementos and plans lovingly detailing each phase of the battle.

A little further on is the city's **main square**, a fountain-splashed expanse of flagstones, flowers and shrubs dominated by the Russo-Byzantine style **mausoleum** (daily 8am–noon & 2–6pm), built to commemorate the Russian soldiers who died at Pleven, although the number of Romanian names on the lists of the fallen makes it clear who saw the worst of the fighting. Garishly modernist grey-and-brown frescoes swirl around inside, while marble necropolitan furniture adorns the crypt. Regular art exhibitions are held on the opposite side of the square in the **old public baths**, a curious pseudo-Byzantine structure whose red-and-white striped facade could be easily mistaken for that of a church.

The historical museum

Follow paths through the park at the southern end of the square and you reach the **historical museum** or *Istoricheski muzei* (Tues–Sun 9am–noon & 1.30–5.30pm), housed in spacious former barracks at ul. Zaimov 3. Natural history occupies the east wing, while the west wing has an enormous history collection, one of the nation's best, beginning with the pick of northern Bulgaria's archaeological remains. A blackened square of earth turns out to be a **Neolithic dwelling** from the fourth millenium BC, excavated near the village of Telish to the west and transferred here in the state in which it was found. It's surrounded by contemporaneous pottery, richly decorated with geometric shapes and animated squiggles.

More pottery comes from the **Roman town of Oescus**, near modern Gigen on the Danube, an important administrative centre and home to the Fifth Macedonian Legion. On show are numerous gravestones and a floor mosaic with abstract patterns swirling around a scene from Menander's comedy *The Achaeans*. The medieval period is represented by finds from another Danube town, Nikopol, whose fortress had a reputation for invincibility under both Bulgarians and Ottomans.

The **ethnographic section** features the hooded cloaks worn by shepherds of the Danube plain, and a couple of blunt-ended boats carved from tree trunks used by fishermen on the great river until very recently. Of particular interest are the reconstructions of local village houses, thatched-roofed dwellings built half above ground, half under, and surrounded by a stockade of twigs. Upstairs are seemingly endless halls filled with weapons and uniforms from the days of the siege, including the samovars presented by Russian officers to the Bulgarian families with whom they were billeted.

Skobelev park

Just to the southwest of the barracks, a lengthy processional stairway ascends towards **Skobelev park**, passing the city **art gallery** on the way. At the top is yet another Bulgarian-Soviet Friendship monument, followed by the gates of the park itself. The park is laid out on a hill formerly occupied by the **Isa Aga Redoubt**, the object of fierce fighting in 1877 and now restored and crowned with an obelisk commemorating the 405 troops who died capturing it. Numerous cannon are secreted within the greenery hereabouts, but the main focus of visitors' attention is the **Panorama** (daily 8am–noon & 2–6pm), an enormous concrete funnel of a building holding two huge panoramas depicting scenes from the siege, each featuring three-dimensional figures set against an enormous circular backdrop.

Kailâka park

Leaving Pleven by the southbound ul. San Stefano it's 2km to **Kailâka park**, laid out around the lush and rocky Tuhenitsa defile, and connected by regular bus to the town centre. Site of a Thracian settlement which the Romans took over and named *Storgosia*, it's here that the citizens of Pleven unwind at weekends, taking advantage of the park's swimming baths, watersports facilities, and open-air theatre. There's also the *Peshtera* restaurant in a cave at the foot of a limestone cliff – and below the baths a monument to the Jews who perished here in 1944 when the camp in which they were imprisoned burned down. (Although anti-Semitism has never been prevalent in Bulgaria, the government gaoled the Salonikan Jews during the latter stages of the war to appease its Nazi allies). Three kilometres upriver, a bronze statue of General Totleben (Russian hero of the 1877 seige) surmounts the **Totleben rampart** which separates two reservoirs: the walls of the smaller one of these were founded upon the remains of a dam erected during the siege to cut off the water that powered Pleven's mills.

Practicalities

You can enquire after **private rooms** in the *kvartirni byuro* at Tsanko Tserkovski 10; otherwise there's little to choose between the city's modern hotels: the 3-star *Pleven*, pl. Republika 2 (☎064/20062; ④); the 3-star *Balkan*, ul. Beshev 68 (☎064/22215; ④); the 2-star *Rostov na Don*, Slava Aleksiev 2 (☎064/27095; ③); or the 2-star *Kailâka* in the park of the same name (☎064/25550; ③).

The nearest **campsites** are the *Kailâka* (open May–Sept), 5km south of town on the Lovech road; and the *Grivitsa* (open April–Nov) in the village of the same name, 8km east of town on the E83 highway to Varna.

Rail and bus tickets can be bought in advance from the *TsKTON* or **transport service bureau** at Zemenhof 2.

Lovech and around

Lying just off the main road and rail routes, **Lovech** is often missed out by those travelling east to west. However, it does lie on one of the important trans-Balkan routes linking Pleven, on the margins of the Danubian plain, with the Valley of the Roses to the south. This can't match crossing the more famous Shipka pass in terms of scenery or sheer excitement (see p.196), but there are compensations. Lusher and less craggy than the mountains further east, the landscape has its own attractions, and **Troyan monastery** merits a visit as much as any of the other ecclesiastical treasures of the *Stara planina*. Lovech has good bus connections with surrounding towns, and is also accessible by rail, lying at the end of a branchline which leaves the main Sofia-Varna line at the otherwise unimportant town of LEVSKI.

Lovech

LOVECH lies an hour's drive to the south of Pleven, dunked between the rolling foothills of the Balkan Mountains. It divides precisely into two sections, the flagstoned walkways and plazas of the modern centre contrasting sharply with the red roofs and protruding *chardaks* of the nineteenth-century **Varosh**, or **old town**, now an architectural preservation area. An important strategic point since Thracian times, standing guard over the northern approaches to the Troyan pass, Lovech has become famous in more recent times for having once been the headquarters of **Vasil Levski**, whose statue and museum are now major attractions.

Nowadays Lovech is notorious for being the site of one of Bulgaria's largest postwar concentration camps, which the inmates dubbed **Slânchev bryag** ("Sunny Beach") in a grimly ironic reference to the well-known Black Sea holiday resort. Prisoners guilty of the most trifling ideological transgressions (such as schoolteachers who failed to instil in their pupils a true understanding of the principles of Marxism) were set to work stonebreaking here, and many perished due to the exacting nature of the labour. Investigators are currently sifting through files to see whether charges can be brought against former camp administrators – and their political bosses.

The old town

Lovech's **rail and bus stations** are on high ground west of the modern town centre, an area of concrete and steel grouped around the pedestrianized ul. Georgi Dimitrov. Follow this southwards to reach the **Pokritya most** or Covered Bridge, of which the locals are extremely proud. Spanning the River Osâm to link new town with old, it was originally designed by National Revival architect Kolyo Ficheto in 1874. The bridge burned down in 1925, and the present reincarnation is the result of successive renovations – most recent of which resulted in the arcade of boutiques, craft shops and cafés which the bridge now holds. At the eastern end of the bridge is **pl. Todor Kirkov**, named after the local revolutionary killed on this spot by the Turks in 1876 after taking part in the April Rising in Tryavna. One block south, the National Revival-style facade of a nineteenth-century school (now a kindergarten) announces the boundary of the Varosh, which stretches up the flanks of the hill from here.

Most of the buildings in the Varosh are in fact modern constructions executed in traditional style, but an attempt has been made to preserve the atmosphere of the previous century in the narrow cobbled lanes which run up the hillside. One of them, ul. Marin Pop Lukanov, leads to a huddle of buildings occupied by the **Museum of Nineteenth-Century Life** (Tues–Sun 8am–noon & 2–6pm). Bulgarians of the period obviously spent their lives close to the floor, eating their food from low wooden tables and sleeping on low beds. The changing lifestyles brought about by turn-of-the-century affluence are shown by the imported Viennese furniture which fills a couple of set-piece rooms here, along with an enormous English iron bedstead. Below in the cellar are a *rakiya* still and a soap-making vessel in which fats were squeezed together and blended with natural perfumes.

Just up the hill from here, a modern concrete structure houses the **Vasil Levski museum**. Between 1869 and 1872, Levski was chiefly responsible for establishing a network of revolutionary cells in Bulgaria, which collected arms and recruits in preparation for a national uprising. The organization's largest base was in Lovech, where Levski usually stayed at the home of Nikola Sirkov, arriving and leaving in disguise. In 1870, the revolutionary committee in Lovech assumed leadership of the nationwide movement, becoming, in effect, the provisional government of the revolutionary underground. In 1872, however, the Turkish intelligence services managed to ensnare many local leaders, ultimately including Levski himself, who was betrayed and arrested at the neighbouring village of Kâkrina. Following interrogation and torture, he was hanged on a winter's morning in Sofia in 1873.

Despite the lack of captions in any language other than Bulgarian, several of the museum's exhibits are self-explanatory. A uniform of the First Bulgarian Legion recalls Levski's days in the 1860s fighting with fellow exiles in Serbia; there are copies of Levski's letters bearing the Lion seal of the revolutionary committee; and the Lovech committee's original printing press – a wooden tray no bigger than a hand into which tiny lines of type were set – accompanied by the amazingly professional-looking documents thus produced. Levski's sabre and dagger lie downstairs, perched atop a shrine-like lump of stone.

Further up the hill, beyond the Uspenska church, steps ascend to the tall and heroic **Levski statue** on Stratesh hill, where townsfolk come to admire the view. The partly reconstructed walls of a medieval Bulgarian **fortress** occupy the summit: Byzantine attempts to strangle the Second Bulgarian Kingdom at birth ended here in the 1190s, when they were forced to sign a peace treaty in Lovech castle recognizing Bulgarian independence.

Practicalities

There are no campsites in the vicinity, but hotel **accommodation** is reasonably plentiful, with the 3-star *Lovech*, ul. Târgovska 12 (☎068/24338; ④), and 2-star *Hisarya*, Georgi Dimitrov (③), in the modern town; the 2-star *Varosha* (☎068/25950; ③) and 2-star *Pokrit most* (③) are both on pl. Todor Kirkov on the other side of the river.

The *Varosha mehana* on ul. Poplukanov has a summer garden and is one of the most pleasant places to **eat and drink**; otherwise restaurants and cafés are in plentiful supply around pl. Todor Kirkov, or along Georgi Dimitrov in the new town. There's a wine-bar with food in the *Orbita* complex on pl. Todor Kirkov, and a late-night bar and nightclub in the *Hotel Lovech*.

Troyan

The journey south from Lovech takes you through wooded hills to **TROYAN**, a ramshackle town ranged along the banks of the River Osâm. Troyan amounts to little save a main square, site of a **town museum** (Tues–Sun 8am–1pm & 2–5pm) which displays many of the craft artefacts for which Troyan and its near-neighbour Oreshak are renowned. The displays include copperware, textiles and a host of vases, bowls and goblets. Next door is a reconstructed National Revival-style house (same times) containing period furnishings in turn-of-the-century rooms.

Troyan's main appeal lies in its proximity to the eponymous monastery secreted in a neighbouring valley, accessible by bus from Troyan's **bus terminal**, a couple of blocks east of the town centre on the other side of the river. You can visit both Troyan and its monastery in a day trip from Lovech, although there's a decent 2-star hotel here, the *Troyan* (☎0670/24323; ③), and dormitory beds are available at the *turisticheski dom* above town just to the east on Kâpincho hill.

Around Troyan monastery

Beyond Troyan the main road climbs the Beli Osâm valley towards the Troyan pass (see opposite), while a lesser road heads up a side valley to the settlements of Oreshak and Cherni Osâm, passing Troyan monastery on the way. Half-hourly buses from Troyan serve the latter route. Five kilometres beyond Troyan, the commune of **ORESHAK** has a long-standing tradition in wood- and ironworking, the subject of a permanent exhibition at the **National Fair of Arts and Crafts** on the village's northern outskirts. If you're interested in learning the rudiments of pottery, ironmongery or woodcarving, contact the Bulgarian National Tourist Office about the eight-day craft courses held here.

The monastery and Cherni Osâm

A further 5km up the valley, on the west bank of the Cherni Osâm river, lies **Troyan monastery** (*Troyanski manastir*). Shaded by trees, the bulky white-washed outer walls of Bulgaria's third largest monastery surround a church, built in 1835 (roughly 135 years after the monastery was founded) and filled with sonorous chanting during mass, when visitors are discouraged. The porch of the church contains a particularly vivid *Last Judgement* – including a suitably macabre figure of Death bundling unfortunates into the gaping mouth of hell. Inside, a series of splendid frescoes executed by Zahari Zograf during the 1840s is richly offset by his brother Dimitâr's icons, placed within an iconostasis made by Tryavna woodcarvers in the 1830s.

The ubiquitous Vasil Levski encouraged the monks to set up a branch of the revolutionary underground at Troyan, and a small "hiding-place museum" is located among the monastery living quarters on the third floor. The table and food bowl offered to the itinerant patriot on the occasion of his visits stand beside the wooden cupboard in which he supposedly hid whenever agents of the Sultan came calling. An adjacent room displays icons, archiepiscopal robes and church regalia, including the surviving doors of an eighteenth-century iconostasis from the previous monastery church.

A couple of kilometres beyond the monastery, buses come to rest in the village of **CHERNI OSÂM**, at the head of the valley of the same name. It's the unusual venue for an extensive modern **natural history museum** (daily 8am–noon & 2–5pm) at the southern end of the village, which aims to document the local wildlife. Stuffed stags, bears, jackals and wolves feature prominently, some of which are mounted on pedestals which suddenly begin to revolve as a background tape plays the appropriate bark or growl. This quiet, unspoilt logging community is these days becoming increasingly popular with Bulgarian trippers and hikers, many of whom stay over at the *turisticheska spalnya* in the heart of the village.

The Troyan pass
South from Troyan, buses begin a slow climb through dense forests towards the **Troyan pass**, where a wonderful panorama suddenly appears as the road crosses the mountains at a height of 1450m. The Stryama valley recedes towards the Sredna Gora, where you can see Mount Bogdan, its highest peak (1714m); beyond lies the Plain of Thrace and the blueish silhouette of the distant Rhodopes. At the foot of the mountains lies KÂRNARE, a nondescript town where you can catch regular buses or trains into the neighbouring **Valley of the Roses** (see Chapter Four).

Between Lovech and Veliko Târnovo

Regular buses make the two-hour journey between Lovech and Veliko Târnovo, picking their way between the wheat- and pasture-covered foothills of the main Balkan Range. Forty kilometres east of Lovech the road joins the main E771 highway at **SEVLIEVO**, a small rural centre whose nineteenth-century buildings have largely escaped the mania for reconstruction and renovation lavished elsewhere. Ul. Skobelevska, the main street, bears a decrepit-looking **church of the Prophet Elijah** with icons by Tryavna masters; next door the **historical museum** at no. 10 (Tues–Sun 8am–noon & 2–6pm), housed in the former village schoolhouse, has displays detailing the various craft industries which characterized town life before the Liberation. One of the more important trades was leatherworking, memories of which are preserved in the **Tabahana**, Tabashka 3 (same times as the museum), a nineteenth-century tannery decked out with original tools and animal skins. There's no reason to stay overnight in Sevlievo, but if you have to there's the *Momina sâlza* **hizha** southeast of town in the Baadalata district.

For those with plenty of time, a car, and a pathological desire to ride the backroads of Bulgaria, a couple of interesting sights lie hidden away to the south of Sevlievo. Minor roads lead to **Gradnitsa** 15km to the southwest, where a medieval fortress tumbles down the slopes of Prechista hill on the south side of the village. Lower layers of the remaining walls are sixth-century Byzantine, but most of the remains date from the Second Bulgarian Kingdom. More intrepid travellers may consider a trip to **Batoshevo monastery** 27km to the south on the old road to APRILTSI, situated high above the west bank of the River Rositsa midway between the villages of Batoshevo and Stokite. Low, barn-like monastery buildings surround the church of the Assumption, whose grey slate roof slopes down over a richly frescoed porch.

Veliko Târnovo

The precipitously perched houses of **VELIKO TÂRNOVO** seem poised to leap into the chasms that divide the city into its separate quarters. Medieval fortifications girdling the Tsarevets massif add melodrama to the scene, yet even more transfixing are the huddles of antique houses that the writer Ivan Vazov likened to frightened sheep, bound to the rocks by wild lilac and vines, forming picturesque reefs veined by steps and narrow streets. Le Corbusier raved about Târnovo's "organic" architecture, and even the dour Prussian field marshal Helmut Von Moltke was moved to remark that he had "never seen a town of more romantic location".

But for Bulgarians the city has a deeper significance. When the National Assembly met here to draft Bulgaria's first constitution in 1879, it consciously did so in the former capital of the Second Kingdom (1185–1396) whose medieval civilization was snuffed out by the Turks. Reclaiming this heritage was an integral part of the National Revival, and since independence (especially during the socialist era) archaeologists have been keenly uncovering the past of Târnovo "the Great" – not only the medieval citadel of **Tsarevets** but also the churches of **Sveta Gora** and **Trapezitsa**. Nor is the city an isolated case, for in the hills and valleys **around Târnovo** are several monasteries and small towns founded during the Second Kingdom or in the aftermath of its collapse, which make great excursions from town.

Târnovo's convenience as a touring base is backed up by the city's **train and bus links** with towns like Dryanovo, Tryavna and Gabrovo to the south – all of which are easy day trips from here.

Practicalities

All trains between Sofia and Varna stop at GORNA ORYAHOVITSA to the north, whence eight local trains daily cover the remaining 13km to Veliko Târnovo. In the middle of the day there's a large gap between services, so you can save time by hopping on the bus shuttle to Gorna Oryahovitsa's bus terminal, from where there's a connection every fifteen minutes (#10 or #14) to Veliko Târnovo.

Târnovo's **train station**, on the Stara Zagora–Ruse line, is 2km south of the centre – bus #4 runs to the main thoroughfare, bul. Levski, but these are so few that it's best to start walking: turn left out of the station yard and keep bearing left until you reach the centre. The **bus terminal** is southwest of town at the end of Nikola Gabrovski: take bus #12 or trolleybus #7 to reach the centre. Advance bus and rail bookings as well as timetable information are available at the *TsKTON* (transport service centre, Mon–Sat 6.30am–noon & 1–6pm), Hristo Botev 12. International rail tickets should be booked through *Rila*, Stamboliiski 1A.

Accommodation

Private rooms are in theory available from a desk in the *Hotel Etâr*, at Ivailo 1, although there seldom seem to be vacancies. Of the **hotels**, the *Etâr* itself (☎21890; ③), an imposing tower block with good views of the old town, has the cheapest beds; the *Yantra*, Velchova Zavera 1 (☎20391; ③) is slightly nearer the sights but slightly more pricey; while the 4-star *Veliko Târnovo*, Emil Popov 2 (☎30571; ④) is of international business standard. The *Orbita* hotel at Hristo Botev 15 is being refurbished and remains an unknown quantity.

Of Târnovo's two **campsites**, *Sveta Gora* (open June–Oct) lies just behind the hill of the same name, fifteen minutes' walk from the railway station; while *Bolyarski stan* (open all year round; ☎40094), just off the Sofia-Varna highway at the western entrance to town, also has cheap **motel rooms**.

Eating and drinking
All of the town's hotels feature reasonably good **restaurants**, usually featuring live music. The folksy *Samovodska sreshta* on the corner of ul. G. Rakovski and pl. G. Kirkov is popular with locals and tourists alike; the *Suhindol*, around the corner at G. Mamarchev 14, offers cheap and filling grills as well as good draught beer. The *Grill-restorant Veliko Târnovo* on pl. Sâedinenie – above the museum of the National Revival – has a limited menu but is very good value.

Most evening **drinking** takes place in the numerous private bars in the old town – try the *Café Bolyarka* at Blagoev 14, or *Simeon i Sin* opposite the entrance to Tsarevets. The *Veliko Târnovo*, Emil Popov 2, has a popular café on a terrace overlooking the river, and also hosts occasional discos. Over the summer, Tsarevets is illuminated by a nightly *son et lumière*, with seating for spectators set out just opposite the entrance to the fortress.

The old town

Lying on an incline, the city's smart modern centre holds most of Târnovo's downtown shopping area along boulevards Levski and Dimitrov. From here you can proceed eastwards on foot and let yourself be drawn gradually into the **old town**. This is fascinating, not so much for its specific sights, of which there are relatively few, but for the feel of the place generally: there's always a fresh view of the city poised above the gorges or some new, unexpected detail.

Heading eastwards along ul. Blagoev, the small **pl. Pobornicheski** or "Combatants' Square" has a monument to local rebel Bacho Kiro and other revolutionaries of 1876, whom the Turks hanged from gallows erected on what was then a rubbish tip. Just above the nearby **pl. P.R. Slaveykov** at ul. Dragoman 15 is the **museum–birthplace** (Tues–Sun 8–10am & 2–5.30pm) of the pedagogue and poet of the same name (1827–95) who, among other things, campaigned for the autonomy of Bulgaria's Orthodox church. But most visitors prefer the **"House of the Little Monkey"** at Vâstanicheska 14, which gets its nickname from the grimacing statuette over the balcony, although the bay windows and deeply pointed brickwork contribute more to the total effect. Like many old Târnovo houses, it sits precariously above a limited groundspace, with orieled living quarters above what used to be a shop or warehouse.

The Ethnographic Museum
As visitors are allowed inside, the former **Inn of Hadzhi Nikolai Minchev** at ul. Rakovski 17 is more satisfying, since it nowadays serves as an **Ethnographic Museum** (daily 10am–5pm). The size of the ground-floor caravanserai reflects Târnovo's commercial upsurge following the Crimean War, which forced the Ottoman empire to accept Western products; the airy, undulating arcades are delightful. Among the woodcarvings, pewter and silverwork on the first floor, the

The telephone code for Veliko Târnovo is ☎062.

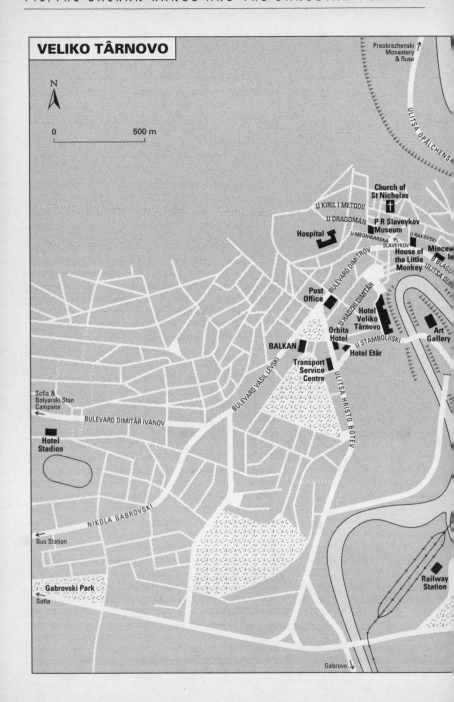

VELIKO TÂRNOVO

N

0   500 m

Preobrazhenski Monastery & Ruse

ULITSA OPÂLCHENS

Church of St Nicholas

U KIRIL I METODII

U DRAGOMAN

Hospital

P R Slaveykov Museum

U MEDNIKARSKA   PL SLAVEYKOV

U RAKOVSKI

House of the Little Monkey

Mincev

B BLAGO

ULITSA GUR

BULEVARD DIMITROV

Post Office

U HADZHI DIMITÂR

Hotel Veliko Târnovo

Orbita Hotel

BALKAN

U STAMBOLIISKI

Hotel Etâr

Art Gallery

Transport Service Centre

BULEVARD VASILLEVSKI

ULITSA HRISTO BOTEV

Sofia & Bolyarski Stan Campsite

BULEVARD DIMITÂR IVANOV

Hotel Stadion

NIKOLA GABROVSKI

Bus Station

Gabrovski Park

Sofia

Railway Station

Gabrovo

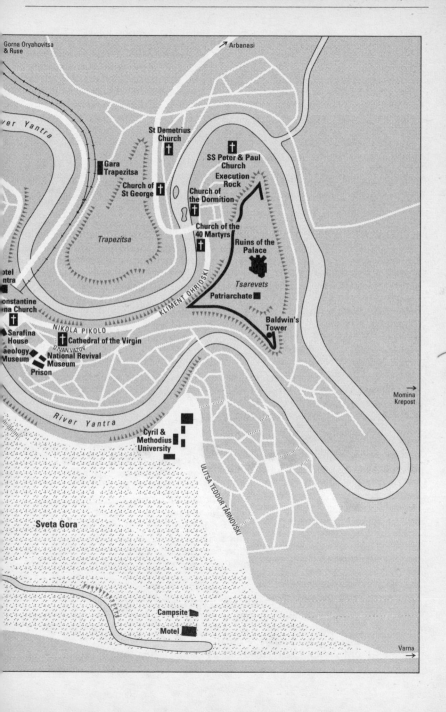

jewel-encrusted belt-clasps are outstanding, and others bearing images of eagles can be seen upstairs together with ecclesiastical art, lace, woollens, bagpipes and peasant wedding costumes. Exhibits on the top floor relate the story of Bulgarian education from the foundation of the first university at Kilifarevo monastery in 1350 to the nineteenth-century campaign for secular Bulgarian-language schooling.

The bazaar and the Varosh quarter

Various restored workshops and an olde-worlde café and pastry shop make up the *Samovodska Charshiya* or **bazaar** at the junction of ul. Rakovski and pl. Georgi Kirkov. It's a good place to observe craftspeople at work, and highly photogenic too, with its wrought-iron garnished facades and cobbled slopes, but it lacks a real bazaar's bustle and hustle. Starting from the square you can follow ul. Vâstanicheska up into the narrow streets of the peaceful old **Varosh quarter**, whose two nineteenth-century churches are verging on the decrepit. The **church of Sveti Nikolai** has, it's said, a carving on the bishop's throne which shows a lion (representing Bulgaria) in the coils of a snake (the Greek church) being devoured by a dragon (Turkey), and up the hill from here the **church of Saints Cyril and Methodius** – with its belfry and dome by the noted architect Fichev – still serves worshippers on ul. Kiril i Metod. If you climb onto the plateau above the Varosh, you can pick up a fairly obvious trail to Preobrazhenski monastery (see p.151).

Heading downhill from pl. Kirkov instead, you're likely to come upon pl. Velchova Zavera (literally, the "Square of Velcho's Plot"), where the glassblower Velcho, Nikola the braid maker, Ivan the furrier and other conspirators were hanged for rebelling against the Turkish authorities in 1835. It's possible to take the stairway behind the *Hotel Yantra* down to the pedestrian **walkway over to Trapezitsa**, but sticking to ul. Ivan Vazov will take you past more of the old town's attractions.

The Sarafina house

To the right you'll catch sight of the **church of Saints Constantine and Elena**, skulking behind foliage at the bottom of a steep flight of steps. From here you can descend to what is perhaps the most characteristic of Târnovo's streets, **ul. General Gurko**, where the houses – mainly dating from Ottoman times – look cunningly picturesque, perched along the curve of the gorge. Don't miss the *Sarafinova Kâshta* or **Sarafina house** at no. 88 (Tues–Fri 8.30am–noon & 1–6pm), which is so contrived that only two floors are visible from General Gurko but a further three overhang the river. The interior is notable for the splendid octagonal vestibule with wrought-iron fixtures and a panelled rosette ceiling which, like the elegantly furnished rooms upstairs, reflects the taste of the architect and owner, the moneylender Dimo Sarafina. The emergence of bourgeois culture in nineteenth-century Târnovo is recalled in the collection of sepia family photographs displayed downstairs.

The museum of the National Revival and the Constituent Assembly

Returning to Ivan Vazov and continuing southwards, you'll soon arrive at pl. Sâedinenie and a spacious blue and white building that houses the *Muzei "Vâzrazhdane i Ureditelno sâbranie"* – the **museum of the National Revival and the Constituent Assembly** (daily 10am–5pm). Designed by Nikolai Fichev in 1872 as the *Konak* of the Turkish governor, Ali Bey (who mounted the trials of the rebels of 1876 here), the building subsequently hosted the first Bulgarian *sâbranie* (parliament), which spent two months in 1879 deliberating the country's first post-Liberation constitution – afterwards known as the *Târnovo Constitution*. The union of Bulgaria and Eastern Roumelia (1885) was also signed here, and this hallowed building was exactly reconstructed (after being devastated by fire) in time to allow the proclamation of People's Power from the premises on September 9, 1944. Exhibits on the ground floor pay tribute to successive generations of Bulgarian patriots, telling the story (mostly through pictures and Bulgarian-only texts) of successive rebellions against the Turks – notably the locally based uprisings of 1598 and 1686. Icons and devotional objects are grouped downstairs, including one sixteenth-century embroidered shroud depicting the Deposition of Christ; there are also nineteenth-century Târnovo metalwork, weights and scales used by the moneylenders and tradesmen of the *charshiya*, and a big still for *rakiya*-brewing. On the first floor is the hall in which the Provisional Assembly sat, its timber-beamed ceiling supported by wooden pillars.

More museums

The adjoining block mounts an **archaeological exposition of medieval Târnovo** (Tues–Sun 8am–noon & 1.30–5.30pm) with lapidry, ceramics, seals, and so on in four halls. Around the corner and lower down the hill, the erstwhile **Museum of the Revolutionary Movement**, housed in the former Turkish **prison**, may by now have been converted to some non-ideological use. Above the square, the modern **cathedral of Sveta Bogoroditsa** stands aloof on a terrace. From here, either ul. Ivan Vazov or Nikola Pikolo leads directly down to the entrance of Tsarevets, the medieval fortress.

Tsarevets

Approaching **Tsarevets** (daily 8am–dusk) along the stone causeway that was erected after the original drawbridge collapsed beneath the Bey's harem, you can appreciate how the boyars Petâr and Asen were emboldened enough by possession of this seemingly impregnable citadel to lead a rebellion against Byzantium in 1185. Petâr's proclamation of the Second Kingdom and his coronation occurred when the empire was already preoccupied by the Magyar and Seljuk Turk menace, and when a punitive Byzantine army was eventually sent in 1190 it was utterly defeated at the Tryavna pass. Now restored and spotlit at night, the ramparts and the Patriarchate (plus the ruins of the palace and various churches) convey something of Tsarevets's grandeur during the Second Kingdom, when travellers deemed Târnovo "second after Constantinople".

Gates and towers

Artisans and clerics serving the palace and the Patriarchate generally resided in the Asenova quarter below the hill, and entered Tsarevets via the **Asenova Gate** halfway along the western ramparts; foreign merchants, invited to settle here by Tsar Asen II, had their own entrance, the "Frankish" or **Frenkhisar Gate** near the southern end of the massif. Rapidly becoming a regional power, the Second Kingdom intervened to help Byzantium overthrow the first Latin Emperor of the East, Baldwin of Flanders, in 1205, the former emperor ending his days as a prisoner in the bastion overlooking the Frenkhisar Gate, thereafter known as **Baldwin's Tower**.

The old palace and the Patriarchate

The **ruins of the palace** seem insignificant compared to the ramparts, but contemporary chronicles and modern excavations suggest that the royal complex was once splendid and opulent. Delicate columns divided the 105ft-long throne room into aisles, which were adorned with green serpentine, Egyptian porphyry and pink marble, and mosaics and murals depicting the rulers of three dynasties. The church of the Blessed Saviour or **Patriarchate**, built early in the thirteenth century, was, significantly, the only structure permitted to surpass the palace in height. Ribbed with red brick and inset with green and orange ceramics, the church – and Tsarevets in general – is now a favourite location for the filming of historical epics.

Execution Rock and the Terterid dynasty

The **Lobna skala** ("Execution Rock") at the sheer northern end of Tsarevets is associated with the dynasty that followed the brief reign of the swineherd **Ivailo** (1277–80). Proclaimed tsar after a popular anti-feudal revolt, Ivailo successfully organized resistance against invading Tatar hordes but neglected to guard against a coup by the *bolyari* (nobles), who had him flung off the rock. The **Terterid** dynasty which followed was chiefly concerned with its own survival and willing to suspect anyone – even the Patriarch, Yoakim III, who was also executed – of collusion with the Tatars; and it was only during the later, four-teenth-century reign of Todor Svetoslav that was there much progress or security.

However, Bulgarian culture – strongly influenced by that of Byzantium – revived during the Shishmanid dynasty (1323–93), and the enlightened rule of Ivan Aleksandâr and his son Ivan Shishman created the conditions whereby medieval Târnovo attained the zenith of its development. Trade with Genoa, Venice and Dubrovnik flourished; hospitals and hospices were maintained by the public purse; students came from Serbia, Russia and Wallachia to study at the university; and Târnovo became one of the Balkans' main centres of painting and literature.

Nonetheless, by the late fourteenth century the Second Kingdom had frag-mented into several semi-autonomous states, and the hegemony of the Kingdom had been dissipated: individually, the states were no match for the expansionist Ottoman Turks, who besieged Târnovo for three months before capturing, plun-dering and burning the city in July 1393.

The Asenova quarter, Trapezitsa and Sveta Gora

To the west of Tsarevets on both banks of the Yantra lies the **Asenova quarter**, where chickens strut and children fish beside the river. During the Middle Ages this was the artisan quarter, which it remained until 1913, when it was struck by an earthquake which levelled most of the medieval buildings and did great damage to the (much reconstructed) churches.

The **church of the Forty Martyrs** (*chetirideset mâchenitsi*), near the bridge – the church with the richest historical associations – is a barn-like edifice founded by Tsar Ivan Asen II to commemorate his victory over the Byzantine rulers of Epirus at Klokotnitsa on Forty Martyrs' Day in 1230. Subsequently much altered, to the extent that it has, apparently, baffled restorers, the church was the burial place of the Serbian Saint Sava* and several Bulgarian tsars, and the Bulgarians saw God's hand behind the collapse of the minaret built when the Turks impiously transformed this into a mosque. Among the pillars within stands Khan Omturag's Column, filched from another site, whose Greek inscription reads in part: "Man dies, even though he lives nobly, and another is born. Let the latest born, when he examines these records, remember him who made them. The name of the Prince is Omurtag, the Sublime Khan". Not to be outdone, Asen had another column inscribed with a list of his conquests from Adrianople to Durazzo (Durrës in Albania), whose inhabitants were spared "by my benevolence".

Further north, the early twentieth-century **church of the Dormition** (Wed–Mon 9am–noon & 1–5.30pm) isn't intrinsically interesting, but stands on the site of the monastery of the Virgin of the Prisoners, where Tsar Ivan Aleksandâr confined his wife as a nun in order to marry the Jewess Sara. The **church of saints Peter and Paul**, 200m beyond, is more remarkable: it contains several capitals in the old Bulgarian style (carved with vineleaves in openwork) and some well-preserved frescoes of which the oldest – dating back to the fourteenth century – is the *Pietà* opposite the altar. On the south wall, opposite the entrance, the church's saints' namesakes are portrayed in a lively manner. The church was the site of the massacre of the *bolyari* in 1393 (only Patriarch Evtimii's intervention dissuaded the Turks from killing the entire population) and, much later, the place where the Ottoman-appointed Greek Patriarch of Bulgaria was evicted by the citizenry.

On the other side of the river are two more venerable and recently restored churches. It was during the consecration of the **church of Sveti Dimitâr** that the *bolyari* Petâr and Asen announced their rebellion against Byzantium, and Sveti Dimitâr (who, legend has it, came from Salonika to help the oppressed Bulgars) became the patron saint of the Second Kingdom. With its red-brick stripes and trefoil windows inlaid with orange plaqucs, Saint Demetrius is the best-looking of the surviving medieval churches, although most of the original frescoes were painted over during the sixteenth and seventeenth centuries. The **church of Sveti Georgi**, further to the south, is smaller but has better-preserved frescoes.

Trapezitsa

Overhead rises the massif known as **Trapezitsa**, where the *bolyari* and leading clergy of the Second Kingdom built their mansions and some forty private churches, sixteen of which are currently being excavated. To be honest, there isn't that much of interest up here, but even today, medieval rings, crosses and other artefacts are being discovered. You can reach the hill by steep footpaths from the Asenova quarter or, more easily, by walking across the railway bridge below the Yantra Hotel, at the end of which there's a path leading onto the massif. From the northwestern side of Trapezitsa, another trail heads off towards the convent of Sveta Troitsa (p.152), about an hour and a halfs' walk northwards into the hills.

The body of **Saint Sava**, founder of the Serbian Orthodox church and a leading figure of the medieval Serbian state, was taken from the church to the monastery of Mileševa (on the border of what are now Serbia and Montenegro in erstwhile Yugoslavia). In 1594 his remains, a potent symbol of Serbian nationalism, were desecrated and destroyed by the occupying Turks.

THE BOGOMILS

Târnovo was the venue for a famous synod of the Bulgarian church in 1211, which tried (unsuccessfully) to curb the growth of a notorious medieval heresy which plagued the Second Bulgarian Kingdom – **Bogomilism**.

The movement is thought to have emerged from the teachings of a tenth-century priest named Bogomil (literally "beloved of God"), who inherited the concept of dualism from the earlier Manichaean and Paulician heresies. This held that the material world was the creation of the devil, and only the soul could be good. The growth of the Bogomils coincided with the fall of the First Bulgarian Kingdom to the Byzantines, and the movement was strongly critical of the Bulgarian establishment; especially the clergy. Left-wing historians have been quick to emphasize Bogomilism's social impact, especially its appeal to the poor.

Our only real knowledge of the Bogomils, however, comes from the movement's enemies – critics like the monk Cosmas, who described them as "lamblike and gentle, and pale from hypocritical fasting", but really "ravening wolves" who "sowed the tares of their preaching" among "simple and uneducated men".

Cosmas was not the only person worried by the spread of the heresy throughout the Balkan peninsula. Byzantine chronicler Anna Comnena relates how her father Emperor Alexius I had the Bogomil leader Basil publicly burned in the Constantinople hippodrome somewhere around 1100. Imperial propaganda accused the Bogomils of all manner of unnatural practices, most common among which was sodomy – the adoption of the word "bugger" by the English language derives from confusion over the terms "Bogomil" and "Bulgar".

Sveta Gora

Sveta Gora ("Holy Hill"), on the south bank of the Yantra, used to be a centre of monastic scholasticism, and nowadays provides the site for the **Cyril and Methodius University**, which can be reached by bus #15 or a bridge to the south of Tsarevets. The rocky spur, linked by footbridge to the *Hotel Veliko Târnovo*, is adorned with an obelisk commemorating the 800th anniversary of the foundation of the Asenid dynasty, but visitors are generally more interested in the contents of the large, copper-roofed **art gallery** nearby, whose theme is "Târnovo through the eyes of diverse painters". A jumble of unchallenging townscapes and lionizations of medieval tsars for the most part, the collection is enlivened by a couple of naive exercises in mid-nineteenth-century portraiture by local artists Nikolai Pavlovich and Georgi Danchov.

Listings

Airlines *Balkan*, Stamboliiski 1A (☎21545). There are two daily flights from Gorna Oryahovitsa airport to Sofia.

Hospital ul. Buzludzha 1 (☎23833).

Markets The main food-buying location is the *Pazar*, an open-air market on the corner of Vasil Levski and Nikola Gabrovski.

Pharmacies Centrally located ones are at pl. Velchova zavera, bul. Levski 23, and bul. Dimitrov 44 – at least one of these will be open at night.

Post office and telephones The main post office is at Hristo Botev 1.

Rail and bus tickets Advance bookings and timetable info from *TsKTON* (transport service centre, Mon–Sat 6.30am–noon & 1–6pm), Hristo Botev 12. International rail tickets from *Rila*, Stamboliiski 1A.

Travel Agencies *Pirin*, Dimitâr Blagoev 79, offers info and bookings on regional *turisti-cheska spalnya* and hikers' chalets.

North of Veliko Târnovo

The terrain **north of Târnovo** is a wild confusion of massifs sundered by the River Yantra and its tributaries, abounding in rocky shelves rendered almost inaccessible by forests and torrents. Nearly twenty monasteries were established here during the Second Kingdom, and several survived the Turkish invasion. These formed a symbiotic relationship with the later towns and villages founded by refugees after the sack of Târnovo. With a car it's feasible to visit the main sites within a day, but relying on public transport (or hiking), one expedition a day seems more realistic.

Arbanasi

Hiding high on a plateau 4km northeast of Târnovo, and overlooking Tsarevets and Trapezitsa to the south, **ARBANASI** is one of Bulgaria's most picturesque villages, resembling a cross between a *kasbah* and the kind of *pueblo* that Clint Eastwood rids of bandits. People vanish into their family strongholds for the siesta, and at high noon only chickens stalk the rutted streets.

The origins of Arbanasi have presented scholars with a characteristically Balkan ethnological puzzle. The village's name has led some to suggest that it was founded by Albanian refugees fleeing Turkish reprisals after a failed fifteenth-century uprising, although this is disputed by modern Bulgarian historians eager to establish the continuity of Slav settlement in the area. What's beyond doubt is that the people who lived here in the village's eighteenth-century heyday belonged to the Greek cultural orbit, speaking Greek and giving their children Greek names. The inhabitants grew rich on the proceeds of cattle-droving, drying meat for their own consumption and selling the fat to the local Muslims, who considered it a delicacy. The leather was loaded onto caravans and taken east, where it was exchanged for Asiatic luxury goods like silk and spices.

Arbanasi's merchants invested their wealth in the big, fortress-like stone houses for which the village is famed, but they also endowed churches, chapels and public drinking fountains, turning the town into a lively urban centre for the local Christian population, hidden from the eyes of Ottoman-dominated Târnovo below. In the nineteenth century, however, commerce became increasingly centred on Târnovo and other lowland towns, forcing Arbanasi's merchants to relocate their businesses, and sending the village into decline.

Practicalities

Despite Arbanasi's proximity to Târnovo, both the gradient and the amount of traffic on the road make it an unappetizing walk – it's easier to take one of the seven daily **buses** from Târnovo's main terminal, or one of the privately owned minibuses which shuttle sporadically up to the village from bul. Levski (these are often unmarked, so you'll have to rely on local knowledge). A kiosk on Arbanasi's main square sells all-inclusive **tickets** to the town's museum-houses and churches, which tend to be open from Tuesday to Sunday from 10am to noon and from 2pm to 6pm – although be prepared for unpredictable closures out of season.

Although most visitors base themselves in Târnovo and come up to Arbanasi for the day, the village does have two **hotels**: the small, family-run *Konstantin i Elena* (well signposted upon entering the village; ②), and the more luxurious *Arbanasi Palace* (⑥) which occupies one of Todor Zhivkov's former villas. The latter is a white concrete monstrosity on the southern edge of the village commanding splendid views of the Tsarevets massif immediately below. A brief visit to the timber-ceilinged hotel bar will be sufficient to give you an idea of the former dictator's taste for opulence.

Around the village: some churches and the town history museum

Squatting on high ground just above Arbanasi's main square is the **church of the Archangels Michael and Gabriel** – the pair are depicted in a mural above the western portal. Dating from 1600, the church is a solid brick structure adorned with irregular lines of blind arcading, its gloomy interior illuminated by tiny, iron-grilled windows. Local schoolmaster Hristo was called on in the early eighteenth century to execute most of the surviving frescoes, including a panoramic *Nativity* scene in the apse, but look out also for the later *Virgin Horanta* painted jointly by itinerant masters Georgi of Bucharest and Mihail of Salonika.

A cobbled path leads south of the main square towards the asymmetrical, red-tiled roof of the **church of Sveti Dimitâr**. The original church perished in the earthquake of 1913, and the pale, unweathered stones of its modern reconstruction make it look more like a suburban bungalow than a place of worship. Some of the interior frescoes have been restored, and vibrant portraits of the two archangels preside over the adjoining chapel of Sveti Nestor. Richly carved Greek and Bulgarian headstones are propped up against the outer walls.

From here you can't miss the pristine white plasterwork of the neighbouring **Hadzhiiliev house**, where a small **town history museum** details the various disasters that befell Arbanasi and presaged its fall from prosperity. The town was sacked three times in the early nineteenth century by the *kârdzhali*, Turkish outlaws who menaced the townsfolk of the Balkans, and mass emigration in the war-ravaged winter of 1877 served to confirm Arbanasi's decline. Further along, the diminutive **church of Sveti Atanas** sits on a spur of the hillside, where more rough-hewn, slanting tombstones litter the churchyard. Inside, the best of the frescoes are to be found in the Haralampi chapel, where an eighteenth-century *Last Judgement* (painted by another brace of local schoolmasters, Tsoyu and Nedyo) shows hordes of halo-gilded righteous folk trooping off to the walled garden of paradise.

Returning to the village square and taking the main road west soon leads to the most sumptuously decorated of Arbanasi's churches, the **church of the Nativity** (*Rozhdestvo Hristovo*). Like the others it's outwardly plain, but inside you'll find richly coloured frescoes. On the north wall is a genealogy of Christ, and in the gallery a frieze of Greek philosophers. The iconostasis contains notable scenes of the Creation and the Fall, and an extravagantly colourful pietà. Both the main body of the church and the chapel of Saint John the Baptist have separate areas for men and women to pray, and at the end of services it was customary for the local nobles to distribute alms in the wide corridor behind the portico.

The Kostantsaliev house

Beyond the church a path leads to the **Kokona fountain**, built in 1786 on the orders of Mehmed Said Ali, author of its Arabic inscription: "He who looks upon me and drinks my water shall possess the light of the eyes and of the soul". About 100m further on is arguably the finest of Arbanasi's mansions, the **Kostantsaliev house**. Like other dwellings erected after the conflagration that gutted Arbanasi in 1798, the ground floor (with servants' quarters and store-rooms) is built of stone and entered via a nail-studded gate, while the upper floor is made of wood. Many of the rooms have beautiful panelled ceilings and ornate plaster cornices bearing geometric or floral motifs. It's not hard to imagine the former owner, the Kokona Sultana (a relation of the Bey), greeting her guests on the wooden staircase that ascends to the reception hall, from which one door leads to the "winter room" or communal bedroom. The other opens onto a corri-dor leading to the dining room and the office of her merchant husband, furnished with a low table or *sofra* topped with a coffee set.

The monasteries

Tracks lead downhill from here to the **monastery of Sveta Bogoroditsa** at the northwestern end of town, whose church presides over a tranquil courtyard frequented by the occasional nun. The church itself is unremarkable, a product of successive destructions and rebuildings, but some seventeenth-century frescoes still survive in the naos and the adjoining chapel of Sveta Troitsa. To the west, beside the main road leading out of town to Veliko Târnovo, is the **monastery of Sveta Nikola**, a predominantly modern-looking complex completely refurbished in the 1890s. The chapel of Sveta Iliya inside the monastery church retains some eighteenth-century murals – the richly coloured scenes from the life of Christ are as fine as any in Arbanasi.

Preobrazhenski monastery and Sveta Troitsa convent

Four kilometres north of Târnovo, lurking high in the crags above the main E85 road to Ruse, is **Preobrazhenski monastery** – the monastery of the Transfiguration. Although the original monastery (founded in 1360 and situated further to the south) was destroyed in the early 1800s, its successor almost looks old enough to be medieval, with a canopy of vines strung between the spartan cells and small churches surrounding the courtyard.

Aping the vines, a flowery motif runs beneath the roof of the **Transfiguration church**, whose south wall bears a remarkable painting of the *Wheel of Life*. The stages of human existence correspond with allegorical representations of the four seasons: bleak winter is accompanied by Death with a scythe, a monster's mouth claims sinners, while in the centre of the circle a woman holding an empty chal-ice symbolizes the negation of the material world. Rose- and green-hued **frescoes** predominate in the esonarthex, where an eye in a circle (traditional symbol of the Holy Ghost) is a recurrent motif, whereas the lower naos (formerly reserved for men) is darker, with saints surrounding Christ beneath the dome and submissive dragons flanking the crucifix. Evil-doers are thrust across a river of fire and stran-gled by demons in the *Last Judgement* by Zahari Zograf, whose portrait hangs in the esonarthex beside that of Vasil Levski. Levski hid away in the caves above the monastery – Bulgaria's monks could always be relied upon to aid the revolution-ary struggle. Preobrazhenski's patriotic credentials were advanced further when the monastery served as a field hospital for Russian troops during the Liberation War, and was rewarded by Tsar Aleksandâr's presentation of a crystal chandelier which still hangs in the Transfiguration church.

Practicalities

There are two ways of **getting to the monastery** – by road or on foot. Number 10 buses from Târnovo to Gorna Oryahovitsa take you past the monastery turn-off 4km north of town, from where a minor road zigzags 3km uphill through a lime forest to Preobrazhenski, passing a **campsite** (with a restaurant and chalets) on the way. The two-hour **footpath** to the monastery begins on the plateau above Târnovo's Varosh quarter and meanders northwards through gullies that get steadily more wooded and choked with mossy boulders. Although you should eventually catch sight of the monastery nestled beneath a cliff, there doesn't appear to be any path covering the last stretch, so you'll probably have to steer a course for the road to the monastery instead.

Samovodene

Two kilometres north of the monastery is the village of **SAMOVODENE** (midway between Târnovo and Gorna Oryahovitsa, it's visited by the #10 bus), an unremarkable village save for an ancient **tell** a few metres east of the main road, where layer upon layer of archaeological remains have been left by successive settlements dating back to the sixth millennium BC. With excavation still in progress there's little to see save for a series of trenches cut into the crest of a knoll, but a small kiosk at the site entrance has info about recent finds.

Sveta Troitsa convent

More or less opposite Preobrazhenski on the other side of the valley, a narrow shelf provides the site for **Sveta Troitsa convent**, which can *only* be approached on foot. It should take you about an hour and a half to walk, following the path that starts on the northwestern side of Trapezitsa (near the Trapezitsa railway halt) and runs along the cliff. Possibly founded as early as the eleventh century, Sveta Troitsa was actually a monastery rather than a nunnery during the Second Kingdom, when Patriarch Evtimii established a school of translators here. Although Holy Trinity's church (also built during the nineteenth century by Nikolai Fichev) is less impressive than the principal one at Preobrazhenski monastery, the nuns dress more austerely than their male counterparts, in a black veil, robe and round hat.

Nicopolis ad Istrum

The **ruins of Nicopolis ad Istrum**, 17km north of Târnovo as the crow flies, attest that the Yantra Valley was settled long before the Bulgars arrived. Founded by Emperor Trajan in 107 and named after his victory over the Dacians, Nicopolis ad Istrum was an important administrative centre and garrison town in the Roman empire's lower Danubian province, *Moesia Inferior*. During the second and third centuries the town commanded the Danube-Constantinople and Sofia-Black Sea roads, and its commercial opportunities attracted merchants, artisans and retired legionaries from all over the empire. Within its walls, the town was centred around a forum with temples dedicated to an eclectic pantheon of deities and a covered theatre that was unique in the Balkans – though the onslaught of the Goths and Avars in the third and seventh centuries respectively have left comparatively little to see. The best-preserved structure is the reservoir to the east, originally fed by a 25km-long aqueduct running from a cave near Mustina, but otherwise there are only steps, stumps of walls, various columns and altars, and a few marble statues.

The site lies 3km west of the E85 Târnovo-Ruse highway just short of the modern village of NIKYUP. Three buses a day run from Târnovo to the village (check carefully the times of return services before setting out), after which it's a 25-minute walk to the ruins themselves.

South of Veliko Târnovo

The mill town of **Gabrovo** is the main urban centre **south of Târnovo**, although it's in the smaller towns and villages, where rural architecture and crafts have been best preserved – notably **Tryavna**, **Bozhentsi**, and the museum-village of **Etâr** – where the main attractions lie. Several historic **monasteries**, such as Kilifarevo, Dryanovo and Sokolski, are within easy striking distance of these places. Veliko Târnovo, Gabrovo and Tryavna are equally convenient as bases from which to explore the region, and even if you're reliant on **public transport** you'll find that several destinations can be reached within the space of one day. Both Dryanovo and Tryavna are linked directly to Veliko Târnovo by rail, although travelling on by train to Gabrovo involves an awkward change at TSAREVA LIVADA. Buses, too, are plentiful, with hourly services linking the area's major towns. Less well served by public transport are the little-visited monasteries near the historic town of **Elena** to the southeast, although they present an easily digestible cluster of rustic sights to those with access to a car.

Travelling onwards to the Valley of the Roses (see Chapter Four) from here involves two of Bulgaria's most scenic mountain routes. The Veliko Târnovo-Tryavna railway winds its way southwards through the densely wooded **Tryavna pass** (where Petâr and Asen defeated the Byzantine army in 1190, preserving the independence of the Second Kingdom), before joining the Sofia-Burgas line at DÂBOVO. If travelling by road, the E85 aims for the impressive **Shipka pass** just above Gabrovo (the place to catch buses over the pass), then drops down towards Bulgaria's rose capital, Kazanlâk.

Southeast of Veliko Târnovo: Kilifarevo and Elena

The nineteenth-century crafts centre of **Elena**, 40km southeast of Târnovo, lacks the concentration of historic buildings offered by Tryavna, Bozhentsi or Etâr, but the various monasteries which are scattered along the route make for an interesting trip. Travellers dependent on the region's rural bus services will find it difficult to visit more than one or two of these sights in the space of a day; but for car-drivers at least, an itinerary taking in Elena and neighbouring monasteries provides access to a rural Bulgaria relatively untouched by the restorers and rebuilders of the heritage industry.

The main road between Târnovo and Elena leaves the E771 6km northeast of town at LYASKOVETS, crossing arable farming land before reaching the village of MERDANIYA, site of the **monastery of the Forty Martyrs**. Founded on the spot where Patriarch Yoakim II rode out to greet Tsar Ivan Aleksandâr after his victory at Klokotnitsa in 1230, the monastery was abandoned until the nineteenth century, when it was rebuilt around a lumpish neo-Byzantine church, its domes bristling with rusting wrought-iron crosses.

There's more to see, however, on the **old road to Elena**, which leaves the Târnovo-Gabrovo road at Debelets. The monasteries of **Plakovo** and **Kapinovo** lie en route, while that of **Kilifarevo**, a major seat of learning during the Second Kingdom, is only a short detour away.

Kilifarevo

Seventeen kilometres due south of Veliko Târnovo and served by nine daily buses, **KILIFAREVO MONASTERY** was a favourite retreat for the tsars of the Second Kingdom. It was also the site of the famous college established by Teodosii Târnovski in 1350, which translated literary works from Greek into the Slavonic script, making them legible to scholars far beyond Bulgaria. Important Russian patriarchs and metropolitans were among the students here, and the School of Kilifarevo might have achieved parity with the great European universities had it not been destroyed during the Turkish invasion.

Like other monasteries around Târnovo, Kilifarevo was rebuilt during the nineteenth century around a principal church – dedicated to the Virgin – designed by Fichev, containing an iconostasis by Tryavna craftsmen. An icon of Teodosii can be seen on the right inside the second chapel, to the northeast of the main church, while the third chapel (to the southwest) dates back to the fourteenth or fifteenth century. You'll find the monastery roughly 2km south of KILIFAREVO village in the Belitsa dell, visible from the Nova Zagora road, from which a track leads 500m to a wooden bridge opposite the monastery gate.

Onwards to Elena

Another monastery lies seven kilometres to the east of Kilifarevo in a wooded valley near the commune of PLAKOVO, which some buses from Târnovo visit after calling at Kilifarevo. Father Sergius, **Plakovo Monastery**'s superior, was involved in the Velcho conspiracy (see p.144) and tortured to death by the Turks after its discovery; a plaque on the stone fountain in the courtyard commemorates him and his fellow conspirators. Tracks continue 2km beyond Plakovo monastery to the more impressive **Kapinovo Monastery**, where the timber verandahs of the monks' cells overlook a courtyard shaded by vines. Sofronii Vrachanski was head monk here before being elevated to the bishopric of Vratsa in 1794, putting the monastery at the forefront of the revival of Bulgarian language and scholarship. Outwardly unremarkable, the monastery church contains an unmissable *Day of Judgement* painted by Razgrad master Yovan Popovich in 1845, with lurid scenes of the dead emerging from their graves.

ELENA, 20km further east, was similar to towns like Tryavna, Kotel and Koprivshtitsa in providing a rural base, sufficiently distant from the centres of Ottoman power, in which Bulgarian crafts and culture could re-emerge. The painters and woodcarvers of nineteenth-century Elena decorated the churches of the surrounding countryside, and patriotic local merchants financed the restoration of nearby monasteries Kapinovo and Merdaniya. However, much less money has been lavished on Elena than on similar centres of the National Revival, and although you'll see plenty of nineteenth-century structures in the town centre – especially just south of the main square – you're unlikely to encounter much in the way of tourist facilities or foreign visitors. **Accommodation** is limited to the basic *Hotel Elena* (☎06151/3732; ②) in the centre of town, or dorm beds at the nearby *turisticheska spalnya Dr Momchilov*.

Beyond Elena, buses head east through lonely highland villages towards the wooded **Kotel pass**, on the far side of which lie the historic settlements of **Kotel** and **Zheravna** (see Chapter Four).

Dryanovo

Thirty kilometres southwest of Târnovo on the main road to Gabrovo, **DRYANOVO** is by no means as pretty as its near-neighbours Bozhentsi and Tryavna, but it does retain a limited core of nineteenth-century architecture around the northern end of ul. Shipka, the town's main street. The area is dominated by the **Perevata kâshta**, an all-timber building dating from the 1840s and the last surviving example of the houses which used to line the street, hiding the ground-floor *dyukyani* or artisans' workshops behind heavy wooden shutters.

A few steps beyond, on pl. Kolyo Ficheto, a more contemporary structure houses the **Nikolai Fichev museum** (Tues–Sun 8am–noon & 1–5pm), honouring the locally born architect. Popularly remembered as "Kolyo Ficheto", he was the most versatile of nineteenth-century Bulgaria's builders, responsible for town houses in Târnovo, bridges at Lovech and Byala, and numerous churches. The museum also includes material on the history of Dryanovo, which was founded during the late fourteenth or early fifteenth century. Deriving its prosperity from vineyards and the silkworms which proliferated in the surrounding dogwood trees (*dryani*), Dryanovo's economy was crippled late in the nineteenth century by outbreaks of phylloxera and a disease striking cocoons. Only over the past few decades has it revived, with the introduction of new industries and the replanting of the vineyards.

Opposite the museum is an early nineteenth-century **Kiliino uchilishte** or elementary school, a fragile little structure of wood and stone; and beyond that, the 1845 **church of Sveta Troitsa**, noted for its delicate timber-framed porch.

Dryanovo monastery

Set in a gorge beneath high crags, **Dryanovo monastery** was chosen as the place from which to launch a local uprising in May 1876, while the fires of rebellion were still smouldering elsewhere after the suppression of the April Rising. Under the leadership of Bacho Kiro and the monk Hariton, several hundred rebels defended the monastery for almost a week against 10,000 Turkish troops rushed from Shumen, whose commander Pasha Faslâ offered to spare Kiro if he publicly repented – and hanged him when he refused. The rebels' bones are contained within an ossuary, and the monastery owns a collection of 150 icons, best of which are the sixteenth-century *St Zosim Greets Holy Mary from Egypt* and *The Prophet Daniel*. A short way beyond the monastery lies the **Bacho Kiro cave**, where Palaeolithic remains have been discovered.

The monastery is 4km south of the town itself, accessible via a track which branches off the main E85 road to Gabrovo. Buses to Gabrovo should drop you off at the end of the track (ask for *spirkata za manastir*) if you want to avoid the walk.

Practicalities

Dryanovo's train and bus stations are both to be found a couple of blocks east of the main thoroughfare, ul. Shipka. Be warned, however, that some buses on the Târnovo-Dryanovo-Gabrovo route only stop on the main street. You can **stay** in town at the 2-star *Hotel Milkana*, ul. Bacho Kiro (☎0676/2261; ③), although there's more tourist accommodation near the monastery in the shape of the *Momini Skali* complex, comprising hotel (☎0676/2471; ③), motel and campsite (open June–Aug).

Tryavna

The old crafts centre of **TRYAVNA** may be a byword for icon painting and wood-carving and feature no fewer than 140 listed buildings, yet it happily lacks the feel of a museum-town. Most of its visitors seem to be Bulgarians rather than foreigners, and you're likelier to encounter art students sketching than coach parties jostling for a photo opportunity. For car-less travellers, trains from Târnovo or regular buses from Gabrovo provide the best means of **getting there** (travelling by rail from Gabrovo entails a change at VÂRBANOVO, which makes it quicker to go by bus).

The town's narrow streets are evocative of the nineteenth century: although Tryavna was founded by refugees from Târnovo 400 years ago, the oldest buildings all post-date the establishment of an official Guild of Master-builders and Woodcarvers in 1804. Often carved with birds and flowers, the wooden houses in the **old quarter** have an asymmetrical structure that disguises the essential similarity of their interiors. Traditionally, the large room containing the hooded *kusti* (hearth) was the centre of domestic life and led directly to the *chardak* or covered terrace; guests were received in a separate room and household goods stored in the ground-floor *odaya*.

Tryavna's museum-houses are open Wed–Sun 8am–noon & 1.30–6pm in summer and Wed–Sun 8am–noon & 1–5pm in winter, unless otherwise stated.

Arriving – and the north end of town

Tryavna is pretty easy to find your way around: turn right out of either **rail** or **bus stations**, both north of the centre, and by walking straight on you'll pass most of the town's sights along the way. Most of the northern end of town is modern, although the **birthplace of Angel Kânchev** at ul. Dimitrov 39 is a prime example of the nineteenth-century Tryavna housebuilder's art. Most of it was the work of Kânchev's father, Kâncho Angelov Popnikolov, his skilled handiwork revealed in details such as the wooden panels and fitted cupboards lining many of the rooms. Born in 1850, Kânchev's patriotism led him to join Belgrade's Artillery School at the age of seventeen, and later spurn a lucrative job offer to work for Bulgaria's liberation. Sent to assist Levski in constructing the revolutionary underground, Kânchev had completed two clandestine "tours" by 1872, when he was caught boarding a steamer at Ruse without a passport. Fearful of betraying secrets under torture, he shot himself, crying "Long live Bulgaria!" – in Levski's words, "the most honourable death for justice that should be considered sweetest for every proud Bulgarian of today".

Around the main square

Before long ul. Dimitrov hits **pl. Kapetan Dyado Nikola**, a set-piece square which retains most of its nineteenth-century character. Dominating the scene is the **clock tower**, a solid stone pillar topped by a half-timbered octagonal structure which supports a dainty wooden bell tower. The **church of Archangel Michael** (daily 8am–noon & 3–6pm) stands to one side, a low-lying edifice sheltering under the shallow overhang of its slate roof, from which a slender minaret-like tower emerges. Inside, the iconostasis is wonderfully rich and dark, with twelve intricate tableaux surrounding the crucifix and a carved pulpit wound around one of the columns. At the rear of the church, originally founded by the *bolyari* Petâr and Asen to commemorate their successful twelfth-century rebellion against Byzantium, memorial photographs of the recently deceased are stuck into candelabras, part of the Orthodox forty-day mourning rite which Bulgarians also observe by putting up posters in the streets.

Immediately next door is the **Staroto uchilishte** or old school, its heavy wooden doors leading to a cobbled courtyard surrounded by a timber gallery draped with ivy. A downstairs gallery showcases the work of Tsvetan Dobrev, a local contemporary architect who presented the town with his watercolours – mostly documenting his travels in east European cities such as Berlin, Warsaw and Wroclav. On the first floor is another gallery, this time devoted to sentimental images of Bulgarian womanhood by modern Veliko Târnovo painter Nikola Kazakov; and several museum collections, including an exhibition of the time-pieces imported by wealthy Tryavana families of the last century.

Between the school and the church, an alley leads to **Raikova kâshta** at Ivan Yonkov 1. Originally the home of scientist Pencho Raikov, the "father of Bulgarian chemistry", exhibits within concentrate on the domestic life of Tryavna's late-nineteenth-century middle class, displaying the mass-produced furniture and crockery which began to penetrate Bulgaria from the west.

Along ul. Slaveikov

A bridge leads from the square to the cobbled ul. Slaveikov, possibly the best preserved National Revival-period street in all Bulgaria. Unusually for a Tryavna building, the **Daskalov house** at no. 27 has a symmetrical plan with two wings joined by a curved verandah. The rooms inside are brightly carpeted, with arched windows and inbuilt *minder*, and also contain superb panelled ceilings – sun motifs made from walnut wood, with fretted rays inlaid within a frame decorated with floral and bird shapes. The ground floor holds a small museum of woodcarving, displaying the products of the State Woodcarving School, established in Tryavna in the 1920s to ensure the craft's survival.

Further along ul. Slaveikov are a couple more exhibitions of works donated by local artists: the **Totyu Gâbenski Picture Gallery** at no. 45, and the **Ivan Kolev Exhibition House** (open Monday to Friday only) at no 47. The personal effects

---

WEIRD BULGARIAN HOUSE-BUILDING RITUALS

There were a number of unusual **customs and rituals surrounding house building** in Bulgaria. It was considered unlucky to build a house near an empty well, an old watermill or a graveyard, and when doubts arose about a prospective site a bowl of water would be left there for bad omens (impurities or clouding) to appear overnight. Before the foundations were laid an animal was slaughtered on the site of the hearth or threshold, and the outlines of the walls were marked by dripping blood as an additional magical precaution. When the house was complete, blessings were shouted and the owners presented the builders with gifts before moving in themselves, preferably on a Monday, Thursday or Sunday at the time of a new moon. By custom, the eldest man would pour water over the threshold and scatter coins and wheat around the hearth in the hope of a future life "as smooth as water", prosperity and full barns. Once he had kindled the first fire with embers from the old family hearth, the woman of the family completed the occupation by breaking a loaf over the flames and hanging up a copper vessel.

of the influential writer and teacher Petko Slaveikov (who taught the young Kânchev) and his son, the poet Pencho Slaveikov, are displayed in the **Slaveikov museum** at no. 50 – Petko's residence for 26 years and Pencho's birthplace. Petko Slaveikov began a distinguished career in patriotism by editing Bulgarian newspapers in Constantinople, his texts fulminating against enemies of the people such as the Greek clergy and the native *chorbadzhii*. In the War of Liberation, he guided Russian troops over the Simitli pass in Macedonia. Settling down to life as a teacher in Tryavna he presided over a precocious brood; quite apart from the poet Pencho, Petko's children included a future minister of education, a minister of justice, and a general in the Bulgarian army. As usual, captions are in Bulgarian only but the house itself is worth seeing: the rooms are quite comfortable, but features such as the low table in the kitchen, and the simple, functional *minder* in the living room, point to a lifestyle rather more ascetic than that enjoyed by rich merchants like Daskalov.

By heading west from ul. Slaveikov, across the railway line and up ul. Breza, you'll reach a stairway which climbs to a church-like edifice housing the **Museum of Icon-painting and Woodcarving**. Inside are numerous sumptuous products of the nineteenth-century **Trevnenska shkola** or "School of Tryavna" – a guild with a distinctive style of cutting the wood back until acanthus leaves, birds and other favourite motifs were rendered in openwork like lace covering the surface of the iconostasis.

Practicalities

Tryavna has a couple of good **hotels**: the 3-star *Tryavna* in the town centre (☎0677/3448; ④) and the 2-star *Ralitsa* (☎0677/2219; ③); although dorm beds at the *turisticheska spalnya*, ul. Dimitrov 58, are significantly cheaper. There are numerous small cafés on pl. Kapitan Dyado Nikola and along ul. P.R. Slaveikov; the *Balabanovata kâshta* at Slaveikov 33 is a good place to **eat**.

Bozhentsi

Lying roughly between Gabrovo and Tryavna, **BOZHENTSI**'s cluster of two-storey houses with stone roofs and wooden verandahs gives some idea of the museum-village Tryavna could so easily have become. According to legend, Bozhentsi was founded by survivors of the fall of Târnovo, led by the noblewoman Bozhena and her nine sons. During the second half of the nineteenth-century, Bozhentsi grew prosperous through the enterprise of its smiths, potters and weavers, and local merchants who traded as far afield as Hungary and Russia. It's now a holiday resort for the architects', artists' and writers' unions.

There are well over a hundred listed buildings in the village, but the main highlights are the **Kâshtata na Doncho Popa**, the early nineteenth-century home of a wool merchant; the **Baba Kostadinitsa house**, a much more humble dwelling which showcases the frugal lifestyle of the rural majority; and the various **workshops** used by village artisans (all the houses are open daily summer: 8am–7pm, winter: 8am–5pm).

There's no tourist accommodation in Bozhentsi so it's inevitably a day excursion from elsewhere. There are occasional buses direct from Gabrovo to Bozhentsi during the summer: more regular are the Gabrovo-Tryavna services which call at the *Torbalbuzh* stop about 2km downhill from Bozhentsi.

Gabrovo

People in every country tell jokes about the miserliness of a particular community, and in Bulgaria the butt of the gags is **GABROVO**. According to such **jokes**, *gabrovtsi* invented the one-stotinka coin, gliding, short skirts, narrow trousers, and matchboxes with only one side for striking; they stop their clocks at night and carry their shoes to reduce wear and tear; let a cat down the chimney rather than hire a sweep; and dock the tails of these luckless creatures so they can shut the door a fraction sooner, conserving warmth. One *gabrovets* says to another, "Whenever I see you I immediately think of Stoyan". "Why?" "Because he owes me 60 leva, too". Another thinks, "Hmm, Pencho has been put on a strict diet. . . we can invite him to dinner". Two *gabrovtsi* have a wager on who can give least when the collection plate comes around; the first donates one stotinka, whereupon the other crosses himself piously and tells the sexton, "That was for both of us". And so on . . .

The *gabrovtsi* themselves apparently relish this reputation, and with their legendary skill for profit-making have turned wit into an industry. Long known for producing leatherwork and textiles which earned Gabrovo the sobriquet of the "Manchester of Bulgaria", the town now attracts thousands of visitors every year to its "Louvre of Laughter", the **Dom na Humora i Satirata**, the House of Humour and Satire, opened on April Fool's Day 1974 on the initiative of one Stefan Furtunov – the man also responsible for twinning Gabrovo with Aberdeen. Gabrovnian jollity reaches a climax in **May** every odd-numbered year, when masked carnivals, folk music, pop, dixieland jazz, comedy films, animated cartoons, prize-givings and the ritual "cutting off the Gabrovnian cat's tail" enliven the town during the **Biennial Festival of Humour and Satire**.

Around town

Standing at the northern end of Gabrovo's thin, straggling town centre, the **Dom na Humora i Satirata** (daily 9am–noon & 2–6pm) will probably be your first port of call if arriving at the nearby bus and train stations. Inside is a collection of 113,000 cartoons, humorous writings and photos, carnival masks and costumes drawn from scores of countries across the world. Since exhibits are changed regularly, you'll hopefully encounter something other than the barrage of anti-Reagan and sexist caricatures displayed here during the pre-1989 period (when very few visitors seemed to be laughing) – selections of which appear in *A Propos* magazine, published in several languages twice a year. The museum is also home to Gabrovo's **Experimental Satirical Theatre**, a cabaret centre occasionally showing films and videos, which opened in 1985.

As usual, the older quarters are the nicest part of town, covering both banks of the River Yantra beyond the **Igoto Bridge**. A statue of Gabrovo's legendary sixteenth-century founder, Racho the Blacksmith, stands on a rock in midstream. The main downtown area is on the east bank grouped around ul. Radetska, although specific sights really boil down to a row of renovated **craft workshops** along ul. Opâlchenska and the **historical museum** (Tues–Sat 9am–noon & 1.30–5.30pm) at ul. Genev 3. An absorbing archaeological section displays the results of a dig carried out at nearby Gradishte in the 1920s, the site of both Thracian and medieval Bulgarian fortresses. Finds include functional Thracian pottery and a suit of medieval chain mail armour.

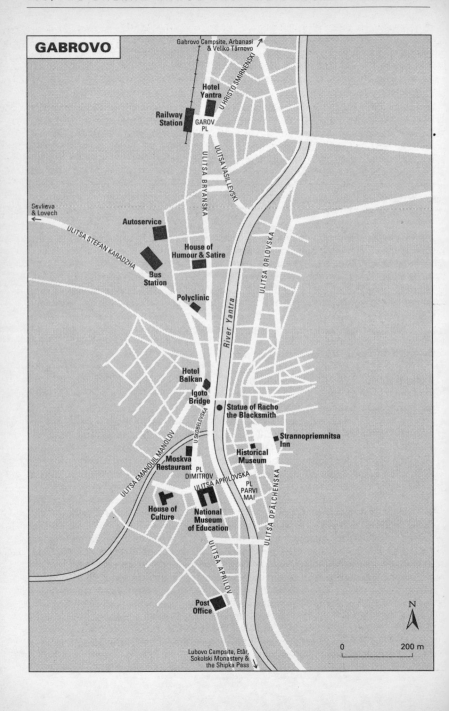

GABROVO

Gabrovo Campsite, Arbanasi
& Veliko Tårnovo

U HRISTO SMIRNENSKI

Hotel
Yantra

Railway
Station

GAROV
PL

ULITSA VASILEVSKI

ULITSA BRYANSKA

Gevlievo
& Lovech

ULITSA STEFAN KARADZHA

Autoservice

House of
Humour & Satire

ULITSA ORLOVSKA

Bus
Station

Polyclinic

River Yantra

Hotel
Balkan

Igoto
Bridge

Statue of Racho
the Blacksmith

U SOBELEVSKA

ULITSA EMANQUIL MANOLOV

Strannopriemnitsa
Inn

Moskva
Restaurant

Historical
Museum

PL
DIMITROV

ULITSA APRILOVSKA

PL
PARVI
MAI

ULITSA OPALCHENSKA

House of
Culture

National
Museum
of Education

ULITSA APRILOV

Post
Office

N

Lubovo Campsite, Etår,
Sokolski Monastery &
the Shipka Pass

0   200 m

Crossing the river by ul. Aprilovska brings you to the **Aprilov School**, founded
by Vasil Aprilov in 1872 and one of the first schools in the country to offer a
secular education in the Bulgarian language. It now houses the **national
museum of education** (Mon–Thurs & Sat 9am–noon & 1–6pm; Fri 9am–noon),
two floors of didactic displays which begin with pictures and texts outlining the
civilizing mission of the medieval Bulgarian state – bearer of the new Slavic
alphabet developed by SS Cyril and Methodius. Upstairs are a series of
reconstructed nineteenth-century schoolrooms (often filled with parties of
schoolchildren), showing the trays of sand which, in the absence of slates, were
used by the pupils for writing on.

Pl. Georgi Dimitrov, Gabrovo's showpiece square, opens up beyond the
building, the site of an archetypal piece of heroic socialist sculpture: the
monument to **Mitko Palaouzov**. Only 14 years old when he was killed fighting
fascists in 1944, Palaouzov is honoured as "an example to be followed by all
Bulgarian children", his monument flanked by two youngsters bearing
kalashnikovs.

Practicalities

Balkantourist are at Opâlchenska 2 (Mon–Fri 8am–noon & 1–6.30pm). Vacancies
can be scarce during the Biennial, but otherwise there shouldn't be any problem
with **accommodation**. Both the 3-star *Hotel Balkan*, ul. Emanuil Manolov
(☎066/21911; ④); and the 2-star *Yantra* on pl. 9 Septemvri (☎066/24812; ③) are
high-rise, mod-con places. The nearest campsites are the *Lyubovo* on the road to
Etâr (open May–Oct; take trolleybus #32 from central Gabrovo to the terminus,
then bus #7); and the *Hemus* (open May–Sept) 9km north of town on the Veliko
Târnovo road.

Gabrovo's east bank boasts several "folk-style" **restaurants and mehanas**:
Mogilyov on Pl. Pârvi Mai; *Karagyozova kâshta* on ul. Genov; and the
Stranopriemnitsa (with excellent summer garden) on ul. Opâlchenska, the most
convenient.

Though it's easy enough to buy tickets at the station, **rail and bus reservations** can also be made from the *TsKTON* (Transport Service Centre) in the bus
station.

Etâr and Sokolski monastery

Workaday Gabrovo is easily outshone by two attractions immediately south of
town: the ethnographic complex at Etâr and the nearby Sokolski monastery –
both of which are within reach of urban transport.

Since Racho the blacksmith set up his smithy beneath a large hornbeam
(*gabâr*, hence the town's name), Gabrovo has been a **crafts** centre, gaining fresh
impetus at the beginning of the nineteenth century when waterwheels were introduced from Transylvania. By 1870 the town had more than 800 workshops
powered by water, making iron and wooden implements, clothing, wool and blankets sold beyond the frontiers of the Ottoman empire; today it produces textiles
in quantities exceeded only by Sliven, and half the leather goods in Bulgaria. To
preserve traditional skills, Gabrovo has established the museum-village of **ETÂR**
(summer: 8am–5.30pm; winter: 8am–5pm), 9km from town on the banks of the
Sivek, a tributary of the Yantra.

The Etâr complex

Strung out along the valley bottom, the Etâr complex falls into three sections. Traditionally, crafts were inseparable from the *charshiya*, and a reconstructed bazaar of the type once common in Bulgarian towns forms the heart of the complex. Throughout much of the day artisans are at work here, hammering bells, throwing pots, sewing braid and sheepskin jackets and so on, and it's possible for visitors to sign up for **crafts courses**. Arranged by Gabrovo's tourist office, these last thirty hours spread over one week, and supposedly impart the rudiments of copper working, rug weaving, pottery, tailoring, flute making, forging and wood turning. Even if your interest in crafts is minimal it's difficult not to admire the interiors of the old houses, which achieve great beauty through the skilful use of simple materials. Besides dwellings and workshops, the bazaar includes several places for wetting one's whistle, and a bakery whence folks emerge clutching fresh *simitli* (glazed buns made of chick-pea flour), a speciality of Gabrovo's baker. Another section contains a watermill (*karadyekia*) and hydro-powered workshops for cutting timber, fulling cloth, and making braid (*dolapkinya*), wine flagons (*buklitsi*) and *gavanki* (round wooden boxes); the third section, intended to show village life, is still being constructed.

Sokolski monastery

An hour or so's walk upstream from Etâr, **SOKOLSKI MONASTERY** perches on a crag above the village of VODITSI. During Ottoman times the monks offered succour to Bulgarian outlaws, putting up the *cheta*, or band, of local haiduk Dyado Nikola in the 1850s, and providing the local rebels with an assembly point during the Rising of 1876. Nowadays it's a discreet, little-visited place, with rose bushes and privet shrubs laid out in a courtyard dominated by an octagonal stone fountain. The small church, dating from the monastery's foundation in 1832, lies at the bottom of a flight of steps to the right. The dome is supported by an unusually large drum of bright blue – also the dominant colour of the frescoes inside (primitively painted by the original pastor, Pop Pavel, and his son Nikolai), which include a vivid *Dormition of the Virgin* above the main entrance.

Practicalities

You can reach Etâr by taking trolleybus #32 from central Gabrovo to the end of the line (currently named *Bolshevik* after the engineering works nearby, although this may have changed by the time you visit), where you change to bus #7.

Etâr and Sokolski can easily be digested as a day trip from Gabrovo (or even from Veliko Târnovo), although the *Etâr* hotel (☎066/42026; ③) at the north end of the complex is a refreshingly tranquil place in which to stay. The hotel has a café and restaurant, and there's also a *mehana* at the other end of the village.

Shumen

Lying midway between Veliko Târnovo and Varna, **SHUMEN** is the obvious base from which to explore the historical sites at Madara, Pliska and Preslav. The city itself has a fair share of ancient monuments and memorial houses, not least a spectacular **medieval fortress** which once guarded the road to Preslav. As Turkish *Shumla*, Shumen was one of the four heavily garrisoned citadel towns which formed the defensive quadrilateral protecting the northern frontier. Although the imposing Ottoman fortifications are no more, the thriving market town which existed within is still present in the shape of one surviving mosque, the **Tombul Dzhamiya**. Modern Shumen presents a good example of what state socialism brought to urban Bulgarian life. Well-built, prestigious civic buildings line a show-case main boulevard, only seconds away from neglected, potholed side streets, where single-storey shacks rub shoulders with greying tower blocks. Dubbed "Red Shumen" by its detractors, the city was nevertheless the only large urban area in Bulgaria to choose a socialist council in the elections of October 1991.

The town

Buses #1, #10 or #12 will take you from the rail and bus stations as far as the east-ern end of the largely traffic-free bul. Slavyanski, where a blend of stately central European and smart modern architecture gives downtown Shumen an expansive air. Occupying a modern red brick building on the boulevard's south side is the **historical museum** (Tues–Sat 8.30am–noon & 1.30–5.30pm), where the pick of the region's archaeological finds have been concentrated. A Bronze Age site at nearby Smyadovo yielded bone-carved idols of the fourth millennium BC; while the Thracian period is represented by silverware from two local burial sites, at Vârbitsa and Branichevo. Also here are many of the best medieval artefacts from Pliska and Preslav, the cultural achievements of the latter revealed in the abstract floral patterns adorning the capitals of stone pillars, and in the delicacy of a tenth-century gold necklace. A crumbling turn-of-the-century pile a couple of blocks further west holds the regional **art gallery** (Tues–Sat 9am–noon & 2–5.30pm), a fairly unchallenging collection of local work.

Along Tsar Osvoboditel

Opposite the art gallery, ul. Layosh Koshut leads down to **Tsar Osvoboditel**, home to much of what's left of Shumen's old quarter. Standing at no. 35 is the so-called **Kossuth house** (Tues–Sat 9am–noon & 2–6pm; Sun 9am–noon), a warren of panelled rooms with divans linked by creaking corridors, where the Magyar revolutionary Lajos Kossuth stayed for three months after fleeing Hungary in 1849, before the Turks interned him in Asia Minor. Ten minutes' walk to the east at Ennio Markovski 42 is the **memorial house of Panaiot Volov** (officially Tues–Sun 8am–noon & 2–5pm, but liable to random and prolonged closures), fellow conspirator of Vasil Levski and leader of the local revolutionary committee.

The biggest concentration of nineteenth-century houses lies along Tsar Osvoboditel to the west. The **Ivan Radev house** at no. 56 (Tues–Sat 9am–noon & 2–6pm; Sun 9am–1pm) houses a collection of graphics and sculpture presented to the city by artist Radev on the occasion of the 1300th anniversary of the Bulgarian state in 1981. Directly opposite is another museum-house, this one commemorating **Pancho Vladiguerov** (Mon, Wed–Sat 9am–noon & 2–6pm; Sun 9am–1pm), a Spaniard who settled in Shumen and became Bulgaria's first composer of classical music, now honoured by tagging his name to an annual **Festival of Piano Music** – held towards the end of September. Further on at no. 87 is the **house of Dobri Voinikov** (Mon–Fri 9am–noon & 2–6pm), crammed with memorabilia relating to this nineteenth-century author of the plays *Princess Raina* and *Civilisation Misunderstood*. At the end of the street, the **Srebrov house** at no. 76, a two-storey symmetrical structure reminiscent of the best of Plovdiv's National Revival architecture, now houses a local artists' club.

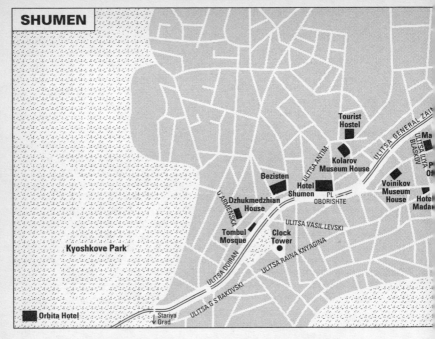

Across the River Poroina from here are several old residences preserved in honour of their former occupants, not least the house of postwar Bulgaria's deputy leader **Vasil Kolarov** at Todor Ikonomov 11 (currently closed while the city authorities consider what to do with the property, a fine turn-of-the-century town house). Born into the bourgeoisie and educated at Geneva University, Kolarov fled to the USSR after the 1923 uprising and took Soviet citizenship. He survived Stalin's purges, and in 1944 returned to supervize the expurgation of non-Communist parties and "home-grown" Communists like Traicho Kostov.

The Tombul Dzhamiya and around

West of Tsar Osvoboditel the broad asphalt sweep of ul. Rakovski – subsequently ul. Doiran – cuts past two impressive relics of Ottoman *Shumla*. Sheltering beneath trees is the **Bezisten**, or covered market, built to cater for the needs of Dubrovnik merchants who established a trading post here in the sixteenth century. Constructed from heavy blocks of stone retrieved from the ruins of Pliska and Preslav, nowadays it serves as an arcade of boutiques and souvenir shops.

From here you will be able to see the proud minaret and bulbous domes of Shumen's main sight, the **Tombul Dzhamiya**. Built in 1744 on the initiative of Sherif Halil Pasha, a native of Shumen who rose to become deputy Grand Vizier in Constantinople, the complex aimed to meet both the spiritual and educational needs of the community. A *mektep*, or primary school, occupied the east wing, while a *medrese* (Koranic school) and *kitaphane* (library) surrounded the cloistered courtyard to the east. This is dominated by the *shadirvan* or fountain,

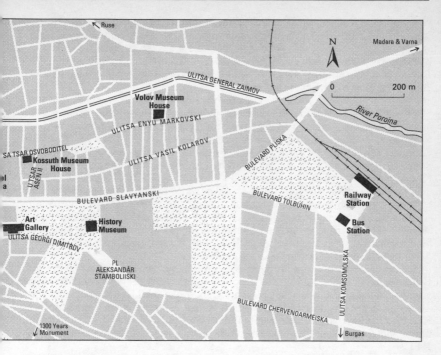

an eclectic structure mixing Moorish arches with classical, Corinthian pillars. Inside the prayer hall, carpets cover the floor beneath the flowery dome and pentagonal lights. The mosque was converted into a museum during the Communist era, but has now reverted to its original role, catering for the spiritual needs of Shumen's considerable Islamic community (the prayer hall and courtyard may be shut outside regular prayer times). The city is once more an important religious centre for the Muslims of northeast Bulgaria, with believers from far and wide annually descending on the Tombul Dzhamiya to celebrate *Kurban bayram*, one of the major festivals of the Islamic calendar (see *Basics*, p.27). Apart from a forlorn eighteenth-century **clock tower** standing amid residential streets immediately south of the mosque, little else remains of the old Turkish town – demolished along with its impressive fortifications after the Liberation.

Among the hillside suburbs to the north of the mosque is the walled **Dyukmedzhian house** at Stara planina 2, arguably Shumen's finest National Revival building. Built in 1851 for a family of rich Armenian merchants, the house is now occupied by various civic organizations; if the big wooden gates are open you can enter the courtyard to admire its impressive, double-winged frontage. The area above the house remains predominantly Armenian and is still called the *Armenskata mahala* – a reminder of the Ottoman period when most Bulgarian towns were divided into *mahali* or neighbourhoods, each grouped around the local mosque, church or synagogue. Non-Muslim groups, whether Bulgarian, Armenian or Jewish, tended to stick to their own *mahala*: Shumen is one of the few places where vestiges of the old system still persevere.

The medieval fortress and the 1300 Years monument

Shumen is surrounded to the south and west by the *Shumensko plato* national park, a tableland of dense woodland. The most accessible part of it is the **Kyoshkove park** at the western end of town (a fifteen-minute walk beyond the Tombul Mosque, or buses #1, #10 or #11), where tracks lead up into the hills past the sites of World War II partisan bunkers.

Immediately above Kyoshkove (and reached by walking 2km uphill from the *Shumensko pivo* brewery at the entrance to the park) is the **Stariyat grad** or medieval fortress (summer: daily 7am–7pm; winter: daily 8am–5pm), whose monumental, part-reconstructed walls are reminiscent of Tsarevets in Veliko Târnovo. The Thracians were the first to fortify the site, followed swiftly by Romans, Byzantines and Bulgars, but it was during the Second Bulgarian Kingdom that the fortress developed its current monumental shape. Ruins of medieval houses outside the fortress walls show that the slopes of the hill harboured a sizable civilian population during the thirteenth and fourteenth centuries; they were subsequently driven from their homes and sent to live in the valley by the Ottomans. A small pavilion displaying finds from the fortress stands by the entrance, with an abundant collection of Thracian ceramics and brightly decorated tableware from the Second Kingdom.

Roadways lead eastward through the forest towards the **1300 Years of Bulgaria** monument – more easily accessible from a processional concrete stairway which begins just above bul. Slavyanski, between the historical museum and the art gallery. A bewildering juxtaposition of Khans, monks, haiduks and Mother Heroines rendered in concrete by a sculptor with Cubist inclinations, this extraordinary hilltop structure was unveiled on the nation-state's 1300th anniversary in 1981.

Equally incongruous but potentially more interesting as an excursion is the **Buffalo and Horsebreeding Centre** just outside town where Indian *Murra* buffalo – noted for their high milk yield – are cross-bred with other species from the former Soviet Union, Romania and Venezuela. Information on visits to the farm can be found in the lobbies of the *Shumen* and *Madara* hotels.

Practicalities

The *Balkantourist* bureau on ul. G.S. Rakovski is the likeliest source of **information and maps**, and it's worth enquiring here whether they handle **private rooms** – a town of Shumen's size is likely to develop this option sooner or later.

Travellers of modest means will find the town's two major **hotels** a little steep; the 4-star *Hotel Shumen*, ul. Rakovski (☎054/58009; ⑤) and the 3-star *Madara*, pl. Bâlgariya 1 (054/57595; ④) are both plush, showcase establishments. Two possible sources of mid-price beds, the *Orbita* in Kyoshkove park (☎054/56374) and the *Ko-op* on the corner of Tsar Osvoboditel and Hristo Botev (☎054/52156), may now be open following restoration but remain unknown quantities. For the time being, bare rooms at the modest *Hotel Ticha*, Slavyanski (①); or dorm beds at the *turisticheska spalnya* on ul. Antim I remain the only sure budget alternatives. The nearest **campsite** is at *Osmarski koloni* (open June–Sept, no chalets), situated 12km southwest of town just off the Preslav road – take the Troitsa and Osmar turn-off in the village of HAN KRUM.

The restaurants in the *Shumen* and *Madara* hotels provide the best range of **food**, and meals here will not break the bank. The folk-style *Popsheitanovata kâshta*, Tsar Osvoboditel 76, has a nice summer garden; while the *Rigoletto*, on

Slavyanski below the *Hotel Ticha*, is favoured by a stylish youthful crowd. For cheaper grill-type fare try *Grozd* on ul. Blagoev.

Daytime **drinking** takes place in the several *sladkarnitsi* along the northern side of bul. Slavyanski, of which *Bâlgariya* and *Prolet* have the widest range of cakes and sweets. In the evening, the alleys linking Slavyanski and Tsar Osvoboditel are the best places to look for small, privately owned *café-aperitif* bars. One of the liveliest, although slightly further afield, is the *Café Hawaii*, opposite the *Hotel Shumen*.

Around Shumen

The northeastern fringe of the Balkan Range is distinguished by three archaeological sites, all easily accessible from Shumen. The ruins of **Pliska** are less interesting to look at than read about, but enough remains of **Preslav** to justify a visit if your taste inclines towards hunky masonry, while the rockscapes around the so-called **Madara Horseman** make up for the eroded face of this unique and ancient bas-relief.

Preslav

Founded by Khan Omurtag in 821, **VELIKI PRESLAV** acquired the prefix "Great" after it was made the capital of the First Kingdom, during the reign of Tsar Simeon (893–927) – although it began to eclipse the original capital, Pliska, at an earlier date. According to contemporary accounts, tenth-century Preslav was the most populous town in the Balkans, with extensive suburbs surrounding a walled inner town containing "large buildings of stone on both sides, decorated with wood". It also held a palace, a royal School of Translators, the Patriarchate and other "churches ornamented with stones, wood and paintings, marble and copper, silver and gold". Preslav's downfall began when it was captured by the Kievian prince, Svetoslav, causing the Byzantine empire to respond by razing the town in 972, and although it later revived (the palace was occupied as late as the Asenid dynasty), Preslav never regained its former size and was subsequently surpassed by Târnovo. Eventually it was burned down by the Turks, who used the remains to construct their own buildings, including the Tombul Mosque in Shumen.

The town and the ruins

The **ruins of Preslav** are scattered over the farmland to the south of the modern town. A signposted lane leads from Preslav's main square towards the site, which lie beyond the town park. Beyond the crest of a hill lurks a modern concrete bunker holding an **archaeological museum** (Tues–Sun 8am–6pm), where plans and diagrams can be consulted before venturing out into the relic-strewn fields. Although the most prestigious artefacts have been moved to the historical museum in Shumen, the display here includes examples of the ceramic tiles used to decorate the medieval town's buildings showing the swirling abstract patterns which characterized decorative arts during the Second Kingdom.

Approaching the ruins from here you'll pass through the northern gate, first sign of the cyclopean **walls** which envelop the medieval city – reconstructed with modern breeze-blocks to something approximating their original height. To the west are the bare ruins of the **palace** where the tsar held court. Further west, the traces of a vast monastery complex lie raked across the hillside. Beyond the south portal is the relatively well-preserved **Zlatna tsârkva** or Golden church, also known as the Round church. Several arches, the bulk of its walls and twelve marble columns (some truncated) still remain, and the church itself – sited on a hillock in what used to be the outer town – now provides the setting for pageants and poetry readings associated with the Veliki Preslav **Literary Days**, normally held around the middle of May.

Practicalities

Modern Preslav offers few inducements to spend longer than an afternoon here, and regular bus services to Shumen and Târgovishte happily mean that you don't need to. If you do get stuck, **accommodation** boils down to the 2-star *Hotel Preslav* (☎0528/2508) in the town square, and a motel near the southern entrance to the ruins.

Târgovishte

If travelling westwards from either Preslav or Shumen towards Veliko Târnovo you're certain to pass through **TÂRGOVISHTE**, which gets its name from the old Slavic word for "fair" – a reference to the largest cattle market in the Balkans, which took place here ever since the settlement was founded by the Turks in the fifteenth century. Nowadays, few signs of the Ottoman period remain: Târgovishte has been extensively rebuilt in concrete, and the town's historical sights are limited to a derelict **mosque** lurking in the backstreets to the west of bul. Levski, and the **school** where P.R. Slaveykov taught (on the west bank of the Varna River), preserved as a museum. Should you wish to **stay**, there's the 2-star *Hotel Miziya* on pl. Svoboda (☎0601/2433; ③). Eight kilometres west of town beside the E771 highway are *Beliyat Kon* motel (☎0601/27858; ③) and the *Lyulyaka* campsite (open May–Oct).

The Madara Horseman

The most popular destination for excursions from Shumen is the village of **MADARA**, 10km to the east and served by frequent trains, where a range of cliffs show signs of human occupation dating back to the third century BC. A concrete stairway constructed immediately outside the station points the way to the village's most famous sight, the mysterious bas-relief known as the **Madara Horseman** (8am–dusk). Carved into the rockface at a height of 95m, this is so eroded that details are only apparent by the light of a setting sun, but the carving is said to represent a horseman whose mount is trampling a lion with the assistance of a greyhound, while he holds the reins in one hand and a wine cup in the other. Various Greek inscriptions next to the carving provide ambiguous clues to its age: the oldest inscription, recording a debt owed by the Byzantine Emperor Justinian II to Khan Tervel, suggests that the Bulgars carved the horseman in the eighth century. However, some scholars believe it is far older than that. The figure, they argue, represents the nameless rider-god of the Thracians, and is of Thracian or Getae origin, the inscriptions merely evidence that it was later appropriated by Bulgarian rulers.

Around the Horseman

To the right of the relief, a path winds off towards the **Large Cave** (*Golyamata Peshtera*) beneath a giant overhang of rock. Various finds from here – Thracian votive plaques, amphorae bearing the stamp of Thasos, Roman candlesticks and Proto-Bulgarian ceramics – are now exhibited in the small **museum** outside the entrance to the complex, and the cool, moss-streaked cave serves as the venue for the **Madara Music Days** in June and July (contact *Balkantourist* in Shumen

THE PROTOBULGARIANS

Known to English-speaking historians as the **Bulgars**, and to the Bulgarians themselves as the *prabâlgari* or **Protobulgarians**, the rulers who founded Pliska and Preslav, and who may have been responsible for commissioning the Madara Horseman, started out as Turkic nomads from the Eurasian steppe.

Originating in western Siberia, the Bulgars coalesced into three warlike tribes in the sixth century; the **Onogurs**, **Utigurs** and **Kutrigurs**. The latter were the first to descend on the Balkans, reaching the walls of Constantinople twice in the mid-500s AD before being pushed back by the armies of Emperor Justinian. For the next half century Byzantine diplomacy concentrated on keeping these three tribes at each other's throats, in an attempt to preserve the balance of power in the territories north and east of the Black Sea. Eventually, however, they began to cultivate the friendship of the Onogurs, who by this time ruled a swathe of steppe north of the Caucasus mountains – subsequently called **Old Great Bulgaria** by Byzantine chroniclers. The alliance was cemented in 619 with the baptism of the Onogur Khan Organa, together with his son Kubrat in Constantinople.

Nevertheless things went awry when the Onogurs were driven from their lands by another Turkic tribe, the rapidly expanding Khazars. Kubrat's successor **Asparuh** led his people southwest to the Danube expecting hospitality from his Byzantine ally Emperor Constantine IV, who instead sent an army to prevent Asparuh from crossing the river. The Byzantine attempt failed, and by 681 Constantine was forced to recognize the existence of an **independent Bulgar state** ruled by Asparuh from his capital at Pliska.

The new kingdom was initially limited to the flatlands either side of the Danube, stretching from the Balkan Range in the south to the Carpathians in the north. However, the Bulgars began to expand beyond the Balkan Mountains and put down urban roots under Asparuh's successor, Khan **Tervel**, and the centuries-old culture of these Turkic-speaking steppe dwellers began to die out. An aristocratic elite ruling over a population of Thracians and Slavs (the latter, valued by the Bulgars as frontier settlers, became increasingly numerous), the Bulgars gradually lost their separate ethnic identity and became assimilated by their subjects. The process was confirmed by Tsar Boris's conversion to Christianity in 865 and the suppression of paganism that followed – many of the old Bulgar families, unwilling to break with the old faith, were simply wiped out.

Little is known about the beliefs and customs of the Bulgars. Byzantine chroniclers have provided us with a few scraps, telling us that they worshipped their ancestors, practised shamanism, sacrificed steppe wolves in times of trouble, and probably indulged in polygamy. Some Turkic-speaking Bulgars still exist, the so-called **Volga Bulgars** who survive in isolated pockets south of Kazan in Russia. They converted to Islam in the tenth century and enjoyed independent statehood until the thirteenth, when they were submerged beneath the advance of their fellow Muslims, the Tatars.

for details). Beyond is a smaller cave, where flints, bones and pottery were discovered; while just above, you'll catch sight of the remnants of a fourteenth-century **rock monastery**, its crudely dug cells pitting the cliff face.

Not far away you'll find the source of the Madara River where Thracian period plaques and statues honouring the Rider-god, Dionysus, Cybele and three Water Nymphs have been discovered; and remains of an early medieval **grain store** where enormous clay vessels were sunk into the ground to keep cool.

Early Bulgarian remains, and the fortress

Most of the early Bulgarian finds are located to the left of the Horseman, where the barest outlines of eighth- and ninth-century churches and monastic complexes lie scattered at the foot of the cliff. Many of the churches were adapted from or built on top of earlier pagan structures – a sign that Madara was an important religious site from the earliest times. Paganism remained ingrained among the Bulgars long after Christianity became the official religion in 865, and although the precise nature of their beliefs remains shrouded in mystery, the discovery of the eighth-century **Old Bulgarian baths** points to the existence of water-based purification rituals.

A rough-hewn pathway works its way up the cliff face to the plateau above. Roughly 500m to the west lies a **ruined fortress** of fifth-century origin, although the remaining walls mostly date from the Second Kingdom. There are also two **tumuli** left by the Getae – who buried their dead in ceramic urns – 300m north of the fortress, but the real attraction is the **view from the plateau**. Roman ruins are scattered about at the foot of the massif, while the surrounding plain is cut off by the Balkans to the south and the Ludogorie Hills to the north – where sharp eyes might be able to discern the ruins of Pliska (see below) amid the acacia groves.

Practicalities

It's pretty easy to see the site and return to Shumen in the space of a morning or afternoon, though there is **accommodation** near the Horseman should you wish to stay. The *turisticheska spalnya* near the entrance to the Horseman complex is usually occupied by groups, but there should be bungalows for rent in the *Madara* campsite (open May–Sept) about 200m to the south. There's nowhere to **eat or drink** in Madara village save for the café and restaurant just outside the complex.

Pliska

Ten kilometres north of Madara, the ruins of **Pliska** are less well preserved than those in Preslav, but in its heyday during the First Kingdom (681–1018), Pliska was a sophisticated and important settlement, covering 23 square kilometres and protected by citadels on neighbouring hills. It was sacked by the Byzantine Emperor Nicephorus in the early 800s, but retained its status as the capital, and it was to Pliska that the disciples of Cyril and Methodius, Naum and Kliment, came in 885 to help spread the Slav alphabet. Pliska's days of glory were over by 900, after Tsar Boris I had come out of monastic retirement to stamp out a return to paganism sponsored by his son Vladimir – one of Boris's acts was to move the capital to Preslav in order to make a fresh start.

THE BESSARABIAN BULGARIANS

Walking between Pliska railway station and Pliska village, you're sure to pass through a building site bearing the name of **Kompleks Besarabiya**, a brand-new suburb designed specifically to house ethnic Bulgarians from the former Soviet Union.

An estimated 90,000 Bulgarians fled the country during the Russo-Turkish War of 1830, finding refuge in **Bessarabia**, the territory northwest of the Black Sea recently seized from the Ottomans by the expanding Russian empire. The descendants of these **Bessarabian Bulgarians** are mostly scattered throughout the ex-Soviet republics of Moldova and the Ukraine, and are thought to number about half a million. Families have tenaciously clung to the Bulgarian language and culture, despite attempts by Stalin in the mid-1930s to close down the community's schools and newspapers.

The uncertainties brought about by the collapse of the Soviet Union have caused many Bessarabian Bulgarians to begin planning a return to their original homeland. Numbers of would-be migrants are likely to increase due to the situation in Moldova, where Bulgarian villages are caught in the middle of a dispute between the Romanian-speaking majority and Russian and Ukranian ethnic minorities.

Drawn to the region's rich agricultural land, Bessarabian Bulgarians first started arriving in the Pliska area in September 1991. The first batch of settlers immediately set about collecting money to cater for the needs of future immigrants, and it's hoped that the planned Besarabiya suburb will provide houses and jobs for about 5000 newcomers.

The ruins
The ruins (entered by a minor road which runs 3km eastwards from the village of Pliska) still occupy a considerable area, although most of the buildings have been reduced to low walls. As you can see from the exhibits in the **museum**, Pliska originally had three lines of defences: a ditch, behind which was the outer town (with workshops and basic dwellings), a stone wall with four gates, surrounding the inner town, and finally a brick rampart around the so-called Little Palace. Between the brick and stone walls lay the two-storied Large Palace, and the yet larger Royal Basilica, the former being supplied with piped water and central heating.

Practicalities
Unless you have a car, **getting to Pliska** from Shumen entails a couple of awkward changes. You can either approach the village by rail, changing to the Varna-Ruse line at Kaspichan and alighting at the Pliska halt (it's important to remember to check timetables carefully: only about three trains a day stop here), from which it's a 4km walk over the hills to the village itself; or take a bus or train to NOVI PAZAR, where local bus services cover the remaining 8km to Pliska village.

Allowing time for these changes, plus the walk to the site itself, a visit to Pliska may require a long day trip from Shumen, though this shouldn't deter you from making the journey in the first place. However, if you are without a car and do get stranded, there's a run-of-the-mill **motel** at the ruins and a **hotel**, the 2-star *Bereslav* (☎0537/2162; ③), in Novi Pazar.

Razgrad and the Ludogorie hills

North of Shumen, the low-lying **Ludogorie hills** separate the Balkan Range proper from the flatter terrain of the Danube plain and the Dobrudzha beyond. The region harbours a large Muslim population of Turkish and Tatar descent, and Islamic architecture distinguishes the Ludogorie's main town, **Razgrad**. There's little of specific interest elsewhere, although the **Thracian tomb at Sveshtari** near Isperih will provide the area with a major tourist draw once it's made ready for the public.

Razgrad

Situated midway between Shumen and Ruse, **RAZGRAD** sprawls messily around the banks of the Beli Lom. Since the Liberation in March 1878, the narrow lanes and artisans' stalls that characterized the town during Ottoman times have gradually succumbed to modern urban planning. Apart from a restored *Varosh* quarter north of the river, where a succession of whitewashed National Revival-style houses provide homes for various artists' and writers' unions, Razgrad remains fairly lacklustre – save for an impressive mosque and some Roman ruins, both worth taking time out to visit.

The town

Commanding immediate attention at the northern end of an otherwise uncompromisingly modern main square, Bulgaria's largest mosque, **Ibrahim Pasha Dzhamiya**, combines forms which succeed in conveying both elegance and power. An imposing block of heavy masonry topped by a graceful dome and tapering minaret, it's a lasting tribute to the skills of its Albanian and Bulgarian builders – and to the Turkish governor Ibrahim, who commissioned it in 1614. Currently undergoing renovation (Razgrad's faithful have to make do with a smaller mosque out on the Ruse road for the time being), the edifice is held up by a web of rusting scaffolding, and the mural-rich interior remains inaccessible. You can, however, see the elaborate Arabic calligraphy decorating the porch on the northern side.

The remaining sights of central Razgrad are quickly exhausted; opposite the mosque is a small **art gallery** hosting changing exhibitions of local work, while pl. Ludogorie immediately to the north revolves around a nineteenth-century clock tower.

The ruins of Abritus

East of town on the Shumen road, just beyond a large pharmaceutical factory, lie the remains of **Abritus**, the fortified Roman town which guarded the road between the Danube and Odessos (now Varna) on the Black Sea. Part of the walls that once surrounded the town (originally standing 12–15m high) can be seen by the roadside, while near the site of the town's eastern gate stand the foundations of the so-called **Peristyle building**, a 23-room complex grouped around a columned courtyard, once used by shopkeepers and artisans. A small, irregularly open **museum** at the site displays pottery fragments and grave inscriptions, plus a collection of bronze tablets depicting the variety of deities – ranging from familiar Graeco-Roman figures such as Zeus and Hera to more exotic rider gods and mother goddesses from the Middle East – worshipped by the cosmopolitan bunch of troops used to garrison the area.

Practicalities

Razgrad's **railway station** lies 5km north of town: although all arrivals are met by buses into the centre, it's not the most convenient point of arrival. The **bus terminal** is on the eastern edge of town, within walking distance of both the Ibrahim Pasha Mosque (about fifteen minutes west) and the ruins of Abritus (about fifteen minutes east). You should be able to see both the above sights while en route between Ruse and Shumen, although Razgrad has two **hotels** if you get stranded: the rather spartan *Abritus*, bul. Beli Lom 33 (②), or the modern, ziggurat-like, 3-star *Razgrad* on ul. Laipzig above the main square (☎084/20751; ③).

The Thracian tomb at Sveshtari

Forty kilometres northeast of Razgrad, just beyond the market town of Isperih, is the village of **SVESHTARI**, site of what is arguably the finest **Thracian tomb** yet discovered in Bulgaria. Discovered in 1982 in a mound of earth known locally as *Ginina mogila*, it is the largest of a group of 26 *tumuli* which stretch for a couple of kilometres on the southwestern fringes of the village. Facilities for visitors are still in preparation: archaeologists had planned to envelop the site in a protective building and open it to tourists by 1987, but the project is way behind schedule – further progress being hamstrung by Bulgaria's current economic difficulties. It's worth contacting the Bulgarian National Tourist Office in your home country to see what the state of play is before departure. In the meantime, the coffee-table books sporadically available in Ruse and Sofia are the closest you can get to the tomb.

The tomb

The burial took place in the late fourth or early third century BC. A corridor lined with well-cut slabs leads to three chambers united by a semi-cylindrical vault: the central one is occupied by two stone couches on which once lay a Thracian king and his wife (five horses were buried in the antechamber to ensure them a mount in the afterlife). The ten stone caryatids and Doric semi-columns which line the walls of the tomb show obvious Hellenistic influences. However, their sturdy upraised arms and full skirts suggest that they represent aspects of the Thracian Mother Goddess, mistress of fertility and of plants, this world and the afterlife. Faint traces of a wall painting occupy one end of the chamber, depicting a mounted horseman – presumably the deceased – being offered a wreath by a female deity, another possible representation of the Mother Goddess.

Archaeologists believe that the tomb was part of a necropolis associated with a large town belonging to **the Getae** (see p.174), and ruins elsewhere in the vicinity have led many scholars to identify the Sveshtari neighbourhood with *Dausdava*, a famous stronghold mentioned in the works of Alexandrian geographer Ptolemy.

Getting to Sveshtari

Once the tomb is open, look out for tourist **excursions** to Sveshtari from either Ruse or the Black Sea resorts. Otherwise, Razgrad is the most convenient place from which to approach the site. There are regular buses from Razgrad to the town of ISPERIH, from where you can pick up a local service running to the village of Sveshtari 6km to the north. You can also reach Isperih by train from a branch line which runs between Samuil on the Ruse-Varna line and Silistra. Beware, however, that only three trains a day run each way, and with no tourist accommodation near the site, a day trip will have to be carefully timed.

THE GETAE

It's hoped that examination of the remains found in the Sveshtari tomb will shed new light on the civilization of **the Getae**, who inhabited both banks of the lower Danube in classical times. Ancient authors disagreed on whether to classify the Getae as Thracians or as Dacians (who lived north of the Danube in what is now Romania), although it seems safe to assume that they were culturally and ethnically very close to both.

Thucydides alluded to their skill as horsemen, and they proved more than a handful for successive invaders – from Darius's Persians in the fifth century BC to the Romans in the first. In 335 BC **Alexander the Great** chased the Getae north of the Danube and destroyed some of their settlements, but failed to subdue them; and his successor Lysimachus was notoriously captured by Getae ruler Dromichaetes in 292 BC, only to be lectured on the value of peace and sent home. However, their period of greatest glory came in the first century BC, when King **Burebista** presided over a short-lived Danubian empire which exercised control of the whole western seaboard of the Black Sea – from what is now the Ukraine in the north to Apollonia (present-day Sozopol) in the south.

It's assumed that, besides believing in a traditional mother goddess, the Getae practised a certain amount of sun worship, and accorded semi-divine status to their chieftains, who ruled as priest-kings. Herodotus relates how they worshipped a certain **Zalmoxis** (thought to be a north-Balkan version of Orpheus, see p.227), who hid himself in an underground chamber for several years before re-emerging, much to the surprise of his contemporaries, to proclaim that he had died and come back to life again. Herodotus also tells of how the Getae sent "messengers" to Zalmoxis by choosing a suitable courier, then tossing him onto a forest of upturned spear-points.

travel details

Trains

From Berkovitsa to Boichinovtsi (7 daily; 1hr); Mihailovgrad (7; 45min).

From Boichinovtsi to Dimovo (6; 2hr); Vidin (6; 2hr 30min).

From Dobrich to Kardam (3; 1hr 15min); Varna (6; 2hr).

From Gorna Oryahovitsa to Pleven (14; 1hr 30min); Ruse (6; 2hr 30min); Shumen (5; 1hr 30min); Sofia (6; 4hr 30min); Târgovishte (5; 2hr); Veliko Târnovo (6; 30min).

From Lovech to Levski (6; 1hr 30min).

From Pleven to Levski (7; 30min); Shumen (2; 4hr 30min); Sofia (hourly; 3hr).

From Ruse to Ivanovo (3 daily; 30min); Pleven (4; 3hr 30min); Samuil (5; 1hr 30min); Sofia (5; 7hr); Varna (3; 3hr 30min).

From Samuil to Isperih (3; 45min); Silistra (3; 2hr 30min).

From Silistra to Isperih (3; 1hr 30min).

From Sofia to Cherepish (6; 2hr); Eliseina (6; 1hr 30min); Lakatnik (7; 1hr); Lyutivbrod (6; 2hr); Vidin (5; 5–7hr); Zverino (8; 1hr 30min).

From Veliko Târnovo to Tsareva Livada (8; 50min); Dryanovo (6; 30min).

From Vârbanovo to Gabrovo (7; 30min); Stara Zagora (2; 2hr); Tryavna (5; 15min); Tulovo (2; 1hr 30min).

Buses

From Belogradchik to Lom (4 daily; 1hr 30min); Rabisha (5; 30min).

From Gabrovo to Kazanlâk (10; 2hr); Pleven (4; 2hr); Razgrad (2; 3hr); Stara Zagora (5; 2hr 40min); Tryavna (hourly; 50min).

From Lom to Oryahovo (2 daily; 2hr); Kozlodui (2; 1hr).

From Lovech to Teteven (2; 2hr); Troyan (hourly; 1hr).

From Ruse to Burgas (1 daily; 5hr; Dobrich (2; 5hr); Isperih (3; 2hr); Pleven (2; 2hr 30min); Razgrad (6; 12hr 15min); Silistra (hourly; 2hr 45min); Svishtov (3 daily; 2hr); Varna (1; 3hr 45min).

From Silistra to Dobrich (4; 2hr 15min); Varna (5; 3hr 30min).

From Shumen to Burgas (4; 3hr); Novi Pazar (10; 1hr); Preslav (hourly; 30min); Razgrad (5 daily; 1hr); Ruse (4; 2hr 15min); Silistra (5; 3hr); Sliven (2; 3hr); Varna (6; 2hr).

From Sofia (*Avtogara Poduyane*) to Botevgrad (every 30min; 45min); Etropole (8; 1hr 30min); Koprivshtitsa (1; 1hr 30min); Kozlodui (1; 3hr); Lovech (3; 3hr); Oryahovo (2; 3hr); Plovdiv (1; 2hr);

Pravets (10; 1hr); Teteven (5; 2hr); Troyan (3; 3hr); Veliko Târnovo (2; 4hr).

From Teteven to Ribaritsa (5; 30min); Pleven (2; 2hr 30min); Vratsa (2; 2hr).

From Troyan to Cherni Osâm (hourly; 30min).

From Veliko Târnovo to Elena (8 daily; 1hr 15min); Gabrovo (6; 1hr); Kazanlâk (2; 2hr 30min); Kotel (1; 3hr); Lovech (4; 2hr); Plovdiv (1; 4hr); Sevlievo (7; 1hr); Sliven (2; 3hr); Svishtov (hourly; 2hr 45min); Teteven (1 daily; 3hr 15min).

From Vidin to Belogradchik (4; 1hr 45min); Berkovitsa (2; 2hr 20min); Kula (hourly; 45min); Lom (8 daily; 45min); Pleven (2; 4hr); Mihailovgrad (4; 1hr 50min).

CYRILLIC PLACE NAMES

ARBANASI	АРБАНАСИ	MIHAILOVGRAD	МИХАЙЛОВГРАД
BELOGRADCHIK	БЕЛОГРАДЧИК	NIKOPOL	НИКОПОЛ
BERKOVITSA	БЕРКОВИЦА	NOVI PAZAR	НОВИ ПАЗАР
BOTEVGRAD	БОТЕВГРАД	ORYAHOVO	ОРЯХОВО
BOZHENTSI	БОЖЕНЦИ	PLAKOVO	ПЛАКОВО
BYALA	БЯЛА	PLEVEN	ПЛЕВЕН
CHERVEN BRYAG	ЧЕРВЕН БРЯГ	PLISKA	ПЛИСКА
DOBRICH	ДОБРИЧ	PRAVETS	ПРАВЕЦ
DRYANOVO	ДРЯНОВО	PRESLAV	ПРЕСЛАВ
ELENA	ЕЛЕНА	RAZGRAD	РАЗГРАД
ETÂR	ЕТЪР	RUSE	РУСЕ
ETROPOLE	ЕТРОПОЛЕ	SEVLIEVO	СЕВЛИЕВО
GABROVO	ГАБРОВО	SHUMEN	ШУМЕН
GIGEN	ГИГЕН	SILISTRA	СИЛИСТРА
GORNA ORYAHOVITSA	ГОРНА ОРЯХОВИЦА	SVESHTARI	СВЕЩАРИ
		SVISHTOV	СВИЩОВ
KAPINOVO	КАПИНОВО	TÂRGOVISHTE	ТЪРГОВИЩЕ
KARDAM	КАРДАМ	TETEVEN	ТЕТЕВЕН
KILIFAREVO	КИЛИФАРЕВО	TROYAN	ТРОЯН
KOZLODUI	КОЗЛОДУЙ	TRYAVNA	ТРЯВНА
LAKATNIK	ЛАКАТНИК	VELIKO TÂRNOVO	ВЕЛИКО ТЪРНОВО
LOM	ЛОМ		
LOVECH	ЛОВЕЧ	VIDIN	ВИДИН
MADARA	МАДАРА	VRATSA	ВРАЦА
MEZDRA	МЕЗДРА	YABLANITSA	ЯБЛАНИЦА

CHAPTER FOUR

THE SREDNA GORA AND THE VALLEY OF THE ROSES

T he most direct route between Sofia and the Black Sea coast cuts straight across central Bulgaria, passing two areas of unique historic interest on the way. Both main road and railway squeeze their way between the mountains of the Balkan range to the north, and the **Sredna Gora**, or "central highlands", to the south. Lining the valleys of the latter are some of Bulgaria's most historic villages, renowned for both folkloric and revolutionary traditions. **Koprivshtitsa** is the most famous: venerated by Bulgarians as the starting point of the ill-fated April Rising of 1876, it's also the site of some of the country's best-preserved nineteenth-century architecture. Nearby are the museums and memorials of **Panagyurishte**, another centre of the Rising, and the ancient Roman spa town of **Hisarya**. The eastern stretches of the Sredna Gora are gentler and less dramatic, but cities such as **Stara Zagora**, site of one of Bulgaria's greatest archaeological treasures, the 7000-year-old Neolithic dwellings; and **Yambol**, home to a couple of Ottoman architectural gems, provide an excuse to break your eastward journey.

Between the Sredna Gora and the *Stara planina* lies the so-called **Valley of the Roses** (*Rozovata dolina* – in fact two valleys; the upper reaches of the Stryama and the upper reaches of the Tundzha), named after the endless rose

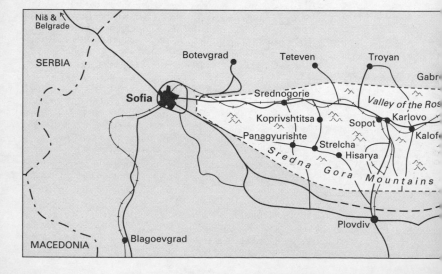

plantations to which the area owes its wealth. It's at its best when the rose crop is harvested in May, but interest is provided throughout the year by the historic settlements lining the valley floor. Those most deserving of attention are **Sopot**, former home of Bulgaria's "national" novelist Ivan Vazov; **Karlovo**, birthplace of seminal freedom fighter Vasil Levski and the best-preserved of the valley's market towns; and the region's most convenient touring base **Kazanlâk**, known both for the Rose Festival, a folkloric bash which attracts visitors in early June, and the Thracian tomb, a remarkable monument to Bulgaria's ancient antecedents. To the north of Kazanlâk lies the **Shipka pass**, slung between some of the highest peaks of the Balkan range, and scene of fierce fighting in the Russo-Turkish War of 1877–78.

Midway between the valley and the Black Sea coast lies **Sliven**, obvious starting point for excursions to the highland craftworking towns of **Kotel** and **Zheravna**. Strictly speaking these places occupy an eastern spur of the Balkan range, but are included in this chapter because they're more easily visited by those travelling the Sofia-Black Sea route.

Getting into and around the area couldn't be easier. The main Sofia-Burgas highway and railway line both skirt the north of the Sredna Gora, but Koprivshtitsa, Panagyurishte and Hisarya have good bus connections with settlements along the main west–east route. Both road and rail pass directly through the towns of the Valley of the Roses, before pressing on to Sliven. Stara Zagora and Yambol lie a little to the south, but are easy to reach from Kazanlâk and Sliven to the north, or Plovdiv (see Chapter Five) to the south.

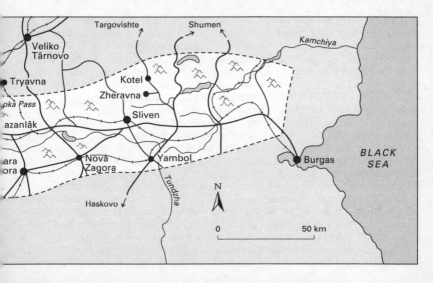

THE WESTERN SREDNA GORA

. . . So, proudly you may gaze
Unto the Sredna Gora, the forest's single queen,
And hear the ring of swords, and all this song can mean . . .

Pencho Slaveykov, *The Song of the Blood*

The **Sredna Gora** separating the Valley of the Roses from the Maritsa Valley stretches from the Pancharevo defile outside Sofia almost as far as Yambol on the Thracian plain. With its forests of oak and beech and numerous caves and hot springs, the region was inhabited by humans as early as the fifth millenium BC. The Thracians subsequently left a hoard of gold treasure at **Panagyurishte** (since moved to the National Historical Museum in Sofia), and the Romans a crop of ruins at **Hisarya**, but for Bulgarians, the Sredna Gora is best known as the "land of the April Rising", an event for which Panagyurishte and **Koprivshtitsa** will always be remembered. The latter, harbouring an unparalleled collection of nineteenth-century village architecture, should certainly not be missed.

Lying roughly between Sofia and Plovdiv, the Sredna Gora is a popular destination for excursions from both. Koprivshtitsa is best reached from the main route between Sofia and Burgas: there's a halt named Koprivshtitsa on the coast-bound **railway line**, and each train stopping here is met by a bus which ferries you 12km south to the village itself. Panagyurishte is well served by regular buses from the capital, or by train from Plovdiv. Hisarya also has a rail link with Plovdiv; otherwise it can be reached by bus from Karlovo or Kazanlâk in the Valley of the Roses. Bear in mind, however, that **bus services** between the Sredna Gora villages themselves are pretty sparse.

Koprivshtitsa

KOPRIVSHTITSA looks almost too lovely to be real, its half-timbered houses nestled in a valley amid wooded hills. It would be an oasis of pastoral calm were it not for the annual descent of summer visitors, tourists drawn both by the superb architecture and the desire to pay homage to a landmark in the nation's history. From the Place of the Scimitar Charge to the Street of the Counter Attack, there's hardly a part of Koprivshtitsa that isn't named after an episode or participant in the **April Rising of 1876**, when Bulgaria's yearnings for freedom from the Ottoman yoke finally boiled over (see p.180). It was Koprivshtitsa's status as a centre of commerce which provided the material basis for such an upsurge in national consciousness. Sheep and goat farming formed the backbone of the village's wealth, and the resulting wool (as well as byproducts, notably carpets and socks) was traded throughout the Levant. By the time of the April Rising Koprivshtitsa had a population of 12,000. After the Liberation, however, Bulgaria's commercial life began to be centred on the lowland towns, and places like Koprivshtitsa ceased to develop – with the result that this typical nineteenth-century mercantile village has been preserved virtually unchanged. Despite its status as a museum-village, however, Koprivshtitsa remains a working agricultural community, with mule-drawn carts still labouring through the narrow cobbled streets.

Every five years the rural quiet is rent by the **Koprivshtitsa folklore festival**, a huge gathering of musicians from all over the country – of which more on p.184.

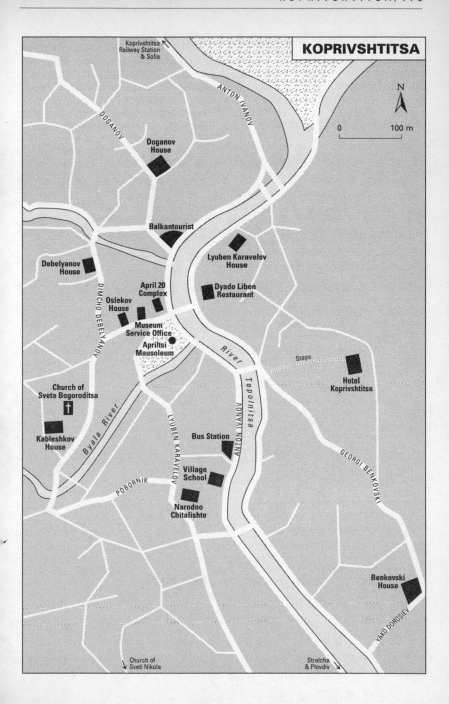

The village and the memorial houses

Koprivshtitsa's stone houses straggle for a couple of kilometres along either side of the River Topolnitsa. A central square stands at the village's northern end, grouped around the greening dome of the **Apriltsi mausoleum**, inscribed "Let us keep the national liberty for which the heroes of the rising of 1876 fell." A street running off to the west leads to the **Oslekov house**, one of the finest in Koprivshtitsa, with pillars of cypress wood imported from Lebanon supporting the

THE APRIL RISING

The 1870s were a time of trouble in the Balkans, with a tired and corrupt Ottoman empire trying to stem the tide of protest both from subject nationalities eager for independence and people within the governing elite angling for reform. In Bulgaria, the rise in education and literacy brought about by the nineteenth-century National Revival had engendered a corresponding upsurge of national consciousness, and a generation of idealistic revolutionaries – people like Vasil Levski, Angel Kânchev, Lyuben Karavelov and Hristo Botev – succeeded in placing the idea of a liberation struggle at the forefront of Bulgarian life.

The strategy of the Bulgarian Revolutionary Central Committee

Formed in 1870 by various nationalist groups, the Bucharest-based **Bulgarian Revolutionary Central Committee**, or **BRCK**, agreed that violent revolution rather than peaceful negotiation was the only way to effect change. Agents like Kânchev (who killed himself to avoid capture in 1872), Levski (hanged by the Turks in 1873) and Zahari Stoyanov (who survived to become the historian of the Rising) travelled the length and breadth of the country setting up revolutionary cells, each of which was responsible for organizing local rebel action once the call for armed struggle eventually came.

The loss of Levski in 1873, and the failure of an uprising in Stara Zagora in 1875, persuaded many on the committee that the kind of insurrection planned by the BRCK was doomed to failure. However, the more hawkish members (led by Botev) won the day: encouraged by the Bosnian Uprising in the summer of 1875, and believing that Serbia and Russia were simply waiting for an excuse to declare war on Turkey, the BRCK leadership decided that the time was ripe for armed rebellion.

Their strategy was based on the time-honoured guerilla methods of the haiduks, Balkan outlaws who could survive for months in the mountains and forests, harrying Turkish positions and relying on the goodwill of the local populace for food and shelter. A series of *cheti*, or highly mobile armed groups, were to be formed, which would move through the countryside, keeping away from heavily defended Ottoman positions, and gathering support where they could – eventually, it was hoped, snowballing into a popular revolt which would provoke the expected foreign intervention.

The Rising begins

The Rising was scheduled for May 1876, and Bulgaria was divided up into four revolutionary regions (centred on Târnovo, Sliven, Vratsa and Plovdiv), each of which was responsible for organizing its own military action. In addition, Hristo Botev collected Bulgarian émigrés living in Serbia and Romania, crossed the Danube in a hijacked Austrian steamboat, and tried to lend support to the Rising by marching south towards Vratsa. The Rising provoked acts of extraordinary heroism everywhere, but hopes of sparking a mass insurrection were dashed. Cowed by Turkish reprisals, the local population failed to support the rebels, and the progress facade. The owner, much-travelled entrepreneur Nincho Oslekov, employed Samokov craftsmen Mincho and Kosta Zograf to decorate the exterior with fanciful scenes of classical cities. Inside, the Red Room (originally the guest room) is particulary impressive, with a wooden ceiling carved with geometric motifs. One of the medallions painted on the wall shows the original, symmetrical plan of the house, never realized since Oslekov's neighbours refused to sell him the necessary land. You can imagine Oslekov brooding over the rebuff while reclining on the cushioned *minder*, taking solace from his pipes and an enormous hookah.

of each *cheta* degenerated into a march into death and martyrdom. That of Botev was the most celebrated, and he was eventually killed on Mount Okolchitsa (see p.102) on June 2.

However, it was the **Fourth Revolutionary Region** (based in Plovdiv and including Koprivshtitsa) that saw most of the action. It was here that the Rising was launched: a tragically botched job in which the seeds of the Rising's ultimate failure were sown. It all began in Koprivshtitsa ahead of schedule on April 20, when the conspirators learned that their plans had been betrayed. Capturing the *Konak*, the rebels dispatched the celebrated "**Bloody Letters**", written in the blood of the first dead Turk, imploring other towns to join them, and began fortifying the village while rain played havoc with their home-made gunpowder and "cherry-tree" cannons (see overleaf).

The Ottoman governor of Plovdiv used irregular troops to restore order in the region. These were either *pomaks*, Bulgarian-speaking Muslims eager to settle private scores with their Christian neighbours, or *bashibazouks*, ill-disciplined groups of freebooters often drawn from the Tatar and Circassian populations, only recently expelled from Tsarist Russia and therefore pretty hostile to Slavs in general. As the *bashibazouks* burned neighbouring towns, refugees flooded into Koprivshtitsa spreading panic, and the local *chorbadzhii* (the rural middle class) attempted to disarm the insurgents. The rebels eventually took to the hills (where most were killed), and it's ironic that – thanks to the *chorbadzhii*, who bribed the *bashibazouks* to spare the village – Koprivshtitsa survived unscathed to be admired by subsequent generations as a symbol of heroism.

The aftermath
The expected intervention of Serbia and Russia never materialized, and before long the Rising fizzled out. The Serbs fought a short war with Turkey in the summer of 1876 (in which many Bulgarian exiles participated), but it was of little use to the immediate needs of Bulgaria. However, the ferocity with which the Turkish "punished" Bulgaria's civilian population (see "Batak", p.229) in the aftermath of the Rising convinced the Great Powers of Europe that the Ottoman empire could no longer be allowed a free hand to discipline its Balkan subjects. As scandalized talk of "Bulgarian atrocities" spread across the continent, Turkey's traditional supporters (like France and Britain) lost the political will to shore up the Ottoman empire against its critics. This suited the Russians, who were angling for the creation of an independent Bulgarian state, which they saw as a convenient vehicle for spreading their own interests in the region.

Ordinary Russian civilians were in any case affronted by the treatment meted out to their fellow Slavs by the Turks, and pressed for war: the April Rising ultimately *did* succeed in giving the Russians the excuse they needed to attack Turkey. Tsar Aleksandăr II finally declared war on April 12, 1877, almost a year after the outbreak of the Rising. By the following January, Ottoman forces had been driven out of Bulgaria, never to return.

MEMORIAL HOUSES' OPENING HOURS

Koprivshtitsa's numerous **memorial houses** are each open Tues–Sun 7.30am–noon and 1.30–5.30pm. A combined entrance ticket valid for all the houses can be bought at the Museum Service office on the main square, although its hours of business depend largely on the whims of the employees. If it's shut, the larger of the memorial houses (such as the Oslekov or the Kableshkov) should be able to sell you a ticket.

The Dimcho Debelyanov house and around

Keep heading west and you run into ul. Debelyanov, which straddles a hill between two bridges and boasts some more lovely buildings. Near the Surlya Bridge at no. 6, the **birthplace of Dimcho Debelyanov** recalls the tragically short career of this early twentieth-century poet with a fairly routine sequence of photographs. Debelyanov's grave is in the yard of the hilltop **church of the Holy Virgin**. There, Lazarov's statue of a seated woman recalls Debelyanov's old mother, who waited in vain for Dimcho to return from the battlefields of Greece, where he was killed in 1916. The inscription is from one of his poems: "Delaying in a gentle dream she becomes her own child." The church – built in 1817, partly sunken into the ground to comply with the Ottoman requirement that no Christian building should be taller than the local mosque – acquired its domed belfry at a later date, and contains an iconostasis with some of Zahari Zograf's best works.

The Kableshkov house

On the same street as the church, the decision to launch the Uprising was taken at the house of the Conspiracy at no. 18, after Turkish troops came to arrest the ringleader, **Todor Kableshkov**, whose **birthplace** lies on a parallel street, accessible via a gate at the rear of the churchyard. Born in 1854, Kableshkov studied French in Constantinople before catching malaria and returning home, where he met revolutionary activist Vasil Levski and began his revolutionary career. Captured near Troyan after the April Rising, he managed to kill himself with a police revolver in Gabrovo.

The ground floor of the house preserves the simple living quarters of a reasonably prosperous nineteenth-century family, including the "women's work room", where spinning wheel and weaving loom were employed to produce some of Koprivshtitsa's renowned woollens. Militaria is displayed upstairs, including the insurgents' silk banner embroidered with the Bulgarian Lion and the words *svoboda ili smârt* ("Liberty or Death!"); and one of the twenty secretly manufactured **cherry-tree cannons**. These home-made artillery pieces were made from the only suitable locally available wood, that of the cherry tree, and cauldrons traditionally used for the distillation of rose oil were melted down in order to provide the copper lining of the barrels. Although one bore the engraved slogan "End of the Turkish Empire, 1876", the cannons soon became a liability to the insurgents, as they tended to explode once the barrel linings had worn away.

The Lyutov house and around

Near the **Bridge of the First Shot** spanning the River Byala where the Uprising began stands a striking example of Bulgarian Baroque, the **Lyutov house**, built in 1854. It's best known for its wealth of murals: palaces, temples and travel scenes splashed across the walls and *alafranga* (niches); wreaths, blossoms and nosegays in the Blue Room; and oval medallions adorning the ceilings. The side-street running southeast away from the bridge leads back towards the river and a handsome pair of ochre-clad nineteenth-century public buildings: the **village school**, built in 1837 and now holding an international centre for the study of Byzantine aesthetics; and the **Narodno chitalishte** of 1869. Ostensibly a public reading room, the *chitalishte* was a crucial aspect of village life, promoting the Bulgarian language, spreading literacy, and nurturing a sense of national identity.

The church of Sveta Nikola and the Benkovski house

From here it's only a few minutes' walk to the **church of Sveta Nikola**. Despite the dedication the emphasis seems to be on Saint Spiridion, whose life is told in ten medallions surrounding a figure of the saint. To the left of the church is a fountain donated by the Moravenovs, one of Koprivshtitsa's leading families in the early eighteenth century.

Following the Kosovo stream down to the main street, and then walking up ul. Dorosiev, brings you to the museum-house of another major figure in the Uprising, **Georgi Benkovski** (1844–76). A prominent revolutionary activist, he helped to reconstruct the clandestine networks built up by Vasil Levski after the latter's execution in 1873. A tailor by profession and leader of a local *cheta*, Benkovski made the insurgents' banner and uniforms – long jackets of white homespun cloth and caps with the Bulgarian lion badge. Benkovski's *cheta* wheeled south via Panagyurishte and Mount Eledzhik trying to rally the locals to the cause, but they were chased northwards by the Turks and eventually wiped out near Teteven. Benkovski's career is covered in usual didactic style by the period photographs and (Bulgarian-only) texts on the first floor, including one declamatory quote by chronicler of the Rising Zahari Stoyanov which helps to crystallize the Koprivshtitsa legend: "Koprivshtitsa was a republic for centuries, without senators, ministers or presidents; ten times more liberal than France, and a hundred times more democratic than America". A monument to Benkovski stands on the hillside above the house; depicting him in the form of a kitsch Socialist-Realist horseman, does much to detract from an otherwise unsullied village skyline.

The Karavelov house

Returning towards the village square along the east bank of the Topolnitsa you eventually reach the **birthplace of Lyuben Karavelov**. Born in 1834, the son of a butcher and sheep merchant, Karavelov's itinerant career was typical of the many patriots who spent long years in exile trying to garner support for the Bulgarian cause. Educated in Moscow, Karavelov was a strong believer in the need to attract Russian and Serbian help in the struggle to liberate Bulgaria from the Turks, and accordingly based himself in the Serbian capital Belgrade. However, his enthusiasm for the idea of a Balkan Federation proved too radical for his hosts, who forced him to flee across the border to the then Habsburg-controlled town of Novi Sad. The Austrians, in a conciliatory gesture towards the Serbs, imprisoned Karavelov in Zemun for a while. He eventually found refuge in Bucharest, where he organized a revolutionary Central Committee in 1860, and for ten years advocated armed struggle against the Turks in the columns of the émigré newspapers *Svoboda* and *Nezavisimost*. After Levski's execution, however, he repudiated direct action in favour of change through reform and education, and was ousted from the leadership of the committee by Hristo Botev.

Built in several stages and surrounded by a high wall, **the house** contains the usual examples of nineteenth-century domestic interiors; and an old printing press, bought in Belgrade in 1871 and shipped to Bulgaria after the Liberation. An adjoining summer house contains the personal effects of Lyuben's younger brother Petko, a prominent liberal politician after the Liberation and twice prime minister.

Practicalities

Koprivshtitsa's small **bus terminal** is a couple of hundred metres south of the main square. Just beyond the square, a *Balkantourist* office at Anton Ivanov 42

THE KOPRIVSHTITSA MUSIC FESTIVAL

Simon Broughton visited the Koprivshtitsa festival in 1991. His account is taken from World Music: The Rough Guide *(Penguin 1993).*

Imagine a cross between a pop festival and a medieval fair: 18,000 people singing and playing music in the mountains of central Bulgaria surrounded by traders exploiting the new free-market potential, the smell of grilling kebabs, beer tents, plastic trinket sellers, stalls with the latest in Bulgarian CDs and Gypsies weaving through the crowds with performing monkeys and dancing bears. This is the festival that takes place every five years on the hillside above the picturesque village of Koprivshtitsa.

It began in 1965 as a showcase for Bulgarian folklore financed by the Ministry of Culture. The Bulgarian Communists were generous in supporting *their* idea of folk music: state song-and-dance troupes presenting a "rich national heritage" abroad and professional dance ensembles going into villages to show the locals how Bulgarian dances *should* be performed. Compared with this, Koprivshtitsa was one of the better ideas. Here the music is performed in its raw style by ordinary villagers.

The 1991 festival was a microcosm of Bulgaria itself: a confused halfway house between a centrally controlled state and a market economy where private cafés have sprung up to serve the petrol queues. The competitive element in which performers were awarded insulting pseudo-gold medals had gone, but the former jurors were still there at their tables observing and taking notes "for research purposes". Around them instrument makers and record dealers had moved in with their stalls and were doing a roaring trade selling bagpipes, gadulkas and tamburas. For those with hard currency these were on offer at bargain prices.

The Ministry of Culture, strapped by the severe economic crisis, only came up with half the money needed and the festival was saved by other government departments providing transport, tents and medication free of charge. The organizers also hoped to recoup costs by selling records and videos. If the recordings are as good as the ones from previous festivals they'll be worth getting, but the prospect of a video of all those stout Bulgarian women linking arms and strutting their open-throated stuff without the distraction of grilling kebabs and dancing bears is daunting.

Bulgaria is host to a large Turkish minority population who were persecuted by the former regime. Officially there were no Turkish groups participating in the festival, although they intend to invite Turkish, Gypsy, Jewish and Armenian performers next time round. But going off in search of a kebab I stumbled across a clutch of Turkish musicians at the centre of a ring of dancers playing "zurna", the (opening hours are unpredictable and the office may close up completely out of season) may be able to help with **accommodation** in one of the village's old mansions, although these are often booked solid by groups – if so, you can try asking around for private lodgings with local people: you'll be expected to negotiate for these. On the hillside east of the main square, rooms at the *Hotel Koprivshtitsa* (☎997184/2182; ②–③) aren't too expensive and have sweeping views of the valley. Travellers with wheels may also consider the *Hotel Barikadite* (☎997184/2091; ③), located in a popular highland recreation area 18km from town; take the road heading south, then the left-hand fork, and then the turning to the left 12km on.

strident Turkish oboe and drum. "Ear fucking" is what they call it when, for a few leva, you can have the dubious thrill of the zurna blown directly into your ear. With the rhythms insistently pumping out, the dancers too were in a sort of sexual frenzy. Some of the men had beer bottles tucked into their wide waistbands, and thrusting their groins they carefully controlled their movements until the climax of the dance, when the beer frothed over and sprayed the crowd.

Its supporters say that the Koprivshtitsa festival shows Bulgarian music at its most authentic – even if this means performing a mid-winter dance on a concrete platform in August with men dressed in woolly bear-suits in a temperature of 30°C. Really they mean that the music, if not the event, is genuine. This is village music as performed by the villagers, not arranged and cleaned up by professional ensembles. Still, I suspect that nowadays most mid-winter rituals in Bulgaria are performed at Koprivshtitsa in August rather than at their proper time. The social changes since the war have changed the nature of village life forever.

Unlike Romania where the music has kept its original function in spite of the regime, in Bulgaria it has rather lost its true meaning thanks to sponsorship by the state. Now it needs to find a natural life again, but whether it can when the link between the music and everyday life is broken is a moot point: it may have become permanently "festivalized".

The best music at Koprivshtitsa happens offstage away from the PA systems. You can find little groups just singing to themselves, or solitary bagpipe and fiddle players on the hillside. This is where the music belongs and where it sounds at its best. But it's hard to see how it can continue without some sort of semi-official structure.

"It's interesting that Bulgaria is practically the only country in the Balkans in which there is no connection between today's popular music and folk music. You find it in Serbia or Greece, but not Bulgaria since the war. That's the effect of the Communist Party trying to impose its rigid patterns so the music has nothing to do with everyday life." So says the new Bulgarian leader, Filip Dimitrov, elected in October 1991; and government policy, in as much as they have one, is to let folk music find its own role and place again with state support where necessary.

After a visit to Koprivshtitsa there's no doubt that there is incredible musicality among ordinary people. Bulgaria only has a population of nine million: head-for-head it's as if 112,000 people turned up in Hyde Park to play and perform – something that's almost impossible to believe could happen in Britain. For the moment the Koprivshtitsa tradition endures and many of Bulgaria's professional musicians go to the festival to keep in touch with music at the roots. As Elena Stoyin, an eminent musicologist and one of the now redundant judges told me, "We are a small and poor country, but we are rich in these traditions and happy that people are preserving these things themselves."

A couple of obvious places at which to **eat and drink**: there's a café and restaurant in the *April 20 Complex* on the main square; while just across the river is the *Dyado Liben Inn*, occupying the beautiful Dragilska house built in 1860, with a restaurant upstairs, and an animated bar in the courtyard below.

Panagyurishte

By keeping control of STRELCHA in 1876, the Turks prevented the insurgents in Koprivshtitsa from linking up with their fellows in **PANAGYURISHTE** – which, as the headquarters of the Fourth Revolutionary Region, had been envisaged as the centre of operations. This contributed to the failure of the April Rising and ensured that Panagyurishte remained isolated until Ottoman forces arrived from Pazardzhik and Plovdiv to set the town ablaze, hence its predominantly modern appearance nowadays. It is less touristy than Koprivshtitsa, visitors are less well provided for here, and its sights can be digested within the space of a day trip – unless the woods and pasturelands of the surrounding hills provide a motive to stay longer.

The town

Panagyurishte's train station lies among modern suburbs on the southeastern fringes of town, a short walk down A. Shishkov into the centre. The bus terminal is a couple of blocks south of the centre, modernist civic buildings grouped around the flagstones of pl. Pavel Bobekov – site of the 2-star *Hotel Kamengrad* (☎0357/2877; ③).

Around pl. Pavel Bobekov

A hill overlooking the square from the east is dominated by the **memorial to the April Rising**, a towering concrete construction typical of the part-modernist, part-socialist realist style that characterized Bulgaria's public monuments in the 1970s and 1980s. A processional stairway leads up to the memorial, passing on the way the early nineteenth-century **church of Sveta Bogoroditsa** (daily 8am–noon and 2–5pm). Partially burnt in the aftermath of the Rising, most of the church's original frescoes perished; patches of blackened and blistered paintwork (immediately on the left as you enter) have been left *in situ* as a reminder of the conflagration. The rest of the interior was colourfully decorated by Samokov painters in the 1890s, covering the walls with a pictorial history of the life of the Virgin Mary consisting of well over a hundred individual scenes – each inscribed with the name of the local benefactor who paid for it.

West of the main square, ul. Raina Knyaginya heads uphill into what remains of the old town. The two towers of the colonnaded, turquoise-plastered church of Sveti Georgi precede the **Shtârbanova Kâshta** at no. 26, home to a prominent member of the local provisional government during the Rising. The house forms one part of a complex of buildings holding the town **museum** (Tues–Sun 8am–noon & 2–5.30pm) that bristles with antique militaria – including the obligatory cherry-tree cannon. Opposite the church of Sveti Georgi, across a small square, ul. Oborishte leads to the **Raina Knyaginya museum-house** at no. 5 (Tues–Sun 8am–noon & 2–6pm). As a young girl, Raina was the flag-bearer of the local insurgents, and was sarcastically accorded the sobriquet *knyaginya* (literally "princess") by her mocking Turkish captors. Severely tortured in Plovdiv, Raina was sent into exile in Russia, returning to Bulgaria after the Liberation to become a schoolteacher in Veliko Târnovo. The house contains sepia family portraits along-side a "Liberty or Death" flag woven by Raina herself in 1901, in memory of the one she carried during the Rising. She's buried in the garden together with her mother and father – the latter a casualty of the Rising.

Out of town

Finally, there's another **monument** in a wooded valley several kilometres north of OBORISHTE, 7km west of Panagyurishte, marking the place where leaders of the Sredna Gora underground agreed to launch the 1876 Uprising on May 1. Unfortunately, there was a spy among them, Nenko Stoyanov, who tipped off the Turks about Kableshkov's group in Koprivshtitsa, and thus unwittingly precipi-tated the Rising in April.

Hisarya

At the foot of the Sredna Gora range between Plovdiv and Karlovo stands one of the great watering-holes of antiquity, **HISARYA** (the name, dating from the Turkish occupation, literally means "the fortress" – although you'll often see the town referred to on road signs and bus timetables by a shortened form, *Hisar*). As gold treasures and other less glamorous finds in neighbouring villages have proved, the area was inhabited as long ago as 5000 BC, and formed part of the Macedonian empire before the arrival of the Romans. But it was the Romans who really developed Hisarya, building marble baths, aqueducts, temples and – after raids by the Goths in 251 – fortifications to protect the town, which they called *Augusta*. Subsequently an episcopal seat, it was devastated by Crusaders despite their appreciation of this "fair town", 150 years before its conquest by the Turks, who restored the baths in the sixteenth century.

The town

A short distance to the south of the railway and bus terminals, a sizable chunk of this history confronts visitors in the form of the damaged but still imposing **fortress walls**, originally between 2m–3m thick and defended by 43 towers. The Roman builders employed the technique of *opus mixtum*, bonding stone and brick with red mortar – hence the sobriquet *Kizil Kale* ("red fortress") which the Turks coined when they besieged the town in 1364. The northern wall consists of a double rampart, but the most impressive section is the huge southern **Kamilite Gate**, so called after the camels which once passed through it. Beyond the gate, 100m west and 125m south are two **ruined basilicas** dating from the fifth and sixth centuries, while beyond a breach in the southwestern corner of the ramparts lies a fourth-century **Roman tomb**, with frescoed walls, a mosaic floor and two fixed "beds".

Stonework, coins and other finds are displayed in the **museum**, within the walls at ul. Stamboliiski 8, but the town's baths are of more interest. The **Havuz mineral baths**, on the opposite side of the main street to the museum, were particularly admired by Roman women on account of their efficacious effects on gynaecological disorders. The other main bathing complex, *Momina Banya*, yields radioactive water recommended for liver and gastric complaints, while the produce of another spring is bottled and sold throughout Bulgaria as mineral water (*Hisar Banya*).

Practicalities

For information on treatments and opening times, enquire at the **tourist office** at ul. Augusta 16. Wealthier convalescents patronize the 3-star *Hotel Augusta* (☎0337/3800; ④); while the *Apriltsi*, bul. Ivan Vazov 66 (☎ 0337/2467; ③) is more down to earth.

THE VALLEY OF THE ROSES

Lying midway between Sofia and the coast, the **Valley of the Roses** is perhaps the most over-hyped region of Bulgaria. A sunbaked and dusty place for most of the summer, in May and early June it's magically transformed by the blooms which give it its name. Outside of this period, however, its towns can seem unexciting – "ramshackle collections of unplastered cottages which might have dropped off a lorry" thought Leslie Gardiner, and he wasn't far wrong. The major towns strung out through the valley – **Klisura**, **Sopot**, **Karlovo** and **Kalofer** – all occupy honoured niches in Bulgarian history as the scene of heroic events or the birthplace of writers or national heroes, but have little that's worth seeing beyond the memorial museums.

The only exception to this rule is **Kazanlâk**, whose geographical position straddling both north–south and east–west routes makes it the obvious place in the region to stay. The venue for the Festival of Roses after the harvest in May,

---

ROSES: "BULGARIA'S GOLD"

The **rose-growing area** between Klisura and Kazanlâk produces 70 percent of the world's attar – or extract – of roses. Considering that perfumiers pay more than £30 million a year for this, it's not suprising that roses are known as "Bulgaria's gold". Rose-growing began as a small cottage industry during the 1830s (supposedly started by a Turkish merchant impressed by the fragrance of the wild Shipka rose), and initially involved small domestic stills comprising a copper cauldron from which water-cooled pipes dripped the greenish-yellow rose oil. It became big business early in the twentieth century but virtually ceased during World War II when Nazi Germany discouraged the industry in order to sell its own *ersatz* scents, but since then Bulgaria's rose-growers have vastly expanded their operations.

Each acre planted with red *rosa damascena* or white *rosa alba* yields up to 1400 kilograms of blossom, or roughly 3 million rosebuds; between 3000 and 6000 kilos are required to make one litre of attar, leaving a residue of rosewater and pulp used to make medicaments, flavourings, *sladko* jam and *rosaliika* liqueur. The rose bushes (covering over 14,000 acres) are allowed to grow to head height, and are harvested during May between 3am and 8am before the sun rises and evaporates up to half of the oil. Nimble-fingered women and girls do most of the picking, while donkeys are employed to carry the petals away to the modern distilleries around Rozino, Kârnare and Kazanlâk. Kazanlâk also has a research institute where pesticides are tested and different breeds of rose developed; according to the director, its gardens contain every variety in the world.

Kazanlâk features a remarkable Thracian tomb. Within easy reach of the town to the north is the rugged **Shipka pass**, heroically defended by Russian and Bulgarian troops during the War of Liberation in 1878.

Regular **trains** from Sofia to Karlovo or Burgas make it easy enough to travel along the valley (although express services don't stop at the smaller places en route, and there are few trains of any description between late morning and early evening). Coming down from the Balkan range via the Troyan or Shipka pass, you can pick up the valley route at Kârnare or Kazanlâk; Srednogorie and Karlovo are linked by buses or branch-rail lines to both the Sredna Gora and Plovdiv.

Between Sofia and Kazanlâk

Heading eastwards from Sofia there's little of great note for the first hundred kilometres or so, although the settlements along the route provide useful jumping-off points for the Balkan range to the north or the Sredna Gora to the south. Things become more interesting once you hit the Valley of the Roses proper, the western stretches of which contain a clutch of towns associated with famous Bulgarian patriots. **Sopot**, **Karlovo** and **Kalofer** were the birthplaces of Ivan Vazov, Vasil Levski, and Hristo Botev respectively; and memories of these men provide the main reason for visiting. Karlovo is the principal market centre on which the others depend, and it's here that the atmosphere of a turn-of-the-century rose-harvesting town has been best preserved. It's also a useful transport hub, with a branch line heading south towards Plovdiv and regular buses to its smaller neighbours in the valley itself.

Sofia to Karlovo

Beyond the broad plain to the east of Sofia, the neighbouring mountains slope down to a succession of saddles and spurs, which the road climbs, passing a *motel/campsite* near MIRKOVO. Non-express trains usually stop at the Zlatitsa and Pirdop suburbs of SREDNOGORIE, a mining town from where a road heads north over the Zlatishki pass towards Etropole monastery (p.130), and buses run south to Panagyurishte (p.186). North of Anton village, you'll see Baba and Vezhen, the first great peaks of the Balkan range; just beyond the railway halt for Koprivshtitsa (12km from the village itself, see p.178), trains enter a long tunnel beneath the Koznitsa spur, emerging into the Stryama Valley, the upper part of the Valley of the Roses. Despite having a bleached and arid look from the end of the rose harvest until the autumn, the valley looks surprisingly lush throughout the rest of the year. Groves of fruit trees give way to pastures dotted with wild flowers, while the surrounding hills are covered by deep forests.

Despite its dramatic situation at the head of the valley, there's little reason to stop at **KLISURA**, although this small town "of tiles and flowers" is lauded for having been burned down during the April Rising, as described in Ivan Vazov's epic *Under the Yoke*. From here onwards it's roses all the way – at least during May – with fading posters from the Communist period exhorting the erstwhile collective farmers of ROZINO, an isolated Turkish-speaking village, to produce more of the valuable blooms. The next small town, KÂRNARE, is the point of departure for **buses to Troyan**, which take the highest road in Bulgaria, crossing the scenic Troyan Pass (see p.139).

IVAN VAZOV (1850–1921)

Born in 1850 to the family of a Sopot merchant, **Ivan Vazov**'s youthful patriotism took him into exile in Romania, where he met other Bulgarian revolutionaries (the poet Hristo Botev was one of Vazov's drinking partners in Galati), and began writing for émigré journals. On returning to Sopot he threw himself into revolutionary politics, but was forced to flee the town on the eve of the April Rising because of the threat of imminent arrest. The events of April 1876, perhaps because of the fact that he was unable to participate in them himself, inspired Vazov to write his best poetry.

After the Liberation he was appointed magistrate in Berkovitsa, where he found that the foibles of the *chorbadzhii* and petty bureaucrats provided material for satirical pieces, and he later devoted himself to editing newspapers in Plovdiv, then the capital of Eastern Roumelia. Fleeing to Odessa after Stambolov's coup in 1886, Vazov wrote the classic tale of small-town life before and during the April Rising, *Pod igoto* (*Under the Yoke*), subsequently acclaimed as Bulgaria's "national novel". Returning home later, he entered Parliament and became minister of education (1897–79), continuing to write a stream of novels, articles and poems until his death in Sofia in 1921, where he was buried on Aleksandår Nevski Square.

Sopot

A machine-building works and modern flats have vastly altered the appearance of **SOPOT**, whose main square features a bronze statue of the small town's most famous son, **Ivan Vazov**. On the western side of the square is Vazov's birthplace, now a **museum** (Tues–Sun 8am–noon & 1–5.30pm). The buildings, grouped around a vine-shaded courtyard, suggest a comfortable upringing in the home of a middle-class merchant – although the study of Vazov's father is frugal and most of the domestic utensils are reasonably functional, save for the imported porcelain in the guest room. An adjacent modern building contains a pictorial history of Vazov's career, including photographs of those of his Sopot contemporaries who provided the basis for characters in *Under the Yoke*.

There's little else to see in Sopot save for a parade of reconstructed **craft workshops** which extend along the western side of the square, and the town's proximity to Karlovo (accessible by buses #5, #6 and #7 from the main square) suggests that you'd do better to base yourself at the latter. Sopot does have one **hotel**, the 2-star *Stara Planina* (☎03134/2123; ③) on the main square.

Karlovo

Set against a backdrop of lofty, arid crags and hollows descending to slopes partly covered with cypresses and fig trees, **KARLOVO** initially looks unimpressive by comparison with its surroundings. However, its old quarter, the subject of much recent renovation, is worthy of exploration; and the birthplace of Vasil Levski provides a popular destination for modern-day pilgrims.

You should be able to see all of Karlovo's sights (and make the short bus trip to Sopot into the bargain) in the space of a day. If you need to stay the night, however, your choice is between the 2-star *Rozova Dolina* (☎0335/3380; ③) on pl. 20 Yuli, or the significantly cheaper *turisticheska spalnya* at ul. Levski 4. The nearest campsite is the *Byala Reka* just west of Kalofer (see p.192).

Around the town

Karlovo's **rail and bus stations** are located at the southern end of town, from which ul. Levski gently ascends towards the town centre. Halfway up, the street passes through pl. Vasil Levski, an ensemble of nineteenth-century houses grouped around a statue of the town's most famous son – shown here accompanied by a small lion. On the northeast corner stands the **Aleksandrov House**, whose pillared porch and curved gables make it a triumph of National Revival architecture. To the south, the colonnaded basilica of Sveti Nikolai squats opposite the **town museum**, housed in a former school (closed for reorganization at the time of writing, but likely to contain an extensive folkloric collection).

Continuing further along ul. Levski, alleys to the right lead off into a quarter of the town full of nineteenth-century houses and spruced-up turn-of-the-century mansions, bisected by cobbled alleys. One of the nicest of the houses (most are still lived in and therefore not open to the public) is the house of **Hristo Pop Vasiliev** on ul. Geshev, now a local teachers' centre, where the building's orieled upper storeys and symmetrical appearance show the influence of Plovdiv styles. At the northern end of ul. Levski is the **Kurshum dzhamiya** ("lead-roofed mosque"), dating from 1485 and featuring an ornate porch supported by cedarwood pillars, and a stunted red-brick minaret, its upper reaches shorn off just above roof level.

Just northwest of here, the flagstoned expanse of pl. 20 Yuli forms Karlovo's modern centre. Ul. Petko Sâbev continues west, past a whitewashed nineteenth-century clock tower, to the **Vasil Levski museum-house** (Tues–Sun 8am–noon & 1–5.30pm), hiding behind a low wall just downhill from the main road. A plain rectangle with a small verandah, the houses has sparse living quarters, the only ornamentation provided by a single shelf running along the wall almost at ceiling-

VASIL LEVSKI (1837–1872)

Born in 1837 and raised by his widowed mother, Vasil Levski briefly considered the priesthood and medicine before dedicating himself to the cause of Bulgaria's liberation. Choosing exile like many patriots, he joined Rakovski's Bulgarian Legion in Belgrade. The Legion's raids across the border into Bulgaria infuriated the Turks but won little sympathy from the local population – leading Levski to conclude that Ottoman rule could only be overthrown by a revolutionary organization based within Bulgaria. Levski and fellow-exile Lyuben Karavelov took control of the Bucharest-based Bulgarian Revolutionary Central Committee in 1867, where they began elaborating the theory that an elite group of committed activists, or "apostles", should carry out the task of constructing a revolutionary network within the country. From 1869 on Levski set about establishing just this: gathering recruits as he ranged across the country in a variety of disguises. Captured near Lovech at the end of 1872, Levski was executed the following February in Sofia – at the spot now marked by the Levski monument.

Inspired by a vision of liberation that transcended frontiers, Levski (the "Apostle of Freedom") became a legend within his own lifetime. Although adopted as a national hero by subsequent generations, Levski would not necessarily have felt at home in the Bulgaria which came into being after the Liberation. His sense of justice made him a convinced republican (hence the exploitation of his legacy by the equally anti-royalist Communists), and also a believer in racial harmony – he made it clear more than once that he was fighting against Ottoman power on behalf of Bulgarians of all races, and not just the Slavs.

level, with pewter dishes arranged along it. At the side of the house is the *boyad-zhiinitsa* (the dyeing shed, where Levski's mother worked), a small alcove filled with big earthenware pots, a brazier, and balls of coloured cord. Behind the house, an exhibition hall harbours photographs of Levski and his comrades in the First and Second Bulgarian Legions in Belgrade; and among other slogans and texts, a list of the various pseudonyms used by Levski when travelling incognito.

Between Karlovo and Kazanlâk

Whether travellers **heading east** see the vineyards, tobacco plants or roses depends on the season, but whatever the time of year you'll pass some of the grandest peaks in the Balkans. Crossing the Staga ridge joining the Sredna Gora to the Balkan range, the road enters **KALOFER**, where numerous water-wheels used to revolve in the River Tundzha, which emerges from a nearby gorge to flow through this small town. Architecturally undistinguished, Kalofer has only one tourist attraction, or rather, place of pilgrimage – the childhood home of another revolutionary, **Hristo Botev**.

Perhaps the most romantic figure in Bulgaria's pantheon of heroes, Botev (1848–76) imbibed patriotism from his father and radical ideals while studying at Odessa, after which he gravitated towards the Bulgarian émigré community in Bessarabia before returning home in 1867. Scornful of compromise, he was soon exiled for preaching "Stop buying and selling, bickering and cheating, strutting and grovelling!", and went to Bucharest in search of the Secret Revolutionary Committee. There he shared a garret with Levski and subsequently worked with Karavelov on *Budilnik* ("Alarm"), *Zname* ("Banner") and other radical papers, writing stirring eulogies to liberty and Hadzhi Dimitâr. A utopian socialist, and a man of action, Botev responded to news of the April Rising by hijacking a steamer and landing with 200 men to aid the rebels, but was killed in action near Vratsa. The highest peak in the Balkan range (2376m), looming to the north of town, now bears his name.

Kalofer's **railway station** lies a couple of kilometres southwest of town, but all trains are met by a bus into the centre. The 2-star *Hotel Roza* (☎234; ③) has reasonably priced **rooms**, but cheaper chalets can be had at *Byala Reka campsite* (open May–Sept; ☎213) 2km west of town. Continuing eastwards the valley begins to level out, although the uncompromising presence of the Balkan Mountains remains to the north. The main item of interest before reaching Kazanlâk is the **Georgi Dimitrov Dam**, built by convict labour between 1947 and 1955 in order to create an artificial lake holding 21 billion gallons of water, which permits the irrigation of 100,000 acres of land around Stara Zagora and Kazanlâk.

Kazanlâk

Principal town of the upper Tundzha valley and capital of the rose-growing region, **KAZANLÂK** is at its liveliest during the first half of July, when it hosts the annual **Festival of Roses**. Rich in folkloric displays and "rose-picking ritual", this is basically a tourist event – the rose crop has already been harvested during May. Should you wish to attend it's advisable to book rooms in advance, and try to ascertain precise dates of what's on from the Bulgarian National Tourist Offices abroad. At other times, Kazanlâk can be fairly dormant, but the discovery

KAZANLÂK

↑ The Shipka Pass, Gabrovo & Kazanlâshka Roza Campsite

■ Museum of the Rose Industry

Tyulbeto Park

■ Hotel Zornitsa

Turbe of Lala Shahin Pasha ■

■ Thracian Tomb

■ Ethnographic Complex

STARATA REKA

GENERAL SKOBELEV

ULITSA ISKRA

■ Iskra Museum

■ Post Office

■ Hotel Kazanlâk

Karlovo ←

N

↑ Church of the Assumption

Sliven & Stara Zagora →

■ Hotel Roza

ROZOVA DOLINA

0   200 m

■ Bus Station

SOFRONII VRACHANSKI

Railway Station

of a fourth-century BC **Thracian tomb** just north of town renders it an essential stop-off for anyone remotely interested in the Bulgarians' ancient antecedents. Plentiful transport connections make it a good place to stay if visiting the Shipka pass to the north or Stara Zagora to the south.

Some history

The area around Kazanlâk has attracted successive waves of settlers and invaders, not least because of its strategic importance in controlling the southern approaches to the Shipka pass. In ancient times the Tundzha valley was the domain of the Thracian **Odrysae**, who exploited the vacuum left by the retreat of Persian power in the fifth century BC to forge a powerful tribal state on the southern slopes of the Balkan range. The power of the Odrysae was temporarily broken by Philip II of Macedon in 342 BC, but they re-emerged a generation later under **King Seuthes III**, an unruly vassal of Alexander the Great's successor Lysimachus, who built a new capital, *Seuthopolis*, 7km west of present-day Kazanlâk – now submerged beneath the lake created by the Georgi Dimitrov dam. *Seuthopolis* soon fell into decline, and a deluge of **Celts** occurred some-where around 280 BC, many of whom settled in the plain just east of Kazanlâk. There was a fortified medieval Bulgarian settlement at *Krân*, just to the north-west, but the town of Kazanlâk itself is relatively modern, dating from the Ottoman occupation. The name itself loosely translates as the "place of the copper cauldrons", a likely reference to the giant stills in which rose oil was prepared. By the turn of the century Kazanlâk's streets were filled with the shops and store-houses of the rose merchants – a breed of Balkan trader which has long since disappeared, squeezed out by social ownership and state control.

The town

The hotels and civic buildings of Kazanlâk's central square present an uncompromisingly modernist face to the rather drab remnants of the prewar town, which straggle untidily westwards. Lurking just behind the *Hotel Roza* is the nineteenth-century **church of the Assumption**, with an exquisite iconostasis carved by Debâr craftsmen. Ul. Iskra leaves the square's northern end, passing before long the **Iskra museum** (Tues–Sun 8am–noon & 1.30–6pm) at no. 13. The archaeological section downstairs is rich in finds from *Seuthopolis* – diagrams of the city's street plan show it to have been an ambitious undertaking, built from scratch on a grid pattern based on the theories of Hippodamus of Miletus, doyen of Hellenistic town planners. Weapons, functional pottery, and coins minted by King Seuthes III help to illustrate life in his capital; while the reconstructed floor plans of domestic houses reveal the bowl-like depressions which served as cult hearths – at which the family would make appeals to the tribal deities. An upstairs picture gallery harbours mediocre local works and a collection of icons from local churches.

    Tyulbeto Park, the site of two renowned funerary monuments, lies a further ten minutes' walk to the northeast, on the far bank of the *Starata reka*. A stairway behind the park gates ascends to the skeletal remains of the **turbe of Lala Shahin Pasha**, conqueror of much of Bulgaria and first Ottoman governor of Rumelia. He fell in battle here, and it's thought that his entrails were interred on the spot before the rest of him was carried back to Bursa (probably embalmed in honey) to be buried in a much finer *turbe* (a small mausoleum) closer to home.

The Thracian tomb

Immediately behind the *turbe* is a protective structure built over Kazanlâk's **Thracian tomb**, site of a late fourth- or early third-century burial unearthed by chance in 1944 during the construction of an air defence observation post. Unfortunately, its frescoes are so delicate that only scholars with authorization from the Ministry of Culture may enter (and even then only if they have a good reason), but the **replica** (daily 8am–noon & 1.30–6pm), built some 50m to the east, is an atmospheric enough recreation.

    Once inside, the domed burial chamber is approached through a narrow corri-dor decorated by two bands of murals – one ornamented with plant and architec-tural motifs, the other displaying battle scenes. The floor and walls are stained a deep red, while in the cupola are the paintings for which the tomb is famed. They depict a procession of horses and servants approaching the chieftain for whom the tomb was built, who sits behind a low table laden with food. His wife, face downcast in mourning, reposes on an elaborate throne beside him, and the couple touch hands in a tender gesture of farewell. A bowl of fruit is offered to the deceased by a female figure to the right, who has been linked with both the Great Mother Goddess common to Thracian tribes, and the queen of the Underworld in the Greek pantheon, Persephone. Racing chariots wheel around the apex of the dome, a possible reference to the games which often accompanied a Thracian funeral. With its graceful composition and naturalistic details, the painting is a masterpiece of Hellenistic art, although opinions differ as to whether the frescoes are the work of an itinerant Greek master or an inspired local.

Folklore and roses

Just below the park, ul. Knyaz Mirski leads down to an **ethnographic complex** (daily 8am–noon & 1–5pm), consisting of a group of nineteenth-century houses furnished in period style, and at no. 24 the museum-house of **Dechko Uzunov** (same times), an accomplished realist painter active in the inter-war years. To the west of the park, just off the Gabrovo road, stands the **museum of the rose industry** (May–Oct daily 9am–noon & 1–5pm), which (despite the lack of captions in foreign languages) conveys an idea of how rose jam, toothpaste, eau-de-cologne, jelly, *rosaliika* and, of course, attar of roses are produced. Bulgarians recall nostalgically how the rose industry was before modernisation, and relish the adventures of Baya Ganyu, the rascally pedlar of rose oil and rugs invented by nineteenth-century writer Aleko Konstantinov.

THE THRACIAN WAY OF DEATH

Large tracts of the Bulgarian countryside are dotted with Thracian *mogili*, or **burial mounds**, the majority of which remain unexcavated. They were erected by a society which obviously thought it important to honour the illustrious dead with the construction of a fitting tomb, and which may have practised a form of ancestor-worship which involved the deification of tribal kings and chieftains.

According to Herodotus, deceased Thracian nobles were laid out for three days before a funeral feast of "various sacrificial animals" which followed "a short period of wailing and mourning". After the corpse was buried or cremated, a "tumulus of soil" was raised, and "various competitive games" were organized, "the biggest prize being awarded for wrestling".

Herodotus notes elsewhere that in those tribes where polygamy was practised, the wives of a dead warrior would compete for the honour of being buried with him. This assertion is borne out by the evidence of some excavated *tumuli*, where the bones of speedily dispatched young females have been found lying near to those of the chieftain. In many cases, however, the deceased had to make do with the company of his favourite horse.

Herodotus's comments about the willingness of widows to follow their husbands suggest that the Thracians did not fear death overmuch. According to many ancient sources, the Thracians believed in the existence of a soul which, separate from the body, was capable of enjoying an afterlife. It is not known whether this conception of life after death applied to everybody, or merely to an elite group of tribal chieftains and priest-kings; but Herodotus relates how certain tribes mourned the birth of children, and celebrated the death of their elders – as if the latter event represented release from the misery of the material world.

Thracian beliefs about the immortality of the soul undoubtedly spread southward to Greece, where they contributed to the development of cults such as **Orphism** (p.227).

Practicalities

Kazanlâk's **rail** and **bus stations** are located on the southern fringes of town, a five-minute walk along ul. Rozova dolina from the central square. Of Kazanlâk's three **hotels**, two are on the square, the 3-star *Kazanlâk* (☎0431/27210; ④) and the 2-star *Roza* (☎0431/14703; ③); while the *Zornitsa* (☎0431/20084; ③) occupies a fine hilltop site just east of the Thracian tomb. The nearest **campsite**, *Kazanlâshka roza* (open May–Oct; ☎0431/24239), is 4km north of town on the Gabrovo road, reachable by bus #5 or #6 from the southern end of ul. Rozova dolina; otherwise camping *Sevtopolis* (open May–Oct; ☎0431/3940) occupies a pleasant spot beside the Georgi Dimitrov dam 13km to the west, near the village of DOLNO SAHRANE (all westbound buses should pass by; otherwise, several local trains stop at the nearby Sahrane halt).

The *Hotel Kazanlâk* presents the best **eating and drinking** opportunities in town, with a *mehana* in the basement, posher restaurant upstairs, and a late-night bar on the top floor; otherwise there are a number of cheaper restaurants and *sladkarnitsi* around the main square. The *Hotel Zornitsa* hosts the occasional disco.

The Shipka pass

Whether you hitch, drive or catch a bus, few routes in Bulgaria match crossing the **SHIPKA PASS** for drama and majestic vistas. Particularly at sunset, when the mountains darken and a chill wind disperses the tourists, you can feel something of the pass's potent historical significance. Ever since Alexander the Great drove back a force of *Triballi* here in 335 BC, control of Shipka has been an important strategic imperative.

When most present-day Bulgarians think of Shipka, however, they probably think of the Russo-Turkish War, when 6000 Russians and Bulgarians resisted a 27,000-strong Ottoman force that had been despatched northwards to break the siege of Plevna in August 1877. Snow exacerbated the hardships of Radetsky's ill-equipped Bulgarian volunteers (many of whom had been civilians in Gabrovo only days before), and despite the local women who brought supplies, the defenders' ammunition was exhausted by the third day of the **battle** and they resorted to throwing rocks, tree trunks and finally corpses at the Turks. But the pass held and in due time Plevna surrendered, whereupon the Russians reinforced Radetsky's army and ordered it to fight its way down the snowy mountainside to defeat the remaining 22,000 Ottoman troops outside Kazanlâk – which it did.

The journey across the mountains **between Kazanlâk and Gabrovo** takes about an hour and a half **by bus** and it's wise to book seats when leaving either town even if you're planning to stop halfway and then continue on by a later service (there are usually a few seats empty by the time buses reach the pass). Most visitors head for three major localities around Shipka: the scenery and war memorials of the **summit** itself; the neighbouring peak of **Mount Buzludzha**, where renowned *haiduk* Hadzhi Dimitâr bit the dust; and the **Shipka Memorial church** which, only 12km north of Kazanlâk, is the easiest of the pass's attractions to reach.

The Memorial church

Bus #6 leaves from Kazanlâk (it can be picked up at the southern end of ul. Rozova dolina, near the railway station) every thirty minutes for SHIPKA village, a rustic huddle of buildings occupying the point at which the Balkan Mountains reach the plain. From the wooded hillside north of the village rise the distinctive golden domes of the **Shipka Memorial Church** (daily 8.30am–4.30pm), built after the Liberation as a monument to both Russian and Bulgarian dead. Conceived by philanthropic Russian aristocrats and paid for by public donations, the church was built on the model of Russian seventeenth-century churches.

The result is a vibrantly coloured confection of pinks and greens, topped off with the distinctive 50m-high spire of the bell tower. The **interior**, the work of Bulgarian artists under the direction of the Russian painter Pomerantsev, is perhaps the best example of the academic realist style which flourished in Bulgaria around the turn of the century. Folk-influenced floral and geometric patterns rich in primary colours weave their way around naturalistic depictions of Bulgarian saints and tsars. Many of the Tsars are dressed up in Byzantine costume, a reminder of the pre-World War I days when Bulgaria's desire to extend its frontiers towards the former Imperial capital was reflected in a passion for all things Byzantine.

At the western end of the church, murals portray great figures in Russian history, including fourteenth-century ruler Dimitri Donskoi being blessed before going off to smite the Tatars; and an allegorical scene of Cyril and Methodius bringing literacy to the Slavs.

The pass

Bulgarian and Russian tourists still place bouquets honouring their sacrifice beneath the bronze Bulgarian Lion that surveys its putative homeland from the towering **Freedom Monument** on Mount Stoletev, from where there's a magnificent **panorama** of the Valley of the Roses and the Sredna Gora. A symbolic sarcophagus graces the interior, surrounded by inscriptions alluding to the "eternal friendship between Bulgarians and Russians".

Three hundred metres northwest of the monument is the extensive **Russian cemetery**, merely the largest of the many concentrations of cannon and gravestones scattered across the slopes of surrounding hills. The pass's small *Shipka* hotel (☎2006; ③) is often occupied by groups, but you can always **sleep** at the campsite (open mid-May–Sept) 2km north of the summit, which has heated chalets – worth taking (it gets very cold at night).

Mount Buzludzha

Twelve kilometres east of the Shipka pass, **Mount Buzludzha** is topped by a bizarre structure resembling a spaceship come to earth. Hadzhi Dimitâr and his rebels died here fighting the Turks on August 2, 1868, though the museum inside the spaceship also commemorates the **founding of the Bulgarian Socialist Party** on the same day in 1891, after a clandestine congress. It can be reached by road from the pass, and there are sometimes buses to the site from KAZANLÂK (see p.192).

BEYOND THE VALLEY OF THE ROSES

East of Kazanlâk the Tundzha valley broadens out, although it continues to be framed by the wall of the *Stara planina* to the north and the lower, wooded hills of the eastern Sredna Gora to the south. Lurking on the far side of the latter is **Stara Zagora**, Bulgaria's sixth largest city, and home to one of the most important Neolithic sites in Europe. This alone makes it worth a brief detour, especially for those travelling southward from the Valley of the Roses towards Plovdiv, Haskovo, Kârdzhali or Turkey, all of which are easily accessible by rail from here. If heading east from Stara Zagora towards the coast you'll pass through **Yambol**, a fairly unremarkable industrial town which attracts few visitors. Two examples of early Ottoman architecture together with various Thracian finds provide the interest if you're passing.

A much more obvious place to stop off en route towards the coast is **Sliven**, the most important town between the Valley of the Roses and the sea. Lying snug beneath the southern shoulders of the *Stara planina*, Sliven's a good base from which to explore the historic craft villages of the nearby mountains – the carefully preserved nineteenth-century settlements of **Zheravna** and **Kotel** are both worth an excursion.

Stara Zagora

Lying on the southern flanks of the eastern Sredna Gora, **STARA ZAGORA** developed at the crossroads of two ancient trade routes, commanding a fertile area still noted both for its wheat and its fruit orchards. Under Turkish rule it was one of the centres of the Bulgarian renaissance – the school here attracted pupils from far and wide, including, briefly, Vasil Levski, Raina Knyaginya and Hristo Botev. Burned down by the Turks in 1877 for welcoming the forces of Russian General Gurko, and subsequently rebuilt on a strict grid-iron plan, the city has an urbane, modern appearance. The spacious boulevards and extensive parks of the city centre make it an easy and relaxing city in which to stroll and explore.

The town

Downtown Stara Zagora zeros in on the **city garden**, a small patch of greenery located at the point where the main east–west and north–south thoroughfares, ul G. Dimitrov and bul. Ruski respectively, cross each other. Near the intersection itself stands the venerable **Eski Dzhamiya**, or old mosque, nowadays surrounded by a gaggle of street traders who drape their wares over the surrounding paving stones. Built in 1409, it features a central dome with a diameter of 17m, a great architectural feat for the time. An inscription in Arabic script above the entrance to the prayer hall remembers the local worthy who paid for it, Emir Hamza Beg, in glowing terms: "shadow of God on earth, glory of the state and of the Faith".

The **district history museum**, just north of here at bul. Ruski 42, is currently undergoing extensive reorganization, but seems to be the most likely place in which to find pottery, funeral *stelae* and bronze jugs from the Roman era. Much of the ethnographic collection is housed in the **museum of nineteenth-century town life** (Tues–Sun 10am–noon & 2–5pm), one block east on ul. Asen Velchev. Dominating the park immediately to the west of bul. Ruski is the sad spectacle of Stara Zagora's **opera house**, gutted by fire in September 1991 just as the autumn season was about to start. Further west, marble slabs litter the **archaeological reserve** just behind the *Okrâzhen naroden sâvet*, or town council building, where a sizable portion of the Roman theatre is being painstakingly restored.

Southeast of the centre at ul. Geo Milev 37 is the **Geo Milev house-museum**, birthplace of the poet whose verses on the subject of the 1923 Uprising caused his untimely death (p.105). Besides several recreated turn-of-the-century interiors, there's also a section dealing with the literary history of Stara Zagora as a whole.

The Neolithic dwellings

Stara Zagora's major attraction, the **Neolithic dwellings** (*Neolitni zhilishta;* Tues–Sat 8.30am–noon & 2–5.30pm), were unearthed in 1969 behind the district hospital. Of the several buildings excavated, the remains of a settlement destroyed by fire somewhere around 5500 BC, two houses were preserved in the state in which the archaeologists found them and covered over by a custom-built pavilion, which now serves as a museum. Once inside, visitors are confronted by a moonscape of crumbling walls and pottery, but familiar domestic details become recognizeable on closer inspection.

Each of the settlement's families would occupy a single-roomed dwelling, usually detatched; although the two preserved here were built back-to-back – possibly the sign of an extended family. In one corner of the house stood a basic stove, in which bread would be baked from flour ground on a nearby millstone. Another corner of the room was a cult area, where idols of the household gods would be kept. A **gallery** in the basement holds the artefacts unearthed by the excavation, covering several millennia – the earliest ones include household implements such as sickles and spoons made out of bone – although most objects belong roughly between the sixth and fourth millennia BC. Pottery contemporaneous with the dwellings upstairs shows a high degree of sophistication, with diagonal lines and geometric patterns adorning the bulky vessels used for storing grain. An abundant collection of clay cult figures include the ample forms of female fertility goddesses alongside various zoomorphic figures: cats, goats, hedgehogs, and an enigmatic pot in the shape of an animal body with a human head. A delicate child's bracelet from the fifth millenium BC is one of the oldest pieces of gold jewellery ever found.

To **reach the site**, head west along ul. General Stoletov (the main east–west boulevard which runs along the back of the museum and opera house) for about twenty minutes – alternatively, ride a couple of stops on any of the buses which run along it – until you pass the district hospital (*okrâzhna bolnitsa*). Turn left when you see a sign bearing the legend *Neolitni zhilishta* and you'll come across the easily missed pavilion lurking at the rear of the hospital, just behind a basketball court.

Practicalities

Stara Zagora's **railway station** lies on the city's southern edge, at the end of bul. Ruski: the **bus terminal** is a couple of hundred yards east of here on bul. Slavyanski; it's a straightforward ten-minute northward walk into town from either. A bureau handling **train tickets and information** is nearer the town centre at bul. Lenin 7.

Private rooms are, in theory, available from the *Tourist Service Bureau* at bul. Dimitrov 100 (☎042/29195), although this has somewhat irregular opening times. There's a reasonable range of **hotels**: the 3-star *Vereya*, bul. Dimitrov 98 (☎042/26798; ④); the 2-star *Zheleznik*, on bul. Slavyanski opposite the bus station (☎042/22158; ③); the *Zagorka* (☎042/53015; ③) has a pleasant lakeside location, but is some distance from the centre, north of town in the Septemvriitsi park on the Kazanlâk road. A couple of unclassified hotels previously off limits to non-Bulgarians, the *Beroe* and *Moskva*, both on bul. Lenin, may be worth checking out.

The **forested uplands** on the fringes of town are a popular recreation area. An extensive park at the northern end of bul. Ruski covers the foothills of the most accessible peak, "Doe Wood Mountain". Perfumed with lime trees and planted with diverse shrubs, the park is a nice place to relax, featuring an open-air theatre and a restaurant, the *Gorski kât*.

East of Stara Zagora

Road and rail routes from Stara Zagora towards the coast hug the southern flanks of the steadily receding Sredna Gora, the expanse of the Thracian plain spreading to the south. Nine kilometres east of town, Bulgaria's largest chemical fertilizer plant sprawls over 370 acres, a depressing harbinger of the next major settlement along the way, **NOVA ZAGORA**. It's a predominantly modern town devoted to agri-business, and there's little to detain you here save for its usefulness as a **transport hub**, start of a branch line which runs south to SIMEONOVGRAD on the Sofia-Svilengrad route.

Travelling east from Nova Zagora by road, you'll rejoin the main Sofia-Black Sea route at Sliven. Travelling by rail you'll bypass Sliven and pass through Yambol instead, before rejoining the coast-bound route at Karnobat.

Sliven

A sprawl of flats and red-roofed buildings, **SLIVEN** lies at the feet of mountains that once sheltered so many bands of *haiduti*, or outlaws, that Bulgarians called this the "town of the hundred *voivodes*" after the number of their chieftains. It's rather less notorious nowadays, and makes a good stopoff between Sofia and Burgas on the coast. There's a fair amount to see – and the memorial houses of renowned *haiduti* like Hadzhi Dimitâr and Panaiot Hitov ensure the town's place on the list of revolutionary pilgrimages.

Whereas vineyards, tanneries and silkworms provided the impetus for a new town to rise from the ashes of the medieval one (demolished by the Turks and replaced by a garrison) during the seventeenth and eighteenth centuries, Sliven's subsequent development has largely gone hand in hand with that of Bulgaria's textile industry. The country's first factory was established here in 1834 by one **Dobri Zhelyazkov** (remembered hereabouts as *Fabrikadzhiyata*, "the gaffer"), who acquired parts and plans of looms by smuggling them home from Russia in bags of wool.

The town

Modern Sliven huddles around a messy central square, **pl. Hadzhi Dimitâr**, where contemporary concrete buildings mix with restored nineteenth-century monuments in unhappy juxtaposition. Focus of the square is a memorial to Sliven's most famous son, **Hadzhi Dimitâr** himself. Born in 1840, Dimitâr had become standard-bearer in the haiduk detatchment of local outlaw Panaiot Hitov by the time he was 20. During exile in Romania he teamed up with fellow patriot Stefan Karadzha to form a *cheta* (guerilla group) that raided Ottoman territory. Turkish forces caught up with them at Mount Buzludzha in 1868: Dimitâr fell in battle, while Karadzha was clapped in irons and taken to be hanged in Ruse.

Just south of the main square, a bridge over the Asenovska River leads to the **Hadzhi Dimitâr museum-house** (Tues–Sun 9am–noon & 2–5.30pm) at Asenova 2. A wooden-canopied well presides over the cobbled courtyard of the building itself, an inn run by Dimitâr's father. Frugal bedding on a bare floor denotes the spartan sleeping quarters of the guests: the family lived in more comfortable rooms towards the rear, taking their meals on a balustraded balcony carpeted with rush matting. Exhibits inside the house include faded photos of the insurgents, and a couple of contemporary prints of the "martyrs" Karadzha and Dimitâr.

The historical museum

Sliven's main shopping thoroughfare, Tsar Osvoboditel, forges eastwards from the main square, passing the ochre and white facade of the **history museum** at no. 6 (Tues–Sun 8.30am–noon & 1.30–5.30pm), whose main attractions are the **Thracian burial finds** from the nearby village of Kaloyanovo. Here a chieftain was buried together with his favourite horse and a prized collection of imported Greek pottery, fragments of which are on display alongside some fearsome Thracian armour. Elsewhere a collection of antique *shishane* rifles showcases the artistry of Sliven's nineteenth-century gunsmiths – one piece is decorated with over 11,500 pieces of inlay.

Into the suburbs

Leaving the northeastern corner of pl. Hadzhi Dimitâr, ul. G.S. Rakovski runs along the fringes of Sliven's nineteenth-century residential suburbs, a quiet, leafy area of narrow alleyways and brilliantly whitewashed one-storey houses. High garden walls conceal neat flowerbeds, vegetable plots and vines. Many of Sliven's 100 or so National Revival-style houses are in this part of town, although few are open to the public, either remaining in the hands of private families or pressed into service as rest homes for members of the arts unions. One exception is the **museum of nineteenth-century town life** at Simeon Tabakov 5, recreating the lifestyles of well-to-do families whose homes manifested the Bulgarian genius for combining wood and textiles to create beautiful interiors. Paradoxically, this class produced dozens of the haiduk chieftains, whose outlaw bands ranged the spectrum of behaviour from brutal banditry to populist chivalry.

Continue along ul. Rakovski past the confluence of the Selishtna and Novoselska rivers and you'll come across the former house of **Panayot Hitov**, Grand Old Man of the haiduk movement, just behind the church of Sveta Sofia at Cherno More 7 (enquire at the history museum about opening times). Owner of nineteenth-century Bulgaria's most extravagant moustache, Hitov personified the ideal of the haiduk as a courageous rebel fighting oppression on behalf of the poor – in contrast to the pure brigandry practised by many of his contemporaries. After spending the 1860s hiding out in the Balkan Mountains with his *cheta*, Hitov headed for Belgrade in the 1870s, where he helped organize guerilla incursions into Ottoman territory. After the Liberation he represented Sliven in the *sâbranie* for a while, and was briefly imprisoned by autocratic prime minister Stefan Stambolov for his pro-Russian sympathies. He eventually died in Ruse in 1918, having outlived all his contemporaries.

Practicalities

Sliven's **train station** is way out east at the end of ul. Georgi Kirkov, at the end of trolleybus route #1. The **bus terminal** is slightly nearer to the town centre on the same street. The pricey, high-rise *Hotel Sliven* (☎044/27065; ④) has a tourist services desk where it may be worth enquiring about **private rooms**; otherwise two other **hotels** on the main square offer cheap if rather frugal accommodation: the *Zora* (②) and the *Sinite Kamâni* (②). About 9km southwest of town is the *Aglika* campsite (open mid-May–Sept; with chalets) near the Turkish-built **thermal baths** of SLIVENSKI BANI, accessible by bus from Sliven.

Cafés and patisseries line Tsar Osvoboditel, Sliven's main promenading ground. Hotels *Sliven* and *Sinite Kamâni* have restaurants with frequent live music, although the *Deboya* complex on pl. Hadzhi Dimitâr is the smartest place to eat. Originally an arsenal, it served as a caravanserai during the eighteenth century, and later as a wool store, until it was totally refurbished. The complex also contains a coffee-shop, wine-cellar and disco, which makes it the focus of **nightlife**.

Bulgaria's first **Formula-1 Racing** track is currently taking shape 2km east of Sliven just off the Burgas road, although the completion date is uncertain. Whenever it opens, the complex should include motor racing, motorcycling and karting tracks, with a motel and campsite, pool and volleyball grounds for visitors.

Around Sliven

At certain times of the year Sliven experiences the blast of a cold, dry *bora* blowing at over 20m per second, which strikes the mountains to the north of town, where the light imparts a blueish tinge to the porphyry massif known as the **Sinite Kamâni** or Blue Rocks. There are regular buses from town to the lower cable-car terminal, from which you can hike north to the rock formation known as "the Ring" (*halkata*), or ride up to the summit in eighteen minutes, the latter affording passengers fine views of the plain, a distant beech forest, and the sheer slopes of Mount Tyulbeto (topped by a TV tower), from where hang-gliders launch themselves. Alternatively, by turning left outside the terminal and crossing the Dyuleva rivulet, you can climb a well-marked path up to the Ring in twenty minutes.

Jaggedly arched and nearly 8m tall, the Ring is associated with several **legends**. Ancient mariners supposedly moored their boats here during the flood, while fairy tales have it that a girl passing through will turn into a boy (and vice versa), and a couple doing so will fall in love forever. From the upper terminal you can walk to a meadow offering a panoramic view, or follow asphalted roads to the isolated Bird's Spring (*Ptichyat Izvor*) or the popular KARANDILA resort, which has a direct bus-link with Sliven, and **dorm accommodation** in the *Karandila* tourist chalet (☎044/82021).

Roads lead north from Sliven to the picturesque mountain settlements of **Kotel** and **Zheravna**, and south to the less-interesting **Yambol** on the fringes of the Thracian plain. After excursions to all or some of these most travellers continue the eastward journey **towards Burgas and the coast**, about 120km distant. None of the settlements along the way really merits a stop, and the increasingly arid nature of the terrain discourages further exploration. Once beyond Sliven, the wheatfields and vineyards of the Tundzha valley begin to give way to sun-bleached pasture lands with big herds of sheep kicking up dust as they graze.

Kotel

Several buses a day head north from Sliven towards **KOTEL** (which literally means "cauldron" – a reference to the springs that bubble hereabouts), a small town renowned both for the number of famous patriots born here and for the wealth of surviving vernacular architecture. The trip is worth taking for the scenery alone, zigzagging over the Sinite Kamâni massif before descending into the pine-clad valleys of the eastern Balkan range, home to dusty villages full of geese and wooden shacks.

Founded by sixteenth-century migrants seeking refuge from the Ottoman-dominated plains, Kotel was another of the highland towns where Bulgarian customs and crafts survived centuries of Turkish rule only to re-emerge with new verve during the National Revival. Local wealth was derived from sheep- and goat-farming, and Kotel-based herders crisscrossed the eastern Balkan Mountains seeking pastures for their flocks – often heading for the Dobrudzha in the summer, then wintering on the plain of Thrace far to the south. Although almost totally destroyed by fire in 1894, the town's timber-framed central quarter was spared to become the subject of twentieth-century preservation orders. The enduring ambience of old Kotel has also been kept alive by the state's encourage-ment of the town's traditional industry – **carpetmaking**. Local carpets (*chergi*) often have lozenge- or diamond-shaped geometrical patterns, which are some-times worked into a broken weft; and the basic colour (usually red, blue or green) determines the secondary use of scarlet, wine red, indigo, black, olive green or light blue. Tufted goat-hair *guberi* with simpler patterns, traditionally used as blankets, are also made here.

The town

The town centre lies two blocks uphill from the bus station, where a flagstoned plaza is dominated by the **Pantheon of Georgi Sava Rakovski**, a monumental structure of heavy stone, punctuated by panels of modernist stained glass, built to house the bones of the locally born revolutionary. Rakovski was instrumental in the formation of the Bulgarian Legions based in Belgrade, and remained preemi-nent in émigré politics until his death in 1867.

Ul. Izvorska leads downhill, past the plain nineteenth-century church of Sveta Troitsa, towards the best-preserved parts of the old town, where squat, vine-covered wooden houses cluster around cobbled alleys. The town **history museum** (Tues–Fri 9am–noon & 2–5pm) on Izvorska is housed in the timber schoolhouse of 1869 and contains momentos of local boy Petâr Beron, another prominent National Revival figure credited with being the founder of Bulgarian medicine. On the opposite side of the road, ul. Shipka leads up the hill to the **ethnographic museum** (Mon–Fri 8am–noon & 2–6pm, Sat 8am–noon).

Accommodation in the town is limited to the small 2-star *Hotel Kotel* (☎0453/ 2762; ③), and the even smaller motel *Starata Vodenitsa* (②) in the Izvorite park at the western edge of town. The latter is also the site of a lively *mehana* with outdoor wooden tables, and the restaurant *Izvorite*.

Zheravna

Smaller and more picturesque than its neighbour, the village of **ZHERAVNA** can be difficult to get to unless you have your own transport. Lying some 6km east of the road between Sliven and Kotel, Zheravna is served by only one daily bus from the former and two from the latter, making an overnight stop here more or less inevitable. The effort is, however, worthwhile. Surrounded by stone walls with nail-studded gates, Zheravna's spacious wooden houses with their broad eaves date from as early as the seventeenth century, when the village earned its living from sheep-breeding and diverse crafts. The living room ceiling of **Sava Filaretova house-museum** (nowadays a museum, honouring the local-born educationalist, situated on Zheravna's single street) is a triumph of the wood-carver's art, and colourful carpets and tufted rugs may also been seen at the **birthplace of poet Yordan Yovkov**, and the **Rusi Chorbadzhii house** (which serves as an art gallery). **Rooms** can be found at the *Zlatna Oresha* – a group of ten walled houses on a slope slightly apart from the village.

Yambol

Thirty kilometres southeast of Sliven, **YAMBOL**'s unprepossessing modern face conceals a history of considerable pedigree: founded by the Romans, this became a crucial strongpoint on the Imperial frontier under the Byzantines, fending off successive waves of barbarian invaders sweeping down from Dobrudzha to the north.

However, it was under Turkish occupation that the city acquired both its current name and its only worthwhile monuments: the fourteenth-century **Eski Dzhamiya** or old mosque, one of the oldest Turkish buildings in Bulgaria, put up very soon after the conquest; and the nearby **Bedesten**. An elongated market hall topped off with four domes, this sixteenth-century structure was largely the initiative of Grand Vizier Hadim Ali Pasha, a wily benefactor who recouped the cost of building the Bedesten with the rent he charged for the shops within it. The centrally located **history museum**, at Izrael Dzhaldeti 12, has a notable collection of Thracian relics from nearby Kabile. Having digested these sights it's best to press on, although there is one **hotel** should you need to stay: the *Tundzha* on ul. Drazhev (☎046/24433; ③).

travel details

Trains

From Hisarya to Plovdiv (5 daily; 1hr).
From Kazanlâk to Burgas (5; 3hr); Sliven (5; 1hr 30min); Sofia (6; 3–4hr); Varna (2; 4–6hr 30min).
From Karlovo to Burgas (5; 4–6hr); Kalofer (7; 45min); Kazanlâk (8; 45min–1hr 15min); Plovdiv (8; 1hr 45min); Sliven (4; 2–3hr); Sofia (6; 2–3hr).
From Nova Zagora to Burgas (3; 2–3hr); Simeonovgrad (5; 1hr 45min); Yambol (9; 30min).
From Sliven to Burgas (5; 1hr 45min); Varna (4hr 30min).
From Sofia to Koprivshtitsa (5; 1hr 40min).

From Stara Zagora to Burgas (3; 2hr 30min–3hr 30min); Dimitrovgrad (3; 1hr 15min); Plovdiv (4; 1hr 30min–2hr); Tulovo (5; 30min); Varna (1; 4hr).

Buses

From Karlovo to Hisarya (hourly; 45min); Kalofer (hourly; 30min); Klisura (7 daily; 50min); Panagyurishte (2; 2hr 15min); Pleven (2; 3hr); Troyan (5; 1hr 30min); Sopot (every 30min; 30min).

From Kazanlâk to Gabrovo (hourly; 2hr 15min); Hisarya (4 daily; 2hr); Haskovo (4; 2hr 30min); Karlovo (4; 50min); Kârdzhali (2; 3hr 30min); Pleven (2; 3hr 15min); Stara Zagora (every 30min; 45min).

From Koprivshtitsa to Panagyurishte (2 daily; 50min); Plovdiv (1; 2hr 15min); Sofia (1; 1hr 30min).

From Kotel to Burgas (4; 3hr); Zheravna (2; 45min); Veliko Târnovo (1; 3hr).

From Panagyurishte to Plovdiv (3; 2hr).

From Sliven to Kotel (6; 1hr 45min); Shumen (2; 3hr); Zheravna (2; 1hr 30min).

From Sofia (*Avtogara Yug*) to Panagyurishte (7; 2hr); Stara Zagora (1; 3hr 30min).

From Stara Zagora to Harmanli (8; 2hr); Haskovo (5; 1hr 15min).

CYRILLIC PLACE NAMES

HISARYA	ХИСАРЯ	SINITE KAMÂNI	СИНИТЕ
KALOFER	КАЛОФЕР		КАМЬНИ
KARLOVO	КАРЛОВО	SLIVEN	СЛИВЕН
KAZANLÂK	КАЗАНЛЪК	SOPOT	СОПОТ
KLISURA	КЛИСУРА	SREDNOGORIE	СРЕДНОГОРИЕ
KOPRIVSHTITSA	КОПРИВЩИЦА	STARA ZAGORA	СТАРА
KOTEL	КОТЕЛ		ЗАГОРА
NOVA ZAGORA	НОВА ЗАГОРА	STRELCHA	СТРЕЛЧА
PANAGYURISHTE	ПАНАГЮРИЩЕ	YAMBOL	ЯМБОЛ
SHIPKA PASS	ШИПЧЕНСКИЯ	ZHERAVNA	ЖЕРАВНА
	ТПРОХОД		

CHAPTER FIVE

THE RHODOPES AND THE PLAIN OF THRACE

Few parts of Bulgaria are as closely associated with antiquity as **the Rhodopes and the Plain of Thrace**. If the Balkan range was the cradle of the Bulgar state, then the fertile plain between the Sredna Gora and the Rhodope Mountains was the heartland of the Thracians and the magnet that drew conquerors like Philip of Macedon and the Romans, whose legacy to the present consists of the graceful ruins that embellish **Plovdiv**. Bulgaria's second city, and a fair rival to the capital in several respects, Plovdiv never fails to charm with its old quarter – a wonderful mélange of Renaissance mansions, mosques and classical remains, spread over three hills. The region is full of memories of the Turks, whose descendants still inhabit the region around **Kârdzhali**, while the mosques and bridges built by their forebears constitute the chief sights of **Pazardzhik**, **Haskovo**, **Harmanli** and **Svilengrad**, strung out along the route between Sofia and Istanbul, nowadays busy with convoys of Turkish *gastarbieter* bound for Germany or Turkey.

Also here is the **Bachkovo monastery** and small towns like **Shiroka Lâka** and **Batak**, whose fortified houses testify to the insecurity of life in the old days, when bandits and Muslim zealots marauded through the Rhodopes. The spa-town of **Velingrad**, and **Pamporovo**, Bulgaria's premier ski resort, attract thousands of tourists, but otherwise foreigners rarely venture into the Rhodopes, where poor roads and an absence of hotels form an effective deterrent.

THE PLAIN OF THRACE

Watered by the Maritsa and numerous tributaries descending from the Balkans and the Rhodopes, the **Thracian plain** has been a fertile, productive land since antiquity. The ancient Greeks called it Upper or Northern Thrace, to distinguish it from the lush plains on the far side of the Rhodopes in Greece and Turkey, collectively known as Thrace after the tribes who lived there. A Bulgarian legend has it that God, dividing the world among different peoples, forgot them until a delegation of Bulgars mentioned the oversight. God replied, "There is nothing left, but since you are hard-working folk I will give you a portion of Paradise". And so the Bulgars received part of Thrace.

The E80, which now links Istanbul and Sofia, essentially follows the course of the Roman Serdica-Constantinople road, past towns formerly ruled by the Ottomans for so long that foreigners used to call this "European Turkey". The most important town, of course, is **Plovdiv**, which dominates southern Bulgaria so much that the other towns along the route appear quite unexciting in comparison. Really only **Pazardzhik**, **Haskovo** and **Harmanli** warrant extensive investigation.

Communications along this route are all fairly straightforward. Roughly every hour, trains depart **from Sofia** bound for Plovdiv – a journey which takes two to two and a half hours by express (*bârz*), or three to three and a half if you use *pâtnicheshki* services. By road, Plovdiv is two hours from Sofia, and is easily hitched. **From other parts of Bulgaria**, branch rail lines and buses connect Karlovo and Panagyurishte with Plovdiv; while travellers coming from Ruse, Gabrovo or Varna will probably need to change trains at Stara Zagora. Coming **from Istanbul**, you'll cross by road at Kapitan Andreevo (see p.226), or by railway at Svilengrad; the *Istanbul Express* arrives in Plovdiv at around 8.30am, the off-season *Istanbul-Hellas* three hours earlier.

Sofia to Plovdiv

Travelling west to east along the E80, the first town you come across after leaving Sofia is **IHTIMAN**, set amid beautiful scenery, with a **hotel**, the *Eledzhik* (☎0724/2405; ③), in the centre and a costlier motel out on the highway. If you're driving in a hurry, or riding on one of the direct bus services, you'll follow the dual carriageway almost as far as Plovdiv, bypassing all the towns along the way. Along with the Sofia-Plovdiv railway line, the old E80 winds its much more leisurely way through the hills which precede the Maritsa valley, passing the *Leshta han* (where lentil dishes are said to be the speciality) 9km beyond Ihtiman, before entering **KOSTENETS**, a small town encroaching on **Momin Prohod**, or the "Virgin's Pass". This gets its name from the daughter of a rich merchant of Philppopolis, whose long-standing paralysis vanished when she bathed in the **mineral springs** here – claimed to be the 25th most radioactive in the world, and nowadays used to treat diabetes, ulcers, rheumatism and skin diseases. **BELOVO**, the next town, like Kostenets a stop for most express trains, has a **campsite** (open May–Sept) and a mineral swimming pool situated 5km to the east beside the highway. From the next proper town, **SEMPTEMVRI**, you can catch trains to Velingrad in the western Rhodopes (p.228) and Bansko in the Pirin Mountains (see Chapter Two).

Pazardzhik

A market town founded by Crimean Tatars during the reign of Sultan Bajezid II, **PAZARDZHIK** was the site of the third largest fair in the Ottoman empire, capable of stabling 3000 horses and 2000 camels in its caravanserai, and until the late nineteenth century commercially more important than Sofia. Many of the Bulgar artisans who began settling here towards the end of the sixteenth century adopted Islam, and Pazardzhik remained a predominantly Turkish and Muslim town until comparatively recently. In 1971, the state's policy of assimilation by foisting "approved" names on Muslims provoked outbursts of rioting (reportedly, two Party officials were murdered), followed by a police crackdown on the

Turkish and *Pomak* (Bulgarian Muslim) communities. But if tension still remains it's unlikely to be apparent to casual travellers: the evening promenade has all the relaxed good humour of small-town Bulgaria, and buildings are decked out in grapevines, giving Pazardzhik an abundant, welcoming feel.

The town

Although this predominantly modern town has long since lost the appearance of an Ottoman bazaar, Pazardzhik's mercantile traditions live on in one of Bulgaria's liveliest street markets, which lines the alleys of the pedestrianized downtown area just west of the main square, Cherven ploshtad. Directly behind the square at Georgi Kirkov 34 is the **city museum and art gallery** (Tues–Sun 9am–noon & 2–6pm), largely concentrating on Thracian oddments.

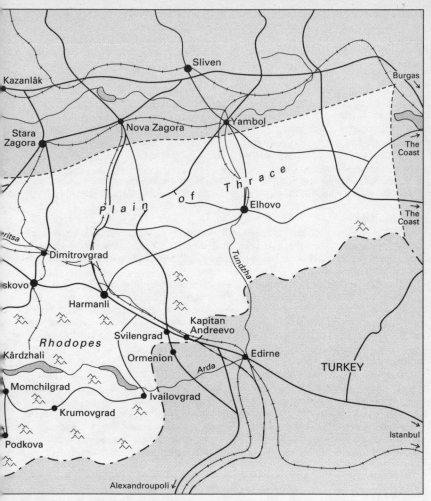

Ul. 9 septemvri heads south from the centre, leading shortly to the **Cathedral of Sveta Bogoroditsa**. Built in 1837 of pink stone, it's an example of the National Revival style applied to church architecture, partly sunk beneath street level to comply with the Ottoman restrictions on Christian places of worship. Its walnut iconostasis is perhaps the finest product of the nineteenth-century School of Debâr, whose craftsmen endeavoured to show the psychological relationships between human figures rather than fill the icon screen with plant and zoomorphic motifs in the manner of the Samokov woodcarvers.

Zahari Zograf aside, Bulgaria's most famous nineteenth-century painter was probably **Stanislav Dospevski** (1826–76), whose former house and studio opposite the cathedral at bul. Dimitrov 50 is now a **museum** (Mon–Fri 9am–noon & 2–5pm). Born in Pazardzhik and educated at the Academy of Fine Art in Saint

Petersburg, Dospevski drew extensively during visits to Odessa and Constantinople, but is best remembered for his icons, portraits and murals, several of which decorate the walls of the house. A participant in the April Rising, he was flung into the dungeons of Constantinople and died before Bulgaria's liberation.

Most of Pazardzhik's surviving nineteenth-century houses lie near the Dospevski museum, where squat pastel-coloured structures huddle along either side of a stream; or among the tree-lined residential streets just west of the cathedral. Here, at Kiril i Metodi 4, is an **ethnographic museum** (Tues–Sun 9am–noon & 2–6pm), which has the usual selection of exhibits remembering the costumes and crafts of the National Revival period. Another block west is the rather delapidated walled **church of saints Konstantin i Elena**, with faded murals of the saints above the portal.

Pazardzhik's remaining sight is the *Kurshum* or **bullet mosque**, built in 1667, which stands just north of the centre, on the far side of the town park.

Practicalities

Pazardzhik's **railway station** is about 5km south of the centre, and all arrivals are met by buses into town. The **bus terminal**, a couple of blocks north of the town centre, is a more convenient point of entry. Rail and bus **reservations** can be made in advance at the *TsKTON*, ul. Esperanto 9.

With regular buses to **Plovdiv, Panagyurishte** in the Sredna Gora, and **Peshtera** and **Batak** in the Rhodopes, Pazardzhik is the kind of place you spend an afternoon in en route to somewhere else. For those who wish **to stay**, however, there's the central *Hotel Trakiya*, Cherven pl. 2 (☎034/26006; ③); and the *Elbrus*, pl. Olimpiiski 2 (☎034/26530; ③), the latter featuring a late-night bar and disco.

Beyond Pazardzhik

The road **between Pazardzhik and Plovdiv** runs "straight as perhaps the Romans had built it" across the widening plain beside the River Maritsa, flanked by acres of trees bearing apples, plums and pears. Bulgarians say that by custom, passers-by may pick fruit from roadside orchards providing they eat it on the spot, but removing any constitutes theft in the eyes of the law. Twenty-seven kilometres east of Pazardzhik, the highway passes the *Maritsa motel-campsite* complex, followed shortly by *Trakiya campsite*, and then the northern suburbs of Plovdiv.

Plovdiv

Lucian the Greek called **PLOVDIV** "the biggest and most beautiful of all towns" in Thrace; he might have added "and Bulgaria", for the country's second largest city (with a population of 360,000) is one of its most attractive and vibrant centres – and, arguably, has more to recommend it than Sofia. Certainly, there's plenty to see: the old town embodies Plovdiv's long and varied history – Thracian fortifications utilized by Macedonian masonry, overlaid with Byzantine walls, and by great timber-framed mansions erected during the Bulgarian renaissance, looking down on the derelict Ottoman mosques and artisans' dwellings of the lower town. But Plovdiv isn't merely a parade of antiquities: the city's arts festivals and trade fairs rival Sofia's in number, and its restaurants and promenade put the capital's nightlife to shame.

Some history

An ancient Thracian site, rebuilt and renamed by Philip II of Macedonia in 342 BC, classical **Philippopolis** was initially little more than a military outpost designed to keep a watchful eye over the troublesome natives. It was a rough frontier town which the Macedonians deliberately colonized with criminals and dropouts – Roman writer Pliny later identifying Philippoplis with *Poneropolis*, the semi-legendary "City of Thieves". Under Roman rule urban culture developed apace, with the town's position on the Belgrade-to-Constantinople highway bringing both economic wealth and a strategic role in the defence of Thrace.

Plovdiv was sacked by the Huns in 447, and by the seventh century, with the Danube frontier increasingly breached by barbarians, the city was in decline. With the arrival of the Bulgars, Byzantine control over the area became increasingly tenuous. "Once upon a time", lamented Byzantine chronicler Anna Comnena in the twelfth century, "Philippopolis must have been a large and beautiful city, but after the Tauri and Scyths (i.e. Slavs) enslaved the inhabitants . . . it was reduced to the condition in which we saw it". In Comnena's time Philippopolis was a notorious hotbed of heretics, a situation usually blamed on local Armenians, who migrated to Thrace en masse in the eighth and tenth centuries, bringing with them the dualistic doctrines of Manichaeanism and Paulicianism. Although these heresies eventually fizzled out, Plovdiv's Armenian population has endured to this day.

The Byzantine town was further damaged by the Bulgarian Tsar Kaloyan in 1206, and it was a rather run-down place that the Turks inherited in the fourteenth century, renaming it *Filibe*. It soon recovered as a commercial centre, with a thriving Muslim quarter, complete with bazaars and mosques, growing up at the base of the hill where Plovdiv's Christian communities continued to live. Many of the latter were rising members of a rich mercantile class by the mid-nineteenth century, and they expressed their affluence in the construction of opulent town houses which showcased the very best of native arts and crafts. Plovdiv's urban elite also patronized Bulgarian culture, and had the Great Powers of Europe not broken up the infant state of Bulgaria at the Congress of Berlin in 1878, Plovdiv would probably have been designated as its capital. In the event, it became instead the main city of **eastern Rumelia**, an Ottoman province administered by a Christian governor-general. Much of the Christian population naturally wanted union with the rest of Bulgaria, which was finally attained in 1885.

Plovdiv has continued to rival Sofia as a cultural and business centre ever since, not least because of the prestigious international trade fairs held here in May and September. Close proximity to Bulgaria's capitalist neighbours Turkey and Greece ensures that Plovdiv is well placed to take advantage of recent changes – and private enterprise seems to have taken root here more quickly than anywhere else in the country.

Arrival and information

Trains arrive at the *Tsentralna gara* on central Plovdiv's southern fringe, and the two main **bus terminals** are nearby: *Rodopi*, serving the mountain resorts of the south, is just on the other side of the railway tracks (accessible via the underground walkway from the station), while *Avtogara Yug*, serving the southeast, is one block east. If heading straight into town from here, a brisk walk down Ivan Vazov will bring you to Tsentralen square, immediately north of which is the town centre, although travelling three stops on buses #1 or #7 will save time.

PLOVDIV

N

International Fair

BULEVARD MOSKVA → Svilengrad

Trakiya Campsite & Sofia

BULEVARD MOSKVA

Leningrad-Park Hotel

Păldin Tours

Hotel Maritsa

Novotel-Plovdiv

River Maritsa

Imaret Mosque

Archaeological Museum

PLOSHTAD SAEDINENIE

Natural History Museum

Market

ULITSA LYUBEN KARAVELOV

ULITSA IZTOK

ROZA LYUKSEMBURG

BULEVARD GEORGI DIMITROV

ULITSA HAN KUBRAT

ULITSA HRISTO DANOV

OLD PLOVDIV

ULITSA MAKSIM GORKI

PL STAMBOLIISKI

ULITSA RAIKO DASKALOV

ULITSA GENERAL VLADIMIR ZAIMOV

ULITSA ANTIM I

BULEVARD R

BULEVARD PERUSHTITSA

See 'Old Plovdiv' map

ULITSA PETKO PETKOV

BULEVARD
KONSTANTIN VELCHIKOV

Asenovgrad

ULITSA BOGOMIL

KAPITAN RAICHO

ULITSA IVANA DIMITROVA

400 m

0

BULEVARD GEORGI DIMITROV

Hotel
Trimontsium

University

Hotel
Bălgaria

Hotel
Republika

Railway
Bookings Office

A KNYAZ ALEKSANDAR

TSENTRALEN

Post
Office

Dental
Polyclinic

BALKAN

Clock
Tower

Freedom
Park

ULITSA NIKOLA VAPTSAROV

BULEVARD HRISTO BOTEV

Rhodopi
Bus Station

ULITSA IVAN VAZOV

Yug
Bus Station

ULITSA SASHO DIMITROV

BULEVARD RUSKI

Hotel
Leipzig

Central
Railway Station

Monument to the
Liberators

Soviet Army
Memorial

BULEVARD VASIL APRILOV

Hill of Youth

BULEVARD YORDANKA NIKOLOVA

Peshtera
& Batak

Accommodation

For **information**, head for *Puldin Tour* (daily 8.45am–12.30pm & 1.30–6.30pm) at bul. Moskva 34 – take bus #1 or #7 from the station and alight once you've crossed the river. They will provide brochures and maps, and can book you into **private rooms**, which despite being the most pricey in Bulgaria (£5 a double, £8 during the Trade Fair in the second half of September), are usually quite central and still a bargain compared to Plovdiv's **hotels** – which are almost as expensive as those of the capital. Plovdiv's three **campsites**, all of which have two-person bungalows, are located some way from town along the Sofia-Plovdiv-Istanbul E80 highway – too far away for those who want to be at the centre of things.

Hotels

Bålgariya, Patriarh Evtimii 13 (☎26064; ③). Average 2-star hotel, probably the best mid-price choice by virtue of its central location.

Laipzig, bul. Ruski 70 (☎232 251; ③). Modern high-rise hotel, near the station and a couple of blocks west of the town centre.

Leningrad, bul. Bålgariya 97 (☎55803; ④). A soulless tower block located amid modern suburbs some distance from the centre (bus #11 from the railway station).

Maritsa, bul. Vâzrazhdane 42 (☎552 735; ④). Modern business hotel situated next door to the international fairgrounds on the north bank of the Maritsa (bus #1 or #7 from the station).

Novotel, Zlati Boyadzhiev 2 (☎55892; ⑤). Plush establishment on the north bank of the Maritsa, featuring swimming pool and tennis courts.

Republika, Knyaz Aleksandâr 39 (☎222 133; ②). Cheapest of the hotels and centrally located, although rooms are basic and without en-suite facilities.

Trimontsium, Kapitan Raicho 2 (☎225 561; ⑤). Old-fashioned big rooms, and near to the modern centre.

Campsites

Chaya (open mid-April–mid-Oct). 15km east of Plovdiv just off the E80 to Istanbul, on the banks of the Chepelarska River.

Maritsa (open April–Nov). 10km west of town.

Trakiya (open April–Nov). Most convenient of the sites, lying on Plovdiv's western outskirts. Bus #4 from bul. Georgi Dimitrov or pl. Sverdlov; or bus #23 from pl. Sverdlov.

The city

Most of Plovdiv's sights are compact enough to be explored on foot, although the town is divided into two distinct parts, quite different from each other in atmosphere: the nineteenth-century **Stariyat grad** or old town, which occupies the easternmost of Plovdiv's three hills; and the **lower town** – predominantly modern with a scattering of Turkish relics – which spreads itself across the plain below.

The modern centre

Modern Plovdiv revolves around the large **Tsentralen ploshtad**, an arid concrete plaza dominated by the ponderously Stalinist **Hotel Trimontsium**, whose restaurant-garden with its brass lamps has a faded Thirties ambience. During the development of the area remnants of the **Roman forum** were discovered – you can explore this marble-paved, once-colonnaded square by descending into a sunken area in front of the hotel.

To the west is **Freedom Park**, a shaded area of lawns and fountains which marks the tail end of the evening *korso*, an animated promenade bringing hundreds of people onto Plovdiv's main downtown street, **Knyaz Aleksandâr**, at the close of every working day. Knyaz Aleksandâr (some maps and street signs may carry its former name, Vasil Kolarov) is lined with shops, cinemas and bars with terraces from which folk watch life go by. At Knyaz Aleksandâr 15 is the **City Art Gallery** (Sat–Thurs 9am–12.30pm & 2–6pm), one of Bulgaria's better collections, with some fine nineteenth-century portraits including one deeply reverent, almost iconic, *Portrait of Bishop Sofronii of Vratsa*, painted in 1812 by an unknown artist. Look out too for Tsanko Lavrenov's pictures of nineteenth-century Plovdiv, painted in the 1930s and 1940s and suffused with a dreamlike nostalgia.

Around pl. Stamboliiski

Further north, Knyaz Aleksandâr gives onto the arresting **pl. Stamboliiski**, surrounded by small cafés packed with a variety of students, whiskery elders and corpulent bon viveurs. The **ruins of a Roman stadium**, visible in a pit beneath the square, are but a paltry fragment of the original, horseshoe-shaped arena where the Alexandrine Games were held during the second and third centuries: as many as 30,000 spectators watched chariot races, wrestling, athletics and other events from the marble stands which once lined the slopes of the neighbouring heights.

Among the variously styled buildings around here, the **Dzhumaiya dzhamiya** or "Friday mosque", with its diamond-patterned minaret and lead-sheathed domes, steals the show. Its thick walls and the configuration of the prayer hall (divided by four columns into nine squares) are typical of the so-called "popular mosques" of the fourteenth and fifteenth centuries, although it's believed that the Dzhumaiya mosque might actually date back to the reign of Sultan Murad II (1359–85). The mosque tends to be locked up outside prayer times, so you'll have to time your visit carefully if you want to admire the fountain, floral motifs, and medallions bearing Koranic texts that reportedly adorn its interior. A plaque on the western wall commemorates the five Communists shot here in 1919, thus explaining the name borne by the square for many years during the Communist period: ploshtad 19 Noemvri.

Immediately northeast of the mosque lies the site of the old *charshiya*, or **bazaar quarter**, where narrow streets still bear the names of the trades that used to operate from here: ul. Zhelezarska, for example, was the preserve of the ironmongers; Abadzhiiska, that of the weavers and cloth merchants. The name *abadzhiya* derives from *abas*, the coarse woolen cloth which the Plovdiv merchants bought from Rhodopi shepherds before re-exporting it throughout the Levant. In Ottoman times Plovdiv's main commercial district stretched from here northwards to the River Maritsa, roughly following the course of the modern ul. Raiko Daskalov – around which, in the sixteenth century, Arab traveller Evliya Chelebi counted 880 shops raised "storey above storey". You won't find much of the area's erstwhile bazaar atmosphere these days – except for the usual gaggle of street traders selling products unobtainable in the shops – but it's a nice experience to wander along the street, shaded by red awnings and dusty foliage.

The Imaret mosque and the archaeological museum

Nearer the river are a number of further relics of Turkish rule, many of which are in a bad state of repair and have long been closed for restoration. With an eye for leaden domes and sturdy masonry, you can identify the *Chifte Hamam* (several blocks east of Raiko Daskalov at the end of Hristo Danov) as an original **Turkish bath**, but you don't have to be an expert to recognize the **Imaret mosque** on Han Kubrat. Zigzag brickwork gives the minaret a corkscrew twist, jazzing up the ponderous bulk of the building, which a frieze of "sawtoothed" bricks and a row of keel arches with tie beams fails to do. Built on Sultan Bajazet's orders in 1444, it contains the tomb of Gazi Shahabedin Pasha, and got its name from the pilgrims' hostel (*imaret*) that formerly stood nearby.

Opposite Milenkov's surreal monument to the union of 1885 on pl. Sâedinenie, there's the **archaeological museum** (Mon 2–5pm, Tues–Sun 9am–noon & 2–5.30pm). Although the region's greatest treasure, the Gold Treasure of Panagyurishte, has been carried off to the National History Museum in Sofia, there's still ample evidence of the culture of Bulgaria's Thracian forebears, much of it drawn from excavations of tribal burial grounds at Duvanli, 20km north of Plovdiv. Austere, locally made earthenware stands in stark contrast to a series of exquisitely decorated pots imported by Thracian warlords from Greece. Abundant weaponry, including a bronze helmet found near the village of Brestovitsa, points to the more down-to-earth concerns of daily Thracian life. Life in Roman Trimontsium is well documented with a range of bronze and terracotta artefacts; while the medieval period is represented by a twelfth-century Byzantine coin hoard found near Asenovgrad and the vibrant, expressive pottery of the Second Bulgarian Kingdom, decorated with multicoloured swirls and coils punctuated by the occasional bird or animal figure.

The **natural history museum** (Tues–Sun 10am–noon & 1.30–5pm), five minutes' walk away at 34 ul. General Zaimov, isn't particularly interesting, so if you haven't already made a beeline for it, it's better to head back towards the old town.

The old town

With its cobbled streets and orieled mansions, Plovdiv's old quarter is a painter's dream and a cartographer's nightmare. Attempting to follow – let alone describe – an itinerary is impractical given the topography and the numerous **approaches**, each leading to a different point in the old quarter. Glimpses of ornate facades or interiors tempt visitors to stray down the occasional alleyway, or into a courtyard – and generally speaking, that's much the best way to see the area.

National Revival architecture

Blackened **fortress walls** dating from Byzantine times can be seen lurking beyond several streets, sometimes incorporated into the dozens of **National Revival-style houses** that are Plovdiv's speciality. Typically, these rest upon an incline and expand with each storey by means of timber-framed oriels – cleverly resolving the problem posed by the scarcity of ground space and the nineteenth-century merchants who demanded roomy interiors. The most prominent oriel on the facade usually denotes the grand reception room inside, while the sides of the upper storeys sometimes feature blind oriels containing kitchen niches or

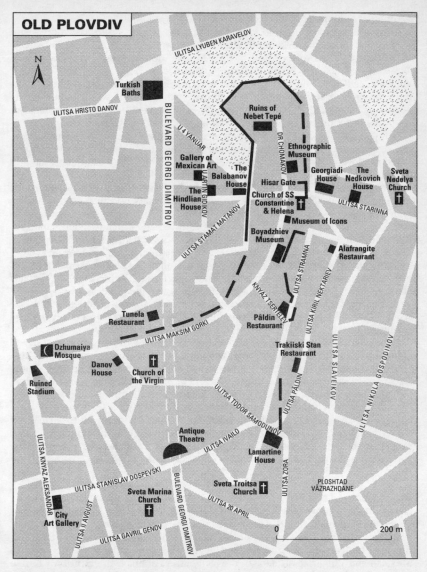

OLD PLOVDIV

cupboards. Outside and inside, the walls are frequently decorated with niches, floral motifs or false columns painted in the style known as *alafranga*, executed by itinerant artists. The rich merchants who lived here also sponsored many of the artistic developments which made up the Bulgarian National Revival, and much of Plovdiv's cultural role is reflected in the numerous small art galleries and concert venues which crowd into the houses of the old town – most of which is designated as an "Architectural-Historical Reserve".

Along ul. Maksim Gorki

Most people approach the old town from pl. Stamboliiski, from which the slight incline of ul. Maksim Gorki gently draws you upward into old Plovdiv. Accessible via a flight of steps to the right is the **Danova house** (Mon–Fri 9am–noon & 1.30–6pm) at Hainrih Haine 2, former domicile of Bulgaria's first large-scale publisher and how home to a museum of Bulgarian printing. Danov was one of those eminent nineteenth-century Bulgarians who regarded distribution of the printed word as a patriotic duty: a crucial step in the peoples' struggle against five centuries of Ottoman darkness. As well as printing books he opened the country's first bookshops in Plovdiv and Ruse; made globes, thermometers and weighing scales (a selection of which are on display) for the nation's schools; and founded Plovdiv's first daily newspaper, *Maritsa*, in 1878 – a title resurrected in modern times after the changes of November 1989.

Occupying a bluff just beyond the house is the **church of Sveta Bogoroditsa**, an imposing hulk of a church which holds some icons by the Samokov master Stanislav Dospevski. Continuing up Maksim Gorki there's a branch of the City Art Gallery at no. 14 (times vary according to what's on show), the venue for thematic exhibitions in the summer, and just beyond, the **Chomatov house** (Tues–Sun 9am–noon & 1.30–5.30pm), now an exhibition gallery devoted to the work of **Zlatyu Boyadzhiev**, one of postwar Bulgaria's best-loved painters. It's easy to see how his work won official favour, pieces such as 1945's *Pernik Miners* showing his marriage of a folk art style with a genuinely felt sympathy for the struggles of working people. Later works such as *Orfei* ("Orpheus") and *Dve svadbi* ("Two Weddings"), use Breughel-like peasant scenes to convey a more earthy national pride.

Retaining the style of a nineteenth-century shop is the **old pharmacy** at no. 16 (Mon–Fri 8am–6pm, Sat 8am–2pm), although you'll need a working knowledge of medical Latin to recognize the archaically labelled concoctions on sale. A little further on is the **museum of icons** (Tues–Sun 9.30am–12.30pm, 2–6pm), rich in fifteenth- and sixteenth-century works rescued from the region's churches; next door to the walled **church of saints Konstantin and Elena** (8am–noon & 1.30–6pm). The frivolous floral patterns adorning the porch gives way to a riotously colourful interior, with brightly painted geometric designs of the ceiling held aloft by pillars topped with Corinthian capitals. Scenes from the gospels cover the surrounding walls, and there's a fine gilt iconostasis by Debâr master Ivan Pashkula, partly decorated by Zahari Zograf.

Around Nebet Tepe

Occupying the corner of Stamat Matanov and 4 Yanuari is the **Balabanov house** (Mon–Fri 9am–noon & 1–6.30pm), once the home of merchant Luka Balabanov, now the venue for modern art shows. Nearby, the curious **permanent exhibition of Mexican art** at Artin Gidikov 11 displays contemporary works by both Mexican and Bulgarian artists. On the same street at no. 4, the **Hindlian house** (summer: Mon–Fri 9am–noon & 1–6.30pm; winter: Mon–Fri 9am–noon) harbours some of Plovdiv's most sumptuous interiors. The Hindlians were Armenian merchants, and the *alafranga* cityscapes painted into the niches of upstairs rooms recall the mercantile cities in which they moved: Constantinople, Alexandria and Venice among them. A wide-ranging collection of furniture collected from the city's wealthy households fills much of the house, including a couple of Biedermeier-period sitting rooms packed with trinkets imported from

Vienna. Downstairs, the Hindlian family bathroom is designed to look like a miniature *hamam*, complete with marble floor and fountain. Many of Plovdiv's surviving Armenian families still live in the surrounding streets, and steps at the end of Armen Gidikov lead up to a modest Armenian church, an Armenian school and the *Erevan* cultural centre. A monument in the courtyard remembers the Plovdiv Armenians who died for "Mother Bulgaria" in the Balkan Wars and World War I.

Ul. Chomakov ascends northwards to the summit of the hill on which the old town is built, passing Plovdiv's most photographed building, the **Kuyumdzhioglu house** (Tues–Sun 9am–noon & 1.30–5.30pm), still known after the Greek merchant who commissioned it in 1847. It was built by Hadzhi Georgi of Constantinople, who combined Baroque and native folk motifs in the richly decorated facade, painted black with yellow trim, its undulating pediment copying the line of the *kolbitsa* or carrying yoke. Now an **ethnographic museum**, the mansion's lower rooms display a mundane tool collection partly redeemed by the inclusion of a rose-still and a splendid oil painting of Plovdiv streetlife during the nineteenth century – but upstairs lies a visual feast. The elegant rooms opening off the grand reception hall, with its rosette-and-sunburst ceiling, are furnished with objects reflecting the *chorbadzhii's* taste for Viennese and French Baroque, and filled with showcases of sumptuous jewellery (the paste-gem-encrusted silver belt clasps are particularly lovely) and traditional Rhodopi costumes, worn by wealthy women and peasants of both sexes, respectively. During June and September, **chamber music** can be heard in the courtyard.

At the head of ul. Chomakov, beyond ramshackle nineteenth-century houses which, still occupied by Plovdiv families, have not benefited from the restoration lavished on others, lies the ruined **Nebet Tepe Citadel**. Although it's difficult to discern precise historical features among the pits and abundant rubble, the site is an archaeologically rich one. Fortified by the Thracian Odrysae tribe as early as the fifth century BC, the hilltop and the settlement of *Eumolpios*, below, were the beginnings of modern Plovdiv, captured by Philip of Macedon in 342 BC, who ordered the former rebuilt in tandem with the new town modestly named *Philippopolis* – which his son, Alexander the Great, abandoned in search of new conquests in Asia. Over the following centuries, the inhabitants must have often resorted to the secret **tunnel** linking Nebet Tepe with the river bank, as the town and citadel were sacked by Romans, Slavs, Bulgars, Byzantium and the Ottoman empire, to name but a few.

From Hisar Kapiya to the Roman theatre

Downhill from ul. Chomakov is the doomy-looking **Hisar Kapiya** or fortress gate, which has been rebuilt countless times since Philip of Macedon had it raised to form the citadel's eastern portal. On the far side, it's the structure rather than ornamentation that makes the **Georgiadi house**, Tsanko Lavrenov 1 (Wed–Mon 9.30am–12.30pm & 2–5pm), so remarkable: the architect has combined "box" oriels with bay windows on a monumental scale. Originally built for a rich Turk in 1846–48, the mansion contains a gallery where musicians once played, plus various salons nowadays occupied by the **Museum of National Liberation**. Pride of place is given to replicas of the bell that tolled and a cannon that fired during the April Rising, when the *bashibazouks* (see p.181) hung Plovdiv's streets with corpses that the population were forbidden to bury. For her relief-work, Britain's Lady Strangord has a street named after her and her picture in the museum; Disraeli, on the other hand, is execrated for condoning the atrocities and ensuring that one-third of newly liberated Bulgaria was returned to the Turks in the form of Eastern Roumelia. The next-door **Nedkovich house** (Mon–Fri 9am–noon & 1–6.30pm) is renowned for the wood-carved ceiling of the enormous first-floor salon, which contains another collection of nineteenth-century furnishings.

The alleyways running downhill behind the Georgiadi and Nedkovich houses lead to several **craft workshops** and many humbler dwellings that have yet to be renovated despite their *obraztsov dom* (listed) status. Looking particularly folorn is the **church of Sveta Nedelya**, a three-aisled basilica said to contain a delicately carved wooden iconostasis and bishop's throne, although the delapidated structure looks set to be closed for some time. Descend much further and you'll find yourself in Plovdiv's **Gypsy quarter**, a shantytown of one-storey one-room dwellings bisected by narrow alleys, stretching between the southern slopes of the old town and bul. Lilyana Dimitrova.

Most visitors, however, head south from here along Kiril Nektariev, one of old Plovdiv's best: although few façades can match that of the house at no. 15, embellished with swags, medallions and intricate tracery in a vivid shade of blue. Follow Nektariev to the end and you'll arrive at the Mavrudi House at the corner of Knyaz Tsertelov and Todor Samodumov, a large buff-coloured mansion with dozens of windows and sturdy ribs supporting the oriels. Popularly referred to as the **Lamartine house** after the French poet who stayed in 1833, writing *Voyage en l'Orient* and recovering from the cholera that killed his daughter in Constantinople, it now contains a small **museum** (in deference to the families that still live there, opening times are limited to Sun, Mon & Tues 9am–noon). There's little to see save for a few pictures of the poet and the places he visited on his travels, accompanied by a few lines of appropriate text, but it's worth peeping inside merely to admire the unusual circular lobby of the house itself.

Tsar Ivailo continues south from here to the **Roman theatre**, whose stands provide a wonderful view of the distant Rhodopes; **classical plays** are staged here during May, June and September. These imposing ruins are practically the only remains of an acropolis which the Romans built when they raised Trimontium from the position of a vassal town to that of provincial capital during the second century. The acropolis, like the residential districts below, was devastated by Kiva's Goths in 251, and later used as building material when the town revived. From here, paths descend to bul. Georgi Dimitrov, at the point where it enters the tunnel beneath the hill, beside which stands the **church of Sveta Marina** (entered from Dospevski or Genov Street), with boldly coloured murals beneath its porch and beguiling devils, storks and other creatures peeping out from the wooden foliage of its intricate iconostasis.

The fair – and other parts of town

A trade centre of long standing, Plovdiv became Bulgaria's principal marketplace during the 1870s, when the railway between Europe and Istanbul was completed and the great annual fair held at Uzundzhovo since the sixteenth century was moved here. Plovdiv's first international trade fair (1892) was a rather homespun affair – a man from Aitos proposed to show his hunting dogs, while Bohemia exhibited beehives – but since 1933 the event has gone from strength to strength, and nowadays claims to be the largest of its kind in the Balkans. There are actually two annual **fairs**: the spring event, devoted to consumer goods in early May, and the larger autumn industrial fair, during the second half of September, both held at the complex on the north bank of the river. Members of the public are free to come along, and there's a special bus service laid on between the railway station and the fairground.

As well as the three hills covered by the old town, there are three more heights ranged across the southwestern quarter of the city. The one nearest to the centre, **Sahat Tepe**, provides a great view of Plovdiv, and the site for what some believe is the oldest **clock tower** in Eastern Europe, restored by the Turks "with divine blessings" in 1809, with an inscription enjoining visitors to "look upon" it "and admire!" From here one can gaze levelly across to **"Alyosha"** (the nickname for this monument to the Red Army) on the neighbouring **Hill of the Liberators**, which also has a pyramidical memorial to the liberators of 1878 on a lower peak. A Thracian temple dedicated to Apollo once stood here, while during the 1950s the Party honoured its demigod by proclaiming this "Stalin Hill" (although locals continued calling it *Bunardzhika*, "Hill of the Crystal Springs"). Further to the southwest lies the **Hill of Youth** (*Hâlm na Mladezhta*), the largest and most park-like of the three.

Eating

Plovdiv is full of privately run kiosks which provide coffee and *hamburgeri* throughout the day, and numerous street vendors sell **snack food** along ul. Knyaz Aleksandâr. The latter also harbours a self-service patisserie useful for breakfasts, *Alen Mak*.

For evening meals, Plovdiv has a wide choice of possibilities. All the hotels have restaurants, more often than not featuring live musical entertainment; the *Bâlgariya* and *Trimontsium* are among the best, while the *Novotel* has a "folk-style" restaurant, the *Evrydika*. However, the most stylish places in which to dine are located in the renovated National Revival-style houses of the old town. Among the best in Bulgaria, these restaurants are expensive by native standards, but a slap-up meal is still within the capabilities of most Western wallets – if not, it's worth popping in just for a drink and a salad merely to enjoy the sumptuous surroundings.

The old town

Alafrangite, Kiril Nektariev 17. Basic Bulgarian nosh served up in elegant nineteenth-century surroundings, with a nice summer garden.

Kambanata, Maksim Gorki. Modern restaurant built into a cellar beneath the church of Sveta Bogroditsa, popular with the stylish young.

Pâldin, Knyaz Tseretenev 3. Most exclusive of the restaurants in the old town, with a wide choice of traditional Bulgarian dishes. A three-course meal with drinks should still cost under £8.

Trakiiski stan, Pâldin 7. Another beautifully refurbished National Revival interior. Often overrun with tour groups enjoying folklore performances.

The new town

Chuchura, Otets Paisii. Modern family restaurant.

Kamenitsa, ul. Knyaz Aleksandâr Batenberg 34. Straightforward mid-price food with a terrace overlooking the city's main promenading street. Good place for a drink too.

Republika, Knyaz Aleksandår 39. Cheapest of the city-centre restaurants serving no-nonsense grilled meats. Loud folk/pop bands most evenings.

Ribkata, Patriarh Evtimii 5. Renowned for its excellent grilled fish dishes.

Tunela, Georgi Dimitrov. Near the northern end of the road tunnel. Lively outdoor venue, worth a try when folk/pop bands are performing.

Trifon Zarezan, Otets Paisii 14. Good food; but a rowdy, male-dominated place with night-club-style floor show.

Zlatnoto Pile, Raiko Daskalov 52. Basic grilled chicken.

Drinking

As elsewhere in Bulgaria, you can snatch a quick coffee or fruit juice almost anywhere in the downtown area during the daytime. There are a growing number of European-style bars catering for evening drinkers, a scene which seems set to grow as a result of Plovdiv's burgeoning private enterprise culture. After 11pm, diehards can try the late-night bars in the *Trimontsium*, *Leningrad* and *Novotel* hotels.

Hisar Kapiya, Kiril Nektariev. No more than a kiosk selling spirits and beer, but the surrounding summer garden is a nice oasis of liveliness in an otherwise quiet area of the old town.

Filipopol, on the corner of Georgi Dimitrov and Gavril Genov. Lively café catering for a mixture of youngsters and daytime shoppers.

Roma, Maksim Gorki. Stylish venue for evening drinking in the old town.

Sinyata house, Kiril Nektariev. Cosy bar housed in a National Revival mansion.

Sladkarnitsa Orfei, Knyaz Aleksandår. Best of the many patisseries around pl. Stamboliiski, serving good ice cream and cakes. Closes at about 9pm.

Yunaid, Maksim Gorki. Outdoor terrace perched above the northern end of the road tunnel running beneath the old town.

Entertainment

Plovdiv takes its culture seriously, and there's a comprehensive diet of music and theatre all year round. Classical concerts take place at the *Plovdiv Philharmonic Orchestra*'s concert hall on the south side of Tsentralen; the *Opera* is based at Sasho Dimitrov 23; while the *Mesalitinov Theatre* at Knyaz Aleksandår 36 is the venue for classical drama. Bookings for musical events can be made at the **concert bureau** at Knyaz Aleksandår 35 (daily 8am–7pm).

There's a busy schedule of festivals too. During the first half of January, the **Winter Festival of Symphony Music** allows the Philharmonic Orchestra to flex its muscles; international virtuosi participate in the prestigious **Festival of Chamber Music**, held in the courtyard of the ethnographic museum in June every odd-numbered year (native ensembles play on until September, and during even-numbered years). Numerous recitals take place in the old town throughout the summer, and in May, June and September (coinciding with the fairs), **opera and drama** can be enjoyed in the spectacular surroundings of the Antique Theatre.

On fine evenings, citizens gather in Freedom Park to admire the play of fountains and coloured lights known as the "Water Music", carefully choreographed to a soundtrack of western pop and traditional Bulgarian tunes. The biggest **cinemas** – the *Balkan* and the *Republika* – are both on Knyaz Aleksandår.

Listings

Airlines *BALKAN*, Sasho Dimitrov 4 (☎233 031).

Car hire from the *Novotel* (☎5892) and *Maritsa* (☎52736) hotels.

Car repairs from *Autoservis*, near the *Trakiya* campsite.

Consulates *Greece*, Preslav 10 (☎232 003); *Turkey*, Filip Makedonski 10 (☎232 309).

Dental treatment at the *Stomatological Polyclinic* on the corner of Ul. Dondukov and Emil de Lavele.

Emergencies Ambulance (☎ 150); police (☎2-22-10).

Filling stations out along the Svilengrad and Sofia highways.

Football The town's premier outfit, *Lokomotiv Plovdiv*, consistently finish near the top of the first division. The *Lokomotiv* stadium is south of the centre on Konstantin Velichkov (bus #4 from Tsentralen or #24 from the railway station).

Markets Plovdiv's liveliest fruit and vegetable market is just off ul. Perushtitsa, west of pl. Sâedinenie. There's a smaller affair just below the old town at pl. Nikola Ginev.

Pharmacies 24-hour chemist on Patriarh Evtimii.

Post and telephones Main post office, Tsentralen 1.

Rail tickets Domestic and international bookings from *Rila*, General Gurko 13.

Taxis ☎142.

Travel agents *Orbita*, Ivan Vazov 23; *Pirin*, General Zaimov 3.

Moving on from Plovdiv

From Plovdiv there are frequent trains to **Sofia** plus four daily expresses to **Burgas** and two to **Varna**. Reaching **central or northern Bulgaria** often entails a change of trains at Stara Zagora, but direct services run to Karlovo, Asenovgrad, Panagyurishte and Hisarya.

Travelling to Turkey from Plovdiv, the *Balkan Express* runs daily to Istanbul throughout the year, while an additional service, the *Istanbul Express*, operates between May and September. A ticket to Istanbul costs about £30 (you can pay in Bulgarian currency), though it's near-impossible to buy tickets to Svilengrad on the border and then buy a Turkish ticket on the other side – people buying tickets on the Svilengrad line are often asked to produce their passport. If travelling to Greece from Plovdiv, there's a connecting service to Thessaoníki at Svilengrad.

Plovdiv to the Turkish border

There are good reasons why so many visitors travel between Plovdiv and Turkey non-stop. The settlements along the way are predominantly workaday places lacking in specific attractions, and there seems little interest in catering for tourists. The Bulgarians have become accustomed to the sight of foreigners speeding through their country en route for either Turkey or Greece (especially young ones who, they feel, spend insufficient time or money here in passing), and travellers on this particular route shouldn't be too surprised if the hand of friendship is not always extended. In the past, stories used to abound of Bulgarian militia hassling those travellers with transit visas who attempted to stray off the E-80 highway: hitting them with petty fines for "safety violations" or demanding that tourists change money into non-convertible leva. Nowadays cases such as these seem to be the exception rather than the rule, and you should perhaps be more wary of unscrupulous traders who expect payment in hard currency for refreshments sold along the route.

Travelling **by road** you'll pass KLOKOTNITSA village just west of Dimitrovgrad, famous as the site of Ivan Asen's victory over Theodor Comnenus, the usurper of Byzantium, in 1230, thereby forcing the empire to recognize him as "Tsar of the Bulgarians and Greeks" and accept the betrothal of Ivan's young daughter to Baldwin, Byzantium's teenage emperor. **Hitching** is pretty good, but be sure not to overshoot the motel (4 km before the Haskovo slip-road) if you aim to stay there. Approaching the border **by rail** means a brief encounter with DIMITROVGRAD – full of power stations and reeking chemical *kombinats* – before catching a bus or train south.

Haskovo

However you manage to get there, **HASKOVO**'s appeal lies in its "Turkish character" – amounting to some vestiges of Ottoman architecture and an atmosphere that's subtly different from the usual Bulgarian ambience. The town was founded in around 1395 and named *Haskoy* by the Turks, who predominated here for the next 500 years, until the development of the tobacco industry and the war of 1912 greatly increased the number of Bulgarians, who now form the majority. Turkish and Islamic cultural influences are still evident, mostly in minutae like the berets and headscarves worn by Muslims now that fezes, *shavlari* and veils have gone out of fashion or been proscribed. Despite all-too-obvious signs of demolition elsewhere, Haskovo still retains its **fourteenth-century mosque**, the oldest in the country, as well as an attractive nineteenth-century **Bulgarian quarter** in the western outskirts.

The town

Haskovo revolves around a modern town square, the usual flagstoned expanse fringed by civic buildings, centred on a memorial to the dead of successive wars. Along the square's southern flank is the town **museum** (Tues–Sun 9am–noon & 2–6pm), with a fine collection of pre-Ottoman artefacts (especially Roman, Byzantine and medieval coins). Five centuries of Turkish rule are passed over relative silence; more noticable is the commemoration of a tobacco workers' state of 1927.

South of the main square is the **Eski Dzhumaya Mosque**, an ancient block of whitewashed stone built immediately after the Ottoman conquest. This is quite a change from the usual delapidated, little-used structures elsewhere in Bulgaria: a carpeted room where the *hodja* reads silently and men pray, footwear and "immodest" attire are taboo, and women are only admitted against Islamic custom to conform with Bulgarian law.

West of the main square bul. Vasil Levski curls round a quiet suburban area, following the course of the Haskovska River, before arriving at the **church of Sveta Bogoroditsa**, a simple basilica of heavy brick filled with fussy woodcarving, most notably the intricate floral capitals of the pillars in the nave. The next-door **chapel** (Tues, Sat & Sun 9am–noon & 2–6pm) holds a collection of icons. Two hundred metres south of the church, at Yanko Sakâzov 4 is the **birthplace of Aleksandâr Paskaliev** (same times), a pioneer of Bulgarian publishing; but the more attractive buildings are immediately behind the church on ul. Bratya Minchev. At no. 9 is **Shishmanova house** (same times) with an ethnographic collection documenting the region's domestic crafts; while next door is Haskovo's finest surviving National Revival building, nowadays the House of Children's Art – not always open to the public, though you can usually admire the symmetrical facade and galleried first floor.

Practicalities and moving on

The town's bus terminal is a few minutes' walk east of the central square, whereas the railway station is about twenty minutes' walk in the same direction. Haskovo has good bus connections with Plovdiv, Kârdzhali and Harmanli if you're using public transport to tour around; otherwise there are several places **to stay**: the 3-star *Aida* (☎038/25033; ③), the slightly less comfortable *Republika*, Otets Paisii 25 (②), or *Rodopi*, bul. Vasil Levski (②). Failing that, take a #102 bus from bul. Dimitrov to the *motel/campsite* (ask for the *Spirka Hancheto*) – but beware that some buses turn uphill at least 3km short.

Harmanli

HARMANLI gets its name from the threshing mills (*harman*) that once abounded on the surrounding plain, nowadays given over to growing cotton, mulberries (for silkworms) and tobacco. A few minutes' walk from the bus terminal, the centre of town clusters around the *Hotel Hebros*, not far from both of Harmanli's "sights". The chunky, ruined caravanserai wall dates from the sixteenth century like the town itself, whose Turkish founders also constructed the hump-backed **Gurbav Bridge**, with its typically flowery dedication:

> *As a token of his gratitude to God the Grand Vizier ordered an arch like a rainbow to be built over the River Harmanli . . . and alleviated rich and poor alike from their sorrows. The world is a bridge which is crossed by both king and pauper. When I saw the completion of this bridge, in praying to God, I spoke this inscription.*

Besides having a sizable ethnic-Turkish population like Haskovo, Harmanli is noted for its Gypsies, who practice the traditional *tsigani* trades at **horsefairs** (sometime in August; ask locals for details).

Practicalities

Harmanli's centrally located bus terminal is preferable as a point of arrival to the rail station, some way out to the southeast and connected to town by a bus. The central *Hebros* **hotel**, ul. Osvoboditel 1 (☎0373/6991; ④) seems to be the best place to eat and drink; while there's also a surprisingly lively **disco-bar** 150m from the *Gergana* **campsite** (open May–Nov), 4km southeast of town – the last reasonably priced accommodation before Turkey. The **Gergana Fountain** within the vicinity is said to have been built by a vizier of Constantinople to win the heart of a Bulgarian woman, a legend used as the theme of P.R. Slaveykov's poem "The spring of the maiden with snow-white feet".

Svilengrad – and leaving Bulgaria

The only place to stay in **SVILENGRAD** is the costly 3-star *Hotel Svilena* (☎0379/2609; ④), which features restaurant, bar, tourist information bureau and car-rental facilities; but to be honest there's little for visitors to stop here for – except the *Stariya Most* beyond the railway station. Also known as the **Mustafa**

Pasha Bridge, this 295m-long structure of Karabag stone supported by thirteen arches is an even finer achievement than the Gurbav Bridge at Harmanli, and was likewise built during the sixteenth century.

There's a handful of antiquities near MEZEK, a village 6km southwest of Svilengrad: a signposted **Thracian tomb**, consisting of a 21 metre-long corridor leading to two rooms and a circular funerary chamber where bronze artefacts were found, probably dating from the fourth century BC. A similar distance west of the village, the **ruined Neutzikon fortress** is perhaps the best preserved of the many *kreposti* (fortresses) raised to guard against Byzantine incursions during the eleventh and twelfth centuries. Unfortunately both attractions used to languish in an off-limits border zone in Communist times, and although the zone no longer exists, there's still uncertainty about whether either of the above attractions is in a position to admit visitors. Ask at the *Hotel Svilena* in town first.

Crossing into Greece and Turkey

From Svilengrad, it's possible **to enter Greece** or Turkey. A train, leaving Svilengrad around 10am, reaches ALEKSANDROUPOLIS four hours later, or there's a 24-hour road crossing just outside town, leading to Greek ORMENION. However, most traffic crosses **the Turkish border** at KAPITAN ANDREEVO (15km from Svilengrad; open 24 hours), where vehicles entering Bulgaria are liable to rigorous examinations depending on narcotics intelligence reports and the current state of Bulgar-Turkish relations. Because trains entering or **leaving Bulgaria** get worked over by customs and immigration at Svilengrad station (rather than at Kapitan Andreevo), it might be possible to board there – at around 1am or 5am, depending on the seasonal schedule of the *Istanbul Express* – and ride on to Istanbul **by rail** without incurring the cost of an international ticket.

Inside Turkey (where motorists and railway passengers undergo customs at KAPIKULE), everything you're likely to need can be found 19km further east in **EDIRNE**. The town's splendid mosque and the chance to witness camel-wrestling (on Thursdays) might stop you from heading straight for Istanbul.

> If you intend travelling into Greece or Turkey, *The Rough Guide* to each of those countries is an essential purchase.

THE RHODOPES

According to Thracian mythology, the mortal lovers Hem and Rhodopis dared call themselves after the divine Zeus and Hera, who duly punished the couple by turning them into mountains separated by the River Maritsa – Hem the Balkans and she **the Rhodopes**. Straddling Greece and Bulgaria, the Rhodopes are the land where panpipes, Orpheus and the Orphic Cult originated, a region rich in gems and ores, but otherwise not fit for much beyond raising sheep and growing tobacco in the arid valleys. Unlike the rest of Bulgaria, whole communities

---

* Herodotus records a Greek legend that the Pyramid of Mycerinus in Egypt was built at the instigation of a Thracian courtesan, Rhodopis, who charged a building block for each act of intercourse – since the pyramid consists of at least 200,000 blocks, her exertions must have been considerable.

converted to Islam after the conquest, and of the numerous Turks who settled here many outstayed the empire's collapse – their descendants now constitute Bulgaria's largest ethnic minority. Over the last thirty years, tourism and hydro-electric schemes have also pushed the Rhodopes into the twentieth century, and the region is today, as Leslie Gardiner noted, a weird mixture of opposites: "donkeys and turbo-generators, Alpine flowers and tropical foliage, bikinis in winter and thick Turkish woollens in summer".

The massacre of its population made **Batak** notorious in the late nineteenth century, but if foreigners have heard of anywhere in the region nowadays it's probably Bulgaria's premier ski resort, **Pamporovo**, from which tourism has spread to lap at **Smolyan** and the picturesque village of **Shiroka Lâka**. Closer to Plovdiv, **Bachkovo monastery** has already established its place on the tourist trail, and the town of **Kârdzhali** is also attempting to get in on the act. Yet the brochures and guidebooks still refer to the "unknown Rhodopes" with some justice, for there are scores of mountain villages off the beaten track (roadbuild-ers were sometimes attacked by locals in the old days), many of which are rarely visited by outsiders.

Given the dearth of public transport (limited to the main roads – most others qualify as tracks) and tourist accommodation, we've covered only the most obvi-ous routes. The **railway** linking Septemvri on the plain with Bansko in the Pirin Mountains serves as the basis for journeys to Velingrad, Yundola and Batak in the western Rhodopes; **buses** from Plovdiv provide the means to reach Asenovgrad, Bachkovo monastery, Pamporovo and Smolyan in the central Rhodopes; to reach Kârdzhali, use buses and trains from Haskovo.

THE ORPHIC MYSTERIES

The **legend of Orpheus** originated in ancient Thrace, where he was supposedly born of a Muse (perhaps Calliope, patron of epic poetry) and King Oeagrus of the Odrysae tribe (Apollo in other versions of the story). His mastery of the lyre moved animals and trees to dance, and with his songs – which had previously enabled the Argonauts to resist the Sirens' lure – Orpheus tried to regain his dead wife, Eurydice, from the underworld. His music charmed Charon, the ferryman, and Cerebus, the guardian of the River Styx, and finally Hades himself, who agreed to return Eurydice on the condition that neither of them looked back as they departed – but emerging into the sunlight of the overworld, Orpheus turned to smile at Eurydice and so lost her forever. Thereafter, Orpheus roamed the Rhodopes sing-ing mournfully until he was torn apart by "the women of Thrace" (whom Aeschylus identifies as followers of Dionysus having a Bacchic orgy). His head continued sing-ing as it floated down the River Mesta to Lesbos, where it began to prophesy until its fame eclipsed that of the Oracle at Delphi.

Despite prohibition by the authorities, an Orphic cult was well established by the fifth century BC, and itinerant priests offering initiation into the **Orphic Mysteries** wandered about Thrace. Original texts codifying Orphism's basic tenets have been lost, although later Hellenistic writers held that initiates were vegetarians and that they regarded the material world as evil (describing the body as a "prison", accord-ing to Plato), and the spiritual world as divine. Little is known about the cult's prac-tices, but it's thought that the ritual involved the mimed – or actual – dismemberment of a person representing Dionysus, who was then "reborn" as a free soul after death. Another theory has it that the cult's true, secret purpose was to bestow upon its adherents longevity, or even physical immortality.

Velingrad, Batak and the western Rhodopes

Like the Rila and Pirin mountains west of the Mesta valley, the **western Rhodopes** are covered by coniferous forests and sparsely populated, with fewer than a dozen settlements along the road from Velingrad to Gotse Delchev, and none at all between Dospat and Batak. Discounting the reservoirs built to trap rivers for the benefit of lowland agriculture, and the shepherds tending their flocks on the alpine pastures, the highlands still belong to their **wildlife**: stags, mouflon, deer, wild boar and all manner of birds inhabit a dozen protected reserves.

Although there are limited bus services from places like Blagoevgrad and Plovdiv, the most reliable means of **approaching from the Pirin Mountains or the Thracian plain** is probably the *Dobrinishte-Septemvri line*, calling at Bansko, Razlog, Yakoruda and Velingrad en route. Velingrad is three hours' journey from Bansko or ninety minutes' ride from Septemvri – slow going, but the sheer beauty of the route makes the journey worthwhile.

Velingrad

With its diverse springs, excellent climate and many trees and parks, **VELINGRAD** is a popular spa town made up of three former Pomak villages, originally named Kamenitsa, Lâzhdane and Chepino – lumped together in 1948 and renamed after local partisan heroine Vela Peeva. Both the rail and bus stations are a few minutes' walk east of the modern centre, which in turn lies just to the east of **Lâzhdane**, where Velingrad's oldest baths, the **Velyova banya** (founded in the sixteenth century, although the buildings are modern), stand in a park beside the Yundola road. Just to the north of the centre is **Kamenitsa**, fringed by wooded parks which harbour the town's open-air baths, most of the modern spa facilities, and a small Ottoman-period *hamam*, the **Kremâchna banya** or "Flint Baths".

Velingrad's third cluster of baths is situated 2km south of the centre in the **Chepino** quarter (bus #1 from the centre), where mineral water flows free from taps in the streets. Above Chepino to the south lies the Kleptuza spring, waters from which flow down to the **Kleptuza lake** just east of Chepino: with pedalos, rowing boats and lakeside walkways, this is the most popular of Velingrad's resort areas.

Practicalities

Reasonably priced **accommodation** is available at the 2-star *Hotel Zdravets* in the modern centre (☎0359/2682; ③), while the 3-star *Velina* in Chepino (☎0359/3412; ④) is more plush. Cheaper chalets are for hire at *Kleptuza camping*, near the spring, and *Velingrad* just outside town on the Yundola road. Most eating and drinking opportunities are in the modern centre's main square. In Chepino, there are restaurants and cafés around the Kleptuza lake, and the *Hotel Velina* has a good restaurant and café-bar.

Besides regular **buses to Batak**, there are three or four daily **trains to Bansko** in the Pirin range.

Southwest of Velingrad

A short bus ride to the northwest of Velingrad, **YUNDOLA** is another small health resort 4560ft above sea level, set amid rounded hills and copses of trees. Yundola used to be a popular rest-home for trade unionists and Young Pioneers, and from a tourist's standpoint Yundola is chiefly remarkable for its inhabitants' longevity. The prevalence of **centenarians** in Bulgaria (some 2000 were recorded in 1969, two-thirds of them women) is ascribed to features of life in the highlands, where "Nature takes years off the weak and adds them to the strong" – as Leslie Gardiner was told. Human longevity is supposedly extended by pure air, climatic extremes, a lack of stress, and a spartan diet with little meat and plenty of yoghurt.

The railway line meanwhile continues eastwards towards Bansko and the Pirin Mountains (see Chapter Two), leisurely winding its way through sandy-soiled pine forests and occasional sub-alpine meadows. Most of the area is *pomak* territory (p.181), although there are few settlements along the route save for the workaday logging town of YAKORUDA.

Batak

Several daily buses from Velingrad traverse 26km of highland pasture, Pomak villages and oak and beech forests to reach the town of **BATAK**: a name which once reverberated across Europe. During the April Rising of 1876 the Turks unleashed the *bashibazouks* and *pomaks* to rape, pillage and slaughter the populace of Batak. Five thousand people – nearly the entire population – were hacked to death or burnt alive – an act for which the Turkish commander responsible was decorated.

Abroad, Britain's Prime Minister Disraeli cynically dismissed the **atrocities** to justify the continuing alliance with Turkey, until the collective weight of reports by foreign diplomats and J.A. MacGahan of *The Daily News* became impossible to ignore. Even so, only a sustained campaign by trade unions, Gladstone and public figures like Victor Hugo and Oscar Wilde prevented British military intervention during the Russo-Turkish War of 1877–78. In addition, at the Congress of Berlin Disraeli managed to ensure that the Ottomans retained control of a third of Bulgaria (Eastern Roumelia) – in return for which Turkey rewarded Britain with Cyprus.

The town

As a bloody milestone on the road to liberation the massacre is still commemorated, and the town reverberates with memories of the dead. One wall of the town **museum** on the main square (Tues–Sun 8am–noon & 2–6pm) is inscribed with a seemingly endless roll-call of those who died, and sepia photographs of the time show old women who survived the massacre sitting besides piles of skulls and bones – some of the latter carefully set out on a table to form the words *Ustanak ot 1876*: "the Rising of 1876". Display cabinets are filled with foreign press reports and savage denunciations of the Turks and those who seemed to lend them support – including Turgenev's attack on Disraeli and Queen Victoria, *Croquet at Windsor*. A burnt tree trunk commemorates local rebel leader Trendafil Kerelov, who was lashed to it before it was set alight.

Second-floor exhibits concentrate on Batak's contribution to the Balkan and both world wars, including documents from the nearby partisan camp of *Tehran* – so-named in honour of the Allies' summit in 1943 – and a gruesome photograph of partisans' heads left on a wall in the village. Partisan dead are also honoured by a marble cenotaph in the crypt in a calculated attempt to demonstrate that the Communist-led rebels of the 1940s were the spiritual descendants of the rebels of 1876.

Immediately opposite lies the low, roughly hewn **church of Sveta Nedelya** (enquire at the museum if it's closed), where MacGahan found naked corpses piled three feet deep; the bloodstains on the walls have never been expunged. The church's bare interior contains stark reminders of the violence: signs point to bullet holes in the walls; a glass case holds one of the heavy woodsmen's axes used to bludgeon the *Batachani* into submission; while in a sunken chamber at the end of the church lie the bones of the massacred.

After all this you may not have much stomach for further sightseeing, although there's a small **Ethnographic Museum** (opened on request: ask at the historical museum) one block north of the church; and an **art gallery** (Wed–Sun 2–6pm) occupying a National Revival-style house east of the main square on ul. Apriltsi.

Practicalities, and moving on

Batak's small **bus station** is at the eastern end of the main street, ul. Apriltsi, along which anything of significance is situated. Head west along here to reach the main square.

Although there's a murky hotel, the *Tekstil* (previously off limits to Westerners, and in any case inexplicably closed when this book was being researched) on ul. Apriltsi, you'd do better to check out the **accommodation** possibilities around Lake Batak, a popular beauty spot west of town. Here you'll find the tourist complex of TSIGOV CHARK about 6km out of town, featuring a **campsite** (open June–Oct) and the *Orbita* **hotel** (③) – Batak-Velingrad buses pass by.

Moving on from Batak, public transport definitely inclines towards Velingrad, Peshtera and Plovdiv: if you're aiming for the eastern Rhodopes it's best to aim for the latter and pick up connections there.

South of Plovdiv

The northernmost spurs of the Rhodopes rear up abruptly from the plain barely 10km south of Plovdiv. Numerous routes lead up the narrow valleys of the various Rhodopi streams which gush down to feed the Maritsa, rendering several mountain resorts within easy reach of the city. One road heads southwest up the Vâcha valley where, beyond the town of KRICHIM, the river has been dammed to form the Antonivanovtsi reservoir – at the northern end of which stands the *Anton Ivanov* chalet (☎03145/2246). From here a reasonable well-surfaced road heads over the hills to the isolated highland communities of Devin and Dospat. More popular as a weekend escape for Plovdivites is the town of TSAR KALOYAN, lying at the foot of the **Chernatitsa massif**. Walkers in the area are catered for by the *Zdravets* chalet just beyond town, while three hours' walk to the east is another chalet, the *Ruen*, lurking below the 1326m-high peak of the same name.

However, the main route south from Plovdiv into the Rhodopes heads up the ruggedly beautiful valley of the River Chepelarska, en route for Bulgaria's premier winter sports area around Pamporovo and Smolyan. The road passes one of the country's most historic monasteries, near the village of Bachkovo. The town of Asenovgrad, standing at the point where the mountains meet the Thracian plain, is the obvious starting-point for expeditions to the monastery.

Asenovgrad

Half-hourly buses speed across the dusty plain between Plovdiv and **ASENOVGRAD** 20km distant, a light and breezy town built around a large park. Rail and bus terminals lie on the northern outskirts, from which it's a short walk through the park and across the river to a modern town square. Two church spires are visible on the hill immediately above: the resplendently ochre-coloured Sveti Dimitår on the left and the smaller Sveta Troitsa on the right. More interesting, however, is the town's main shopping thoroughfare running south from the square, where a small **historical museum** (Mon–Sat 9am–noon & 2–5pm) holds local Neolithic and Thracian finds – including a fine bronze helmet and the iron wheel rims of a Thracian chariot. The Thracians were the original inhabitants of the fortified hill overlooking the entrance to the Chepelarska gorge 2.5 km south of town – now the site of a ruined **medieval fortress**. Founded during the eleventh century, it was enlarged after Asen II's victory over the Byzantine empire in 1230, hence the town's medieval name, *Stanimaka* – "protector of the mountain pass". What little remains of the fort can be seen just as easily from the window of a bus, although devotees of Byzantine architecture might consider it worth climbing up to the nearby **church of the Virgin** which has stayed relatively intact.

The only **accommodation** in town is the 2-star *Hotel Asenovets* on the main square (☎0331/23288), and it seems better to take one of the regular buses up the valley towards Bachkovo, Chepelare and Smolyan.

Towards Bachkovo

Just beyond Asenovgrad the road enters the impressive **Chepelarska gorge**, its river nowadays harnessed to produce electricity. Heavy trucks bound for the mines around Ardino are another sign that modernization has come to the Rhodopes, but you can still see goatherds with their flocks and mule-trains bearing packs. Throughout the centuries of Ottoman rule, the Rhodopes was the region most consistently infested with outlaws: *haiduks*, whom the Bulgars now romantically view as precursors of the patriotic *chetis*, but also bandits of Turkish origin known as *kårdzhalii*, who spread terror among the villages.

The last wave of armed resistance to authority occurred in 1947–49, when anti-Communist partisans operated in the hills around Asenovgrad; and if Amnesty International's report on events in Dolni Voden (just northwest of town) is accurate, the memory of this may well have influenced the state's decision to send in troops to ensure that the ethnic Turkish and Bulgarian Muslim villagers submitted to the "name-changing campaign" in 1984.

Bachkovo monastery

Nine kilometres south of Asenovgrad, **Bachkovo village**'s fortress-like stone houses, overgrown with flowers, are no indication of what to expect at **BACHKOVO MONASTERY**, a kilometre or so further up the road. Gardiner's description of it as "a mixed bag of buildings – chapels, ossuaries, cloisters, cells –

daubed with frescoes more naive than artistic" doesn't really do justice to Bulgaria's second largest monastery, which, like Rila, has been declared a "world monument" by UNESCO.

The story goes that it was founded in 1038 by two Georgians in the service of the Byzantine empire, one of whom, Grigoriy Pakuryani, renounced the governorship of Smolyan and Adrianople to devote the remainder of his life to meditation. A great iron-studded door admits visitors to the cobblestoned courtyard, surrounded by vine-wreathed wooden galleries and kept free of grass by sheep. Along one wall of the courtyard, **frescoes** provide a narrative of the monastery's history, showing Bachkovo roughly as it appears today, but watched by God's eye and a celestial Madonna and child, with pilgrims proceeding to a hill in the vicinity to place icons. Other frescoes show in gory detail the slaying of the dragon: a powerful archetype in ancient European and Chinese cosmology, appropriated by Christianity to be vanquished by Saint George and symbolize the demise of paganism.

Sveta Bogoroditsa
Beneath the vaulted porch of Bachkovo's principal church, **Sveta Bogoroditsa**, are more frescoes, all expressing the horrors in store for sinners: among many scenes of retribution, a boyar is tormented on his deathbed by a devil brandishing a female doll-figure (presumably representative of past infidelities), while women look on in terror. The entrance itself is more cheerful, with the Holy Trinity painted on strips set at angles in a frame, so that one sees God or Christ flanking a dove, depending on which side you approach from, like a medieval hologram. Floral motifs in a "naive" style decorate the beams of the interior, where a fourteenth-century icon of the Virgin, of Georgian origin, is displayed to your right as you enter. August 25, the name-day of the church's patron, is the occasion for ritual devotions – and there's reportedly another **religious festival** held 25 days after the Orthodox Easter.

Saint Nicholas
Bachkovo's other church, **Saint Nicholas**, was founded in the nineteenth century and has recently been restored. There's a fine *Last Judgement* covering the porch exterior, which includes portraits of the artist, Zahari Zograf, and two colleagues in the upper left-hand corner. In the old **refectory** you can see *The Procession of the Miraculous Icon* (executed by Zograf's pupils), which repeats the pilgrimage portrayed on the wall of the courtyard; the accoutrements of a monk's life are neatly displayed in a former cell off the first gallery. More striking is the **museum**, where carved spoons, broken teapots and ecclesiastical hats are jumbled together with filigreed crosses, books bound in gold and the odd Thracian bas-relief, as if inviting visitors to choose at a jumble sale. Finally, there's **Sveta Troitsa**, standing 300m from the main gate: a church which contains numerous early medieval frescoes and life-sized portraits of Tsar Ivan Aleksandâr (1331–71) and the royal family, who lavishly endowed the monastery.

Practicalities
An easy day trip from Plovdiv, the monastery can be reached by taking either one of the five-or-so daily **buses** from Asenovgrad to Bachkovo, or a Plovdiv-Chepelare or Plovdiv-Smolyan bus, both of which run past the monastery drive. It's often difficult to predict the times of buses returning in the opposite direction, so you may be in for a long wait.

There are two **restaurants** in the immediate vicinity of the monastery, so there's no difficulty in obtaining refreshment. There's a fairly rudimentary **campsite** (May–Sept) just outside the monastery; otherwise the nearest accommodation is the *Asenovets* back in Asenovgrad, or the small **motel** about 3km south of Asenovgrad.

Around Narechenski Bani

Fourteen kilometres south of Bachkovo, the old village of Narechen has been subsumed by the **mineral baths** of NARECHENSKI BANI – efficacious for treating metabolic disorders, obesity, gout and diabetes. Sufferers usually benefit from a stay at the *Hotel Zornitsa* and balneotherapy, and there's also a campsite (open all year round) located in tranquil scenery 3km upriver from the town. Otherwise it's difficult to think of reasons for stopping here. However, travellers with private transport might consider a detour to so-called **Rock Bridges**, which can be reached by turning west off the main road 14km south of Narechenski Bani, and taking the right-hand fork 10km later, from where it's a further 5km to the *Skalni Mostove*. These weird rock formations consist of a "bridge" almost a hundred yards long, overhanging an abyss, 200m below which is a deep, natural tunnel. Two well-appointed **chalets** are on hand for those who wish to explore further: the *Chudnite mostove*, and the *Skalni mostove* (☎03051/2927) slightly beyond.

Cave-buffs might also enjoy the **Speleological Museum** in CHEPELARE, a small mountain town with a 2-star **hotel**, the *Zdravets* (☎2177; ③) situated on the main road 6km north of Progled. If you take the right-hand fork after Progled, it's only another 3km up to Pamporovo, the "Gem of the Rhodopes".

Pamporovo

Bulgaria's largest ski resort creeps up the wooded mountainside like a partisan column determined to sabotage the TV tower on Mount Snezhanka. PAMPOROVO is a user-friendly type of ski-centre. Everyone sees action, casualties are minimal, and veterans and rookies alike return to revel in the base-camp hotels come evening, exchanging their adventures and mishaps on the slopes above. Mild weather and good snow-cover make **skiing** conditions near perfect from mid-December until mid-April, and there's a range of classes and pistes to suit everyone from absolute beginners up to the pros who compete for the Rhodopa Cup each year around mid-March. Beginners' slopes are close to the resort centre, while the other runs – including the giant slalom – begin higher up the mountain, above the *Studenets* way-station (which will hire you equipment) and the outlying *Malina* chalet-complex. Both places are linked to the summit by chair-lifts (operating 8.30am–5pm), and Malina can be reached by bus or on foot (20min) from the grouping of hotels and restaurants which comprises Pamporovo's "centre".

Planning a trip

However, Pamporovo is the kind of place you should make up your mind to visit well in advance. Independent travellers are charged considerably more for rooms, tuition and equipment than people on **package-holidays** (and might find that everything's booked up anyway), so would-be skiers are strongly advised to take one of the cheap deals offered by foreign tour operators (see p.6), plus the optional "ski pack" which covers all rentals and lift rides. If you do just turn up, the *Rozhen, Prepsa, Panorama, Orfei* and *Snezhanka* hotels, and the Malina chalet-colony, have the cheapest **beds**; the **tourist office** in the *Hotel Murgavets* will probably ring around and help with bookings if requested. Once there, traditional **Rhodope dishes** like spit-roasted lamb (*cheverme*), stuffed peppers (*sarmi*), white bean stew (*Smolenski bob*) and a local variation on the cheese-filled *banitsa* are on offer at "folk-style" restaurants such as the *Chevermeto, Malina* – and *Vodenitsata* in STOYKITE village, 7km west – which feature music and dancing. Otherwise entertainment is pretty much as you'd expect. Discos in the *Rozhen, Prepsa, Perelik* and *Snezhanka* hotels operate until the small hours; plus there's a "Ball of Nations", a "ski carnival" which starts on the slopes and moves to the *Perelik*, and the saccharine ritual of choosing and crowning a "Miss Pamporovo".

Independent travellers who fancy a spot of skiing may find it preferable to stay down the valley in Smolyan, from whence there are regular buses up to the pistes of Pamporovo during the winter season – a hut handling ski and boot hire lies just behind the Pamporovo bus stop. Chair lifts take you from here to the *Studenets* chalet, then onwards to the 1926-metre-high summit of Snezhanka, starting-point of many of the ski runs. It's also the site of the **Snezhanka Tower** (daily 9am–4pm), a futuristic structure with a café and an observation gallery giving a marvellous view of the Rhodope Mountains and, on clear days, parts of the Pirin and Rila, too. Twenty minutes' walk from here are the **Orpheus Rocks** (*Orfeevi Skali*), the vantage point for a superb panorama of the mountains surrounding the Smolyan valley.

Smolyan

Like many Bulgarian settlements, **SMOLYAN** represents a triumph over adversity. It was raised on the ruins of three villages – Smolyan, Raikovo and Ustovo – which the Turks destroyed when their inhabitants refused to become Muslims. Situated 1000m above sea level, it's the highest town in Bulgaria, an expanding industrial and winter tourism centre with a population of almost 40,000. The result is a long, straggling town stretching for about 10km along the banks of the Cherna River.

The town

The western end of town (the part you're likely to see first if approaching from Sofia or Plovdiv) is the most modern, a tastefully laid-out mixture of chalet-style residential blocks and modern civic buildings. It's here that all the shops and amenities are located, including prestige structures such as the Rhodope Drama Theatre, Evridike shopping centre, and the **planetarium** (about two shows daily, usually in the early evening).

More historic are the older quarters of Raikovo and Ustovo to the east, the former holding Smolyan's only major attraction, the **Pangalov house** on ul. Veliko Târnovo. A splendid National Revival-style mansion with timber-framed oriels and the customary trimmings, the house now contains a superb **ethnographic museum** (Tues–Sun 8am–noon & 2–5.30pm; may well close erratically out of season). The inhabitants of the Rhodopes were once noted for their distinctive costumes: men wore relatively sombre attire with a modicum of braiding, but the women let rip with red and yellow plaid aprons, deeply slit *soukmans*, and elaborate ear-covers, tiaras and diadems – variously known as *trepki*, *kossichniki* and *kruzhila*. Sadly, traditional dress is nowadays rarely worn, even for village festivals. However, carpets (*chergi*) and tufted goat's-hair rugs (*halishta*) – of which the museum has a fine collection – are still manufactured around Smolyan.

Another two or three kilometres east of the museum (past the turn-off for Rudozem) one enters **Ustovo**, which still partly resembles the village it once was, sited higgledy-piggledy on the hillsides around the confluence of the Cherna and Bepar rivers.

Practicalities

Smolyan is served by three **bus terminals**. Most coaches from Sofia, Plovdiv and all other points to the north and west arrive at the *Avtogara zapad* on ul. Minyorska, a ten-minute walk west of the modern centre. Some other services from Plovdiv (those which bypass Pamporovo and come instead via the Rozhen pass) arrive instead at the new *Avtogara iztok* in Ustovo, 8km east of the centre. Also in Ustovo, to make matters worse, is the old *Avtogara iztok*, where Rudozem, Madan, Zlatograd, Ardino and Kârdzhali services arrive and depart. Timetable information and advance reservations are available from the *TsKTON*, ul. Lenin 41 (usually 8am–6.30pm, with a break for lunch). Bus #3 (pay the conductor on board) runs from one end of Smolyan to the other, linking the bus stations and passing the modern town centre on the way.

There's a **tourist office** (Mon–Fri 8am–noon & 1.30–6pm) in the modern centre which deals in **private rooms**, but will often pretend that they are all booked up in order to press-gang you into staying at the next-door, 3-star *Hotel Smolyan* (☎0301/23293; ④). The high-rise 2-star *Sokolitsa*, ul. Pârvi Mai (☎0301/33085; ③) is a cheaper alternative; as is the *Ezerata* (☎0301/32272; ③), 3km up the hill on the Pamporovo road in **Smolyanso ezero**, a picturesque mountainside suburb where a sequence of small lakes is surrounded by crags and coniferous forests – reach it with bus #4 from *Avtogara zapad*. The latter service also passes Smolyan's two **campsites**: the *Panorama* (open all year round), and the *Kolibata* (open May–Sept) which has chalets.

Heading west

Easily accessible from Smolyan or Pamporovo, **SHIROKA LÂKA** is where folks go to see a genuine Rhodope village. With its rambling streets and tall, asymmet-rical stone houses built steeply into the mountainside, this settlement of 2000 souls could have been lifted off a picture-postcard – and is, remarkably, unspoilt, despite increasing numbers of package-trippers who arrive in coaches to invade its humble tavernas. The advantage of coming here on a tour is that you get to see a performance by the students of the **School of Folk Instruments and Music** (situated in an alpine meadow up behind the village) – something you might otherwise miss should you turn up on spec. Old residences like the **Sugurov house** and the **Kalamdji house** (which contains the local Ethnographic Museum) are open to visits if the curators are around. By evening most foreigners have gone, although there is **dorm accommodation** in a small *turisticheska spalnya* in the village, and two more in the neighbouring villages of SOLISHTA and GELA.

Devin and around

Further west of Shiroka Låka the road leads through a typically Rhodopian land-scape of weathered rocks and luxuriant vegetation, to the spa of **DEVIN**. You can do this trip by bus from Smolyan, or on one of the excursions organized by *Balkantourist* in Pamporovo or Smolyan, who also run day-trips to the **Yagodinska cave** and the **Trigrad gorge** (both of which lie at the end of minor roads radiating southwards from TESHEL, a village 11km from Devin). A village down here was allegedly the last refuge of the Russian royal family. According to local **legends**, they escaped the massacre at Ekaterinburg, fled south across the Urals, the Caspian and the Black Sea, stayed for a while in Plovdiv and finally settled in a remote Rhodope village. There the Tsar, the Tsarina and the sickly Tsarevitch died, whilst the four Grand Duchesses lived on as peasant women, two of them marrying local people. From a practical standpoint, the chance of **buses** going this far south is pretty slim, but the destinations to look for are YAGODINA (for the *Yagodinska peshtera*) and TRIGRAD (for the *Trigradski skali*). If you make it this far, there's a mountain *hizha* above Trigrad village, the *Trigradski skali*.

Around Dospat

The main road continues westwards from Devin to the Pirin mountain town of GOTSE DELCHEV (p.90), 59km beyond **DOSPAT**, a small town once noted for its folk costumes and festivities but nowadays better known for its reservoir. Bus services in these parts are unreliable but with a car you can make detours to isolated Rhodope villages. **Goats** are still the basis for life in many such communities: every family owns several, which are entrusted to the village goatherd, or *manzardji*. Their milk is drunk or turned into yoghurt and cheese, which together with salted goat's meat (*pasturma*) forms the villagers' wintertime staple; goat's hair is woven into rugs which can last for eighty years; and their skin can be made into everything from wine-sacks and sandals to bagpipes (*kaba*). During the Ottoman occupation, when Bulgarians were forbidden to carry arms, goat's horns served as daggers, and many of the country's most famous haiduks (including the female outlaw Rumena Voivoda) started their careers as goatherds.

Outsiders – let alone foreigners – are rare birds in these **villages**, and should you pay a visit, be prepared to accept the locals on their own terms. You might be offered hospitality (including lodgings, which is okay if there's no police in the village), but if you're made to feel unwelcome, clear out fast. Reportedly, two of the most beautiful villages are **DOLEN** and **KOVACHEVITSA**, the first 4km off the road between Dospat and Devin, the second, way up in the mountains along the awful road running between Gotse Delchev and Velingrad.

Smolyan to Kårdzhali

Fairly regular buses run from Smolyan to Kårdzhali, 91km away, following the road past numerous *pomak* and Turkish villages before running past the **Arda gorge**, a beautiful spot for riverside walking and picnicking if you have your own transport. Sixty kilometres beyond Smolyan is the predominantly Turkish mining town of **ARDINO**, a recently industrialized town with little to recommend it save for the vacation complex of **Belite Brezi**, incorporating campsite and hotel, a few kilometres further on. Getting its name from the surrounding silver birches, it's the starting-point for numerous hikes, including a seven-hour trail to the 90m-high **Ardino waterfall** on the River Arda, and should you make it, not much further to *Dryavolskiyat Most*, one of the old hump-backed **Turkish bridges** which span several of the Arda's tributaries.

Another road from Smolyan approaches Kârdzhali by way of Momchilgrad (p.238), running closer to the Greek border. This little-travelled route (before 1990 you needed a special permit to journey this close to the border) takes you past or close to several large mining centres – **RUDOZEM, ZLATOGRAD** ("Gold Town") and **MADAN** (from the Arabic for "mine") – whose zinc and lead is so pure that the London Metal Exchange accepts it without certification. Much of the area is inhabited by Muslims, and the nearby villages of **BENKOVSKI** and **GORSKI IZVOR** were said by Amnesty International to have been the scene of violent clashes between locals and the security forces during the "name-changing campaign" of 1984 (p.315). PODKOVA, 25km northeast of Benkovski, is the terminal of a branch line up to Kârdzhali, Haskovo and Stara Zagora.

Kârdzhali and the eastern Rhodopes

The **eastern Rhodopes** were the Ottomans' first conquest and their last foothold in Bulgaria before the Balkan Wars of 1912–13, and to this day a sizable number of the inhabitants are of ethnic Turkish origin. Geographically, the region displays special features, having 2500 hamlets and villages (far more settlements than exist in either the central or the western Rhodopes) and comparatively low highlands, the slopes of which are covered with deciduous rather than coniferous forests. Most characteristic of all are the expanses of eroded, deforested waste-lands, which, seen by moonlight, resemble deserts or lunar surfaces. The land, with its Mediterranean climate and dry sandy soil, has always needed irrigation to produce crops, and the minerals in the mountains – zinc, lead, gold and silver – made mining more profitable than agriculture until the Turks introduced the cultivation of tobacco. Traditionally, this was the poorest and least developed area of Bulgaria – a condition that's only begun to be remedied since dams and non-ferrous metal plants were established in the 1950s – and today there's still a great disparity between thriving towns like **Kârdzhali** and the remote highland villages.

Kârdzhali

One of the last Bulgarian settlements to remain in Turkish hands, **KÂRDZHALI** had fewer than 3000 inhabitants when it was handed back in 1913. But during the last thirty years the construction of large dams to supply water for irrigation and hydroelectricity for industry has given its fortunes a prodigious boost, inspiring copywriters to dub this the "city of two reservoirs". More recently, Kârdzhali has set about attracting tourist lucre by building a luxurious hotel in the town centre and promoting watersports on the *Kârdzhali* and *Studen Kladenets* reservoirs, though whether the investment will pay off is anybody's guess. With hourly buses and six trains a day from Haskovo, and a fairly regular bus service from Plovdiv's *Yug* terminal, **getting there** is easy, anyway.

Approaching town from the east, trains run alongside the *Studen Kladenets* reservoir, almost within sight of the **Pyramids of Kârdzhali**. Tinted pink, yellow and rust-coloured by the presence of manganese, iron and other ores, these strange rock formations covering an area of five hectares are known by locals as the "Stone Wedding Procession", and can be reached by bus from the town's terminal. If you're driving from Haskovo you might like to take the minor road to Kârdzhali (which leaves the E85 at Manastir), as this runs past another geological oddity situated near the village of Solishte, the **stone mushrooms** (*skalni gâbi*).

Around town

Kârdzhali itself consists of reefs of low-rise housing set amid greenery, with a main street running the length of town roughly parallel to the river. From the station or the bus terminal you simply follow the broad sweep of ul. Dimitrov to reach the centre. Despite a well laid-out **Gradska gradina** or city garden with elegant floral arrangements there's very little specific to see, save perhaps for the **historical museum** (Tues–Sun 8.30am–noon & 2–5pm), ul. Ivailo 18. Much better, therefore, to escape to the surrounding countryside.

Five kilometres west of town lies the **Kârdzhali reservoir**, a developing water-sports centre with facilities for windsurfing, water-skiing, rowing, fishing and power-boat racing – the venue for annual outboard motor racing and angling tournaments (dates vary). For the more sedentary, there are regular trips around the reservoir by **hydrofoil**, not to mention a **restaurant boat**, the *Emona*, brought from Varna at the behest of Bulgaria's first round-the-world yachtsman, Georgi Georgiev. For bookings and details of buses to the reservoir, enquire at the *Hotel Arzepos*, which can also arrange **excursions** in the eastern Rhodopes.

Practicalities

The 3-star *Arzepos*, ul. Republikanska (☎0361/28801; ④), occupying pleasant riverside gardens, may well be the only reliable place to **stay** in town – the cheaper *Bâlgariya*, Georgi Dimitrov 13, seems to have closed down, though it's worth trying. There are two *hizhi* on the shores of the Kârdzhali reservoir: the *Metalurg*, 3km west of town; and *Borovitsa*, another 7km beyond that. The nearest campsite is the *Gorichkata* (open May–Sept), 3km north of town on the E85 Plovdiv road.

Good local **food** can be sampled at the *Rusalka* restaurant in the city garden, or the restaurant in the *Hotel Arzepos*. The hotel is noted for Kârdzhali's **regional specialities**: mutton *kurban*, sausages (*suzdurma*) and *shashlik*, *baklava* and figs, and *Armira* wine from the Ivailovgrad district.

Around Momchilgrad and Ivailovgrad

Fifteen kilometres south of Kârdzhali stands the small one-hotel town of **MOMCHILGRAD**, which earns its living by growing an aromatic strain of tobacco called *dzhebel basma*, a name deriving from *djebel*, the Arabic word for hill. Used by the Turks to describe the surrounding region, where the sandy soil forms hundreds of ridges and mounds, the name has clung to the neighbouring town of DZHEBEL, where a research institute seeks to improve the crop. Seven kilometres from here is a curious freak of nature beside the village of **VODENICHARSKO**. The ridge of the **Broken Mountain** (*Yanuk Tepe*) looks like God has taken a cleaver to it, terminating midway in a precipitous drop with huge riolite columns strewn around – the result of a landslide at the end of the nineteenth century. **Accommodation** in the area is provided by the *Hotel Osetiya* (☎0363/2414; ②) in the middle of Momchilgrad; and the hillside *Momchil* chalet thirty minutes' walk to the northeast.

The borderlands east of Momchilgrad are craggily overgrown or parched and sandy, dotted with **ruined fortresses** built by both Bulgars and Byzantium, when the area was a borderland, hotly contested between the two empires. One of the castles stands near the village of ZVEZDEL halfway along the road to **KRUMOVGRAD**, a pretty similar town to Momchilgrad, with an unpretentious **hotel**, and the point of departure for buses on to **IVAILOVGRAD**. It's said that **camels** still serve as beasts of burden in villages around Ivailovgrad, but if anything tempts travellers to come this far it's more likely to be the **remains of a Roman villa**, situated 4km from town off the Ivailovgrad-Lyubimets highway. The villa was built during the second century, probably for a Roman landowner from Adrianople (Edirne), and some idea of its original sumptuousness may be gained from the large mosaic floors, which depict the owner and his family, mythological creatures (including the gorgon), and bird and animal figures. Visitors can stay at the small *Hotel Trakiya* in Ivailovgrad, but remember that there's **nowhere to cross the frontier** around here; the nearest border-checkpoint is at Svilengrad (p.225).

travel details

Trains

From Asenovgrad to Plovdiv (every 30min; 25min).

From Harmanli to Dimitrovgrad (5 daily; 1hr); Plovdiv (5; 3hr 30min); Simeonovgrad (6; 15min); Svilengrad (6; 30min).

From Haskovo to Dimitrovgrad (6; 30min); Kârdzhali (6; 1hr–1hr 45min); Momchilgrad (6; 2hr–3hr 15min); Stara Zagora (3; 1hr 30min–2hr 30min).

From Hisarya to Plovdiv (5; 1).

From Momchilgrad to Dimitrovgrad (5; 2hr 15min–2hr 45min); Kârdzhali (7; 30min); Stara Zagora (3; 2hr 15min–4hr 30min).

From Kârdzhali to Dimitrovgrad (5; 2hr); Momchilgrad (9; 30min); Podkova (3; 30min); Stara Zagora (3; 3hr–4hr).

From Panagyurishte to Plovdiv (4; 1hr 45min).

From Plovdiv to Asenovgrad (every hour; 25min); Burgas (4 daily; 3hr 45min); Dimitrovgrad (10; 1hr–1hr 30min); Harmanli (5; 2hr–3hr 15min); Hisar (5; 1hr); Karlovo (9; 1hr 45min); Panagyurishte (4; 1hr 45min); Pazardzhik (20; 30–45min); Septemvri (20; 45–60min); Sofia (20; 2hr–3hr 30min); Varna (2; 6hr).

From Podkova to Dimitrovgrad (1; 3hr 30min); Kârdzhali (2; 1hr); Momchilgrad (7; 30min).

From Septemvri to Bansko (2; 4hr 15min); Plovdiv (17; 45–60min); Sofia (18; 1hr 30min–2hr 15min); Velingrad (7; 1hr 30min).

Buses

From Asenovgrad to Bachkovo (every 2hr); Plovdiv (every hour).

From Dimitrovgrad to Haskovo (every 30min).

From Haskovo to Dimitrovgrad (every 30min); Harmanli (5 daily); Ivailovgrad (3 daily); Kârdzhali (8 daily); Svilengrad (5 daily).

From Pamporovo to Smolyan (every hour).

From Pazardzhik to Batak (7 daily); Gotse Delchev (2 daily); Panagyurishte (every 45min; 1hr 30min); Peshtera (5 daily); Septemvri (5 daily).

From Plovdiv (*Avtogara Yug*). to Asenovgrad (every 30min); Batak (3 daily); Blagoevgrad (1 daily); Haskovo (10 daily); Pazardzhik (every 30min); Sliven (2 daily); Sofia (1 daily).

(*Avtogara Rodopi*) to Kârdzhali (8 daily); Haskovo (10); Pamporovo (6); Smolyan (hourly); Zlatograd (3).

From Smolyan to Ardino (hourly); Devin (8 daily); Kârdzhali (5); Madan (hourly); Pamporovo (hourly); Rudozem (hourly); Zlatograd (hourly).

From Velingrad to Batak (5 daily); Blagoevgrad (2); Yundola (every 45min).

Flights
From Kârdzhali to Sofia (5 weekly during the summer; 1hr).

International trains
From Plovdiv to Belgrade (1 daily; 10hr 30min); Istanbul (1; 1hr 30min).
From Svilengrad to Alexandroupolis (1; 4hr).

CYRILLIC PLACE NAMES

ARDINO	АРДИНО	KRUMOVGRAD	КРУМОВГРАД
ASENOVGRAD	АСЕНОВГРАД	MADAN	МАДАН
BACHKOVO	БАЧКОВО	NARECHENSKI	НАРЕЧЕНСКИ
BATAK	БАТАК	BANI	БАНИ
BELITE BREZI	БЕЛИТЕ БРЕЗИ	PAMPOROVO	ПАМПОРОВО
CHEPELARE	ЧЕПЕЛАРЕ	PAZARDZHIK	ПАЗАРДЖИК
DOLEN	ДОЛЕН	PESHTERA	ПЕЩЕРА
DOSPAT	ДОСПАТ	PLOVDIV	ПЛОВДИВ
HARMANLI	ХАРМАНЛИ	PODKOVA	ПОДКОВА
HASKOVO	ХАСКОВО	RUDOZEM	РУДОЗЕМ
IHTIMAN	ИХТИМАН	SEPTEMVRI	СЕПТЕМВРИ
IVAILOVGRAD	ИВАЙЛОВГРАД	SHIROKA LÂKA	ШИРОКА ЛЬКА
KAPITAN	КАПИТАН	SMOLYAN	СМОЛЯН
ANDREEVO	АНДРЕЕВО	SVILENGRAD	СВИЛЕНГРАД
KÂRDZHALI	КЪРДЖАЛИ	VODENICHARSKO	ВОДЕНИЧАРСКО
KOSTENETS	КОСТЕНЕЦ	ZLATOGRAD	ЗЛАТОГРАД
KOVACHEVITSA	КОВАЧЕВИЦА		

CHAPTER SIX

THE BLACK SEA COAST

The Bulgarian **Black Sea coast** has quietened down a bit since its heyday in the Seventies and Eighties, when it served as the playground for the entire Eastern bloc. The big tourist complexes built to garner west European package tourists still do good business, but the flood of Russians, Poles, former East Germans and Czechs who used to descend on Bulgaria's seaside towns has dwindled to a trickle since 1989. Bulgarians too are taking fewer holidays than in the past, with the result that the Black Sea is quieter now than at any time since the Sixties. In many ways this makes it a good time to visit: beaches are much less crowded than before, and you'll rarely have problems finding accommodation, but the local small businessmen are less enthusiastic about the current state of affairs. Private enterprise has taken off here quicker than anywhere else in Bulgaria, but many Black Sea café-owners, restauranteurs and hoteliers exist in a kind of limbo, eagerly awaiting an upsurge in the tourist trade which many privately believe may not happen for some years yet.

Many continue to think of the Bulgarian coast in terms of its big package-oriented complexes, the biggest of which have discouragingly ersatz names like **Sunny Beach** and **Golden Sands** and are correspondingly characterless once you arrive there. Newer resorts like **Albena** are more pleasant, and the most recent "holiday villages" like **Elenite** and **Dyuni** compare favourably with villa settlements in the Mediterranean. Holidays here are cheap and beaches are clean, but none of these purpose-built resorts reveals much of what the Black Sea is really about – and they are sited sufficiently far away from centres of population to prevent you from finding out for yourself. Independent travellers would be well advised to stick to the main seaside towns, where **private rooms** are plentiful, family-run **guesthouses** are on the increase, and out-of-town **beaches** are easy to reach on foot or by bus. The ideal base for exploring the northern coast is the riviera town of **Varna**, which after Sofia and Plovdiv is Bulgaria's most animated metropolis. North of Varna crumbling rock formations and imposing cliffs characterize the coast around **Balchik** and **Kaliakra**, while to the south lie quieter seaside backwaters and the **Longoza**, a dense riverine forest which lines the lower banks of the **River Kamchiya**.

Controlling access to the southern half of the Black Sea coast is the rough-edged trawler port of **Burgas**, but it's far outshone by the historic peninsula towns immediately north and south – old Greek fishing villages like **Sozopol** and **Nesebâr**, the latter noted for its ruined Byzantine churches. The coast beyond Sozopol and the Turkish border offers a succession of glorious white sand beaches and a wide variety of flora and fauna, ranging from the near-tropical forest around **Ropotamo River** to the wildfowl-infested marshes just inland from the coast. If all this fails to impress, numerous local museums* recall the Greek settlers who colonized the area six centuries before the birth of Christ.

---

*Once beyond Varna and Burgas, many museums and tourist attractions on the coast open only during the summer season, and hours become erratic as tourist numbers begin to slacken off in September.

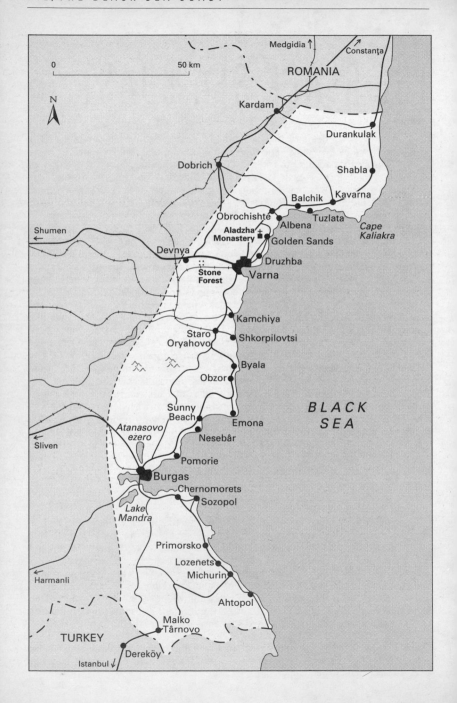

0   50 km

N

Medgidia ↑   ↗ Constanţa

ROMANIA

Kardam

Durankulak

Dobrich

Shabla

Balchik   Kavarna

Obrochishté   Tuzlata

Shumen ←   Albena   *Cape*
Aladzha   Golden Sands   *Kaliakra*
Monastery

Devnya   Druzhba

Stone   Varna
Forest

Kamchiya

Staro   Shkorpilovtsi
Oryahovo

Byala

Obzor

Sunny   *BLACK*
Beach   *SEA*
Emona

Atanasovo   Nesebâr
ezero
Sliven ←   Pomorie

Burgas
Chernomorets
Sozopol
Lake
Mandra

Primorsko
Lozenets
Harmanli ←   Michurin

Ahtopol

Malko
Târnovo

TURKEY   Dereköy

Istanbul ↓

HOTEL ROOM PRICES

For a fuller explanation of these codes, see p.16 of *Basics*.

① £4–6 ② £6–12 ③ £12–25 ④ £25–40 ⑤ £40–60 ⑥ over £60

However you travel, your likely **point of arrival** on the coast will be either Varna or Burgas, whence **buses** take you to the smaller towns and resorts. From mid-May to the end of September public transport is augmented by a number of **hydrofoil** and **hydrobus** services, which link the main points of tourist interest from Sozopol in the south to Balchik in the north. However, the decline in tourist business has led to serious cutbacks in services over recent years, and departures may be restricted to one or two a day.

At the time of writing it's difficult to say definitely whether you will be able to travel **on from Bulgaria by boat** to anywhere else in the Black Sea, although it seems safe to predict that there will be **ships to Istanbul** (maybe continuing to Mediterranean ports like Cairo or Genoa) run by the successors to the former Soviet shipping company, *Morflot*. Their agents in Bulgaria are *Interbalkan*, whose addresses are included in the text where relevant.

VARNA

Back in the days when **VARNA** was a cholera-ravaged Ottoman garrison town British troops passed through here on their way to the Crimean War; one of them, Major General J.R. Hume, described the town as "no paradise . . . a wretched place with very few shops". Until recently many foreign visitors may have said the same, but over the past few years Bulgaria's third city has struggled more than most to catch the train to Westernisation. Signs of change are everywhere: old state-owned shops stand empty, while the streets around them sprout fashion boutiques, exchange bureaux, Japanese car showrooms, video-rental stores, and fast-food outlets staffed by prancing miniskirted waitresses. Crop-haired youths practice skateboarding manoeuvres in the main square, or stroll along the main boulevards in a range of pseudo-designer summer threads more reminiscent of west-coast USA than some far-flung eastern outpost of the European continent.

Varna still has its problems – loss-making **shipyards** southwest of the centre give the place a hard industrial edge – and it's worth bearing in mind that most of the consumer goods on offer in the town centre are still beyond the means of those who inhabit the high-rise suburbs. Nevertheless, the self-confident riviera-town swagger of the place comes as a breath of fresh air after the more austere appearance of much of inland Bulgaria. It rivals Sofia and Plovdiv in providing a wide range of sights and **museums** (whether you're attracted to the outstanding archaeological treasures in the Museum of History and Art, or the more off-the-wall ghoulishness of the Museum of Medical History), and offers cultural attractions too, most notably the annual **Varnensko Leto** (Varna Summer): a summer-long festival of classical music which attracts world-class performers.

As well as being a **beach resort** in its own right Varna offers access to quieter spots up and down the coast, and attractions like the nature reserve at **Kamchiya**, the rock monastery of **Aladzha**, or Queen Marie of Romania's former palace at **Balchik** can all be treated as day trips from here.

↑ Bus Station, Shumen & Dobrich

BULEVARD VL VARNENCHIK

DIMITĂR BLAGOEV

Hotel Orbita

Georgi Velchev Museum

Dentists' Clinic

Museum of History & Art

Art Gallery

LYUBEN KARAVE

MAKSIM GORKI

City Hospital

Post Office

KNYAZ BORIS I

DIMITĂR BLAGOEV

SLIVNITSA

Hotel Cherno More

Fetsi Ha

Asparuhovo & Galata
←

Cathedral of the Assumption

PL VARNENSKA KOMUNA

ASEN ZLATAROV

SHIPKA

SHENOVO

21 YULI

KNYAZ BORIS I

Hotel Odesa

Market

Clock Tower

BALKAN

National Revival Museum

PL EKZARH IOZIF

BULEVARD PRIMORSK

Theatre & Opera House

PL NEZAVISIMOST

KNYAZ BORIS I

Roman Fortress Wall

M KOLONI

PLEVEN

Balkantourist Accommodation Bureau

Hotel Musala

Armenian Church

HAN ASPARUH

ODRIN

MUSALA

Ethnographic Museum

PANAGIURISHTE

AVRAM GACHEV

KNYAZ AL BATENBERG

HAN KRUM

HAN KLIMENT

KRALI MARKO

Aquar

DEBĂR

Church of Sveta Bogoroditsa

Roman Thermae

Church of Sveti Atanas

Naval Museum

DRAZHKI

SAN STEFANO

GRAF IGNATIEV

Museum of Medical History

Balkantourist

VARDAR

PLISKA

HAN OMURTAG

Museum of the City of Varna

8 NOEMVRI

Railway Station

PL SLAVEIKOV

Roman Baths

BULEVARD PRIMORSKI

Port

↓ Hydro Statio

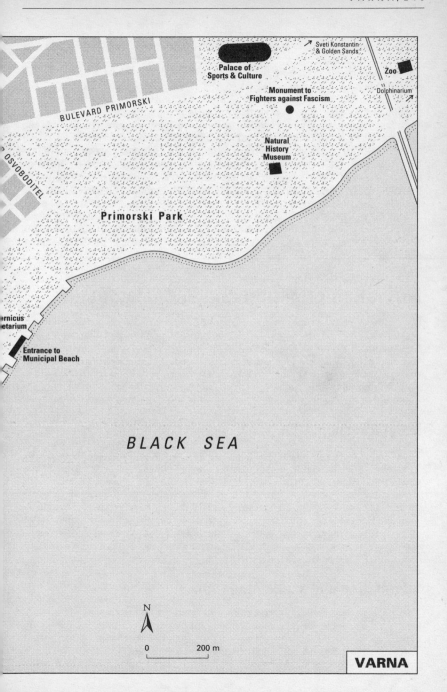

Sveti Konstantin
& Golden Sands

Palace of
Sports & Culture

Zoo

Dolphinarium

Monument to
Fighters against Fascism

BULEVARD PRIMORSKI

OSVOBODITEL

Natural
History
Museum

Primorski Park

ernicus
etarium

Entrance to
Municipal Beach

BLACK   SEA

N

0   200 m

VARNA

Some history

Highly skilled gold- and coppersmiths lived around the Gulf of Varna 6000 years ago, and their Thracian descendants littered the interior with burial mounds, but Varna's importance as a port really dates from 585 BC, when a mixed bag of Apollonians and Milesians established the Greek city-state of **Odyssos**. The town's best years came in the second and third centuries when it was the Roman province of Moesia's main outlet to the sea, a bustling place where Greek and Thracian cultures met and mingled. Devastated by the Avars in 586 AD, and repopulated by Slavs (who were probably responsible for renaming it *Varna*, or "Black One"), it nevertheless remained the region's biggest port and an important staging-post for the Byzantine fleet on its way to the Danube. Declining somewhat under the Turks, Varna recovered as an important trading centre in the nineteenth century, when a population of Bulgarians, Greeks, Turks and Gagauz (Turkic-speaking Christians, see p.254) made it one of the coast's more cosmopolitan centres. To the Turks, Varna was the key to the security of the western Black Sea, and the town's military role is still reflected in the students of Varna's Naval Academy, who stride around town in uniforms belted with ceremonial daggers.

Arrival, information and accommodation

Both Varna's **railway station** and passenger dock are located just south of the centre, and a ten-minute walk up ul. Avram Gachev will bring you into town. The **bus terminal** is 2km to the northwest on bul. Vl. Varnenchik, from which you take bus #1, #22, or #41 to reach the centre; while Varna **airport** on the city's western outskirts is served by bus #50. These buses zero in on an area known as *Tsentâr* (literally "the centre") comprising the streets grouped around the Cathedral of the Assumption, a few paces north of the main downtown area.

Local transport

You'll find central Varna easy to explore on foot, although **local buses and trolleybuses** come in handy if you're heading for the southern suburbs or the seaside resorts to the north – in which case *Tsentâr* is the place to catch them. Varna's bus network has recently been deregulated, meaning that privately owned buses and minibuses operate many of the same routes as the municipal vehicles. For the latter you'll need to buy **tickets** (bought in kiosks and validated by perforating them in the on-board machine) in advance, while on private services you'll pay cash to the driver or driver's mate (a flat fare of two or three leva, more for the resorts to the north).

Information and accommodation

There are several **Balkantourist** offices in town (although they're now run by local firm *Varnenski bryag*, so watch out for a possible name change in the future), all of which seem reasonably happy to hand out **maps** and **information**. The main offices are just opposite the train station at Avram Gachev 10 (☎222389) and in the centre at ul. Musala 3 (☎225524). The latter (Mon–Fri 8.30am–

12.30pm & 1–6pm) serves as the **accommodation bureau**, allocating **private rooms** for around £6 a double, many of which are very well appointed and reasonably central. Several **independent travel agencies** are beginning to enter the private room market if you fancy shopping around: most central is *Terziiski*, ul. Sheinova 8.

There's one **campsite** (mid-June–mid-Sept) within striking distance of the city, 6km away in the southerly suburb of Galata; it's on the seafront near the Galata lighthouse. To reach it, take bus #17 from bul. Hristo Botev to the Galata terminal, and walk downhill past the naval installation.

Balkantourist won't give you any information about the increasing numbers of **private hotels** and family-run **guesthouses** springing up in the Varna area – to find these you'll have to travel around and look for roadside advertisements. The best places to look are along the E87 coast road heading north out of Varna towards Sveti Konstantin/Druzhba, and in the suburb of Galata (bus #17) to the south.

Hotels

Musala, ul. Musala 1 (☎223925; ②). A bit dingy, and rooms are without en-suite bathrooms, but the cheapest of the central hotels.

Cherno More, bul. Slivnitsa 33 (☎232115; ④). Modern 3-star place in the centre of town.

Grand Hotel Varna, Sveti Konstantin (☎861491; ⑥). 5-star bastion of luxury and privilege, with swimming pool and bowling alley.

Odessa, bul. Primorski 4 (☎228381; ③) Pretty nondescript 2-star place just next to the Primorski park.

Orbita, Tsar Osvoboditel 25 (☎225162; ③). Average 2-star tower block, within walking distance of the central sights.

Sandrovo, Sveti Konstantin (☎0861/241; ⑤). Pleasant 3-star hotel next door to the *Evksinograd Palace*, some 6km to the north of town. Bus #8 or #9 from the centre.

The town

Varna's social life revolves around **pl. Nezavisimost**, where the opera house and theatre provide a backdrop for an ensemble of restaurants and cafés. The square is the starting point of Varna's evening promenade, which flows eastward from here along bul. Knyaz Boris I, passing a ruined **Round Tower and fortress wall** dating from Roman times (and currently inaccessible in the middle of a building site) at the corner of ul. Shipka.

To the north of pl. Nezavisimost, Varna's main lateral boulevard, Dimitâr Blagoev, cuts through pl. Varnenska Komuna, an important traffic intersection dominated by the domed **Cathedral of the Assumption**. Constructed in 1886 along the lines of Saint Petersburg's Cathedral, this contains a splendid iconostasis and bishop's throne carved by craftsmen from Debâr in Macedonia, and murals painted after the last war. South of the cathedral in the city gardens stands the **Old Clock Tower**, a fairly unremarkable structure paid for by the city guilds in the 1880s, whose silhouette nevertheless serves as something of a trademark for the city.

The phone code for Varna is ☎052.

In general, however, the downtown area is a place in which to stroll and enjoy the vigour of emergent enterprise culture rather than visit specific sights. Most of the latter are to the south and east, among the residential streets between the centre and the port, although the otherwise undistinguished ul. Blagoev is the home of the biggest of the city's museums.

The history museum and around

The **Museum of History and Art** (Tues–Sun 10am–5pm) occupies Varna's former girls' high school on the corner of Dimitâr Blagoev and Slivnitsa. A display of nineteenth-century icons has recently been installed upstairs, but it's the archaeological collection, scattered throughout innumerable halls on the ground floor, which commands most attention.

The Chalcolithic necropolis

Bulgaria's claim to be one of the cradles of European culture was bolstered by the discovery of a **Chalcolithic* necropolis** on the outskirts of town in 1972. Dating from the fourth millennium BC, the necropolis was unusual in that it contained many graves in which effigies, rather than human dead, were buried – probably to ensure the continuing health and rejuvenation of the living. The gold trinkets with which these symbolic corpses were adorned are displayed extensively in the museum: baubles, bracelets, and pendants in the shape of animals. Many pieces are simply executed; others display an incredible degree of skill considering that they were made as long as 6000 years ago. They're possibly the oldest examples of gold jewellery ever discovered, and have led many to assume that metalworking techniques were developed in Bulgaria independently of the other *loci* of civilization in the Near East.

Greek, Thracian and Bulgarian artefacts

No less impressive is third-century BC jewellery from Greek Odyssos: a magnifying lens reveals a perfectly shaped Hermes-like deity surrounded by a golden shell on one of a pair of earrings – to the naked eye the details of the tiny figure are imperceptible. However, most space is devoted to Bulgaria's finest assemblage of Roman-period **funerary sculpture**. Prominent Greek and Roman citizens were honoured with a tombstone depicting scenes of funeral feasts, usually showing the deceased reclining on a couch surrounded by wife and kids. Townsfolk of Thracian origin preferred a grave plaque decorated with a relief of the so-called **Thracian horseman** (see opposite), the rider god whose worship became universal among the natives from the Hellenistic era onwards.

Bulgarian gold and silver from the fourteenth century introduces a collection of medieval weaponry and ecclesiastical art; while the National Revival and revolutionary periods are represented by the usual banners and manifestoes.

Two nearby art museums

Round the corner from here at Karamfilova 8 is the **Georgi Velchev museum-house** (Tues–Sun 8.30am–noon & 2–5.30pm), honouring a local painter of seascapes, many of whose canvases grace the early twentieth-century interior. A couple of hundred metres to the east on Lyuben Karavelov is the **City Art Gallery**

---

*"Chalcolithic" is the name given to the era when Neolithic man began to smelt copper.

THE THRACIAN HORSEMAN

Even the smallest of Bulgaria's historical museums devote at least some space to a display of stone tablets portraying the principal deity of Thrace during the Roman era, the **Thracian horseman** (*Trakiiski konnik*; sometimes also translated as the "Thracian rider" or the "Thracian hero").

The ancient Thracians had a thing about equine beasts from the earliest times, and the neighbouring Greeks spoke enviously of their stockbreeding expertise and excellent horsemanship. A **cult of horse and rider** was common to the lands bordering the Black Sea, shared by the plain-dwelling Scythian nomads to the north as well as Asiatic peoples across the Bosphorus to the east. The horse was (possibly for its swiftness) regarded as an animal capable of reaching the underworld and communicating with the dead, while the rider was a protector of both nature and the souls of the departed. An early manifestation of the rider cult is included in Homer's *Iliad*, in which an archetypal horseman figure, the Thracian King **Rhesus**, has his prized herd of horses stolen by wily Greeks Odysseus and Diomedes.

Stone tablets bearing reliefs of a spear-wielding horseman, often accompanied by a hunting dog, began appearing in Thrace in the third century BC, and soon became universal throughout the eastern Balkans. Tablets were placed in sanctuaries and sacred caves, often those linked with deities associated with health or the protection of nature like Asclepius and Apollo; and they were increasingly used as **funerary monuments**, implying that bereaved families were eager to identify the deceased with the person of the rider god himself.

The stylised iconography of the Thracian horseman probably found its way into the subsequent Christian art of the Balkans; with the familiar, spear-wielding, mounted hero re-emerging in medieval icons of **Saint Demetrius** and **Saint George**.

(Tues–Sun 10am–7pm), which hosts high-profile temporary exhibitions downstairs. Visitors to the permanent collection on the first floor are greeted by a row of seventeenth-century diplomats painted by Flemish portraitist Anselmus von Hulme; beyond these are several rooms of contemporary art. Beside a few lionizations of the Bulgarian peasantry courtesy of Vladimir Dimitrov-Maistor (see p.71) and Stoyan Venev, most room is taken up with works by previous winners of the Varna Graphics Biennale, held in the summer during odd-numbered years.

Between bulevard Knyaz Boris I and the sea

Many of Varna's attractions lie amid the crumbling turn-of-the-century buildings which lie between bul. Knyaz Boris I and the port, where the commercial bustle of the city centre gives way to quiet residential streets lined with chestnut trees. Huddled among the town houses are several excellent museums, a couple of churches, and the best of Varna's Roman remains. Careful map-reading is often required to find them, but it's worth the effort.

The ethnographic museum

The **ethnographic museum** (Tues–Sun 10am–5pm), one of Bulgaria's finest, occupies an old house on ul. Panagyurishte. Downstairs lie reminders of the region's traditional trades and occupations, with a variety of fishing nets, wine barrels, wattle-and-daub beehives and a nineteenth-century *yamurluk* or hooded cloak – as worn by the shepherds who roamed the hills of the interior.

On the first floor there's a fine display of **regional costumes**, showing great diversity of styles, largely because the area inland of Varna was a crossroads of migrating peoples. One distinct local group were the *chenge*, represented here by a wedding scene from the village of Asparuhovo 50km west of Varna. Costumed dummies are grouped around a ceremonial wooden wedding sledge, with the bride surrounded by men in black hats wreathed with flowers and accompanied by the slightly menacing figure of the village matchmaker holding aloft a black cockerel. Items relating to regional folk beliefs include the embroidered **masks** worn during *Kukeri* (spring) and *Survakari* (new year) rites, and a couple of the **New Year camels** paraded through the streets in some areas – approximations of the humped beast were made from sheepskin and mounted on skis. Also on display are a variety of **ritual loaves** baked to mark specific occasions: the *Kravai* for New Year or Saint John's Day; the "Pony" (*Konche*) for Saint Theodor's Day; or the *Proshtupalnik* – shaped like a baby's foot – to celebrate a child's first steps.

The National Revival museum

Five minutes' walk east at the southern end of ul. 27 Yuli stands the **National Revival museum** (Tues–Sun 10am–6pm), occupying the former church of Archangel Michael and the premises of Varna's first Bulgarian school. Both school and church were established here in the 1860s, much to the chagrin of the local Greeks, who were accustomed to controlling the town's educational and ecclesiastical affairs. A preserved schoolroom includes the balustraded pulpit from which the teacher surveyed his pupils, the latter sitting in wooden pews and using sand trays to write in. Discipline was ensured by placing older boys at the end of each row of pews to supervise the younger ones.

The former girls' classroom upstairs now holds photographs and texts telling the history of nineteenth-century Varna, including one photograph of British and French troops marching into town in 1854 en route for the Crimea: the local Bulgarians reacted to the foreign troops with "unconcealed hatred", according to the accompanying caption.

The Armenian church and the church of Sveta Bogoroditsa

South of here is pl. Ekzarh Iosif, where elderly *Varnentsi* gather for an evening chat, and locals bring jerry cans and flagons to collect the hot mineral water gushing from a public fountain. Just beyond at the junction of Han Krum and Kliment is a small nineteenth-century **Armenian church**, squeezed into the corner of a schoolyard. Serving a local population of about 3000, the church contains naive, child-like icons covered in Armenian script. Outside, a small tablet commemorates the genocide of 1915, when up to one and a half million Armenians lost their lives at the hands of the Ottomans – suggesting a shared history of suffering in which both Armenians and Bulgarians can find common cause.

Of more historical value, however, are the intricately carved iconostasis and bishop's throne of the seventeenth-century **church of Sveta Bogoroditsa** at Han Krum 19, a partly sunken church whose tower was added later once Ottoman restrictions had been removed.

The Roman thermae and the church of Sveti Atanas

Across the road from the church stands a vast tower of crumbling red brick, once the western wall of the **Roman thermae** (Tues–Sun 10am–5pm), a sizable complex thought to have been built in the late second or early third century –

coins found on the site bear the visage of the then emperor, Septimus Severus. Scrambling among the ruins, it's possible to imagine the ritualized progress of the bathers from the *apodyterium*, or changing room, through the rising temperatures of the *frigidarium*, *tepidarium* and *caldarium*; and then back again. The daily visit to the baths was an important part of social life, and bathers would circulate and exchange gossip in a large central hall, the solid walls of which cut through the middle of the ruins.

The adjacent **church of Sveti Atanas** used to be an exhibition hall displaying the icons now relocated in the Museum of History and Art. It's recently reopened as a church, and is a classic example of National Revival architecture. An arcaded porch precedes a sumptuous interior, with a rich, gilt iconostasis, carved wooden ceiling, and painted marble-effect pillars.

The City Historical Museum

Nearby at ul. 5 noemvri 8 is another beneficiary of changing times, the recently relaunched **City Historical Museum** (Tues–Sat 10am–5pm), formerly a dour museum of revolutionary history. Ancient sepia photographs showing a skyline bristling with (now demolished) minarets are among many reminders of the town's past, where exhibits emphasize the transformation of Varna from Balkan backwater to comfortable bourgeois European town. On the basement floor original copies of French fashion mag *Marie Claire* lie strewn over a reconstructed tailor's workshop of the 1940s, while upstairs lie further re-created interiors, including that of an inter-war photographer's studio – complete with cumbersome, ancient camera. Varna's development as a seaside resort in the 1920s is documented in numerous photographs, including pictures of the annual **beauty contests** – a competition which *Varnentsi* claim the dubious honour of inventing. Initially contestants were dubbed "Sea Hyenas" (perhaps because of their long, stripy bathing suits), and as costumes got skimpier during the 1920s they were renamed "Sea Nymphs".

A few paces further south are the overgrown remains of more **Roman baths**, this time dating from the late fourth century, and far less extensive than the better-preserved *thermae* on Han Krum.

The museum of medical history

Considerably more interesting is the **Museum of Medical History**, ul. Paraskeva Nikolau 7 (Mon–Fri 10am–4pm), sheltered within the sandy-coloured nineteenth-century building which once housed Varna's first public hospital. Inside a words-and-pictures display adopts a patriotic tone, attempting to show how the medieval Bulgarian state inherited the medical wisdom of the ancients and transmitted it to the rest of Europe – only to have their standards of public hygiene ruined by the Turks, who made everybody live in smelly and unsanitary cities. However, the early Bulgarians were not without their forays into perversity. An array of tenth-century **skulls** on the ground floor reveal that one in three of the local population had been subjected to a symbolic form of trepanation (the practice of drilling holes in the skull) – in which the bone had been scratched and dented but not actually pierced. Archaeologists presume that this had some kind of ritual purpose – but quite what, no-one knows.

Less macabre but equally disconcerting are the ferocious-looking early twentieth-century surgical instruments on display upstairs, along with a reconstructed turn-of-the-century dentist's consulting room and antiquated x-ray machines.

Primorski park

The massed flowerbeds of Varna's seaside gardens, the **Primorski park**, were laid out at the end of the nineteenth century by Czech horticulturalist Anton Novak (invited here by those other Bohemian Bulgarophiles the Škorpil brothers; see p.263), who supposedly modelled them on the Baroque palace gardens of Belvedere and Scönbrunn in Vienna. The park's tree-lined pathways are patrolled from dawn to dusk by young families and courting couples, although you'll occasionally come across chained **dancing bears** resting in the shade, brought here by their Gypsy owners to be photographed alongside tourists in return for a few leva.

The Navy museum and the aquarium

At the western end of the park, the gunboat responsible for the Bulgarian navy's only victory lies honourably embedded outside the **Navy museum** (9am–noon & 1.30–5pm). The boat in question, the *Drâzhki* ("Intrepid"), sank the Turkish cruiser *Hamidie* off Cape Kaliakra during the First Balkan War of 1912. Since Bulgaria's navy was reduced to a rump by the Neuilly Treaty of 1919, and later collaborated with Hitler's *Kriegsmarine*, there's little else for it to take pride in, and the exhibits inside trace seapower and commerce on the Black Sea and the lower Danube back to its earliest days, devoting special attention to the Russian Black Sea Fleet's campaign against the Ottomans in 1877–78.

Just beyond is the **aquarium** (Mon 2–5pm, Tues–Fri 9am–5pm), a small collection of fresh- and seawater creatures whose habits are frustratingly explained in German-language texts. Most interesting specimens are the sea-needles, who reproduce when the female of the species deposits her eggs in a pouch on the male, who is expected to do the brooding; the Black Sea turbot, a denizen of the sea bed which assumes the colouring of rocks to disguise itself against predators; and the freshwater sturgeon, which can grow to a length of 9m in the wild. Those confined to the bubbling tanks here are significantly smaller, but still magnificent enough to be the star attractions.

A little way to the east, the grandly named **Copernicus astronomy complex** (Mon–Fri 8am–noon & 2–6pm) offers regular planetarium-type shows as well as a chance to look at a reconstruction of Foucault's pendulum. You can descend from here to Varna's *Morski bani* or municipal **beach**, where bathers can look out at the shoals of tankers and cargo vessels anchored in the bay. The beach stretches northwards for a couple of kilometres: at the far end steaming mineral water spews out of the hillside, collecting in a pool often used by elderly bathers well into winter.

The natural history museum, the zoo and the dolphinarium

Back to the park: tree-lined avenues drive eastwards towards an angular **Monument to Fighters against Fascism**, to the south of which lurks an unassuming **Natural History Museum** (Tues–Sun 10am–5pm), which provides a useful introduction to the coast's flora and fauna if you can make out the Bulgarian captions. Live specimens prowl their spartan quarters in a small **zoo** just beyond (daily 8am–5pm) featuring camels, lions, Shetland ponies and wolves – the latter being the most animated of a generally sorry-looking bunch. A little further on is the **dolphinarium** (daily 11am–3pm: shows on the hour), where the birth of the establishment's first baby caused much excitement in June 1992. A little short on cash, the dolphinarium invited private citizens to donate the funds necessary for the upkeep of specially quarantined nursery quarters – it will be interesting to see whether the creature survives. On the other side of bul. Primorski looms the ultra-modern **Palace of Sports and Culture**, venue for concerts and indoor sports such as wrestling and basketball.

The park of Fighting Friendship

Among the housing estates that mark the city's northwestern margins lies the bizarrely named **park of Fighting Friendship** on Varna's northwestern margins (bus #22 from *Tsentâr*), where a granite monument tops a Thracian tumulus marking the site of the **battle of Varna**. In November 1444, 30,000 Crusaders preparing to sail for Constantinople were surprised when 120,000 Turks landed on the coast, and during the subsequent clash King Ladislas III of Poland and Hungary (known to the Bulgarians as *Vladislav Varnenchik*) recklessly led a charge to capture Sultan Murad in his tent. Ladislas was cut down by a janissary and his army wavered, forcing János Hunyadi to order an inglorious retreat, marking the end of Christendom's last attempt to check the Ottoman advance.

There's a small **museum** (daily 9am–5pm) built into the mound displaying medieval armour and tributes to the various east European races that made up Ladislas's army.

The northern suburbs and Evksinograd

Varna's northeastern suburbs have always been favoured by city folk as the venue for relaxation; the villas and holiday cottages of the more affluent cling to vine-covered hillsides overlooking the sea, or nestle in small gardens rich in fruit. The one specific sight in the region is **Evksinograd Palace**, former residence of monarchs Aleksandâr and Ferdinand. Less interesting to visit but worthy of mention is the suburb of VINITSA 10km northeast of town (bus #31 from the centre), still inhabited by one of the Black Sea's more elusive and mysterious minorities, the **Gagauz** (see p.254).

Evksinograd

Built under the name of *Sandrovo* by Prince Aleksandâr Batenberg in 1882, and renamed **Evksinograd** (combining the Greek word *euxine* – hospitable – with the Slavonic *grad* – town or fortress) by his successor Ferdinand, the palace is nowadays notorious for being the former holiday home of the Bulgarian Politburo. It still belongs to the state, and foreign dignitaries stay here when visiting Varna, but the construction of a new hotel (the *Sandrovo*) in the palace grounds seems designed to place Evksinograd on the international conference circuit.

You can't visit the palace itself, but there are extensive guided tours of the grounds. These lead past the **vineyards** where Bulgaria's most sought-after wines and brandies are produced and descend towards the seafront through the **botanical gardens** layed out for Ferdinand by French horticulturalists at the turn of the century. The Communist Party hierarchy built themselves a deluxe **beach complex** in the woods overlooking the shore, complete with state-of-the-art health clinic and sports hall – the latter including a rather unnecessary bowling alley. Each member of the Politburo had his own beach house, all linked by secret tunnel to a central command bunker – in the unlikely event of them being taken unawares by the apocalypse while bathing. Party Secretary Todor Zhivkov's beach house was, of course, bigger than the rest, isolated from those of his comrades on the other side of the headland.

The entrance to the palace lies on the main coast road running north out of Varna (bus #7 or #8 from Tsentâr). **Tickets** for the guided tour are bought at the reception desk of the *Sandrovo* hotel (☎861241) beside the entrance. First tour of the day kicks off at 10am and lasts about ninety minutes, but ring and check for further details (no-one in central Varna will know).

The southern suburbs and the Lake of Varna

Buses #2 and #17 lead from *Tsentâr* southwards across the Asparuh bridge towards the southern suburbs of **Asparuhovo** and **Galata**, passing port and ship-building facilities on the way. Travel to the fjord-like Lake of Varna to the east is best accomplished by suburban trains. These stop at the satellite towns strung out between Varna and the brutish industrial town of **Devnya**, providing access to the strange rock formations known as the **Stone Forest**.

Asparuhovo and Galata

The suburb of **ASPARUHOVO** on the south side of the Asparuh bridge is a pretty uninspiring, sleepy place, bordered on the east by a wooded town park. Concealed in the latter is Khan Asparuh's eighth-century **defensive embankment**, a vast earthwork with a stone core built to ward off Byzantine attacks. On the far side of the embankment is a good sandy beach, quieter than the main one in Varna, and a jetty with views of Varna docks. Bus #17 continues to **GALATA**, a quiet residential quarter occupying the wooded flanks of a rocky headland. Varna's **naturists** frequent the beach at Fichoza just beyond the cape, and are currently agitating for it to be recognized as the city's nudist beach. Galata's new private hoteliers don't like the idea, fearing that it will scandalize their guests.

The Stone Forest and Devnya

Roughly 18km due west of Varna on either side of the Devnya road, the desolate scrubland is interrupted by scores of curious stone columns standing up to 7m high. These are the so-called *pobiti kamâni* or "standing stones", usually rendered into English as the **Stone Forest**. These strange, snake-haunted formations were created around fifty million years ago when fragments of two chalk strata gradually bonded together in the intervening sand layer, by a process analogous to stalactite formation. **Getting there** involves taking a suburban train to Strashimirovo or Beloslav on the shores of the Lake of Varna, and heading northwards into the hills.

There's nothing else of note to detain you on the Lake of Varna, and **DEVNYA**, the town at its western end, is a place to be avoided at all costs. The gargantuan chemicals factory bequeathed to the town by its erstwhile Communist bosses produces a variety of plastic products, subjecting its workforce to a wide range of carcinogenic toxins in the process.

Eating, drinking and entertainment

Most of Varna's eating and drinking venues are found along the route of the evening *korso*, which stretches east from pl. Nezavisimost along bul. Knyaz Boris I, before turning down Slivnitsa towards the Primorski park. Plenty of pavement cafés line the route, while the lower reaches of Slivnitsa are the best places to look for inexpensive restaurants. Another popular locale is the area around ul. Drâzhki a couple of blocks south of Knyaz Boris I, where restored nineteenth-century town houses provide the setting for a handful of restaurants and bars.

Snacks

The snack bars around pl. Nezavisimost and along Knyaz Boris I are the best places to grab **breakfast**; while a succession of *sladkarnitsi* along bul. Knyaz Boris I sell pastries, *banitsa*, small pizzas and other snacks throughout the day. The 24-hour *banitsa* and pizza bar at ul Sheinovo 2; *restorant M* at Knyaz Boris I 40; the German delicatessen selling hot dogs at Knyaz Boris I 44; and the hamburger kiosk at Slivnitsa 32 are the best places to grab a quick bite.

ROMA: VARNA'S GYPSIES

Leaving Varna on the Devnya road you'll pass a shanty town sprawled over slopes on the city's western outskirts – Varna's **Gypsy quarter**. Bulgaria has for centuries been the home of both sedentary and nomadic Gypsies (*Roma* as they call themselves; *Tsigani* to the Bulgarians), whose lifestyle and tribal organization puts them at odds with mainstream society. Tribes like the *Kalburdzhi* (sieve-makers) and *Kalaidzhi* (tinners) have essentially been made redundant by modern industry, while the freedom for nomadic horse-dealers, bear-tamers (*Ursuri*) or criminal tribes (*Grebenari*) to operate as their forbears did was greatly reduced during the socialist era. Many Gypsies have found work in industry or as municipal labourers, but for various reasons "assimilation" hasn't gone very far. Meanwhile they complain that they're given the worst jobs and housing, and Bulgarians retort that the *Tsigani* are "naturally lazy" and "keep animals indoors if they're given proper flats".

Restaurants

Bistro Rimska Terma, 8 Noemvri. A small, privately owned place worth trying for the home cooking.

Galera, Drâzhki 17. Better-than-average choice of dishes, becomes a disco after 10pm.

Evksinograd, Anton Ivanov 2. The folksy wooden interior suggests tourist exploitation, but in fact it's a good source of basic cheap grills and good draught beer.

Morska Sirena, hydrofoil passenger terminal. Fairly unatmospheric, but the food is good; a good stop off if you're nosing around the port area.

Morsko Konche, pl. Nezavisimost 4. Popular seafood restaurant on the main square.

Panorama, top floor of the *Cherno More* hotel. Excellent food in elegant surroundings, chamber music most nights. More traditional Bulgarian fare can be had in the *Stara Varna* restaurant on the first floor of the same hotel.

Rostock, bul. Vl. Varnenchik 20. Hearty meat dishes in a "beer-hall" atmosphere.

Starata kâshta, Drâzhki 14. Mid-price place with good schnitzel-type pork and veal dishes.

Zlatno Pile, Slivnitsa 7. A pretty basic menu centred around grilled chicken and chips, but the draught beer is excellent.

Drinking and nightlife

Popular daytime *sladkarnitsi* include *Palma*, Nikola Vaptsarov; and *Espresso Balkan*, Knyaz Boris I 49, both of which serve excellent cakes. The café inside the *Festivalen komplex*, Slivnitsa 2, is renowned for its ice cream. The outdoor coffee garden at Slivnitsa 30 is the liveliest of the daytime drinking venues.

The pavement cafés tend to close around 9–10pm, although several privately owned bars in the streets north of Knyaz Boris (such as ul. Libkneht and ul. Telman) stay open longer. Otherwise head for the bar of the *Hotel Cherno More*; or choose one of the **discos** which stay open until around 1–2am: in the *Morsko Kasino* in Primorski park; the *Café-Teatâr* in the *Festivalen kompleks*, on Slivnitsa; or the *Kosmos* disco in the Palace of Sport and Culture.

Entertainment

The opera on pl. Nezavisimost is the seat of Varna's main cultural institution, although many major events, including orchestral concerts, take place in the open-air theatre in Primorski park; the modern *Festivalen kompleks*, Slivnitsa 2; or, on occasion, the Palace of Sport and Culture. All of the above are pressed into service during the annual **Varnensko leto** or "Varna Summer" of symphonic, operatic and chamber music (mid-June–mid-July), which attracts some of the world's finest orchestras and companies.

The cinema in the *Festivalen Kompleks* presents an interesting range of popular and cult films.

Listings

Airlines *Aeroflot*, bul. Knyaz Boris I 45 (☎231082); *Balkan*, Shipka 2 (☎331451).

Car repairs Try the big city centre depots at bul. Vl. Varnenchik 262 (☎449885); and Vl. Varnenchik 184 (☎441252), although in the past they have concentrated on east European models. Fiat, Lada and Zastava from the repair shop beside the petrol station in Druzhba/Sv. Konstantin (☎861377).

Dentist Maksim Gorki 24.

Hospitals The *Poliklinik* at Maksim Gorki 46. Foreign-language staff at polyclinic on bul. Knyaz Boris I.

Pharmacies *Apteka no. 12*, bul. Knyaz Boris I 29, is open 7am–9pm seven days a week. The privately owned *Hadzholyan* pharmacy, Dimitâr Kondov 11, may have a wider choice of imported drugs.

Post and phones Main post office at Maksim Gorki 36.

Radio News in English and other foreign languages on *Radio Varna* between May and September, on medium wave 774khz.

Rail tickets Domestic bookings from *BDZh*, 27 Yuli 13 (☎221137); international, *Rila*, Shipka 3 (☎226273); sleepers from *Wagons Lits Cook*, 27 Yuli 13 (☎227036).

Taxis In front of the rail station, or around the junction of bul. Knyaz Boris I and Slivnitsa. For airport or other out-of-town destinations, ☎440760.

Travel agents *Interbalkan* (agents for *Morflot*), lobby of the *Cherno More* hotel; *Pirin*, Knyaz Al. Batenberg 13 (☎222710).

North of Varna

When people think of the coastline north of Varna they normally think of sprawling tourist complexes like **Golden Sands** (Zlatni pyasâtsi) and **Albena**, and the first 50km of the E87's northward progress can seem like an endless procession of tower-block hotels and dusty building sites. Once you get away from the main road, however, even the biggest of the resorts can be quite peaceful and relaxing, making good use of the sandy beaches lining the shore and the forests which form their immediate hinterland. **Sveti Konstantin** (formerly *Druzhba*) and Golden Sands are both near enough to Varna to be on the urban bus network – those staying in town can come out here to use the beach or explore the bars and discos (and late-night taxi fares back into town aren't too expensive).

Beyond Albena the atmosphere changes, with the less crowded towns and villages of the Dobrudzhan littoral perched above an increasingly rocky coast – a coast which culminates in the dramatic cliffs of **Cape Kaliakra**. The picturesque town of **Balchik** is the centre most likely to appeal to the non-package tour crowd, although all the settlements along this stretch of the water make good **day trips by bus** from Varna.

Sveti Konstantin (Druzhba)

Immediately beyond Evksinograd, suburban Varna fades imperceptibly into the first of the great tourist complexes built in the postwar drive to develop the coast. **SVETI KONSTANTIN** (originally known as *Druzhba*, or "Friendship") first admitted Western tourists in 1955, and has since served as a prototype for others. Most of *Sveti Konstantin*'s hotels are clustered in the southern half of the resort, while to the north are rest homes for trade unionists, the Militia, *Balkan Airlines* staff and journalists. The overall impression is quite cosy, with an abundance of oaks and cypresses, and a number of small beaches and coves. The luxurious new Swedish-built *Grand Hotel Varna* (see Varna accommodation listings, p.247) reflects *Druzhba*'s recent move up-market, and the resort is increasingly being promoted as suitable for international conferences.

Any spare **rooms** are assigned at the **Balkantourist** bureau in the *Hotel Rubin* (☎61020), or the accommodation bureau in Varna – but you'll be lucky to pay less than £20 a head. Buses #8 and #9 run into Varna *Tsentâr* every 10 to 15 minutes.

Golden Sands

Tourists generally baulk at pronouncing *Zlatni pyasâtsi*, so most Bulgarians along the coast will understand if you say *Goldstrand* or **GOLDEN SANDS** instead. It's a polyglot place: of all the nationalities here, Germans predominate, and two members of the 2nd of June terrorist group were actually arrested here in 1978 after being recognized by a West German prison warder who, like them, was on holiday. The resort's 81 hotels and 128 restaurants occupy a wooded, landscaped strip behind Zlatni pyasâtsi's greatest asset, its **beach**: a soft, pale golden expanse 4km long, free of jellyfish and rubbish, sloping gently into an undertow-less sea. Golden Sands offers a wide range of bars, restaurants and discos (recent additions to the panoply of delights on offer are the *Samudra* Indian restaurant and *Golden Lion* pub), and if you're looking for the kind of Costa del Sol nightlife with which the rest of Bulgaria is badly served, this is the place.

Practicalities

Independent travellers are charged much more for hotel **rooms** than those who have booked a package holiday, but if you do fancy the idea of spending the odd night here then your first port of call should be the **accommodation bureau** (☎052/855681) on the main E87 highway. They will fix you up with rooms in 2-star hotels for about £10 per person, or in 3-star hotels for £15 per person; as well as checking vacancies at the resort's *Panorama* campsite. **Buses from Varna** (#9 from opposite the cathedral) arrive near the sea front in the centre of the resort – to get to the accommodation bureau from here, work your way up the lanes which zigzag their way uphill to the main road.

There's both a **polyclinic** (☎855352) and a **pharmacy** (☎855689) behind the *Diana* hotel; a **post office** beside the *International* hotel; and **taxis** can be summoned by dialling ☎855675.

Aladzha Monastery

In the Hanchuka Forest, 4km to the southwest of Golden Sands, dozens of cells and chambers hewn into a friable cliff comprise what remains of **Aladzha Monastery** (Tues–Sun 9am–5pm). The caves to the west were occupied during the Stone Age by people whom Strabo called "pygmies", and served as a place of refuge during the Dark Ages. A Christian church may have existed here as early as the fifth century, though the monastery itself was probably established during the thirteenth century like the Ivanovo rock monasteries (see p.124).

Aladzha's monks were *hesychasts*, striving to attain union with God by maintaining physical immobility and total silence. However, they did get round to painting several exquisite murals in the chapels (at the end of the first and second galleries). Nowadays they're scrappy and faded, although in olden times they were sufficiently impressive to earn the monastery its name – *Aladzha* means "multicoloured" in Turkish.

You might, however, enjoy poking around the various catacombs and surrounding woods – the latter a place of many **legends**. Its mythical guardian, Rim Papa, is said to awake from a cotton-lined burrow every year to ask whether the trees still grow and women and cows still give birth, and go back to sleep upon being answered affirmatively.

A **museum** at the entrance displays models of how the monastery used to look when occupied, alongside ornaments, weapons and other artefacts dating from around 5000 BC, discovered in a Chalcolithic necropolis on the western outskirts of the city in 1972. You can reach the monastery by bus from either Varna or Golden Sands (the #33 Varna-Kranevo service); although the walk up the hill from the resort can be quite pleasant providing you avoid the midday heat.

Around Albena

Just beyond the northern end of Zlatni pyasâtsi the E87 passes through KRANEVO, where several privately run small hotels and numerous rooms (the *kvartirno byuro* in the centre may be closed due to lack of custom, so ask around) cater for those who prefer the tranquility of village life to the bustle of the big resorts. Kranevo is set back slightly from the sea and lacks a good beach, but those staying here can head for the nearby sands of **ALBENA**, the next resort up the coast. The step-pyramid architecture of Albena's hotels mark it out as one of the newer resorts, originally designed to attract a more stylish, youthful crowd than Zlatni pyasâtsi. Albena is bypassed by the main road, but is well served by buses from Varna and Balchik (see below). Arriving at the terminal near the post office, see the **tourist bureau** across the way (☎2152) about vacancies in any of the forty hotels, or check out the campsite with deluxe bungalows (off the entrance road) if you're hoping **to stay**. The resort covers a large area, and the other two campsites are farther away, so get a map and directions before seeking either.

The Tekke at Obrochishte
Beyond Kranevo the E87 swings eastward to follow a coastline dominated by pale, powdery rocks and arid scrub. Another road heads northwest towards Dobrich (see p.127), passing through the town of OBROCHISHTE 3km inland. Just outside town is the site of a **ruined Turkish monastery** known as *Ikazalubaba* or *Arat Tekke*, dating from the sixteenth century and consisting of two seven-sided structures roughly 50m apart. Pilgrims would thrust their hands through a special opening in the *turbe* to acquire good fortune from proximity to the head of a saintly Muslim buried within, or hang their clothes on the tree nearby as a means of "casting out evil". After the last Dervish departed in the nineteenth century this became a place of veneration for Christians, too: in the belief that it was really Saint Athanasius who was buried here, pious Bulgar shepherds sacrificed hundreds of sheep here on Saint George's Day – hence the name *Obrochishte*, "place of sacrifice".

Balchik

Occupying a succession of sandy cliffs and crumbling sugarloaf hills, **BALCHIK**'s whitewashed cottages hover precipitously above a series of ravines running down to the sea. It's the kind of scene beloved of artists, and Balchik-inspired seascapes are a regular sight in provincial art galleries throughout Bulgaria. Founded by the Milesians in the sixth century BC and named *Krounoi* ("The Springs"), the town was a valued haven for Greek merchants attempting to pass the treacherous waters around Cape Kaliakra, as well as an important centre for viniculture – hence its later name, honouring the god of the vine, *Dionysopolis*. The harbour had silted up by the sixth century AD, and the Turks were subsequently to dub the town *Balchik* – town of clay.

Balchik was a predominantly Muslim town until the present century, home to many of the Turkish-speaking **Tatar tribes** settled here by the Ottoman authorities in order to guard the northern frontier of the empire. Many left town after Turkey's defeat in the war of 1877–78, but most Tatars remained for the simple reason that they had no homeland to which they could flee, and you'll still hear Turkish widely spoken on the streets.

Despite being popular with Bulgarians who take advantage of numerous private rooms and trade-union-owned rest homes, Balchik doesn't see many foreign tourists, largely because it lacks a good beach. Inmates of Albena (see p.259) are, however, bused into town during the day to stroll around the streets and visit Balchik's main attraction: the **summer palace of Queen Marie of Romania**, a memory of the inter-war years when Balchik was ruled from Bucharest.

The town

Heading downhill from Balchik's **bus station** you'll soon come across the **History Museum** (Mon–Fri 7.30am–noon & 1.30–5pm) on the town square, which naturally enough contains marble and bronze statuary from Dionysopolis, including busts of the deity himself. Opposite is a small **Ethnographic Museum** (same times) showing nineteenth-century domestic trinkets alongside local peasant crafts. From here the main street winds down to the port, passing on the way a flight of steps leading up to an **art gallery** at ul. Otets Paisii 4 featuring icons from local churches. At the bottom of the hill, a small whitewashed mosque stands inland from the port, where the hydrofoil passenger terminal abuts a lively seafront square.

From here an esplanade stretches westwards, passing the misshapen concrete lumps that form Balchik's sea defences. There are a few areas of sand (shipped in every spring to create an artificial beach), although most bathers prefer to position themselves on the various piers and jetties protruding into the bay.

The palace of Queen Marie

Two kilometres west of town, ranged on a hillside overlooking the sea, is the **Quiet Nest**, summer residence of Queen Marie of Romania. English-born Marie ordered the construction of a series of follies here, presided over by a whimsical-looking villa topped by a minaret (the reconciliation of her Christian and Muslim subjects was one of Marie's pet projects). The surrounding **botanical gardens**, home to over 600 varieties of trees, shrubs and cacti, are dotted with pavilions now used as rest homes by the Union of Bulgarian Artists. Descending towards the sea just behind the villa are six terraces – one for each of Marie's children, the sixth one (truncated by the cliff) symbolizing Mircea who died of typhus at the age of two. To the east of the villa are several set-piece follies, including a water mill, a rose garden, a Roman bath, and culminating in a small chapel, where naively executed frescoes include a picture of Marie herself in Byzantine garb. Marie left instructions for her heart to be buried within the chapel in a jewelled casket – the latter was hurriedly removed from Balchik in 1940, when Bulgaria regained the southern Dobrudzha.

You can see the Quiet Nest's minaret clearly from Balchik's seafront esplanade: unfortunately, it's not accessible from here, its lower gates locked to discourage bathers from picnicking in the grounds. The main entrance is at the northern end of the palace garden, just off the Balchik-Albena road – best reached by following ul. Primorski westwards from the port, or taking the hourly Balchik-Albena bus (ask to be put down at *dvoretsa*, "the palace").

Practicalities

The *Balkantourist* office (☎0579/2455) on the main street – midway between the bus station and the port – should have **private rooms**. Otherwise, the 2-star *Hotel Dionysopolis* (③) on Primorska, just west of the port; or the *Esperanta* guest-house at ul. Dimitrov 16 (③), represent the alternative accommodation possibilities.

Opportunities for **eating and drinking** tend to be concentrated near the seafront, where several outdoor cafés serve coffee and spirits until late. A complex of arcaded whitewashed buildings next to the port hold a couple more cafés and a touristy *mehana*. One block inland is the folk-style *Ribarskata sreshta* restaurant, offering the mackerel-based dishes universal to the coastal resorts.

Quarter-hourly buses to Albena run past *Biser* campsite on the beach 2km south of Balchik, and there are also services to a huge campsite run by the Bulgarian Automobile Club, *Belyat Bryag*, on the road to the TUZLATA spa, renowned for its **therapeutic mud** scraped from Balchik's salt lake.

Kavarna and Cape Kaliakra

Eighteen kilometres along the coast from Balchik, **KAVARNA** was probably founded by the Mesembrians in order to challenge the importance of the harbour at Krounoi just down the coast. It's a quiet place nowadays, lying a couple of kilometres inland from the seafront, where there's a small beach resort, the **Morska zvezda**, and a port used for the export of Dobrudzhan grain. It's a good spot from which to explore the coastal cliffs just to the east which culminate in the dramatic **Cape Kaliakra**.

Around Kavarna

Ul. Chernomorska heads from the **bus station** into the town centre, where steps behind the *Hotel Dobrotitsa* descend to an old mosque containing the town **museum** (summer: Tues–Sun 8am–noon & 1–6pm; winter: Tues–Fri 8am–noon & 2–6pm). Exhibits within tell of the local noble Balik, who set up an independent principality based on Kavarna in the 1340s, extending his power southwards as far as the river Kamchiya. His son Dobrotica wrested independence from his nominal suzerains the Bulgarian tsars, and severed links with the Târnovo patriarchate, accepting the writ of Constantinople instead. Further down Chernomorska there's a small **art gallery** (same times) with temporary exhibitions of works inspired by the sea. Although lacking in further specific sights, Kavarna does still possess a few squat, single-storey stone-built houses which used to characterize the northern coastal towns.

There's one hotel in town, the *Dobrotitsa* on ul. Chernomorska (③); and a campsite, the *Morska zvezda*, 2km away on the beach – signposted from the centre of town.

Cape Kaliakra

Bulgarians make much of the "Beautiful Headland" – as **CAPE KALIAKRA** was dubbed during the Middle Ages – and this reddish crag rearing 70m above the sea has something of the mystique of Tintagel. Along the shore are ruined fortifications raised as early as the fourth century BC (according to Strabo) and subsequently enlarged by the Roman and Byzantine empires, which reached their zenith during the fourth century when the *bolyari* Balik and Dobrotitsa ordered shafts dug through the rock so that the garrison could be supplied by sea. Legend has it that during the Ottoman conquest forty women tied their hair together and jumped from the rocks rather than be raped by the Turks, and other bodies have been washed up after naval battles off the cape. A **museum** (June–Sept daily 10am–5pm) in one of the caves (a restaurant occupies another) commemorates Admiral Ushkov's defeat of the Turkish fleet in 1791 and the sinking of the *Hamidie* in 1912, but the **seals** that frequent Kaliakra are undisputably the main attraction.

Boat excursions may operate from Albena and Golden Sands over the summer; otherwise you'll need either your own transport or an appetite for walking to reach the cape. Served by four buses a day from Kavarna, the village of BÂLGAREVO 6km short of Kaliakra is the closest you can get by public transport.

Around Shabla, and the Durankulak border crossing

From Bâlgarevo, midway between Kavarna and Kaliakra, a minor road runs northwards to SVETI NIKOLA, where the land slopes down to *Taouk Liman*, the **Bay of Birds**, recently developed as the **Rusalka Holiday Village**. A villa complex accompanied by the usual bars, restaurants and an open-air cinema, Rusalka boasts good facilities for young children and may be a quieter alternative to the bigger resorts to the south. *Yailata* is the name given to the picturesque rocks and caves 5km further up the coast near KAMEN BRYAG village, but buses along the coastal road are infrequent.

There's likelier to be more transport heading south from TYULENOVO (literally the "place of seals") where **oil** was discovered in 1951, precipitating high expectations and lots of drilling, although so far large deposits have proved to be expensively elusive. The majority of buses heading north from Kavarna take the main road further inland and aim for **SHABLA**, a small farming town frequented by many varieties of birds, principally ibises, herons and grebes. From here buses run to the muddy, faintly radioactive **Shabla Tuzla lake**, separated from the coast by a strip of sand, whereupon sits the pretty basic *Dobrudzha* campsite.

A couple more beachside campsites are signposted off the main E87 northwards: the *Karvuna*, on the far side of the Shabla lake; and the *Krapets* a little further on, just outside the seaside village of KRAPETS, known for its dunes and bird life. However, the main reason to venture this far is to cross **the border** at **DURANKULAK**, the 24-hour checkpoint located 6km north of the commune of the same name. Accessible by bus from Balchik, Kavarna and Shabla, Durankulak is famous for being the epicentre of the 1900 peasant rebellion against the *desyatâk*, a crippling tax imposed on agricultural produce by the Radoslavov regime. To the east of here is a fish-rich lake, with a **campsite**, the *Kosmos*, situated between the village and the beach.

South of Varna

Although there's no direct rail link along the coast it's possible to travel from Varna to Burgas by train, but it's a time-consuming inland journey, usually involving at least one change. It's far better to take one of the regular buses running **south of Varna** along the E87 highway, a road which winds its way across the coastal hills, occasionally offering glimpses of the sea. Ultimately you hit the mega-resort of Sunny Beach some 100km to the south, but the towns you pass along the way are among the quietest of the Black Sea coast. They're seldom visited by anybody but Bulgarians, and are visibly suffering from the decline in tourism of the past two years. You'll find a scattering of campsites, and plenty of families offering **rooms**, but the accommodation bureaux which used to handle them will probably have closed down for want of customers – be prepared to ask around.

Kamchiya and around

South of Lake Varna the highway swings inland to climb the Momino plateau, and you won't catch sight of the sea again for another 55km unless you take one of the minor roads which branch off towards the coast. The first of these, approximately 25km out from Varna just beyond the village of Bliznatsi, descends to the mouth of the **River Kamchiya**, where a small resort sits beside the wooded estuary.

The main attraction is the **Kamchiya nature reserve** slightly upstream, an area of marshy forest and luxuriant vegetation known as the Longoza, which covers about twenty square miles. The waters are rich in pike and carp, and wild pigs run free in the woods. In high season **boat trips** commence from the river's mouth, although the Longoza's elusive pelicans, kingfishers and waterfowl tend to make themselves scarce when they hear the tourists coming.

About five buses a day run from Varna to Kamchiya, making it a feasible day-trip destination. There's a **campsite** at the estuary should you wish to stay, and a couple of formerly Bulgarian-only **hotels** which are probably open to allcomers these days – *Balkantourist* or *Interbalkan* in Varna should have current information. Several kiosks serve up grilled fish, and look out for the *Nestinari* restaurant which entertains its clientele with displays of walking barefoot on red-hot coals.

Shkorpilovtsi

Further south a minor road leaves the E87 at Staro Oryahovo for **SHKORPILOVTSI**, 8km away on the coast. A modest resort with a dune beach and two campsites, *Izgrev* and *Horizont*, the town was named after the Czech Škorpil brothers who "founded" Bulgarian archaeology in the late nineteenth century. Karel and Herman Škorpil came to Varna in 1882 and immediately began sorting out and cataloguing the region's antiquities, a collection which formed the basis of the Varna History Museum. They were pioneers in the field of medieval Bulgarian archaeology too, and Karel was honoured by being buried among the ruins of the medieval capital Pliska (see p.170).

Byala, Obzor and beyond

Seven kilometres beyond Staro Oryahovo, the highway itself veers eastwards, passing vineyards whose grapes are made into *Dimyat* **wine** at **BYALA**, a small town facing Cape Atanas. South of this, the last wooded foothills of the Balkans descend to meet a 6km-long **beach** backed by the *Luna*, *Prostor* and *Slântse* campsites, where buses will halt on request before entering **OBZOR**. Broken columns in a large park to the left of Obzor's main square show that this small resort, the *Naulochos* of the ancients, was once graced by a Temple of Jupiter, but its principal asset nowadays is the **beach** to the north. Private **rooms** are usually available from a *kvartirno byuro* in the town centre, but this may be closed outside the peak season.

Heading south, the road turns inland once more, ascending the ridge of a mountain that slopes down to **Nos Emine**, Bulgaria's stormiest cape. On the way you'll pass through BANYA, a pleasant highland village presiding over a carpet of vineyards. From here a slow climb through dense forest leads to the *Lovno Hanche*, a popular roadside **restaurant**, after which the main road descends for a magnificent view of Nesebâr, the southern coastline and the distant Strandzha massif.

Sunny Beach and its satellites

Slânchev Bryag – called *Sonnenstrand* by the Germans and **SUNNY BEACH** by the Brits – is Bulgaria's largest coastal resort, with room for 25,000 tourists in its 112 hotels and 3 campsites, and yet more accommodation in the neighbouring holiday villages of **Zora** and **Elenite**. It's a vast, only partly shaded expanse of hotels interspersed with restaurants, snack bars and other places to spend money, and on (rare) rainy days its soullessness quickly becomes apparent. Having said that, Sunny Beach does possess all the essentials for a lazy holiday, not least its 6km-long expanse of fine sand sloping gently into the sea. Numerous restaurants, nightclubs and discos provide a wide range of nightlife, but Sunny Beach's principal drawback is its sheer size: it's impossible to explore the resort's facilities without shuttling up and down the main strip by bus, and the grid-iron housing-estate-style layout of the place soon induces feelings of disorientation and alienation.

Practicalities

Varna–Burgas buses pass through Sunny Beach, although most people approach the resort from Burgas, from which there are bus services every twenty minutes. You'll be dropped at the "Centre", where there's an **accommodation bureau** (☎2106) assigning hotel rooms for £10–15 per person. Apartments, sleeping four people, are also available for £35–40 per night. The least expensive option of all is to stay at the *Slânchev bryag* or *Emona* **campsites** at the northern end of the resort.

Zora and Elenite

The **ZORA HOLIDAY VILLAGE** just north of Sunny Beach prefigured the kind of self-contained, self-catering tourist complexes that are currently springing up along the southern coast, providing guests with villa accommodation complete

SUNNY BEACH: HOLIDAYS IN HELL?

In January 1992 **Sunny Beach** was featured in a list of the "Ten worst resorts in the world" by the consumer magazine *Holiday Which*. Criticism concentrated on the crime wave which had allegedly engulfed the resort in the post-1989 era, when the disintegration of the Communist regime led to a decline in public discipline – muggers, pickpockets, pimps and crooked moneychangers providing the main hazards. Part of Sunny Beach's raison d'être was to concentrate a large number of hard currency-wielding foreigners in one place and make money out of them, so it's hardly surprising that Bulgaria's newly emboldened underworld descended on places like this in order to take advantage of the rich pickings to be found here. Although it's true that crime in Bulgaria is on the increase, it still hasn't reached the levels which are taken for granted in the cities of the West. Take the usual precautions therefore (and don't change money on the streets no matter how good the offer seems), and you shouldn't have much to fear.

Since the *Holiday Which* report was compiled two good things have happened in Sunny Beach: first, the management, faced by the threat of declining profits, have been forced to clean up the resort and keep it litter-free (dirty beaches and seawater was *Holiday Which*'s other complaint); and second, the complex is increasingly attracting Bulgarian custom, making it less of a hard-currency lager and more of a balanced family resort.

with local nightclub, shops, tennis courts, bike-hire and tourist office. In 1985, the classier **ELENITE HOLIDAY VILLAGE** opened further up the coast, divided into two villa colonies sharing a nightbar, disco and sports facilities. Both places are normally booked by tour groups, but there could be vacancies. If not, there's always the windswept **campsite** by the shore 200m from VLAS, midway between Zora and Elenite.

Nesebâr

Three kilometres south of Sunny Beach, a slender isthmus connects the old town of **NESEBÂR** with the mainland, ensuring a constant stream of visitors to what was once undoubtedly a beautiful spot. Harbouring the best of the coast's nineteenth-century wooden architecture, as well as a unique collection of medieval churches*, it's easy to see why Nesebâr has become the most heavily publicized of Bulgaria's Black Sea attractions. At the height of summer the town can be a little oppressive, with street hawkers and souvenir sellers thronging the narrow streets, but a willingness to put up with the crowds is rewarded by Nesebâr's many fine sights.

---

*Although they're usually referred to as "Byzantine" by art historians outside the country, Nesebâr's churches are understandably regarded as masterpieces of medieval Bulgarian culture by the locals. The churches date from a period when control of Nesebâr changed hands many times, and the ethnic origin of the people who commissioned and built them is pretty hard to discern. It's probably fairest to regard them as products of a great Orthodox civilization – both Slav and Greek – which flourished in the Balkans during the late Middle Ages.

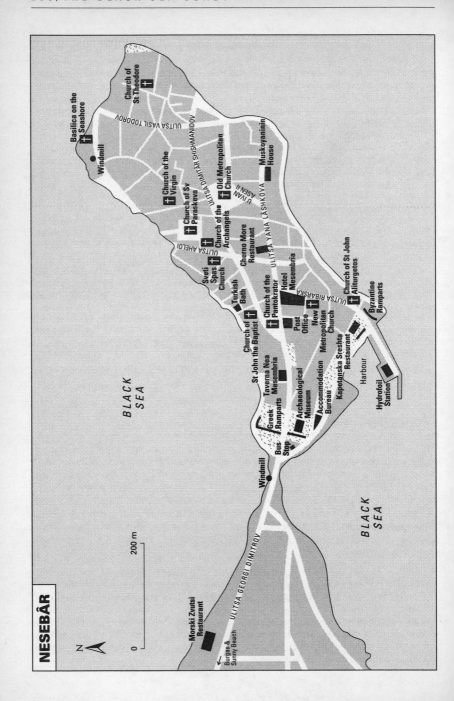

NESEBÂR

BLACK SEA

BLACK SEA

Church of St Theodore

Basilica on the Seashore

Windmill

ULITSA VASIL TODOROV

Church of the Virgin

Church of Sv Paraskeva

ULITSA DIMITÂR SHISHMANDOV

Old Metropolitan Church

Muskoyaninin House

Church of the Archangels

UTÂN ASEN II

Sveti Spas Church

Cherno More Restaurant

ULITSA AHELOI

ULITSA YANA LÂSHKOVA

Turkish Bath

Hotel Mesembria

Church of St John Aliturgetos

Church of St John the Baptist

Church of the Pantokrator

ULITSA RIBARSKA

Byzantine Ramparts

Post Office

St John Nea Mesembria

New Metropolitan Church

Taverna Nea Mesembria

Kapetanska Sreshta Restaurant

Greek Ramparts

Archaeological Museum

Accommodation Bureau

Harbour

Bus Stop

Hydrofoil Station

Windmill

200 m

ULITSA GEORGI DIMITROV

Morski Zvutsi Restaurant

Burgas & Sunny Beach

N

0

Some history

A thriving port in Greek and Roman times, Nesebâr really came into its own with the onset of the Byzantine era, when it became the obvious stopoff point for ships travelling between Constantinople and the Danube. The Byzantines used Nesebâr as a base from which to assail the First Bulgarian Kingdom during the eighth century, provoking Khan Krum to sieze it in 812 after a siege of two weeks. The bellicose Bulgar captured tons of booty in the process, including the formula for "Greek Fire", a highly explosive mixture which the Byzantines relied on for their military superiority over the "barbarians".

Nesebâr, as the Slavs now called it, passed from Byzantine to Bulgarian ownership several times throughout the Middle Ages, but commerce and culture continued to thrive whoever was in control. Under the Ottomans, Nesebâr remained the seat of a Greek Bishopric and an important centre of Greek culture, thus explaining why many of its ecclesiastical monuments remain. In the long run, however, places like Varna and Burgas were to grow at Nesebâr's expense, hastening the town's decline into an unassuming fishing port. By the nineteenth century, a much-reduced population was earning a living by importing wood from the lower Danube and building humble caïques. Nowadays Nesebâr depends on **tourism**: its fishing fleet can't employ enough of the town's 7000 inhabitants (of whom approximately 3000 live on the peninsula, the remainder on the mainland), and its importance as a one-time mercantile power and city-state belongs to a distant past.

The town

Fragments of Hellenic-period walls lie beneath the Romano-Byzantine fortifications which grace the entrance to the peninsula, and a brand-new **Archaeological Museum** just inside the town's west gate includes further evidence of Nesebâr's classical past. From here ul. Yana Lâshkova, the town's main artery, leads past a bazaar-like gaggle of street traders and stallholders towards the first of the town's numerous churches, the ruddy, gingerbread-coloured **church of Christ the Panokrator**. Completed during the fourteenth-century reign of Tsar Aleksandâr, the church is chiefly notable for its exterior decoration. Panokrator's blind niches, turquoise ceramic inlays and red brick motifs (occasionally alternating with marble) are characteristic of latter-day Byzantine architecture, although the frieze of swastikas (then a symbol of the sun and continual change) is quite unusual.

The church of Saint John the Baptist

Across the road, the **church of Saint John the Baptist** (daily 9am–noon & 2–6pm) also has a cruciform plan, but the drum supporting the dome is extraordinarily large, and its plain, undressed stone exterior dates it as a tenth- or eleventh-century building. Inside are several frescoes: the portraits of the donor and his contemporaries – on the west part of the south wall, and beneath the dome – date from when the church was built, the others from the sixteenth and seventeenth centuries. One depicts Saint Marina pulling a devil from the sea before braining it with a hammer – possibly representing local merchants' hopes that their patron saint would deal with the Cossack pirates who raided Nesebâr during the mid-seventeenth century.

More churches

Though the small, towerless **church of Sveti Spas**, further down the peninsula, is unremarkable, **ul. Aheloi** on which it stands is lovely, overhung by half-timbered houses carved with sun-signs, fish and other symbols. This leads from the seafront to the impressive **church of the Archangels Michael and Gabriel**, which features a chequered pattern of brick and stone on the blind niches not unlike the Panokrator church. The nearby ruined **Sveta Paraskeva** is similarly studded with green ceramics. Nowadays worshippers use the **church of the Virgin** to the northeast: a comparatively modern (and ugly) building by Nesebâr standards, heated by a long, protruding stovepipe. Occupying the historic centre of town, now a small plaza occupied by artists and picture-sellers, is the ruined **old Metropolitan church** (*Starata Mitropoliya*). Dating back to the fifth or sixth century, it was here that bishops officiated during the city-state's heyday, when Byzantine nobles demonstrated their wealth and piety by endowing Nesebâr with over forty ecclesiastical buildings. Several of them were concentrated at the northern tip of the peninsula, where you'll stumble upon the remains of the so-called **Basilica by the Seashore**, and a keep suggesting the frequency with which this exposed church (originally dedicated to the Virgin of Tenderness) was sacked by pirates and invaders.

The thirteenth-century **church of Saint Theodor**, nearby, is rather dull and the old houses along the streets leading back into the centre are far more eye-catching. The **Muskoyanin house**, on ul. Yana Lâskova, now contains an **Ethnographic Museum** (daily 9am–noon & 2–6pm), enabling visitors to appreciate its asymmetrical interior and the fine view from the residential quarters, which overhang the ground floor of undressed masonry.

The new Metropolitan church

Some time during the fifteenth century, power passed to the **new Metropolitan church** (also known as *Sveti Stefan*; daily 9am–1pm & 2–6pm), an eleventh-century three-aisled basilica whose exterior decoration is less assured than the frescoes inside – mostly added in the sixteenth and seventeenth centuries. So alike are the faces of the seven handmaidens who accompany the Virgin to the Temple (painted on the southwest pillar) that legend has it that the unknown artist was infatuated with his model. The patron who financed the church's enlargement during the fifteenth century is given pride of place among the *Forty Martyrs* on the west wall. Also note the bases of the marble columns, which originally formed the capitals of pillars in a pagan temple; and the opulently carved eighteenth-century bishop's throne, one of the best of its kind in Bulgaria.

Finally there's the ruined **church of Saint John Aliturgetos**, standing in splendid isolation beside the shore. Although tradition has it that the church was never consecrated, it represents the zenith of Byzantine architecture in Bulgaria. Its exterior decoration is strikingly varied, employing limestone, red bricks, crosses, mussel shells and ceramic plaques, with a representation of a human figure composed of limestone blocks incorporated into the north wall.

Practicalities

Buses shuttle between Sunny Beach's centre and Nesebâr every 15–20 minutes, arriving beside the harbour. This is also the site of Nesebâr's **accommodation bureau** (daily 8am–7pm): their private rooms, many of them in fine old houses,

THE BLACK SEA GREEKS I: ANCIENT COLONISTS

Why the ancient Greeks ever bothered to ventured north into the Black Sea remains the subject of much conjecture. Initially they called it the *Axeinos*, or "inhospitable", sea; and heroic legends exemplified by the tale of the **Argonauts** suggest that it was perceived as a hostile place where only adventurers dared to tread. By the sixth century BC, however, Greeks from Asia Minor were beginning to establish a string of colonies in the region, first along the coast of northern Turkey, subsequently moving on to the shores of what is now Bulgaria, Romania and the Ukraine.

Overpopulation and political upheaval at home obviously helped to precipitate this sudden burst of outward migration, but opportunities for trade played a part too. Pioneers in colonizing the Black Sea were the Greeks of **Miletus** (a city-state on the Aegean coast of Turkey), although some Bulgarian historians reckon that they merely followed in the footsteps of their neighbours the Carians: a race from Asia Minor (closely related to Bulgaria's Thracians) who had developed mercantile contacts in the Black Sea several generations earlier.

Apollonia (now Sozopol) was Miletus's first colony on the Bulgarian coast, soon followed by **Odyssos** (Varna), **Anchialos** (Pomorie) and **Krounoi** (Balchik). In many cases the colonists settled on or near an existing Thracian port: this was certainly the case with **Mesemvria** (Nesebâr), where the natives were ejected by newcomers from the Greek mainland city of Megara. Having settled down and established a network of maritime trade, the Greeks renamed the sea *Euxinos*, or "hospitable" – which remained its name throughout the Classical era.

These colonies couldn't have survived without friendly contacts with the Thracians, and a mutually beneficial system of **trade** developed. The Thracians obtained wine and salt (salt-pans are still a feature of the regional economy, especially around Pomorie) in return for grain and livestock – which the Greeks then re-exported at a tidy profit. **Intermarriage** must have been common from the earliest days, and cities such as Odyssos developed a thriving hybrid culture where colonists and natives lived cheek-by-jowl, observing each other's customs and paying homage to each other's gods.

begin at a mere £3 a double. It's difficult to get a room at the 2-star *Hotel Mesambriya* on ul. Ribarska (☎0554/3255; ③) during the summer season, since it's usually fully booked by groups.

There's a surfeit of places to **eat**, beginning with the kiosks beside the harbour selling mackerel and chips, mussels, and other snacks. The old town is crammed with small, privately owned restaurants trying to attract tourists with "schnitzel" and "pork chop"-dominated menus. For authentic fish dishes, however, try *Stariyat ribar*, ul. Ivan Asen.

More seafood can be sampled at the *Balkantourist*-run *Kapetanska sreshta* above the harbour, a theme restaurant complete with waiters in maritime stripey shirts and an accordion-driven band assailing the diners with Slavic sea shanties. The *Nea Mesembria* taverna at the western end of town serves Bulgarian food in a Greek ambience, while live music in otherwise soulless surroundings can be sampled in the restaurant of the *Mesambria* hotel, or the *Cherno More* on Yana Lâshkova.

Café Rumi on Ivan Asen serves the best cake and ice cream to be found in town; while the *Bar Burgas*, Meha 10, is the place to enjoy an intimate evening drink.

Pomorie

Continuing south from Nesebâr, beyond AHELOI, the road passes the salt-pans surrounding Lake Pomorie, one of Bulgaria's main sources of salt, and nowadays renowned for its therapeutic **mud baths**. Sited upon a peninsula beside the lake, **POMORIE** itself would probably resemble Nesebâr if it hadn't been gutted by fire in 1906 and subsequently rebuilt in concrete. Pomorie's ancient precursor, *Anchialos*, was founded by the Apollonians, became rich through the export of salt and wine, and found favour in the Roman era as an exclusive health resort. The lakeside sanatorium remains an important element in the local economy, as does another speciality of long standing, the locally produced aromatic *Pomoriiski Dimyat* **wine**. The ancient cult of wine-god Dionysus metamorphosed in Christian times into the cult of **Saint Trifon**, whose feast day was celebrated by sprinkling the vines with holy water – a task carried out by youths on horseback. Such rites are still celebrated both here and in other wine-producing regions of Bulgaria as the festival of *Trifon Zarezan*, on February 1.

The town

Pomorie's **bus station** is separated from the town by a 3km stretch of industrial and suburban horror (bus #1 to the centre cuts out a dull walk) enlivened only by the **Monastery of Saint George**, 500m east of the bus station. A medieval foundation re-established by Ottoman governor Selim Bey (who according to legend converted to Christianity after being cured of illness by a miraculous spring), the monastery now occupies a rather functional set of nineteenth-century buildings, brought to life by the shrubs and pot-plants which fill the central courtyard.

FISHING IN THE BLACK SEA

The harbours of old peninsula towns like Nesebâr, Pomorie and Sozopol (see p.274) remain clogged with the small boats which traditionally provided most local families with a livelihood – **fishing**. Although the numbers of full-time fishermen are in decline, most people still have access to a boat and augment their incomes by fishing in the coastal waters.

The working year is dictated by the seasonal migration patterns of the fish. Most activity takes place in the spring and autumn, when shoals of *skumrii* (mackerel) and *palamudi* (brown-striped tunny fish) pass along the Black Sea coast on their way between the waters of the Crimea and their wintering grounds in the Sea of Marmara and the Aegean. The *hamsiya*, or Black Sea anchovy, also makes fleeting appearances off the Bulgarian coast during its extensive circuits of the Black Sea, but the rest of the time people hunt *barbun* (mullet), *safrid* (scad), *kalkan* (turbot) and *tsatsa* (sprat) – piles of the latter, deep-fried and crispy, are a staple of coastal snack bars.

In recent decades it's become increasingly difficult to actually make a living from fishing due to the **gradual exhaustion** of the Black Sea's stocks, and harvests are getting smaller every year. Those with small fishing operations feel particularly threatened by the big state-owned trawler fleets operating out of Burgas, and are agitating for a complete ban on trawling in coastal waters. Such a ban would help preserve the small-town economy of places like Pomorie and Sozopol, but may not be enough to save the Black Sea's fish: hunting for turbot has (at least officially) already been suspended until its numbers improve, but you'll find it on the menues of most local restaurants all the same.

East of here lies a quiet, relaxed seaside town, although Pomorie's **centre** really boils down to a small pedestrianized area around the main street, Nikolai Lâskov, with a colourful fishing port a block to the south. The town's spa facilities lie a kilometre or two to the north on the shores of the lake, where there's also something of a **beach**.

Private rooms can be rented from the *kvartirno byuro* at Lâskov 56, a welcome alternative to the rather costly 3-star *Hotel Pomorie*, bul. Yavorov 3 (☎0596/2440; ④) at the southern tip of the peninsula. Nearest **campsite** is the *Evropa*, 2km west along the Burgas road.

Atanasovsko ezero

Midway between Pomorie and Burgas the road passes **Atanasovsko ezero**, a 10km-long stretch of shallow inland water frequented by herons in the spring. The lake serves as the midway point on the "Via Pontica" – the route used by birds migrating between Scandinavia and Africa. Its status as a nature reserve is supposed to ensure a kind of ecological quarantine, but locals throw their rubbish on the lake shore all the same – there's not enough money to employ wardens to enforce the regulations.

Burgas

Any preconceptions you may have had about eastern Europe will probably be confirmed by **BURGAS**. Encircled by crumbling high-rise suburbs and punctuated by weed-covered pavements and rubble-strewn patches of waste ground, Burgas presents a hard face to casual interlopers. In many ways it's the riviera town that never was, with a city centre patrolled by raffish-looking moneychangers and hustlers, bordered by an unkempt and overgrown stretch of seaside park – a pale reflection of the sea gardens in Varna.

The site of an oil refinery and associated chemical plants, Burgas is much more industrial than any of its neighbours on the coast, and its deep **harbour** is the home of Bulgaria's oceanic fishing fleet. The presence of numerous visiting ships ensures that the downtown streets possess a certain raw vigour, and the existence of a decent archaeological museum and a couple of boisterous restaurants provides reason enough to linger awhile – before utilizing Burgas's good transport connections with the more appetizing destinations further south.

Arrival and accommodation

All the main points of **arrival**, including train, bus and hydrofoil stations, are located just south of the centre on Garov ploshtad – half-hourly buses from the airport end up here too, and it's the best place to pick up a **taxi**. The main street, Aleksandrovska, strikes north from here into the main downtown area. **Rail tickets** for *TsKON* and *Rila* can be booked and bought at Aleksandrovska 106 (☎056/47023), and there's an *Interbalkan* **travel agent** in the foyer of the *Bâlgariya* hotel, Aleksandrovska 21 (☎056/42147).

Accommodation

There's a *Balkantourist* office opposite the rail station at Aleksandrovska 2 which offers **private rooms** in town for as little as £2 a double, and rooms are also avail-

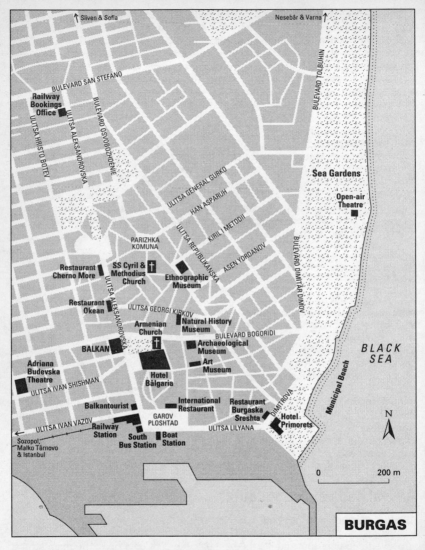

↑ Sliven & Sofia

Nesebâr & Varna ↑

BULEVARD SAN STEFANO

BULEVARD TOLBUHIN

Railway
Bookings
Office

ULITSA HRISTO BOTEV

ULITSA ALEKSANDROVSKA

BULEVARD OSVOBOZHDENIE

Sea Gardens

Open-air
Theatre

ULITSA GENERAL GURKO

HAN ASPARUH

KIRIL I METODII

ULITSA REPIBLIKANSKA

ASEN YORDANOV

BULEVARD DIMITÂR DIMOV

PARIZHKA
KOMUNA

Restaurant
Cherno More

SS Cyril &
Methodius
Church

Ethnographic
Museum

ULITSA ALEKSANDROVSKA

Restaurant
Okean

ULITSA GEORGI KIRKOV

Armenian
Church

Natural History
Museum

BALKAN

ULITSA ALEKSANDROVSKA

BULEVARD BOGORIDI

Archaeological
Museum

Art
Museum

BLACK
SEA

Adriana
Budevska
Theatre

ULITSA IVAN SHISHMAN

Hotel
Bâlgaria

Municipal Beach

Balkantourist

International
Restaurant

Restaurant
Burgaska
Sreshta

DIMITROVA

Hotel
Primorets

N

ULITSA IVAN VAZOV

Railway
Station

GAROV
PLOSHTAD

South
Bus Station

Boat
Station

ULITSA LILYANA

Sozopol,
Malko Târnovo
& Istanbul

0   200 m

BURGAS

able from a scattering of newly opened private tourist offices along ul. Bogoridi. They're likely to prove better value for money than the town's three **hotels**: the luxurious 3-star *Bâlgariya*, Aleksandrovska 21 (☎056/45336; ④); the 3-star *Kosmos*, out towards the airport in the northerly suburb of Osvobozhdenie (☎056/35901; ④); the 2-star *Primorets*, Liliana Dimitrova 1 (☎056/44117; ③); or the 1-star *Briz*, Garov ploshtad (☎056/43180; ②).

The nearest campsite is at *Kraimorie*, signposted from the coast road 14km south of town.

Around town

Most daytime activity takes place along ul. Aleksandrovska, a shopping street without any shops, and the adjoining, café-lined **ul. Bogoridi**, which heads eastwards from the town centre towards the sea gardens. Cowering beneath the hotel *Bâlgariya* at the street's western end is the small **Armenian church of Sveti Hach**, a modern structure with curious bell tower, ministering to the needs of a local population of a few hundred.

Archaeological museum

Further along ul. Bogoridi at no. 21 is the **archaeological museum** (Tues–Sat 9am–noon & 2–6pm), crammed with Roman-period votive tablets depicting the Thracian rider god. One Greek-language inscription from Mesembria serves as a reminder of the atmosphere of cultural exchange in which the coastal cities existed, recording a peace treaty between the city and the local Thracian ruler Sadala which accorded him the right to parade around town in a golden laurel wreath on the occasion of the annual festival of Dionysus. Classical-era burial finds include the gold jewellery of a Thracian priestess, and a second-century BC wooden sarcophagus complete with the deceased's preserved sandals and burial shroud.

Other museums

One block south of the archaeological museum at Vodenicharov 22 is the **art gallery** (Mon–Sat 7.30am–noon & 2–6pm), housed in an old synagogue: the fine display of eighteenth- and nineteenth-century icons are on the top floor just below the dome.

North of Bogoridi, turn-of-the-century residential streets huddle around the **church of Saints Kiril i Metodii**, built between 1894 and 1905. The saints themselves are depicted in peeling murals above the entrance, framed by some interesting Art Nouveau-inspired stained glass. The nearby **ethnographic museum** (Mon–Sat 8.30am–noon & 2–5.30pm), Slavyanska 19, shows off *Kukeri* costumes and regional textiles. Displays documenting the local flora and fauna fill three floors of the **natural history museum** (Mon–Fri 8am–noon & 2–6pm) at Fotilov 30, among which is a diorama of bird life at the Atanasovo ezero (see p.271). It's difficult to tell whether the tableau of two hyenas fighting over a toy dolphin has any local relevance.

Eating and drinking

Burgas's main promenading area, along ul. Aleksandrovska and ul. Bogoridi, is lined with outdoor cafés. *Bistro Victory* on ul. Bogoridi is among the liveliest of the daytime drinking venues. In the evening drinkers tend to congregate in the numerous city-centre restaurants, the majority of which feature live music. *Morski vâlni*, Aleksandrovska 12, offers seafood and loud Gypsy music, although it seems to be a predominantly male preserve; while the clientele of the equally rowdy *Cherno More*, Aleksandrovska 88; and *Briz*, Garov ploshtad, appear more mixed.

For more relaxed dining try the summer garden of the *Burgaska sreshta* on Lilyana Dimitrova, opposite the *Hotel Primorets*.

Around the Gulf of Burgas

Road traffic southwards is borne by a thin finger of land which separates the gulf itself from the land-locked Burgasko ezero to the west. The latter was long used as a dumping ground by the Neftohim oil refinery and chemicals plant which blights its northern banks (see box below), and has nothing of the natural beauty of **Mandrensko ezero** (Lake Mandra), lying beside the main E87 road 10km south of Burgas. Surrounded by reedy grass, the lake is a good place to look out for wildfowl, especially **spoonbills**, who nest here in May and June.

There are only two settlements of any size on the south side of the bay: **KRAIMORIE**, a naval town serving a big base on the nearby peninsula of Aitia, and, 25km out from Burgas, **CHERNOMORETS**, a small beach resort with a neatly manicured park, a campsite and numerous private rooms. Both towns are served by hourly buses on the Burgas-Sozopol route, but it's better to press on to the relative clean air and calm of Sozopol.

POLLUTION IN THE GULF OF BURGAS

Arriving at Burgas you'll see both the best and the worst of what the coast has to offer: while glorious beaches and wildlife-infested lakes lie a few kilometres away both north and south, the city itself is one of the **most polluted** in Bulgaria.

The **Black Sea** as a whole is in a sorry state. Rivers such as the Don, Dniestr, Dniepr and Danube carry the waste products of a vast industrial hinterland into a sea which is largely closed – only the Bosphorus to the south provides an outlet for the accumulated gunk. The depths of the Black Sea have always been low on oxygen, leaving only a thin upper layer of water capable of sustaining life. Twentieth-century pollution is rendering this layer thinner than ever, and intensive fishing threatens to reduce even further the stock of marine animals this once-rich sea contained. **Dolphins**, previously a common sight off the Bulgarian shore, are increasingly rare: the fish they used to feed off are gone.

Burgas's problems are compounded by the presence of a vast chemicals plant, **Neftohim**, on the western outskirts of town (you're sure to pass it if entering or leaving the city by train). Neftohim's waste products used to be diluted in a series of water tanks before being released into the gulf, but during the Communist period few paid attention to the kind of toxins which were allowed to seep into the sea this way. Nowadays emissions of this kind are more closely monitored and stiff fines imposed on transgressors, but the Gulf of Burgas remains pretty ugly. The tankers and cargo ships frequenting the port here all shed a little oil from time to time, and the currents in the gulf tend to circulate within the bay itself instead of diluting these concentrations of waste in the open sea.

Naturally enough, few people patronize Burgas's municipal **beaches** these days, but neighbouring resorts don't seem to have been affected by the city's environmental problems. Coastal waters around Nesebâr to the north or Sozopol to the south are remarkably pure, and you shouldn't have any qualms about bathing here.

Sozopol

Hourly buses link Burgas with **SOZOPOL** 35km to the south, an engaging huddle of nineteenth-century houses occupying a rocky headland. The town's architectural attractions are backed up by a brace of excellent beaches, but

Sozopol lacks the excessive crowds of Nesebâr, and the tranquility of fishing-village life remains surprisingly unruffled. Sozopol's uniquely relaxing atmosphere made it the favoured holiday resort of Bulgaria's literary and artistic set, and although they descend on the town in ever decreasing numbers, sketch pad-wielding students can still be seen in the narrow lanes and alleys of the old town. Slightly incongruously, Sozopol harbour also serves as one of Bulgaria's most important **naval bases**, with ranks of gunboats anchored off the neighbouring island of Sveti Kirik. The townsfolk (seeing the navy as an obstacle to the development of the town's full tourist potential) are keen to eject the military altogether and convert the harbour into a yachting marina.

Some history

Stone anchors displayed in the local museum suggest that traders were visiting Sozopol harbour as early as the twelfth century BC, although the identity of these early seafarers remains the subject of much conjecture. More certain is the town's status as the first of the **Greek colonies** along the coast, founded somewhere around 610 BC by a party of adventurers from Miletus. They named the town *Apollonia Pontica* after **Apollo**, the patron of seafarers and colonizers, and prospered by trading Greek textiles and wine for Thracian honey, grain and copper. Apollonia's major customer was Athens, and the decline of the latter in the fourth century BC ended the town's brief reign as a minor maritime power.

Having spent a couple of centuries existing quite happily on the fringes of much more powerful Thracian and **Macedonian** states, the Apollonians flirted with various anti-Roman alliances in the first century BC in order to try to stave off the inevitable advance of Latin power. Their attachment to the Black Sea empire-builder **Mithridates of Pontus** was punished by Roman general Marcus Lucullus in 72 BC, who sacked the town and carried off the treasured statue of Apollo which formerly graced the harbour.

Apollonia disappeared from the records of chroniclers during the Dark Ages, re-emerging in 431 under the name of **Sozopolis**, the "City of Salvation". Under the Byzantines the town soon developed a reputation for the good life, and rebellious nobles and troublesome bishops were "retired" here by emperors unwilling to see their peers too harshly punished. However, marauding armies returned during the fourteenth and fifteenth centuries, and following the Turkish invasion Sozopol sunk into anonymity, replaced by Burgas as the area's major port.

The town

Sozopol divides into two parts: the **old town** confined to the peninsula, and the modern, **Harmanite** district (literally "The Windmills", although only one of the contraptions still survives) on the mainland to the southeast. The main **beach** lies below the latter, nestling within the curve of a sheltered bay, while there's a second, much more extensive beach beyond the headland to the south. Between old and new towns lies the town **park**, carpeted with cotton-like wads of blossom throughout the early summer. Sheltering among the trees is the pale sandstone **Chapel of Sveti Zosim**, honouring the saint who, as the protector of seafarers, was in many ways the Christian Church's answer to Apollo. The whitewashed bulk of the **church of saints Kiril i Metodii** lies immediately to the north, used as an exhibition hall during the Communist era and now awaiting the funds necessary to return it to its former spiritual purpose.

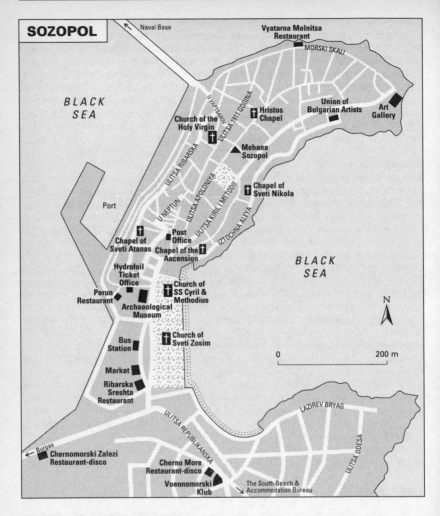

The Archaeological Museum

Immediately opposite the church is Sozopol's **Archaeological Museum** (Mon–Fri 8am–noon & 1–5pm, Sat & Sun 9am–noon & 2–4.30pm), where you'll see forests of *amphorae* dredged up from ancient wrecks on the seabed. Also here is arguably Bulgaria's best collection of Greek vases, including twelve Attic *kraters* with vibrant red-figure depictions of mythical scenes. At least five of them show Dionysus, god of wine and lustful celebration, a reminder that each *krater* was originally used for the mixing of wine and water during feasts. The Thracians who lived inland – and mined the copper so profitably shipped overseas by the Greeks – are remembered in an extensive collection of weaponry and functional pottery.

The old town and the church of Sveta Bogoroditsa

North of the museum ul. Apoloniya leads into the **old town**, where cypress trees rustle in the breeze and old ladies brandishing lace tablecloths prepare to ambush stray tourists. The best examples of Sozopol's **old houses** lie towards the head of the peninsula along ul. Apoloniya, and along the parallel ul. Kiril i Metodii. Boats and fishing tackle were housed in the stone-built lower storeys during the winter, while families lived in creaking wooden upstairs rooms – which project so far out that houses on opposite sides of the narrow streets almost meet.

Several garden shed-like *paraklisi* or **chapels** can be found scattered throughout the town, usually bare inside save for a picture of the saint to whom they're dedicated, but Sozopol's principal eccelesiastical gem is the **church of Sveta Bogoroditsa** (same times as the museum), nestling within a walled courtyard on ul. 1911 Godina. Inside the subterranean nave are a finely carved iconostasis and bishop's throne – both executed by anonymous local masters in the early 1800s – and a wooden screen behind which female worshippers were required to stand.

Sozopol's former high school at the northern end of Kiril i Metodii now contains a small **art gallery** (Tues–Sun 8am–noon & 2–6pm), although most of the works on the ground floor look suspiciously like the garish daubs dashed off by holidaying artists in between drinking bouts at the local *mehana*. Things are more interesting upstairs, where works by local marine artists Aleksandâr Mutafov and Yani Chrisoupolis document pre-World War II Sozopol and the working lives of its fisherfolk.

Inland from Sozopol: the Copper Ridge

Immediately inland from Sozopol lies the *Meden rid* or **Copper Ridge**, the wooded peaks of which are crowned by a series of Iron Age hill forts once occupied by Thracian chieftains. The latter grew rich by trading the local copper with the Greeks of Apollonia, although they occasionally descended to the Black Sea shore to prey on shipwrecks washed up here by frequent storms. The hills stretch southwards for some 20km, but the highest point of the range, 376m-high **Bakârlâk**, can be reached from Sozopol by walking to the *Zlatna Ribka* campsite and heading directly west from there. Allow about five hours to get there and back.

Practicalities

Sozopol's bus station is on pl. Han Krum opposite the town park, from which it's a fifteen-minute walk to the *Balkantourist* bureau on the south beach. Here you can choose between **private rooms** in the old houses of the peninsula or in the more spacious chalet-style buildings of Harmanite. Sozopol (mercifully) lacks a big tourist hotel, but there's a small pension, the *Radik*, at Republikanska 4 (☎05514/1706; ③); and the *Voennomorski klub* (literally the "navy club", ☎05514/245307; ②) further south along Republikanska, formerly intended for visiting Bulgarian naval officers, is now a hotel open to all-comers. The *Zlatna Ribka* **campsite** 3km north of town is one of the south coast's best, situated on a part-sandy, part-rocky coastline – the bus from Burgas passes the site on its way into town.

THE BLACK SEA GREEKS II: THE MODERN ERA

Occasionally you still come across elderly residents of Sozopol speaking **Greek** amongst themselves – a reminder that the Greek population of the coast remained an important feature of local life well into this century.

The Greeks of the coastal towns had maintained some degree of wealth and influence under Turkish rule, and therefore seemed well poised to take advantage of the upsurge in commerce that occurred in Ottoman lands in the wake of the Crimean War. However, the decline of Turkish power and the rise of **modern national movements** had a detrimental effect on the cosmopolitan culture of the Black Sea towns, with subject peoples squabbling among themselves rather than uniting to challenge the decaying Ottoman empire. The Greeks, inspired by the existence of an independent Greek state from 1830 onwards, came under the influence of the **Megáli Idhéa** ("Great Idea") of liberating all the Hellenes within Turkish territory and forging a new Byzantine empire.

The idea that the Black Sea towns formed an integral part of the Hellenic world was of course anathema to the **Bulgarians**. Increasingly numerous in the coastal towns due to immigration from the countryside, they saw the Greeks – who controlled the Church, education, and most local trade – as mere agents of the ruling Ottoman elite. The Ottoman authorities played one group off against the other, eventually acquiescing to Bulgarian demands for the establishment of a Bulgarian Orthodox Church independent of Greek control – a move which infuriated the Greeks.

With the foundation of a Bulgarian nation-state after 1878, mistrust between the two groups faded into the background, only to re-emerge when Bulgarian and Greek governments squabbled over the fate of Macedonia in 1905. Bulgarian citizens vented their frustrations by indulging in a spate of **anti-Greek riots**: the defenceless townsfolk of Sozopol and Pomorie bore the brunt of their anger as Greek-owned shops and houses were destroyed.

After World War I both governments agreed to settle their differences with an exchange of populations. According to the **Molov-Kafandaris Agreement** of 1924, Black Sea Greeks would quit the coastal towns to be replaced by ethnic Bulgarians from Aegean Macedonia and southern Thrace. Greeks in Sozopol, Pomorie, Nesebâr and elsewhere were given a straightforward choice: they could declare themselves to be Bulgarians and adopt Bulgarian names, or they could leave. In practice, the poorer Greek families stayed behind because they lacked the resources to contemplate uprooting themselves and building a new life elsewhere, but their descendants have largely been assimilated by the Slav majority over the last seventy years.

Despite the population exchange, the atmosphere of the coastal towns didn't necessarily change that much – most of the new arrivals tended to be vine-growers and fisherfolk, very much like the people who moved out, and locals still joke that the incoming Bulgarians from southern Thrace usually spoke better Greek than the Hellenes they were replacing.

The bitterness which used to characterize relations between Greeks and Bulgarians on the coast has these days largely disappeared, especially now that the straitjacket of Communist educational policy – which trumpeted Bulgarian achievements at the expense of everyone else's – has been cast aside. Many Bulgarian families of the Black Sea coast can dredge up a Greek ancestor or two from somewhere or other – nowadays the subject of fond reminiscences rather than ethnic angst.

Eating and drinking

A compact cluster of **cafés** lines the southern stretches of ul. Apoloniya, and there are several outdoor drinking venues along the main beach. Most of the residents of Harmanite seem to be converting their garages and front gardens into *café–aperitif* bars – useful if you're shuttling between beaches and need refreshment.

The *Mehana Sozopol* on Apoloniya and the *Vyatarna Melnitsa* on Morski Skali are both touristy folk-style **restaurants** with generous outdoor seating and regular live music. Slightly more elegant is the restaurant of the Union of Bulgarian Artists at the northern end of ul. Kiril i Metodii, whose dining room juts out above the sea. *Perun*, near the harbour, and the *Druzhba* ship restaurant immediately opposite, are good places to sample grilled fish in a lively outdoor setting; although the smaller family-run restaurants can be much more friendly and intimate. Best of the latter are the *Amfora*, hidden away in the backstreets but well signposted off the main ul. Apoloniya; and *Neptun*, Morski Skali, with a terrace overlooking the sea. The *Ribarska sreshta*, just south of the bus station, is a handy mackerel-and-chips takeaway.

Two restaurants in the modern part of town which turn into discos after 10pm are *Cherno More*, ul. Republikanska, and *Gâbite* near the south beach.

South of Sozopol

South of Sozopol, the coast offers some of Bulgaria's most glorious stretches of **sandy beaches**. A whole string of semi-deserted beaches are punctuated by areas of coastal wetland, notably the lush woodlands around the estuary of the **River Ropotamo**, while the sandy soil of the coastal hills provides a tenuous base for clusters of prickly conifers. Hugging the Turkish border just west of the coast are the mountains of the **Strandzha**, covered by Bulgaria's deepest and least-explored **forests**.

The modern complex of **Dyuni** excepted, the resorts along this stretch of the Black Sea were largely frequented by Eastern bloc tourists in the past, and are nowadays fairly empty. This has given rise to a familiar Bulgarian paradox: private rooms in quiet seaside towns like **Primorsko**, **Michurin** and **Ahtopol** are cheap and numerous, but the accommodation bureaux which allocate them are rarely open. Make use of local knowledge – private café-owners and restauranteurs are bound to know a near-neighbour who has a room to spare.

Those with their own **transport** can cruise the area and pick their spot for bathing, but travellers reliant on local buses will have to time things carefully. There are seven buses a day between Sozopol and Michurin, calling at Kavatsite, Dyuni, Ropotamo and Primorsko on the way; and two of these continue all the way to Ahtopol. In summer, however, services fill up quickly, and drivers won't stop to pick up travellers waiting at minor roadside halts if the vehicle is already packed.

Kavatsite, Dyuni and around

Four kilometres south down the coast from Sozopol, the **KAVATSITE** tourist complex includes a deluxe **motel** (☎05514/261; ③) and the *Kavatsite* **campsite**, a shaded woody area with bungalows huddled together like a partisan camp in the forest.

Not far to the south is one of Bulgaria's newest tourist developments, the **Dyuni Holiday Village**. The village specializes in offering self-catering units in a wide range of vernacular buildings, some built in imitation of the wooden houses of Sozopol. The small size and relative quiet of the resort make it a good venue for family holidays.

Dyuni's **accommodation bureau** is at the entrance of the villa complex – a right turn off the coast road if you're heading southwards. The marina, surrounded by many of the resort's cafés and restaurants, is off to the left.

Rooms at Dyuni are expensive for independent travellers arriving on spec (expect to pay the equivalent of around £20 a double), but the reward is a marvellous stretch of **beach**: a long bar of sand which extends southwards for 3km, protecting an inland plain of marsh and reed and **Lake Alepu**, a lagoon surrounded by dunes and sand lilies. About one hour's walk due west of Alepu is **Malkoto Kale** ("The Little Fortress"), the best-preserved of the Iron Age forts of the Copper Ridge. Halfway up the hill you'll pass the **Robinson fountain**, named in remembrance of the local Crusoe-style hermit *Ignat*, who tended the lighthouse at nearby Cape Maslen (see below) and lived off the local waterfowl.

Arkutino and the Ropotamo River

ARKUTINO, 3km south of Dyuni, used to be the favoured holiday destination of the Communist elite, although the rest homes that once belonged to the Party aren't yet open to the general public. Former dictator Todor Zhivkov spent vacations at **Perla**, a holiday villa on the seashore where **Robert Maxwell** was subsequently entertained by Bulgaria's post-1989 "socialist" rulers. The tubby tycoon had Perla's harbour measured up to see whether it could accommodate his private yacht, and sweet-talked his hosts with improbable tales about how he wanted to turn the Black Sea coast into the California of eastern Europe.

The Ropotamo River

A few kilometres to the south is the mouth of the **Ropotamo River**, whose upper reaches have been designated a **nature reserve** into which small boats (departing from Dyuni a couple of times a week) venture. They don't go very far upriver, however, so if you're particularly keen to see the Ropotamo's famous waterlilies it's probably better to walk along the banks, lined with oaks, beech, willows and creeping lianas. Since the Ropotamo abounds in grey mullet, whitefish, barbel and carp, it's popular, too, with amateur fishermen; dragonflies, small black turtles and (non-poisonous) watersnakes also abound here. Sozopol-Michurin buses stop at the point where the E87 crosses the river, but drivers seem to have an aversion to picking up passengers here – be prepared to hitch back.

To the south of the river mouth rises **Cape Maslen**, where the sea has hollowed out caves that are sometimes frequented by **seals**.

Primorsko, Kiten and Michurin

On the other side of the cape lies the village of **PRIMORSKO**. It's a dusty, tired-looking place, but a glorious curve of a beach runs along the bay to the south, culminating in a gargantuan white elephant of a holiday resort which used to rejoice in the name of the **Georgi Dimitrov International Youth Centre**. Conceived in the days when young people and students from all over the

Communist world came to be coralled together in purpose-built holiday camps, the *Orbita*-run centre has lost its *raison d'être* now that the socialist regimes of eastern Europe have dissolved. What's left is a forest of rusting parasol stands and a hotel complex overgrown with weeds, but it's bound to be redeveloped into something nicer eventually. In the meantime, a couple of open-air snack bars cater for the beach bums still drawn here by the vast expanse of sand. The neigh-bouring *Les* and *Kitenski zaliv* **campsites**, the latter with a good position on the shoreline, are both signposted from the road.

A minor road heads ten kilometres inland from Primorsko to the village of **Yasna Polyana** below the northern flanks of the hills known as the Strandzha (see overleaf). Disciples of the novelist and vegetarian pacifist **Leo Tolstoy** chose this then-isolated region as the site for a commune, naming it after the Russian village where their guru spent his latter years. Continuing southwards down the coast, there are plenty more camping possibilities just beyond the one-horse town of KITEN, where four **campsites** – *Kiten*, *Yug*, *Koral* and *Oasis* – are well sign-posted from the main E87 highway.

Michurin

Judging by the cluster of individual letter boxes hanging outside the town's post office (one for each of the former socialist countries), **MICHURIN** once attracted considerable numbers of summer visitors. It's difficult to see why: it's a fairly unremarkable fishing port high on a rocky promontory, with a beach on the northern side, a harbour on the south, and nothing very much in between. There's one **hotel**, the *Chaika* (③), on the main square just above the bus station. Limited nighttime revelry takes place in the open-air café and the *Pasat* floating bar, both in the harbour.

Towards Ahtopol

Beyond Michurin the E87 swings *inland* towards the Strandzha and the frontier crossing at Malko Târnovo (see overleaf), while a well-surfaced minor road continues along an increasingly rocky coastline before reaching the last town of any size, Ahtopol. Occasionally forced inland, the road dives between coastal hills, where herders watch over grazing sheep and pigs.

Ahtopol and beyond

Surrounded by a girdle of trade-union rest homes belonging to factories in Sofia, Plovdiv and elsewhere, **AHTOPOL** is a tranquil, sea-battered little place whose peninsular position echoes that of Sozopol and Nesebâr. From the bus station at the western end of town, the main street leads down towards a small fishing harbour. Just above is a small town **museum** (Tues–Sun; irregular hours) and a flight of steps lead from here into the **old town**, whose narrow streets preserve a few examples of the vernacular architecture already seen in Sozopol; but, aside from a lighthouse brooding at the end of the peninsula, Ahtopol's sightseeing potential is soon exhausted. There's a *kvartirno byuro* doling out **rooms** just next to the bus station, and a rudimentary campsite, the *Delfin*, on the beach 3km north of town.

SINEMORETS, 5km south on the other side of the Velika River, has a fine beach. From here it's another 10km to the village of REZOVO beside the Turkish border, though it's *not* possible to cross the frontier here.

The Strandzha

The interior west of the south coast is dominated by the wooded **Strandzha**, a region of plateaux and hills interrupted by rift valleys, where the Ropotamo and other rivers flow. It's a captivating area of untouched forests, thick with oak, beech, alder and elm trees, and would be perfect hiking territory were it not for the fact that distinct paths are rare, tourist accommodation hard to find, and good maps of the area nonexistent. Plenty of traffic passes through the Strandzha en route for the border crossing into Turkey at Malko Târnovo, but only two buses a day make the trip here from Burgas. If you want to explore the Strandzha, you emphatically need your own **car**.

Routes into the Strandzha, and fire dancing

There are two main **routes into the area**: the southbound E87 heads inland from Michurin, winding its way slowly over the hills towards the frontier 80km distant. However, most traffic from Burgas (including buses) takes a more direct route, turning inland at Kraimorie and using minor roads from there on.

Both routes climb through increasingly beautiful terrain, but neither of them pass settlements of particular size or interest. Lying on the E87, however, are **Kondolovo** and **Bâlgari**, villages renowned for the ancient custom of *nestinarstvo* or **fire dancing**. Traditionally associated with the feast day of saints Konstantin and Elena on May 21, the ritual involves initiates falling into a trance and dancing on hot embers, to furious bagpipe accompaniment. Ethnologists have suggested that fire dancing is directly descended from the Dionysian rites of the ancients, and thus constitutes a direct link with the ecstatic religion of the Thracians. Unfortunately, genuine *nestinarstvo* no longer forms part of village life, and these days is only performed for the benefit of tourists along the coast.

Malko Târnovo and the frontier

MALKO TÂRNOVO, situated 10km from **the border**, is a small mining town lying in a bowl formed by the surrounding hills. The town's central role in the 1903 Ilinden Uprising against the Turks assured it of a historical pedigree, and much of the town's nineteenth-century architecture is in a good state of preservation, but in the past tourism was never encouraged here due to the proximity of what used to be a highly sensitive border. There's a **motel**, the *Strandzha* (③), midway between Malko Târnovo and the frontier, and a tourist service office at the frontier itself.

If travelling **by car**, traffic at the frontier is pretty light, and clearing Bulgarian customs shouldn't involve lengthy queueing. Things can be more time-consuming at the Turkish end, where you'll have to wait behind files of coach passengers in order to purchase an entry visa (have £5 in sterling ready).

Crossing the border **by coach** is a different matter. Malko Târnovo is overrun with Bulgarians, Romanians and Ukranians on the way to Istanbul (many carrying holdalls stuffed with goods they hope to sell on Turkish markets), and their baggage gets a thorough going-over by officials on both sides. Coach passengers will probably be stuck here all night, but the wait is worthwhile – the descent into Turkey through the scrub-covered slopes of the Strandzha is highly scenic.

> If you're thinking of heading on into Turkey, then *Turkey: the Rough Guide* (Penguin: £8.99) is an essential investment.

CYRILLIC PLACE NAMES

AHELOI	АХЕЛОЙ	GOLDEN	ЗЛАТНИ
AHTOPOL	АХТОПОЛ	SANDS	ПЯСЪЦИ
ALADZHA	АЛАДЖА	KAVARNA	КАВАРНА
MONASTERY	МАНАСТИР	MALKO	МАЛКО
ALBENA	АЛБЕНА	TÂRNOVO	ТЪРНОВО
ARKUTINO	АРКУТИНО	MICHURIN	МИЧУРИН
ASPARUHOVO	АСПАРУХОВО	NESEBÂR	НЕСЕБЪР
BALCHIK	БАЛЧИК	OBROCHISHTE	ОБРОЧИЩЕ
BURGAS	БУРГАС	OBZOR	ОБЗОР
BYALA	БЯЛА	POMORIE	ПОМОРИЕ
CAPE KALIAKRA	НОС КАЛИАКРА	SHABLA	ШАБЛА
CHERNOMORETS	ЧЕРНОМОРЕЦ	SHKORPILOVTSI	ШКОРПИЛОВЦИ
DEVNYA	ДЕВНЯ	SOZOPOL	СОЗОПОЛ
DRUZHBA	ДРУЖБА	STONE	ПОБИТИ
DURANKULAK	ДУРАНКУЛАК	FOREST	КАМЬНИ
DYUNI	ДЮНИ	SUNNY BEACH	СЛЬНЧЕВ БРЯГ
ELENITE	ЕЛЕНИТЕ	SVETI	СВЕТИ
EVKSINOGRAD	ЕВКСИНОГРАД	KONSTANTIN	КОНСТАНТИН
GALATA	ГАЛАТА	VARNA	ВАРНА
KAMCHIYA	КАМЧИЯ	ZORA	ЗОРА

travel details

Trains

From Burgas to Karnobat (18 daily; 45min–1hr 30min); Kazanlâk (4; 7hr); Plovdiv (3; 4hr 30min); Sofia (5–6; 5hr 30min); Stara Zagora (4; 3hr).

From Varna to Burgas (7; 4hr 15min); Karnobat (7; 3hr–3hr 30min); Plovdiv (2; 6–7hr); Ruse (2; 4hr); Sofia (5; 8–9hr); Dobrich (6; 2hr 45min).

Buses

From Balchik to Albena (hourly; 30min); Dobrich (8 daily); Durankulak (2 daily); Kavarna (7 daily); Shabla (6 daily).

From Burgas to Ahtopol (2 daily); Malko Târnovo (2 daily); Michurin (6 daily); Pomorie (every 30min); Ruse (1 daily); Sozopol (hourly); Sunny Beach (every 20min); Varna (6 daily).

From Druzhba to Golden Sands; Varna (every 10–30min).

From Golden Sands to Albena (every 15–30min); Druzhba and Varna (every 10–30min).

From Kavarna to Bâlgarevo (6 daily); Dobrich (hourly); Durankulak (2 daily); Shabla (hourly).

From Sozopol to Ahtopol (2 daily); Michurin (6 daily); Primorsko (6 daily).

From Sunny Beach to Nesebâr (every 15–20min); Obzor (1 daily); Varna (1 daily); Vlas (8 daily).

From Varna to Aladzha Monastery (hourly); Balchik (10 daily); Byala (2 daily); Dobrich (every 30min); Druzhba (every 10–30min); Kamchiya (5 daily); Galata (every 30min); Golden Sands (every 10–30min); Kavarna (4 daily); Obzor (6 daily); Silistra (4 daily); Shabla (3 daily); Shkorpilovtsi (1 daily); Shumen (5 daily).

Hydrobuses (May–Sept only)

From Varna to Balchik (2 daily; 2hr); Druzhba (2; 30min); Golden Sands (2; 1hr).

Hydrofoils (May–Sept only)

From Varna to Nesebâr (2 daily; 1hr 30min); Pomorie (2; 2hr); Sozopol (2; 2hr 30min); Burgas (2; 3hr).

Flights

From Burgas to Sofia (1–2 daily; 1hr).
From Varna to Sofia (2; 1hr).

International trains (June–Sept only)

From Burgas to Budapest (1 daily; 23–27hr); Craiova (1; 10hr); Warsaw (1; 42hr).

From Varna to Bucharest (1; 7hr); Budapest (1; 27hr); Buzău (1; 9hr); Warsaw (1; 59hr).

International buses

From Burgas to Istanbul (1 daily; 12hr).

PART THREE

THE
CONTEXTS

THE HISTORICAL FRAMEWORK

National history is a serious business in a country that was virtually effaced for 500 years – when this part of the Ottoman empire was referred to by Westerners as "European Turkey". Since the Liberation in 1877–78, successive regimes have tried to inculcate a sense of national pride among their citizens, emphasizing historical continuity between the modern state and the medieval Bulgarian empires of the past.

NEOLITHIC BEGINNINGS

Despite several Palaeolithic finds in the caves of the Balkan Mountains, the early inhabitants of the Bulgarian lands don't really enter the limelight of history until the sixth millennium BC, when the Balkans were a major centre of the so-called **Neolithic Revolution**. This came about when Stone Age hunters began to be replaced by a more settled, agricultural population – probably the result of a wave of migration from the Near East. This sudden flowering of organized urban culture is best observed at the recently excavated Neolithic village at **Stara Zagora** (see p.198), famous for its decorated pottery, clay figurines and fertility symbols. By the fourth millennium BC mining and metallurgy took off in a big way:

copper and gold objects found in the **Chalcolithic necropolis** near **Varna** (see p.248) show that the Balkan peoples were developing smelting techniques independently of the civilizations of the Near East.

Chalcolithic culture went into decline at the end of the fourth millennium BC, a process hastened by a worsening of the climate. Civilization in the Bulgarian lands was revitalized by the arrival of newcomers from central Europe, bringing with them the metalworking techniques of the **Bronze Age**. By the end of the second millennium BC these migrant groups, together with the original tribes of the eastern Balkans, were coalescing into an ethnic and linguistic group subsequently known to history as the **Thracians**.

THE THRACIANS

Ruled by a powerful warrior aristocracy rich in gold treasures, the ancient Thracians inhabited an area extending over most of modern Bulgaria, northern Greece and European Turkey. Close ethnic links with their neighbours in both the Danube basin to the north (such as the Getae, see p.174) and in Asia Minor to the east placed them at the centre of an extensive Balkan-Asian culture. Despite their subsequent absorption by a whole host of invaders and their eventual assimilation by the Slavs, the Thracians are regarded as one of the **bedrock peoples** of the Balkans whose ethnic stock (though much diluted) has endured – and the present-day Bulgarians are proud to claim them as ancestors.

We're largely dependent on ancient Greek authors – notably Herodotus, Xenophon and Strabo – for knowledge of the Thracian world. Herodotus, in a famous passage you'll see quoted in museums throughout Bulgaria, claimed that the Thracian population was "greater than that of any country in the world except India", and would have been a force to be reckoned with had it not been for their tribal disunity.

Although the Thracians were admired for skills such as archery and horsemanship, many of their **customs** seemed slightly barbaric to their southerly neighbours. Certain tribes practiced polygamy, others allowed their young women unlimited sexual freedom before marriage, while tattoos for both males and females were *de rigueur* in most areas. Strabo relates how one group of Thracians was nick-named the *Capnobatae* (literally the "smoke treaders"), suggesting that they burned hemp seeds indoors and got high on the fumes. Dope-crazed hopheads or not, the Thracians *did* practice an ecstatic, **orgiastic religion**, honouring deities closely linked with the Greek god Dionysus. Themes of death, rebirth and renewal figured highly in their religious rites, providing a corpus of belief from which the Greeks borrowed freely – most notably in the case of the legendary Thracian priest-king **Orpheus** (see p.227).

GREEKS, PERSIANS AND MACEDONIANS

Certain Thracian tribes developed close links with the **Greek colonists** who began settling the Black Sea coast from the seventh century onwards. The Greek presence turned the Black Sea into an extension of the Mediterranean world, and while bounteous harvests of wheat and fish were shipped southwards to the Aegean to feed cities like Athens, exquisite sculpture and pottery came in the other direction, enriching the culture of the eastern Balkans.

The **Persians** invaded the area in the late sixth century BC, disrupting the lively system of trade which linked the Black Sea Greeks with the Thracians inland. However their departure allowed the emergence of powerful Thracian tribal kingdoms such as that of the **Odrysae**, which brought stability to the region in the mid-fifth century BC and allowed Greek-Thracian mercantile contacts to flourish anew.

The Odrysae briefly threatened to become the nucleus of a powerful Balkan empire, but this role was taken up a century later by the neighbouring **Macedonians** under Philip II – who invaded Thrace and founded Philippopolis (present-day **Plovdiv**). It took Philip and his son Alexander the Great (who marched to the Danube in 335 BC) a lot of time and men to subdue the Balkans, but their empire (under Alexander's successors the *Antigonids*) proved lasting. It was during this period that the Thracian interior was opened up fully to the ideas, goods and culture of the Hellenistic world, and the **tombs** of local Thracian rulers (most notably the one at **Kazanlâk**, see p.192) were sumptuously kitted out with Greek-inspired frescoes and luxurious furnishings.

ROME AND BYZANTIUM

The **Romans** became the dominant power in the region after their defeat of Macedonia in 168 BC, but it took almost two centuries for the empire to subdue the Thracians, who were in constant revolt. It wasn't until about 50 AD that the conquerors were finally able to carve out secure administrative units, creating the province of **Thrace** to the south of the Balkan range and **Moesia** to the north. Using slave labour, the Romans built garrisons, towns, roads and bridges across their domain, and conscripted many Thracians into their legions.

Military strongholds and neighbouring civilian settlements sprang up along the **Danube frontier** (relics of which can today be seen in the museums of Vidin, Pleven and Sofia), while prosperous new towns like **Nicopolis ad Istrum** (near Veliko Târnovo, see p.140) commanded the trade routes inland. Many of the old Greek towns along the coast continued to thrive, and although they now hosted a population of mixed Greek and Thracian descent, Greek language and culture remained dominant throughout the region.

From the third century onwards the empire's contraction and decline was hastened by recurrent invasions of the Danubian provinces by the Goths (238–48), Visigoths (378), Huns (447) and other so-called **barbarians** – civilization in Moesia and Thrace suffered greatly as a result. However the division of the empire into two parts, with **Byzantium** inheriting the mantle of Rome in the east, meant that the authorities in nearby Constantinople could (for a while at least) concentrate their military resources more effectively here.

Both the Danubian frontier and the stronghold of Thrace were reinforced by Emperor **Justinian** in the sixth century, allowing urban life in the region a brief reprieve. Both Philippopolis (Plovdiv) and **Serdica** (Sofia) flourished during his reign. Even under Justinian, however, the **sklaveni** (ancestors of the Balkan Slavs) found a way of breaching the empire's defences, and indulged in big looting trips into Thrace in the 540s. By the seventh century increasing numbers of Avars and **Slavs** were crossing the river with impunity, leaving the Byzantines with little choice but to allow them to settle and employ them as irregular frontier troops.

SLAVS AND BULGARS

The **Slavs** who migrated into the Balkan peninsula from the late fifth century onwards were one of the indigenous races of Europe, the distant forebears of the Russians, Poles, Czechs, Slovaks, Slovenes, Croats and Serbs – and, of course, the Bulgarians. Many of them came in the wake of the Avars, a warlike central Asian people who briefly forged a central European empire in the sixth century and press-ganged the Slavs into their all-conquering armies. However they got here, the Slavs who settled south of the Danube soon began to outnumber any remaining Thracians in the area and established a linguistic and cultural hegemony over the region.

The Slavs were later to fuse with a new wave of migrants, the warlike **Bulgars*****. These mounted nomads, possibly originating deep in central Asia, swept down towards the Balkans after being driven out of "Old Great Bulgaria" – a swathe of territories over which they briefly ruled lying between the Caspian and the Black Sea. They were a Turkic people, ethno-linguistically akin to the Huns, Avars and Khazars. Under pressure from the latter, the Bulgars began a great **migration** into south-eastern Europe, where the largest group (some 250,000 strong) led by **Khan Asparuh** reached the Danube delta around 680 and shortly afterwards entered what would soon become Bulgaria.

THE FIRST KINGDOM

Theophanes the Confessor records that in 681 the Byzantine emperor Constantine IV was forced to recognize the independence of a "new and vulgar people" north of the Balkan range. Asparuh's new **Bulgar Khanate**, subsequently known as the *Pârvo Bâlgarsko Tsarstvo* – the **First Bulgarian Kingdom** – was centred at **Pliska** and ruled over a Danubian state which stretched from the Carpathians in the north to the Balkan range in the south.

---

*Usually, the term "Bulgar" refers exclusively to the Turkish-speaking nomads who came to the Balkans in the seventh century, while the term "Bulgarian" is used to denote the Slav people south of the Danube into which the Bulgars were eventually assimilated. We've observed this convention throughout the book.

Although the Khanate was very much reliant on Slav strength, the Bulgars – whose society was geared to movement and war – definitely provided the impetus for its expansion over the next 150 years.

THE KHANATE – AND THE GROWTH OF CHRISTIANITY

The Khanate's growth was greatest during the reign of **Khan Krum** "the Terrible" (803–14), who collected goblets fashioned from the skulls of foes, and pushed his boundaries as far as the Rila Mountains in the west and the Rhodopes in the south. Finally, having conquered all that he could, **Khan Omurtag** (816–31) signed a 30-year treaty with the Byzantine empire, and in the ensuing peace the Bulgar state was increasingly opened up to Byzantine culture. The most obvious manifestation of this process was the decision of **Khan Boris** (852–89) to adopt Orthodox **Christianity** as the official state religion in 865. The move was a pragmatic one, recognizing that a rapprochement with Byzantium was in the First Kingdom's long-term diplomatic interests, but Boris's son **Simeon** feared that the Orthodox Church could be used as a vehicle for Byzantine interests in Bulgaria: he therefore established a separate **Bulgarian Patriarchate**, thus ensuring the Bulgars full ecclesiastical autonomy.

The **majority Slav population** over which the Bulgars ruled was largely Christianized well before 865, and Boris's decision to adopt the new religion bolstered the growing influence of the Slavs in the Bulgar state. Many Bulgar nobles agitated for a return to **paganism**, and their defeat only served to confirm the gradual eclipse of the Turkic culture of the original Bulgars – although the name of the former ruling class has been perpetuated in the name **Bulgaria**.

LANGUAGE AND THE CYRILLIC ALPHABET

The position of Slavs in the Bulgarian Kingdom was also enhanced by the decision to adopt the **Slav tongue** (rather than Greek) as the official language of the Bulgarian church. The Byzantines themselves were eager to promote this, as they thought that their missionaries, armed with a Slavonic translation of the gospels, would be able to go forth and convert the entire population of central and eastern

Europe. Thessaloniki-based missionaries **Cyril and Methodius** began the job of creating an alphabet suited to the needs of the Slav language, initially opting for a rune-like script subsequently known as Glagolitic. However, the task was completed by their disciples **Kliment** and **Naum**, who named the script (still used in varying forms by the modern Bulgarians, Serbs, Ukranians and Russians) **Cyrillic** in honour of their mentor.

ZENITH AND DECLINE

Armed with the Cyrillic alphabet, Bulgaria became the main centre of **Slavonic culture** in Europe. The "golden age" of literature and arts coincided with the reign of **Tsar Simeon** (893–927), whose defeat of the Byzantine army at Aheloi in 917 allowed the annexation of sizable chunks of Macedonia and Thrace, and the haughty claim to be "Tsar of all the Bulgarians and Byzantines".

But the tsars' perennial exactions and wars bred discontent with the feudal order. Thus arose the **Bogomils** (see p.148), a sect whose "heretical" doctrines amounted to a rejection of church and state, which took fright wherever Bogomilism appeared in the Balkans, and in France and Italy where like-minded movements emerged during the twelfth and thirteenth centuries.

Besides such class conflicts, the reigns of Petâr I (927–69) and Boris II (969–71) were also marked by increasingly violent conflicts between the nobility, or **bolyari**. Byzantium, too, posed a constant threat, and an invasion by Prince Svyatoslav of Kiev gave the Byzantines the pretext they needed to launch a full-scale onslaught. Bulgaria was reduced to a rump, known as the **Western Kingdom**, governed from Ohrid in Macedonia. **Tsar Samuel** was partly successful in restoring the old kingdom until the Byzantine emperor Basil Bulgaroctonos – the **"Bulgar-Slayer"** – defeated his army at Strumitsa in 1014 and blinded the 14,000 prisoners taken. Samuel died of horror after seeing the maimed horde fumbling its way into Ohrid.

Following Ohrid's capture in 1018 the whole of Bulgaria fell under **Byzantine domination**. As a result, the Orthodox Church was largely Hellenized, and Bulgarian architecture and art were increasingly influenced by Byzantine styles. The authorities in Constantinople visited savage repression upon heretics like the Bogomils, and retaliated violently to various eleventh-century rebellions. However their power didn't extend to protecting the local populace against marauding **Magyars** and **Pechenegs**, who plundered south of the Danube in the eleventh and twelfth centuries.

THE SECOND KINGDOM

In 1185 the *bolyari* Petâr and Asen led a successful popular uprising against Byzantium, proclaiming the **Second Kingdom** in Veliko Târnovo, henceforth its capital. Byzantine forces under Emperor Isaac Angelus confidently expected to be able to crush the rebel state at birth, but after two attempts in 1187 and 1190, were finally forced to accept Bulgarian independence. Asen's brother and successor **Tsar Kaloyan** (1197–1207) extended Bulgaria's borders further, recapturing Varna and parts of Macedonia and Thrace from Byzantium. However it was the **fall of Constantinople** to the **Crusaders** in 1204 that gave the Second Kingdom the chance it needed to consolidate and grow. Exiled Byzantine aristocrats, having established statelets in Epirus and Nicaea, proceeded to make war on both each other and the Crusaders' self-styled **Latin Empire of the East**. Tsar Kaloyan sought to exploit this fragmentation of Byzantine power in the Balkans, dreaming of one day setting up a Slav-Greek empire of his own.

The Bulgarians initially put out peace feelers towards the new Latin rulers of Constantinople, but were from the start distrusted by the latter because of their adherence to the Orthodox faith. Bulgaria inflicted a stunning defeat on the Latins in 1205, capturing Emperor Baldwin and holding him prisoner in Târnovo (see p.140). However Kaloyan died before he could take advantage of this success, and a period of anarchy ensued under Tsar Boril before **Ivan Asen II** (1218–41) could restore order and continue the expansion of Bulgaria's frontiers. His victory over Theodore Comnenus of Epirus at **Klokotnitsa** in 1230 won him territories from the Adriatic to the Aegean, and ushered in an era of prestige and prosperity which marks the zenith of medieval Bulgaria's development.

THE MONGOLS

This period of plenty was cut short by a completely unexpected disaster. After 1240 **Mongol hordes**, fresh from their campaigns in central Europe, withdrew through Serbia and Bulgaria, desolating the countryside. The ensuing chaos provided the Byzantines with an opportunity to win back some of the ground they had lost in the plain of Thrace.

One batch of Mongols – subsequently known as the **Tatars** – settled in southern Russia and the Crimea, from whence they mounted continuous raids on the lands bordering on the Black Sea. The presence of this powerful and unpredictable warrior-state on its northeastern borders considerably weakened Bulgaria's freedom of manoeuvre – perpetually threatened by enemies on both sides, the Second Kingdom increasingly had to compromise with its neighbours in order to avoid their wrath.

THE LATE THIRTEENTH CENTURY

The latter half of the thirteenth century saw a return to internecine feuding and punitive taxation, producing a **peasant rebellion** which led to the crowning of **Ivailo the Swineherd**, whose brief reign (1277–80) was largely devoted to fighting off the Tatars. Dethroned by the nobility, Ivailo was replaced by the first of the **Terterids**, a dynasty whose only remarkable tsar, Todor Svetoslav (1300–21), succeeded in making peace with the Tatar khans. By threatening to secede from the kingdom, the feudal ruler of Vidin, **Mihail Shishman**, managed to have himself crowned tsar in 1323, inaugurating the new **Shishmanid dynasty**. However, Mihail was fatally wounded at the battle of Velbâzhd (modern Kyustendil) in 1330, when the Bulgarian army was smashed by that of **Serbia** – by now the ascendant power in the Balkans.

IVAN ALEKSANDAR – AND THE TURKISH VICTORY

During the reign of Mihail's successor, **Ivan Aleksandâr** (1331–71), Bulgaria almost regained the prosperity and level of civilization attained during Asen II's time, with literature, sculpture and painting displaying a harmonious fusion of Bulgar and Byzantine styles. However, the rest of the fourteenth century was a confused story of disintegration and decline. Over-powerful *bolyari* asserted their autonomy

from Tsar **Ivan Shishman** (1371–96), weakening the central authority of the kingdom just when it was needed to organize resistance to a new threat: the **Ottoman Turks**.

Possessing a disciplined war machine and superior numbers, the Turks proved unstoppable; mutual distrust between Balkan and Byzantine rulers prevented any meaningful concerted action against the invaders, and the defeat of a powerful Serbian army at **Kosovo** in 1389 effectively sealed the fate of the whole Balkan peninsula. Most of Bulgaria had been overrun by 1393 and the anti-Turkish **crusades** of 1394 and 1444 failed to reverse the situation. With the fall of Constantinople, last bastion of the Balkan Orthodox world, in 1453, any remaining hope of outside help against the Turks disappeared for good.

"UNDER THE YOKE"

It's estimated that almost half of Bulgaria's population was massacred or enslaved and transported to another part of the empire within a few years of the Turkish conquest, whose long-term effects were equally profound. The **Ottoman empire** not only isolated Bulgaria from the European Renaissance, but imposed and maintained a harsher system of **feudalism** than had previously existed. Muslim colonists occupied the most fertile land and prosperous towns, while the surviving Bulgars – mainly peasants – became serfs of the Turkish *Spahis* (land-holding knights), who gouged them for their own profit and for numerous state taxes. In northern Bulgaria and the Rhodopes some Bulgars succumbed to forced **Islamicization** and, as converts (*pomaks*), gained rights denied to the Christian *Rayah* or "Herd", notably exemption from the hated **blood tax** or *devshirme*, whereby the oldest boys were taken from their families and indoctrinated before joining the élite Ottoman janissary corps.

The Turks looted monasteries and subordinated the native **Orthodox Church** to the Patriarchate of Constantinople, which imposed Greek bishops and ignorant, grasping clergy on the faithful. Worst of all was the perpetual insecurity, for Bulgars were raped and robbed by Turkish troops or "visiting" dignitaries, cheated by tax collectors and Greek merchants, and had no way of getting **justice** through the Ottoman courts

After the failure of several popular **rebellions** (in 1402–03, 1598, 1686 and 1688), for which the Turks took brutal reprisals, many Bulgars became **haiduks**, or outlaws. Banditry often coincided with, or matured into, a concern for social justice; haiduks who robbed landowners or killed rapacious soldiers could usually count on being secretly helped by the local peasants, whose **ballads** preserved the folk memory of resistance.

Meanwhile, spiritual and artistic values predating the conquest were nurtured in the monasteries, which restored contact with **Russia** after the sixteenth century. Having rid itself of Tatar domination, re-enshrined Orthodoxy, and started to expel the Turks from Caucasia, Russia came to be viewed as the great hope of the subject Christians of the Balkans.

THE NATIONAL REVIVAL

The role of Bulgaria's monasteries in preserving ancient traditions ensured that memories of the medieval empire never died out altogether. Interest in Bulgaria's past began to express itself with the publication (outside Ottoman territory) of a *History of Bulgaria* written by Peter Bogdan Bakshev, seventeenth-century catholic Bishop of Sofia, and a *History of the Serbs and the Bulgarians* written by Hristofor Zhefarovich a century later. However neither of these had the impact of **Paisii of Hilendar**'s *Slav-Bulgarian History*, written in 1762. Circulated in manuscript form (because the Greeks who controlled the church wouldn't countenance the printing of Bulgarian-language texts), Paisii's work inspired a generation of nationalists, and became the spiritual cornerstone of the Bulgarian renaissance, the **National Revival**.

The material base for such an upsurge in national feeling was provided by the economic changes of the nineteenth century. Bulgaria was increasingly supplying the Ottoman empire with wool, cloth and foodstuffs, giving rise to a prosperous **mercantile and artisan class** based in the towns and villages of both the Balkan Mountains and the Sredna Gora. Economic development speeded up after the Crimean War, when Turkey's French and British allies demanded that the Ottoman empire should be opened up to western European trade.

Bulgaria's cultural reawakening expressed itself in protests against the **Greek church**, which controlled all ecclesiastical affairs in the country and ran most of the schools as well. The Greeks opposed Bulgarian efforts to establish churches and schools of their own, and **riots**, in which the local Greek priest was chased out of town, were a popular feature of mid-nineteenth-century life.

Community leaders had to bargain hard with the Ottoman authorities in order to gain concessions on the issue of Bulgarian-language schooling, but by the 1840s Bulgarian **education** was beginning to take off. The growing middle class endowed schools offering a modern, secular education; in addition, there were *chitalishta* or "reading rooms" – cultural centres that offered courses for adults. Both helped to make the Bulgarian peasantry among the most literate in Europe. The campaign for church autonomy was rewarded in 1870, when a decree from the Sultan permitted the foundation of the **Bulgarian Exarchate** – a stunning success which emboldened the Bulgarians to extend their struggle further into the political sphere.

Whereas their elders had sought reforms, "second generation" nationalists increasingly pursued Bulgarian independence through armed struggle, and émigrés in the Serbian capital Belgrade, led by **G.S. Rakovski**, began organizing a **Bulgarian Legion** in 1861. Its members fought alongside Serbia in its wars with the Ottoman empire, while other Bulgarian exiles formed *cheti* or armed groups which raided Turkish-controlled territory from sanctuaries in Serbia and Wallachia.

THE REVOLUTIONARY UNDERGROUND

The *cheti* received little support from the Bulgarian peasantry, however, and their unpopularity convinced **Vasil Levski** and the Bucharest-based **Bulgarian Revolutionary Central Committee (BRCK)** that a mass uprising could only be inspired by an indigenous **revolutionary underground**, which they set about creating. Levski himself led the way, travelling the length and breadth of the country in order to establish clandestine revolutionary cells: Levski and the other agents charged with setting up the BRCK network were henceforth known as the **apostles** due to the almost evangelical nature of their work. Levski himself was captured and executed in 1873, a setback which neverthelss provided the liberation struggle with its first great martyr, inspiring idealistic and patriotic youngsters everywhere to rally to the cause.

THE APRIL RISING

Culmination of the BRCK's organizational efforts was the **April Rising of 1876**, which after exhaustive (but, as it turned out, insufficient) preparation was launched in the Balkan Mountains and the Sredna Gora – an heroic attempt answered by savage Ottoman reprisals, which took an estimated 29,000 Bulgarian lives.

THE "EASTERN QUESTION"

Despite these valiant efforts, the fate of Bulgaria didn't really rest with the Bulgarians themselves. The gradual stagnation of Ottoman power in Europe had raised the problem – dubbed the **"Eastern Question"** by contemporary politicians and journalists – of who would profit from the empire's demise. The main contenders in the area were Austria-Hungary and tsarist Russia, the latter nursing a longstanding ambition to extend its influence as far south as Constantinople and thereby gain control of the Bosporus. Both the French and the British were horrified by the prospect, and tended to support Turkey in order to frustrate Russian expansion. In the cynical environment of Great Power diplomacy, the aspirations of the nationalities languishing under Ottoman rule counted for little.

The Russians exploited the ideology of **Pan-Slavism** – the belief that Slav peoples everywhere should be freed from foreign domination and united under the authoritarian guidance of the Russians – in order to stir up anti-Ottoman sentiment in the Balkans and exert control over the liberation movements thus produced. It was therefore taken for granted by Russia's opponents that any future Bulgarian state would merely be a vehicle for the Balkan ambitions of its big Slav brother. However, the Western powers found it difficult to give the Turks their unqualified support: public opinion in the West was often deeply sympathetic to the demands of the Ottoman empire's Christian subjects – of which Russia fancied itself to be the protector.

Russian troops had temporarily expelled the Ottomans from parts of Bulgaria during the 1810–11 and 1828–29 **Russo-Turkish wars**, but were consistently unwilling to provoke the Western powers by pressing their advantage in the region too far. Britain and France had even laid siege to Russia's Black Sea ports in the **Crimean War** of 1854–56 in order to demonstrate their support for the Ottoman empire – which they hoped would survive in its present form if only they could persuade it to introduce "reforms".

THE CONSTANTINOPLE CONFERENCE

In 1876, however, the **massacres** which followed the April Rising sent a wave of revulsion throughout Europe, and the Russian army prepared to teach the Turks a lesson. The British and French, faced by an angry public enraged by tales of **Bulgarian atrocities**, were no longer in a position to back up the Turks. The British tried to diffuse the situation by bringing the Turks to the negotiating table, but after assenting to the **Constantinople Conference** in November 1876, the Ottoman government rejected its draft proposals for an autonomous Bulgarian province.

The Russians were initially cautious about embarking on a war with Turkey because they feared an armed response from Austria. By the time the Constantinople Conference broke up, however, the Russians had reached a secret agreement with the Austrians; promising them Russian support for their claim to Bosnia-Hercegovina if they remained neutral in any Russo-Turkish conflict. Free to act, the Russian tsar Alexander II (subsequently known to Bulgarians as **Tsar Osvoboditel** – the "Tsar-Liberator") declared war on Turkey in April 1877.

THE WAR OF LIBERATION

Romanians and Bulgarian volunteers fought alongside the Russians in the 1877–78 **War of Liberation**, which would have been a total rout had the Turks not fought belated rearguard actions at the siege of Plevna (modern-day Pleven) and the battle of the Shipka pass.

The defeated Turks signed the **Treaty of San Stefano** in March 1878, recognizing an independent Bulgaria incorporating much of Macedonia and Thrace. This so-called "**Big**

Bulgaria" was too much for the Western powers to swallow, and was promptly broken up by the speedily summoned **Congress of Berlin** (July 1878). The outcome of the Congress reflected the desire of British Prime Minister Benjamin Disraeli to "keep the Russians out of Turkey, not to create an ideal existence for Turkish Christians". Macedonia and southern Thrace were returned to the Turks, and the rest of Bulgaria was split into two chunks: land south of the Balkan Mountains became **Eastern Roumelia**, an autonomous province of the Ottoman empire; while land to the north became an independent **Principality of Bulgaria** owing nominal suzerainty to the Turks and paying annual tribute to the sultan.

FROM INDEPENDENCE TO WORLD WAR I

In the immediate post-Liberation years, attempts to build a stable **democracy** were hampered by continuing Great Power interest in Balkan affairs. Particularly damaging was the tension between pro- and anti-Russian elements within the country, the latter all too often regarding Bulgaria as a mere instrument of tsarist policy.

Russian advisers hoped to help the country to its feet by drafting an autocratic constitution, but this was rejected by the Constituent Assembly which met at Târnovo in 1879. Dominated by the Liberal Party (in which many leading lights of the liberation struggle were gathered), the Assembly drew up the so-called **Târnovo Constitution**, which envisaged a single chamber parliament elected by universal male suffrage. This went down badly with Bulgaria's newly chosen prince, the autocratically minded Aleksandâr Battenberg – a German aristocrat who had served with the Russian army during the Liberation War. Encouraged by the accession of reactionary monarch Alexander III to the Russian throne in 1881, Prince Alexander suspended the constitution and convened a special assembly in the Danubian town of Svishtov – which he blackmailed into voting him emergency powers by threatening to abdicate if they refused. However, even Alexander's Russian backers became alarmed at the Prince's subsequent drop in popularity, forcing him to accept a return to democratic government in 1883.

UNIFICATION – AND THE SERBO-BULGARIAN WAR

Many of the Liberal politicians who fled Alexander's so-called **personal regime** ended up in Eastern Roumelia, which since 1878 had been ruled by local governor-generals eager to advance the Bulgarian cause in the region, despite its continuing status as a province of the Ottoman empire. Growing popular agitation for **unification with Bulgaria** culminated in an uprising within Eastern Roumelia and the declaration of union in September 1885; a *fait accompli* which Turkey accepted after much sabre-rattling.

Serbia, offended that changes of Balkan borders could be made without its permission, and afraid that Bulgarian unification could be followed by territorial gains elsewhere, launched a punitive attack on Bulgaria – in the ensuing **Serbo-Bulgarian war of 1885** a ramshackle Bulgarian army scored an heroic victory at Slivnitsa.

INTERNATIONAL INTRIGUE

More serious, however, was the displeasure expressed by Russia at Bulgaria's failure to consult its big Slav cousin on the issue of unification. In a complete **turn-around of international attitudes**, Bulgarian expansion was now opposed by the Russians, because they were constrained by an agreement with Germany and Austria promising to preserve the status quo in the Balkans. The British, slowly becoming aware that Bulgaria wasn't necessarily the subservient Russian creature they had feared it to be, responded to Bulgarian unification with glee. It didn't take long before Bulgaria's internal politics were thrown into confusion by these international intrigues. Pro-Russian officers deposed Prince Aleksandâr and spirited him out of the country in 1886, before themselves falling victim to a counter-coup organized by leading Liberal politician **Stefan Stambolov**. Stambolov secured Aleksandâr's return, but increased Russian threats persuaded the Prince that it would be best for all concerned if he abdicated for good. Acting as the head of a **Council of Regents**, Stambolov attempted to sever the Russian connection entirely by realigning Bulgaria's foreign policy with Austria and Germany, and inviting the Habsburgs' favourite

German toff **Ferdinand of Saxe-Coburg Gotha** to become the new monarch.

Stambolov, however, had to initiate a repressive regime in order to get these changes accepted by the country, and his **dictatorship** lasted until he was ditched by former protegé Ferdinand in 1894. Ferdinand sought a rapprochement with Russia, and set about creating a more **absolutist monarchy** which relied on state terrorism to achieve its aims: Stambolov, killed by Ferdinand's assassins in 1895, was merely the first of its many victims.

THE BALKAN WARS

By the turn of the century, growing turmoil in the Ottoman empire left the Great Powers of Europe increasingly unable to control events in the region – however desperate they were to do so – giving the small states of the Balkans more room for independent action. Ferdinand exploited the chaos created by the **Young Turk** revolution in July 1908 to declare Bulgaria's full independence from Ottoman suzerainty, crowning himself **king** in the same year. Political crisis in the Ottoman lands meant that the future of **Macedonia and southern Thrace** was once more back on the agenda, and Bulgaria and its neighbours began discussing ways of driving the Turks from the area for good.

The **First Balkan War** of 1912 gave Bulgaria the chance it had been waiting for to try and reclaim some of the territories taken away by the Congress of Berlin. In alliance with Serbia and Greece, Bulgaria launched an attack on Turkey, coming within a whisker of capturing Istanbul. Bulgarian troops also occupied the Pirin region of eastern Macedonia, but found that the Serbs and the Greeks had beaten them to the rest. Unable to agree on an equitable division of the spoils, the former allies fell out, Greece and Serbia defeating Bulgaria in the **Second Balkan War** of 1913.

Bulgaria was forced to renounce claims on the bulk of Macedonia and surrender the southern Dobrudzha to Romania, but still managed to finish the Balkan Wars with a positive balance. Allowed to keep the Pirin, it also obtained Thracian lands in the south, including access to the Aegean Sea at the port of Dedeagach (now the Greek town of Alexandroupolis).

WORLD WAR I

Following the outbreak of **World War I**, much of Bulgarian opinion sided with the Entente Powers of Britain, France and Russia, largely due to ties of Slavic kinship with the Russians and a common dislike of the Turks. However, the Entente's commitments to Bulgaria's major Balkan rival, Serbia, dissuaded Bulgaria from joining the alliance. Instead, German promises to restore **Macedonia** persuaded King Ferdinand and Prime Minister Radoslavov to enter the war on the side of the Central Powers.

Hoping to gain large amounts of territory at very little human cost, Bulgaria waited until September 1915 before joining the action, with Radoslavov confidently boasting to his compatriots that it would all be over by Christmas. Three years of agony ensued: anti-war politicians like the Agrarian leader, Stamboliiski, were gaoled; and countless thousands of Bulgarians were dispatched to die in the trenches and mountains of Macedonia.

1918–1944

With the country bled white, Bulgaria's army collapsed beneath the Allied offensive along the Salonika front in September 1918. Deserting soldiers hoisted red flags and converged on Sofia, soon to proclaim the **"Radomir Republic"**, while the cabinet declared an **armistice** and released **Aleksandâr Stamboliiski**, hoping to avert a revolution. Though the mutineers were swiftly crushed, Ferdinand was forced to abdicate in favour of his son, **Boris III**, leaving Stamboliiski's **Bulgarian Agrarian National Union** or **BZNS** the most powerful force in the country.

The Agrarians emerged as the largest party in the 1919 election – the general desire for radical change was reflected in the fact that the Communists came second – and Stamboliiski became prime minister of a country whose wartime allegiance the Allies punished by the **Treaty of Neuilly** (1919). Under its terms, Bulgaria was bound to pay crippling war reparations, Romania reoccupied the southern Dobrudzha, Serbia claimed most of Macedonia, while southwestern Thrace – and with it, access to the Aegean – went to Greece.

Unlike previous governments the **Agrarians** favoured the countryside rather than the towns, exalting "peasant power" to the dismay of Bulgaria's traditional elite. The bourgeoisie became alarmed by Stamboliiski's dictatorial radicalism, and nationalists everywhere were outraged by his attempts to build peaceful relations with neighbouring Yugoslavia – a policy which entailed renouncing Bulgarian claims on Macedonia. Bulgaria had been flooded with Macedonian refugees since the end of the war, many of whom owed their allegiance to the **Internal Macedonian Revolutionary Organization**, or **IMRO** – a group committed to effecting the unification of Macedonia and Bulgaria and therefore implacably opposed to Stamboliiski's new direction in foreign policy.

THE IMRO COUP

In June 1923, IMRO gunmen joined right-wing military officers in staging a bloody **coup d'état** against the Agrarians, assassinating Stamboliiski in the process. The reactionary "**Democratic Concord**" coalition under Aleksandâr Tsankov assumed power, which it monopolized until 1931. Having stood aloof in June, the **Communists** staged an **uprising** in September 1923, provoking the army and police to savage repression and anti-Communist terror. The Communist Party was banned, and many of its leaders who fled to the Soviet Union later perished during the Stalinist *Ezhovshchina*, or Great Purge.

THE 1930s

The Thirties were a time of stagnation and political unrest, epitomized by the murderous feuds within the IMRO. The June 1931 election brought to power a left-of-centre coalition, the "People's Bloc", but faced by the constraints of the **Great Depression**, the new government was unable to carry out its radical social programme. Economic slump provoked an increase in political extremism, which mirrored the growth of authoritarianism elsewhere in Europe. The Communists re-emerged in the shape of a front organization, the **Bulgarian Workers' Party**, banned by the government in 1932; while Aleksandâr Tsankov made up for the demise of the Democratic Concord by forming the Hitler-inspired **National Socialist Movement**.

Disintegration of the body politic encouraged the **Military League** to assume power in May 1934 in a coup inspired by the ideas of **Zveno** ("Link"), another elitist organization whose programme included the customary hotch-potch of militant left- and right-wing ideologies. Parliament was dissolved, all parties were abolished and the IMRO was brought to heel: Bulgaria was "depoliticized". But in government the League proved as faction-ridden and ineffectual as its civilian predecessors, and after November 1935 **King Boris III** established his own **dictatorship**, periodically erecting a parliamentary facade.

WORLD WAR II

Nazi Germany's economic penetration of the Balkans during the late 1930s provided the Third Reich with considerable influence over Bulgaria and its neighbours, and despite the country's declaration of neutrality on the outbreak of **World War II**, Bulgaria inexorably succumbed to the Reich, which required it as a "land bridge" across which German troops could cross in order to mount the invasion of Greece. In return for Hitler's offer of Macedonia, Boris committed Bulgaria to the Axis in March 1941, although he baulked at declaring war on the Soviet Union due to Bulgaria's traditionally good relations with the Russian people (it was long believed that Boris's death, following a visit to Berlin, was the result of Nazi poisoning, although a team of pathologists examining the Tsar's heart in 1991 finally put an end to these rumours).

Many Bulgarian Communists exiled in Moscow returned home to foment resistance, but Bulgaria's wartime **partisan movement** was a relatively small affair. However, the Communists did manage to infiltrate and manipulate other opposition groups, combining them into the **Fatherland Front** (*Ochestven Front*) in 1942. Events moved towards a climax with the Red Army's advance and Romania's escape from the Axis in August 1944. On September 8 the USSR declared war and crossed the Danube; that night, junior officers acting with the connivance of the Minister of Defence, Gregoriev, seized strategic points in Sofia, while partisan brigades swept down from the hills. This virtually bloodless putsch was repeated across Bulgaria the next day, making September 9 **Liberation Day**.

THE PEOPLE'S REPUBLIC

After September 9, the Bulgarian Communist Party emerged from two decades of clandestine existence to become the leading political force in the country. Initially their radicalism was hidden behind the ostensibly moderate **Fatherland Front government** fronted by Gregoriev. Within six months, however, the **Communists** had passed a law expropriating foreign capital and increased their membership from 15,000 to 250,000; obviously the party with a future, they welcomed all comers while manipulating the Ministries of Justice and the Interior to cow right-wing collaborators, and drove the left and centre parties into opposition by repeated provocations. Dominant in government, they then staged a referendum on the **monarchy**, abolished it, and proclaimed the **People's Republic** on September 15, 1946.

Now controlled by **Georgi Dimitrov**, **Vasil Kolarov** and **Anton Yugov**, the state apparatus was turned against the opposition. Many of the political parties left outside the Communist-controlled Fatherland Front had boycotted Bulgaria's first postwar elections in 1945, convinced that the presence of the Red Army on Bulgarian soil would intimidate voters into backing the Front.

A more organized campaign was mounted for the general elections of October 1946, producing a parliament which included a small but vociferous number of anti-Communist MPs. The opposition centred around the Agrarian party or BZNS, heir to the popular radical tradition of Stamboliiski, and leaders of peasant resistance to enforced collectivization of the countryside. The Communists claimed that they were traitors sabotaging the economic recovery of the nation: hundreds of BZNS party workers were purged and their leader, **Nikola Petkov**, was hanged for "treason" after a show trial in 1947. Other parties outside the Front were snuffed out at the same time. The same year, Bulgaria acquired the new "Dimitrov" **Constitution** (modelled on the USSR's) and the **nationalization** of 2273 enterprises struck the "bourgeoisie" a mortal blow.

The following year saw a power struggle within the Party, largely over **economic links with the Soviet Union** and **relations with Tito's Yugoslavia**. The Tito-Stalin row of 1948 and Yugoslavia's subsequent expulsion from the Soviet camp gave communist leaders everywhere the chance they needed to get rid of comrades who they found troublesome. Moscow-trained cadres targeted "homegrown" Communists, i.e. those who had chosen to remain in the country during the inter-war years rather than flee to the USSR, in an attempt to settle old scores.

Some of the more patriotic Bulgarian Communists criticized the terms of Bulgaro-Soviet trade (80 percent of Bulgaria's tobacco crop was purchased at below market prices and then undersold abroad), leaving themselves open to accusations of nationalism at a time when blind loyalty to the Soviet Union was the order of the day – as good a reason as any to launch a purge of "Titoists". Ten ministers, six Politburo members (including **Traicho Kostov**, shot after renouncing his "confession" to having been a fascist spy since 1942) and 92,500 lesser Party members were arrested or dismissed in the purge of 1948–49, while the nation was paralyzed by **police terror**. Stalinism pervaded Bulgaria, and for his total sycophancy the Party leader who succeeded Dimitrov, **Vâlko Chervenkov**, was dubbed "little Stalin".

THE ERA OF "SOCIALIST CONSTRUCTION"

With opposition both outside and inside the Party effectively crushed, the government could embark on the transformation of Bulgaria into a modern industrial state. Average Bulgarians, however, gained little from the first **Five-Year Plan**, though this gave a great boost to heavy industrial production (up 120 percent from 1949–55). While factories mushroomed, workers were expected to meet ever-rising production targets, and consumer goods and foodstuffs grew increasingly scarce. Agricultural production remained at roughly its 1939 level, despite an increase in the population and Bulgaria's acquisition of the grain-producing southern Dobrudzha. Unlike elsewhere in eastern Europe, there were few large estates to be expropriated – on the contrary, economists bemoaned the mass of smallholdings and the individualism of their owners.

Following the **death of Stalin** (1953), Moscow gradually withdrew support from hardliners in the satellite states, and advocates of less spartan policies replaced them. In Bulgaria, Chervenkov lost the position of Party

Secretary (1954) and Prime Minister (1956) to **Todor Zhivkov** and Anton Yugov. The separation of these offices reflected the Kremlin's new policy of "collective" leadership, and Bulgaria's dutiful purge of "Anti-Party" elements in 1957 followed their example by avoiding bloodshed. China, however, seems to have inspired Zhivkov's sudden announcement of the "**Big Leap Forward**" in October 1958, whereby the economy aimed to fufill the Five-Year Plan in three years, and smallholdings were pooled into 3290 **collective farms**. Industrial dislocation was considerable but the effect on agriculture was mitigated by the private plots which peasants were allowed to retain (unlike in China, where famine followed Mao's Great Leap Forward).

THE ZHIVKOV ERA

For much of the **Zhivkov era**, Bulgarian conformity to Soviet wishes became a cliché of east European politics, with the country jokingly referred to – even by Bulgarians themselves – as the sixteenth republic of the USSR. However, this pliability did have its advantages: Bulgaria obtained cut-price Soviet oil, electricity and raw materials, and was relieved of the duty of hosting significant Soviet garrisons.

With access to education and employment consistently denied to people who failed to conform, most Bulgarians had no choice but to grudgingly accept rigid party control of public life, although this passivity was made easier to bear by the Communist system's achievements in the social sphere. Given adequate food, guaranteed work, schooling and medical care, and the prospect of a flat in the future, people were generally prepared to tolerate low wages, shortages of consumer goods and the lack of many liberal freedoms.

The West's image of Bulgaria under Zhivkov was almost wholly negative, coloured by the country's slavish adherence to Soviet foreign policy, and the fearsome reputation of the *Dârhavna Sigurnost* or *DS*, the state security police. The assassination of dissident writer **Georgi Markov**, who was killed after being stabbed by a poison-tipped umbrella on a London street in 1978, gave the Bulgarian security services a reputation for subterfuge and cruelty. Subsequent allegations that the DS had abetted a **plot to kill the Pope** in 1981 suggested that Bulgaria did the kind of dirty work with which not even the KGB would wish to soil its hands.

However, it was the Party's manipulation of **nationalism** which seemed in Western eyes to be the most distasteful aspect of the regime. On the surface, attempts by the Party to present socialist Bulgaria as a homogeneous national state, the logical culmination of centuries of struggles for freedom, seemed to start off innocently enough. Vast amounts of money were spent on the monuments and festivities celebrating the **1300th anniversary of the founding of the Bulgarian state** in 1983, and resources were channelled into the restoration of historical monuments associated with Bulgaria's past greatness.

However there wasn't much room in Zhivkov's Bulgaria for people of different ethnic origin. Ever since the 1950s smaller minorities like Vlachs (see p.113) and Islamicized Gypsies had been encouraged to drop their traditional names and adopt Bulgarian ones. The campaign moved on to the **pomaks** (Muslim Bulgarians) in the 1970s, and to the million-strong **Turkish minority** in the 1980s. Those who refused to Bulgaricize their names were refused work, housing, or worse still, sent to concentration camps like Belene and Lovech. Opposition to the **name-changing campaign** sparked violence in 1984, and led to a mass exodus of Bulgarian Turks in summer 1989, provoking outrage from human rights groups across the world. All this led to a further deterioration of relations between Bulgaria and the outside world – even Bulgaria's socialist allies were increasingly embarrassed to be associated with it.

THE DEMISE OF THE COMMUNIST REGIME

Bulgaria's socialist economy was beginning to stall well before the emergence of **perestroika** in the Soviet Union began to raise fundamental questions about the continuing viability of the whole system. Summer droughts in 1984 and 1985 had harmed agriculture and reduced hydroelectric power (which usually accounts for much of Bulgaria's needs) at a time when Soviet oil supplies were cut back, causing widespread energy shortages. Prices skyrocketed with hardly any corresponding wage increases, and for the first time in many years a note of testiness entered Bulgaro-Soviet relations.

As Gorbachev increasingly toyed with the idea of wide-reaching democratic reform in the USSR, the hard-line leaders of his Soviet bloc allies became more and more of an embarrassment. Zhivkov was particularly unpopular with the new Soviet leadership, not least because they found his anti-Turkish policies repugnant. Aware of this, high-ranking Bulgarian officials began jostling for position in preparation for the day when they could (perhaps with Gorbachev's backing) oust their aging leader. However, they had to wait until the end of the decade for their opportunity to do so, by which time they were almost as discredited as he was.

THE JULY CONCEPTIONS

The Bulgarian Communist Party's initial reaction to Gorbachev's innovations was predictably cautious, and it wasn't until July 1987 that Zhivkov announced the **July Conceptions**, an attempt to give the Party a patina of perestroika-esque credibility. Although it promised decentralization of state-run businesses and democratization of party structures, it was difficult to find examples of these fine-sounding commitments ever being carried out. A Party Conference in January 1988 was almost euphoric in its support of dynamic change, but senior figures like Zhivkov and chief ideologist Yordan Yotov emphasized that changes had to be introduced "slowly and carefully".

By January 1988 Bulgarians were being allowed to form private firms providing that they employed no more than ten people, and the government increasingly advocated a departure from rigid state planning and a tentative move towards **market economics**. Enthusiasm for political change continued to be lukewarm, however, and for some while Bulgarians moved in a strange political limbo, where talk of glasnost and perestroika was officially sanctioned, but any practical application of them merely invited the usual hassles from the security police.

PROTEST

Ecological protesters from the city of **Ruse** were the first independent citizens to organize themselves into pressure groups outside Party control in spring 1988. Encouraged by their example, intellectuals in Sofia formed the **Club for the Support of Glasnost and Perestroika** in November of the same year, an organization which united both dissidents and moderate Party members, but the Club's supporters were subjected to petty harassment, denied meeting space and forbidden even to use photocopiers.

The Communist Party itself was split between those around Zhivkov who favoured caution, and those eager to rush ahead with political change. Zhivkov was obviously worried about the events his July Conceptions had set in motion, and rounded on his opponents at a Party **Plenum** in **July 1988**. Among the Central Committee members who lost their posts were his heir-apparent Chudomir Aleksandrov, whose demise was attributed to his wife's involvement in the ecology movement; and Svetlin Rusev (head of the Artists' Union), a prominent member of the Club for the Support of Glasnost and Perestroika.

The regime's determination to remain in control of Bulgarian society was further demonstrated in January 1989, when on the eve of a visit to Sofia by President Mitterand, members of the **Independent Association for the Defence of Human Rights** were placed under house arrest. Throughout 1989 opposition organizations like **Podkrepa**, the new independent trade union federation formed in February 1989, and **Ecoglasnost**, a green pressure group (which did much to unite disparate strands of the opposition around a cause which they could all share), were allowed to operate after a fashion, but their members never knew from one day to the next what the precise limits to their political freedom were.

One government-inspired anti-dissident campaign chose to make an example of Podkrepa's leader **Konstantin Trenchev**, who was slung in gaol and charged with anti-state activities in May. As the year progressed Zhivkov attempted to win support by stoking up nationalist fervour, with renewed repression of Bulgaria's Turks. The resulting **mass exodus** of Bulgarian Muslims into neighbouring Turkey merely served to convince many in the country that the Communist regime had finally lost all legitimacy to rule.

THE FALL OF ZHIVKOV

In October 1989 Sofia's police were still beating up members of Ecoglasnost with impunity on the capital's streets, but in the end the forces of conservatism were overtaken by events. On **November 10 1989** (the day after the Berlin Wall came down) reformers within the Party seized their chance and called a meeting of the Central Committee, which forced Zhivkov's resignation. The former dictator was arrested on charges of inciting racial hatred and, soon afterwards, embezzling state funds, and new Party leader **Petâr Mladenov** promised free elections, market reforms, and an end to the corruption and gangsterism of the past. Opposition leaders took advantage of the new atmosphere to form the **SDS** or *Sâyuz na demokratichnite sili* (Union of Democratic Forces) on December 7, an impressive assemblage of dissidents, greens and human rights activists which non-Communist Bulgarians everywhere pressed forward to join.

POST-COMMUNIST BULGARIA: A SLOW START

The reformist wing of the Bulgarian Communist Party had obviously thought that by ditching Zhivkov and committing themselves to the idea of a multi-party system, they stood a good chance of being perceived as the authors of democratic change, thereby winning back the trust of the populace. Initially, however, their strategy ran into trouble. Throughout December of 1989 the Bulgarian parliament was regularly under siege from protesters demanding a speeding up of democratic reforms, most notably the abandonment of the Communist Party's **leading role** in society, hitherto enshrined in the constitution. The Party was also under pressure from its own hardliners, who tried to sabotage democratization by organizing **nationalist demonstrations and strikes** throughout the country in protest at the government's retreat from Todor Zhivkov's anti-Turkish policies.

In 1990 the dismantling of Communist power structures began in earnest. Separation of party and state was symbolized when Petâr Mladenov became state president and relinquished the Party chairmanship to **Aleksandâr Lilov**, previously the victim of one of Zhivkov's purges. Former hardliners were removed from government, Mladenov's protegé **Andrei Lukanov** became prime minister, and the Party itself changed its name to the **Bulgarian Socialist Party (BSP)**.

Multi-party elections were called for **June 1990**, too early for either the BSP or the opposition SDS to establish themselves as credible democratic movements. The BSP despite verbal commitments to democratic socialism, still included far too many dyed-in-the-wool Communists for people to take its new identity seriously; while the SDS, a loose coalition of newly-formed parties and citizens' pressure groups, could agree on little save for a hatred of Communism and a desire to speed up market reforms.

Public uncertainty over the economic changes proposed by the SDS played into the hands of the BSP, which garnered 45 percent of the vote and an absolute majority in the *Veliko Narodno Sâbranie* or **Constituent Assembly**. Much of this success was attributed to the conservative nature of the Bulgarian countryside, where the Socialist Party machine was much more effective in reaching potential voters than its cash-starved opponents. The other main beneficiary of the poll was the **Movement for Rights and Freedoms** – *Dvizhenieto za prava i svobodi* or **DPS**: formed to protect Bulgaria's Muslims, the DPS gained solid support from the country's Turks and *pomaks*, giving it 23 MPs in the new chamber. However, Bulgaria's urban population had voted en masse for the SDS, and many suspected that the BSP's majority had been artificially inflated by **vote rigging**.

THE SUMMER OF 1990 – AND AFTER

The SDS leadership was split on the issue of whether to accept the election result or stage some kind of protest, but the potentially volatile nature of Bulgarian society persuaded them to refrain from anything which might provoke violence. Nevertheless, **discontent** smouldered on throughout June, with regular street demonstrations in the capital, and student-manned **barricades** going up outside Sofia University. Frustration at the BSP's victory boiled over with the discovery of an old **video tape** which showed President Mladenov threatening to use tanks against opposition demonstrators in Sofia the previous December. Mass meetings called for his resignation, a demand echoed by Socialist Party members themselves after an expert panel of video-watchers pronounced the recording to be genuine.

Mladenov bowed to pressure and resigned on 7 July, but this only encouraged further demonstrations by opposition groups dissatisfied with the slow pace of change. In Sofia, university lecturers and students established the "**City of Truth**" – a tent settlement near the mausoleum of Communist Bulgaria's founder, Georgi Dimitrov – to demand a removal of all former Communist MPs and a speeding-up of the criminal proceedings against Todor Zhivkov. Similar "cities" soon sprang up in provincial capitals as well. In the meantime, **conservative forces** egged on by hardline Communists continued to protest against the new freedom accorded to Bulgaria's ethnic Turks, outraged by the thought that national unity might be compromised by the presence of Turkish deputies in parliament.

By the time the Constituent Assembly convened in Veliko Târnovo in mid-July political authority within the country was in a serious state of disintegration, prompting dark rumours of a return to hardline government with possible help from the military. The Assembly's first and most urgent task was to elect a new president who could somehow hold the country together. Despite their parliamentary majority, BSP MPs realized that they would provoke serious divisions in the country if they opted for one of their own candidates, but they were initially unwilling to accept anyone put forward by the opposition. After over a month of deadlock, however, the Assembly awarded the presidency to the leader of the SDS, **Zhelyu Zhelev**, a respected dissident academic who had been sent into internal exile by the former regime for writing a book entitled *What is Fascism* – a work which embarrassed Bulgaria's erstwhile rulers by demonstrating the similarity between both left- and right-wing forms of totalitarianism.

Zhelev faced a potentially dangerous breakdown in public order almost immediately upon his election. A decision by parliament ordering the removal of Communist symbols from all public buildings was interpreted by the Sofia mob as an invitation to **set fire** to the Socialist (i.e. Communist) **Party headquarters** – where a big red star was prominently displayed – on August 26. Socialist Party bosses exploited the situation by accusing the opposition of unleashing the forces of "neo-fascism", and it was rumoured that Podkrepa-leader and SDS-ally Konstantin Trenchev had encouraged the violence. Zhelev established his presidential impartiality by swiftly denouncing the vandals, and things began to calm down. The "Cities of

Truth" were dismantled by opposition activists as a sign that the tactics of political confrontation had, for the time being, been abandoned.

Plummeting confidence in the socialist system had, however, produced a crisis in the Bulgarian **economy**. The cabinet of BSP Prime Minister Andrei Lukanov courted the likes of Robert Maxwell in an attempt to attract foreign investment into the country, but unwillingness to adopt necessary market reforms soon led to the government's collapse. Made nervous by a nationwide wave of **strikes** and **student protests**, the socialist-dominated Assembly consented to the formation of a **coalition government** in December 1990. Led by nonparty lawyer Dimitâr Popov and including SDS members in the key ministries of industry and finance, the new administration was charged with the task of speeding up the transition to capitalism and preparing the ground for **new elections**. Stiff medicine was applied to the Bulgarian economy with the **liberation of prices** in February 1991. Subsequent massive inflation and high interest rates caused bankruptcies, growing unemployment, and widespread **social misery**.

OCTOBER 1991 AND AFTER

As the **elections of October 1991** approached, Bulgarian society appeared to be as divided as at any time in its history. The most visible results of post-Zhivkov change – rising prices, declining social services, and the ostentation of those who grew fat on the proceeds of private enterprise – were an affront to people on fixed incomes, especially pensioners and employees of ailing state firms. The BSP tapped these resentments by proposing a slowed-down model of economic reform and the retention of some measure of state planning. More ominously, the BSP increasingly posed as the party of **discipline and order** to Bulgarians left bewildered by collapsing public morals (a huge rise in crime had accompanied the decay of the Communist system); and exploited the nationalist sentiments of those disquietened by the sudden appearance of Bulgaria's Muslims as important players on the political scene. By emphasizing the need for **national unity**, the socialists seemed to be offering a return to the certainties of the past. For the SDS and other non-socialists, however, Bulgaria's salvation depended on a further

purge of Communist influence, and the wholesale adoption of a **free market** – whatever the social cost.

There was clearly an anti-socialist majority in the country, but **political infighting** threatened to destroy the opposition's chances of victory. Dismayed by the motley collection of right-wingers, monarchists and messianic capitalists increasingly drawn into the fringes of the SDS, Social Democrat and Green splinter groups left to form mini-SDS coalitions of their own. The presence of two **Agrarian parties** (the *Unified BZNS* and the *BZNS-Nikola Petkov*, both of which claimed descent from the *BZNS* originally created by the great Agrarian leader Aleksandâr Stamboliiski) split the anti-socialist vote even further.

In the end the election was a **close-run thing**. The SDS received 34 percent of the vote and 110 seats in the new 240-seat Assembly; the BSP 33 percent and 106 seats; the DSP 7.5 percent and 24 seats. All other parties failed to exceed the 4 percent barrier necessary for representation in parliament. Despite the narrow margin of victory, the result was hailed as a turning-point in Bulgarian history by the BSP's opponents – Bulgarian socialism had been finally laid to rest.

Failure to win an **outright majority** meant that the SDS was dependent on the support of the predominantly Turkish DPS in order to form a government. The Socialist Party tried to reverse the election result by taking the DPS to court, arguing (unsuccessfully, as it turned out) that the DPS were an exclusively ethnic party of a type prohibited by the Bulgarian constitution. Many Bulgarians (including SDS supporters) were horrified by the idea that the "Turks" now held the balance of power in the Assembly, but it was clear that the SDS and the DPS had much in common: a shared hatred of Communism and a desire to dismantle its heritage as quickly as possible.

Prime Minister-designate **Filip Dimitrov** opened negotiations with DPS leader **Ahmed Dogan**, who was careful not to offend Bulgarian nationalist sentiment by demanding places in the new cabinet in return for his support. Nevertheless it was clear that Dogan exercised a veto over ministerial appointments, and the knowledge that secret bargains were being struck behind closed doors got the new administration off to an undignified start.

POST-SOCIALIST BULGARIA

The new government initiated a crash programme of economic reform, removing barriers to foreign investment, speeding up the **privatization** of state-run firms, and establishing the ground rules for *restitutsiya* or **restitution** – the process by which property and land nationalized by the Communists could be reclaimed by its former owners. Public spending was slashed and wages in the state sector were held down, producing much social hardship and polarizing the country even further. The winter of 1991/92 was characterized by extensive **power cuts**, after former Soviet republics began to demand hard currency for the electricity they used to supply so cheaply.

The first challenge to the post-socialist order came in the **presidential elections** of January 1992, when Zhelyu Zhelev only narrowly beat off the challenge of BSP-sponsored candidate Velko Vâlkanov. Vâlkanov had exploited growing unease about alleged "Turkish" influence in Bulgarian affairs resulting from the DPS's central position in political life.

Suspicions about the DPS's loyalty to the Bulgarian state were raised in February, when it was claimed that Ahmed Dogan had provided the Turkish Embassy with a list of Bulgarian intelligence agents serving in embassies abroad. The resulting furore, dubbed the affair of *tozi spisâk* or "**that list**", was denounced by the government as an attempt to discredit the DPS, thereby disrupting its parliamentary alliance with the SDS. A subsequent debate about the future of the intelligence services, and whether they should be subject to presidential or prime-ministerial control, led to a split between Zheliu Zhelev and Filip Dimitrov; and Defence Minister Ludzhev – much favoured by Zhelev – was forced out by the Prime Minister.

President Zhelev was also being targeted by those who favoured the return of Bulgaria's **monarchy**. Many Bulgarians believed that **Simeon**, the Madrid-based son of Tsar Boris III, would be an ideal figurehead capable of healing some of Bulgarian society's wounds: having lived in exile for the last 45 years, Simeon was entirely uncompromised by the Communist era. There was also a strong legalistic argument in his favour: the referendum which had abolished the monarchy in 1946 had been rigged by the Communists and was there-fore – according to some – null and void.

Support for the monarchy came from the radical wing of the Bulgarian **Orthodox Church**, an institution catapulted to the fore-front of national life when reformist priests occupied the offices of the Holy Synod in May. Led by former human rights activist and SDS MP **Bishop Hristofor Sâbev**, the occupiers demanded the resignation of current head of the Church **Patriarch Maksim**, whom they accused of **collaboration** with the Zhivkov regime. Although Bulgaria's constitutional court declared that the state had no right to interfere in religious disputes, the aggressive nature of Sâbev's action clearly irritated both the government and the President. Sâbev's support for the monarchist cause ("Orthodoxy and the monarchy are inextricably linked, historically and spiritually", according to the Bishop) was calculated to offend the earnest **republicanism** of Zhelyu Zhelev.

Throughout 1992 the economic reform programme had done little to improve living standards for the bulk of the population. In order to demonstrate that Bulgaria's economic collapse was the fault of the outgoing regime rather than the ruling SDS, the government developed a new taste for **anti-Communist witch hunts**. Throughout the summer the SDS newspaper *Demokratsiya* ran daily articles detailing the pilfering activities of former Communist functionaries, who allegedly emptied state coffers in order to provide them-selves with country villas, luxury cars, and expense-account trips abroad.

August 1992 saw the court appearances of Todor Zhivkov, as well as former prime minis-ters Georgi Atanasov and Andrei Lukanov, to answer charges of **embezzlement** – Zhivkov himself was sentenced to a seven-year prison term. Dossiers on their more serious misde-meanours – responsibility for concentration camps, repression of ethnic Turks, and so on – looked, at the time of writing, set to take many more months to prepare.

BULGARIA'S POSITION IN THE WORLD

Before the removal of **cold-war certainties**, Bulgaria's priorities were close links with the USSR and the maintenance of strong defences against nearby NATO countries Turkey and Greece. After November 1989 Bulgaria was free to develop relations with its Balkan neigh-bours regardless of ideological constraints, but the situation was complicated both by worsen-ing conditions in Yugoslavia and political infighting at home.

The BSP, increasingly nationalist in its atti-tude to Bulgaria's Turkish minority, considered the Muslim communities of the Balkans, and the growing role of Turkish diplomacy in bind-ing them together, to be the biggest threats to regional peace. For the BSP, therefore, Bulgaria's natural allies were Serbia and Greece. Many on the right of Bulgarian politics shared similar views.

The elections of October 1991, however, produced a strongly **pro-Western govern-ment** which depended on the ethnic Turkish MPs of the DPS for support. Relations with Turkey were normalized, not least because of Turkey's status as the USA's most important ally in the region, but also because it was an increasingly dynamic capitalist power capable of providing Bulgaria with much-needed invest-ment. The war in Yugoslavia had disrupted a lot of Bulgaria's overland trade with western Europe, thus making it natural that much of the country's commerce should flow southwards instead – in the words of DPS leader Ahmed Dogan, "the road to Europe leads through the Bosphorus". However, pro-Western elements in the governing SDS feared that rapprochement with Turkey would ultimately lead Bulgaria away from the main currents of European life. When President Zhelev signed up to the **Black Sea Economic Zone** – one of Ankara's pet projects – in June 1992, critics complained that Bulgaria's integration into Europe might be postponed if the country engaged itself too deeply in the "Euro-Asiatic economic sphere".

The danger of the **Yugoslav civil war** eventually spreading to **Macedonia** repre-sents the biggest threat to Bulgaria's security. The disintegration of the Macedonian republic – inhabited by people whom the Bulgarians regard as their ethnic kin – would place intoler-able pressures on Sofia and threaten the stabil-ity of Bulgaria's fledgling democracy. Such fears have led to worsening relations between Bulgaria and Greece, whose refusal to recog-nize Macedonia is regarded as irresponsible; and to the demonization of Serbia, whose expansionism is seen as the root cause of the conflict.

THE POLITICAL PRESENT

Bulgarian politics continue to be dominated by the left-right struggle between the BSP and the SDS. The BSP regards the government's pursuit of Western capitalism and "collaboration" with ethnic Turks as a betrayal of national interests; while the SDS sees its rival as a hang-over from the totalitarian regime and a barrier to democratic development. It's debatable whether this **extreme polarization** is in itself a threat to Bulgarian democracy, with the political centre, too fragmented to secure representation in parliament, largely excluded from public life.

The development of a rigid **two-party system** along current lines might actually stabilize Bulgarian politics in time, but a great deal depends on whether the BSP can convincingly throw off its Communist past, and whether the SDS survives as a unified right-of-centre movement – or disintegrates into its constituent parts.

Relations within the SDS in Autumn 1992 were characterized as a **"war of all against all"**, with different factions jockeying for power. Some of its members began flirting with the OSD or Social Democratic Alliance, a group of deputies on the right wing of the BSP, in an attempt to build a new parliamentary majority – but these secret negotiations were denounced by their SDS colleagues.

Criminal proceedings against Zhivkov and his cronies provided the government with a spurious veneer of anti-Communist unity, and helped to detract public attention from stalling economic reforms. However, the zeal with which the government prosecuted former Communists was criticized by President Zhelev, for whom SDS policy contained the roots of a **new authoritarianism**. A serious rift between president and prime minister developed, raising important questions about the precise constitutional role of both these offices of state. By September 1992 relations between Filip Dimitrov and Zhelyu Zhelev reached an all-time low, with the supporters of each one being accused of mounting plots to unseat the other.

Such intrigues damaged Bulgaria's attempts to promote itself to the West as a healthy post-Communist democracy worthy of political and financial support. Bulgaria had nevertheless achieved the transition from totalitarianism to multi-party pluralism without the degree of social unrest and political disintegration experienced by many of its erstwhile Eastern bloc allies. Hailed as **"an island of stability in the Balkans"**, Bulgaria has more reason than most to be optimistic about the future.

THE MACEDONIAN QUESTION

The name "Macedonia" is a geographical term of long standing, applied to an area which has always been populated by a variety of races and cultures. For centuries an area of discord between Balkan peoples, it's currently divided between three states – Bulgaria, Greece, and the former-Yugoslav Republic of Macedonia – each of which has deep-seated historical reasons for regarding the Macedonian name and the Macedonian heritage as something exclusively its own. Bulgaria has gone to war over Macedonia three times this century, only to end up on the losing side on each occasion. As a symbol of the nation's unfulfilled destiny in the Balkans, Macedonia continues to occupy an important place in the Bulgarian psyche.

HISTORICAL MACEDONIA

The original **Kingdom of Macedonia**, which attained its zenith in the fourth century BC under Philip II and Alexander the Great, was governed by Greek-speaking kings and inhabited – from what historians can gather – by a predominantly Greek-speaking population. Its early borders spread from Mount Olympus in the south to the upper Vardar basin in the north, and it was this core area which provided the basis for the subsequent **Roman** and **Byzantine provinces of Macedonia**, preserving the idea of the region as a cohesive administrative unit. Although the ethnic composition of Macedonia was constantly changing (in ancient times Greeks lived cheek-by-jowl with Thracians and Illyrians, and from the sixth century onwards they were increasingly joined by **Slavonic tribes**), medieval chroniclers continued to refer to its inhabitants as "Macedonians" regardless of their racial origin – thus bolstering the concept of a specific Macedonian identity.

Under **Turkish rule** Macedonia was broken up into separate units, but as the empire went into decline and Ottoman possessions in

Europe shrank, the area was reunited under the name of the "**Three Provinces**", with administrative centres at Thessaloniki and Monastir (present-day Bitola in ex-Yugoslav Macedonia). Turn-of-the-century Macedonia was one of the most cosmopolitan provinces of the empire, peopled by Slavs, Greeks, Turks, Albanians and Jews. Cities like Thessaloniki were centres of **revolutionary intrigue**, rocked not only by the increasing national consciousness of the subject peoples of the empire, but also by Turkish reform movements which hoped to liberalize the archaic institutions of the Ottoman state.

In the late nineteenth century the newly independent **nation-states** of Greece, Serbia and Bulgaria all coveted Macedonian territory, but their claims were complicated by the confused ethnic map of the area. The races who lived here didn't inhabit clearly defined geographical units: towns with predominantly Greek or Turkish populations were often surrounded by exclusively Slav or Albanian rural areas. To make matters worse, people were also divided along **religious lines**. Local Slavs who had converted to Islam in the fifteenth century (known hereabouts as *pomaks*, *torbeshes* or *poturs*, they're still very much in evidence) often identified with Macedonia's Turks and Albanians more strongly than with the Christian Slavs. It's not surprising, therefore, that the Greek, Albanian and Slav **armed bands** which roamed the countryside in the early years of this century were often implacably opposed to each other – each fighting for a "Free Macedonia" which would exclude the national aspirations of its rivals.

Education was one way in which the struggle for the allegiances of the Macedonian people was waged. By raising money to establish schools in the area, Bulgarian, Serb and Greek cultural societies could impose modern **literary languages** on people whose patchwork of regional dialects had hitherto confused their sense of ethnic belonging. Macedonia's Slavs, who were concentrated in the north of the province, but also formed substantial communities in the south along the Aegean seaboard, spoke a language grammatically very close to Bulgarian, but local dialects often shaded into neighbouring Serbian. Both states were eager to claim the Macedonian Slavs as

MACEDONIA

SERBIA   ● Sofia

Shar Mts.   ● Kyustendil   BULGARIA

● Skopje   Blagoevgrad (Gorna Dzhumaya)

Pirin Mountains

● Veles

Debar   REPUBLIC OF MACEDONIA   ● Gotse Delchev

● Strumitsa   Melnik

ALBANIA   Ohrid   Bitola (Monastir)   ● Petrich   ● Dhrama

● Serres

N

Thessaloniki

0   100 km

Mt ▲ Olympus

GREECE

R Struma

R Vardar

– · – · Modern State boundaries

The historic region of Macedonia

their own; provoking the formation of the Bulgarian **Saints Cyril and Methodius Society** and the Serbian **Society of Saint Sava** in the 1880s, both of which intended to carry out educational work throughout the province and win local hearts and minds.

THE BULGARIAN CLAIM

It's axiomatic to Bulgarian thinking that the Slavs who inhabit Macedonia are, in fact, Bulgarians. They speak the same language (or at the very least, a dialect exceedingly close to it), and are descended from tribes which came to the Balkans at around the same time.

In the medieval period Macedonia was closely linked to Bulgaria, thus bolstering the latter's **historical claims** to the area. Northern Macedonia was conquered by the Bulgar Khans in the ninth century, and remained within the orbit of the First Bulgarian Kingdom until 1218, when the western Macedonian town of **Ohrid** – by that time the Bulgarian capital – finally fell to the Byzantines.

Under the Second Bulgarian Kingdom (1185–1396) things were more confused, with the emergent power of **Serbia** increasingly extending its influence in the area in the 1300s. The central Macedonian town of Skopje was

briefly the capital of the greatest of medieval Serbia's rulers, **Tsar Dušan**. The feudal princedoms into which Macedonia fragmented immediately before the **Ottoman conquest** are claimed by both Serbian and Bulgarian historians as their own; and the Macedonian-based **Krali Marko**, a semi-legendary figure who fought vainly to stem the Turkish advance, is a popular figure in the folk literature of both countries – an example of how modern ideas of ethnicity don't always conform to the complex racial goulash which prevailed over much of medieval Europe.

Under Turkish rule links between Bulgaria and Macedonia remained strong. The needs of Bulgaria's Christian population were served by the **Archbishopric of Ohrid**, a town which became synonymous with Bulgarian spirituality and learning, until the church was eventually placed under the jurisdiction of Constantinople in 1767.

During Bulgaria's nineteenth-century **National Revival**, Bulgarians and Macedonians shared a common upsurge in Orthodox culture and art. Woodcarvers from **Debâr** in west Macedonia, a town famed for its craft traditions, worked in churches throughout Bulgaria. Bulgaria's struggle to free ecclesiastical affairs from the control of the Greek Patriarchate was accompanied by assumptions that any future Bulgarian church would extend to cover the Orthodox Slavs of Macedonia as well. When the Ottoman authorities acquiesced to the creation of an autonomous **Bulgarian Exarchate** in 1870 they included within it much of central Macedonia, and promised that it would have jurisdiction over any other areas where at least two-thirds of the population voted to join. Those around Skopje, Ohrid and Bitola did so – a move regarded by the Bulgarians as an implicit recognition of their claims to the region.

Bulgarian designs on Macedonia found a powerful sponsor in the shape of **tsarist Russia**. After the Russo-Turkish War of 1877–78 the Ottomans agreed to the creation of an independent Bulgarian state, which included the lion's share of Macedonia, at the **Treaty of San Stefano**. This didn't just antagonize the many non-Slav nations who lived within the borders of this so-called "Big Bulgaria" – it also struck fear into the hearts of the European Great Powers, who saw the new country as a vehicle for Russian ambitions in the Balkans. The subsequent **Berlin Congress** promptly returned Macedonia to the Turkish Empire, on the condition that the Ottoman authorities carried out a vague programme of "reforms". The Bulgarians have always regarded the Berlin Congress as a cynical move to frustrate their legitimate national aspirations, and the desire to regain control of Macedonia has been a recurring theme in Bulgarian politics ever since.

MACEDONIAN REVOLUTIONARY POLITICS: THE IMRO

Whatever the peoples of Macedonia felt about the idea of being incorporated into a "Big Bulgaria", most of them were pretty unhappy to find themselves once again languishing within the borders of the decaying Ottoman empire. The ensuing frustration helped to fuel a growing **Macedonian separatist movement**, characterized by a plethora of clandestine groups who specialized in terrorist action and political assassination. Most influential of these was the *Vâtreshnata Makedonska revolutsiyonna organizatsiya* or **Internal Macedonian Revolutionary Organization** – more commonly known by the acronym of

VMRO or **IMRO** – founded by schoolteachers **Gotse Delchev** and **Dame Gruev** in 1893.

Inspired by Bulgarian freedom fighters like Vasil Levski and Hristo Botev, and adopting the "Liberty or Death" slogan beloved of Bulgarian insurgents, the IMRO clearly saw themselves as the inheritors of the **Bulgarian revolutionary tradition**. However, none of the IMRO's early leaders thought that Macedonia's interests would be served by straightforward incorporation into Bulgaria.

Delchev, a committed republican, was disillusioned by post-Liberation Bulgaria's degeneration into monarchical dictatorship, and saw the creation of an **autonomous Macedonia** within some future **Balkan federation** as the best possible antidote to the wave of authoritarianism currently sweeping the infant nation-states of the region.

He also accepted that the ethnic collage of turn-of-the-century Macedonia would be difficult to reconcile with the creation of an enlarged Bulgarian nation-state, without recourse to either mass coercion or the forced migration of entire populations – something which a man of his socialist convictions was unwilling to countenance.

Delchev and the IMRO insisted on the creation of a clandestine organization within Macedonia itself in order to ensure the movement's independence from the interference of outside powers. However, many of the **Macedonian emigrants** who found refuge in Sofia after the Berlin Congress began to look towards the Bulgarian state as their most likely means of liberation. They gravitated towards the **Supreme Macedonian Committee** (whose members came to be known as the *vârhovtsi*, or **Supremists**), a group formed by Bulgarian court circles in order to gain control of the Macedonian freedom movement.

Supporters of both IMRO and the Supremists began to infiltrate each others' organizations, and Macedonian activists became increasingly **split** – between those who saw Macedonia as an entity in its own right and those who favoured its incorporation into Bulgaria. These two strands in the Macedonian revolutionary tradition were exploited by future Bulgarian and Yugoslav governments, each eager to secure historical legitimacy for their diametrically opposed policies in the region.

THE ILINDEN UPRISING

IMRO leaders particularly resented incursions by Supremist-sponsored armed bands into Ottoman territory. Ill-starred adventures such as the **occupation of Melnik** in 1896 and the attempted **uprising** in **Gorna Dzhumaya** (now Blagoevgrad) in 1902 merely served to provoke Ottoman repression and hamper the work of the underground IMRO network within Macedonia. Eager to demonstrate their independence from the Sofia-based Supremists, and fearful that a reform programme forced on Turkey by the Great Powers might take the limelight away from the revolutionary movement, the IMRO opted to launch a premature and hurriedly planned uprising. Leaders like Delchev were against the idea, but eventually had to go along with the argument that the IMRO had to do something in order to regain the initiative in the anti-Ottoman struggle.

Named **Ilinden** ("Saint Elijah's Day") after the day on which it was launched – August 2, 1903 – the uprising was centred on the town of Krushevo high in the mountains southwest of Skopje. Intended as a beacon of hope to the surrounding populace, the so-called **Krushevo Republic** fell in a matter of weeks.

Fierce Ottoman reprisals followed, and surviving IMRO members retreated into despair and impotence. Gotse Delchev had been killed three months before the uprising in a chance run-in with police, and Dame Gruev fell three years later in an isolated guerrilla action. The left-wing, autonomist traditions of the movement were subsequently inherited by **Yane Sandanski** (after whom one of Bulgaria's Pirin towns is named), but his fiercely anti-monarchist sentiments earned the wrath of Tsar Ferdinand, who had him assassinated in 1915. With the bitter failure of Ilinden still hanging over the IMRO, power increasingly passed into the hands of the pro-Bulgarian wing of the organization.

FROM THE BALKAN WARS TO WORLD WAR II

In the aftermath of Ilinden, Serbian organizations had taken advantage of IMRO's failure by flooding the area with cultural workers and priests. The government in Sofia increasingly sought a rapprochement with Serbia in order to preserve what was left of Bulgarian influence in Macedonia. Planning a joint attack on Turkey, the two states agreed in March 1912 to split Macedonia between them, with Bulgaria being promised the west-central portion around Bitola and Ohrid. Greece joined the alliance soon afterwards, and in the **First Balkan War** of 1912 Greek and Serbian troops occupied most of Macedonia, while the bulk of the Bulgarian army was tied up fighting the Turks in the east. The Serbs were particularly unwilling to give up any portion of land thus acquired: the creation of an independent state of Albania had frustrated Serbian dreams of westward expansion, and so Macedonia – renamed "**South Serbia**" by government propagandists – became a legitimate target of Serbia's imperialist ambitions.

Bulgaria protested, but its attempt to drive its erstwhile allies from the region in the **Second Balkan War** of 1913 ended in defeat. The subsequent carve-up of the historic province created divisions which endure to this day. The Bulgarians were allowed to keep the eastern part, known as **Pirin Macedonia**; while **Aegean Macedonia**, comprising the port of Thessaloniki and its hinterland, fell to Greece; the Serbs grabbed **Vardar Macedonia** to the north and west, including the towns of Skopje, Bitola and Ohrid. Each of the three states regarded their newly acquired inhabitants respectively as Bulgarians, Greeks or Serbs – expressions of any other ethnic identity were either ignored or suppressed.

After a brief period of Bulgarian occupation during the First World War, predominantly Slav-populated Vardar Macedonia ended up in a Serb-dominated **Yugoslav state** which had no place for a separate Macedonian identity. Serbian administrators, priests and school-teachers descended on the region to run local affairs, and Serbian settlers were encouraged to settle on land vacated by emigrating Turks. In Greek-controlled Aegean Macedonia, many Slav communities moved north into Bulgaria during the inter-war years, thus consolidating Greek ethnic dominance of the region.

Bulgaria found itself **diplomatically isolated** after 1918, and therefore unable to press any claim to the Macedonian territories of which it felt unjustly deprived. However, a resurgent IMRO, sustained by the refugees who poured into Bulgaria to escape Serbian rule in Vardar Macedonia, put pressure on politicians to take a tough line on the Macedonian question. The presence of such a vociferous (and heavily armed) Macedonian lobby, with strong clandestine networks in both Sofia and the Pirin town of Petrich, was a serious threat to internal stability at a time when Bulgarian governments were eager to build bridges with their Balkan neighbours.

IMRO IN THE INTER-WAR YEARS

Years of guerrilla struggle in the Balkans had turned IMRO into a disciplined revolutionary force, and armed bands continued to harry the Yugoslav authorities in Vardar Macedonia from their sanctuaries in the Pirin. The organization also carried out **terrorist attacks** in Bulgaria itself, occupying Kyustendil in 1922 in protest at the government's pro-Yugoslav policies, and threatening the lives of political opponents. Bulgarian nationalists initially thought that they could use IMRO as a private army, enlisting their support to topple the Stamboliiski regime in 1923. However, successive governments regarded IMRO as an obstacle to good relations with Yugoslavia and Greece and worked to neutralize its influence.

In Moscow the newly established Communist International, or **Comintern**, saw the IMRO as a potential partner, imagining that the creation of a revolutionary situation in Macedonia would be a prelude to the toppling of reactionary regimes throughout the Balkans. Discussions in Moscow and Vienna in 1924 led to the **May Manifesto**, a document calling for cooperation between IMRO and the Comintern signed by IMRO leaders **Todor Aleksandrov**, **Aleksandâr Protogerov** and **Petâr Chaulev**.

Communist strategy for the Balkans, however, envisaged the creation of a free Macedonia – not its incorporation in an enlarged Bulgarian monarchist state – and therefore ran counter to the wishes of many of IMRO's right-wing, pro-Bulgarian activists. Aleksandrov and Protogerov bowed to pressure by disowning the *Manifesto*, launching a purge of "socialist" elements from the organization, and expelling Chaulev. However, Aleksandrov was still regarded as a traitor by more reactionary IMRO colleagues, who had him assassinated in August 1924.

Confined to "exile" in Pirin Macedonia and unable to find a proper role for itself, the IMRO spiralled downwards into **self-destruction**. In July 1928 veteran leader Protogerov was shot on the instructions of fellow Central Committee member **Ivan Mihailov**, a particularly ugly piece of internecine strife from which the organization never recovered. Mihailov ran IMRO like a mafia boss, liquidating opponents and funding arms purchases by trading in opium grown in the valleys of the Pirin Mountains.

By the 1930s IMRO had become completely ineffectual as a Macedonian liberation movement. IMRO's last great act of wanton terrorism came in 1934, when – in a plot hatched together with Croatian fascists – Yugoslav **King Alexander** was shot dead in Marseille by Macedonian Vlado Chernozemski. As far as the Bulgarian government was concerned, IMRO was simply a **criminal organization** which needed to be got rid of – a task carried out the same year when troops were sent into the Petrich region to destroy the IMRO network.

The demise of IMRO meant that, for much of the inter-war period, the denizens of Vardar Macedonia were left without any effective political leadership, and had to endure **Serbian repression** alone. This created a vacuum into which other political forces could move: former IMRO member Dimitâr Vlahov, who had been involved in the preparation of the *May Manifesto* in 1924, emerged at the head of pro-Comintern "**United IMRO**" which agitated for Gotse Delchev's original aim: the formation of an autonomous Macedonia within a Balkan Federation. Vlahov's organization was never very popular within Macedonia itself, but it helped to keep autonomist traditions alive – something which Yugoslavia's Communists were subsequently to exploit.

THE SOCIALIST REPUBLIC OF MACEDONIA

With the outbreak of **World War II** Bulgaria was invited to occupy Macedonia in return for supporting the Axis powers. Having endured two decades of heavy-handed Serbian rule, the locals greeted the Bulgarian army with open arms, but the imposition of a military government – often staffed by officials with little knowledge of the area – soon led to disillusionment.

Eager to exploit the rumbling discontent, Yugoslav Communist and partisan leader **Josip Broz Tito** sent his able sidekick **Svetozar Vukmanović Tempo** southwards to help organize a Macedonian resistance movement, which would act in concert with the Yugoslav partisan army. Not all of the local Communists agreed with Tito's avowed aim of creating a Macedonian Republic within a federal Yugoslavia, and a purge of "Bulgarophiles" – who included Macedonian party boss Metodije Šatorov Šarlo – had to be carried out.

The success of Yugoslavia's partisans in combatting Nazi aggression gave them an enormous amount of prestige among fellow Communists after the war, and their Bulgarian comrades were very much the junior partners in an unequal relationship. Tito hoped that the creation of a Macedonian Republic would be a good way of enticing Bulgaria into a Balkan Federation which he himself could then dominate.

The Bulgarian leadership felt obliged to open negotiations on the subject of a **merger between the two countries**, not least because the idea had the backing of Stalin, although they were suspicious of Tito's ambitions. Most importantly, they feared that any Macedonian component of a future federation would seek to remove the Pirin region from Bulgarian control, thus weakening their own power and importance. For the time being, however, the laws of Communist solidarity decreed that such reservations had to remain unvoiced: Bulgaria recognized the right of the Macedonians to have their own republic, and *de facto* recognized the existence of a Macedonian nationality – something which all previous Bulgarian governments had refused to do.

Plans for Bulgarian-Yugoslav union ultimately came to nothing, and Bulgaria retained the Pirin region, but the inhabitants of the Pirin were from 1945 onwards accorded the status of a **national minority**, and were positively encouraged to declare themselves as Macedonians – not Bulgarians – in state **censuses**.

Greece's rulers, on the other hand, were horrified by the creation of the Yugoslav Republic of Macedonia. The government in Athens feared that the Greek Communists, currently waging a guerrilla war in the north of the country, had come to a secret agreement to turn over parts of Aegean Macedonia to the Yugoslavs in the event of a Communist victory. It became apparent that the Greek Communists

were themselves divided on the issue, and such plans came to nothing. However, the Greeks have accused Yugoslav Macedonia of harbouring **territorial pretentions towards Aegean Macedonia** ever since.

One episode serves to illustrate the extent to which people were kicked around in the name of **proletarian internationalism** in the aftermath of the war. In 1945 about 5000 Aegean Macedonians from the area around Dhrama and Serres fled north to Bulgaria in order to escape the ravages of the Greek civil war. They were refused entry by Bulgarian officials who, eager to tow the current Party line, informed them that as Macedonians, their place was not in Bulgaria but in the new Yugoslav republic of Macedonia to the west. On arrival in Yugoslavia, they were promptly shipped by the authorities not to Macedonia but to the Serb province of Vojvodina far to the north – part of a policy of bolstering the multi-ethnic character of the Yugoslav state. Apparently these Macedonians are still there, marooned among a predominantly Serb population who no longer look so kindly on the presence of national minorities on their soil.

FORMING A MACEDONIAN NATION

Having established the Socialist Republic of Macedonia, and having won from the Bulgarians an admission that such a state had the right to exist, the Yugoslav authorities set about building a Macedonian **national identity**. Most important was the creation of an official **written language**, which was based on a dialect far enough removed from literary Bulgarian to be just about credible as a separate tongue.

Leaders of the original, autonomist IMRO – most notably Gotse Delchev – were elevated to the status of national heroes in order to provide the new republic with **historical legitimacy**. The Macedonian Empire of Alexander the Great was claimed as the state's ancient precursor, and pro-regime academics argued that although Alexander may have been Greek-speaking, he belonged to a distinct Macedonian race whose bloodlines had been preserved through intermarriage with the Slavs.

Although Yugoslavia's federal constitution permitted the republics a certain degree of autonomy, Tito's League of Communists ensured that manifestations of national feeling were never allowed to get out of hand. Macedonians who advocated outright independence or, worse still, expressed overly warm feelings towards neighbouring Bulgaria, were swiftly silenced. In **1967**, however, the Communist authorities supported the local clergy in the establishment of an autonomous **Macedonian Orthodox Church** (ecclesiastical affairs in the republic had hitherto been under Serbian jurisdiction). This was a typical example of Tito's management of Yugoslavia's nationality problems: throwing a concession or two to the Macedonians was a good way to prevent the Republic of Serbia from becoming too cocky.

In Bulgaria, worsening relations with Yugoslavia following the **Tito-Stalin split of 1948** produced a turn-around in official policy towards the Pirin Macedonians. Initially they continued to be classed as an ethnic group in their own right, with the Bulgarians demonstrating to Yugoslavian Macedonians that they would be treated with sympathy should they ever choose to rebel against the benighted Tito regime. By the early 1960s, however, Bulgaria's rulers were increasingly keen to emphasize the ethnic homogeneity of the Bulgarian nation. The authorities henceforth refused to issue personal identity documents to inhabitants of the Pirin region who failed to declare themselves as Bulgarians, and the version of history taught in schools once again drove home the message that the true boundaries of the Bulgarian people extended from the Black Sea in the east to Ohrid in the west.

In Yugoslav Macedonia, the change in Bulgarian attitudes assisted the process of nation-building. By playing on people's fears of Bulgaria as an expansionist power, the authorities succeeded in uniting people around a sense of regional Macedonian pride.

THE 1990s

With the collapse of Communism throughout eastern Europe and the disintegration of the Yugoslav state, the unresolved ethnic problems of the Balkans were once more up for grabs. Initially, however, the Yugoslav Republic of Macedonia entered **the 1990s** as one of the most conservative forces in the region. Home to a Communist bureaucracy which owed its existence to the regime in (and tax income

from) Belgrade, and too poor to be viable as an independent state, Macedonia joined Serbia in opposing the reformist and secessionist doctrines emanating from northerly, Westernized republics like Slovenia and Croatia. A gradual **change of heart** occurred when it became clear that the Serbian struggle to preserve the Yugoslav state would inevitably lead to Serb domination of those parts of the federation which chose to remain. Throughout 1990, **fear of Serbia** was the prime factor in mobilizing Macedonian national sentiment.

Several nationalist parties were formed to contest the republic's first democratic elections, timetabled for November 1990. Prominent among these was the **VMRO-DPMNE**, led by 25-year-old poet Ljupčo Georgievski, which claimed descent from the original IMRO of Gruev and Delchev. Together with an allied nationalist group, the *Macedonian Action Party* or **MAAK**, *VMRO-DPMNE* called for the reunification of all Macedonian peoples – an open challenge to the governments of Bulgaria and Greece. Even during the Communist period, the authorities in Yugoslav Macedonia had protested at the treatment of Macedonian minorities in neighbouring states, but had refrained from jeopardizing inter-Balkan relations by pressing these complaints too far. Now that these resentments were out in the open, the emergence of a boisterous democratic Macedonian state threatened to become a destabilizing influence on the region.

VMRO's popularity forced the adoption of a nationalist agenda upon other parties, including the Macedonian League of Communists or **SKM**, which had thrown its former leadership overboard and adopted a social democratic programme. The *SKM* was able to form a coalition government after the elections of November 1990, but the emergence of the *VMRO-DPMNE* as the strongest party in the *sobranie* or Assembly forced the government to adopt a nationalistic line. The Assembly issued a declaration of Macedonian **sovereignty** in January 1991, to be followed by a full declaration of **independence** in April 1992 once the collapse of Yugoslavia had become an unavoidable reality. Bulgaria recognized the infant state at once, but objections by **Greece** prevented the European Community and other Western powers from doing the same.

The ostensible reason for Greek intransigence was the **name** of the republic: seeing as much of northern Greece went under the same title – and had done so since before the days of Alexander the Great – how, insisted the Greeks, could a foreign state call itself "Macedonia" and thereby usurp the rich heritage that went with it? Lurking behind this objection lay Greek concern over the future of remaining pockets of Slavs (the so-called "**Slavophone Greeks**") who still lived in Aegean Macedonia. The presence of a newly independent Macedonian state threatened to reawaken demands for minority rights in northern Greece, perhaps calling into question the unitary nature of the Greek state. The Greeks invited their northern neighbours to rename their state *Vardar Macedonia* or *Skopje-Macedonia*, but despite EC mediation no compromise was found. Certain **symbols** adopted by the republic led to increased Greek disquiet. A picture of the **White Tower**, a famous landmark in Thessaloniki, found its way into Skopje's official publicity literature; while a **sun motif** previously associated with the Empire of Philip II and Alexander became the centrepiece of the Macedonian flag. Both cases suggested that the Republic of Macedonia nursed territorial pretensions far beyond its current borders, although this was strenuously denied by the authorities in Skopje.

Consigned to the **limbo** of independence without international recognition, Macedonia spent most of 1992 teetering on the brink of economic collapse. Observers argued that any prolongation of this state of affairs would lead to the republic's disintegration from the inside, possibly provoking intervention from neighbouring powers. The biggest potential threat to the republic's stability came from the presence of a large **Albanian minority** in western Macedonia. If the Yugoslav civil war were to spread to the adjacent Serbian province of Kosovo – also predominantly Albanian – then the Albanians of Macedonia would have to rethink their options in a rapidly changing Balkan environment, perhaps rising up in support of the creation of a Greater Albanian state. If that happened, Greece, Bulgaria and Serbia would find it hard not to become involved.

Ethnic Albanian MPs occupy a quarter of the seats in the Macedonian Assembly, and the Skopje authorities are keen to project an image of tolerance and inter-communal calm. However, most of the republic's parties are engaged in a contest to prove who is the most vociferous defender of national interests, and accusing one's opponents of having pro-Bulgarian sympathies is still a good way of stirring up Macedonian sentiment. The Macedonian government tried to smear the *VMRO-DPMNE* in June 1992 by putting seven of the party's regional activists on trial for hoarding firearms and plotting a coup. Sources in Sofia claimed that the trial was intended to signal a witch hunt of Bulgarophiles – and citizens of the Bulgarian town of Blagoevgrad began raising money to support the families of the accused.

BULGARIAN RESPONSES

Despite recognizing the Republic of Macedonia and offering it economic and political support, the Bulgarian government continued to stress that it couldn't recognize the existence of a Macedonian nation. To do so would have had serious consequences for the Pirin region – if the inhabitants of the Pirin were allowed to think of themselves as Macedonians, the unity of the Bulgarian state would be seriously compromised.

So far, however, the removal of totalitarian restrictions has failed to produce any great outpouring of Macedonian consciousness. April 1990 saw the emergence of the *Obedinenata makedonska organizatsiya* (United Macedonian Organization) or **OMO-Ilinden**, which called for recognition of Macedonian nationhood and autonomy for the Pirin region. Ilinden was accused of receiving funding from Skopje, and a clause in the Bulgarian constitution which forbade ethnic-based parties ensured that the organization was driven underground.

Pro-Bulgarian traditions in Macedonian political life were reawakened in the shape of the *VMRO-Sâyuz na makedonskite druzhestva*, or **IMRO-Union of Macedonian Societies**, an organization which denounced the very idea of a separate Macedonian nation as being an anti-Bulgarian plot sponsored by a whole host of international enemies – predominantly Communists, Titoists and Serbs.

Throughout 1992 Bulgaria's rulers remained sympathetic to the plight of ex-Yugoslav Macedonia, believing that its recognition by the West would help reduce the risk of conflict in the area. However, most, ordinary Bulgarians continue to regard the Macedonians as long-lost kin, who are perfectly entitled to toy with the idea of an independent state for the time being, but will probably return to the fold some time in the future.

Despite the obvious ethnic and linguistic links between the two states, however, over a century of separate development has provided Vardar Macedonians with a distinct national consciousness of their own; and their faith in Macedonian uniqueness may one day spread to infect the people of the Pirin too. A lot depends on the shifting alliances of the Balkans; Macedonia's strategic position in the centre of the peninsula makes it far too important for any of its neighbours to allow their rivals a commanding role in the region. It's too early to say whether Macedonia will once more be partitioned by surrounding powers or will survive as a buffer state keeping rival Greek, Bulgarian, Albanian and Serbian ambitions apart.

BULGARIA'S MUSLIM MINORITIES

Despite a proud Slavonic heritage forged through centuries of national struggle, Bulgaria is far from being an ethnically homogeneous state. As well as Gypsies, Vlachs, Armenians and Jews, the country contains about a million Muslims of varying origins – mostly Turk, Tatar and Slav. Bearing in mind that Islam is associated with the Ottoman empire, under which Bulgarian Christians languished for 500 years, it's not surprising that Bulgaria's Muslims have on occasion been regarded as a threat to national unity and have suffered state repression as a result.

During the 1980s Todor Zhivkov's Communist regime attempted to forcibly integrate Muslims into mainstream Bulgarian life by pressing them to abandon their traditional culture and adopt Slavonic names – attracting widespread international outrage in the process. Democratic changes after November 1989 brought an end to such blatant abuses of human rights, but the question of inter-ethnic relations remains a touchy subject for all concerned.

ORIGINS

Some sources estimate that Muslims constituted up to a third of Bulgaria's population on the eve of the Liberation. Many of them fled in the wake of the Ottoman collapse, but the descendants of those who stayed are scattered throughout the country. Today, the heaviest concentrations of Muslims are found **near the Turkish border** around Kârdzhali, Harmanli and Haskovo; **throughout the Rhodope mountains**; **northwest of the Balkan Range** near the towns of Shumen, Razgrad, Târgovishte and Isperih; **on the Black Sea coast** between Burgas and Varna; and north of Varna in the **Dobrudzha**.

During the 1980s Bulgarian historians argued that almost all of the surviving Muslims were descended from **ethnic Bulgarians** who adopted the religion, and in many cases the language, of their Ottoman conquerors in the

fifteenth century. However, a constant stream of **settlers** came from Asia to Europe in the wake of the Ottoman advance, and it's impossible to believe that their blood lines are not in some way preserved in the Muslim communities of the Balkans.

Many of Bulgaria's 700,000-strong **Turkish population** are likely to be descended from **Yörük tribespeople**, nomadic sheep-rearers from central Anatolia who were introduced to the Balkans by the Turkish sultan in order to guard the frontiers of his European domains. These newcomers put down roots throughout Bulgaria, especially in lowland regions where the native Christian population was either wiped out or put to flight.

Tatars had been frequenting the Dobrudzha and the Black Sea coast since the thirteenth century, and their Islamic religion and Turkic language made them natural allies of Bulgaria's Ottoman conquerors. Their numbers were augmented in the nineteenth century by refugees fleeing from Turkey's wars with tsarist Russia. Large numbers of Crimean Tatars were settled here in the 1850s, but they found it hard to adapt to a sedentary lifestyle, continued to practice nomadism, and in lean years pillaged Christian and Muslim farmers alike. Similarly unruly were the **Circassians**, also refugees from the tsarist empire, who were given lands along the southern banks of the Danube. The Circassians were recruited as irregulars by the local Ottoman gendarmes, and soon earned a reputation for arbitrary cruelty among the local Bulgarians. Both Tatars and Circassians were gradually assimilated by the more numerous Turks, and soon lost many of their specific racial characteristics – nowadays, Dobrudzhan Tatars are usually referred to as Turks by the local Bulgarian population.

Some fifteenth-century Bulgarians **renounced Christianity** in favour of Islam. It's unclear whether these conversions were forced, or whether landholding peasants willingly adopted Muslim ways in order to retain their privileges under a new regime. In many cases village priests went over to Islam and took their flock with them, despairing at the way in which Balkan Christianity had collapsed so quickly. Subsequently known as **pomaks** (derived from the word *pomagach*, or "helper" – they were viewed as collaborators by their

Christian neighbours), about 300,000 of these Slavic Muslims still live in compact communities throughout the western Rhodopes. Under the Ottoman empire, *pomak* irregulars were often used by the authorities to police the local Christians. It was a *pomak* leader from Dospat, Ahmed Aga Barutanliyata, who was allegedly responsible for the **Batak** massacre in 1876 (see p.229).

MUSLIMS UNDER THE MODERN BULGARIAN STATE

Muslims tended to occupy a privileged position under Turkish rule, and fear of Bulgarian reprisals caused many of them to flee during the War of Liberation in 1877. The Bulgarian government undertook to preserve the religious rights of Muslims that remained, paying for the upkeep of mosques and providing Turkish-language teaching in some schools. Isolated cases of **revenge** did occur, with ethnic Turks being burned out of their villages by irate Slavs, but few of these incidents are documented.

During the **inter-war years** Muslims were left largely unmolested by the state, although several Turkish settlements were awarded Bulgarian names in the 1930s – the northwestern town of Târgovishte, *Eski Dzhumaya* until 1934, is one example. Local government officials habitually doled out Slavonic names to ethnic Turks when registering births, although there was no consistent, government-sponsored campaign to do so.

The Soviet-inspired **constitution of 1947** paid lip service to minority rights, although Bulgaria's Communist bosses seemed eager to facilitate **emigration** of Muslims to Turkey during the immediate postwar years. Around 155,000 Turks departed between 1949 and 1951, and were followed by a second wave in the late Sixties. The early years of the **Zhivkov regime** were characterized by attempts to encourage Turks to join the Party and participate in Bulgarian political life. In 1964, Todor Zhivkov made a notorious speech calling for an improvement of Turkish-language schooling and a widening of minority cultural activities; but with hindsight this appeared to be the swan song of Bulgaria's enlightened nationality policy rather than the herald of some new dawn.

TURNING MUSLIMS INTO BULGARIANS

Educational facilities for ethnic Turks were being wound down by the late Sixties, marking a radical change in the government's attitude towards Bulgaria's minorities. From now on the emphasis was to be on outright **assimilation**. Bulgaria's atheist leaders were frustrated by the way in which Turks and *pomaks* clung to religious traditions – of all the country's inhabitants, the Muslims were the most impervious to the propaganda of secular education – and began to wonder whether they could ever be turned into loyal citizens of the socialist state.

To make matters worse, Muslim fertility was increasing at a time when the Bulgarian birth rate was in decline. Anxieties about Bulgaria's changing demography were coupled with the Party's growing exploitation of **nationalism**. The Zhivkov regime was eager to camouflage its subservience to the Soviet Union by posing as the guardian of patriotic values, and the ideology of the integral nation-state – in which there was little room for ethnic minorities – began to brush aside the proletarian internationalism of Marx and Lenin.

The *pomaks* were the first to experience the effects of the **name-changing campaign**, which aimed to coerce the bearers of traditional Islamic names into adopting Bulgarian alternatives. Beginning in 1971, official ceremonies took place in villages throughout the western Rhodopes, in which *pomaks* were awarded fresh identity papers bearing their new Bulgarified names. The vast majority had little choice but to accept them without complaint, as any dissent was harshly dealt with. Riots in Pazardzhik, in which two Communist Party officials were reportedly killed by an angry mob, resulted in mass arrests and deportations. Opposition to the campaign in the Gotse Delchev region led to a military clampdown, accompanied – it is alleged – by public hangings of *pomak* leaders.

The unexpected strength of resistance probably led to a lull in name changing over the next decade, but **the winter of 1984** saw the full force of the campaign directed against Bulgaria's ethnic Turks. This time the campaign was accompanied by a full-scale attack on Muslim traditions. Mosques were closed down or demolished, local religious leaders were replaced with party stooges, circumcision was discouraged, and use of the Turkish language in public places was forbidden. The speed and ferocity of the campaign was surprising, but it was part of the Communist mentality to believe that wholesale social change could be achieved through administrative decisions from above. The Party leadership had been shaken by events elsewhere in the Balkans – in Yugoslavia, the emergence of Muslim Albanian sentiment in Kosovo posed a threat to that state's continued existence – and Zhivkov obviously wanted to deprive Bulgarian Turks of their ethnic identity before they developed separatist aspirations of their own.

The campaign, going under the sanitized name of the *Vâzroditelniyat protses* or **Regeneration Process**, was presented to the Bulgarian public as another glorious chapter in the country's progress towards national rebirth. Sycophantic academics were employed to argue that the Turkish minority had in fact been Bulgarians all along: forcibly Islamicized in the fifteenth century, they were merely fulfilling their destiny by adopting Bulgarian names and returning to the fold. Repressive aspects of the campaign were often conducted under the smokescreen of social progress. Well-intentioned Bulgarians were led to support the measures against the Turks when it was argued that Muslim women, denied access to educational and career opportunities by the bonds of patriarchal society, would benefit from forced assimilation.

The campaign met with **fierce resistance** from the Turks themselves. Numerous demonstrations in towns in the Kârdzhali district ended with security forces firing on angry crowds; and eight civilians were shot dead during one peaceful protest in Momchilgrad in December 1984. Such events soon attracted the attention of human rights organizations abroad, but the regime turned a deaf ear to foreign criticism. The government turned the crisis to its own advantage, garnering domestic support by accusing Amnesty International and the Western press of participating in a plot to destabilize socialist Bulgaria.

SUMMER 1989: THE "GREAT EXCURSION"

With the Zhivkov regime increasingly relying on nationalist excesses in order to detract attention from the Communist system's failings,

anti-Turkish policies were stepped up in the **spring of 1989**. This time the action moved on to Bulgaria's northwest, where strikes and demonstrations in the Razgrad area gave vent to Muslim anger.

Growing numbers of Turks sought to emigrate rather than change their names, and the Turkish government declared its willingness to accept as many Bulgarian Muslims as wanted to leave. Sofia called Turkey's bluff by issuing passports to any Muslims requesting them, and by June 1989 the Bulgarian-Turkish border was jammed with people trying to leave, many taking their entire worldly possessions with them. Official sources claimed that the crowds gathering at the frontier were "tourists (*ekskurziyanti*)" taking advantage of the new freedom of travel, unintentionally providing the phrase by which 1989's exodus of Turks came to be known – the *golyama ekskurziya* or **"Great Excursion"**.

Between May and August up to 300,000 Turks and *pomaks* crossed the border. Initially Turkey promised to provide sanctuary to Bulgaria's entire Muslim population if necessary, but by August the flood of refugees was placing impossible strains on the Turkish economy. There was insufficient accommodation or work for the newcomers, many of whom were housed in tent cities along the border, and the special treatment accorded to them (however meagre it may have been) was resented by local people. Many *ekskurziyanti* were beginning to return home after a couple of months, dismayed by Turkey's inability to provide them with a life better than the one they had left. Turkey had in any case **closed the border** by the end of August, unable to take any more.

The Great Excursion was beginning to have serious consequences for Bulgarian society. Whole areas had been depopulated, and entire towns and villages had been deprived of highly trained professional people like teachers and doctors. Most importantly, the economically vital **tobacco crop**, traditionally concentrated in areas of Muslim settlement, lay unharvested in the fields. Urban Bulgarians were organized into work brigades and sent to the countryside to save the crop – for many of them, this was their first experience of the havoc wrought by Todor Zhivkov's nationality policies.

Inspired by the progress of glasnost in the Soviet Union, Bulgarian intellectuals were increasingly eager to join persecuted Turks in denouncing the totalitarian nature of the state, and organizations like the *Independent Committee for the Defence of Human Rights* brought leaders of both groups together for the first time. Sharing a common hatred of Communism, Bulgaria's ethnic Turks and urban liberals seemed to be at the start of a fruitful political friendship when the Zhivkov regime came to an end on November 10, 1989.

THE POST-ZHIVKOV ERA

Conservative fears that rapidly emerging democratic forces would sell the country out to the Turks initially provoked a nationalist backlash. When new Party leader Petâr Mladenov admitted that the name-changing campaign had been a big mistake, hardliners tried to undermine him by organizing protest strikes and demonstrations in mixed-race towns like Haskovo and Kârdzhali, where Bulgarian-Turkish relations were sensitive. A big nationalist demonstration in Sofia on December 7 called for a referendum on the issue of whether Bulgaria's Muslims should be permitted to have their old names back.

Muslims themselves responded to the demise of totalitarianism by reclaiming their culture. *Pomaks* took to the streets of Gotse Delchev to demand the right to wear *shalvari*, the baggy trousers banned during the dark days of the name-changing campaign; nowadays traditional dress is worn with pride, even by Westernized younger women, in many parts of the Rhodopes. The Turkish language – and Turkish music – were loudly flaunted in those areas where ethnic Turks lived; and attendance at the local mosque once again became de rigueur for respectable members of the community.

THE DPS

Nationalist unrest flared once again in July 1990, when protestors tried to prevent newly elected Turkish MPs from taking their seats in the Grand National Assembly in Veliko Târnovo. Originally, ethnic Turk leaders had joined the main opposition coalition, the SDS, but personality clashes within the movement had persuaded them to form a political party of their own in early 1990. Named the "Movement for Rights and Freedoms" – *Dvizhenieto za prava i svobodi* or **DPS** – the

party was led by Ahmed Dogan, a former university lecturer imprisoned by the Zhivkov regime for his opposition to the name-changing campaign.

The DPS made every effort to present itself as a multi-racial human rights organization, although it was clear that most of its supporters were Turks and *pomaks*. Bulgaria's Muslims voted en bloc for the DPS in June 1990, leaving its critics to claim that the Movement would lead to the ghettoization of the country's minorities, not their rehabilitation into national life. Others feared that the DPS's monopolistic hold over the Muslim population, especially in the Kârdzhali area where ethnic Turks form a majority, would lead to demands for regional autonomy and, eventually, outright secession. The BSP, increasingly the natural home for conservative forces within the country, portrayed the DPS as an exclusively Turkish national party which owed its allegiance to Ankara rather than Sofia. The DPS's dominance over Bulgarian Muslims would also lead, they argued, to the gradual Turkification of Bulgaria's *pomaks*, who would slowly lose their Slavonic roots.

The first real chance for the DPS to flex its political muscle came in September 1991, when the Ministry of Education went back on its pledge to introduce four hours of Turkish-language lessons a week in towns with a sizable Turkish population. Local DPS leaders launched a **schools boycott**, which achieved a high degree of unity and discipline throughout the campaign – although opponents accused DPS activists of intimidating schoolkids into staying at home. At the beginning of October parliament relented and voted to restore the four hours of language schooling originally promised – on condition that it took place outside regular school hours.

THE OCTOBER 1991 ELECTIONS AND AFTER

As the **elections of October 1991** approached it became clear that neither of Bulgaria's main parties – the SDS and the BSP – were capable of winning an outright majority, and the DPS would in all likelihood hold the balance of power. The BSP knew that an SDS–DSP coalition was the likely outcome of such a situation, and began to play on public fears of a "Turk-dominated" parliament in an attempt to win support.

The BSP's eagerness to pose as the "keep the Turks out" party led to a dangerous polarization of attitudes in areas with a sizable Turkish population. In cities such as Shumen and Razgrad, Muslims and Bulgarians voted en masse for the DPS and the BSP respectively; and people like the SDS, who tried to play down the national issue, were totally squeezed out.

The election **result** confirmed the BSP's worst fears, with DSP deputies agreeing to support an SDS administration committed to market reforms and "de-Communization". In November the DSP's legitimacy was challenged in court by BSP members who argued that the Bulgarian constitution prohibited the formation of purely ethnic or religious parties. The court found that the DPS was sufficiently multi-ethnic to be acceptable.

Conditions for Bulgaria's Muslims have **radically changed for the better** since November 1989, and the country's new leaders are eager to portray the relationship between SDS and DPS as an example of Bulgarian democracy's maturity and good sense. However, it's clear that many in the new society – including members of the government itself – feel threatened by the sudden reappearance of Muslim influence at the very heart of Bulgarian politics, and regard the Muslim minorities as potentially disloyal to the Bulgarian nation-state. The DPS's importance may wane if changes occur in the ruling coalition, or if future elections produce a parliamentary majority which no longer requires its support – thus inviting a return to the anti-Muslim policies of the past.

BOOKS

There is more writing on Bulgaria than might initially be imagined – though, understandably, it appears more in books on the Balkans as a whole than forming the central subject of either travel writing or fiction. Sadly, much of it is no longer in print. What follows is a collection of books on or about the country either currently in print or (when indicated o/p) out of print and available in larger libraries or specialist secondhand bookstores. Otherwise, *Collets Bookshop*, 40 Great Russell Street, London WC1 (☎071 637 7598) is the main outlet in Britain for books about eastern Europe. For some examples of contemporary writing from Bulgaria, see p.322.

TRAVEL BOOKS AND GENERAL ACCOUNTS

Claudio Magris, *Danube* (Collins Harvill). This highly praised account of the Danubian countries interweaves history, reportage and highbrow literary anecdotes in an ambitious attempt to illuminate their cultural and spiritual backgrounds. Only one section is devoted to Bulgaria, naturally enough, but the rest is a fascinating read.

Leslie Gardiner, *Curtain Calls* (Readers Union 1977: o/p). The last six chapters deal with Gardiner's experiences in Bulgaria – including a slow-burning flirtation with his *Balkantourist* guide, Radka – recounted in an amusing style.

Bernard Newman, *The Blue Danube* (Jenkins 1935: o/p); *Bulgarian Background* (Travel Book Club 1961: o/p). The latter is marginally livelier – and contains a lot more about Bulgaria –

than Newman's earlier book, relating his epic bicycle ride alongside the Danube. Solid stuff, but hardly riveting.

Lovett Fielding Edwards, *Danube Stream* (Travel Book Club 1940: o/p). This book on the Danube and its influence on southeastern Europe is chiefly interesting for its account of life amongst the polyglot boatpeople. Includes descriptions of Vidin, Lom and Ruse, but otherwise only marginally relevant to Bulgaria.

George Savas, *Donkey Serenade* (Travel Book Club 1941: o/p). Savas did his travelling on foot along the backroads of Bulgaria, accompanied by the roguish ex-IMRO fighter Vasil Levski. Rather twee, but includes a couple of fine Bulgarian poems and the odd notable vignette.

Stowers Johnson, *Gay Bulgaria* (Hale 1964: o/p). More earnest than Newman and prosier than Savas, Johnson voyaged by Dormobile across Bulgaria just before the country became a tourist destination, which constitutes the book's main attraction.

A.L. Haskell, *Heroes and Roses* (Dartman, Longman & Todd 1966: o/p). Potted biographies of Bulgarian revolutionaries, sections on the arts and chunks of travelese, combined with diatribes against pop music and other things that this pompous ballet critic dislikes most.

Claire & Brophy, *Residence in Bulgaria* (o/p). Travelling through "European Turkey" in the second half of the nineteenth century, these two Brits formed a low opinion of the Bulgarians, whom they considered lazy, superstitious curs. Why couldn't they learn to appreciate the benefits of Ottoman rule and stop bleating about independence, dash it? Long winded, but a mine of historical anecdotes.

HISTORY, POLITICS AND SOCIOLOGY

Mercia Macdermott, *A History of Bulgaria, 1393–1885* (Allen & Unwin 1962: o/p); *The Apostle of Freedom*; *Freedom or Death*; and *For Freedom and Perfection*. Written sympathetically and with obvious enjoyment – all in all, probably the best histories of Bulgaria in the English language. The last three (published by Journeyman) are biographies of famous nineteenth-century revolutionaries – Vasil Levski, Gotse Delchev and Yane Sandanski.

R.F. Hoddinott, *The Thracians* (Thames & Hudson 1981). Thorough introduction to the Bulgarians' ancient antecedents, although descriptions of archaeological evidence sometimes seem a bit too technical for the lay reader. Excellent book for those who have seen Thracian treasures in Bulgarian museums and wish to find out more.

D.M. Lang, *The Bulgarians* (Thames & Hudson: o/p). Traces the Bulgars from Central Asia until the Ottoman conquest, neatly complementing Macdermott's history. Illustrated.

Steven Runciman, *History of the First Bulgarian Empire* (1930: o/p). Though long out of print, this is the classic account of the rise and fall of Bulgaria's first medieval kingdom, by a respected scholar of Byzantine and Balkan history.

R.J. Crampton, *A Short History of Modern Bulgaria* (Cambridge University Press). Easy-to-read standard history widely available in public libraries. A good introduction to the intrigues of Bulgarian political life after the Liberation.

Stanley Evans, *A Short History of Bulgaria* (Lawrence & Wishart 1960: o/p). Slightly turgid and inevitably dated, but a useful general history, including coverage of the periods before the collapse of the Second Kingdom and after unification.

Dimiter Markovski, *Bulgaria: A Brief Historical Outline* (Sofia Press 1981). A succinct if not exactly lively account of Bulgarian history from a Marxist standpoint.

Stephen Constant, *Foxy Ferdinand* (Sidgwick & Jackson 1979). Readable but over-deferential biography of Bulgaria's unlamented tsar, who privately referred to his subjects as *mes bufles* – "my buffaloes".

Stephane Groueff, *Crown of Thorns* (Madison 1987). Boris III, Ferdinand's successor, is the subject of this slavish work – complete with endorsements by William Buckley and other right-wing nutters – written by an émigré whose dad served Boris.

J.D. Bell, *Peasants in Power* (Princeton UP 1977). Before, during and after World War I, the Agrarians were the largest radical opposition party in Bulgaria and were the "Greens" of southeastern Europe. Bell discourses on the brief period of Agrarian government and their charismatic leader, Stamboliiski, in a scholarly but uninspiring manner.

Christo Anastasoff, *The Bulgarians* (Exposition Press 1977: o/p). Academic essays on diverse aspects of Bulgarian history. Typically, while the diplomacy, religious schisms and Byzantine feuds of centuries are minutely dissected, women don't even rate a mention in the index, let alone a monograph.

Georgi Markov, *The Truth that Killed* (Weidenfeld 1983). Disillusioned by constraints on his literary career in Sofia, Georgi Markov defected for a new life in England, where he began broadcasting for the BBC World Service. Both autobiographical and a sermon à la Solzhenitsyn, this book apparently so enraged the Politburo that they ordered his murder. Jabbed with a poison-tipped umbrella on Waterloo Bridge, Markov died of a rare fever a few days later. Essential reading.

Claire Stirling, *Time of the Assassins* (Angus Robertson 1984). Readers' Digest bankrolled Stirling's hunt for the "Bulgarian Connection" whereby Mehmet Ali Agca's attempted murder of the Pope in 1981 was stage-managed by the KGB, and her tendentious account is couched in the Digest's breathless right-wing house style. Similar assertions are made in *The Plot to Kill the Pope* by **Paul Henze**. "Communist subversion" was its justification, and in an earlier book, *The Terror Network* (Holt & Reinhardt), Stirling accused Bulgaria of smuggling arms and narcotics into Turkey.

Amnesty International, *Bulgaria: Imprisonment of Ethnic Turks* (1986). Reports on the forced "assimilation" of Bulgaria's largest minority group, using documentary, eyewitness and hearsay evidence.

Hugh Poulton, *The Balkans: Minorities and States in Conflict* (Minority Rights Group 1991). Exhaustively researched compendium of information on the national minorities of Bulgaria and its neighbours.

ETHNOGRAPHY

Penko Puntev, *Bulgarian Folk Art* (Septemvri/Collets). An illustrated rundown on traditional costumes, jewellery, ceramics, ironware and other native crafts, worth the investment if you're interested in such things.

Margarita Vassileva, *Lazarouvane: Bulgarian Folk Customs and Rituals* (Septemvri 1982). Before its disappearance early this century, the *Lazarouvane* ritual (named after the feast of

Lazarus Day) combined pagan and Christian beliefs and symbolism. Details are described in this booklet (available from Collets Bookshop, address on p.319), which has nice illustrations.

FICTION AND POETRY

Yordan Yovkov, *The Inn at Antimovo and Legends of the Stara Planina* translated by John Burnip (Slavica 1989). Twentieth-century novelist Yovkov was born in Zheravna in the eastern Stara Planina (the Balkan range), and this collection of short stories recalls the atmosphere of small-town life under the Ottoman occupation.

Ivan Davidikov, *Fires of the Sunflower* translated by Ewald Osers (Forest 1988). A representative range of works by this well-respected contemporary lyric poet.

Lyubomir Levchev, *Stolen Fire* translated by Ewald Osers (Forest 1986). Levchev was a Central Committee member and President of the Writers' Union under the old regime, but despite occasional flashes of ideological content most of his work is unashamedly personal and emotional.

Geo Milev, *Roads to Freedom* translated by Ewald Osers (Forest 1988). Milev's death at the hands of the reactionary Tsankov regime in 1925 made him into one of socialist Bulgaria's favourite left-wing martyrs, but it's often forgotten that he was a ground-breaking modernist poet who borrowed from expressionism and other Western styles.

Young Poets of a New Bulgaria (Forest 1990). A collection of over twenty poets, mixing those who did well under the old regime with those who suffered for their anti-Communist convictions. Other anthologies published by Forest are **Poets of Bulgaria** and **The Devil's Dozen**, a collection of women poets, including work by the current vice-president of Bulgaria, Blaga Dimitrova.

BULGARIAN POETRY AND FICTION

Outside Bulgaria itself, knowledge of the country's literature is scant. Unlike major Slavonic tongues like Russian, Bulgarian is rarely studied abroad, and English translations of the best Bulgarian writers are scarce. Bulgarian poets and novelists have never shied away from political involvement, and, as the selection here shows, have played leading roles in struggles for liberation and democracy.

GEO MILEV

Killed by Bulgaria's military rulers in a purge of left-wing sympathizers, **Geo Milev** (1895–1925) posthumously became the darling of the postwar literary establishment. Although largely remembered for politically committed works like *September*, an epic poem based on the 1923 Uprising, Milev was also a modernist and an innovator who put Bulgarian literature in touch with the European avant-garde. The following poem, taken from *A Little Expressionist Calendar for 1921*, is reproduced from *The Road to Freedom* (Forest Books 1988).

November

When the great human wave gigantically and alarmingly
engulfs buildings, roofs, towers – O the crash and
crack of beams and tiles under its weight – and the
mighty roar of the last surge – and the despairing,
frightened scream. Rebellion!

We are building barricades: boxes, casks, bales of
paper: O jerking of wiry muscles – barricades with
red flags over them.

High above the roofs chatter the insolent machine-guns:
dizzy gyration – crowds, squadrons, cannon, armoured
cars – in the streets, squares, courtyards . . .

Suddenly in front of the Guards' barracks: two terrible
ranks of riflemen with red bands on their arms.

We are building barricades, we are digging a trench:
between Yesterday and Tomorrow.

Spartacus!

Translated by Ewald Osers

NIKOLA VAPTSAROV

Nikola Vaptsarov (1909–42) was another revolutionary firebrand who died at the hands of an authoritarian regime. Growing up among Macedonian revolutionary circles in the Pirin town of Bansko, Vaptsarov trained as an engineer and worked on merchant ships before becoming a full-time Communist activist and proletarian poet. Reminiscent of Italian futurism and Russian Constructivism, Vaptsarov's work exudes a love of factories and machines. *Epoch* is taken from the anthology *Poets of Bulgaria* (Forest Books 1988).

Epoch

Machines, steel, machines
and oil and steam and stink.
In the sky, concrete chimneys.
In the hovels, ghostly hunger.
In Mexico the golden corn is burned
in steam boilers to keep it dear
and slaves with cracked lips
harvest it night and day.
Elevators roar, the engine shakes its fist
in time's old face.
Man has broken gravity's spell
and today flies
faster than the free bird.
But still life weighs on us,
shackles our wings mercilessly
with tough rope,
chokes us on the poison mould
of old rust.
The surge of our lives is pressed down
by the steel helmet sky.
And, below, the people's dark sea
swirls turbulently.
Vain slogans of brotherhood –
life builds a wall.
Life, the inveterate spender
replies cynically – war! war!

And what about the countless starving?
War! What about the purposeless death?
And what about our wellspring of youth
which shakes the world?
An epoch of savage cruelty
galloping insanely forward.
Epoch of molten steel
on the brink of a new world.

Translated by William Meredith

BLAGA DIMITROVA

Born in 1922, **Blaga Dimitrova** is one of
Bulgaria's best respected contemporary poets.
A human rights activist during the Zhivkov
years, Dimitrov is now vice-president of the
Bulgarian Republic. *Travelling Alone*, also
taken from the anthology *Poets of Bulgaria*,
seems to express something of the long-term
solitude of the dissident writer.

Travelling Alone

Until I reach the future
countless roads must be traversed.
Will you be waiting for me still?
The wind and my hair are as one,
the sun beats red in my blood;
as soon as my arms wrap around you,
the whole hot country of me
will assimilate you.
But when will that day come?
Space and his partner time,
those relentless amortizers
of even the longest-lasting feelings,
will dwindle your love and betray me!
Yet, I have confidence
in the rigorous, exacting roads
and set out upon them alone.
At all points I am accompanied
by the tender, true, and majestic
dear profile of the Balkans.
It whispers to me on the roadway
with a voice I remember from childhood,
it whispers ancient tales
and legends freshly coined.
Solitude cannot be borne
away from home.
Only in my own land
can I be heroine enough
to travel always alone.

Translated by John Updike

VLADIMIR LEVCHEV

Vladimir Levchev (born 1957) was a prominent member of Ecoglasnost, the environmental pressure group formed to coordinate
opposition to the Zhivkov regime. His poem
November 3rd, a breakneck journey through
Bulgarian history, commemorates the day in
1989 when Ecoglasnost protestors petitioned
parliament, causing one of the biggest anti-
government protests ever seen in Sofia. The
poem is included in *Young Poets of a New
Bulgaria* (Forest Books 1990).

November 3rd

A "group of citizens" came from the East –
Asiatic centaurs
waving their tails in the air.
They mixed with another group of citizens
from the North –
fair-haired heroes
with honey-combs for shields
and sickles for swords.
A group of citizens ruled
over the Balkans –
from the dark west of the Franks
to golden Constantinople.
A group of citizens were Baptized
and they ploughed the souls of Slavs
with the Cross
from Ohrid to the Baltic.
A group of citizens survived
the Ottoman Empire
with their Bulgarian names,
verandah houses
and fatted herds.
A group of citizens adopted in Târnovo
the most democratic
Belgian constitution.
A group of citizens
survived two national catastrophes –
around the First World War,
and a second catastrophe
after the Second World War.
A group of citizens kept silent by day
and cried in their sleep
suffocated by fumes and demagogy,
and their number decreased,
and their children died of cancer
and hopelessness,
and they were beaten and cheated
and patted amiably on the shoulder.
On the third of November

a group of citizens
flooded the square –
from the church of 'Sveta Sophia'
to the Parliament,
and the bells of 'Sveti Alexander Nevski'
were ringing
and the group of their thousands
was crying:
We want clean air
and pure water!
Democracy,
glasnost
and a referendum! . . .

Meanwhile another group of citizens
(former peasants)
deaf and blind in their old age
were popping their heads out of two windows
at the Parliament House
surrounded by the militia.
And on the next day 'Rabotnichesko delo' –
the Party organ – wrote
that a group of citizens put forward
a petition to the Parliament.

Translated by Belin Tonchev

EDVIN SUGAREV

Another Ecoglasnost activist, **Edvin Sugarev**
(born in 1953) was a prominent literary critic
before opposition to the Zhivkov regime thrust
him into the maelstrom of politics. An MP for
the Union of Democratic Forces, he currently
serves as the vice-president of the Bulgarian
parliament. The following poem is too taken
from the *Young Poets of a New Bulgaria*
anthology.

A small anonymous song about the big Old Organ-grinder

(any similarity to Stalin is coincidental)

I know the Old Organ-grinder
     Old Organ-grinder
     Old Organ-grinder
He pulls on his Black Gloves
     Black Gloves
     Black Gloves
For he wouldn't like the Gold Handle
     Gold Handle
     Gold Handle
To hurt him while telling us Rich Fables
     Rich Fables
     Rich Fables

And they each Bear a Moral
     Bear a Moral
     Bear a Moral
For years on end we Thought he was Playing
     Thought he was Playing
     Thought he was Playing
But what did it turn out to be? A Grinding Mill!
     To Grind the People
     To Grind the People

Translated by Belin Tonchev

YORDAN YOVKOV

Yordan Yovkov (1880–1937) was born in
Zheravna, a sheep-farming community in the
eastern Balkan Range – the mountains known
as the *Stara planina* in Bulgarian. Despite
moving away from Zheravna in his youth – he
completed his education in Sofia before working as a schoolteacher in the Dobrudzha – he
remained fascinated with the folk tales associated with the area, and ultimately compiled
his own cycle of Zheravna-based stories,
Legends of the Stara Planina. His use of a
colloquial, rather than a literary style, made
him a respected observer of the Bulgarian
countryside and one of the most popular writers in the country.

Shibil

> *Radka was standing at the gates,*
> *up came Mustafa...*

             – Folk-song

Shibil, the terrible brigand, sought by guards
and watch 'neath tree and rock, was coming
down from the mountains and going to give
himself up. Tomorrow this piece of news would
be heard everywhere; who would believe it!
Shibil took little reckoning of that. He was in a
hurry and was thinking of other things.

He was thinking how, a month or two ago,
from the high peaks of the Blue Rocks,* where,
amidst the nests of the eagles, he too had his
brigand's nest, he saw women coming along
the road below. The molestation of women was
not among the brigands' rules, nor was there
room for women in the heart of a brigand. But
Shibil had broken many laws, and no longer
knew, or wanted to know, what was sin and
what was not. "Women here, amid the

---

*Crags north of Sliven (see p.202).

Dzhendem,*" thought he to himself, "that's good loot as well!" And up he got, not in the least concerned as to where curiosity might lead him. The brigands set off after him, laughing and their teeth gleaming like those of hungry wolves.

They dropped down the mountain, traversed the wood, which was not yet in leaf, and came out on to the road amid the Dzhendem. This was a very terrifying spot. Here the road dipped deep into the defile, twisted now to one side and now to the other, described two arcs, two hoops of a snare, in which many men had found death. And, as they had done on other occasions, the brigands barred the road, standing there, frightening, bearded, dressed in black Albanian hooded cloaks, bristling with guns. The women appeared at the turning, and when they saw them, halted as if dumbfounded; then they made a rush, some upwards, some downwards, and began to flee. But their legs collapsed under them, and they only fluttered around in one place, like wounded birds. Sinking with fear, they fell to the ground and set to weeping.

The brigands were not touched. They didn't even look at the women. Their attention was elsewhere: still standing on the road was one woman, young and beautiful. And how she was dressed up! A blue taffeta dress, a jacket of scarlet satin, a bright apron from the Sepulchre, silver buckles. And at her throat heavy necklaces, a row of large gold pieces, a row of small gold coins and *mahmuds.*** Whither had she been going, dressed up like this – to her wedding? Was this father crazy to let her out alone among these mountains?

Shibil took a pace forward. The girl looked at him calmly and straight in the eyes. A single plumbline had halted between the ribbons of her brows, her scarlet lips quivered.

"Well" she called, her gentle voice sounding oddly amid the weeping of the women. "Be about your business, or else you'll know about it. Are you not ashamed, what do you wish from a group of women?"

At these words, the brigands, who had not taken their eyes off the coins on her neck,

rushed towards her, reaching out their sinewy hands from afar. Shibil waved his arm and stopped them. Then he turned, drew himself up to his full height, and looked down on the girl, measuring her with his eyes. What a fair complexion! And slim in the waist, with wide skirts, like a doll. And what courage! His eyes gleamed merrily, he swelled with laughter. But the girl had laughed aloud before him. Her face shone, she became even more beautiful, and it could be seen that her eyes were blue and her teeth white. Shibil looked at her in amazement: what sort of devil was this?

How all came about that happened later, Shibil himself could not understand. The women came to, and, though still as timid as deer, thronged towards him. The mountains seemed to cheer up, the river roared below, a small bird called from the wood. Shibil himself had sat down on a rock, smiling and listening to the girl's chatter. What was she saying? God alone knew – words which meant nothing, words which are forgotten. But how her eyes shone, and how pleasant it was for a man to look at her! At one side, the brigands, tamed as by a miracle, had sat down and were calmly smoking.

"So you are Veliko the Crier's daughter," Shibil was saying. "Rada you are called. But how did your father come to let you loose on your own? And dressed up with gold coins and these strings of mahmuds. I shall take them!"

"You just try! Come on, give me some more, because I haven't enough! Look now," she called, pointing, "look how you've torn your sleeve. Wait a minute, I'll sew it up for you."

Shibil looked at his arm, lying on the stock of his musket; the red cloth was indeed torn. And before he could realise whether she was joking or no, he saw her right in front of him – he was looking at the down on her white face, at her red lips, and, as she looked at him, her eyes bathed him in a soft, gentle light. She was smiling and looking at him mischievously, gathering the torn edges of the sleeve, and holding needle and thread between her lips.

"Don't move," she scolded him, "I'm starting. And put something in your mouth, or I'll sew up your mind too. At least if you have one!"

They all laughed.

"Listen," went on Rada, "you ought to get married, to have somebody to do your sewing for you. Not to go about torn, like..."

---

*An Arab/Turkish word meaning "hell", *Dzhendem* is used here to describe a rocky, arid place.

**Gold coin struck in the reign of Sultan Mahmud II (1808–39).

"Like what?"

"Like a gipsy!"

Shibil frowned. The women looked at each other fearfully.

"To get married," said Shibil, "but the girls don't want me."

"But of course they'll want you. A bachelor like you!"

"All right then, you have me yourself!"

"Who, me! 'He flees through the glen, tying up his boots.' Who is he? A brigand! No, he's no use to me. I don't want a brigand."

Shibil frowned again. Rada met the pleading eyes of the women and quickly decided to correct herself.

"Maybe, maybe... I might have you. Only you'll have to ask Veliko the Crier."

And when she had paused a little, she added:

"And Murad Bey the Watch... That's done. Look how I've sewn it up for you," she said, and put down the sleeve. "Wear it in life and in health, to remember me by."

Shibil looked at her and laughed. They chatted a little longer, and then the women went on their way, and Shibil accompanied them to where the wood ended and the fields began.

It was spring when all this happened. Just here and there in the valleys had the new beech-leaves shown green, and there were only buds on the other trees. Shibil was going back to the mountains and was still smiling. The brigands followed after him, looked at the ground and stayed silent. A black raven flew over them and croaked – a bad sign! Shibil did not notice, but the brigands gathered in a group and whispered something. A woman had barred their path, a beautiful woman, and all this boded no good.

A little time passed, it grew warmer. The wild plums blossomed, the pears came into leaf, and one day, in the warm air and the sun, the cuckoo was heard. As was the custom, Shibil began to count how many years he would live, but then he fell to thinking about his age, and he felt he was old. He remembered Rada and he smiled: "What an odd mixture," he reflected, "of a woman, a child and a devil! And how everything she did was right; she said something, and it was sensible, she did something, and it was good!" And he saw her as he had seen her when she was holding the needle and thread in her lips,

looking at him and smiling. "Not a needle," thought Shibil again, and sighed, "but a knife she could have been holding like that, in her lips, and on that knife a man would willingly have died!"

Just at that time some merchants were going by, and the brigands stopped them. Terrified, turning yellow as jasmine, they could scarce hold on to their saddles, and waited to hear what Shibil should say. But Shibil did not compel them to open their saddle-bags, nor did he seek what there was in their money-belts. From a distance, he started a conversation about this and that, mentioned Veliko the Crier, and finally began to speak of Rada. The brigands looked at the ground and burned with shame. Shibil let the merchants go their way, accompanied them so far, and loudly ordered them to give his best wishes to Rada.

The brigands no longer spoke to Shibil nor dared to look him in the eyes. And when, at evening, they got back to the mountain at the top of the Blue Rocks, amid the eagles' nests, and Shibil had lain down and gone to sleep, they stayed around the fire and talked. The mountain was the same one, their refuge was safe. And yet they were restless, and kept looking around fearfully. A fox barked somewhere – and it seemed to them that a man coughed; a twig snapped – and they thought that somebody was coming. And they bent closer to each other, whispered, and watched Shibil twisting in his sleep, groaning and saying something. Then they rose and prepared to set off on their way. They did not kill him, but they fled from him as from the plague.

Shibil was left alone. And then the moneys of which he had robbed the royal treasury, the rings taken from the hands of the living and of the dead, the gold and silver from churches and monasteries – all the treasure he had accumulated and hidden in caves and hollow trees, all this flowed into the house of Veliko the Crier, all as gifts to Rada. Rich gifts in exchange for every good wish from her. But then, lo!, he received tidings which astounded him: Rada summoned him to come down to the village; her father gave them his blessing, Murad Bey pardoned him. And as a sign that his word was true, the Watch was sending him a rosary of amber, from the Sepulchre.

For long Shibil pondered whether this were a trap. Everything he possessed he had given.

And the whole wood was green now, grown heavy and dark, the glades were covered with tall grass, the peonies had flowered, the dittany blossomed, flower of the fairies. The scent of lilac and of lime wafted through the valleys. And when the roar of the stag echoed through the dark recesses, and the crested dove began to call in the Old Wood – the rock upon which Shibil laid his head at evening seemed hard, and his musket seemed heavy. He could endure no more, and set off for the village.

When he set off from the Blue Rocks it was already noon; when he got down to the road and looked back, the peaks of the mountains and the crags along them had turned pink from the set of the sun. But the eagles were still wheeling before the white scree and the rocky walls of the precipices. Those eagles, which had grown accustomed to carrion and which often, perched on some cliff, tore at human flesh. It was growing dusk, bluish mist was dropping into the valleys, long shadows were creeping over the hill-sides. The mountain had concealed itself, calm, lost in thought, as though it was looking at Shibil as he went, and asking: whither? Shibil felt sad, doubt gnawed at his heart like a worm. He sat down on a rock and thought.

And he passed everything through his mind, thought over everything. When he raised his eyes, the moon had begun to shine. Shibil saw another world in front of him, and the mountain had also become other – spread out wide, blurred, smoothed like a blue wall, wrapped in a white veil. The woods were hidden in black shadows, a chill was coming from the meadows and white mist crawled among them and wound like a serpent. Somewhere in the dark a firefly glowed, writing out with its fiery line some sign or other, some secret word, and then died out. And deep in the gorge something was singing – was it a river perhaps? – singing so peacefully, so beautifully.

Shibil was looking before him and thinking. In his eyes the rays of the moon seemed broken into short, yellow slivers, sparkled and wove themselves into some kind of confused image, which now appeared and now vanished. But Shibil clearly saw two eyes which looked at him, a smile which enticed him. He arose, set off towards those eyes and that smile, and no more looked back.

Three cautious knocks, a cautious whisper: "It's me, Mustafa," the door opened and he entered his parents' house. A fire burned in the hearth, shadows played on the walls. Reflections shone on the hilts of Shibil's pistols, on his pouches and on the tassels of his knapsack. Tall and well built, he made the house seem small for him. He met his mother's eyes and understood all the alarm which troubled her.

"Mustafa," said she, "why did you come? Will you go there?"

"I'll go."

"You'll go! When?"

"Tomorrow."

The old woman knew her son well, and knew that it was useless to insist, to reason with him. She sat by the fire, held her knees with her arms, sank her eyes in the ground, and lamented:

"Mustafa, for three days the Watchman's men have been pouring leaden bullets and sharpening their knives; they try them with their fingers to see if they are sharp, so that if they drop a hair on them they will cut the hair. And they twist their moustaches and look towards us... Mustafa, something evil is going to happen."

Shibil turned and looked at her, but his look was such that she did not know whether he had heard her and whether he had understood her. She fell silent and said nothing more.

And Shibil took off his belt, took off the pistols with the goldchased butts, the knives with the *Kulah** handles, the pouches worked in silver – everything which for him was now a heavy and useless burden.

Above, at the cafe by the church, by the open window, sat Murad Bey the Watch and Veliko the Crier. The Bey was frowning, silent, and pensively sucking his long pipe. But Veliko the Crier was jolly, he walked about the room, sweeping the floor with the bottoms of his wide trousers, again and again took out of his brightly coloured silk sash a watch as big as a ball, looked at it and put it back again. Then he rubbed his hands and said:

"Everything is organized, Bey *Effendi;* don't worry, the wolf is in the trap..."

On the table before the Watch were placed two kerchiefs: a white and a red. These were

---

*Ear-shaped handles on a knife.

the signals for the men hidden in the ambush. If the Bey waved the white kerchief from the window, it meant mercy, if he waved the red, it meant death. And they waited and peeped at the street. Nobody was to be seen. Neither had Rada gone out to the gate, nor had Mustafa been seen approaching. Veliko the Crier could not restrain himself and made a dash for home.

"Well?" asked the Bey when he returned.

"Everything is in order. She has dressed in her finest clothes, a scarlet satin jacket and a blue taffeta dress. Just the same as she dressed herself when we sent her into the mountains. And she's a woman — looking at herself in the mirror, pencilling her brows and laughing."

"What has she to laugh at," said the Bey crossly, "doesn't she know what's going to happen?"

"She knows, how could she not know?"

"Did you tell her everything?"

"Mm... I didn't tell her everything, how could I? Oh, no! As a matter of fact, I did tell her everything. Effendi, don't look for worries. It's all fixed up."

Another hour passed. Nobody came. Veliko the Crier ran back home again, stayed there longer this time, and finally came back.

"Well?" asked the Bey.

"To cap it all, now there's something else. She's crying. She says that old witch of a mother of his came. If I caught her I'd teach her a lesson. She came, Effendi, and who knows what she babbled to her. Now she's wringing her hands and crying. 'I won't allow a hair of his head to be hurt,' she shouts. 'I'll elope with him. I'll run away to the mountains with him.' Oh, women, women! That's what they are like. Never mind. I put her in order. She'll come out. You'll see her at the gate any minute now..."

The Watch stroked his beard and stayed silent. Blue smoke rings folded and twisted round his head.

But there, Rada was standing at the gate, and Mustafa was coming up the road. The Watch and Veliko the Crier ran towards the window, hid behind the curtain, and watched with bated breath.

Mustafa was walking up the middle of the street. On roofs, on fruit trees the sun was shin-ing. Far away at the bottom of the street could be seen the mountains where Mustafa was king. He was not armed. But how he was dressed! His clothes were of blue Brashov* cloth, embroidered in gold. Slim and tall, a little emaciated, a little dark, but handsome and dashing. In his hands were an amber rosary and a single red carnation — the rosary from the Bey and the carnation from Rada. He was near now, looking at Rada, looking at her and smiling.

The Bey crumpled his white beard and said:

"What a gallant fellow! How handsome!"

"The kerchief, Bey Effendi, the kerchief!" called Veliko the Crier.

"What a gallant fellow," repeated the Bey, entranced, "how handsome!"

Veliko the Crier grabbed the red kerchief and ran to the window. The Bey caught his arm.

"No, squire, such a man should not die!"

"But my girl! My honour!" shouted Veliko the Crier, broke free, went to the window and waved the red kerchief.

Muskets cracked. The panes of the windows rattled, the houses rocked, something like a black shadow fell over the earth. Shibil halted, terrifying, handsome. He broke the rosary, but did not cast aside the carnation, crossed his arms on his chest and waited. A moment or two — enough for the men to re-load their muskets. A sharp scream rose from the direc-tion of the lower ward. Shibil did not quiver. Another scream from the gate of Veliko the Crier. Shibil turned: it was Rada. She was running towards him and holding out her arms as if to protect him; he unfolded his arms, as though to embrace her. The muskets cracked again. Shibil fell, he fell at first on his face, and then turned on his back. By him fell Rada also.

And everything fell silent. The sun warmed the cobbles of the roadway. Like a spot of blood, between the two bodies, the carnation glowed red.

From the cafe by the church, from the window, somebody was desperately waving a white kerchief.

Translated by John Burnip

---

* City in Transylvania famed for its textiles.

BULGARIAN MUSIC

Until very recently all aspects of **Bulgarian musical life**, from musicological research to composition and teaching to recording and broadcasting, were under the control of the state. Although this helped to preserve the music and encourage certain developments, it also introduced distortions and affected the natural growth of the music. This has led to the paradoxical situation that the beautiful recordings of the Women's Choir of RTV Bulgaria, sold in the UK under the title of "Le Mystere des Voix Bulgares", were thought of here as folk music, when they are in fact postwar pieces by the country's leading modern composers. On the other hand, the band of Ibraim (Ivo) Papazov is seen as that of a unique Balkan jazz genius – when he is actually the most remarkable representative of a movement that managed to flourish *outside* official encouragement or censorship. Both are products of the postwar era and examples of growth from village roots, yet are utterly different in aesthetic and ideology.

OPEN THROAT

There is something about Bulgarian music that at once proclaims itself: both its matter and manner are powerfully individual. To the Western ear one of the most immediately recognizable characteristics is the vocal timbre of such singers as Nadka Karadzhova, Yanka

Rupkina and Konya Stojanova, a rich, direct and stirring sound, referred to in the West as **"open-throated"**. In fact the throat is extremely constricted and the sound is forced out, which accounts for its focus and strength and which allows the complex yet clean ornamentation that is such a striking feature of this style of singing. The only songs which the villagers dignified with the name of "folk songs" are the slow, heavily ornamented solo songs which are particularly the province of women and which used to be sung at the social events called *sedyanki*, evenings when unmarried women would gather together to sew and embroider, gossip and compare fiancés, or at the table on the occasion of various parties of one sort or another. Songs for dancing, or for various rites, were seen as being "practical" or "useful", and weren't felt quite worthy of being called music. The ornamentation, although subtly varied with each performance, was always considered a vital part of the tune, and the only time you will ever hear a song without such decoration is when the singer is too old to manage it.

Much Bulgarian music, both sung and played, was performed with no harmony, or with (at most) a simple drone like that of a bagpipe. Nonetheless, in some districts a most extraordinary system of **polyphonic performance** grew up. In the Shop area near Sofia women in the villages of Plana, Bistritsa and others sing in two- and three-part harmony, though not a harmony that Western ears readily recognize, as it is full of dissonances and tone clusters and decorated with whoops, vibrati and slides. The singers themselves say that they try to sing "as bells sound". In the Pirin district, in the southwest, the villagers sometimes sing two different two-voiced songs with two different texts simultaneously, resulting in a four-part texture. This polyphonic style of performance is normally the domain of women, although in Pirin men also sing in harmony, but with a different repertoire and in a rather different and simpler style.

The **rhythmic complexity** of Bulgarian music is also striking, and for the Hungarian composer and collector of folk songs **Bela Bartok** (1881–1945), the discovery of these irregular rhythms was a revelation. The most widespread is probably the *Ruchenitsa* dance, three beats arranged as 2 2 3, closely followed by the *Kopanitsa* (2 2 3 2 2). More complex patterns like 2 2 2 2 3 2 2 (*Bucimis*) or 3 2 2 3 2 2 2 2 3 2 2 (*Sedi Donka*, also known as *Plovdivsko Horo*) are also common. These patterns, foreign to us, are ingrained in the people, who snap their fingers in such rhythms while queueing for a bus or hanging around on the corner of the street.

Even though Bulgaria is a small country, there are several clearly defined regional styles: the earthy, almost plodding dances from Dobrudzha, in the northeast, are quite different in character from the lightning-fast dances of the Shop people, and the long heart-rending songs from the Thracian plain contrast with the sweet and pure melodies from the northeast. In the remote mountains of the Rhodopi, in the south, you can still hear the distant sound of a shepherd playing the bagpipe to his flock of a summer evening, and in the villages or small towns of the valleys groups of people sing slow, broad songs to the accompaniment of the deep *kaba gaida*, a large, deep-voiced bagpipe.

RITUAL MUSIC

The yearly round of peasant life was defined by the rhythm of the seasons, sowing and harvest, and many of the **ancient rituals** intended to ensure fertility and good luck still survive, though more as a folk tradition than in the belief that they will produce any kind of magical effect. All these customs, such as *Koleduvane*, which normally involves groups of young men going in procession around the village and asking for gifts from the households; *Laduvane* at the New Year; and *Lazaruvane* on Saint Lazarus Day in spring (the most important holiday for the young women, when they take their turn to sing and dance through the streets) have particular songs and dances connected with them. The songs are usually simple, repetitive and very old. The most startling of these rites, *nestinarstvo* from the villages of Bulgari, Kondolovo and Rezovo in Strandzha, has died out in its original form, when its exponents would fall into a trance and dance on hot coals to the sound of bagpipe and drum to mark the climax of the feast of saints Konstantin and Elena, but it's sometimes presented at festivals and folklore shows. The wild stirring music remains the same.

These days the two most important rites of passage in Bulgarian life, whether in the country or in the town, are **getting married** and **leaving home** to do military service. Both these occasions are marked by music. Every aspect of a wedding – the arrival of the groom's wedding party, the leading out of the bride to meet it, the procession to the church and so on – has a particular melody or song associated with it. The songs sung at the bride's house the night before the wedding are by no means joyful celebrations of marriage: on the contrary, they are the saddest songs in the whole body of Bulgarian music, because the bride is leaving home, never to return to her parents' house.

Parties to see the young men off to the army are more cheerful. In the town the family of the recruit hires a restaurant and a band, normally some combination of accordion, violin, electric guitar, clarinet/saxophone and drum kit which plays a haphazard mix of folk, pop and other melodies, and the guests eat, drink and dance. In the country the feast is often held in the evening and out of doors. In the village of Mirkovo the guests were entertained by a little band of two clarinets, trumpet and accordion, who played the slow melodies called *na trapeza* (at the table) while the guests ate. Later the young soon-to-be soldier is led round and presented with gifts of money, flowers or shirts. (Shirts in fact play a great role in Bulgarian folk life. At weddings each member of the party wears a handkerchief pinned to their breast, but the more important relatives are permitted an entire shirt, sometimes still in its cellophane wrapping.)

After all the food has gone, the band strikes up a set of local dance tunes, and everyone rushes to join in a *horo* whose leader capers and leaps, all the while flourishing an enormous flag on a long pole. Dancing is very popular, especially among villagers; and at the end of a festival or similar event, if the band starts to play a bit for pleasure you can see people – from grannies to young children – literally racing across the grass to join the circle.

In most of the country the bands for weddings and so on are made up of modern, factory-made instruments often amplified, but around the town of Yambol in the Strandzha area, in the east, many people prefer the old folk instruments and if they can afford it, will even hire a band from Sofia to come and play them.

FOLK INSTRUMENTS

Such a band will almost invariably consist of *gaida* (bagpipe), *kaval* (end-blown flute), *gadulka* (a bowed stringed instrument) and *tambura* (a strummed stringed instrument), sometimes with the addition of the large drum, the *tapan*. They always were common throughout the country, but when after World War II the state founded its own ensembles for folk songs and dances, these instruments were the ones chosen to make up the huge orchestras thought necessary to accompany them. As a result they have undergone certain developments and refinements to aid reliability of tuning and tone, while some players have brought their skill to a quite unbelievable peak of virtuosity.

The **gaida** is maybe the most famous of all these instruments, although it's fairly simply made: a chanter for the melody, a drone and a mouth-tube for blowing, all attached into a small goatskin which acts as a reservoir for air. It's capable of a partly chromatic scale of just over an octave, and in the hands of a master such as Kostadin Varimezov or Nikola Atanasov its wild sound has an astonishing turn of speed and rhythmic force. These players also have the ability to use the possibilities that the gaida has for rich ornamentation to perform beautiful versions of slow songs and other *na trapeza* melodies. In the Rhodopi they have a huge bagpipe, the deep-voiced *kaba gaida* which accompanies singing or plays for dancing, sometimes alone and sometimes in groups of two, three, four or even more. There is one group called rather literally *Sto kaba gaidi* (One hundred kaba gaidi), and although this could be thought excessive the sound is undeniably impressive.

Like the gaida the **kaval** was originally a shepherds' instrument, and some of its melodies, or rather freely extemporized meditations on certain motifs which are specific to it, go by such names as "Taking the herd to water", "At noon", "The lost lamb". The modern *kaval* is made of three wooden tubes fitted together, the topmost of which has a bevelled edge that the player blows against on the slant to produce a note. The middle tube has eight finger holes and the last has four more holes which affect the tone and the tuning. They are sometimes called *Devil's holes*, and there is a tale that were made by the Devil who was so jealous of the playing of a young shepherd that

he stole his *kaval* while he was sleeping and bored the extra holes to ruin it. Of course they only made the instrument sound sweeter and the Devil was, as is usual in folk tales, discomfited once more.

The school of *kaval* playing led by Nikola Ganchev, and Stoyan Velichkov that has grown up since the war is extremely refined and capable of all manner of nuances of sound. The sound is sweet and clear (the folk say "honeyed"), the low (kaba) register is rich and buzzing, and in the last ten or so years someone (possibly Nikola Kostov) invented a new technique called *kato klarinet* (clarinet style) where the instrument is played as though it were a trumpet, producing a sound very like the low register of the clarinet.

The **gadulka** is a relative of the *rebec*, with a pear-shaped body held upright on the knee, tucked into the belt or cradled in a strap hung round the player's neck. It has three, sometimes four bowed strings and as many as nine sympathetic strings which resonate when the instrument is played, producing an unearthly shimmering resonance behind the melody. The *gadulka* is unbelievably hard to play – there are no frets and no fingerboard, the top string has to be stopped by fingernails and the whole thing keeps wriggling out of your grasp like a live fish. This makes the *gadulka* players' habit of showing off by playing virtuoso selections from the popular classics both startling and highly irritating. Mihail Marinov and Atanas Vulchev are among the older players of note, and Nikolai Petrov is one of the younger generation.

The **tambura** is a member of the lute family, with a flat-backed pear-shaped body and a long fretted neck. Its original form, found in Pirin and in the central Rhodopi, had two courses of strings, one of which usually provided a drone while the melody was played on the other. These days the common form of the instrument has four courses tuned like the top four strings of a guitar, and in groups it both strums chords and plays melodies.

STATE CONTROL

The extent to which music was controlled by the former Communist government and the extent to which the musicians themselves were able to escape this control is an integral part of the development of music in Bulgaria. In the early Fifties the Communists set up the **State**

Ensemble for Folk Songs and Dances under the leadership of **Philip Kutev**, an extraordinarily talented composer and arranger whose style of writing and arranging became the model for a whole network of professional and amateur groups across the country. His great gift was the ability to take the sounds of village singers, drone-based and full of close dissonances but essentially harmonically static, and from this forge a musical language which answered the aesthetic demands of western European concepts of form and harmony without losing touch with the particularly Bulgarian feeling of the original tunes. If you compare his work with the attempts of earlier arrangers to force the tunes into a harmonic system which they really didn't fit, his success is as obvious as their failure. This is what you hear on the "Le Mystere des Voix Bulgares" recordings, and from the Trio Bulgarka and the instrumental group Balkana.

It is impossible to over-estimate the tight grip that the state had on every aspect of life, and this is as true of music as of anything else. What began as a praiseworthy attempt to preserve and enrich folklore became a straitjacket to which all musicians had to conform or else stop working as musicians. It reached even such ridiculous extremes as prescribing a certain percentage of Russian songs to be played in the course of an evening's entertainment in a restaurant, say, to demonstrate the eternal friendship of the Bulgarian and Soviet peoples. And you couldn't ignore this insanity, because there were people around whose job it was to make sure that you were doing it. One musician told me with rage how he had had to audition all his new songs and dances to a committee which he called "The Committee of Pensioners" before he was permitted to perform them on the radio. If they were "not Bulgarian enough" then permission was refused. Even if it was granted, then the style of performance had to be acceptable. "Once they told me that I was playing too fast, and that Bulgarian music is not played so fast. This was a tune that I myself had written, it was I that was playing it, and I am a Bulgarian musician. How should they tell me the way to play my own song? But they could. I tell you, Bulgarian music used to be behind closed shutters — but now the shutters have been opened."

This doesn't mean that the people working in the field of folklore were all apparatchiks or that they failed to produce beautiful music. The network of regional professional ensembles fed by a stream of talent trained in special schools set up to teach folk instruments and folk singing meant that there were time, money and opportunity available for people to develop the approved language in their own way, and many composers have created their own individual style. Amongst arrangers and composers, Kosta Kolev is one unmistakable voice, and the work of Stefan Mutafchiev and Nikolai Stoikov with the "Trakiya" ensemble in Plovdiv was very progressive. The series of regional competition/festivals held around the country culminating once every five years at the vast gathering of amateur music groups at the **Koprivshtitsa festival** (see p.184), the mass-production of cheap folk instruments and the encouragement shown to amateurs have managed to keep music alive in the villages. Unfortunately, this has been at the cost of alienating many people, particularly young city-dwellers, by means of insisting on such propagandist drivel as "Mladata Traktoristka" ("The young girl tractor-driver") and referring to them as "contemporary developments in folk creativity". No-one now knows what will happen, given the economic crisis in Bulgaria, but there will certainly be less money either to develop or control folk music.

The festival at Koprivshtitsa is particularly important, not merely because of its size (there are literally thousands of performers bused in from all over the country) but because it is the only one devoted to amateur performers. Practically the only recordings of genuine village music that the state record company *Balkanton* has ever released are from this festival – *Koprivshtitsa '76* and the double album *Koprivshtitsa '86* – and they are among the most beautiful and valuable recordings of Bulgarian songs and dances ever made.

Around the end of the nineteenth century factory-made instruments like the accordion, clarinet and violin appeared in the country and were soon used to play dance music and to accompany songs. Modern **accordion style** was pretty much defined by **Boris Karloff** (no relation to the horror-movie star) who wrote a number of elegant tunes which have become standards. Karloff's *Krivo Horo* in particular is famous; every band that plays Bulgarian music knows it. More modern accordionists worthy of note are the Gypsy Ibro Lolov (sometimes known as Ivo as a result of the programme of Bulgarianization of names of Turkish origin under the Zhivkov regime), Traicho Sinapov and Kosta Kolev, also well known as a composer, arranger and conductor who plays in a very unique style which contrasts in its restraint and care with the high-speed acrobatics of some of the younger players. By far the most brilliant of these is the young **Petar Ralchev**, a Thracian, who unlike some of the speed-merchants combines new ideas with a lot of taste and, more importantly, a lot of soul.

WEDDING BANDS

The **wedding bands** are a fascinating example of "underground" folk music that is currently an extremely important part of Bulgarian musical life. Unlike the musicians mentioned above, who were approved by the state (though none the worse for that) they existed outside the framework of official music making, hired to play at weddings, the seeing off of recruits and various village festivities. Because they did not have to conform to the communist idealization of the people and the people's music in order to record or get on the radio, they were free to experiment with new instrumentation, mixtures of folk instruments like *gaida* and *kaval* with electric guitar, synthesizer and kit drums, rock and jazz rhythms, and foreign tunes. As the recording industry in Bulgaria didn't allow the formation of a commercial style like that of the Yugoslav folk-based pop music, they simply took those songs straight across, learning them from radio broadcasts picked up from over the frontier (or from pirate cassette tapes) and performing them to a public that responded to their directness and energy. It was only in the mid-Eighties that officialdom realized the existence of this music, and through the efforts of some quite brave and far-seeing musicologists was persuaded to recognize them as worthy of public support and recording. A tri-yearly festival was set up in the town of **Stambolovo** (hence their alternative name *Stambolovski orkestri*) which presented them in maybe a slightly bowdlerized form – they were subjected to the "assistance" of approved musical directors – but the *Balkanton* record *Stambolovo '88* gives a very good impression of

the amazing revelation of this kind of previously unsuspected music.

Ivo Papazov is the best known of these musicians in the West, thanks to the work of Hannibal Records, who managed to record him with his electric band after a long struggle with the bureaucracy. His flirtations with jazz following his work in the late Seventies and early Eighties with the Plovdiv Jazz-Folk Ensemble are maybe less successful than his startling transformations of traditional Thracian music, but some of his most intriguing achievements lie in the performance of Turkish music. He is of Turkish origin, and even in the period just prior to the fall of the Zhivkov regime when the very existence of a Turkish minority in Bulgaria was denied, you could get home-made recordings of Papazov playing Turkish melodies with a typical small band of the type common today in Istanbul. Now that under the new government *Balkanton* has released tapes and records of "Turkish Music from Bulgaria" he should be producing some interesting music. His second Hannibal release, "Balkanology", begins with a Turkish dance and also includes Macedonian and Greek material.

There are many other modern bands of this type, often Gypsy, now using the new freedom in all kinds of ways. The bands "Sever", "Juzhni Vetar", "Vievska Grupa", "Shoumen" and "Trakiiski Solisti" all have fresh and startling ways of interpreting their traditional music. Some of these have now made commercial recordings, others are still only to be heard live or on poor quality home-made tapes sold in the markets of the small towns where they live.

NEW SOUNDS

It is not only the wedding bands who have lately been pushing back the boundaries. Some of the bands that play purely traditional instruments have been making experiments. Black Crown records in the UK has recently released a record of the band Loznitsa called *Moods*, featuring both the old master of the *gaida* **Nikola Atanasov** and the incredible young *kaval* player Georgi Zhelyaskov: it's a good representation of the new trend. Particularly worth investigating is the work of the *kaval* player Teodosi Spassov who has not only recorded a very beautiful and practically avant-garde folk album, "Dulug Put" in collaboration with composer Mutaftchiev, but also played to great acclaim with the well-known Bulgarian jazz pianist Milcho Leviev on his first concert in Sofia after twenty years' exile. Spassov's album, *The Sand Girl* is successful folk-jazz fusion from one of Bulgaria's most exciting young players.

It's impossible to predict the **future** of Bulgarian music. At the time of writing the country is making a painful transition to democracy and is in the grip of a serious economic crisis. It will probably be impossible to sustain the network of festivals of music, dance and folk art as there simply isn't the money to support them. Koprivshtitsa will

almost certainly survive given its importance, but even the wedding bands are likely to find hard times ahead as people have less money to spend on their marriage festivities. On the other hand, increased opportunities for travel and the new availability of influences and techniques from the rest of the world may result in something remarkable. Some very wonderful music may come from Bulgaria in the next few years.

This article – an edited extract from World Music: the Rough Guide *was researched and written by* Kim Burton.

DISCOGRAPHY

Various: *Le Mystere des Voix Bulgares* **Vol.1**
4 Ad (UK)
From the archives of Radio Bulgaria. Classic melodies and arrangements given a hauntingly beautiful performance by the Women's Choir of the Radio. Indispensable. There are two further volumes.

Trio Bulgarka: *The Forest Is Crying*
Hannibal HNBC1342 (UK)
Various: *Balkana*
Hannibal (UK)
The three singers perform a cappella or accompanied by one of Bulgaria's best instrumental groups, the Trakiiskata Troika (Thracian Trio). The two albums include some Bulgarian favourites re-recorded for a Western audience. The Balkana album has instrumental numbers as well.

Ivo Papazov and his Orchestra: *Orpheus Ascending* **and** *Balkanology*
Hannibal HNBC 1363 (UK)
Both albums are splendid examples of Papazov's irrepressible style. The virtuoso clarinetist and his band play all sorts of goodies from their collection of wedding music. Fast and furious: Gypsies love it, musicologists despair. The *Balkanology* album includes more ethnically diverse material and, with the allusion to Charlie Parker, perhaps a touch more jazz.

Losnica: *Moods*
Black Crown Workalb1
Gaida and *kaval* playing by Nikola Atanasov and Georgi Zhelyaskov: interesting if you enjoy recent Bulgarian music.

Various: *Stambolovo '88*
Balkanton VNA (or BHA) 12367/8 (Bulgaria)
A selection of wild and wonderful experiments by some of the wedding bands who took part in the 1988 Stambolovo festival. They come from all across the country and give some idea of the diversity of Bulgarian styles and their modern development.

Koprivshtitsa '76 & Koprivshtitsa '86
Balkanton BHA 2067 & 11902/903 (Bulgaria)
Recordings of some of the best amateur musicians and groups to take part in the great quinquennial festival at Koprovshtitsa. Highly recommended if you can find them.

Various: *Village Music of Bulgaria*
Nonesuch (USA)
Excellent selection of material including a stunning performance of the song "Izlel e Delyo Haidutin" by Nadja Balkanova which was the first Bulgarian song in space, where it travelled on the spacecraft "Voyager" as one of its examples of earth culture.

Various: *Popular Clarinetists from Thrace*
Balkanton (Bulgaria)
A cracking collection of superb playing from six of Bulgaria's best clarinetists, including Petko Radev and Ivo Papasov. If you can find it, get it !

The Bisserov Sisters & Trakiiskata Troika
Balkanton (Bulgaria)
A well-produced album with some exhilarating songs from the three sisters on side one, accompanied by a selection of dances from the Trakiiskata Troika on side two.

LANGUAGE

Bulgarian is a South Slavonic tongue closely related to Slovene and Serbo-Croat, and more distantly to **Russian**, which most Bulgars learn at school. Although **English** language studies are increasingly popular in Bulgaria, **French** and **German** were taught more widely in the past, and on the whole you'll find that English is widely understood only in Sofia, Plovdiv, and the ski and beach resorts favoured by British holidaymakers. Those who devote their efforts to acquiring some Bulgarian will find that a little goes a long way in endearing yourself to the average person.

Bulgarian National Tourist offices usually supply free **phrase books**, which, together

THE CYRILLIC ALPHABET

Most signs, menus and so on are in the **Cyrillic alphabet**, but along highways you'll also see signs in the Roman alphabet. For easy reference, you'll find **town names** boxed in both alphabets at the end of each chapter. And note that at railway stations, the Roman version won't be visible before the train pulls out unless you sit up front.

There are different ways of **transcribing** Cyrillic into Latin script (for example, "Cherven Bryag" or "Červen Brjag" for ЧЕРВЕН БРЯГ; "Târnovo" or "Turnovo" for ТЪРНОВО) but – with a few notable exceptions like "Bulgaria" and "Sofia" instead of "Bâlgariya" and "Sofiya" – we've tried to adhere to the following system. This shows Cyrillic characters in capital and lower case form, with their Roman transcription and a roughly equivalent sound in English.

It's useful to know that putting the word *da* before **verbs** makes an infinitive (*iskam da kupya*, "I want to buy"); while *ne* is used to form the negative (*ne iskam*, "I don't want"). Use of the particle *li* turns the sentence into a question – *imate li . . .?* is "do you have . . .?".

А а	a as in father	П п	p as in pot
Б б	b as in bath	Р р	r as in rasp
В в	v as in vat	С с	s as in sat
Г г	g as in gag	Т т	t as in tap
Д д	d as in dog	У у	u as in rule
Е е	e as in den	Ф ф	f as in fruit
Ж ж	zh like the 's' in measure	Х х	h as in loch (aspirated)
З з	z as in zap	Ц ц	ts as in shuts
И и	as in bit (or 'b*ee*', at the end of a word)	Ч ч	ch as in church
		Ш ш	sh as in dish
Й й	i 'y' as in youth	Щ щ	sht like the last syllable of 'sloshed'
К к	k as in kit	Ъ ъ	â like the 'u' in 'but'
Л л	l as in like	Ь ь	(this character softens the preceding
М м	m as in met		consonant)
Н н	n as in not	Ю ю	yu as in you
О о	o as in got (never as in go)	Я я	ya as in yarn

In practice there are the odd **exceptions** to this pronunciation: Bulgarians pronounce ГРАД (town) as "grat" instead of "grad", for example. But the system generally holds good and if you follow it you'll certainly be understood.

The most important thing is to work on **pronouncing** certain sounds (Ж, Х, Ц, Ч, Ш, Щ, Ь, Ю and Я in the alphabet) and attuning your ear to Bulgarian's throatily-mellow timbre. Most Bulgars sway their heads sideways for **"yes"** and nod to signify **"no"**, but a few do things "our way", increasing the possibility of misunderstandings which can leave both parties floundering through *das* and *nes*. For more on **body language**, see p.30.

with the vocabulary below, should see you through. Few self-study courses are regularly available, although *A Course in Modern Bulgarian* by Milka Hubenova, published by Slavica in the USA, is one of the most user-friendly if you can find it. *Collets*

International Bookshop (laddress on p.319), will probably be the best place to look. Once in Bulgaria itself, an increasing number of Bulgarian-English dictionaries and phrase books are available from bookshops and street stalls.

BULGARIAN WORDS AND PHRASES

BASICS

Do you speak English/ German/French	*Govorite li angliiski/ nemski/ frenski?*	good morning	*dobro utro*
yes – okay	*da – dobre*	good day/evening	*dobâr den/ vecher*
no/not	*ne*	good night	*leka nosht*
I don't understand	*ne vi razbiram*	goodbye	*dovizhdane*
please – excuse me	*molya – izvinete*	please speak more slowly	*govorete po-bavno, ako obichate*
thank you	*blagodarya* (or *merci*)	please write it down	*bihte li ya napisali?*
you're welcome	*nyama zashto*	what's this called?	*kak se kazva tova?*
how are you?	*kak ste?*	come here!	*ela!*
what's up?	*kakvo ima?*	go on!	*haide!*
hi !	*zdravei*		

REQUESTS

Have you got . . .?	*Imate li. . . ?*	Haven't you a cheaper room?	*Nyamate li po-evtina staya?*
a single/double room	*Staya s edno leglo/ dve legla*	Where can I buy . . .?	*Kâde moga da si kupya . . . ?*
How much for the night?	*Kolko se plashta na vecher za leglo?*	The bill, please	*Smetkata, molya*
It's too expensive	*Mnogo e skâpo*	How many/how much?	*Kolko?*
		Please give me . . .	*Daite mi. . . molya*

For more on *sleeping* and *eating* see p.16 and p.22.

REACTIONS

good, bad	*dobro, loshe*	early, late	*rano, kâsno*
expensive, cheap	*skâpo, evtino*	hot/cold	*toplo/studeno*
difficult, interesting	*trudno, interesno*	my/mine, ours, yours	*moe, nashe, vashe*
beautiful, calm	*hubavo, spokoino*	what, which?	*kakvo?*
big, little/few	*golyamo, malko*	how?	*kak?*
new, old	*novo, staro*	this, that	*tova, onova*

N.B. If you're uncertain about a noun's gender it's easiest to give the qualifying adjective or pronoun a neuter ending (as above).

SIGNS

entrance, exit	ВХОД, ИЗХОД	day off	СВОБОДЕН ДЕН
open, closed	ОТВОРЕНО ЗАТВОРЕНО	pause/lunch break	ПОЧИВКА
		closed for repairs	НА РЕМОНТ
vacant, occupied	СВОБОДНО ЗАЕТО	attention/danger	ВНИМАНИЕ
		no smoking	ПУШЕНЕТО
admission free	ВХОД СВОБОДЕН		ЗАБРАНЕНО

GETTING ABOUT

here	*tuka*	Where do I get off for...?	*Na koya spirka da slyaza za...?*
there	*tam*	Stop!	*Spri!*
How can I get there?	*Kak moga da otida do tam?*	Are there connections for...?	*Ima li vrâzka za...?*
Which bus to the centre?	*S koi avtobus moga da otida v tsentra?*	Where do I change?	*Kâde tryabva da smenya?*
Is this the bus for...?	*Tozi li e avtobusât za...?*	Please reserve me...	*Molya, zapazete mi...*
Is this the boat to...?	*Tozi li e prahodât za..?*	two sleepers/seats	*dve legla/mesta*
Where are you going?	*Za kâde pâtuvate?*	Which platform for the ..... train?	*Na koi kolovoz se namira . . .vlakât za...*
Is it near?	*Blizo li?*		

More help with *transport* on p.12.

TIME AND DATES

What's the time?	*Kolko e chasât?*	March	*Mart*
When?	*Koga?*	April	*April*
today, tomorrow	*dnes, utre*	May	*Mai*
(the day before) yesterday	*(za)vchera*	June	*Yuni*
in the morning	*sutrinta*	July	*Yuli*
in the afternoon	*sled obed*	August	*Avgust*
this week	*tazi sedmitsa*	September	*Septemvri*
from . . .until . . .	*ot . . .do . . .*	October	*Oktomvri*
January	*Yanuari*	November	*Noemvri*
February	*Fevruari*	December	*Dekemvr*

Monday	*ponedelnik*	ПОНЕДЕЛНИК
Tuesday	*vtornik*	ВТОРНИК
Wednesday	*sryada*	СРЯДА
Thursday	*chetvârtâk*	ЧЕТВЪРТЬК
Friday	*petâk*	ПЕТЬК
Saturday	*sâbota*	СЪБОТА
Sunday	*nedelya*	НЕДЕЛЯ

NUMBERS

1	*edin, edna, edno*	11	*edinaiset*	21	*dvaiset i edno*
2	*dve, dva*	12	*dvanaiset*	30	*triiset*
3	*tri*	13	*trinaiset*	40	*chetiriiset*
4	*chetiri*	14	*chetirinaiset*	50	*petdeset*
5	*pet*	15	*petnaiset*	60	*shestdeset*
6	*shest*	16	*shestnaiset*	70	*sedemdeset*
7	*sedem*	17	*sedemnaiset*	80	*osemdeset*
8	*osem*	18	*osemnaiset*	90	*devetdeset*
9	*devet*	19	*devetnaiset*	100	*sto*
10	*deset*	20	*dvaiset*	500	*petstotin*
				1000	*hilyada*

GLOSSARY

ALAFRANGA Term for the combination of native woodwork and textiles with Western fashions in nineteenth-century interior design (from *à la française*); or painted niches and walls in National Revival-style houses.

BANYA Public bath or spa.

BASHIBAZOUKS Murderous bands of *pomaks* (see below) and Turks, employed to punish rebellions against Ottoman rule.

BEY Turkish provincial governor.

BLATO Marsh or reed-encircled lake.

BOLYARIN Medieval Bulgarian nobleman (a *bolyarka* is a noblewoman).

CARAVANSERAI Hostelry for merchants in Ottoman times.

CHARDAK Balcony or porch.

CHARSHIYA A bazaar or street of workshops, once a typical feature of Bulgarian towns.

CHERKVA Church (see also *Tsârkva*).

CHESHMA Public drinking fountain.

CHERNO MORE Black Sea.

CHETA Unit of resistance fighters (originally applied to the Bulgarian Legion of the 1860s).

CHIFLIK Farm, or small administrative unit in Ottoman times.

CHORBADZHII Village headmen (literally, "Soup drinkers") or rich landowners; also perjorative term for those who collaborated during the Ottoman occupation.

DERE Stream.

DVORETS Palace.

DUPKA Hole, den or cave.

DZHAMIYA A mosque (also spelt DJAMI or DZHAMIJA).

ESONARTHEX Short porch before the narthex of a church.

EZERO Lake.

GORA Forest, hill or mountain (*Sredna Gora* – Central Range).

GRAD City or town. The oldest quarter is often known as the *Stariyat grad* or the *varosh* (see below).

GRADINA Garden.

HAIDUK Outlaw, usually considered as a freedom-fighter by Bulgarians and as a bandit by the Turks.

HALI Market hall.

HAN Inn or caravanserai.

HISAR Fortress.

HIZHA Hikers' chalet or mountain hut.

IGUMEN Father-superior of a monastery.

IZVOR A spring.

JANISSARIES An elite military fighting corps raised from foreigners whom the Turks abducted during childhood (under the hated *devsirme* system), and indoctrinated with fanatical loyalty to the sultan.

KÂRDZHALI Turkish outlaws, particularly active in the late eighteenth and early nineteenth centuries.

KÂSHTA House.

KAZA Small Ottoman administrative unit.

KHAN (or HAN) Supreme ruler of the Bulgar tribes and, later, the first Bulgarian state; the title is of Central Asian origin.

KOMITADZHI Another word for *Cheta* (see above).

KONAK The headquarters of an Ottoman *chiflik* or region; including the governor's residence, a garrison and a prison.

KORSO Evening promenade.

KREPOST Fortress.

KVARTAL Suburb.

KVARTIRA Room (*chastni kvartiri* – private rooms).

LIBERATION, THE The attainment of Bulgaria's independence from Ottoman rule, following the Russo-Turkish war of 1877–78.

MAGISTRALA Main highway.

MAHALA Quarter or area of town occupied by a particular ethnic or religious group (*tsiganskata mahala* – the Gypsy quarter).

MALKO Small or little, as in Malko Târnovo – Little Târnovo.

MANASTIR Monastery.

MINDER Couches or seats built into a room.

MOST Bridge.

NAOS Innermost part of an Orthodox church.

NARTHEX Entrance hall of Orthodox church.

NATIONAL REVIVAL Nineteenth-century upsurge in Bulgarian culture and national consciousness. Sometimes called the Bulgarian renaissance.

NATIONAL REVIVAL STYLE Architecture developed during the eighteenth and nineteenth centuries, characterized by the use of oriels and decorative features such as carved wooden ceilings, stylized murals and niches. Best seen in Târnovo, Tryavna and Plovdiv.

NOS Cape.

OSVOBOZHDENIETO The Liberation (see above).

PAMETNIK Monument or memorial.

PÂT Road.

PAZAR Market.

PESHTERA Cave (see also *Dupka*).

PLANINA Mountain.

PLOSHTAD (*Pl.*) Square.

POMAKS Bulgarians who converted to Islam during the Turkish occupation, or their descendants; mainly resident in the Rhodopes.

POP An Orthodox priest.

PROHOD Mountain pass.

PROLOM Gorge or defile.

RAYAH (or RAYA) "The Herd", as the Ottomans called and treated the non-Muslim subjects of their empire.

REKA River.

SELO Village.

SHOSE Avenue or highway (from the French Chaussé).

SOFRA Low table with a circular top of copper or brass.

SVETI (*Sv.*) Saint; blessed or holy (*Sveta* is the feminine form: *Sveta Bogoroditsa* – Holy Virgin).

TELL Mound of earth left by successive generations of human settlement. Tells in the Plain of Thrace provide evidence of Bulgaria's Neolithic and Bronze Age inhabitants.

THRACIANS Inhabitants of Bulgaria during the pre-Christian era.

TSÂRKVA Church.

TURISTICHESKA SPALNYA Tourist hostel, providing cheap dorm-type accommodation.

ULITSA (*Ul.*) Street.

VELIKO Great, as in Veliko Târnovo – Great Târnovo.

VAROSH Central quarter of old Balkan town.

VÂZRAZHDANE National Revival.

VILAYET Large Ottoman administrative unit; province.

VRÂH Summit or peak.

YAZOVIR Reservoir, artificial lake.

ACRONYMS

BKP Bulgarian Communist Party.

BSP Bulgarian Socialist Part (successor to the BKP).

BZNS Bulgarian Agrarian National Union.

DPS (*Dvizhenieto za prava i svobodi*). The Movement for Rights and Freedoms – a party supported by Bulgarian Muslims and ethnic Turks.

DS (*Dâzhavna Signurnost*). State security police.

IMRO (Internal Macedonian Revolutionary Organization). Macedonian separatist organization, predominantly terroristic from 1893–1934.

SDS (*Sâyuz na demokratichnite sili*). Union of Democratic Forces – the governing coalition.

INDEX

DIRECT ORDERS IN THE UK

Title	ISBN	Price
Amsterdam	1858280869	£7.99
Andalucia	185828094X	£8.99
Australia	1858280354	£12.99
Barcelona & Catalunya	1858281067	£8.99
Berlin	1858280338	£8.99
Brazil	1858281024	£9.99
Brittany & Normandy	1858281261	£8.99
Bulgaria	1858280478	£8.99
California	1858280907	£9.99
Canada	185828130X	£10.99
Classical Music on CD	185828113X	£12.99
Corsica	1858280893	£8.99
Crete	1858281326	£8.99
Cyprus	185828032X	£8.99
Czech & Slovak Republics	185828029X	£8.99
Egypt	1858280753	£10.99
England	1858280788	£9.99
Europe	185828077X	£14.99
Florida	1858280109	£8.99
France	1858280508	£9.99
Germany	1858281288	£11.99
Greece	1858281318	£9.99
Greek Islands	1858281636	£8.99
Guatemala & Belize	1858280451	£9.99
Holland, Belgium & Luxembourg	1858280877	£9.99
Hong Kong & Macau	1858280664	£8.99
Hungary	1858281237	£8.99
India	1858281040	£13.99
Ireland	1858280958	£9.99
Italy	1858280311	£12.99
Kenya	1858280435	£9.99
London	1858291172	£8.99
Mediterranean Wildlife	0747100993	£7.95
Malaysia, Singapore & Brunei	1858281032	£9.99
Morocco	1858280400	£9.99
Nepal	185828046X	£8.99
New York	1858280583	£8.99
Nothing Ventured	0747102082	£7.99
Pacific Northwest	1858280923	£9.99
Paris	1858281253	£7.99
Poland	1858280346	£9.99
Portugal	1858280842	£9.99
Prague	185828015X	£7.99
Provence & the Côte d'Azur	1858280230	£8.99
Pyrenees	1858280931	£8.99
St Petersburg	1858281334	£8.99
San Francisco	1858280826	£8.99
Scandinavia	1858280397	£10.99
Scotland	1858280834	£8.99
Sicily	1858280370	£8.99
Spain	1858280818	£9.99
Thailand	1858280168	£8.99
Tunisia	1858280656	£8.99
Turkey	1858280885	£9.99
Tuscany & Umbria	1858280915	£8.99
USA	185828080X	£12.99
Venice	1858280362	£8.99
Wales	1858280966	£8.99
West Africa	1858280141	£12.99
More Women Travel	1858280982	£9.99
World Music	1858280176	£14.99
Zimbabwe & Botswana	1858280419	£10.99

Rough Guide Phrasebooks

Title	ISBN	Price
Czech	1858281482	£3.50
French	185828144X	£3.50
German	1858281466	£3.50
Greek	1858281458	£3.50
Italian	1858281431	£3.50
Spanish	1858281474	£3.50

Rough Guides are available from all good bookstores, but can be obtained directly in the UK* from Penguin by contacting:

Penguin Direct, Penguin Books Ltd, Bath Road, Harmondsworth, West Drayton, Middlesex UB7 0DA; or telephone our credit line on 0181-899 4036 (9am–5pm) and as for Penguin Direct. Visa, Access and Amex accepted. Delivery will normally be within 14 working days. Penguin Direct ordering facilities are only available in the UK.

The availability and published prices quoted are correct at the time of going to press but are subject to alteration without prior notice.

* For USA and international orders, see separate price list

DIRECT ORDERS IN THE USA

tle	ISBN	Price
msterdam	1858280869	$13.59
ndalucia	185828094X	$14.95
ustralia	1858280354	$18.95
arcelona & Catalunya	1858281067	$17.99
erlin	1858280338	$13.99
razil	1858281024	$15.95
rittany & Normandy	1858281261	$14.95
ulgaria	1858280478	$14.99
alifornia	1858280907	$14.95
anada	185828130X	$14.95
assical Music on CD	185828113X	$19.95
orsica	1858280893	$14.95
rete	1858281326	$14.95
yprus	185828032X	$13.99
zech & Slovak Republics	185828029X	$14.95
gypt	1858280753	$17.95
ngland	1858280788	$16.95
urope	185828077X	$18.95
orida	1858280109	$14.95
ance	1858281245	$16.95
ermany	1858281288	$17.95
reece	1858281318	$16.95
reek Islands	1858281636	$14.95
uatemala & Belize	1858280451	$14.95
olland, Belgium & Luxembourg	1858280877	$15.95
ong Kong & Macau	1858280664	$13.95
ungary	1858281237	$14.95
dia	1858281040	$22.95
eland	1858280958	$16.95
aly	1858280311	$17.95
enya	1858280435	$15.95
ondon	1858291172	$12.95
editerranean Wildlife	0747100993	$15.95
alaysia, Singapore & Brunei	1858281032	$16.95

Morocco	1858280400	$16.95
Nepal	185828046X	$13.95
New York	1858280583	$13.95
Nothing Ventured	0747102082	$19.95
Pacific Northwest	1858280923	$14.95
Paris	1858281253	$12.95
Poland	1858280346	$16.95
Portugal	1858280842	$15.95
Prague	1858281229	$14.95
Provence & the Côte d'Azur	1858280230	$14.95
Pyrenees	1858280931	$15.95
St Petersburg	1858281334	$14.95
San Francisco	1858280826	$13.95
Scandinavia	1858280397	$16.99
Scotland	1858280834	$14.95
Sicily	1858280370	$14.99
Spain	1858280818	$16.95
Thailand	1858280168	$15.95
Tunisia	1858280656	$15.95
Turkey	1858280885	$16.95
Tuscany & Umbria	1858280915	$15.95
USA	185828080X	$18.95
Venice	1858280362	$13.99
Wales	1858280966	$14.95
West Africa	1858280141	$24.95
More Women Travel	1858280982	$14.95
World Music	1858280176	$19.95
Zimbabwe & Botswana	1858280419	$16.95

Rough Guide Phrasebooks

Czech	1858281482	$5.00
French	185828144X	$5.00
German	1858281466	$5.00
Greek	1858281458	$5.00
Italian	1858281431	$5.00
Spanish	1858281474	$5.00

ugh Guides are available from all good bookstores, but can be obtained directly
he USA and Worldwide (except the UK*) from Penguin:

arge your order by Master Card or Visa (US$15.00 minimum order): call 1-800-253-6476; or
nd orders, with complete name, address and zip code, and list price, plus $2.00 shipping and
ndling per order to: Consumer Sales, Penguin USA, PO Box 999 – Dept #17109,
rgenfield, NJ 07621. No COD. Prepay foreign orders by international money order, a
eque drawn on a US bank, or US currency. No postage stamps are accepted. All orders are
bject to stock availability at the time they are processed. Refunds will be made for books not
ailable at that time. Please allow a minimum of four weeks for delivery.

e availability and published prices quoted are correct at the time
going to press but are subject to alteration without prior notice.
les currently not available outside the UK will be available by
y 1995. Call to check.

or UK orders, see separate price list

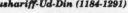

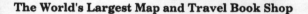

The best of
Bulgaria

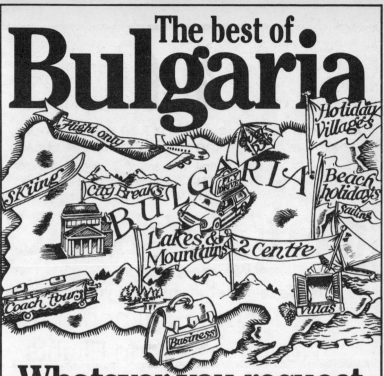

Whatever you request
you'll get the best with

ABTA
14003

ATOL
252

HOLIDAYS

simply the best!

Contact your
ABTA Travel
agent now or call Balkan Holidays direct on 071-493 8612.
Balkan Holidays Limited, Sofia House, 19 Conduit Street,
London W1R 9TD.

You are
A STUDENT

You travel
THE WORLD

You want
TO SAVE MONEY

Here's how

The International Student Identity Card

Available at Student Travel Offices Worldwide.

Entitles you to discounts and special services worldwide.